Working in Ski Resorts

Europe & North America

Working in Ski Resorts

Europe & North America

Victoria Pybus

Distributed in the USA by
The Globe Pequot Press, Guilford, Connecticut

Published by Vacation Work, 9 Park End Street, Oxford
www.vacationwork.co.uk

WORKING IN SKI RESORTS – EUROPE & NORTH AMERICA
by Victoria Pybus

First & second editions 1985 & 1988 by Victoria Pybus & Charles James
Third, fourth, fifth and sixth editions 1993, 1997, 2003 & 2006 by Victoria Pybus

Copyright © Vacation Work 2006

ISBN 13: 978-1-85458-355-0
ISBN 10: 1-85458-355-7

Cover design and maps by mccdesign ltd

Line drawings by John Taylor

Typeset by Brendan Cole

Printed and bound in Italy by Legoprint SpA, Trento

CONTENTS

A JOB BEFORE YOU GO

British Association of Ski Patrollers – The Ski Club of Great Britain
Other Opportunities – Alpine Answers – Free Radicals – Harri's Bar – Hotel
Belles Pistes – Jobs in the Alps – Macdonald Aviemore Highland Resort – Pamper
Off Piste – Pierre et Vacances – Precision Ski Shops – Ski Higher – Snow Fun –

EUROPE – FINDING A JOB ON THE SPOT

(REPORTS FROM THE RESORTS)

FINDING A JOB IN NORTH AMERICA

UNITED STATES OF AMERICA

DIRECTORY OF MAIN UNITED STATES RESORTS

CANADA

MAIN CANADIAN RESORTS

AUSTRALASIA

PREFACE

In the twenty or so years since the first edition of this book was published the skiing industry has undergone a major expansion and gone from being an elite sport to a mass one. By the late 1980s about a million Britons a year had taken to the white stuff. Then came the recession and the number dropped off dramatically until throughout the 1990s. In, this first post millennium decade, the ski industry in Europe is still growing, but at a slower rate of a few percent per year. Meanwhile there has been much speculation on the effect that global warming will have on the European snowline. There is the probability that many lower-lying resorts will become untenable as ski resorts, while the higher ones will be more prone to avalanches as proved the case in the 2005/06 season. There has been a particular upsurge in the number of people heading for the 'beginner resorts' of countries like Bulgaria, and even Turkey, while the experienced powder hounds are looking to ever further horizons and trying Chile, Argentina and Japan. Andorra is the only European area which has declined in popularity as the inexpensive skiing for which it was known, is being undercut by Eastern European areas. However widespread the skiing possibilities are, most British skiers still end up in France, which took over from Austria as the number one destination a few years back; also skiing surveys indicate that the numbers of British skiers going to resorts in Italy and Austria are rising while the number going across the Atlantic to the snow-sure USA, and more particularly Canada continue to rise, and daily direct flights to the USA and Canadian ski entry points are available. A notable growth area has been weekend and mid-week mini catered or self-catering skiing breaks to Europe boosted by no frills airfares, although the classic catered chalet holiday week provided by specialist operators is still much in evidence.

Note that the bulk of skiers and boarders going to North America are handled by centralised agencies or specialist booking agents that do not employ staff in the resorts although a few British companies also employ chalet staff and reps there. American resorts are often desperate for staff and exchange visitor programmes (EVPs) and hospitality trainee schemes have become more flexible so that they cover the winter months as well as the summer. The USA also has a visa for specialised resort staff.

In Europe, by contrast, many ski companies employ teams of resort staff, which is great news for any prospective alpine worker. As well as the usual types of work for just pocket-money and ski perks associated with working for a British tour operator, there are regular jobs involving longer hours and national statutory wages, working for foreign employers in the resorts.

Lastly, there is continuing scope for the entrepreneur who spots or creates a demand and then supplies it. Selling hot, roasted chestnuts in the street or refreshments to drivers stuck in alpine traffic jams are just two examples of the spirit of individual enterprise in action, while mobile massage for aching limbs, and mobile pampering treatments brought direct to guests in their chalets are all making money for their operators.

Besides listing the major British-based tour operators we include reports from the major skiing countries in Europe (including Scotland) and the main north American resorts where job opportunities occur. There is also coverage of Australian and New Zealand resorts. The *Reports from the Resorts* highlight the possibilities for all kinds of work whether for ski bums who just want to earn enough to get by for another month's skiing, for career-minded types who seek a genuine future in tourism or skiing, or for gap students and the newly-graduated who want to spend the winter earning a little money or paying for an instructor's course, while enjoying the international flavour of skiing and après ski in a top European or North American resort.

Working in a ski resort can be the experience of a lifetime, or the beginning of an addiction; we hope this book helps you find the job and all the alpine white stuff you want. *Hals und Beinbruch!*

Victoria Pybus
Oxford, August 2006

ACKNOWLEDGMENTS

We are grateful to Steve Rout who inspired the first edition of this book; also to Phil Nolan for his account of an instructor course in Canada and Laura Clarke of SnowCrazy for her advice to novice chalet cooks.

N.B. The author and publishers have every reason to believe in the accuracy of the information given in this book and the authenticity and correct practices of all organisations, companies, agencies etc. mentioned; however, situations may change and addresses, telephone numbers, wages, websites etc. can alter, and readers are strongly advised to check facts and credentials for themselves. Wages, exchange rates and government employment policies and regulations are particularly susceptible to change, thus the ones here are intended merely as a guide.

If, in the course of your travels and labours you uncover information which might be of use to other readers, please write to Victoria Pybus at Vacation Work, 9 Park End Street, Oxford OX1 1HJ; victoria@vacationwork.co.uk. This book depends very much on up-to-date reports from people who have worked in ski resorts and we welcome all corrections and new information. The best contributions will be rewarded with a free copy of the next edition or any other Vacation Work title (see list at the end of this book).

Introduction

The English bartender who pulls the pints in Verbier, the Scot who makes the beds in St. Anton, the New Zealander who escorts skiers in Courchevel and the Welsh chef in Whistler are all part of a growing group of thousands who live for the winter months on the slopes. For many, skiing has taken over their lives; jobs and travel revolve around a return to the mountains for another season.

For other travellers, a winter spent working in a ski resort is a way to earn a little money and have some fun through the inhospitable months from November to April; for them the skiing is an added bonus.

The route to a job in a ski area differs from person to person. Some arrange a job from home, some make use of contacts from friends who have previously worked in a village and some just head out to the mountains and travel around until they find something.

Steve Rout, who worked in ski resorts for over seven years, found his first job from a conversation on a train in Switzerland, where he had gone to try and save for a trip to North Africa. He recollects:

When I first got to Switzerland I had no intention of skiing – in fact I had no idea what the sport entailed. The only reason I was there was to earn money and paying for equipment and a season ski pass was certainly not one of my priorities.

However, Steve was dragged out on to the slopes by friends and soon became hooked.

Now by September I start getting itchy feet and dreaming about skiing; by November I have to be back on the snow and waiting for the lifts to open.

A JOB BEFORE YOU GO

At the last count there were over 350 British-based companies arranging skiing holidays overwhelmingly in Europe but increasingly in North America. Such operators range from the giants: Airtours (0800-028 8844; www.mytravel.com), Crystal (0870-160 6040; www.crystalski.co.uk), First Choice (0870-754 3477; www.fcski.co.uk), Inghams 020-8780 4433; www.inghams.co.uk) and Thomson Ski & Snowboarding (0870-606 1470; www.thomson-ski.co.uk) who between them go to nearly a hundred resorts in a dozen countries, to the one-hotel or couple of chalet enterprises like Hotel les Belles Pistes (+33 4-50 30 00 17), or the one resort company like Ski Verbier (020-7385 8050; www.skiverbier.com). Each season seems to bring a new crop of companies into business while many existing ones expand their operations, merge with or take over other companies, and only occasionally do they disappear (usually for personal, rather than economic reasons). The overall growth of the market means that the numbers of staff required for the winter season are going up – estimates of chalet staff alone vary between 5,000 and 8,000, compared with 1,000 in 1985. Since many jobs are doubled-up, for instance *plongeur* (washer uppers)/ski guide or, more usually representative/ski guide and sometimes chalet person/ski guide, it is essential to show adaptability as well as skiing (or other skills) in order to land a job in the Alps. Jobs with British tour operators are covered in the first section of the book *A Job Before You Go*, and where possible we have given full details of duties, hours, wages and perks. Also covered in this section are other organisations who, although not all are employers themselves, offer either a job finding service or are able to put applicants in touch with potential employers.

The snow has hardly melted off the mountains before some of the ski tour organisations start recruiting for the next season. However, many applicants who have accepted jobs by mid-year often find themselves unavailable on the brink of the skiing season, so it is always worth looking round in November and December as a surprising number of companies have last minute vacancies. In particular, paying a visit to the Metro Ski and Snowboard Show held at Earls Court, Olympia, in London during the second half of October (see below) may prove fruitful. Otto Karki, a qualified ski instructor from Australia, organised a job in Champéry while at the Ski Show. Another possibility is to look for advertisements for chalet and other resort staff in specialist work and travel magazines; *TNT* aimed primarily at Australasians but useful to anyone who wants to work abroad and *The Lady* magazine can prove invaluable for catering jobs and nanny jobs both of which are likely to be found amongst the copious job listings. Several British ski companies advertise for staff in this weekly magazine. *Ski and Board*, the magazine of the British Ski Club of Great Britain (0845 458 0780; www.skiclub.co.uk); is also worth checking out.

USEFUL ADDRESSES

Metro Ski and Snowboard Show: (www.metroskishow.co.uk). Ticket hotline 08705 900090. Dates for 2006 are 18-22 October. Check website for dates in 2007. Exhibitors include many well-known ski companies.

Global Snowshows: (www.globalsnowshows.co.uk) organise regional ski shows around the UK e.g. NEC Birmingham, Manchester, Calshot, usually in October. ☎01580-201533 for details or look on website.

TNT: 14-15 Childs Place, Earls Court, London SW5 9RX; ☎020-7373 3377; www. tntmagazine.com. Free in London. Published every Monday. Large sits vac section for all kinds of staff and excellent for cheap flights to everywhere.

The Lady: 39/40 Bedford Street, London WC2E 9ER; ☎020-7379 4717; ads@lady.co.uk. Published weekly on Tuesdays. Particularly useful for chalet staff/ski nanny jobs.

FINDING A JOB ON THE SPOT

Besides the positions offered by ski holiday companies or those available through agencies, there are lots of local job possibilities in hotels, bars, nightclubs, lift stations, mountain restaurants, shops and other businesses, which make up a large part of most resorts. You can try writing to employers at any of these in advance but all the reports indicate that you are much more likely to land a job on the spot by presenting yourself in person to the employer. The time to do this is (a) during the previous winter if you happen to be on a skiing holiday or (b) during the summer or (c) in late autumn, say mid-October to mid-November or (d) just before the season starts. Of these (b) and (c) are likely to be the most successful.

If, however, you arrive at your chosen resort after the season has started there are still opportunities for snow-clearing, babysitting, and other free enterprises and as there is a high incidence of replacement due to breakage amongst winter seasonal workers, there is always a variety of jobs becoming vacant at short notice if you can outstrip the competition. This is all dealt with in detail in the second section of this book.

CLAIMING THE UK JOBSEEKER'S ALLOWANCE IN EUROPE

If you are going to look for work in a ski resort in an EU country (e.g. France, Italy, Spain, Germany, Austria, Sweden, Slovenia, Finland etc.), and you have been claiming the Jobseeker's Allowance for at least four weeks in the UK, you can arrange to receive this, paid at the UK rate, for up to three months while looking for work within the EU. In order to do this, you should inform the UK Employment Service Jobcentre through which you

are receiving the allowance, well in advance (usually six weeks), of your intention to seek work elsewhere in the EU. If possible you should give a departure date and a destination. Note that if you go on holiday and then decide to stay and look for work, your benefit cannot be transferred. Your local Jobcentre should provide a leaflet (reference JSAL 22) for people going abroad or coming from abroad and an application form for transferring benefit. In the country where you are going to work you should contact the local office there, which deals with benefits:

○ **Austria:** local office of the *Arbeitsamt.*
○ **France:** local office of *L'Agence National pour l'Emploi (ANPE).*
○ **Germany:** local office of the *Arbeitsamt.*
○ **Italy:** local office of the *Istituto della previdenza sociale.*
○ **Norway:** local employment office *Arbeidformidling.*
○ **Spain:** local office of the *Oficina de Empleo* or *Instituto National de Seguridad Social (NSS).*
○ **United Kingdom:** local Jobcentre.

Once you have informed the UK Jobcentre of your plans, they will supply a letter in English and the language of your destination country explaining that you are eligible to claim benefit. This letter is used to register with the authorities in the destination country which must be done within seven days of arrival. Your UK Jobcentre will also inform the Pension and Overseas Benefit Directorate of the Department for Work and Pensions (DWP), who will decide whether or not to issue an E303 which authorises the authorities in the destination EU or EEA country to pay UK contribution-based JSA for up to three months.

As there may be delays in payments received abroad, even when this procedure is meticulously followed, it is advisable to have some emergency financial resources of your own to fall back on.

Please note that anyone tempted to chuck in their present job to go on the dole for the requisite four weeks before going off to a ski resort to look for work, will be disappointed: by making themselves voluntarily unemployed they render themselves ineligible for the Jobseeker's Allowance for 26 weeks!

SKIING COMPETITIONS

Your chances of finding casual work at short notice can increase dramatically if your presence coincides with a major skiing competition. There are a number of important competitions every year, the most significant of which are the World Cup men's and women's series, consisting of a downhill, special, giant slalom and super giant slalom events. These are held mainly in Europe and also North America, Korea, Australia etc. The exact dates and venues of the forthcoming season's events are picked every summer by the Fédération Internationale de Ski (FIS, Blochtrasse 2, 3653 Oberhofen in Switzerland; ☎+41 33-244 61 61; fax +41 33-243 53 53; www.fis-ski.com) which is the highest body for the sport and part of the International Olympic Committee for athletes. Even greater crowd-pullers are the World Ski Championships for alpine skiing which are held every two years anywhere from Austria to America.

The World Cup events do not last for more than a couple of days, but can offer anyone who is on the spot the chance of picking up some lucrative temporary work as the resort is swamped by spectators. The relevant details of the forthcoming World Cup schedule can be obtained from The FIS or the British Ski and Snowboard Federation website (www.snowsportgb.com).

INCOME TAX

The tax position of a British citizen working abroad varies according to where they are working and the nationality of their employer. The situation is most straightforward when someone is working abroad for a British company, as Britain has what are known as Double Taxation Agreements, with most western countries to sort out some of the complications involved in working abroad. These will usually apply to people working in a ski resort and state that a host country gives up its right to tax an individual's income if they are working for a British employer for less than six months. The British worker is then subject only to standard United Kingdom income tax, as if they were working in the UK.

When a British citizen is working in another country for a citizen of that country then they are liable for tax as if they were a local. But, having accepted a low rate of pay in exchange for the chance to spend time skiing, they may be in a situation where their wage is so low that they are not earning enough to make them liable for income tax. Some countries including Germany structure their tax systems so that people on the lowest incomes pay no tax at all: in Britain that threshold is currently about £96 per week for a single person, in France it is slightly less at about £81. In most other western European countries including Austria and Switzerland, all workers pay some tax, although those on the lowest incomes pay only a small amount.

People working abroad for a foreign employer for less than six months are still technically resident in Britain and so are still obliged to pay UK income tax on the money they earned abroad. So a worker may face a further demand for tax on their return to the UK if the country in which they have been working has a comparatively low rate of income tax. This demand will only amount to making up the difference between the two amounts: in general, double taxation agreements ensure that that the total amount of income tax paid in both countries is no more than would normally be deducted in the country which has the higher rate of tax. If, on the other hand, a worker had paid more tax on their income from abroad than they would have done in Britain, the Inland Revenue is interested for information purposes only: you cannot unfortunately reclaim the 'overpayment'.

RECIPROCAL HEALTH AGREEMENTS

People looking for work in ski resorts abroad are entitled to emergency medical treatment provided under reciprocal health agreements. Details are in the leaflet *T5 Health Advice for Travellers Anywhere in the World,* which is obtainable from main post offices in the UK or by telephoning 0800 555 777 any time, free of charge. The leaflet T5 lists the 40 countries with which Britain has a reciprocal health agreement and a summary of what you are entitled to in each of the 40. It also contains the application form for the EHIC (European Health Insurance Card) which will enable you to receive emergency treatment in certain countries including the fifteen countries of the European Union and others including Norway, which are part of the European Economic Area. You can get your EHIC by completing the form and returning it to the PPA (Prescribing Pricing Authority; ☎0845 606 2030). This takes 21 days by post. By telephoning the PPA you can get the EHIC within 10 days. You can also apply online for the EHIC from the Department of Health website (www.dh.gov.uk). On the home page scroll down to 'Health Advice for Travellers' and click.

Note that neither Canada nor the USA have reciprocal health agreements with the UK. In Switzerland, you can use the public health service only if you have paid into a Swiss sickness insurance fund. Even in the countries, which do have reciprocal health agreements with the UK, note that they do not entitle you to repatriation in the event of illness, nor do they provide treatment completely free of charge.

Should you require emergency medical treatment abroad, you may still be liable to pay a portion of the costs depending on the country. In France for instance, 25% of the cost of hospital costs has to be paid by the patient and there may also be a fixed daily hospital charge (*forfait journalier*), while in Austria in-patient costs are largely covered but not outpatient ones which could leave you with a hefty bill for a broken limb. It is for this reason that it is essential to take out private medical insurance to cover the difference.

The EHIC is only for treatment in state hospitals. If there is no state hospital in the resort, you may be taken to the nearest large town in an emergency. However, larger resorts usually have an abundance of private clinics many of which have agreements with the state sector to treat non-private patients. Since such clinics are likely to have wide experience in the treatment of skiing injuries, this can be quite reassuring. Of course if you have private medical insurance (see below) you will have fewer restrictions and wider options.

INSURANCE

Anyone who is working for a British tour operator in a ski resort is normally insured by that company for the duration of employment. It is however advisable to check what the policy actually covers you for *before* you start work. Once you are in employment abroad, the EHIC (see above) no longer applies and you may have to make your own insurance arrangements as the employer's cover may not cover you both for accidents while skiing and working.

Broadly speaking, anyone who is in full time employment abroad with a foreign company or employer and paying health and social security contributions should be covered by that country's social insurance scheme. However those with more precarious employment, e.g. intermittent casual work, should certainly take out private insurance. Regular UK ski insurance packages as sold by travel agents and tour operators to their clients are not appropriate for alpine workers as they are tailored to the holidaymaker and would work out very expensive for five months. Some of the specialist ski insurance companies offer a range of special packages including the all important cover for medical expenses, legal liability, personal accident and loss of earnings. Worldwide and Fogg Travel Insurances have a policy which can be tailored to alpine workers and both companies offer baggage cover to Reps, and also cover for their skis following theft or accidental damage. Premiums with Fogg may be as much as double for North America because of the high medical costs there. The Ski Club of Great Britain has linked with Acumus Insurance to provide an insurance package to cater for the season worker. Another option open to alpine workers is to take out sports insurance in the country where they are working. The Swiss and French have a huge indigenous demand for insurance tailored to mountain sports enthusiasts and their packages are sometimes available through UK agents: Sportscover Direct offers a French sports and leisure package (Multisports Card) that provides mountain sports (skiing and mountaineering) accident insurance for an annual premium. Primarily intended for 'getting you off the mountain' (mountain rescue) and repatriation and third party liability, they are meagre on medical costs (up to £500) so additional medical only cover may still be required if your injuries are not considered severe enough to warrant repatriation back to the UK. For this reason, rescue and repatriation packages may not be as good value as at first glance they may appear. Another thing to watch out for is that the repatriation benefit may have an expiry limit, in the case of Sportscover Direct it is available for up to 60 days only.

Those considering taking out any skiing insurance should note that hazardous variations of skiing (including off-piste, snowboarding, ski jumping, parapente, freestyle etc.) are normally not included and that separate premiums will have to negotiated for these.

USEFUL ADDRESSES

Fogg Travel Insurances Service Ltd.: Crow Hill Drive, Mansfield, Notts. NG19 7AE; ☎01623-631331; fax 01623-420450; www.sales@fogginsure.co.uk.

Ski Club of Great Britain: The White House, 57/63 Church Road, Wimbledon, London SW19 5DQ; ☎020-8410 2000; www.skiclub.co.uk.. Offers insurance package in conjunction with Acumus Insurance. Suitable for season workers in the resort.

www.jsinsurance.co.uk: 10-11 Lower John Street, London W1F 9EB; 0870 755 6101. Offers comprehensive ski insurance from single ski to annual travel insurance with skiing. Also tailor made policies for ski seasonaires.

Snowinsure.com: ☎0870-333 1790; specialises in adventure travel and backpackers' travel insurance for up to one and a half years of cover on a single trip. Suitable for seasonal workers in ski resorts.

Sports Cover Direct: 29 Great George Street, Bristol BS1 5QT; ☎0845 120 6400; fax 0845 120 6401; www.sportscoverdirect.com; e-mail contact@sports cover.co.uk. Offers French Multisports Card insurance for 'getting you off the mountain and repatriation'.

Worldwide Travel Insurance: The Business Centre 1/7 Commercial Road, Paddock Wood, Tunbridge TN12 6YT; ☎0870 112 8100; sales@worldwideinsure.com. Does a long stay insurance. Adding wintersports ups the premium.

SWISS HELICOPTER INSURANCE

Not all regular travel insurance covers skiing accidents and loss or breakage of ski equipment automatically (athough such cover can usually be added for an additional premium). For those who get a job in a Swiss resort, Swiss helicopter rescue insurance is excellent value. It is organised by the REGA Organisation (Swiss national rescue service) and you pay a subscription known as a 'patronage fee' of SFr 30 which is valid from the day of payment until 15 May of the following year. Tourists and seasonal workers are eligible to become 'patrons'. There is also a family cover. If you are injured on the mountain you will be flown from the mountain where you are injured, to the nearest hospital. If you were not a patron (i.e. had not paid your SFr 30 patronage fee) you would be personally liable for the cost of the helicopter and it could be over SFr 12,000! The emergency, 24-hour number is 1414 within Switzerland.

In Switzerland, this form of insurance is available from such outlets as pharmacies in the resorts of the Wallis canton, e.g. in Zermatt from the Pharmacie Internationale, or you can arrange it online www.rega.ch by sending an e-mail stating your requirements.

Note that neither the cost of Swiss helicopter rescue beyond the border, nor air ambulance flights departing from Switzerland is included.

Addresses
Swiss Air-Rescue (REGA) Administration, Rega Centre, PO Box 1414, 8058 Zurich-Airport; ☎01 654 33 11; fax 01 654 33 22; info@rega.ch; www.rega.ch.
Rega patrons information: ☎0844 834 844; fax 01 654 32 48; goenner@rega.ch.

Types of Job Available

AU PAIR

There is a regular demand for au pairs in ski resorts and some British-based agencies, which customarily have such vacancies are listed below. It is also very possible to arrange such a job on the spot in a resort since many of the local people involved in the running of a resort are extremely busy during the season and need extra help in the house and looking after the children. Hoteliers, especially, routinely employ au pairs in the busy season. Try advertising on notice boards (often there will be one in the local supermarket), visit the tourist office or advertise in the local paper.

Lucy Sumner got an au pair job looking after a busy hotelier's children in Monêtier-les-Bains, Serre Chevalier, France. She got the job through Jobs in the Alps (see *Other Organisations*) where she applied in September. Her job was confirmed in October and she worked the whole season from December to May for SFr. 1,500 per month. She cleaned the family's apartment in the mornings and baby-sat from 5pm until her employers returned from the hotel at night. She had most afternoons off for skiing. Of her experience she says:

> *An obvious advantage of au-pairing in a family hotel environment is that there are a number of seasonal workers in the hotel; in this case there was another English girl and it was invaluable to have a companion. Evening free time began after midnight but as we were willing to mix with the locals I soon became totally absorbed in the village life.*

Lucy had all her meals provided, even on her days off and she had her own single room in the hotel so she could come and go as she pleased. She also worked in the hotel during peak periods and earned extra money. During the afternoons when she was skiing she met lots of people, residents and tourists, and as a seasonal worker she paid a reduced price for her lift pass and ski hire. To sum up she says:

> *I thoroughly enjoyed every aspect of my time in France. I became one of the family and made many good friends and I have good memories of my time at Monêtier. I*

returned the next year and was welcomed very much as a local – a lovely feeling.

For further details and a list of useful agencies, see *Other Organisations*.

USEFUL ADDRESSES

Butterfly et Papillon: 5 Ave de Genève, 74000 Annecy, France; ☎+33 4-50 46 08 33; fax +33 4-50 67 0133; aupair.france@wanadoo.fr. Can arrange placements in the region of the French Alps for those aged 18-35 for monthly pocket money.

Childcare International Ltd: Trafalgar House, Grenville Place, London, NW7 3SA; 020-8906 3116; www.childint.co.uk Contact: Sandra Landau. Au pair and au pair plus placements in the French ski resorts for the ski season. Also, with American associates can arrange nanny/au pair placements in/near US ski resorts. Applicants must be age 18-26, drivers and non-smokers with plenty of child care experience. Families pay round trip airfare, medical insurance, two weeks' paid holiday and a salary of up to $170 per week, depending on qualifications.

French Au Pairs: P.O.Box 68, Whitchurch, Shropshire SY13 4WH; ☎01948-665161; www.frenchaupairs.com. Finds childcare positions in EU countries plus Switzerland and Norway, Canada, Australia and New Zealand.

CHALET COOK

The once popular image of the chalet cook is that of a fun-loving, husband-hunting female super Sloane whose only concession to being abroad is to change her main catch-phrase from 'Okay yah' to 'C va ja' is less so today. Chalet companies are only too well aware that being a chalet cook and host calls for considerable skills, stamina, presence of mind and a lot of hard work. Nowadays it is the girls and boys with the right qualities who get the jobs. Actually 'girls' may sometimes be a relative term as at least one company, Crystal Finest (formerly Simply Ski), has employed 'girls' over 50 years old, as chalet cooks.

According to one estimate, there are well over 5,000 chalet staff, the majority of them female, working in Europe each winter season and although the tour companies begin recruiting as early as May, late, last minute and mid-season applications still stand a reasonable chance of succeeding. There are always some dropouts right up to the commencement of the season in mid-December. A surprising percentage of staff fail to last the gruelling five-month stint of cooking, cleaning, budgeting, skiing and partying. Natural resilience may give way to a variety of aggravating factors (pining for partner, sacked, broken limbs or hearts, etc.) and cause them to leave their jobs. It is estimated that 25% drop out in the first few weeks so after Christmas is probably as good a time as any to ask about vacancies, but, there is no harm ringing round the companies at any time during the season to see if any emergency vacancies have come up. There have also been many cases where suitably skilled people on a skiing holiday have been employed on the spot by making it known to the reps that they would be available for work at the drop of a hat (or chalet employee). This happened to a guest at one chalet who offered to take over when the chalet girl dislocated her knee and she ended up working in Verbier until the end of the season.

Generally speaking, all Chalet Hosts require a good cooking qualification (Cordon Bleu or equivalent) or considerable experience catering for parties. The requirements of various tour operators vary considerably in this respect and some will ask potential staff to cook a meal as part of their selection process, whilst others organise their own cookery courses as Crystal Holidays does through Natives.com. Languages are also useful and skiing ability is an advantage. The problems chalet hosts are likely to be dealing with are guests eating the allocated food in the fridge and using the next week's allocation of laundry. With this in mind chalet hosts need to be resourceful and resilient.

Chaleting, as it is usually known amongst the *cognoscenti*, is a very demanding job for startlingly low pay and although there is usually some form of overseeing either by the local rep to whom problems can be referred, there are still endless minor decisions to be made each day beyond what to cook for supper. In resorts where a company does not have a rep, chalet hosts will often be responsible for getting the clients fixed up with ski boots, passes etc. and may also be expected to ski with them several times a week. Again, the responsibilities vary considerably from one company to another, but in all cases it is an exacting job. Bladon Lines (now part of Inghams), was one of the original chalet operators and used to issue their chalet girls with a sixty-page staff manual to cover every contingency from the finer points of delivering a first night speech to chalet guests to providing gluten free diets. They also provided chalet girls with a cookbook containing over 100 recipes and an accompanying recipe manual containing suggestions for keeping the punters' taste buds from terminal boredom. For instance it included 20 different ways of preparing potatoes! Useful 'cooks' bibles' are just one of the ways the companies ensure standards are likely to be adhered to. Most usually demand a dinner party demonstration for the directors before hiring and provide several days' pre-season training in the resort and any host for Crystal or Thomson has to have read a manual of about 150 pages before they begin the two weeks of pre-season training. Bladon Lines' manual is also famous for having contained a warning that any chalet girl found spending the night with someone in her bedroom will be instantly dismissed even if it is her mother or, more surprisingly, the vicar!

It says a great deal for the chalet staff that they are able to take on all these tasks and still have a great time. They soon get the routine down to a fine art and can be free to ski by about 11am and not have to be back until about 4.30pm. Changeover day begins early, sometimes at 5am, and is all work and no skiing. However, virtually all chalet staff get a complete day off a week.

Samantha Creasey and Kathryn Nightingale who worked together in Verbier both emphasise that aspiring chalet staff should be aware that in spite of the long afternoons free for skiing it is a stretched day starting at 7am and not finishing until about 9.30pm or 10pm. It is also hard work: Samantha and Kathryn shopped twice a week for a couple of hours each time and there were always minor problems to see to such as blocked plumbing, cookers reluctant to heat-up, no firewood or the irritation of having to wash up in cold water because the guests had used all the hot water for showers. They were surprised at the high level of responsibility required and felt it was probably easier for girls over 21 when it came to dealing with over-excited parties: punch-ups in the sitting-room are not unknown.

According to Joanna Stapley supervision can however reach uncomfortable extremes

The chalet reps even checked the chalet rubbish bins to make sure the chalet girls were not using any convenience foods. I can understand that established companies have to maintain their edge by ensuring standards remain constant, but I think that the high level of unemployment amongst graduates means that many companies are now dealing with a different kind of chalet person. These days many applicants are graduates and skilled people used to working on their own who can be trusted to call the rep only when needed.

Joanna is however quick to point out that Bladon Lines in particular has its good points

Because the people in the personnel department have worked as chalet staff themselves they know all the chalets backwards and are extremely helpful. For instance it is obviously better to have a new chalet with mod cons which is near to the lifts as possible. Some of the more picturesque chalets, though popular with the guests can make a chalet cook's life miserable; having no dishwasher can affect skiing time considerably as can being twenty minutes from the slopes. If you apply early you will be able to ask for the pick of the 'good chalets'

Whatever the trials involved the pleasures generally outweigh them and the majority of chalet staff enjoy the experience and would do it again.

James Nibloe worked as chalet host for Thomson Ski and Snowboard in Zell am Zee. James, aged 26 was a trainee chef with Best Western Hotels and did an advanced Hospitality and Catering GNVQ. He then had a change of direction, went to university and gained a degree in English and Business Studies. Using the book *Work Your Way Around the World* as a starting point he contacted several ski companies and decided to apply to Thomson Ski and Snowboard as they allow their cooks more flexibility with their menus than some other companies.

James Nibloe describes his recruitment by Thomson, how he got a chalet in Zell am Zee to run on his own and gives advice on how to win over your guests.

We had to attend an assessment day for which we had to take with us a cake we had made. During the morning we were given basic literacy and numeracy tests and a kind of theoretical 'Ready Steady Cook' test. At midday the interviewers conducted a cake tasting and then summoned for interview the best cake makers. I was interviewed and five days later was told I had a job. Two days after that I was in Austria for the 10-day induction which took place in Ellmau.

During the induction they were trying to work out who got on best with each other and who would work well together. Obviously, I didn't get on with anyone because I was given a chalet for 12 to run on my own. However, I was told this was a compliment.

I really enjoyed the season. I felt that the chalet was my home and that it was like welcoming guests to my own house. Most of the time guests got on well but occasionally there were hitches: two burly macho men found that an Austrian twin bed is actually two beds in one frame and spent the whole week terrified of misunderstandings and prefacing their remarks with 'I'm not gay...'

In positively romantic contrast, there were two pairs of British sisters who shared the chalet with a bunch of New Zealand guys who demonstrated the haka (Maori ceremonial war dance accompanied by chanting) for them in the resort car park. It must have impressed as one of the girls and one of the New Zealanders are going on holiday together this year.

> *The highlights were being out in the mountains every day in a beautiful place, affordable mountain restaurants, and the companionship of the guests. I went out drinking with the guests and this level of commitment really impressed them, and also meant that after a hard night they would make their own breakfast while I lay in bed; although I had to put up with being ribbed endlessly for a couple of days afterwards.*
>
> **Asked if his experiences had taught him anything James replied:**
> *I would say that no education or training you have is ever wasted or time spent socialising with the guests – they will appreciate it.*

James is planning another season in a ski resort working for a private chalet company with two chalets in Les Arcs, France. After that he plans to lease his own chalet and run it for himself. Thomson Ski and Snowboard obviously spotted his potential.

Generally speaking the ratio of guests to one chalet host is about 8:1 and bigger chalets may have three or four staff working together, with a trained chef doing the cooking and an MBO/plongeur on hand to do the odd jobs and keep everyone happy.

To summarise: although companies are keen to promote their chalet staff as cooks/hosts par excellence, they load on additional responsibilities including doing all the shopping and providing wonderful dinners on a generally strict budget, making guests' beds (canny chalet staff bribe their guests, usually with snack bars, to do their own), hoovering, polishing, keeping the front porch/steps clear of snow, making laundry arrangements, getting the plumber, carpenter, electrician etc., dealing with breakages to both fixtures and guests and helping with airport transfers all for, in many cases, £80 or less per week. Small wonder then that in 2006/7 ski companies were finding it harder to find recruits where once the supply seemed endless. Other reasons affecting recruitment include the fact that the chalet companies have become pickier about the quality of their staff skills, canny cooks are finding better paid jobs elsewhere, and the general lack of basic cookery skills amongst the first generation that has grown up virtually on convenience foods.

A consolation for chalet staff who do make the grade, might be if satisfied guests showed their appreciation in the form of a tip at the end of the week. Unfortunately only some do this and from a chalet of 20 people £10 might be given, or nothing at all. Sometimes £30 will be given. Most disappointing of all from the chalet staff's point of view is an unwanted gift like chocolates or flowers etc. There are a few unscrupulous chalet staff who seem to have a birthday every two weeks. The poor unsuspecting guest will, at least buy drinks for the 'birthday person' and if they are really lucky a sweatshirt or some gift which can be returned to the shop for cash later on.

Quite a number of chalet staff go on to make a career in tourism and take permanent jobs on the administrative side of a ski tour organisation.

Private Chalets
An alternative to working for a tour operator, is to work for a private chalet owner. This is probably the alpine equivalent of a country house party. The advantages are that you will probably be paid double the tour operator rate of pay, and that working conditions will be better all round. You are likely to have your own room (company staff frequently share spartan accommodation in a dingy basement) and a less stringent budget. If a ski company cook overspends there is no room for manoeuvre; she or he will either have to skimp on the next set of guests and risk complaints and thus the sack, or she/he will have to make up the amount from personal funds. Private employees will probably be provided with a food processor, most company staff have to provide their own. Lastly, a private chalet cook may not have to stay the whole season although this will depend on the employers' arrangements. Many private chalets advertise in *The Lady*.

COOKERY COURSES

Since the chalet host's most prized attribute (apart from personality) is his or her culinary skill, there is a big advantage to be gained in the employment stakes if you have a cookery course under your belt. These vary from a fairly informal one-week course specially geared to chalet cooking, to a fully certificated, internationally recognised cookery qualification such as the Cordon Bleu.

Laura Clarke of SnowCrazy, a chalet company that also runs a cookery course offers advice for making the most of your time while keeping guests happy: *Cooking for a chalet full of guests may seem daunting. A cookery course could help immensely in building up your confidence as well as a repertoire of recipes. The first three weeks of the season will be very busy and you can guarantee your chalet will be full while you are still getting used to cooking for large numbers at altitude (heard of the yoghurt cake recipe?) and trying to keep to a tight budget, often with a restricted shopping list. These are my tips for menu planning to guide you through the first weeks and keep your guests satisfied and ensure you make the most of your time.*

Firstly, learn and practise 7 to 8 options for each meal and course you prepare (breakfast, afternoon tea, high tea for kids and dinner). Breakfast is the easiest meal; most items can be put out for guests to help themselves. A hot option is normally offered and you should choose what you are going to offer, rather than cooking to order. You are normally required to serve porridge everyday as well.

Dinner for an average chalet (8-16 guests) should take no longer than two hours to prepare, especially if there are two of you. You will probably be required to serve meat/fish with two vegetables plus one option from potatoes, pasta, cous cous or rice. Menu options vary depending on the company; for some spaghetti Bolognese is a big no no. The thing is not to set your sights to high; most people do not want to eat fancy cuisine after a hard day's skiing. Filling, tasty, warming meals are what hits the spot. Serve tea and coffee in the lounge, so that you can clear the dining-room and clean and tidy as quickly as possible.

At some stage, you will have to cater for special diets (veggies, vegan, wheat-free, dairy-free, nut-free) Have at least six vegetarian/vegan options. Other intolerances or allergies are fairly easy to adapt to during the week. Make sure the options fit with the veg/carbs you are serving with the meat dish, so you don't have to cook an entirely different meal.

You may also have to cook children's meals separately. Most kids will eat only what they are used to at home and it is useful to talk to the parents at the beginning of the week to see what they want their children to eat, as well as what their children want to eat (there may be a difference). Maintain a stock of frozen pizzas, ice cream, chips etc., but parents will appreciate home-cooked food. It's easy and cheaper to make your own turkey nuggets for example.

Laura Clarke's Top Tips for Menu Planning

- Recipes should be quick and easy. Avoid anything that needs stewing or involves intricate preparation.
- In presentation avoid repetition and vary textures. Make the plates look nice. Colours on the plate should not clash or be bland. Add garnishes.
- Fruit and vegetables deteriorate at different rates at altitude, so be flexible and use ingredients in order of perishability.
- Never serve margarine, long-life milk or stale bread, this will not impress (OK to use in recipes though).
- Filter coffee is often cheaper than instant and guests will love waking up to the

aroma of fresh coffee in the mornings.

- Take into account your storage facilities, e.g. you may only have a tiny freezer.
- Transfer day will be spent mostly cleaning the chalet and guests may arrive late especially if the weather is extreme. Choose a meal that will not spoil e.g. cold salad starters like Tomato and Mozarella salad and a main course than can be successfully reheated such as Beef Bourguignon and for dessert mousse, cheescake etc.
- Familiarise yourself with the supermarket/shopping list (availability, quality, prices, specialist counters such as meat, fish, cheese).
- Keep a back-up meal in case delivery/shopping is delayed, or you have a major disaster.
- Big up your food to your guests, announce dinner every night, make it sound really delicious and use elaborate or foreign names to give dishes an air of mystery.
- Avoid telling your guests in the morning what they are having for dinner just in case you have to do a last minute change because the broccoli has turned yellow.
- Avoid wastage. Go for cheaper recipes which are just as effective as ones with more expensive ingredients. Serving the meat on a plate and the vegetables/carbs in separate dishes causes more wastage. Try serving the whole meal on each plate; allow 150g per person of meat and make sure there is enough for seconds. Freeze reusable items or recycle into soups. Half-used tins of food can be used in other recipes.
- Finally, and most importantly, appear confident and enthusiastic. Guests will often want to relay their day's escapades to you whilst you are cooking, so make sure you walk the walk and talk the talk (and hide the recipe books).

Here is a list of cookery schools and courses that can provide basic and/or full training:

The Avenue Cookery School: 74 Chartfield Avenue, Putney, London SW15 6HQ; ☎/fax 020-87883025; info@theavenuecourses.com; www.theavenuecourses.co.uk. Run by Mary Forde and Diana Horsford who between them have many years' experience working in the catering trade and of teaching cookery. The Avenue is particularly geared to the interests of young people from undergraduates cooking courses to commercially orientated courses for chalet staff and gap year students. The course for chalet cooking lasts 5 days (or two weeks if starting from scratch). There are also chalet cooking evening classes run over six or twelve evenings.

Ballymaloe Cookery School: Shanagarry, Co. Cork, Ireland; ☎+353 (0)21 4646 785; fax +353 (0)21 464 6909; info@cookingisfun.ie; www.cookingisfun.ie. Run by Darina Allen a well-known Irish cookery writer, Ballymaloe has a 12-week certificate course (€8,775) run three times a year and a wide range of short courses lasting from half a day and costing from 95 euros. Residential or non-residential. Accommodation from 95 euros per week (twin shared). Has many contacts amongst chalet companies.

Cookery at The Grange: The Grange, Whatley, Frome, Somerset BA11 3JU; ☎01373-836579; www.cookeryatthegrange.co.uk; info@cookeryatthegrange.co.uk. Run by William Averill. The Grange offers residential or non-residential four-week intensive practical cookery courses from £2,850-£3,320 inclusive of full board and accommodation (Monday to Friday).

Cutting Edge Food & Wine School: Hackwood Farm, Robertsbridge, East Sussex, TN32 5ER; ☎01580-881281; cuttingedge@fsmail.net; new school recommended by Inghams. Range of courses includes cooking on a budget for university students and gap year participants, as well as a chalet cook's course. Principal Ruth Sands Edwards.

Le Cordon Bleu Culinary Institute: 114 Marylebone Lane, London W1U 2HH; ☎020-7935 3503; fax 020-7935 7621; london@cordonbleu.net; www.cordonbleu.net. Institute has branch in Paris and many other cities. Offers Le Cordon Bleu Basic Cuisine Certificate course covers both basic and complex recipes, from traditional meals to vegetarian and ethnic recipes. Course last 10 weeks and costs £4,427, but many shorter full-time and part-time courses also offered. Accommodation not included but available nearby

The original Cordon Bleu cookery school has strong links with some of the top ski companies, many of whom recruit directly from the School.

Edinburgh School of Food and Wine: The Coach House, Newliston, Edinburgh EH29 9EB; ☎0131-333 5001; info@esfw.com; www.esfw.com; Courses for cooks of all levels from basic to 'cordon bleu' standard cookery. Of particular interest to chalet cooks is the Certificate Course – 4-week Intensive Certificate Course – which is geared towards chalet work. Other courses include the 1-Week Survival Certificated Course for those living away from home for the first time. Prices range from £475 (one week) to £8,800 (6-Month Diploma in Food and Wine). The school is located in an idyllic situation and is the only cookery school in Scotland offering this type of cookery course.

Food of Course: Louise Hutton, Middle Farm House, Sutton, Shepton Mallet, Somerset BA4 6QF; ☎01749-860116; louise.hutton@foodofcourse.co.uk; www.foodofcourse. co.uk. Run by professional cook Lou Hutton who has had her own catering business and was principal teacher at Cookery at the Grange for four years before setting up her own school. Suitable for chalet cooks: four-week intensive foundation course teaching classic methods and skills and includes tuition in Foundation Certificate in Food Hygiene. Upon completion of the course Food of Course can put you in touch with ski companies and employment agencies. Course fee is from £2,650 which includes all meals, shared accommodation (single accommodation £50 per week extra), equipment and recipe file.

The Gables School of Cookery: Pipers Lodge, Bristol Road, Falfield, South Gloucestershire GL12 8DF; ☎01454-260444; www.thegablesschoolofcookery.co.uk. One to four-week courses ideal for chalet cooks. Can be taken as a four-week course (up to advanced standard), or from £725 per week including shared accommodation.

Leiths School of Food & Wine: 21 St. Alban's Grove, London W8 5BP; ☎020-7229 0177; www.leiths.com. One of the big name cookery schools, Leiths have a full range of courses. Suitable for potential chalet cooks are 2-week beginners, intermediate or advanced courses in July or 4-week beginners courses in July and September. Alternatively, a longer 10-week course from September to December. Prices range from £1,150 for 2 weeks to £5,350 for ten weeks. Non-residential, but help given to find accommodation if needed.

The school also runs an employment agency, Leiths List, to help you find permanent or temporary employment in the UK or worldwide, after your course. For further information contact info@leiths.com.

The Manor School of Fine Cuisine: Woodpeckers, 35 Lambley Lane, Burton Joyce, Nottingham NG14 5BG; ☎0789 1122616; fax 01159-372181; www.manorcuisine.co.uk. The Manor School is run by Claire Tuttey who holds The Cordon Bleu School of London's Diploma. The School offers courses covering basics and more advanced creative skills suitable for those embarking on a professional catering career. Courses include a 5-day Beginners' Foundation Course (£600) with a graded certificate on successful completion. A follow-up letter of recommendation may be issued for future employment. Skills learned are ideal for careers in chalet cooking, yachts, directors' dining rooms, outside catering, hotels and shooting lodges. The course is non-residential but accommodation can be arranged locally.

Miranda Hall: The Old School, Hambleton, Oakham, Rutland LE15 8JT; ☎01572-723576; e-mail Miranda hall@btinternet.com; website http://uk.geocities.com/mirandahall@ btinternet.com/chaletcookscourse. Run by qualified Home Economics teacher with a Cordon Bleu (Paris) diploma. The Chalet Cooks Course has been run for a decade. The five-day intensive Chalet Cooks Course is held in October and possibly November and is designed to cover three weeks of memorable meals each with an in-built vegetarian option. Course provides each student with confidence in their professional role at the start of the season and the ability to organise their preparation in the mornings so as to maximise their skiing time. Cost of course is £495 including all meals and accommodation.

Natives Cookery Course (www.natives.com): The Natives cookery course is run twice a year (August and October) at St. Teresa's School for Girls, Effingham, Surrey. The course lasts 5 days, costs £399 and includes food and accommodation. The course includes a Basic Hygiene Certificate. For details of how to book, log on to the Natives website or telephone 08700 463377. Natives has connections with many ski companies that take on chalet cooks.

Rosie Davies: Penny's Mill, Nunney, Frome, Somerset BA11 4NP; ☎01373-836210; fax 01373-836018; e-mail info@rosiedavies.co.uk; www.rosiedavies.co.uk.. Offers a 4-week cookery course beginning with essential skills and basic techniques but moving on to more complex aspects. Part of the course will include the specialist skills needed to work as a chalet host. Certificate of completion and Basic Hygiene Certificate. Costs £2,700 including shared accommodation.

Snowcrazy: UK ☎01342-302910; France: +33 (0)4 79 09 14 86; e-mail Gosnowcrazy@ aol.com; www. snowcrazy.co.uk. Offers a week's cookery course (Ultimate Chalet Host Cookery Course) combining learning practical cookery skills with time off to sample the local activities including white-water rafting and paragliding. Course takes place over various weeks in July and August in a luxury chalet in La Rosière at the end of the Tarentaise valley and includes essential tips for maximizing your time on the slopes, correct health and safety in the kitchen, basic language skills for the job and more. £395 per person including accommodation and all cooking ingredients.

Tante Marie School of Cookery: Carlton Road, Woking, Surrey GU21 4HF; ☎01483-726957; info@tantemarie.co.uk; www.tantemarie.co.uk. Offers career and short/gap year courses. Both the 11-week Cordon Bleu Certificate Course (£4,995) starting every January, April and September and the 4-week Essential Skills Course (£2,300) starting every January, April, July, September and October are suitable courses for the chalet cook. Non-residential but accommodation approved by the School can be arranged locally.

DISC JOCKEY

Mainly because of the dominance of British and American popular music, it is generally thought chic by discos in various European countries to have an English-speaking disc jockey. Jobs are sometimes advertised in the music papers but there is scope for approaching the nightclubs direct (get the names from ski operator or ski resort websites). For instance Wasteland Ski (020-8246 6677; www.chalet-travel.co.uk) employ DJs for La Grotte du Yeti bars in the French Alps for a salary of 1000-1500 euros per month. Basically, the line to take is 'give me the job and I'll play some decent music for you'. If you have a really good selection of current releases you will improve your chances of success. Keep an eye open for jobs in *Mixmag* and *Loot*.

FREE ENTERPRISE

Ski bums think of some marvellous ways to keep themselves in sufficient funds to be able to carry on skiing throughout the season. Apart from the basic standbys of work in hotels, bars, restaurants, nightclubs, shops and transfer repping, there are plenty of opportunities for freelance snow-clearing, illicit ski teaching, offering a baby-sitting service and doing a morning fresh bread and croissant round for chalets and apartments. A more elaborate version of this last is the breakfast run. The idea is that you prepare and deliver breakfast to clients throughout the resort. You can advertise your service by posting photo-copied sheets in self-catering apartment blocks and also giving these sheets to the reps to put in the welcome packs given to self-catering clients. As your publicity distribution relies heavily on the goodwill of the reps it is essential as one ski bum put it 'to be in their good books.' Another variation is the beer run, which involves selling and delivering crates of beer to punters. Publicity is again managed by handing out price lists and order forms to reps and punters. Beer is then bought in the nearest hypermarket outside the resort and sold to undercut the resort supermarkets.

Other enterprising people have set themselves up as freelance photographers on the slopes and even make video films with send-up commentaries for enthusiastic punters. The great thing about personal enterprise in the Alps is that you can operate at almost any level: selling hot chestnuts in the street at one end of the scale or, at the other end, setting oneself up in a proper business perhaps by renting a couple of chalets and going into the chalet business or by taking the lease on a nightclub for the season.

Other people have done well by providing entertainment for hotels such as ski races and fondue evenings or by offering to look after children for the day so that parents can go off skiing the more difficult runs without worrying about junior. Although tour operators' staff are mostly not supposed to pay people outside the company to help out, a certain amount of this goes on and for that reason as well as the possibility of being taken on as emergency help, you should always keep in close touch with reps, chalet staff and the rest of the tour operators' teams.

One caveat about operating on a free enterprise basis is that you must be careful to keep a low profile. This is particularly important in Switzerland where you are liable to be deported for not having a work permit. There is also a problem with 'family mafia' in some smaller Swiss and Italian resorts where all local businesses are run by or connected to in some way, one or two local families. It is therefore necessary to carry on business exclusively through the British grapevine. In most resorts the British tour reps are only too keen to help out if your service is regular and reliable, especially if it keeps their clients happy or they get a cut. If you make yourself known to all the reps they can mention you to anyone showing interest. You can most easily make contact with the reps on the evenings when they hold their welcome meetings for clients and exchange mobile numbers with them. You must however be prepared to pursue them, as they will be unlikely to seek you out. Many resorts also have their own radio station and website and you can usually advertise your services for a fee. This is useful if you are organising a weekly event e.g. a piste picnic or a race.

These are a few other tried and tested enterprises, which have kept ski bums in funds and even made them a healthy profit:

Apartment Letting
For those lucky enough to have enough cash at the beginning of the season to rent their own apartment: you can make a good living either running a bed and breakfast from it, or by renting out spare beds to other ski bums. In most resorts there are always people who cannot afford to rent their own place so you should have no difficulty finding people with whom to share.

Babysitting
Babysitting is available in almost every resort. In French resorts the hourly rate is about €12 an hour. The best deals are those where the family provides you with free sustenance while on duty. An affection for and understanding of children is a prerequisite but also useful is somewhere that you can take children to play, such as your own or a friend's apartment. If you are a good skier, you can offer to teach children the basics. Most tourist offices keep a list of babysitters so all you need to do is to register with them on arrival. You will however need a fixed address and a telephone on which you can be contacted. One recommended way to find clients is to offer to do a transfer for one of the big tour operators. This way you could distribute your publicity material to potential clients on the coach and having made contact they are more likely to prefer you to an unseen name on a list. Over the Christmas and New Year period babysitters can find themselves running the equivalent of a crèche or small kindergarten and making themselves a lot of money.

Hairdressing
There is always a shortage of reasonably priced hairdressers in most resorts, so any trained hairdresser, in particular if they are expert cutters, will do a thriving trade once word gets around and you can visit clients at their accommodation. The going rate in France for ad hoc hairdressing is £12+.

Massage and Beauty Therapy
It is a wonder that more ski companies do not employ them. Lotus Supertravel have a masseur/euse but he or she has to double-up as a chalet helper; Purple Ski employs a qualified physiotherapist who also helps with the chalet and driving, and Optimum Ski Courses in Les Arcs (deirdre@optimumski.com) employ a part-time masseur. For free enterprise massage it is better if you can offer a mobile service; i.e. you have a car and a collapsible (but not collapsing) padded table. Pamper Off Piste (www.pamperoffpiste.com) offers a mobile massage and beauty treatments service to clients at 'home' in their chalets. They operate in Courchevel, La Tania and Méribel and employ about a dozen staff (for details see Pamper Off Piste entry in *Other Opportunities* section). Scott Dunn employ five beauty therapists to take bookings from their clients and move around their chalets in the resort. Beauty therapists must have a recognised qualification or extensive experience.

Piste Picnics/Barbecues/
Often the reps in a resort will club together and organise a picnic for their guests. This is an

excellent money-spinner, but it requires much planning and preparation. Some reps will be all too willing for you to take the burden of organisation off their shoulders and will split the profit as they provide the readymade clientele and you provide the food and drink.

Sandwiches

Another variation on the breakfast and beer runs (see above) which involves preparing sandwiches and packed lunches for clients. It is always easy to undercut the local suppliers, especially if you can do your shopping in a hypermarket outside the resort.

T-shirts & clothing

Many an enterprising ski bum with the appropriate fashion flair has made a small fortune designing T-shirts, sweat shirts and rugby shirts and selling them in the Alps. Often they are made up in the UK and transported to the resort in vans. The truly managerial entrepreneur can organise a network of ski bums to sell them in several resorts. Salespersons should however be selected with care. It is advisable to persuade him or her to wear the product regularly. Bartenders make good sales people as they can be seen wearing the item.

Washing

Taking in washing sounds like something from the days of the 1930s Depression, but if you are lucky enough to have a washing machine in your apartment you will be able to undercut the local launderette. In Val Thorens, the going rate was £10 approx. for a load for washing only. Profits are higher if electricity and water are included in the rent.

HOTEL/CATERING STAFF WITH 'JOBS IN THE ALPS'

Jobs in the Alps (see also entry under *Other Organisations*) make no bones about the type of employee they want and the standard of work and hours expected by the employers for whom they find staff. By and large the hotels to which they send staff pay the minimum national wage and expect a proper day's work in return. At busy times (Christmas/New Year, Easter and mid-February) there will be plenty of overtime, which in Switzerland will be repaid by other days off and in France by extra payment. In some instances time off for skiing is not permitted until long after the New Year, and as a general rule these jobs pay more than British tour operators, but involve longer hours and less free time than working for a British tour operator.

None the less Jobs in the Alps have some interesting jobs and more varied than you might expect including the occasional swimming pool attendant, or the more usual night club staff and night auditor/porter, chamber staff, waiting staff and 'a lot of washer-uppers'. For those with languages, receptionist jobs may also be offered.

Bethany Smith took a year out after 'A' levels and applied to Jobs in the Alps; after an interview she was offered a job at Hotel la Cachette run by the French tour operator Nouvelles Frontières in Les Arcs:

Bethany describes getting a job through JITA

Dreaming about a whole winter spent skiing abroad was, I'm sure what got me through the final 'A' level examinations. I didn't know how to go about it until I got hold of a Jobs in the Alps leaflet. JITA have been organising work placements for years, and know exactly the type of employee they are looking for. If you are worried about hard work don't even bother applying, but for those who can handle that side of it, the benefits and fun to be had from a ski season are indescribable. But be warned it's addictive!

Having applied to JITA, I was asked to telephone to arrange an interview, which turned out to be more of an informal chat during which it was stressed that with over four applicants for every job those good with languages or with previous experience were most likely to be placed. Obviously they have to try to send the best employees they can abroad, but having said that, the variety of jobs means that it is worth applying as some posts require a lot of skills and others less.

A week after the interview I was offered a job in Les Arcs, France, as a waitress in a hotel in which nine of the other staff were British people sent by JITA and doing various jobs from dishwasher to receptionist. We all met each other for the first time on our departure from Gatwick airport on December 12th.

After 20 hours of travelling we finally arrived in Les Arcs, a week before the resort was due to open. We were shown our rooms for the winter, four boys shared a room and six girls another (thank God we all got on brilliantly!). Almost immediately after arriving and dropping our bags in the rooms, we joined the other hotel staff for a meal. The next week was spent learning our way around, getting to know the other staff we would be working with, cleaning the hotel for opening and generally settling in.

I worked as a waitress in the hotel's main restaurant along with two of the British lads which helped to make life easier as it meant I didn't have to speak French all the time. I had one and a half days off a week and in general my hours were 9-11am, midday-3pm and 7-11pm; over Christmas and New Year add on about 5 hours a day, and for the quiet times deduct 2 hours per day. This is what JITA meant by hard work! To be honest, the January lull couldn't have come soon enough.

The pay varied per month depending on the job and included full board and accommodation. Our pay was less than the French workers received, but good by comparison with working for most British tour operators. The employer also paid our return flights. JITA sent us pages of guidelines, and gave advice and help with insurance policies.

There was no time to ski until the New Year (except two hours which I was determined to sneak on Christmas Day!) but this was O.K. as it allowed us time to settle in and buy cheap skis (in my case a snowboard) and get a season's lift pass. I got a 66% discount on the normal price. Quite good when you consider what the punters pay for a week.

From January on, the weeks just merged. Work became easier because we settled into a routine and I was able to ski for a few hours every day; other workers I spoke to only managed to ski on their days off. On our days off we were able to ski at other resorts: Val d'Isère, La Plagne and La Thuile.

I have to admit that I was almost permanently in a state of tiredness but this was due as much to the skiing and late night partying as to the long working hours. Excessive doses of Pro-Plus almost kept my eyelids defying gravity. By the time May arrived we could hardly have been more different from the wan-faced, linguistically incompetent college-leavers who had arrived in Les Arcs a mere five months before. We were bronzed, healthy, almost fluent in French and had formed many lasting friendships amongst the French and British, the locals and the tourists. I enjoyed it so much that I have postponed going to university for another year to enjoy another winter in the mountains with my snowboard; this time in Canada. Thanks to JITA for getting me started.

HOTEL/CATERING JOBS THROUGH A UK TOUR COMPANY

Quite a number of tour operators including those that organise school groups' skiing own or take on for all or part of the season whole hotels, bars, nightclubs or hostels, and staff them with their own people brought out to the resort.

These establishments offer the chance for all types of catering, office and domestic staff:

bartenders, receptionists, cleaners, chamber, waiting and maintenance staff and chefs. The jobs are hard work are not well paid, but the atmosphere is informal and there is plenty of free time for skiing. The perks make it possible to ski for free while partying and generally living it up with the guests and co-workers takes up the rest of the time when not working or sleeping.

UK Overseas Handling (0870-220 2148; ukoh@ukoh.co.uk) offers management, trainee and student placements in roles involved in all aspects of hotel and restaurant management with a number of their clients. French is required for positions with a lot of customer contact.

Chefs

Chefs are something of an exception in the hotel and catering field as their professional status is generally recognised by higher pay and longer hours and therefore they have less free time for skiing. Furthermore they are very much the key to the success of clients' holidays and need to be extremely efficient and well trained.

Positions are often advertised in the *Caterer and Hotel Keeper* or on the ski job websites. Or, you can just trawl through the tour operator websites which have chalet hotels or which offer gourmet catered chalets. Hours for chefs are usually 9am-12.30pm and 4-8.30pm with one day off a week. Pay varies among companies but is usually in the bracket of £90-£240 per week plus board and lodging.

Ski companies that employ one or more chefs include: Alpine Tracks, Belvedere Chalets, Crystal, Equity Travel, First Choice, Inghams, Masterski, Optimum Ski Courses, Purple Ski, Ski Chamois, Ski Company, Ski Miquel, Ski Olympic, Snowcoach, TJM, Tops/Ski Plan, Wasteland Ski and YSE. For companies' exact requirements, please see *Working for Tour Operators* section.

Some companies however offer chefs a less strenuous work schedule with more time for skiing and a correspondingly smaller wage. Highest professional standards are however still expected. Veronica Goff and Simon Joyce, the former with a BTEC in hotel management and the latter City and Guilds qualified, worked for Bladon Lines' Hotel de la Fôret in Val d'Isère. Both had worked before for BL in Courchevel at the Hotel Saint Louis. They finished by 10.30am in the morning and were free to ski until about 5pm. Their evening hours were 6pm to 9.30pm. As they pointed out, their hours were shorter than the chalet girls and chalet hostesses who generally finished much later at night. Once the season was under way, and the routine established they were left to run their own kitchens. There is a 10% loyalty bonus for the second season. Head chef appointments are generally paid slightly better. Bladon Lines is part of Inghams.

Useful Contact

Coolworks.com – website for jobs in US ski resorts.

HOTEL/CATERING STAFF – JOBS FOUND ON THE SPOT

Hotels, restaurants, bars, shops and nightclubs are regular standbys for ski bums and others looking for casual work to extend a working holiday. In ski resorts such jobs can be hard to come by and it is worth taking anything you are offered from a few hours washing up in the evening in exchange for a meal (and if you are lucky a room), to a full eight-hour day in a mountain restaurant which will be reasonably paid hard work and may well start off with a trek up the mountain laden down with huge piles of provisions and end skiing down in the dark long after the lifts have closed. With the exceptions of Spain, Andorra and Eastern Europe it is possible to find a catering job in all countries throughout the winter season; experience is a great help and languages pretty well essential (except for washing up).

There can be problems with work permits (details under the specific countries) but where these are needed and not easily forthcoming there are plenty of employers who will still take on help, particularly over Christmas, New Year and the mid-February half-term, on an unofficial basis. You are very likely to receive only board and accommodation and if you are paid it will be at a rate well below the official minimum. In addition you will most likely be uninsured. However, if you are looking for a job that will allow you time to ski as well, this can still work out well so long as you make sure you know exactly where you stand.

The best way to fix up a full-time job of this kind with a permit, if needed, is to actually go out to the resort at the end of the summer or in November and approach employers in person then. This can be done by e-mail (get a list of hotels etc. from the local tourist office website), but application in person is far more effective as employers are more likely to employ someone they have met. If this is difficult, get there in the first two weeks of December before the season starts or as early in the season as possible.

If you are not available in December, mid-January can also be a good time; local students are back at college and after the New Year rush there will be employees who cannot take the pace dropping out.

There is quite a lot of casual work going on in some ski resorts during the summer with chalets and hotels needing redecorating and refurbishing; if you have the time to find a job of this sort during July and August you are perfectly placed to make the necessary contacts for fixing a job for the winter. The golden rule is to pick a resort, which has a high proportion of British skiers in it unless of course you possess linguistic talents.

Besides 'knocking on doors', visit the local tourist office, watch out for notice boards in supermarkets and bars and get the local papers where there are often many advertisements for jobs. Barbara Cameron from Canada had no particular contacts to help her get a job when she arrived in Verbier but she found a job as a chambermaid at the Hotel Fougère in La Tournaz, a little village that shares the Verbier skiing complex, through an advertisement in *La Nouvelliste* (www.nouvelliste.ch), a daily paper distributed in the Valais canton.

It requires hard work and ingenuity to find a job on the spot, but plenty of people succeed; the tourist offices in some resorts have an employment service and it is important to get to know the local reps as they are often the first to hear of a vacancy that comes up.

MAINTENANCE AND BUILDINGS OFFICER/PLONGEUR

Otherwise known as MBOs (also short for muscle-bound oafs), snowmen, *homme tout main* etc, these are essentially jacks of all trades. The job will entail washing up, clearing snow, basic maintenance, getting fresh bread early in the morning, arranging picnics, serving behind the bar, driving, collecting luggage and helping generally with changeovers and transfers. The work is often associated with jumbo chalets, or chalet/hotels, which will sleep upwards of 24 people. There is a good chance for people between school and university, though some companies look for people a bit older. Pay will be £60+ per week plus the usual skiing perks. Electrical, mechanical or plumbing skills as well as a strong physique can help land this kind of job.

There is also scope for getting one of these jobs in the resort during the season. It is surprising how often people get sick or injured and it is always worthwhile being well in with the local reps in case an opportunity arises. Start off by offering to help carry a few suitcases on changeover day or assist an injured customer getting to the doctor or hospital. There are plenty of odd jobs which fully-employed staff are pleased to have help with and while initially your part-time work may only be rewarded with a few drinks or a free meal it can lead to better things and a steady job. Companies that employ MBOs include: Inghams, Ski Total, Skiworld, YSE and Skibound.

MUSICIAN

There are opportunities for good musicians in almost any ski resort if you are prepared to take the chance that the music you play will prove popular and you are of a good professional standard. However, while it may make sense for a single guitarist or fiddle player to take his instrument along and try a few evenings' work in the local bars, the cost of transporting the equipment for an entire group is prohibitive and not recommended unless you have a definite contract.

Nick, Kirk and Colin, known as the 'Cellmates', saw an advertisement in *Melody Maker* and fixed up a job before the season started, to play in Mayrhofen. They received a small weekly wage, board and lodging and a free flight, but subsequently found it more profitable to go freelance. They reported:

> *Don't turn up on spec unless you have really good contacts already, as we did, having worked under contract previously. Competition is very stiff, transport is a problem and it can be really difficult to get equipment repaired as music shops are few and far between.*

There is also a reasonable chance of employment for talented and versatile pianists in the Alps in grand hotels and intimate piano bars. John Carter (of Les Chalets de St. Martin; les.chalets@virgin.net) proprietor of the Pourquoi Pas bar in St. Martin de Belleville, in the Trois Vallées employs a pianist for five evenings a week to work from 4pm-7pm. From 7pm-9pm, the pianist stands in for the chalet staff while they take a break; he or she then has a couple of hours break themselves and plays on from 11pm to 1pm. All this for £100 per week plus tips, shared accommodation, ski pass, insurance and return travel to the UK. The job can be negotiated on the spot or by contacting John Carter in France (☎04 79 08 91 77; fax 04 79 01 08 75). L'Avalanche in Alpe d'Huez is just one of the many Alpine bars with a resident pianist.

British tour companies occasionally recruit musicians: Skibound has employed guitarists with additional flair in the vocal department .

NANNY/CHILDCARE ASSISTANT

Over the last few years a number of British tour operators have been vying with each other for the growing market in family skiing holidays whereby parents can take their children on holiday with them yet be able to ski and dine on their own while their offspring have a whale of a time in the hands of qualified others for most of each day. Around 30 operators now run their own crèches for their clients' progeny. From the employment point of view this is excellent news for qualified NNEBs or SRNs with childcare experience. Such a service is usually provided in the chalet or in a special crèche. The nanny may also have to deliver and retrieve older children from ski school and night-time baby-sitting may also be included in their duties.

Gemma Jobes was aged 21 with an NNEB qualification when she worked as a nanny for Simply Ski (now Crystal Finest) in Bad Hofgastein, Austria for two seasons. She applied for the job through the website Natives.com.

> **Gemma Jobes describes her job as a tour operator nanny**
> *It is much easier being a nanny in ski resort than it is in the UK. In Bad Hofgastein I worked from 8.30am to 5pm, compared with 7.30am-6pm four and half days a week in the UK which I am finding hard work. Sometimes I was the only nanny and looked after 3 children and sometimes I worked with another nanny and we had six children between us. I often got small gifts and tips from parents whose children I was looking*

> *after; and twice I was offered jobs as a family nanny by Simply Ski's guests. I loved the work and the snow and the fact that the job was mainly outdoors. I had two days off a week, Wednesdays and some Saturdays, when I skied all day. The season is a wonderful way of making contact with people from all over the world working in the resort. I am spending holidays this summer in America and New Zealand where I have been invited by friends I met in Bad Hofgastein.*

Gemma was planning to do a business degree this autumn. Ultimately she plans to run her own chalet in Bad Hofgastein.

A specialist training and recruitment agency that places qualified and/or experienced nannies with British tour operators in the Alps and on the Mediterranean is Nannies Abroad Ltd (Abbots Worthy House, Abbots Worthy, Winchester S021 1DR; 01962-882299; fax 01962-881888; michele@nanniesabroad.com) finds UK nannies jobs with ski tour operators throughout Europe. The nannies remain employees of Nannies Abroad rather than the tour operator. The advantage of this for the nannies is that they have the backing of an organisation that takes care of their interests and protects their working conditions. Nannies Abroad also runs its own, purpose-built crèche in the resort of Les Gets, Portes du Soleil, France and recruits nannies holding the relevant childcare qualifications (NNEB or DPP or equivalent). The crèche caters for 21 children from three months to eight years old and it has a staff of eight.

Amongst the chalet companies that employ nannies, Esprit (www.esprit-holidays.co.uk), most of whose chalets are in France, still make a feature of their childcare provision. Other companies providing a childcare service include: Club Med (08453 67 67 67), Collineige (info@collineige.com), Crystal Finest (020 8939 0843), Family Ski Company (enquiries@familyski.co.uk), Le Ski (mail@leski.com), Mark Warner (www.markwarner-recruitment.co.uk), Lotus Supertravel (alice@lotusgroup.co.uk), Meriski (www.meriski. co.uk), Powder Byrne (www.powderbyrne.co.uk), Scott Dunn Ski (ski@scottdunn.com), Simon Butler Skiing (www.simonbutlerskiing.co.uk), Ski Barrett-Boyce (www.skibb. com), Ski Beat (www.skibeat.co.uk), Ski Chamois (www.skichamois.co.uk), Ski Famille (www.skifamille.co.uk), Ski Hillwood (01923-290700), Ski Hiver (www.skihiver.co.uk), Ski Peak (www.skipeak.com), Snowbizz (www.snowbizz.co.uk), Snowline, Thomson Ski & Snowboarding (www.thomson-ski.co.uk) and VIP (www.valdisere.co.uk).

There exist two other possibilities for employment apart from tour operators' chalet crèches. Many resort hotels have their own crèches and there are also independent kindergartens in some resorts principally in France and Austria. However knowledge of foreign languages would be essential to land a job in either of these.

One thing that has changed in the last few years is that ski companies are now insistent on nannies having the relevant childcare qualifications. You can no longer scrape by on a lot of experience working with children without a recognised qualification.

For babysitting, see the *Free Enterprise* section above.

OFFICE STAFF

For British Ski Companies in the Resort

Working in an office is not everyone's idea of an ideal job in a ski resort, but if this is where your skills and you speak more than basic French, German or Italian, lie then it might be worth considering. Few British companies employ full-time office staff in the resort, but worth trying are First Choice (office administrative assistants), Tops/Ski Plan (office administrator), Interski (après ski co-ordinator), PGL (office staff) and Cordon Rouge (office administration assistant).

For British Ski Companies in the UK

Although this category of work does not usually involve working in a ski resort it is worth considering if you are looking for a job which gives office staff the opportunity for subsidised skiing during the winter. Many staff at head offices have graduated from the slopes having previously worked as reps or chalet staff, but it can work the other way too. Soon after leaving university, Colin Mathews saw an advertisement in *The Times* for a job with Snowtime. He managed to get transferred to Méribel where he worked as a guide/rep for two seasons. He then started his own company in Méribel – Meriski.

For Letting Agencies in the Resort.

Many French resorts have a huge selection of self-catering apartments in blocks, many of which are handled by large agencies which have a branch in the resort itself and a chain of offices, or their central office elsewhere in France. It is possible for those with fluent English/French minimum, (additional languages are an asset) to work for them in the resort office dealing with clients and arranging letting contracts.

Those with suitable linguistic skills can contact companies including Maeva, Sogim, Les Domaines du Soleil and Pierre et Vacances in the resorts.

RESORT REPRESENTATIVE

Reps are the linchpin of a tour company's operation; they need to combine charm to keep the customers happy with the ability to be effective in sorting out the chaos which is occasionally inevitable in the package holiday business. If a client's suitcase has gone to Rome instead of Milan or Zürich instead of Geneva, charm will do a lot to alleviate the immediate situation; but if you cannot get it back you have failed.

Ski reps generally speaking will need to be at least 21 years of age with many companies looking for people over 24. They should speak one or more foreign languages, French, German, Italian and Spanish be the most obviously useful, and if possible have experience either as a rep or a chalet person. Some of the larger companies, among them Thomson, Lotus Supertravel, Crystal, Thomson and Simply Travel, Panorama and First Choice, have a major summer programme and can offer the winter rep jobs first to people who have previously worked a summer for them.

A resort representative is responsible for meeting groups at the airport, escorting them to their accommodation and giving customers all the necessary information about the resort they are staying in. They will also deal with the issuing of skiing equipment and ski passes and generally look after the welfare of the customers during the holiday. Reps establish an 'office hour' every evening, usually in some convenient café or bar, or sometimes at the hotel which is accommodating the majority of clients. They also aim to eat with the clients at a different hotel or chalet every evening so everyone knows they are about and has the opportunity to discuss any problems. If the company concerned has catered chalets the rep will very likely be responsible for the chalet staff and have to deal with any problems they cannot solve, and check the accounts.

Another manor function of the reps is to arrange evening entertainment such as fondue evenings, torchlight toboggan races and prize giving parties on the last night after the ski class races. These can be an important source of income for the ski companies and of commission for the reps.

A number of organisers use their reps as part-time ski guides (see below), but whether or not this is so, reps will generally be free to ski most afternoons except on changeover days and the days they are busy repatriating the injured or visiting them in the local hospital. Changeover day is long and tiring, often involving a round trip coach journey to the airport of from four to nine hours, plus all the worries of seeing that everyone is ready to leave on time, dealing with outgoing passenger, Mrs. Smith who has lost her passport, or packed it at the bottom of her suitcase, and incoming passenger, Andrew James, whose luggage has not arrived on the plane and whose father is throwing a wobbly.

Generally, reps are paid from £60 to £150 per week plus free skiing, travel and insurance, plus accommodation always and meals sometimes. The rep relies heavily on commission from ski shops, restaurants and social activities etc. to boost his or her pay.

SHOP ASSISTANT

Shops of any kind in resorts with a high proportion of British skiers will often take on an English-speaking assistant to help serve the customers. Shoe shops, boutiques, photography shops are all worth trying. The problem with shop work is that while the job is usually reasonably well paid, the business hours tend to severely restrict the time available for skiing.

SKI GUIDE

Many British ski companies employ ski guides (also called ski hosts, ski companions, ski socialisers, ski leaders etc) to ski alongside their clients and show them around the the slopes. It is a service intended to help the clients get the most out of their week's skiing holiday without wasting the first two or three days in getting acquainted with the layout of the runs. Companies that employ ski guides include Alpine Tracks (01248-717440), Belvedere Chalets (01264 738257), Discover Verbier (0870 874 6840), Equity Travel (01273-886911), First Choice (0870 750 1204), Inghams (020-8780 4400), Masterski (020-8942 9442), Oxford Ski Company (0870 787 1785), Purple Ski (01885-488799), Ski Chamois (01302-369006), Ski Miquel (01457-821200), Ski Olympic (01302-328820), Ski Peak (01428 608070), Ski Power (01737-823232), Ski Weekend (08700 600 615), Snowline (020 8870 4807), Snowcoach (01727-866177), Specialist Holiday Group (0870 888 0028), Tops/Ski Plan (01273-774778) and YSE (0845 122 1414).

Some companies insist that their ski guides have a BASI III qualification. Others do not demand any qualifications but stipulate only that the guide must be a good/advanced skier. Authorities in the resorts have long objected to British tour operators having their own ski guides on the basis that they take clients off piste without being trained to do so and that the word 'guide' implies an expertise and knowledge of mountain safety, which most do not possess. You can enrol on mountain safety and avalanche safety courses through specialists such as Mountain Tracks (020 8877 5773). Local mountain guides on the other hand are highly qualified and experienced professionals.

Rob Fowler, who is 28 and has a degree in Human Geography from Leicester, formerly worked as a School Programme Manager for Challenge Expeditions. He worked as a ski host for Silver Ski in Val d'Isère, Tignes and Méribel and for Mark Warner in Courchevel. He is also a qualified ski instructor (BASI III).

> **Rob Fowler loves ski hosting and says this makes a good ski host**
> *If you become ski host just because it enables you to get paid for skiing, forget it as you will not make a good host. A host has to be someone who enjoys skiing with people of different levels, and who are often not as good as you are. If all you want to do is practise your skiing or boarding, get a ski bum's job that allows you to ski when, where and how you want.*
>
> *Ski companies vary in their policy towards off piste skiing. Mark Warner is very strict about it and any ski host caught off piste with guests will be fired. Other companies say that if the guests want to go off piste then the ski host is allowed to accompany them on a 'sociable' basis. As an employee of the*

company I would keep to company policy. However, for me the vital issue is good mountain practice; for instance I would not ski off piste with anyone who did not know how to use their transceiver for locating someone buried in an avalanche.

I admit I have a bit of a bee in my bonnet about safety. Ignorance is bliss until it kills you. There are many more deaths in ski resorts, mostly from avalanches off piste than we hear about over here.

Rob also offers some tips to would-be ski hosts
Before you accept a ski host job check whether the company covers the cost of getting you out to the resort and back; some do, some don't. If they don't then you can most probably get a lift through Natives.com by using their website chatroom, which makes organising a lift easy. Also, watch out for whether ski companies expect you to double-up ski hosting and several other jobs such as maintenance or chalet hosting. Companies vary greatly on this: for instance some will have you ski hosting for five full days a week and helping out on transfer days and serving and washing up every evening in the chalets; while others will have you ski hosting every day and dining with the guests and helping out in the chalets just a couple of evenings.

I would recommend anyone going to work in a ski resort as a ski guide or anything else and who intends to ski off piste to take mountain safety very seriously. There are mountain safety courses you can do – in the UK through specialist,s and the Ski Club of Great Britain also run courses. In Val d'Isère you can ask about Henry's Avalanche Courses. You need to know how to use the contents of your safety pack; your life or your buddies' lives could depend on it.

Rob has fixed up a job with Le Ski in Val d'Isère or Courchevel, for a second season in the Alps. He is preparing to take more instructor exams in Tignes to take him to BASI II level and then he wants to do some ski instructing in New Zealand. He says that working in a ski resort has brought many things together for him and he has plans to be running his own multi sports holiday company, possibly in Canada, within the next three years.

Useful Address
Mountain Tracks Alpine Skills: 3 Broomhill Road, London SW18 4JQ; (☎020 8877 5773; fax 020 8877 5771; e-mail Chris@mountaintracks.co.uk.). Experts in guided mountain adventure that run Alpine Skills courses including Introductory and Advanced Avalanche Awareness, Winter Skills, Glacier Travel and Crevasse Rescue, Mountain Awareness and Ski Hosting. Further details from the above address or website.

SKI/SNOWBOARD INSTRUCTOR

Considering this is the glamour job *par excellence* of the ski slopes, it is perhaps incongruous that there has been so much unseemly spatting surrounding the efforts of British ski and board instructors to establish themselves in the Alps. The problems of British instructors were compounded by poor snow records in the Alps in recent years, which meant there were too many instructors chasing too few jobs. This brought grievances between BASI (the British Association of Snowsport Instructors) and the ESF (the French instructors' association) to a head. The root of the problem was that unlike the Austrians and Swiss who virtually grow up on skis, British instructors find the training and qualifications both time-consuming and expensive to achieve. For many years the British qualification, even the top level, was considered inferior to that achieved by Alpine instructors because it did not include off-piste and mountain training. The differences with the ESF were resolved (sort of) by means of a test (*test technique*). Anyone who has reached National Ski Teacher (the top BASI) qualification can work in France for four years after which they have to upgrade to International Ski Teacher. However, in order to satisfy rigorous French requirements the instructor has to pass the Test Technique, which French instructors have to pass before gaining their licence. With this formidable test under their belt in addition to the top BASI qualification, British instructors can operate in France on the same basis as top-qualified French instructors. However, the test is so exacting that success can be elusive for all but a minority.

The French decision to accept the BASI grade has reduced a major obstacle for British Instructors and British ski schools which have been operating in France (perfectly legitimately under European law, which recognises our qualification) but have nevertheless been subjected to some very high-handed behaviour by French counterparts. Gendarmes were seen swooping on British instructors such as those working for Ski Cocktail (run by Yves Lapreyere) in Courchevel and arresting them in front of their horrified class.

Other British ski schools have been set up in the French Alps. The British Alpine School (BASS) is based in Les Gets +33 (0)4 50 79 85 42;lesgets@britishskischool.com; www. britishskischool.com and Morzine and a total of eight schools in the French Alps. New Generation (www.skinewgen.com) was started in Courchevel 1650 in 1998/99 and has ski schools in Courchevel 1850, Méribel, Val d'Isère and Les Arcs. In Serre Chevalier there is Eurekaski (www.eurekaski.com; info@eurekaski.com or telephone 01326 375710 for details). Look out also for the new Development Centre (www.tdcski.com) in Val d'Isère. The newer schools have been set up by small groups of British ski instructors. Older, established ski schools with a preponderance of British staff include: Masterclass (www. masterclass.f9.co.uk) in Alpe d'Huez, Ski Supreme (www.supremeski.com) in Courchevel 1850, and the British Alpine Ski School (see above).

Other Grade I (the highest) BASI qualified instructors with full local qualifications operate on an individual basis in several, mainly French resorts; for instance Ali Ross in Tignes (www.alirossskiingclinics.com). There is now scope for British instructors in France and elsewhere in the Alps as the other Alpine nations follow France's lead. For exact details see the BASI entry at the beginning of *Working for Other Organisations*.

Antonia Lee-Bapty of Snowtec in Val d'Isère highlights the programme in Val d'Isère which will enable people based in that resort to take their ski instructor qualifications while they are working. On most ski instructor programmes you cannot do both at the same time. Details below.

Ski Astons (01905-829200; www.skiastons.co.uk) has ski and snowboard instructor vacancies and offers subsidised skiing, snowboarding and first aid courses, subsidised staff training weeks and performance courses and reduced ski vacations for instructors.

At the height of the season there are some 400 instructors teaching in the Cairngorms alone and many thousands in Europe. There are also opportunities for work further afield including in North America and Australasia. Outbreak Adventure (www.outbreak-adventure.com; rob@outbreak-adventure.com) recruits all types of staff including ski and board instructors for resorts in North America.

EU citizens working in Switzerland will require either a seasonal work permit issued or the new one year residence permit both of which can be applied for on the spot. Although France has agreed to accept British qualified instructors on the same basis as nationals (see above), it will probably be some time before it becomes noticeably easier to penetrate the closed ranks of the Swiss and Austrian ski schools. Other countries where local traditions are less firmly rooted in skiing and where it may be easier to get jobs are Andorra and Spain, especially around the height of the season at Christmas, New Year and February half-term. Full details of these opportunities are given in the section *Finding a Job on the Spot*. For further details of all BASI qualifications and how to get them, see the BASI entry in *Other Organisations*.

A select number of British companies also have a small number of their own professionally qualified ski instructors; these include Fresh Tracks (part of the Ski Club of Great Britain).

Companies that employ large numbers of ski instructors include: Interski and Ski Europe. Ski Gower employs 20 volunteer instructors who work for keep. Other companies employ a handful of instructors; Simon Butler skiing employ four. See *British Tour Operators* section for more details.

BASI News, the newsletter of BASI, is worth looking at for ski instructor jobs and even summer jobs in the Alps.

Useful Website
www.snowsportrecruitment.com – is a free recruitment site for those looking for employment in the snowsport sector. The website has four zones: jobs, training, resources and instructor's directory.

SNOWBOARD INSTRUCTOR
Snowboarding is probably the fastest growing sport in the world and in view of this, anyone who can instruct in snowboarding is employable from the Cairngorms to Cerler and from Norway to New Zealand. It is possible to do snowboarder instructor courses on dry slopes in the UK and on the Kaprun Glacier in Austria. Further details on all aspects of the sport can be obtained from the British Ski and Snowboard Federation (0131-445 7676; www.snowsportgb.com; info@snowsportgb.com).

INSTRUCTOR COURSE ORGANISERS
DEUTSCH-INSTITUT TIROL: Am Sandhügel 2, 6370 Kitzbühel, Austria; ☎53-56 712 74; fax 53 56 723 63; office@deutschinstitut.com; www.gap-year.at. Offers a combination of German language and ski and snowboard instruction in a course specially aimed at gap year people. For further details see the section on Kitzbuhel.

GAP SPORTS: Willow Bank House, 84 Station Road, Marlow, Bucks SL7 1NX; ☎0870 837 9797; info@gapsports.com; www.gapsports.com. 11-week Ski and Snowboard Instructor Courses in Quebec: Mont Sainte-Anne and British Columbia: Whistler. Includes 2 weeks paid work experience.

ICE: Work at the same time as getting your ski instructor training and grade. A permanent BASI (British Association of Snowsport Instructors) training centre is located in Val d'Isère called The International Centre of Excellence for Snowsport Instructors. ICE (www.icesi. org) is a BASI European Business Partner in the Alps, licensed to train and grade BASI instructors to the same high standards as are expected on BASI run courses. Students can form their own courses. This means those working in the resort can take part in modular based courses over a period of time. Alternatively, they can join one of the packaged courses including an extensive Gap Year and Career Break programme which includes the BASI course and training. Call ☎0870 760 7360; ask for Rupert.

THE INTERNATIONAL ACADEMY: King's Place, 12-42 Wood Street, Kingston-upon-Thames, Surrey KT1 IJY; ☎0870 060 1381; fax 020-8939 0411; info@ theinternationalacademy.com; www.theinternationalacademy.com. Organises professional ski and snowboard instructor courses in Canada (Whistler-Blackcomb) and Banff/Lake Louise. Snowsports also available in the summer months at Cardrona, New Zealand. Gain recognised CSIA, CASI or NZSIA qualifications. A five-week ski or snowboard course in Canada costs £4,390 and 12 weeks £6,650. Also organises training towards PADI diving instructor qualifications and private pilot licence.

NONSTOPSKI.COM: Nonstop Ski and Snowboard, Shakespeare House, 168 Lavender Hill, London SW11 5TF; ☎0870 241 8070; info@nonstopski.com. Offers ski and snowboard instructor courses and mountain survival techniques in Fernie Red Mountain and Banff in the Canadian Rockies. Includes intensive avalanche and mountain safety course. Instructor courses last three, six and twelve weeks.

PEAK LEADERS: Peak Leaders UK Ltd., Mansfield, Strathmiglo, Fife, KY14 7QE; ☎01337-860079; fax 01337-868 079 176; www.peakleaders.co.uk; info@peakladers. co.uk. Instructor courses in Canada, Switzerland, France, Argentina and New Zealand.

ROOKIE ACADEMY: PO Box 402, Wanaka, New Zealand; www.rookieacademy.com. Offers ski and snowboard instructor training in New Zealand (info@rookieacademy.co.nz) and Keystone, Colorado USA (Anthony@rookieacademy.com).

SKI INSTRUCTOR TRAINING: offers ski and snowboard instructor training in Queenstown, New Zealand. Courses run from June to September. E-mail www.skiinstructortraining.co.nz or info@snowboardinstructortraining.co.nz).

SKI LE GAP: 220 chemin Wheeler, Mont Tremblant, Québec, Canada J8E 1V3; UK freephone 0800 328 0345; fax +1-819-425 7074; email info@skilegap.com.Based in Canada www.skilegap.com offers an instructor programme at Mont Tremblant for British gap year students.

SKI YOUR BEST: offers summer and winter instructor courses; www.skiyourbest.com.

WARREN SMITH SKI ACADEMY: UK office: ☎01525-374757; Swiss office: ☎07 93 59 65 66; sales@sportssynergy.com. Runs a nine-week Gap Ski Instructor Course in association with BASI which takes place in Verbier. The course is designed to take successful students to BASI III level. Chalet accommodation and meals as well as teaching practice at the Adrenaline Ski School (www.adrenaline-verbier.ch). Successful students are invited back for a full season contract. The courses take place January to March; cost £6,499.

SKI TECHNICIAN

Most ski shops or rental operators hire ski technicians (ski techs) to fit boots and skis correctly for clients as well as for servicing and repairing skis. It is a skilled job but does not take long to learn. A well-known course provider in the UK is Anything Technical

Ltd run by Andy Taylor. His company Anything Technical (01539-734701) offers courses running for 1,2 or 3 days, twelve times a year in Basingstoke at the headquarters of Salomon, or at the Anything Technical workshop in Kendal. Courses cost from £175 per day. The courses are recognised by the main UK retailers and overseas employers and may be helpful in your search for a job as a ski tech as a certificate of attendance is awarded for each day. They are also a great way to try out all the new equipment and to purchase repair equipment at reduced prices. You can enquire and book direct by calling 01539-734701 or book on www.natives.co.uk/skijobs/skitech/.

British ski hire shops may take on school or college leavers. Scottish resorts have a lot of hire shops and may take on one or two helpers each for the winter. If applicants do not have training they are usually sent on a course.

To get a job fitting abroad or for a company like Skibound organising school parties you will have to have had experience or training but there are many English-speaking people (particularly Australians and Canadians), who have got these jobs abroad either full or part-time. Snow Fun which has fifteen shops spread through Val d'Isère and Tignes employ English technicians and non EU nationals with a work permit as do Precision Ski Shops in Val d'Isère. Ski Higher has five shops in the Portes du Soleil and Three Valleys ski areas and operates a mobile ski and board service. Further details on jobs with Snow Fun and Ski Higher in the section *Working Through Other Organisations*. The rule is to pick the resorts with the highest numbers of British punters where being able to speak English is a definite advantage to the shop manager. Obviously, it is extremely useful to have another language as well. Working for a school party organisation will give you more time off for skiing than working in a local shop, but increasingly school group organisers are using local facilities instead of supplying their own equipment.

SNOW CLEARING

This can be an official job like the one Mark Stephenson got in Crans Montana keeping the surrounds of an apartment block clear for which he was provided with a machine, SFr 15 an hour and endless tots of alcohol from sympathetic residents; or it can be unofficial where someone goes round knocking on doors offering his services – another regular stand-by for ski bums. There is a convenient law in Switzerland, which insists that snow shall be cleared off all roofs before it gets two metres deep.

TEACHING ENGLISH

A surprising number of people manage to get jobs in ski resorts teaching English. Once of these, Richard Williams a modern languages undergraduate at Oxford got a job in Kitzbühel. Remember when applying for jobs teaching English that it will not impress if you said that skiing was your motivation in applying. Richard was on a nine-month assignment and had a wonderful time with lots of skiing.

Possibilities include working for language schools in mountain resorts or basing yourself somewhere within easy access to them like Geneva, Munich, Bergamo, etc. For instance, the Centre Andorra de Llengues (centrandorra.lang@andorra.ad) is in Andorra la Vella near the Principality's ski resorts.

Other people have less formal arrangements – just helping out the local English teacher in exchange for board and lodging like David Moore in Norway. There is also scope for advertising locally on notice boards and in newspapers to give private English lessons to visitors or residents at £8-£10 per hour. Try writing polite letters to local schools.

RECRUITMENT AGENCIES & WEBSITES

The following agencies and websites have expertise in ski resort and ski job placements:

Free Radicals: www.freeradicals.co.uk; info@freeradicals.co.uk (☎07968 183848; 1 December-1 May in France ☎+33 (0)613 268 224) is an independent ski recruitment specialist describing itself as a 'one stop shop' for finding ski jobs throughout Europe and America. Ski companies looking for staff advertise on the site and you can apply online. The site also has links for seasonal accommodation, insurance for the season, current chalet chef courses and more. You should contact them by e-mail (info@freeradicals.co.uk),

Jobs in the Alps: (www.jobs-in-the-alps.co.uk; info@jobs-in-the-alps.co.uk) is an employment agency that has been arranging hotel jobs in Alpine resorts since 1972. For details see Other Organisations.

Natives: (☎020-8785 3888 or 08700 463377; www.natives.co.uk; jobs@natives.co.uk). Website includes profiles of ski companies and the positions they have available. There are jobs for cooks, chefs, managers and nannies. Also operates ski cook courses with a job with a ski company guaranteed if you pass the course.

SeasonWorkers: (www.seasonworkers.com). The Season Workers website has a very wide range of ski resort work on offer. You can chat to experienced workers, browse company files, apply direct from the website, and have jobs emailed to you via the free Season Workers newsletter. There is even a Friends Reunited style section for regaining contact with old friends from seasons past. Season Workers has won an award every year since it started in 2003 and with over 120,000 visitors per month is one of the most popular sites of its kind in the UK.

Ski Connection: www.skiconnection.co.uk; e-mail jobs@skiconnection.co.uk; ☎0870 766 9194 or +44 20 73727740. SkiConnection specialises in seasonal winter recruitment. The website has over 100 ski operators advertising approximately 2000 vacancies per season. In addition to jobs vacant, the site has ski operator profiles, job descriptions, resort reviews, chalet girl tips, menu planning advice and visa information. The site is free to use and allows you to apply for posts directly online. For a small fee (£10) candidates are able to create an online CV with photograph and apply for jobs online. Website run by Amanda Zuydervelt.

Skistaff: Farm View House, 45 Farm View, Yately, Hampshire GU46 6HU; ☎0870 432 8030 (office hours only); work@skistaff.co.uk; www.skistaff.co.uk. Specialists in placements Europe-wide.

Voovs.com Ltd: 26 Vine Close, Welwyn Garden City, Herts. AL8 7PS; ☎01707-396511; info@voovs.com; www.voovs.com. Offers ski resort jobs in chalets, hotels, bars, reps, instructors, nannies and technicians from December to April, working with both large and smaller companies to offer a varied range of jobs. Other services offered include online CV registration, useful tips and advice on which ski resort jobs to apply for, interview and menu planning tips etc. plus help with job descriptions and interviews. Wages from £50 per week; six-day week ski pass, accommodation and transfers to the resort. Minimum age is 18. Also offers beach front, camping and activity jobs in summer including beach reps, instructors nannies, chefs, bar and hotel staff from April to October. Also cruise ship and yachting jobs and voluntary work.

A Job Before You Go

**Working for a
tour operator, agency
or other organisation**

Work With Ski Tour Operators

AIRTOURS HOLIDAYS

Airtours Holidays was founded in 1980 and is now part of a parent group MyTravel, which also includes Panorama Holidays. Airtours Holidays employs approximately 900 staff overseas of which over 100 work on the ski programme. The ski programme covers over 50 resorts in eight countries: Andorra, Austria, Canada, France, Italy, Spain, Switzerland and the USA.

According to their overseas recruitment department they no longer recruit externally for the ski programmes and their chalet hosts are provided by NBV (see separate listing for NBV).

ALPINE ACTION LTD

Marine Suite, The Old Town Hall, Southwick, West Sussex, BN42 4AX; 01273-597940; fax 01273-597910; sales@alpineaction.co.uk; www.alpineaction. co.uk.

Family run business CAA/ATOL and AITO credited, with 8 chalets in Méribel and La Tania in the Three Valleys, France. Employs 20-22 in-resort staff. Couples and singles required for hosting chalets, must have chalet cookery course qualifications. Phone or e-mail for an application form and menu plan.

ALPINE ELEMENTS

1 Risborough Street, London SE1 OHF; ☎08700 111360; info@alpineelements. co.uk; www.alpineelements.co.uk.

Alpine Elements arrange chalet and self catering holidays in Chamonix, Morzine, Les Gets, Méribel, Alpe d'Huez, Val d'Isère, Les Arcs, Courchevel and Tignes in France and Whistler in Canada. 65 staff are employed in the resorts annually: **chalet hosts, resort managers, hotel chefs** and **reps**. Staff should be 18+ and be British passport holders. Reps must hold a clean driving licence. Staff get two weeks of training in France and the UK. There is also a Summer Alpine programme in France from May to September and resort staff often stay to work in the summer as well.

Applicants should send a letter and CV to the above address or e-mail for the attenton of Mr. G Niedermann.

ALPINE TRACKS

40 High Street, Menai Bridge, Anglesey LL59 5EF; ☎01248-717440; fax 01248-717441; sales@alpinetracks.com; www.alpinetracks.com.

Alpine Tracks began operating in 1998 and offers chalet, hotel and short breaks in Morzine (France), Champéry (Switzerland), Breckenridge (USA) and Lech (Austria). Up to 30 staff are recruited:

Chefs: chefs to run 18-bed chalet hotel; couples are preferred to run five and six bedroom chalets.

Other staff: **chalet staff, ski guides, drivers, bar persons, ski techs**. All personnel should have the relevant qualifications.

Applications from suitable Britons, Australians, North Americans, New Zealanders etc. welcomed from 1 May for work starting 1 December. Apply to Bethan Scott or Duncan

Gilroy on 01248-717440 or e-mail bethan@alpinetracks.com or Duncan@alpinetracks.com.

ALTITUDE HOLIDAYS
Suite 787, 2 Old Brompton Road, London SW7 3DQ; ☎0870 870 7669; fax 0870-870 7668; Richard@altitudeholidays.com; www.altitude holidays.com.
Altitude holidays is a small, catered chalet company. Several ski staff employed including **chalet chefs**. Most jobs are varied and involve a variety of roles, many of which involve client contact, some of which involve working on your own. If you are employed as a chalet chef you will not stay in one chalet for the season, you will have some weeks cooking one off meals for groups of people in smaller apartments. Other duties include airport transfers (minibus driving), checking clients in and out of apartments, shopping, laundry, ironing, and general administration. Having basic (or better) French would be advantageous, but is not essential. Personality and experience most important.

Applications at any time of year to Richard Evans at the above address.

BALKAN HOLIDAYS
Sofia House, 19 Conduit Street, London WIS 2BH; ☎020-7543 5555; www.balkanholidays.co.uk.
Balkan Holidays has been operating since 1967. Their ski packages to Bulgaria, Romania, Slovenia and Croatia are on a bed and breakfast or half board basis. Their ski staff are mostly recruited locally in the above countries. However, they recruit 'kiddy representatives' and **entertainers** in the UK. The wage is £150-£200 weekly including board and lodging and travel. As they are also a summer holiday operator, ski staff can apply for summer work.

Applications should be sent in September (or February if apply for summer work) to the Customer Services, at the above address. All staff receive pre-season training in the resort.

BARRELLI SKI
19 Sefton Park Road, St. Andrews, Bristol BS7 9AN; ☎0870 220 1500; fax 0870 220 1501; www.barrelliski.co.uk; chalets@barrelliski.co.uk
Barrelli Ski has been going since 1993 and specialises in catered chalets and self-catering chalets in the French resorts of Les Houches, Chamonix, Champagny-en-Vanoise, Paradiski and La Plagne. Nine resort staff are employed annually:
Chefs/cooks: knowledge of French useful, driving licence, friendly up-beat personalities, ability to be flexible and sometimes work long hours.

Applications at any time to Steve Barrell or Emma at the above address/e-mail. Staff get two weeks training in Champagny before the season starts in mid-December. Australians, Canadians with working visas welcome.

BELVEDERE CHALETS
☎01264-738257; fax 01264-738533; e-mail info@belvedereproperties.co.uk; www.belvedereproperties.co.uk.
Since 1999 Belvedere Chalets has been offering top of the range chalet holidays in Méribel, France. Staff are recruited as couples. One of the pair must have a driving licence. Eight staff employed. Staff have complete everyday responsibility for the guests and chalet, calling in maintenance teams when required.
Chef: qualified (706/1 and 706/2). Three years' restaurant experience, or the equivalent. Must be creative, practical and run a very efficient kitchen, but also share other responsibilities of the chalet.
Chalet manager: must be personable, flexible, have computer and basic bookkeeping skills and give strong support to chef. Chef and Chalet Manager share responsibilities in the chalet.

Five days of training given in the resort. Applications to Jane Blount, Director at the above address or e-mail info@janeblount.co.uk. Please send a 6-day menu plan, CVs, photographs by email, or please telephone the above number.

BIGFOOT TRAVEL
Winchcombe House, 123-126 Bartholemew Street, Newbury, RG14 5BN; ☎0870 300 5874; in France: 5B Résidence Le Mummery, 27 Avenue du Savoy, Chamonix Mont Blanc; ☎+33 (0)4 50 53 00 63; cat@bigfoot-travel. co.uk; www.bigfoot-travel.co.uk.
Bigfoot is a Chamonix specialist and employs staff only in the resort of Chamonix. 20-30 staff are employed in the season as **chalet staff**, **reps** and **office staff**. A handful of staff also needed in summer.

Applications to Cat Teasdale at the above address or email cat@big-foot.co.uk.

CLUB MED
Direction du Recrutement, 132 rue Bossnet, 69458 Lyon Cedex 06, France; International recruitment centre ☎08453 676767; e-mail recruit.uk@clubmed. com; www.clubmedjobs.com.
Creator of the holiday club concept, Club Méditerranée is the world leader in all-inclusive holidays, with more than 80 Villages in 40 countries and the cruise liner Club Med 2. In opening up the upmarket, friendly, multicultural segment of the market, Club Méditerranée applies the Club Med signature to products that set the highest standards in terms of comfort and service, and has reestablished itself as the benchmark for prestige vacations, while capitalizing on its ability to create friendship-based relationships and happiness with clients, thanks to the professionalism and constant availability of its welcoming GOs.
Gentiles organisateurs (GOs): all Club Med staff are known as *Gentiles Organisateurs* (G.O.s) regardless of their job. Clients are known as *Gentiles Membres* (G.M.s).

Club Med require qualified and experienced instructors in golf, scuba-diving, sailing, water-skiing, riding and tennis, as well as hosts/hostesses, cashiers, nurses, beauty therapists, playgroup leaders and restaurant, boutique and administrative personnel. Applicants must be aged between 20 and 30, and be fluent in both French and English (for some positions a third language is required); sports instructors must have appropriate instructing qualifications.

Club Med's ski operations include resort hotels (also known as villages); these include L'Alpe d'Huez (2 hotels), Les Arcs (2 hotels), Avoriaz, Chamonix, Flaine, Les Menuires, La Plagne (2 hotels), Tignes Val Claret and Tignes Les Brevieres and Val d'Isère in France, Cervinia and Sestriere in Italy, Pontresina, St. Moritz Roi Soleil, Villars-sur-Ollon and Wengen in Switzerland, Crested Butte in the United States and Sahoro in Japan.

COLLINEIGE SKI
30-32 High Street, Frimley, Surrey GU16 7JD. ☎01276-24262; fax; 01276 27282; info@collineige.com; www.collineige.com
Collineige have been in business in Chamonix and Argentière since 1980/81 and have made a speciality of these resorts where they run nine catered chalets and some self-catering and hotel accommodation. They employ resort reps and chalet chefs. They get over 100 applications a year for these jobs and so if you are applying make sure that you are are appropriately qualified and experienced and have a stunning CV.
Chalet girls/boys: aged 22+. Must be either qualified or have professional cooking experience.
Resort representatives: aged 24+. Must have excellent French, minibus driving skills and experience of working in a ski resort and managerial, supervisory experience.
Applications in writing from early summer onwards to Collineige at the above address.

New staff receive training partly in the UK and partly in the resort. As the chalets are let as self-catering accommodation in the summer there are limited possibilities for casual summer jobs as chalet maids, cleaning (but not cooking) and for repping, office work and administration in the resort.

CONTIKI
Wells House, 15 Elmfield Road, Bromley, Kent BR1 ILS; ☎020-8290 6777; travel@contiki.com; www.contiki.com/jobs.asp.
Contiki Travel has its headquarters in Guernsey, with its United Kingdom base at the above address. The organisation is heavily oriented towards Australasians as 60% of their clients come from there. They are mainly an international adventure holiday company and their winter operation is small and involves one Austrian resort, Hopfgarten situated in the Tirol region, where Contiki organise half-board skiing holidays in Gasthofs exclusive to Contiki clients. The winter staff consists of a resort manager and about ten resort staff to assist in the daily activities and operation of the resort. The winter staff is recruited from the summer employees of which there are about 350, working as campsite reps, tour managers and tour drivers. Contiki stress that it is not possible to obtain winter work unless you have already completed a summer season with. October/November is their main recruitment and interviewing period. Applicants with EU passports or Australian, American, Canadian, South African, New Zealand or Asian applicants with working visas or British passports.
Gasthof staff: Cook for the customers and clean the Gasthofs. They also accompany the clients to ski school, help them hire equipment, buy lift passes etc.

CORDON ROUGE
Suite One, Brendon House, Silverton Road, Matford Park, Exeter EX2 8NL; ☎0870 240 7861; fax 01392-824930; e-mail french.office@frenchskiholidays. com; www.frenchskiholidays.com.
Cordon Rouge used to be known as Ski Red Guide (which no longer exists). Cordon Rouge was created to develop the prestige catered chalet side of the business, which was, and is, a growth area. Cordon Rouge now provide chalet holidays for about 3000 skiers a year, but remain at heart a family-run company. They are specialists in the Three Valleys Ski Area and their chalets are in Courchevel 1650, Val Thorens and Belle Plagne. Where about 30 staff are employed, most of them as chalet hosts.
Chalet host (20): over 21 with proven cooking skills. Able to cook for 6+. Applications from couples and friends welcome.
Resort rep/Ski host (3): multi-faceted job involving much liaison with other resort reps, interaction with guests, regular chalet visits and help with sales of ski hire equipment, ski passes etc. and running a ski hosting programme. Driving resort vehicles also required. Spoken French desirable. Prefer applicants over 25 years old.
Maintenance/Driver/Ski Host: same as above plus DIY skills.
Office admin assistant: must speak French.
Team Leader: with experience of running chalets and although not chalet-based, the TL should be ready to step in and cover for any chalet staff who are ill or injured and so must be competent to cater for up to 20 guests if the need arises. Aged over 23 and with a driving licence.
Mid-season relief staff: (2). To help with any of the above.
Applications to the above address.

CRYSTAL
King's Place, 12-42 Wood Street, Kingston-upon-Thames, Surrey KT1 IUG; ☎0845 055 0255; www.workingwinter.co.uk.
Crystal is one of biggest holiday companies and huge in terms of winter season staff of which 1,000 are employed and 500 for the summer. Countries in which staff work are Austria, Bulgaria, Finland, France, Italy, Norway, Slovenia, Switzerland and the USA and

Canada.

Hotel jobs include: hotel manager/assistant hotel manager, hotel chefs (qualified and experienced head chefs, second chefs and newly qualified chefs), hotel hosts, kitchen porters, night porters. Also chalet chefs, chalet hosts and assistant chalet hosts, resort manager, team leader, resort representatives, ski/snowboard escorts, administration assistants (fluent language skills required for all administration posts), crèche and family nannies (must hold NNEB or equivalent qualification), childcare staff (to supervise activities for children aged 4-10).

Successful applicants will be given a six-day training cours, usually in the country they will be working in. Possession of an EU passport, British National Insurance number and UK bank account essential. Recruitment starts in May and finishes in late October. Applicants should apply on-line or phone 0845 055 0255.

CRYSTAL FINEST
Kings Place, 12-42 Wood Street, Kingston-upon-Thames KT1 1UG; ☎020-8939 0843;fax 020-8939 5030; www.crystalfinest.co.uk.
Crystal Finest was formerly Simply Ski. Crystal Finest is part of the TUI group and offers high quality chalet and hotel holidays in Courchevel, Méribel, Val d'Isère, Zermatt, Verbier and St Anton. For details of recruitment contact the above telephone number or go to the website www.crystalfinest.co.uk/ski/ski/jobs_winter.asp?programme=ski.

DISCOVER VERBIER
Appleton House, Stinchcombe Hill, Dursley, Gloucestershire GL11 6AQ; ☎0870 874 6840; fax 01453-549106; e-mail jobs@discoververbier.co.uk; www.discoververbier.co.uk.
Discover Verbier provides luxury catered chalets and apartments in Verbier, Switzerland with chef and hot tub. Clientele are often families and corporate bookings. Discover Verbier employ a team of 6 staff in the resort:
Chalet host (4): cooking to a good standard.
Chef : with catering qualifications and/or experience.
Ski Guide: must be advanced skier.

All staff must be over 21 years old. Wages are competitive and accommodation and full board are provided. Work period commences 9 December.

Applications should be made to the above address.

EQUITY TRAVEL
One Jubilee Street, Brighton, East Sussex BN1 1GE; ☎01273-886911; fax 01273-203212; recruitment@equity.co.uk; www.equityski.co.uk/ employment.
Equity are one of the UK's leading ski specialists in travel for adult and school groups, and individual holidays. Each season, Equity carry about 25,000 passengers and employ about 150 full season staff and 70 peak season staff to work in resorts across Europe. Positions include:
Resort reps: aged 21+. Fluent Italian/French/German. Reps are responsible for ensuring client requirements are provided (i.e. après ski, ski services etc) and their needs are met (i.e. helping with translation in medical cases etc.). Previous experience as a rep is not essential but relevant experience in dealing with people will assist an application.
Ski companions: aged 21+. French or German an advantage. A good skiing ability and experience of ski fitting and maintenance are essential (qualifications an advantage but not essential). Work alongside the rep in skiing with clients during the day and running the entertainments in the evening. Must be mature and responsible.
Hotel Managers: aged 25+. Responsible for the running of an Equity hotel in France or Austria including staff management, accounting, client care etc. Equity hotels vary in

size from 50 to 176 beds with teams of 8 to 27. Some level of management experience is essential for this role, as is a good sense of leadership.

Hotel staff: aged 18+. Waiting/housekeepers, bar, chefs (all levels) and kitchen/night porters are all recruited to work in Equity-run hotels in France and Austria. Previous experience is essential as is a good attitude and a smile. Language ability is preferred especially for bar positions.

All staff get a competitive employment package with excellent benefits including: travel to and from the resort, full board and lodging and a day off per week etc. Recruitment runs from June to October and continues once the season is underway to replace ill and injured etc. If successful, interviews are held in July, September and October.

All applicants must have an EU passport, UK bank account and UK National Insurance number. All staff attend an intensive, pre-season training course held overseas before going on to their resort for the season where training will continue.

Visit the Equity website www.equityski.co.uk/employment for more information and to complete the online application form.

ERNA LOW
9 Reece Mews, London SW7 3HE; ☎0870 750 6820; fax: 020-7589 9531; info@ernalow.co.uk; www.ernalow.co.uk.
Erna Low take on **ski representatives** in several resorts in France including La Plagne, Les Arcs and Flaine. Reps must speak fluent French and have relevant experience as they are solely responsible for running the resort under the management of the UK office.

ESPRIT HOLIDAYS & TOTAL SKI
185 Fleet Road, Fleet, Hampshire GU51 3BL; ☎01252-618318; fax 01252-618328; recruitment@esprit-holidays.co.uk; www.esprit-holidays.co.uk.
Esprit Holidays is a highly successful company with over 24 years' experience providing quality winter and summer holidays. With two ski brands **Esprit Ski** (for families) and **Total Ski** (for mixed guests, adult groups, individuals and families) plus **Santa's Lapland** and **Alpine Sun** holidays, their programmes offer quality, catered chalets and chalet hotels in resorts across France, Austria, Italy and Switzerland, as well as the Santa programme in Finland. Ski resorts include Val d'Isère, Courchevel (France), St. Anton, Obergurgl (Austria), Saas Fee and Verbier (Switzerland), Selva Val Gardena (Italy). Jobs are also available in Lapland.

Staff are picked for their friendly and outgoing personalities and their skills and experience to run the Chalet Hotels and Chalets featured by both Esprit and Total Ski. Suitably qualified, fun loving people are also recruited to run the Esprit nurseries and Snow Clubs, catering for the younger Esprit/Total guests.

Representatives: age 25+. Good command or spoken French or German. Clean driving licence. Hospitality and customer service experience an advantage.

Resort Manager: age 25+. Good command of spoken French or German. Hospitality and customer service experience. Management and supervisory skills. Competent skier. Clean driving licence.

Chefs: age 20+. Qualification or proven ability in the catering industry.

Chalet Hosts: age 19+. Cooking/catering experience or qualification essential. Hospitality and customer service experience an advantage.

Nannies: 18+. DCE, NNEB, B-TEC or NVQ level 3 required. To care for babies and toddlers in Esprit's nurseries and in Snow Clubs for children aged 3-10 years.

All ski staff are required to work for a full season from late November to late April, although there are some opportunities starting in January. Alpine Sun programme season runs from mid-June to mid-September. Santa's Lapland runs for the month of December, with the opportunity to continue the winter season with either Esprit Ski or Total Ski in the Alps.

Applications for Esprit and Total, by telephone, mail or e-mail to the above address.

FAMILY SKI COMPANY
Bank Chambers, Walwyn Road, Colwall WR13 6QG; ☎01684-540333; fax 01684-540203; enquiries@family ski.co.uk; www.familyski.co.uk.

The Family Ski Company was founded in 1993 to fill a gap in the market for a company offering a childcare package as a priority rather than a gimmicky add on. The company offers catered family chalet holidays with childcare in France: Reberty Village (Les Menuires) in Trois Vallées ski area; Les Coches near La Plagne; Ardent and Les Prodains in Portes du Soleil ski area. There is an alpine staff of 55.

Resort manager: good working knowledge of French and a driving licence essential.

Assistant resort manager: helps the resort manager. Very varied position. Must be flexible, have catering and childcare experience. Will take over on the resort manager's day off.

Cooks: for chalets. Able to cook for up to 14 adults and 10 children. Driving licence an advantage.

Chalet hosts: help cooks prepare evening meal and serve and accompany. Great deal of contact with guests. Driving licence an advantage. Cleaning and maintenance of a designated chalet. Help cooks prepare evening meal and serve and accompany.

Activity leaders: work in a team on a rota basis providing activities for children on holiday. Age range is infant to 12 years. Each resort has its own equipped crèche. Must be enthusiastic, motivated and imaginative. Experience necessary. Qualifications preferred.

Ski school helper: based at the French ski school to help and encourage the younger children to get the most out of their skiing. A familiar and understanding face for younger guests. Also runs the Powder Adventurers Club for children who are more accomplished skiers. Advanced skiing experience and good understanding of French essential.

Applications to the Overseas Personnel Manager at any time of year. The application form can be downloaded from the website or obtained by post. Applications can be e-mailed to miked@familyski.co.uk. All staff are given two weeks pre-season training in the resort specialised to their job.

FINLAYS
2 Abbotsford Court, Kelso, Northumberland, TD5 7RE; ☎01573-226611; fax 01573-229666; info@finlayski.com; www.finlayski.com.
Finlays has been organised catered chalet holidays in Courchevel and Val d'Isère since 1982 and employs 30 staff in the resorts in the following categories: **assistant resort director, handy person, chalet hosts** and **chalet assistant**. Handy person must have practical background for running repairs to chalets and equipment and a driving licence. Chalet staff must have the ability to cook a high quality dinner party menu each evening. Staff get one to three weeks' training in the resort. Applications to Roddy Finlay, the managing director at the above address.

FIRST CHOICE HOLIDAYS AND FLIGHTS LTD
Overseas Ski Department, Jetset House, Church Road, Crawley RH11 OPQ; ☎0870 750 1204; www.firstchoice4jobs.co.uk, or e-mail skijobs@firstchoice. co.uk.
First Choice Ski is one of the leading winter sports operators providing a vast variety of skiing and snow sports holidays from school tours to tailor made holidays in Europe. First Choice leases and runs its own club-hotels and chalets in France and Austria and also run programmes in Italy, Slovenia, Lapland, Bulgaria, Andorra and Switzerland and aims to provide a service to its guests, which is not only efficient and professional but noticeably the winter season and the company looks for positive, motivated individuals who are committed to both customer care and the continued success of the company.
Office administrators: age: 18+. Must have a good command of French, German or Italian and excellent administrative skills.
Representatives: age 20+. Must have at least one year's target based sales experience, be able to speak the relevant language and possess excellent customer service skills.
Chalet cooks, managers and **assistants:** age 18+. Must have excellent catering and housekeeping abilities and flair for socialising with guests.
Bartenders: age 18+. An outgoing personality required together with experience of bar work and French, German or Italian to a good conversational level.
Apply on-line at www.firstchoice4jobs.co.uk. Interviews are held from July onwards. Excellent career prospects available for successful winter employees.

FLEXISKI
The Port House, Port Solent, Portsmouth, Hampshire PO6 4TH; ☎02392 222 329; fax 02392 224 280; flexiski.com.
Started in 1988 as an independent company. Was taken over by First Choice and is now the luxury arm of that company. Flexiski, as the name implies offers some of the most adaptable ski packages: long-weekends, week and ten-day holidays and if none of these suit one can be tailor-made. They offer chalet or hotel accommodation in 13 European resorts, the main focus being on their chalet resorts: Courchevel 1850 (France), Chamonix (France), Verbier (Switzerland) and St. Anton(Austria). A total of 20 resort staff are employed including **chefs, chalet staff, resort managers** and **ski reps/guides**. Staff must be aged 21+. Salaries start from £80 per week plus the usual ski perks. Applications in writing with CV from May or complete the application form on the website.

HEADWATER HOLIDAYS
The Old School House, Chester Road, Castle Northwich CW8 1LE; ☎01606-

720033/720099; info@headwater.com; www.headwater.com.
Headwater Holidays was started in 1986 and organises Cross Country skiing and winter walking holidays in small, unspoilt villages in Austria, France and Norway. They employ staff in the resorts.

Representatives for Cross Country skiing: minimum age 21. Representatives give 'basic tuition' getting everyone on their feet and running a fully guided programme. Applicants must have experience of Cross Country skiing, leading groups and winter driving. Reps are based in the resort and work alone. A Nordic ski pass is provided and an equipment allowance at the start of the season. Wages from £120 per week, includes accommodation and meals.

Applications should be sent to Headwater Overseas Recruitment. Positions start in December. Headwater also recruits winter/summer walking guides and summer representatives to run walking and cycling holidays in France, Italy, Spain and Austria.

HOTEL LA BELLE ETOILE
Le Bettex, St. Gervais 74170 St Gervais les Bains, France; ☎+33 (0)4 50 93 11 83; fax +33 (0)4 50 93 14 91; abi@belleetoile.com; www.belleetoile.com.
La Belle Etoile specialises in hotel-based ski holidays for school groups, individuals and groups of adults. Operations are concentrated on the Megève ski area and based at St. Gervais in France. There are six resort employees, (two permanent and four seasonal) who work in the hotel, which is located on the slopes. The season lasts from December to April.

General Hotel Staff: age 18+. Duties include cleaning rooms/bathrooms/public areas on a daily basis, service at mealtimes, and some bar work. Spoken French preferred. Food and accommodation are provided and a discounted season ski pass. Applicants need to be flexible and helpful and able to work without constant supervision. Some experience in the hotel industry is preferred.

Applications with CV and referees should be sent to the Hotel from May onwards.

HUSKI CHALET HOLIDAYS
14 Warren Road, Nork, Banstead, Surrey SM7 1LA; ☎020-7938 4844; fax 020-7504 3776; e-mail ski@huski.com; www.huski.com.
Huski is a small chalet company that was started in 1985 and operates catered chalet and self-catering holidays in the Chamonix valley, France. They take on six employees in the resort.

Driver/mechanic: (1) age 21+. French-speaking. Clean driving licence. Organisational skills are essential. At least eight weeks skiing experience. Wages: £75 basic per week plus the usual ski perks and the use of a car and fuel allowance.

PA/Resort manager (1).

Chalet host: (2) age 21+. To housekeep. Some cooking skills or training essential. Preferably able to speak French. Clean driving licence or own vehicle preferred. Preferably with some skiing experience. £65 per week and the usual ski perks. May have the use of car and fuel allowance. Some chalet staff positions are live out.

Chef: (2) cooking school certificates/catering degree or City and Guilds essential. Restaurant/kitchen experience essential. Food hygiene certificate. Driving licence and own car. £75-£85 per week and the usual ski perks. Non-British applicants must have the relevant working visas where applicable. Apply any time in writing with a CV and photograph for an application form and questionnaire. New staff have an informal pre-season weekend in the UK.

INGHAMS
10-18 Putney Hill, London SW15 6AX; ☎020-8780 4400; fax 020-8780 4405; e-mail travel@inghams.co.uk; www.inghams.co.uk.

For many years Inghams Travel has been a leader in quality Ski and Lakes and Mountains holidays. With a history dating back to 1934, Inghams is one of the oldest ski tour operators as well as being one of the largest. For the forthcoming summer and winter seasons, they will be looking to recruit 450 staff to work as part of their overseas team. Staff positions include resort managers, overseas reps, chalet managers, clubhotel managers, head chefs, chefs, receptionists, supervisors (for restaurant, bar, housekeeping, kitchen), brasserie staff, chalet hosts, hotel hosts and maintenance staff.

Overseas Representative: to work in resorts in Europe and North America, either working alone in a small resort or part of a team of reps in a larger one. Part of the rep's job is to organise and guide excursions and activities and completing financial and quality control reports. A reasonable fluency in the local language is usually required.

Resort Manager: responsible for the overall running of the resort. Should have previous experience as a representative and possess excellent organisation and leadership skills plus reasonable fluency in the local language.

Clubhotel Manager : must be enthusiastic with skills and experience to manage a hotel and a diverse team. Responsible for overall running of the clubhotel, the welfare of guests, staff training and development, achieving financial targets and have the flexibility to react logically to unexpected situations. Working knowledge of French required.

Chalet Manager: responsible for all aspects of running chalet operations in resort. Duties involve staff management, hygiene and quality control, budget and menu planning supervision, general administration including controlling chalet finances and keeping accurate accounts and in some resorts, maintenance duties. Previous experience working in a resort, preferably running a chalet. Fluency in another language is advantageous.

Receptionist: to create warm, welcoming and friendly atmosphere. Previous experience in the hospitality industry. Fluent French to degree level.

Head Chef: professional with verified experience in the industry. Able to prepare and cost a 12-day menu within budget. Able to train/coach mixed ability team. Knowledge of French useful. Should show passion, flair and initiative.

Chefs: all levels required for preparation and presentation of fresh and varied dishes. Where resort teams are small, there will also be kitchen work including washing pots and cleaning kitchen. Short order/high volume for some positions.

Supervisors (Restaurant, Bar, Housekeeping, Kitchen): to take on responsibility for one or more of the above areas. Must be strong in personnel management skills. Duties include training, stocktaking, cash handling, orders, rotas and staff welfare. French an advantage.

Cactus Café, Méribel: food service personnel. Previous experience in the hospitality industry. Bar experience. Conversational French useful.

Hotel host: for serving meals, wine and drinks, preparing and cleaning rooms, making beds.

Chalet host: responsible for running a catered chalet including catering and cleaning, menu–planning budgeting and basic administration. Chalets vary in size from 8 on your own to larger chalets suitable for friends and couples to run together.

General handyman: responsible for day-to-day maintenance of chalets and clubhotels. Positions vary depending on the resort. Some resorts are heavily maintenance and driving orientated, and others where there is less maintenance mean you will help in the chalets and club hotels. Duties include luggage transfers, laundry distribution, deliveries and clearing snow. Over 21 for insurance purposes. Clean driving licence. Catering skills for some positions.

Inghams offer seasonal work from May to September or December to April. The main recruitment periods stretch from April to October for the winter season, and December to April for the summer, applications are accepted year round as vacancies do arise mid-season.

Due to EC regulations or work permit restriction, it is necessary to be an EC passport holder for work in Europe.

To request an application form for any of the positions email your address to travel@inghams.co.uk or download an application form from www.3.inghams.co.uk/general_pages/job.html or call 020-8780 4400.

INTERSKI
Unit 8, Acorn Park, Commercial Gate, Mansfield, Notts NG18 1EX; ☎01623-456333; fax 01623 456353; mail@interski.co.uk; www.interski.co.uk

Interski is a unique tour operator offering all-inclusive snowsports holidays within the Aosta Valley in North West Italy. As one of the UK's leading schools and adult operators they transport 14,000 clients to the Alps every year. In doing so, Interski has become the market leader and largest UK operator in the region. Interski arranges hotel-based holidays in the resorts of Courmayeur, Aosta/Pila and La Thuile.

After 20 years in the industry Interski has one of the strongest and most dynamic resort teams in the Alps. They recruit individuals with experience in a customer related environment. Candidates must have an approachable nature, be able to demonstrate the ability to work under pressure, both independently and as part of a large team. All positions require the same underlying characteristics of honesty and integrity. They recruit only the best quality staff and in return for hard work and commitment staff will receive superb rewards and have the opportunity to spend time in an environment that will help develop their career in the winter sports industry.

Snowsport instructor: must hold a current BASI III minimum.

Full and part-time course co-ordinator (rep); Resort rescue; Ski hire co-ordinator; Resort assistant; Resort Co-ordinator; Snowco Assistant.

Over 45 staff are employed for the entire duration of the season plus over 1000 snowsport instructors. For more details of intstructor recruitment, see Interski entry in *Jobs with School Ski Party Organisers.*

Applications to Overseas Employment at the UK address.

LES CHALETS DE ST MARTIN
John Carter, Chalet Roussette, 73440 St. Martin de Belleville, Savoie, France; les.chalets@virgin.net.

John Carter who runs two catered chalets in St. Martin de Belleville in France employs **chalet maids/boys** (with some knowledge of kitchen work), **bar staff** two **chalet assistants** and a **pianist** prepared to do some bar work. Wages and ski pass, insurance and return travel to the UK provided.

Applications to John Carter at the above address.

LE SKI LTD
25 Holly Terrace, Huddersfield HD1 6JW; ☎0870-754 4444; fax 0870-754 3333; e-mail recruitment@leski.co.uk; www.leski.co.uk.

Le Ski is a medium-sized, family-run company specializing in quality catered chalet holidays in top French resorts. 2006/07 is its 24th season in the Alps and there are 29 attractive Le Ski chalets in the most popular French resorts of Courchevel 1650, Val d'Isère and La Tania. Approximately 70 resort staff are employed per season.

Chalet staff: cooking experience required but formal qualifications not essential.

Ski guides: no qualifications necessary but a minumum of 20 weeks snow skiing experience. French is an advantage.

Resort and chalet managers: at least a year's experience in a resort and fluent French.

Maintenance: no qualifications needed but good all round knowledge of plumbing, electrics, carpentry and vehicle maintenance. Driving licence essential.

Nannies: for La Tania only, for Le Ski crèche and nanny service. NNEB or equivalent.

In return for hard work all staff get a competitive wage, food and accommodation, season ski pass, equipment hire, Carte Neige mountain rescue insurance, return travel to the UK at the end of the season, no financial bond.

No staff under 21 are employed (managers must be 25+). Applicants to be holders of a British (or other EU) passport. Relevant qualifications are an advantage, but anyone who is practical, positive and has a sincere interest in working in a ski resort is of interest. Visit the website above for further details and download the relevant application form. Alternatively, call Caitlin (0870 754 44 44).

LOTUS SUPERTRAVEL
Sandpiper House, 39 Queen Elizabeth Street, London SE1 2BT; ☎020-7962 1369; ski@lotusgroup.co.uk; www.supertravel.co.uk
Lotus Supertravel, formerly Supertravel the chalet specialist was taken over by Lotus Leisure in 1991. The company is still a leader in upmarket chalet holidays albeit on a smaller scale with an alpine staff of approximately 50. Lotus Supertravel employ staff to work in France and Austria. Lotus Supertravel go to Courchevel and Méribel in France and St. Anton in Austria. They also sell holidays in Zermatt, Switzerland and like many countries they have expanded their operations to North America – namely, Whistler, Banff, Lake Louise in Canada and Aspen, Snowmass, Steamboat, Lake Tahoe, Vail and Winter Park in the USA. The majority of their team comprise chalet hosts reflecting a continuing emphasis on their speciality, but they also organise hotel-based holidays.
Resort manager and chalet manager: age 25+. Must speak good level of French or German, be confident skiing all terrain in all conditions and have a clean driving licence.
Chalet host: age 18+. A confident and able host who must be able to cook three or four course dinners to a high standard, as well as provide a good selection of cooked breakfasts, cakes and canapés.
Chalet assistant: age 18+. Relevant catering and hosting experience preferred.
Handyman/driver: age 25+. Must have clean driving licence and must be confident skiing all terrain in all conditions, together with the relevant maintenance experience.
Nanny: age 21+. Must have recognised qualification e.g. NNEB or equivalent and/or sufficient experience.

Apply via e-mail, fax or post to the Operations Manager, or alternatively call direct for further information. All applicants must have relevant experience and hold British or other EU passport.

MARK WARNER
George House, 61-65 Kensington Church Street, London W8 4BA; ☎020-7761 7300 or visit www.markwarner-recruitment.co.uk.
Mark Warner is a leading tour operator with chalethotels across the Alps including Courchevel, Méribel and Val d'Isère in France, St. Anton in Austria, and Courmayeur in Italy. They need **chefs, chalet staff, kitchen porters, nursery nurses, ski hosts, accountants** and more to work in the Alps every winter.

Applicants should be 18 and over, flexible, team players and prepared for the challenge of a season. In addition to a rewarding and fun season, Mark Warner offer a competitive package including full board, medical insurance, travel expenses, ski/board and boot hire and a season's lift pass. Contact the Resorts Recruitment department at the above telephone number or visit www.markwarner-recruitment.co.uk.

MASTERSKI
Thames House, 63-67 Kingston Road, New Malden, Surrey KT3 3PB; ☎020-8942 9442; fax 020-8949 4396; francesca@mastersun.co.uk; www.mastersun.co.uk.
Masterski is a well-established Christian tour operator of hotel and chalet holidays in resorts including La Plagne, Châtel, La Tania, Tignes (France) and Reschen (Italy).

Destinations vary slightly from year to year. They also have a programme of watersports holidays during summer in Italy, Greece and Turkey. Masterski was set up in 1983 with the aim of providing high quality ski holidays, combining the fun and pleasure of skiing with the benefits of Christian fellowship and teaching. The company has a loyal clientele and is growing rapidly (80% in the last three years). Team size varies from 12 in their larger hotels to 4 in the smaller chalets. As a Christian company, staff are required to be sympathetic to the Christian ethos of the company. All staff get the usual ski perks on top of their wages and pre-season training for all staff lasts five to seven days in the resort. Winter staff can apply for appropriate summer season vacancies if they are available from late April until October.

Resort Manager: (1) age 25+. Overall responsibility for running the resort, including producing weekly accounts. Must have team management experience (ideally hotel/travel background) and good French..

Ski Representative: responsible for the accompanied skiing programme, transfer duties and organisation of evening entertainments. Proven ski ability and BASI or Ski Leader qualification plus valid First Aid required, along with excellent interpersonal skills. At least 2 years previous customer science/client facing experience essential.

Ski Technician: maintenance and issue of skis, boots and poles to guests and operation of accompanied skiing programme. BASI or Ski Leader qualification, First Aid, and previous ski technician experience essential.

Regional Accountant: responsible for producing weekly accounts and managing cash flow for all ski resorts. At least 2 years' previous experience and IT skills essential. French speaker preferred.

Head Chef: responsible for up to 75 guests. At least 3 years' industry experience and qualification (NVQ level 2/equivalent). Previous staff management experience.

Chalet Chef: to be responsible for preparation and cooking for 15-30 guests.

Bar Manager: with at least 2 years' experience.

Host: for table waiting, help in kitchen, washing up and room cleaning.

Gap Year Students: special package for gap year students from September to September the following year. Tailor-made programme includes sun and ski environments.

Applications to Lynette Rhodes, Recruitment Manager at the above address.

MERISKI
1st Floor, Carpenters Buildings, Carpenters Lane, Cirencester, Glos. GL7 1EE; ☎01451-843100; fax 01285-651685; www.meriski.co.uk; sales@meriski. co.uk

Meribel specialist with 10 chalets in this top French resort. Employment available: **chalet chefs and cooks, qualified nannies and drivers.** Also **chalet operations managers, guest services managers, maintenance staff** etc. About 45 staff in all. Must be minimum age 23 (except for nannies). Must be EU national. Employment is for the whole winter season.

Applications to the HR Co-ordinator accepted from May. Training and management support offered throughout the season. All staff get the usual ski perks.

MOUNTAIN HIGHS
Chalet Marcassin, Le Clos de Reneve, Seytroux 74430, France; ☎/fax +33 (0)4 50 79 29 54; e-mail info@mountainhighs.co.uk; www.mountainhighs. co.uk

Tiny company that operates skiing and boarding holidays in Morzine. Portes du Soleil skiing area in France. They employ a **chalet cook** and a **chalet host** and prefer to have a couple. The chalet cook must have catering experience. 25 years is the minimum age for both positions. Pay is according to age and experience, but will be a minimum £90.

Applications should be addressed to Rachel Pullen, Director at the above address.

Applications to the HR Co-ordinator accepted from May. Training and management support offered throughout the season. All staff get the usual ski perks.

NBV LEISURE LTD
Top Floor, Link Line House, 65 Church Road, Hove, East Sussex, BN3 2BD; ☎0870 220 2148; e-mail nbv@ukoh.co.uk; www.nbvleisure.com.
NVB Leisure was set up in 1997 and operates in popular resorts throughout the Alps including French resorts of Val d'Isère, Méribel, Chamonix and Courchevel. NBV leisure works with a range of international tour operators, and recruits catering staff for chalets and resort reps and provided resort-based services to other companies. Hundreds of staff are recruited for the winter season: **chalet managers/hosts/assistants, chefs** (must be qualified), **resort managers/reps, resort accounts assistants, transport administrators, maintenance personnel, drivers, chamberstaff, receptionists** and **bar staff.**

Applicants can be individuals or couples or friends, British or other Europeans with UK bank account and UK national insurance number. Applications at any time via the website or fax. Successful applicants get five to seven days training in resort. There are also a few jobs available in summer on the summer operation and NBV will help anyone interested to find a summer job with their partners.

NEILSON ACTIVE HOLIDAYS
Locksview, Brighton Marina, Brighton BN2 5HA; ☎0870 241 2901; fax 0870 909 9089; skijobs@neilson.com; www.neilson.com
Neilson, part of the Thomas Cook Group, is dedicated to providing active holidays, from beginners to experts alike, and employs staff for their team each winter,. Staff are the company's most valued asset. Each member of the resort team is chosen for their expertise, flexibility and knowledge. Equally important is real enthusiasm and a genuine love of the job. Neilson looks for people who demonstrate a desire to get involved, further skills and a commitment to ensuring that Neilson guests have the time of their lives. The ski season runs from mid-November until mid-April, but part-season jobs are also available from January to mid-April.
Ski representatives: educated to GCSE standard and ideally with knowledge of a second European language. Must be able to ski to an advanced level. A high level of customer service, professionalism and ability to cope under pressure and own initiative are essential.
Chalet hosts: educated to GCSE level or equivalent, with knowledge of a second European language an advantage. Previous relevant cooking/catering experience essential, as is the confidence to prepare meals and maintain a property for up to twelve people.
Chefs – all grades: variety of positions to suit all levels of experience. Generally our kitchen teams are quite small and so all chefs must be prepared to take a hands-on approach to every aspect of kitchen work.
Hotel managers/Food & beverage supervisors: educated to GCSE standard and conversant in either French or German. Managerial experience within the hospitality industry would be an advantage, as would previous experience of managing company funds. These roles are extremely challenging and demand excellent time management and interpersonal skills.
Administrators: knowledge of Microsoft Word and Excel is essential, as is a good knowledge of a second European language.
A competitive salary package is offered, including accommodation, lift pass, equipment hire and medical and personal belongings insurance.

More detailed job descriptions, company information and instructions on how to apply are available on the Neilson website, as is the application form, which should be sent to the Overseas Department at the above address. Written applications are accepted from May and interviews are held from June through September. Ski rep applicants have a ski test. Applicants should be from the EU or hold a working visa for the country for which they are applying to work.

As Neilson is part of the Thomas Cook group, on successful completion of a winter season, Neilson staff may also be considered for a position within Thomas Cook Tour Operations or Neilson Active and Beach plus centres for a variety of summer roles.

OPTIMUM SKI COURSES
Chalet Tarantaise, Le Pre Villaroger, 73640 St. Foy Tarentaise, France; ☎+33 479 06 91 26; fax +33 479 06 93 56; deirdre@optimumski.com; www. optimumski.com.
Optimum was started in 1989 and runs chalet-based ski courses in Les Arcs, France. Seven ski staff are employed for the season: a **qualified chef**, two **chalet staff**, a **bar/video person,** a **part-time masseuse**, and a **ski instructor** (must be fully qualified). All positions include a ski pass, board and lodging plus negotiable pay.

Non-British nationals with EU nationality or in possession of the appropriate visa welcome to apply. Applications with references in June to Deirdre Rowe at the above address.

OXFORD SKI COMPANY
Magdalen Centre, Robert Robinson Avenue, Oxford OX4 4GA; ☎0870 787 1785; info@oxfordski.com; www.oxfordski.com.
The Oxford Ski Company is a very upmarket ski operator organising catered chalet and self catering holidays in 11 resorts across the French, Swiss and Austrian Alps. The standards offered are the equivalent of the levels at a five-star hotel, but provided in the comfort of a privately-run chalet.
Chalet Manager: previous management experience essential. Reasonable French.
Chef: qualified with experience of working in reputable hotels/restaurants. Has to provide breakfast, cake, biscuits and pastries for tea, staff and children's supper and five-course dinner and daily bread baking. Good French needed.
Chalet hosts: to work alongside chalet manager catering to guests' every need. Duties include food service, driving guests around the resort, chalet cleaning and airport transfers. Needs to be flexible and enjoy providing a service.
Ski guides: for Crans Montana. Non ski connected duties same as ski rep/driver. Must have BASI III and be a team player.
Ski rep/driver: responsible for daytime logistics of guests' holidays. Duties include snow clearing, fire laying, vehicle maintenance and cleaning, general chalet maintenance. Good French an advantage.

Driving licence essential for all staff. Applications to info@oxfordski.com at any time of year. All new staff get two weeks' training in the resort and benefits package. ·

PANORAMA HOLIDAYS
Panorama (not to be confused with the resort of that name in the Canadian Rockies), began operations in 1954 and is now owned by Mytravel which is also the parent company of Airtours. Panorama organise all types of holidays throughout the year. The skiing programme revolves mainly around Andorra and also Austria and Italy (Sauze d'Oulx).

According to their overseas recruitment department they no longer recruit externally for the ski programmes and their chalet hosts are provided by NBV (see separate listing for NBV).

POWDER BYRNE
250 Upper Richmond Road, London SW15 6TG; ☎020-8246 5342; fax 020-8246 5321; enquiries@powderbyrne.co.uk; www.powderbyrne.co.uk
Powder Byrne is a specialist in family holidays to four and five star hotels in Switzerland (Zermatt, Flims, Grindelwald, Villars, Arosa, Klosters); Austria (St. Christoph, Zurs) and

France (Courchevel). Powder Byrne employs about 100 resort staff for the following jobs:
Resort managers: age 24+. Clean driving licence, at least twenty weeks skiing experience, previous resort experience, computer literate, language skills preferred.
Ski manager/guide: age 21+. Clean driving licence, and at least twenty weeks skiing experience. Language skills preferred.
Crèche manager/assistant: age 19+. NNEB certificate or equivalent. Previous experience in a child-oriented role.
Driver: age 21+. Clean driving licence, good customer service skills.
Peak season staff: All the above positions are for the full season but for one to two weeks at New Year, February half-term and Easter there are short-term requirements for children's ski club managers/assistants (min age 19 and previous childcare experience), and ski managers/guides (age 21+ and 20 week's skiing experience).

All staff need fluent English and be EU passport holders. The best time to apply is around July but applications are considered any time. Please apply online at the website. Staff have a week's pre-season training in Switzerland.

Powder Byrne also has summer resort jobs in France, Italy, Spain, Cyprus, Portugal and Mauritius.

PURPLE SKI
4 Cruxwell Street, Bromyard, Herefordshire HR7 4EB; ☎01885-488799; fax 0845-345633; karen@purpleski.com; www.purpleski.com.
Purple Ski offers holidays in a handful of quality catered chalets in Méribel, France. Each chalet sleeps 10-14 people. Purple Ski expects very high standards from the 20 or so staff it employs. They are paid more and have better conditions and accommodation than are offered by most other chalet companies. A high proportion of staff each year are returnees. All staff must have EU passports and permanent UK National Insurance numbers, ideally all will also have driving licences. Minimum age is 21 years. All staff must have a driving licence. About 20 staff are employed:
Chefs: (7). Age 24+. From £170 per week. Must be qualified with several years of experience in professional kitchens.
Chalet persons: (8). Age 21+. £120-£140 per week. Must have significant prior hospitality (ideally waitressing and housekeeping) experience.
Masseuse/chalet assistant/driver (2). From 140 per week. Must be qualified physiotherapist with at least four years post-qualification experience.
General assistant: (1). Age 23+. £120-£140 per week.
Administrative assistant (1). Age 23+. About £140 per week.
Supplies manager: (1). Age 23+. £140-£160 per week.

Further details of each job are available from the website www.purpleski.com/jobs/home.htm.

RUSH ADVENTURES
10 Chemin des Enversins, Taconnaz, Les Houches, 74310 France; ☎0121-2886131 in the UK or +33 (0)4 50 91 35 39; e-mail: info@rushadventures.co.uk; www.rushadventures.co.uk.
Rush adventures have two chalets in Chamonix and 2005/06 is their second year of business running catered chalet skiing holidays. As well as skiing and boarding holidays for groups and families, they also provide a whole host of activities to keep their guests entertained during the stay. They employ two chalet staff /ski hosts.
Chalet Hosts/Manager: (2). Age 21+. To cook for up to ten people and provide guests with ski hosting showing them the resort, collecting them from and taking them to the airport etc. Must have clean driving licence. Daily maintenance and cleaning of the chalet also required. Positions are ideal for two friends or a couple. Staff package includes wage of £70 per week plus seasonal bonus (£1330), lift pass and mountain insurance. Must be

available from 3 December to 15 April.

Applications with a CV and full description of applicant, plus a passport size photograph and a telephone number that you can be contacted on.

SCOTT DUNN
Fovant Mews, 12 Noyna Road, London SW17 7PH; ☎020-8682-5087; fax: 020-8682 5090; e-mail: recruitment@scottdunn.com; www.scottdunn.com.
Set up in 1986, Scott Dunn revolutionised the ski chalet market and has been gradually expanding ever since. Starting with two chalets in Champéry, the company has chalets in Zermatt (20 resort staff), St. Anton (12 resort Staff), Courchevel 1850 (35 resort staff), Val d'Isère (40 resort staff) and Méribel (12 resort staff). The company also has a portfolio of villas across the Mediterranean, but is still a small and very personalised company.

Much of Scott Dunn's success is down to its attention to detail. They pride themselves on treating each guest as an individual and have the very highest standards. Staff are selected very carefully to help the company achieve its goals in standards of service. In return staff are well provided for with excellent accommodation and all living and skiing expenses plus a competitive wage.

Applicants should be dynamic, organised and motivated and be available from the beginning of November. There is the opportunity to continue working for Scott Dunn in the Mediterranean villas during the summer. Ski staff totals 175.
Resort Managers: (18). Age 26+. Fluency in French or German and management ability are essential along with basic accounting skills. Strong leadership qualities and sense of humour. Should also be a competent skier. Computer literacy and management experience essential.
Chalet chefs: (36). Age 22+. Must have formal qualification; minimum of three months' course and one year's experience. Driver preferred.
Chalet hosts: (33). Age 21+. £50 per week. Very hard working, friendly and willing to do anything. Hospitality experience and driver preferred.
Nanny: (35) Age 19+. Must have NNEB or equivalent.
Maintenance/driver: (9). Age 23+. Clean licence. Experience in a trade preferable.
Beauty therapists: (5). Age 21+. Must be qualified.

All staff get a ski jacket, fleece, ski pass, hired skis, boots and poles, medical insurance, return travel, one day off a week and great staff accommodation.

Telephone or e-mail for an application form from May. Applications to the Recruitment Department at the above address.

SILVER SKI
Conifers House, Grove Green Lane, Maidstone, Kent ME14 5JW. ☎01622-735544; fax 01622-738550; e-mail: hazal@silverski.co.uk; e-mail karen@silverski.co.uk; www.silverski.co.uk.
Silver Ski have been in business for about twenty-three years. They offer only catered chalet holidays in about 40 chalets spread through several French resorts: La Tania, La Plagne, Courchevel, Méribel, Reberty and Val d'Isère. Each chalet is run by a team, usually of two people. **Chalet teams** are mostly couples i.e. husband/wife or girlfriend/boyfriend and as there are no resort reps, each team is self-sufficient. The men must be over 25 and experienced skiers, drivers and able to handle jobs around the house. Women must be good cooks/housekeepers and experience is more important than qualifications. Minimum age for consideration is 21 years. All staff must be energetic and outgoing. Antipodeans and North Americans are sometimes employed. All staff receive a modest wage and the usual ski perks.

Applications in writing enclosing a c.v. should be addressed to Mr Len Silver at the above address from May onwards.

SIMON BUTLER SKIING
Portsmouth Road, Ripley, Surrey GU23 6EY ☎01483-212726; fax 01483-212725; e-mail info@simonbutlerskiing.co.uk; www.simonbutlerskiing.co.uk.
Simon Butler skiing specialise in instructional skiing holidays based in the French Alpine resort of Megève. Guests are accommodated in two catered chalets and skiing instruction is provided by the company's own ski instructors. Instructors need to have worked at least one season before applying. Simon Butler is himself a BASI Grade 1 instructor. 22 staff including four **ski instructors** are employed in the resort. The other staff are:
Chefs (4): minimum age 21 years. Relevant qualifications.
Nannies (4): minimum age 21. Relevant qualifications.
Chalet girls/boys: (8): experience preferred.
Maintenance (2): experience is essential.
   Wage rates are given at interview stage. Staff get full board and travel to and from the UK and all the usual ski perks.
   Applications to Jay Blatherwick, Manager at the above address.

SKI ACTIVITY
Lawmuir House, Methven, Perthshire PH1 3SZ; ☎01738-840888; fax 01738 840779; www.skiactivity.com.
Ski Activity has been operating for over 23 years in both Europe and North America. They specialise in catered chalets (Europe only) in Méribel, Val Thorens, Les Gets, Val d'Isère and Verbier. Resort staff with tolerance, good humour, enthusiasm and the ability to work hard as part of a team. Guests come first and it is the resort staff that can make their holiday memorable.
Chalet staff: age 21+. Extensive catering experience, smart appearance and outgoing, pleasant personality. High standards of health and hygiene and attention to detail are important.
Resort manager/rep: age 23+. Good team player with exceptional organisational and people skills. Management experience preferred and must be fluent or have conversational French.
   Applications to the HR manager with a CV and menu plan or online at www.skiactivity. com or e-mail recruitment@skiactivity.com.

SKI ADDICTION
The Cottage, Fontridge Lane. Etchingham, East Sussex TN19 7DD; ☎& fax 01580-819354; in France ☎ +33 (0)450733983; www.skiaddiction.co.uk
Started in 1989, Ski Addiction is a two-resort company offering chalet, hotel and self-catering holidays in Châtel and La Chapelle d'Abondance, France. They employ four resort staff.
Chalet staff: age 21+. Ability to speak French and previous experience an advantage. Catering qualification necessary. Wage negotiable.
Ski instructor: age 21+. BASI qualified or equivalent. Must have previous ski school experience. Knowledge of the Portes du Soleil, is an advantage and fluent English is a necessity.
   North Americans, Australasians and other EU nationals considered. Please note that as Ski Addiction employs so few staff their recruitment is completed very early. Two to three days' pre-season training will be provided in the resort.

SKI AMIS
122-126 High Road, London NW6 4HY; ☎020-7692 0850; fax 020-7692 0851; jobs@skiamis.com.
Ski Amis offers catered chalets and self-catered apartments skiing holidays in France.

Catered chalets are in La Plagne and La Tania. Eleven resort staff are recruited: **chalet hosts** (4), **chef** (1), **chalet supervisor/resort rep** (1) and **chalet couples** (2). The summer operation employs two staff – these are permanent positions. Applications from May to Christine Metcalfe. Staff are given three weeks' training in the resort prior to the season.

SKI BEAT
Metro House, Northgate, Chichester PO19 1BE; ☎01243-832510; fax 01243-533748; e-mail alex@skibeat.co.uk; www.skibeat.co.uk
Ski Beat is a small, friendly independent company that has been operating chalet holidays for over twenty years. They have 49 catered chalets in the French alpine resorts of La Plagne, Les Arcs, La Rosiere, La Tania, Méribel and Val d'Isère. They recruit staff for the following positions:

Resort manager: winter season experience essential either in a chalet or as a holiday resort manager/rep. To be responsible to the French office, but able to act on own initiative, to liaise with other managers and to oversee all aspects of the guests' needs. To deal with the week-to-week running of the resort operations and problem solving. Arrange airport or train transfers, lift passes, ski school, weekly staff meetings and evening activities. Fluent French with all the appropriate management/accounting skills and able to ski or board to an advanced level.

Chalet host/cook: singles and couples to run chalets in all Ski Beat resorts and to provide guests with breakfast, afternoon tea, children's high tea and a three-course evening meal six days a week. Cookery certificate not essential, but proof of catering experience and genuine love of cooking is. Please submit a menu plan with your CV. There are **jobs for couples or friends** to run catered chalets together and a **chef** is required for the select service option, which offers guests catering at a higher gourmet standard.

Reserve Chalet Host/Ski Host: Candidates must be able to cook to dinner party standard and be responsible for assisting with the running of the larger chalets. Preparing breakfast, afternoon tea, children's high tea and three course evening meal, six days a week and keeping the chalet clean at all times. You may work in different chalets depending on numbers. Clearing snow and ice from paths and steps. Depending on the resort, you may be expected to offer ski hosting to guests for three days a week.

Nanny: Qualified nannies (NNEB, BTEC, NVQ Level 3) plus previous childcare experience, to work in Ski Beat's crèches and run their afternoon childcare services, or as a private nanny. This is an opportunity to use your skills and training in a fun and varied atmosphere, either working on your own or as part of a team caring for children aged 3 months to 7 years. Nannies work on rota basis and have two days off a week.. **Head Nanny** positions are available to oversee the day-to-day running of the crèche.

Applicants can apply all year round and must hold an EU passport holder and resident in the UK. You can apply online for an application form on website and e-mail (jobs@ skibeat.co.uk) or post it with a CV (and a six-day menu plan if relevant. Or, for recruitment enquiries call 01243-832510.

SKI BLANC
Wick Hill House, Finchampstead, Berkshire, RG40 5SW; ☎/fax 020-8502 9082; e-mail tony@skiblanc.co.uk; www.skiblanc.co.uk.
The small chalet company Ski Blanc began in 1993 and operates in Méribel. They take on ten ski staff: **chefs** (4), **chalet staff** (4) and **MBOs** (2). They welcome couples with combined cooking and driving ability and all staff must be self sufficient, practical types. Lift passes, ski hire, return travel, board and lodging and insurance provided.

Applications to M J Garrett from June. Pre-season training is provided in the UK (one day) and Méribel (seven days).

SKI CHAMOIS
18 Lawn Road, Doncaster DN1 2JF; ☎01302-369006; fax 01302-326640; www.skichamois.co.uk.
Ski Chamois is a small company started in 1980, which specialises in chalet holidays in Morzine. They usually employ the following alpine staff:
Chalet staff: (2) age 21+. No cooking required.
Ski guide: must ski to a high standard.
Bar person: must speak fluent French.
Chefs: head chef and assistant/pastry chef (jumbo chalet has 30-50 persons).
Nanny: must be NNEB, Norland, or RGN qualified.
Ski tech/odd job person.
   Applications from April/May should be addressed to: Ski Personnel Department, at the above address. Contracts are finalised in July. However, last minute vacancies for chefs and a nanny are occasionally available later in the year. New staff are given a briefing in the UK and arrive in the resort a week before the season starts. Australasians with suitable qualifications are welcome to apply.

SKI CUISINE
49 Burses Road, Southend on Sea, SS1 3AX; ☎01702-589543; fax 01702-588671; anne@skicuisine.co.uk
Ski cuisine was started in 1996 and specialises in chalet holidays in Méribel, France where it has 20 resort staff: **chefs** (must be very experienced), **chalet hosts, nannies** (should be experienced and hold childcare and first aid qualifications) and **driver/maintenance persons.**
   Applications by e-mail or post from June to Anne Woolley at the above address. Staff have ten days pre-season training in the resort.

SKI DIRECT CONTROL
Colliford Lake Park, Bolventor, Bodmin Moor, Cornwall PL14 4PZ ☎01208-850051; fax 01208-821597; info@huckslodge.com; www.huckslodge.com
Ski Direct Control offers good value ski and board holidays in the French Alps based on the resorts of La Tania, Vallandry and Tignes. They recruit 15 staff for the resort in the following roles: **Resort manager** (2), **Resort rep** (2), **Chalet chef** (4), **Chalet Assistant** (5) and **Driver** (2).
   The period of employment is from 6 December to 7 April. All the usual ski perks are provided plus wages and bonus scheme.
   Applications to Simon Crowther, Director, at the above address.

SKI ÉQUIPE
Victoria House, 19-21 Ack Lane East, Bramhall, Cheshire SK7 2BE; ☎0161-439 6955; fax 0161-439 6804; info@ski-equipe.co.uk; www.ski-equipe.co.uk.
Ski Équipe offer quality holidays to France, Italy and Austria, as well as to North America. Apart from specialist, gourmet chalets, Ski Équipe also arrange hotels and self-catering holidays to top resorts. Ski Équipe welcome applications from couples and older applicants as well as younger ones, but all must comply with the following:
Chalet hosts: age 21+. Qualified cook or have completed one of the many chalet cooking courses available. Able skier, preferably language proficient and able to work on own initiative.
Resort representative/ski guide: age 24+. Fully conversant in the relevant language and a very competent skier as a minimum two days of guiding is required. At least one year's experience in the Alps, preferably in a chalet environment.
   Applicants should write with CV, photograph and if applying for chalet host, a menu

plan, to the above address.

SKI FAMILLE
Unit 10, Chesterton Mill, French's Road, Cambridge CB4 3NP; ☎0845-6443764; fax 0845-64449385; info@skifamille.co.uk; www.skifamille.co.uk.
As the name implies, Ski Famille specialises in family ski holidays and employs about 40 staff in Les Gets and Morzine (France). There is also a summer programme with opportunities for employment as mountain bike guides, chalet hosts and childcare staff. The winter staff required are:

Chalet hosts: competent cooks with proven commercial experience (not necessarily cordon bleu). Applications from mature people and couples are welcome.

Chalet helpers: assistants without formal skills and training but who possess attention to detail and enthusiasm.

Nannies: must be qualified nurses or childcare professionals with minimum 18 months experience. Childcare operates 5 days a week from 9am-4.30pm.

Assistant nannies: not necessarily qualified, but must be experienced in childcare.

Resort Assistants: to support the chalet and childcare teams. Driving and DIY skills are required.

Staff package includes the usual ski perks and wages according to job and experience. Applications (to the Recruitment Manager) welcomed throughout the year though late summer is the main recruiting and interviewing period.

SKI FRANCE
Third Floor, Link Line House, 65 Church Road, Hove, East Sussex, BN3 2BD; ☎0870 220 2148; e-mail skifrance@ukoh.co.uk; www.skifrance.co.uk.
Ski France is a specialist ski tour operator to the French Alps offering catered chalets, hotels and apartments. Ski France offer just holiday accommodation and optional travel. They operate catered chalets in Alpe d'Huez, Chamonix, Courchevel, Chamrousse, Isola 2000, La Joue du Loup, La Plagne, La Rosière, La Tania, Les Arcs, Les Houches, Les Deux Alps, Les Menuires, Méribel, Montgenèvre, Mottaret, Orcières-Merlette, Peyragudes, Praz-sur-Arly, Serre Chevalier, St. Gervais, St Jean d'Arves, St Sorlin d'Arves, Tignes, Val d'Isère, Valloire and Val Thorens.

Ski France take on a variety of carefully chosen resort and chalet staff for these resorts: **resort manager** (age 23+) **resort rep** (age 21+), **office administrator** (age 23+), **chalet controller** (age 23+). All these positions need fluent French.

Other positions for which fluent French is not essential: **chalet hosts** (age 21+), **chalet assistants** (age 19+), **chefs** (age 21+, **qualified nannies** (age 21+), **maintenance & building officers** (age 21+).

Chalet hosts: age 19+. Previous cooking experience and appropriate qualifications are essential.

Staff package includes ski pass reimbursed at the end of the season, ski hire, full board and lodging and work (but not skiing) insurance. There is a bonus paid to those who stay the whole season.

Applications from July with a CV and covering letter addressed to The Overseas Recruitment Manager at the above address. Staff are given a week's pre-season training in the resort.

In addition to the above ski jobs Ski France through their hotel partners can offer management, trainee and student placements in all aspects of hotel and restaurant management.

SKI HILLWOOD
Lavender Lodge, Chipperfield, Herts. WD4 9DD; ☎01923-290700; fax 01923 290 340; sales@hillwood-holidays.co.uk.

Ski Hillwood are a small family-run operator specialising in family holidays in the Austrian resorts of Söll and Zauchensee, and the French resorts of Les Gets and Argentière. Ski Hillwood have crèches for children as young as nine weeks in all resorts.

Ski Hillwood employ up to twenty staff (**child reps and resort reps**). The minimum age for nannies is 19 years and for reps it is 21 years. Some knowledge of French or German is helpful but not essential. Qualifications for child reps should be NNEB or equivalent although teaching qualifications will also be considered; some snow skiing experience is also helpful. Resort reps need to have a least a season's experience in a summer or winter resort. Accommodation and food allowance provided as well as lift pass.

Applications from September to Howard Webby at the above address. Non-EU nationals (e.g. New Zealanders) must have a valid work permit.

SKI HIVER
29 Place House Close, Fareham, Hampshire PO15 5BH; ☎01329-847788; skihiver@w2392-428586; skihiver@aol.com; www.skihiver.co.uk.
Ski Hiver is a small company started in 1995 which has catered chalets in Les Arcs and La Plagne (Paradiski) in France and employs 6 ski resort staff each season: **cooks** and **helper.** Couples considered ideal. Applicants should be holders of an EU passport. Prefer cooks who are experienced but will train if keen. Age 25+.

Applications from the end of the season to Colin Harvey by post or e-mail.

SKI INDEPENDENCE
5 Thistle Street, Edinburgh EH2 1DF; ☎0845-310 3030; fax 0131-225 4789; jon@ski-i.com; www.ski-i.com.
Ski Independence was started in 1993 and specialises in tailor-made holidays to the USA and Canada. They employ ten resort staff (**resort rep** and **chalet staff**), sourced from the UK and also a number of part-time Americans and Canadians. UK-sourced staff are likely to be placed in Whistler, Vail, Breckenridge, Banff and Tremblant. Must be over 25 years old, have driving licence, health and safety knowledge and cooking experience for chalets. Five days' training given in the resort.

Applications from May to Jon Thorne, Overseas Manager, by e-mail.

SKI MIQUEL
73 High Street, Uppermill, Nr. Oldham, Lancashire OL3 6AP; ☎01457-821200; e-mail ski@miquelhols.co.uk; www.miquelhols.co.uk
Ski Miquel specialise in catered chalet and hotel holidays in Bad Gastein (Austria) and Alpe d'Huez and Serre Chevalier (France), Whistler (Canada), and Lauterbrunnen (Switzerland). This last is conveniently near Wengen and Mürren, but less pricey. They employ 36 alpine staff: chefs, chalet helpers/ski guides and resort managers.
Chefs: qualified chefs looking for an opportunity to run their own kitchen and to enjoy the skiing/boarding. Responsible for cooking for up to 30 guests from menus provided by Ski Miquel. Up to £180 per week.
Resort managers: responsible for all aspects of running the resort. Must have at least two seasons' experience and able to speak the local language. £180 per week.
Chalet staff: to clean chalet hotels, serve the meals and look after the guests. £60 per week.

All staff have plenty of time for skiing and have one day off per week, they also receive full medical insurance. Lift pass, Uniform, ski hire, full board and clothing allowance. Applications in writing with full CV by letter or email to Richard Barton, Operations Director.

SKI MORGINS
The Barn House, 1 Bury Court Barn, Wigmore HR6 9US; ☎01568-770681; fax

01568-770153; info@skimorgins.com; www.skimorgins.com
Ski Morgins was started in 1985 and runs chalet and self-catering winter holidays and caters for adults, families and school groups. They concentrate on Morgins in the Portes du Soleil region (Switzerland). About eighteen winter staff are employed:
Cooks/chefs: up to ten. Wage: £320 per calendar month plus usual ski perks. Must have cooking experience.
Chalet host: up to six. Wages: £280 per calendar month plus usual ski perks. No formal qualification required.
Driver: Wages: £280 per calendar month plus usual ski perks. Must have clean UK driving licence with a minimum of two years' experience and be over 25 years old. Ability to speak French and experience of driving in Europe.

Staff package includes the usual ski perks. Applications to Hilary Markland, at the above address with CV, photograph and covering letter. Pre-season training for one week in the resort. Possibility of summer work. All EU nationals welcome to apply.

SKI OLYMPIC
PO Box 396, Doncaster South Yorkshire DN5 7YS; ☎01302-328820; 01302-328830; info@skiolympic.co.uk; www.skiolympic.co.uk
Ski Olympic started in 1987/88 and specialise in catered chalet holidays in eight top French alpine resorts including: La Rosière, Les Arcs, La Plagne, Val d'Isère, Méribel, Courchevel 1550 and 1650, Tignes and Reberty. The company employs nearly 150 alpine staff for their chalets, hotels, ski fitting and ski guiding:
Chefs and assistant chefs: age 21+. Must be qualified or experienced. Catering for ten to 75 clients in chalets and hotels. May have to demonstrate cooking skills prior to hiring.
Chalet chefs/hosts: age 21+. To clean, wait tables etc. Must be willing to work hard.
Ski guides (Hosts/Reps): must have skiing qualification (BASI or equivalent).
Ski technicians/maintenance staff: (2) must be qualified ski technicians. Also required to carry out maintenance in chalets/hotels: plumbing, joining etc.

Write or telephone for an application form from May. Applications in writing with a CV and small photo or send application via the website. Staff are given a week's training in the resort. Applications from suitably qualified Australasians, North Americans (must be able to get a British National Insurance Number) and other EU nationals welcomed.

SKI PEAK
Barts End, Crossways Road, Grayshott, Surrey GU26 6HD; ☎01428-608070; fax 01428-608071; info@skipeak.com; www.skipeak.com.
Ski Peak was set up in 1988 and operates chalet and hotel holidays in Vaujany/Alpe d'Huez. They employ 24 alpine staff (**chalet girls, reps** and **ski guides**) in Vaujany 'the back door' to Alpe d'Huez.

Applicants should send in their CV and covering letter. Suitable applicants will be interviewed and those taken on board will be given a week's training in the resort just prior to the season.

SKI POWER
The Gables, Coopers Hill Road, Nutfield, Surrey RH1 5PD; ☎01737-823232; fax 01737-821449; info@skipower.co.uk; www.skipower.co.uk.
Ski Power offers luxury chalet and hotel holidays in the French resorts of La Tania and Courchevel 1550 in the Three Valleys Ski Area. They employ 26 resort staff and have a variety of positions to offer. Most staff are required from 1 December to 30 April, except the Hotel Manager (20th November to 30 April).
Chef (8): with chef qualification and experience. To cater for 40 covers per sitting.
Chalet Assistant (6): work includes helping chef and cleaning. People skills most important as job involves much guest contact.

Hotel Manage: must have relevant experience and speak French, preferably fluently.
Barperson (2): must have relevant experience of running a bar, mixing cocktails and good French.
Driver (3): clean licence and proven experience of mountain and minibus driving.
Ski Guide (3): excellent skier to cope with any piste in all conditions.
General Assistant: with DIY/building expertise. Will be asked to demonstrate DIY skills.
Nanny (2): NNEB or equivalent.

Staff get variable, but generous wages depending on role, age and experience: chalet hosts from £70 per week and chef from £100 per week. Staff package includes full ski perks, end of season bonus and generous tips. Drivers, chefs and hosts must be over 21 years old..

Applications to the above address or send full CV and covering e-mail to pip@skipower.co.uk.

SKI PURPLE GOAT
1a Denmark Close, Poole, Dorset BH15 2DB; ☎07711670234; e-mail info@ skipurplegoat.com; www.skipurplegoat.com.
Ski Purple Goat is a small company with two catered chalets in the Morzine, Portes du Soleil skiing area of France. They employ three staff in the resort from 6 December. Staff get competitive wages and skiing perks including snow risk insurance.
Chalet manager: (2) age 25+ with management experience and a 'nothing is too much trouble' attitude. Outgoing, approachable, friendly.
Chef: age 25+ with cooking skills to a very high standard (3 years' experience hotel/ restaurant at chef de partie level). Must have a passion for flavours and presentation. To cook for up to 22 guests.

Applications to Stephanie Murdoch at the above address.

SKI ROYALE
Farm View House, 45 Farm View, Yately, Hampshire GU46 6HU; ☎0870 011 1718; fax 0870 011 1719; info@skiroyale.com; www.skiroyale.com.
Ski Royale was founded in 2001 and is a small, friendly company that employs staff to work in their catered chalets in Megève, France.

Seven staff are recruited annually: qualified chef, qualified chef couple, chalet host with cooking experience, 2 non-cooking chalet hosts and two drivers/ski guides.

Applications from July to September to Ski Royale.

SKITOPIA/TJM
40 Lemon Street, Truro, Cornwall TR1 2NS; ☎01872-272767; fax 01872-272110; shelly@tjmtravel.com; www.skitopia.com.
TJM/Skitopia organises hotel and chalet-based holidays and also school groups skiing holidays in France in Mongenèvre, Serre Chevalier, 3 Valleys and Tignes and they take on over 70 ski staff for the season: **managers** (7), **chefs** (7), **chalet hosts** (8), **domestic servers** (20), **bar staff** (3), **maintenance staff** (4), **driver** (3), **reps** (10), **support staff** (10). Chefs must have NVQs or equivalent and driver should have a clean driving licence. Extra staff are taken on during the schools peak periods (Christmas/New Year, February half-term and Easter).

Applications to Dany Duncan, Operations Director at the above address. Australasians and North Americans welcome to apply if they have a working visa for France.

SKI-VAL
The Ski Barn, Shortlands, Middlemoor, Tavistock PL19 9DY; ☎01822-615440; fax 01822-611400; sarah@skival.co.uk; www.skival.co.uk

Ski-Val is an established independent company with over 25 years experience specialising in skiing holidays in the top resorts of St. Anton in Austria; Courchevel, Val d'Isère and Tignes in France. They pride themselves on their friendly staff, superb food and comfortable, luxurious chalets. Job opportunities include **resort managers**, **chalet managers**, **resort representatives**, **chalet hosts**, **chefs** and **bartenders**. Applicants with previous relevant experience required. Must be holders of a passport from EU member country only, and must have National Insurance number.

SKI VERBIER
Thames Wharf Studios, Rainville Road, London W6 9HA; ☎020-7385 8050; fax 020-7385 8002 laura@skiverbier.com; www.skiverbier.com.
Ski Verbier operates luxury chalet holidays in one resort, Verbier. They employ 40 staff in the resort including **chefs, hostesses, managers, drivers** etc. Ages 21+. Must have relevant qualifications and experience. Manager posts require the ability to speak French. Weekly wage and all usual skiing perks and Patagonia clothing.

SKI WEEKEND
Darts Farm, Darts Farm Village, Topsham, Exeter, Devon EX3 0QH; ☎08700 600 615; fax 08700 600 619; info@skiweekend.com; www.skiweekend.com.
Ski weekend have been operating for over 20 years and specialise in Tailor Made short weekends, Midweek and All Week breaks. They pride themselves on the high level of service they offer. Their main resort is Chamonix, France, although they will book holidays to other resorts in France, Switzerland and Italy. They employ seven staff in Chamonix for the winter season.
Resort manager: aged 25+. Fluent French. Good skier/snowboarder. Clean driving licence. Ideally previous experience in the ski industry, highly organised, team player. £125 per week + commission.
Ski guides (4): excellent skier/snowboarder with at least BASI III or equivalent qualification. French speaker. Clean driving licence, team player, organised, friendly and able to provide high levels of client care. £125 per week + commission.
Chalet staff (2): ideally a couple, 1 chef and 1 chalet manager. Chef must be able to cook to a high standard with qualification and/or proven experience. Chalet manager to run all other aspects of the chalet to include cleaning, accounts, ski pass/ski hire, clients management. Chalet sold on a 3 or 4 night weekend and mid-week holidays. Breakfast, tea, 4 course evening meal.
All staff receive accommodation in Chamonix, ski jacket and trousers and items of other kit, use of skis/snowboard for the season, season ski pass, 1 day off a week.
Formal applications throughout the summer. New employees get a week's training once in Chamonix. Applications should be made to Brett Gregson at the above address or email.

SKI WEEKENDS
4 Post Office Walk, Fore Street, Hertford SG14 1DL; ☎0870 442 3400; fax 0870 442 3401; www.skiweekends.com.
Ski Weekends was started in 1989 and has its own 'club hotel' in Brides les Bains, in the Trois Valleés in France. Ski Weekends employs 12 staff in the resort annually in various hotel jobs: **table waiting staff, reps, drivers, reservations clerk.**
Applications from any suitable UK or other EU passport holder to Frank Harris at any time of year.

SKIWORLD
Overseas Personnel Department, Skiworld House, 3 Vencourt Place, London W6 9NU; ☎0870 4205912; fax 020 8741 1131; recruitment@skiworld.ltd.uk;

www.skiworld.ltd.uk.
Skiworld has a truly fantastic reputation in the ski industry for looking after its staff, a fact proven by its high staff return rate. Staff benefit from the unique experience of working for an experienced, independent company that offers great opportunities in over 25 top European and North American ski resorts. Each applicant is considered individually and matched to a specific resort and property, so you know exactly where you are. In return, you will receive a competitive package and excellent training and support through to the end of the season.

Resort managers (13) Previous ski season experience, previous hospitality experience, previous staff management experience, proven sales experience, demonstrating the ability to meet and exceed sales targets, a flexible, hands on and proactive approach. Fluent French or German.

Resort accountants (9) Excellent customer service & interpersonal skills, a qualified accountant (or demonstrating previous relevant accounting experience), experience being in charge of budgets and handling cash, proven accuracy, highly organized, strong communication skills and good conversational French / German.

Resort representative/chalet managers (45) Fluent French or German, previous staff management experience, previous hospitality experience, Advanced level of skiing/ snowboarding, Excellent customer service and excellent organizational skills.

Hotel managers (7) excellent customer service & interpersonal skills. Previous hospitality experience, previous staff management experience, a flexible, hands-on and proactive approach, highly motivated and able to motivate others, able to work on own initiative and solve problems alone..

Head chefs (7) & second chefs (7) & chalet chefs (14). Extensive cooking experience in catering for large numbers, previous staff management experience, excellent organizational skills and can work well under pressure.

Head chalet hosts (14) Previous staff management, excellent customer service, previous hospitality experience and previous cooking experience (formal qualifications not required).

Chalet hosts (140) & flexi hosts (17) & chalet assistants (21). Previous cooking experience (formal qualifications not required), excellent customer service, excellent organisational skills and able to work on own initiative.

Hotel hosts (24) and kitchen/night porters (15). Excellent customer service and interpersonal skills, highly flexible, good team player and previous hospitality experience.

Maintenance persons (10) Considerable experience within a particular trade e.g. plumbing, electrics, carpentry, etc. Previous direct customer service experience, highly organised and able to work on own initiative.

SNOWBIZZ
69 High Street, Peterborough PE6 9EE; ☎01778-341455; fax 01778-347422; www.snowbizz.co.uk.
Snowbizz Vacances was formed in 1984 and caters for family skiers in the resort of Puy St. Vincent, France. They have their own in-house ski school and recruit English-speaking staff for seasonal opportunities. They look for candidates who are hard working, enthusiastic, friendly and have a genuine desire to work with children, making each child's holiday a special one. It will aid applicants if they have a childcare qualification, ski or speak conversational French. In return for working for this small specialist company you get an above average salary and a generous perks package which includes concessionary travel for friends and relatives. All this, and plenty of free time for personal skiing/boarding.

Resort representative: age 21+. French to 'A' level standard. Previous repping experience is essential.

Junior rep: 18+. Working alongside ski school with ages 5-11 years.

Ski instructors: Fully qualified, English speakers.
Ski nanny: crèche based, also working in ski kindergarten with ages 3-4.
Crèche Manager: Minimum NVQ3 (or equivalent) with previous experience.
Applications to Wendy Lyotier (wendy@snowbizz.co.uk; 01778-348809) or to the above address from June onwards. Applicants must satisfy the minimum qualifications listed above.
Pre-season training is carried out in the UK and the resort.

SNOWCOACH
Holiday House, 146-148 London Road, St. Albans, Hertfordshire AL1 1PQ; ☎01727-866177; fax 01727-843766; info@snowcoach.co.uk; www. snowcoach.co.uk.
Snowcoach specialise in value for money ski holidays by air, coach or self-drive and offer a selection of hotel, chalet and apartment accommodation. They operate in a range of resorts in France and Austria and also provide a special Snowcoach Ski Safari service to give clients the opportunity to ski and enjoy several ski areas in one week. Their resorts include: St Gervais, Chamonix, Megève, Valloire, Val Cenis and Mèribel in France; Kirchdorf, Mayrhofen and Zell am Ziller in Austria.
Snowcoach employ a number of staff and positions include: **chefs, chalet and hotel staff, representatives, ski guides** and **drivers.** All staff get a package that includes travel to the resort, accommodation and meals, staff insurance, season ski pass and weekly wage..
Applications should be sent before the end of August to: Jenny Howard, The Overseas Department at the above address.

SNOWCRAZY LTD
55 Lancaster Drive, East Grinstead, West Sussex RH19 3XJ ☎01342-302910-866177; e-mail gosnowcrazy@aol.com; www.snowcrazy.co.uk.
Snowcrazy offers high quality, fully catered ski chalets with hot tubs in La Rosière, a modern resort at the end of the Tarantaise Valley in the French Alps. They employ (ideally a couple) chalet staff.
Chalet host/Chef: must be trained either NVQ or in-house training and with previous relevant experience of cooking for groups. Should be outgoing, approachable, confident and responsible and possess excellent organisational skills and ability to keep within budget. Also employs a **Chalet host/Resort Assistant.** Staff get a good salary including holiday pay and season completion bonus, season ski pass, equipment hire, medical insurance. Excellent accommodation in a self contained apartment and all meals are provide. Season runs from the first week of December to the first week of April.
Applications should be sent to Laura Clarke at the above address. Snow Crazy also run a week-long chalet cook's course during summer. For more details and cost see *Cookery Courses* in *Types of Job Available*.

SNOWLINE/VIP
Collingbourne House, 140-142 High Street, Wandsworth, London SW18 4JJ; ☎020-8870 4807; fax 020-8875 9235; recruitment@snowline.co.uk; www. snowline.co.uk or www.vip-chalets.com
Snowline Skiing has been in business since 1987 and operates catered chalets in France (Méribel, Morzine, La Tania and Val d'Isère) and Switzerland (Zermatt). They employ a variety of staff in each of these resorts: **resort managers, chalet managers, chalet hosts, driver/handymen, stockmen** and **driver/ski hosts** and sometimes staff for the London office.
Applicants should be over 21 with a bubbly, enthusiastic personality, good sense of humour and relish hard work. Individuals, couples and mature applicants are welcomed.

Candidates need to be available for training in late November and employment lasts until April/May. Only EU passport holders, resident in the UK with a UK National Insurance number need apply for the resort positions.

Applications should be sent to Liz Burland, Snowline and VIP Recruitment to the above address or apply online from the jobs section of the website. New staff are given seven to ten days' training in the resort at the beginning of December.

SNOW and TREK
109, Main Road, Southbourne, Emsworth, Hampshire PO10 8EX; ☎01243-379970; fax +33 (0)4 50 74 16 67; info@snowandtrek.co.uk; www.snowandtrek. co.uk.
Snow and Trek is a small company that offers luxury chalet and apartment ski and summer holidays in Morzine. They employ 5 to 7 staff in the resort.
Chefs (2/3): qualified or with professional experience. Cooking for 8-15 covers a day. Some driving and cleaning also.
Chalet Assistants 2/3: should be proactive with some kitchen skills. Cleaning chalet of 4/5 bedrooms daily and assisting chef. Some driving.
Nanny: NNEB qualified or equivalent and over 25 preferred. For owners children and some nannying for guests. Applications from couples welcome.

For all positions: minimum age is 21 (except nanny, see above) and a driving licence is essential.

STANFORD SKIING
479 Unthank Road, Norwich, Norfolk NR4 7QN; ☎01603-477471; fax 01603-477406, info@stanfordskiing.co.uk; www.stanfordskiing.co.uk.
Stanford is a small, family-run company started over 20 years ago, which specialises in the picturesque resort of Megéve, France. They employ 14 staff in the resort: **chalet hosts**, **driver/ski guides**, **managers** and **chefs** to work in their chalet/hotels and luxury chalets.

Applications should be send to the above address and if applying for a chef position, please send a six-day, 3-course menu plan with your CV.

SWISS TRAVEL SERVICE
1 Tabley Court, Victoria Street, Altrincham Cheshire WA14 1EZ; ☎0161-385 4073; e-mail for recruitment: swiss.ch@bcttravelgroup.co.uk.
Swiss Travel Service have specialised in holidays to Switzerland for over 50 years. They employ resort representatives to assist and advise guests staying in hotels and apartments in the resorts.
Resort representatives: age 21+. Must be able to ski. Knowledge of French or German. The ability to get on with all kinds of people. Must be organised, with common sense and able to work on own initiative.

The majority of resort representatives are drawn from the summer season staff. Written applications only to Jackie Willcocks. Interested applicants must be able to attend an interview in the UK.

THOMSON
Kings Place, 12-42 Wood Street, Kingston upon Thames, Surrey KT1 1SH; ☎0845 055 0255; www.cantwaitforwinter.com.
Thomson Ski is a partner company of Crystal. Vacancy and employment details are the same as for Crystal (see Crystal's entry in this section).

TOPS/SKI PLAN TRAVEL
Lees House, 21 Dyke Road, Brighton, East Sussex BN1 3DG; ☎01273-774778; fax 01273-734042; e-mail info@topstravel.co.uk; www.tops.travel.

co.uk; www.skiplantravel.co.uk.
Tops/Ski Plan organise skiing holidays in Club Hotels, for adult groups and school groups in the French Alps. Resorts include Alpe d'Huez, Les Deux Alpes, Chatel, Vars and Serre Chevalier. About 250 resort staff are employed in the following categories: **hotel manager, assistant hotel manager, head chef, assistant chef, kitchen porter, night porter, bar staff, waiting/cleaning staff, resort representative, ski technician, handyman, driver** and **office administrator.** Knowledge of French is useful, but not essential to all roles. To apply, post or e-mail a copy of your CV to Sue Lloyd, Overseas Recruitment at the above address.

TOTAL SKI
185 Fleet Road, Fleet, Hampshire, GU51 3BL; ☎01252-618309; fax 01252-618328 www.skitotal.com; e-mail recruitment@skitotal.com
Total Ski are a part of Esprit Holidays and recruitment details are the same as for Esprit (see Esprit Holidays entry).

TRAIL ALPINE
Cordelia House, James Park, Dyserth, Rhyl, Denbighshire LL18 6AG; ☎0870 750 6560; 0870 750 6570; www.trailalpine.co.uk.
Trail Alpine specialise in chalet and hotel holidays. Their chalet staff are in Morzine (France). The following staff are taken on: **chefs, cleaners, ski guides** (must have BASI III or in training for BASI III), **driver** (needs mini bus licence). French is an advantage for all staff.
Applications from June to Mrs A G Jones at the above address.

YSE LIMITED
Church House, Abbey Close, Sherborne, Dorset DT9 3LQ; ☎0845 122 1414; fax 0845 122 1415; staff@yseski.co.uk; www.yseski.co.uk.
Founded in 1991 by two experienced ski tour operators, whose aim is to provide gourmet chalet holidays with close personal attention. They specialise exclusively in Val d'Isère, where one of the partners is resident. The majority of their employees are catering staff.
Chalet staff: 20 employed. Cooking qualifications or considerable cordon bleu practical knowledge is essential. Applications from pairs of friends is possible for some chalets.
Chefs: (3) must be qualified with broad experience of cooking for to a high level for top paying guests.
Chalet assistants: (20 employed). Age 21+. To assist with cleaning and serving meals. Must be enthusiastic, hard-working and presentable.
All applicants must be aged 21+. Wages are competitive and vary depending on experience. All staff receive the usual ski perks.
Applicants should telephone for an application form from May. 2-3 week pre-season training in the resort.

OTHER SKI COMPANIES EMPLOYING RESORT STAFF

The following companies also employ resort staff but did not respond to a questionnaire sent asking them to provide their details for this book.

Alp Leisure: +33 479 005942. Chalet.

Bigfoot Travel: 186 Greys Road, Henley-on-Thames, Oxon RG91 1QU; ☎0870 300 5874; www.bigfoot-travel.com. All types of holiday in Chamonix including catered chalets.

Bonne Neige Ski: P.O. Box 42, Crewe CW2 7FH; ☎01270-256966; ukoffice@ bonne-neige-ski.com. Very small company. Offers hotels and chalets in Méribel.

Chalets & Auberge sur la Montagne: La Thuile, Sainte Foy Tarantaise 73640 France; ☎+33 (0)4 79 06 95 83; fax +33 (0)4 7906 95 96. Catered and self-catering chalets and hotel sleeping up to 24 in the Savoy Alps.

Chalet1802: Three catered chalets in Chamonix, France; ☎+33 (0)4 50 90 05 89; info@chalet1802.co.uk; www.chalet1802.co.uk. Has three catered chalets in Chamonix.

Connick Ski: Chalet La Chaumiere, Route de Thonon, 74390 Chatel, France; ☎+33 (0)6 07 13 15 37; nick@connickski.com; www.connickski.com. Large catered chalet. Staff are a mixture of Brits and Irish.

Cooltip Mountain Holidays: Ashcourt, Main Street, Long Riston, Hull, HU11 5JF; ☎020-7384 3854; ski@cooltip.com. Small company. Catered accommodation in Méribel.

Descent International: Riverbank House, Putney Bridge Approach, London SW6 3JD; ☎020-7384 3854; fax 020-7384 3864; www.descent.co.uk; sales@descent. co.uk. Ostentatiously upmarket chalet operator with chalets in Klosters and Val d'Isère and bases in Méribel and Verbier.

The Great Escape: 66, St. Margaret's Grove, St. Margaret's, Twickenham, TW1 1JG; ☎07879-667545; www.thegreatescape.eu.com. Luxury catered chalet in the heart of Chamonix Valley. Contact Fiona Kimber (fionakimber@blueyonder.co.uk)

Oak Hall Skiing and Snowboarding: Oak Hall, Otford, Kent TN15 6XF; ☎01732-763131; office@oakhall.co.uk; www.oakhall.co.uk. Organises Christian holidays to about ten resorts in Austria, Switzerland and the USA. Teams of staff are made up of volunteers.

Ski Adventures: 10 Graham Road, Malvern, Worcestershire WR14 2HN; ☎+33 (0)4 79 07 97 15; andrew@skiadventures.co.uk; www.skiadventures.co.uk. Runs three catered chalets at Les Arcs (Arc 1600). High end catering and childcare offered to guests.

Ski Basics: 95 West Avenue, Oldfield Park, Bath BA2 3QB; ☎01225-444143; www. skibasics.co.uk. Ten catered chalets in Méribel.

Ski Bon: two catered chalets in Méribel. E-mail mik@skibon.com or enquiry@ skibon.com.

Ski Brev: 22 Cambridge Street, Tunbridge Wells, Kent TN2 4SU; ☎01892-618230; www.skibrev.com. Catered chalet ('La Sache)'. in Tignes les Brevieres Contact Chris Wood (chris@skibrev.com).

Ski Moments: Apt B5, La Vizelle, 73550 Méribel, France; ☎+33 (0)6 61 88 10 48; www.skimoments.com. Two chalets in Méribel. Contact Stacey Wright.

Smitten by Snow: 48 Cowan Road (3rd floor), Edinburgh EH11 1RJ; ☎0790 533 0279; info@smittenbysnow.com; www.smittenbysnow.com. Catered chalet in Belle Plagne. Contact Phil McMillan.

Snowflakes Winter Holidays/Snowflakes Lodge: Snowflakes Lodge, 360 Chemin du Planet, 74400 , Chamonix, France; ☎+33 (0)4 50 54 22 29; e-mail louise@ snowflakes.co.uk.; www.snowflakes.co.uk.. Privately catered lodge/chalet for fourteen guests in Argentière, Chamonix. Contact Louise Garland.

Snow Monkey Chalets: Mill Lane, Sharnford, Leicestershire, LE10 3PS; ☎07970-447121; e-mail info@snowmonkeychalets.co.uk; www.snowmonkeychalets.co.uk. Catered chalet in the Paradiski (Les Arcs, La Plagne) ski area of France. Contact Sam Hinton.

Snowfox Holidays: Shepway East Lympne Hill, Hythe, Kent, CT21 4NX ☎01303-230623; e-mail Camilla@snowfoxholidays.co.uk; www.snowfoxholidays.co.uk. Catered chalets in La Plagne, the Paradiski (Les Arcs, La Plagne) ski area of France. Contact Camilla Bryer.

Snowstar Holidays: 38 Nicola Close, South Croydon, CR2 6NB; ☎0870-068 0611; e-mail info@snowstar.co.uk; www.snowstar.co.uk. Two catered chalets in Tignes. Contact Richard Scott.

Wasteland Ski : 9 Disraeli Road, London, SW15 2DR; ☎020 8246 6677; fax 020 8246 6982; www.wastelandski.com. Very large student/group operator, that also does family and other group holidays tailor-made and has a catered chalet section. Employs entertainment reps for groups, a bartender, a DJ and chalet hosts.

Winetrails/Ski Gourmet: Greenways, Vann Lake, Ockley, Dorking RH5 5NT; ☎01306-712111; www.winetrails.co.uk. Catered gourmet chalet operator in Filzmoos, Austria with wine tasting and a cookery course.

Jobs with School Ski Party Organisers

CLUB EUROPE HOLIDAYS LIMITED
Fairway House, 53 Dartmouth Road, London SE23 3HN; ☎020-8699 7788; fax 020-8699 7770; kim.s@club-europe.co.uk; www.club-europe.co.uk
Club Europe began operating in 1980 and offers ski packages in 20 resorts in three European destinations to its ever-increasing client base. Club Europe organises school ski package holidays.
Ski resort representatives: to accompany each group and assist with ski hire, lift passes, the ski school and arrange the evening entertainment and trouble shoot generally.

Applicants should be keen skiers with a friendly outgoing personality and excellent organisational and communication skills. They should be fluent in French, German or Italian and able to work under pressure.

Pay is £250 depending on experience for a nine-day tour, board and lodging, ski hire and lift pass are included. Positions are available from February half-term through to and including Easter.

EQUITY TRAVEL
One Jubilee Street, Brighton, East Sussex, BN1 1GE; ☎01273-886911; fax 01273-203212; e-mail recruitment@equity.co.uk; www.equityski.co.uk/employment.
Equity Ski are one of the UK's leading ski specialists for adult and school groups. They operate on a direct-sell basis from the above Brighton office, so their brochures are not found in travel agents. Each season Equity carries about 25,000 passengers and employs about 150 full season staff plus 70 peak season staff in Europe. Positions include **Resort Rep, Hotel Manager**, **Hotel Staff** and **Ski Companions**.

They also recruit Peak Season Ski Reps, Educational Tour Reps and also have vacancies in their Brighton office as and when they arise. For full details and to apply for a position, visit www.equityski.co.uk/employment.

FIRST CHOICE HOLIDAYS AND FLIGHTS LTD
Overseas Ski Department, Jetset House, Church Road, Crawley RH11 OPQ; ☎0870 750 1204; www.firstchoice4jobs.co.uk, or email skijobs@firstchoice.co.uk.
First Choice Ski is one of the leading winter sports operators providing a vast variety of skiing and snow sports holidays from school tours to tailor made holidays in Europe. First Choice leases and runs its own club-hotels and chalets in France, Italy, Slovenia, Lapland, Bulgaria, Andorra, Switzerland and aims to provide a service to its guests which is not only efficient and professional, but noticeably more friendly and flexible than in traditionally run resorts. About 600 staff are recruited for the winter season over all the ski brands and the company looks for positive, motivated individuals who are committed to both customer care and the continued success of the company. For full details of staff employed throughout their ski brands and for application details see the First Choice entry in the *Ski Tour Operators* previous section.
Schools representatives: age 18+. Must be able to speak the relevant language and possess excellent customer service skills.

HALSBURY TRAVEL
35 Churchill Park, Colwick, Nottingham NG4 2HF; ☎01159-404303; fax 01159-404304; enquiries@halsbury.com; www.halsbury.com.
Halsbury Travel started in 1986 and organises chalet, self-catering and school group skiing in Les Arcs, La Plagne, Tignes, Val d'Isère Les Deux Alpes and many more resorts in the French Alps. Halsbury send reps and staff to accompany each group.
Resort Couriers/Guides: age 21+ with fluent French and outstanding personality. Previous ski rep experience helpful and preferred. Good skiing standard preferred.
  Staff required principally for school holiday weeks: Christmas/New Year, February half-term and Easter. For application details see entry in *British Ski Tour Operators* section.

HOTEL LA BELLE ETOILE
Le Bettex, St. Gervais 74170, France; ☎+33 450 931183; abi@belleetoile. com; www.belleetoile.com.
La Belle Etoile is a friendly hotel with doorstep skiing, known and loved for its relaxed atmosphere and good food. It caters for school groups, large parties and individuals of all nationalities. Operations are concentrated on the Megève ski area and based at St. Gervais in France. Three or four seasonal staff are employed by the hotel each winter in addition to two permanent staff. The season runs from mid-December to mid-April.
General hotel staff: age 18+. Duties include cleaning rooms/bathrooms/public areas on a daily basis, service at mealtimes and some bar work. Spoken French preferred. Board and lodging and a discounted ski pass for the season are provided.
  Applicants need to be flexible, helpful and able to work without constant supervision. Some experiende in the service industry preferred. To apply, please send CV with references, to the hotel from May onwards.

INTERSKI
Unit 8, Acorn Park, Commercial Gate, Mansfield, Notts NG18 1EX; ☎01623-456333; fax 01623 456353; in Italy: Strade Ponte Suaz 14, 11100 Aosta, Italy; ☎+39 0165 304711; fax +39 0165 304716; email@interski.co.uk; www. interski.co.uk
Interski is a unique operator offering all-inclusive snowsports holidays within the Aosta Valley, North West Italy. As one of the UK's leading schools and adult operators they bring over 14,000 clients to this region of the Alps every year. Interski has proven itself a market leader and the largest UK operator in the region. Interski arranges hotel-based holidays in the resorts of Courmayeur, Aosta/Pila and La Thuile.
  Interski has great experience going back twenty years in the industry and they have built one of the most dynamic resort teams in the Alps. Ideally they prefer people with experience in a customer related environment. Candidates must have an approachable manner, be able to demonstrate the ability to work under pressure, both independently and as part of a large team. All positions require the same underlying characteristics of honesty and integrity. They recruit only high quality staff and in return for hard work and commitment they receive superb rewards and have the opportunity to spend time in an environment that will promote career development in the winter sports industry.
Snowsport instructors: must have a minimum of BASI 3 or national equivalent. Considered by the client as probably the most important person on their holiday. Responsible for looking after the clients on the slope, improving their ski/board ability, keeping them safe and supervising a lunch break.
Full and part-time co-ordinator (rep): first point of contact for groups and hoteliers. Must be flexible and eager to provide highest level of customer care. Good team spirit and lots of initiative. Conversational French or Italian an advantage.
Resort rescue: provides caring and supportive back-up for sick/injured clients in resort. Duties include liaising between Italian and British agencies involved in the medical

process. Demanding, often tiring job offers challenge to the right applicant who should be able to communicate effectively in French or Italian.

Ski hire co-ordinator assistant: in constant contact with clients. Must have working knowledge of ski and snowboard maintenance and repair. Duties include keeping accurate control of stock and efficient rental and return system. Should be cheerful and welcoming, methodical and organised.

Resort assistant: one of the most demanding and integral positions within the team. Must be a good all rounder with a range of skills and qualifications. A desire to learn quickly and the ability to think beyond the initial situation are key requirements.

Resort co-ordinator: to oversee the daily off mountain and resort operations. Involves acting as a point of contact for the resort team, group leaders, coach drivers and suppliers. Good organisational skills are essential when planning weekly programmes, booking venues and attending events. Preferably Italian or French language ability.

Snowco assistant: responsible for planning, delivery, collection and upkeep of all resort clothing, including rental suits, helmets and resort staff uniform. Expected to travel regularly between Interski's three resorts. Driving licence essential.

Over 45 staff are employed for the entire duration of the season, plus over 1,000 **snowsport instructors.** Staff package includes uniform, equipment, accommodation, all meals and an opportunity to progress to a BASI Instructor level. Mobile, two-way radio and car provided to chosen positions.

Applications to Overseas Employment at the UK address.

PGL SKI
Alton Court, Penyard Lane, Ross-on-Wye, Herefordshire HR9 5GL; ☎01989-767311; fax 0870 403 4433; skipersonnel@pgl.co.uk; www.pgl.co.uk/skipersonnel.

PGL has over 50 years of experience in the school travel business, carrying in excess of 200,000 children annually to various centres in the UK and abroad. PGL Ski organises a variety of products, adventure holidays in the UK or Europe, school tours, ICT (Information and Communication Technology), Mission Earth, individual children's activity holidays, family active, and of course skiing holidays.

PGL Ski organises school skiing trips to resorts in Austria, France, Italy, Switzerland and the USA, operating mainly in the peak school holidays, therefore most of their positions are short-term; specifically New Year, February half-term and Easter. Many PGL staff are in full-time education, or employment and they use some of their annual leave to work for PGL.

Ski representatives: PGL's front line people in the resort who ensure that all the work carried out in preparation for the trip pays off. Their main role is to ensure that every aspect of the trip runs smoothly. This involves liaison with the hotel, drivers, ski school, evening entertainment venues and, of course, the party leader. Ski reps also have to provide a full evening entertainments programme, which is normally a mixture of non-costing 'in-house' events run by the ski rep, plus the hiring of local facilities (e.g. ice-rink, bowling alley) if the group requires it. Ski reps normally travel to the ski resort with their school group and stay 1-2 weeks, working exclusively with their group(s).

Applicants should be aged 20+, have excellent organisational and communication skills and previous experience working with school/youth groups. Also required are good conversational German, Italian or French and ski or boarding experience on snow.

Reps have to attend a comprehensive, residential training course during autumn, prior to the season. All staff are paid a competitive wage and get travel to and from the resort from a pick up point in the UK, full board accommodation, lift pass, ski hire insurance and uniform.

For further details of how to apply, or request an application form, visit the website www.pgl.co.uk or e-mail skipersonnel@pgl.co.uk or telephone 01989-767311.

SKI ASTONS
Clerkenleap, Broomhall, Worcester WR3 3HR; ☎01905-829200; fax 01905-820850; ski.astons@virgin.net; www.skiastons.co.uk.
Founded in 1953, Ski Astons organises school group holidays to many resorts throughout Europe with the majority in Austria and Switzerland. About 60 ski staff are engaged annually:

Ski tutors/guides: for occasional weeks throughout the winter season. Must hold valid ski instruction qualification. German language useful.

Main weeks for 2004 are 26 Dec-3 Jan, 13-21 Feb, 26 Mar-3 Apr and 2-10 April. There is no full season work.

Applications to Rachel Price, Tours Manager, or Marty Walford at any time of year. Have had applicants in the past from Canada, New Zealand and Australia. Successful applicants receive a ten-day tour in October and two weekends in November (Midlands and Scotland).

SKIBOUND
The Port House, Port Solent, Portsmouth, Hampshire P06 4TH; ☎02392 222 329; fax 02392 224 280; www.firstchoice4jobs.co.uk.
Skibound is the school group ski organising arm of First Choice holidays and all recruitment is done through First Choice (see address above). It is the largest winter sports school tour operator, providing hotel accommodation for primarily school groups and adult groups. Skibound offers a wide range of competitively-priced holidays to suit all requirements. Resorts are in France. A total of 200 employees are recruited for the winter sports programme each year. The ages shown below represent the minimum age for each job.

Representatives: age 18+. Must be able to speak the relevant language and possess excellent customer service skills.

Chefs: age 18+. Must be able to cater for 50-150 covers on a set menu.

Assistant chefs: age 18+. A basic knowledge of catering is required.

Bartenders: age 18+. An outgoing personality required together with experience of bar work.

Waiting/cleaning staff: age 18+. Must be able to work well in a team of young people, Energy and enthusiasm essential.

Hotel managers: age 23+. Must have hotel management experience and a good knowledge of French, German or Italian.

Assistant managers: age 23+. Must have worked in the hospitality/catering industry at a supervisory level.

Handy persons: age 18+. Practical DIY knowledge and self motivation required.

Porter (kitchen & night): a dual role covering a two-week shift in each job role. A mature approach essential.

Candidates should apply online at www.firstchoiceforjobs.co.uk. Interviews are held in July. August and September and jobs are confirmed in October. Pre-season training is provided for reps, hotel managers and chefs. Excellent career prospects available for employment for successful winter employees.

SKI GOWER
2 High Street Studley, Warwickshire B80 7HJ; ☎01527-851411; www.gower.com; peter@gowertours.com
Ski Gower established in 1961 is one of the oldest school group ski organisers. Groups stay in youth hostels and small hotels in most Swiss resorts including St Moritz, Saas Fee Fee, Les Diablerets, Zermatt and Wengen. Positions include course manager and evening activities organiser and four or five ski teachers per resort. All staff get the usual ski perks and free skiing lessons (if needed).

Instructors:(20)volunteers, but get board and lodging and the usual ski perks. Minimum age 20 years. BASI III or equivalent.
Evening Entertainments: Volunteers, but get board and lodging and the usual ski perks plus skiing lessons if needed. Knowledge of relevant languages preferred.

Write or telephone for an application form any time of year. Applications should be sent to Peter Cook, Ski Gower Manager. New staff have a weekend briefing in the UK. Possibility of summer courier work for those who can speak one or two additional European languages.

SKI PLAN TRAVEL
Lees House, 21 Dyke Road, Brighton, East Sussex BN1 3DG; ☎01273-774778; fax 01273-734042; info@ topstravel.co.uk; www.topstravel.co.uk; www.skiplantravel.co.uk.
Tops/Ski Plan organises skiing holidays for school groups and in clubhotels and for adult groups in France in Alpe d'Huez, Les Deux Alpes, Chatel, Vars and Serre. About 250 resort staff are employed. For details see Tops/Ski Plan entry in previous section *Work with Ski Tour Operators.*

SKITOPIA/TJM
40 Lemon Street, Truro, Cornwall TR1 2NS; ☎01872-272767; fax 01872-272110; shelly@tjmtravel.com; www.skitopia.com.
TJM/Skitopia organises hotel and chalet-based holidays and also school groups skiing holidays in France in Mongenèvre, Serre Chevalier, 3 Valleys and Tignes and they take on over 70 ski staff for the season: **managers** (7), **chefs** (7), **chalet hosts** (8), **domestic servers** (20), **bar staff** (3), **maintenance staff** (4), **driver** (3), **reps** (10), **support staff** (10). Chefs must have NVQs or equivalent and driver should have a clean driving licence. Extra staff are taken on during the schools peak periods (Christmas/New Year, February half-term and Easter).

Applications to Dany Duncan, Operations Director at the above address. Australasians and North Americans welcome to apply if they have a working visa for France.

Working Through Other Organisations

OFFICIAL BODIES

BRITISH ASSOCIATION OF SNOWSPORT INSTRUCTORS (BASI)
Glenmore, Aviemore, Inverness-shire PH22 1QU; ☎01479-861717; fax 01479-861718; e-mail: basi@basi.org.uk; www.basi.org.uk

BASI has been the training and certifying organisation for snowsport instructors in Britain for over 40 years. BASI provides teaching qualifications in five snowsport disciplines, Snowboard, Alpine, Nordic, Telemark and Adaptive. Adaptive is teaching where the learner would need to use adapted equipment to facilitate taking part in the sport.

BASI currently has nearly 4,000 members, only 300 of whom hold the coveted National Ski Teacher international licence and highest qualification. On average, it takes five years to achieve this qualification. Qualified members work in 25 different countries and BASI qualifications are continuing to gain a worldwide reputation.

BASI International Ski Teachers can now work in all European countries on a full-time basis. BASI Ski Instructors can also work in France for four years on passing an aptitude test (test technique) after which they must upgrade to International Ski Teacher, and can work in all other European countries on a full-time basis.

Anyone wanting to work outside the EU will need to obtain a work permit. This is not normally a problem for higher levels of BASI qualifications, but lower grades may find some countries and some snowsport schools harder than others. There is more chance of work in the North East of the United States which is a good starting point for lower level qualifications. At the other end of the spectrum, obtaining a work permit to teach as a ski teacher in Canada is harder because of more stringent immigration rules, but it is still possible. The key to gaining a work permit is getting a job offer from a Snowsport school who can get the work permit on your behalf. Normally, a Snowsport school would require you to attend a hiring clinic before considering offering you a job.

Courses

BASI has introduced an exciting new fast track/gap year programme which has a range of courses varying between 10 and 13 weeks duration, and based in 8 different countries around the world. These courses culminate in the BASI Instructor exams and work in partnership with Snowsport schools and local Instructor training organisations to maximise training and development of students. The programme totally immerses students in all the aspects of the Snowsport Resort environment and is a thoroughly exciting and rewarding experience. Most students find that they not only have an Instructing licence at the end of the course, but have gained hugely in their people skills, management skills, and their own personal confidence.

Every year BASI publishes a 75-page comprehensive course directory available from the above address, or the BASI web site www,basi.org.uk. The Directory is also a manual with information on a range of tops of interest to prospective candidates. Approximately 2000 candidates attend courses every year in a variety of countries including Britain (Scotland), Italy, France, Switzerland, Andorra, Argentina, New Zealand and the USA. It is advisable to book early as some of the courses fill up very quickly. Some courses are residential and

BASI can offer a package that includes accommodation, lift pass, travel and insurance.

Courses are also offered on a training fee basis only and are mostly of five or ten days' duration. Training fees for the longer courses work out at about £60 per day which includes five hours on snow, followed by review groups, seminars, video analysis and lectures.

Candidates receive pre-course and on-course work books and various BASI manuals.

Membership
Before joining a BASI training course, candidates have to be paid up members of the Association. Candidates applying for the first level of training should join as associate members. All membership fees are renewable annually on 1 October.

Full membership benefits include regular newsletters, which help keep members up-to-date and is also a valuable source of job advertisements for ski instructors. Other benefits include free contingent liability insurance when ski teaching and equipment discounts.

THE BRITISH ASSOCIATION OF SKI PATROLLERS
c/o The Secretary, 20 Lorn Drive, Glencoe, Argyll PH49 4HR; tel/fax: 01855-811443; e-mail: firstaid@basp.org.uk; www.basp.org.uk.
Although ski patrolling has been practised in Britain for 30 years, BASP was founded as late as 1987 to standardise and integrate the training of ski patrollers in the UK. All ski patrollers in Scottish resorts are members of BASP and have received their training through the Association. The aim of the organisation is to promote safety on the mountain by minimising the risk of accidents and injuries and to provide highly trained patrollers who can handle emergencies when they occur. BASP is an active member of the Federation Internationale des Patrouilles de Ski (FIPS) and contributes to the International conferences on improving ski patrolling with special emphasis on first aid and rescue.

In order to satisfy the entry requirements for training, applicants should be at least 18 years, be qualified in 4-day standard HSE first aid, and a competent parallel skier. It is an advantage to have winter mountain skills. All qualifiers have to be members of BASP. At the end of the basic training a logbook is issued and any further training schemes taken (e.g. advanced first aid, mountain and avalanche skills) are noted. The course is run once a year in December at Nevis Range in Fort William, Scotland and the basic cost is £150 (non-residential). First aid courses cost from £90 and information on other courses is supplied on request. After many years of experience it is possible to achieve the level of Grade 1 Ski Patroller. This qualification enables Ski Patrollers to qualify for similar jobs in Australian and New Zealand ski resorts.

Even before they reach this illustrious stage Ski Patrollers need not be out of a job in summer in Scotland as they can become Trainers, instructing trainees in first aid and other skills during the non-skiing season.

THE SKI CLUB OF GREAT BRITAIN
The White House, 57/63 Church Road, Wimbledon, London SW19 5SB; ☎0208-410 2000; fax 0208-410 2001; www.skiclub.co.uk
The Ski Club of Great Britain dates back over a hundred years and exists to help people get on to the slopes without spending a fortune. The club is open to all skiers and snowboarders of all ages and abilities and offers a wide range of services and organised activities to its 30,000 members. Ski Club members save money, get help preparing for the slopes and have a range of holiday options to choose from. They also get access to a wealth of information and a calendar of events that spans the entire year. The Ski Club also has opportunities to ski for free as a Ski Club Representative (see details below).

Discounts. There are over 1,000 discounts for Ski Club members: from shops in the UK including Fat Face, Ellis Brigham, Snow+Rock, Blacks and White Stuff, to accommodation, ski schools and ski hire shops in resort. Members can also get discounts on car hire, airport parking, transfer services, health and fitness services, at dry slopes and online shops. In addition, over 90 tour operators offer a discount on holidays to Ski Club members.

Information. Comprehensive snow reports are available online at www.skiclub.co.uk, as well as a resort guide to over 250 resorts. The website includes all the latest news from the snowsports world, plus guides to download on fitness for skiing, working in a ski resort, travelling independently, instructor courses etc.

Events. The Ski Club holds two Annual Balls as well as plenty of parties and other special events throughout the year. The Club also runs fun racing events for individuals and families in Verbier and Zermatt during the season.

Holidays. As well as a search engine for finding the right tour operator for the user's requirements, there is also a Travel Service for booking at a discounted price, and Ski Freshtracks (www.skifreshtracks.co.uk), a programme of holidays run by the Ski Club. Freshtracks holidays are tailored to the level and type of skier.

Ski Club Representatives. Members can ski with Ski Club Reps, who are trained volunteers based in 41 resorts across the world. Skiing with a rep is an excellent way to discover the best areas in a resort as well as hook up with other Ski Club members. Different days with the rep cater for different standards. Reps also provide a social focus in the resort.

To become a Ski Club rep you should be aged 22 to 50, with at least 15 weeks' experience skiing or snowboarding. The Club provides board and lodging and a ski pass and covers travel and general expenses. No actual wages are paid. The Club looks for a long term commitment from its reps, preferring that they give a minimum of three weeks to the job every year, or every other year, rather than just staying for one whole season. Reps are required to take part in a two-week training course in Tignes in December (at a cost of £1,400). The course includes safety on all types of snow, avalanches, first-aid, organising and judging British Ski Tests etc.

Reps can also become party leaders who lead the Ski Clubs Ski Freshtracks holidays if they have the required high standard of skiing (i.e. BASI qualified). Party leaders co-ordinate travel arrangements, organise instruction and take groups skiing. On the Club's 'Under 20' holidays, they have responsibility for children. Holidays last up to two weeks. Leaders have one day off on two-week holidays, and a half-day for holidays under two weeks, so it is quite intensive.

For more information on becoming a rep/party leader, see the Ski Club website.

NATIONAL SNOWSPORT ORGANISATIONS FOR ENGLAND, SCOTLAND AND WALES

There are national snowsport organisations in each of England, Scotland and Wales which are the snowsports' (skiing and snowboarding) governing bodies in the United Kingdom which administer the Snowlife Awards (www.snowlife.org.uk) at nine different levels. These organisations also administer a number of other awards including the ASSI (Artificial Slopes Ski Instructor) which authorises the holder to instruct on dry slopes. In Northern Ireland, candidates for training can contact Craigavon Golf and Country Club (see below).

Candidates for the ASSI qualification must have reached the required level, and be registered as a candidate club instructor. For the latest information concerning the training course contact the appropriate national office (addresses below).

Once the skier has attained Club Instructor status he or she is authorised to instruct beginners at the designated club/slope.

The coach qualification is aimed at those who work with young skiers on a regular basis. There are two levels: Artificial Slope Performance Coach (ASPC) and Coach (two types: Development and Racing). Basic entry requirements are ASSI and six weeks' experience on snow plus pre-course completion of various courses including BASP First Aid, or an equivalent. The English Ski Club coach qualification is awarded after further training including a week alpine course, 150 hours of logged teaching, formal approval by a club or ski slope and a one-week residential assessment. The ESC coach award authorises the holder to coach ESC's skiers abroad on snow. If you become a racing coach then you can coach the Club's racers abroad on snow. Ski course organiser courses are in three parts: Ski Course Organiser, Ski Course Leader Training and Ski Course Leader.

Exemptions from some of the above requirements may be granted to holders of British Association of Ski and Snowboard Instructors (BASI) qualifications.

Further details may be obtained from the Ski Councils (see below).

USEFUL ADDRESSES

English Ski Council: Area Library Building, Queensway Mall, The Cornbow, Halesowen, West Midlands B63 4AJ; ☎0121-501-2314; fax 0121-585-6448.
Northern Ireland Ski Council: 43 Ballymaconnel Road, Bangor, County Down, BT20 5PS; ☎028-91450275; www.niweb.com/niid/sport/skiin.
Snowsports Scotland: Caledonia House, South Gyle, Edinburgh EH12 9DQ; ☎0131-317 7280; info@snowsportscotland.org; www.snowsportscotland.org.
Ski Council of Wales: 240 Whitchurch Road, Cardiff CF4 3ND; 01222-619637.

ARTIFICIAL SKI SLOPES

Scotland, has the only reliable skiing season in the UK (usually from December to May) so it is hardly surprising that Britain has the largest number of dry ski slopes in the world at over 140 nationwide. They are very active in running competitions at local and national level. However, they to tend to be used seasonally as there is a surge of bookings leading up to the skiing season from those preparing for a 'real' skiing holiday, including school groups. Most are open from around September until April, with 50 or more open year round. Of these, some are small, only between 60 and 100 metres long, and exist as part of multi-activity holiday centres offering a range of sports to the holidaymaker. Most are between 100 and 200 metres long.

The largest artificial slopes are in Chatham, Edinburgh, Gloucester, Rossendale and Swadlincote. Sheffield's Ski Village, built on the site of a disused mine (0114-276 9459) even offers skiing weekends (with accommodation nearby in hotels). It may sound uninviting, but the 250,000 skiers a year which it attracts, presumably disagree. The slope at Rossendale employs three full-time instructors and, more significantly, a dozen part-time instructors who live within a 30-mile radius. Artificial slopes provide an admirable opportunity for would-be, full-time instructors to gain training, teaching experience and qualifications.

The following artificial ski slopes as listed by the Ski Councils and Snowsport bodies of the United Kingdom are:

Aldershot: Alpine Snowsports Centre. Gallwey Road, Aldershot, Hampshire GU11 2DD; ☎01252-325889; www.alpineski.co.uk.
Alford: Alford Ski Centre, Greystone Road, Alford, Aberdeenshire AB3 8HH; ☎01975-563024.
Aylesbury: Riviera Restaurant Suite, Ski & Watersports, Watermead, Aylesbury, Bucks HP19 3FU; ☎01296-432288.

Barnard Castle: X-Country Ski Track, High Force Training Centre, Forest in Teesdale, Barnard Castle, Co Durham DH12 OHA; ☎01833-622302.

Bebington: Oval Sports Centre, Old Chester Road, Bebington, Wirral, Merseyside L63 7LF; ☎0151-6450551; fax 01511-644-1643.

Birmingham: Ackers Trust, Golden Hillock Road, Smallheath, Birmingham B11 2PY; ☎0121-772 3739; info@ackers.co.uk; www.ackers.co.uk.

Bracknell: John Nike Leisure Sport Ltd.,Bracknell Ski and Snowboard Centre, John Nike Way, Bracknell, Berks RG12 8TN; ☎01344-789002; ski-bracknell@nikegroup.co.uk; www.nikegroup.co.uk/jnl/bracknell.htm.

Brentwood: Brentwood Park Ski and Snowboard Centre, Warley Gap, Brentwood, Essex CM13 3LG; ☎01277-211994.

Burton-on-Trent: John Nike Leisuresport Ltd, Swadlincote Ski Centre, Hill Street, Swadlincote, Burton-on-Trent, Derbyshire DE11 8LP; ☎01283-217200; ski-swadlincote@nikegroup.co.uk; www.nikegroup.co.uk/jnl/swadlincote/htm.

Cardiff: Ski/Snowboard Centre Cardiff, Fairwater Road, Fairwater Park, Fairwater, Cardiff CF5 3JR; ☎029-2056 1793; www.skicardiff.com.

Carlisle: Carlisle Ski Slope, Edenside, Carlisle, Cumbria CA3 9NA; ☎01228-514569.

Catterick: Catterick Indoor Ski Centre, Loos Road, Catterick Garrison, North Yorkshire DL9 4LE; ☎01748-833788.

Chatham: John Nike Leisure Sport, Chatham Ski and Snowboard Centre, Alpine Park, Capstone Road, Chatham, Kent ME7 3JH; ☎01634 827979.

Christchurch: Christchurch Ski Centre: Matchams Lane, Hurn, Christchurch, Dorset BH23 6AW; ☎01202-499155; skicentre@lineone.net.

Churchill: Avon Ski Centre, Lyncombe Lodge, Churchill, North Somerset BS25 5PQ; ☎01934-852335; www.highaction.co.uk.

Craigavon: Craigavon Golf & Ski Centre, Turmoyra Lane, Lurgan, Craigavon, BT66 6NG, Northern Ireland; ☎028-3832 6606; www.craigavon.gov.uk.

Cramlington: Allenheads Northumberland, British Norwegian Ski Club, c/o 4 Yardley Grove, Cramlington, Northumberland NE23 1TW; ☎01670-715719; skiing@brisc.org.uk.

Dundee: Ancrum Outdoor Centre: 10 Ancrum Road, Dundee DD2 2HZ; ☎0382-435911; fax 01382 435915; ancrum.centre@dundeecity.gov.uk; www.dundeecity.gov.uk.

Edinburgh: Midlothian Ski Centre: Hillend, Biggar Road, Nr. Edinburgh EH10 7DU; 0131-445 4433; www.midlothian.gov.uk.

Esher: Sandown Ski School, More Lane, Esher, Surrey KT10 8AN; ☎01372-467132; www.sandownsports.co.uk.

Exeter: Exeter and District Ski Slope, Clifton Hill Sports Ground, Belmont Road, Exeter, Devon EX2 2DJ; ☎01392-211422.

Folkestone: Folkestone Sports Centre, Radnor Park Avenue, Folkestone, Kent CT19 5HX; 01303-850333.

Gateshead: Whickham Thorns Ski Centre, Market Lane, Dunston, Gateshead, Tyne and Wear, NE11 9NX; ☎0191-4601193.

Glasgow: Bearsden Ski and Board, The Mound, Stockiemuir Road, Bearsden, Glasgow G61 3RS; ☎0141-943 1500; fax 0141 942 4705; www.skibearsden.co.uk.

Glasgow: Glasgow Ski/Snowboard Centre, Bellahouston Park 16, Dunbreck Road, Glasgow G41 5BW; ☎0141-427 4991/3; www.ski-glasgow.org.

Gloucester: Gloucester Ski and Snowboard Centre, Robinswood Hill, Matson Lane, Gloucester GL4 9EA; ☎01452-414300.

Glyntawe: Dan-yr-Ogof Ski Slope: Abercrave, Glyntawe, Upper Swansea Valley, West Glamorgan; 01639-730284.

Guildford: Bishop Reindorp Ski School, Larch Avenue, Guildford, Surrey; ☎01483-504988; www.brski.co.uk.

Hailsham: Knockhatch Ski Centre: Hempstead Lane, Hailsham, E. Sussex. BN27 3PR.

Halifax: Halifax Ski and Snowboard Centre, Sportsman Leisure, Bradford Old Road, Swalesmoor, Halifax HX3 6UG; ☎01422-340760.

Hemel Hempstead: Hemel Ski Centre, Wheelers Lane, St Albans Hill, Hemel Hempstead, Herts. HP3 9NH; ☎01442-241321; communicate@hemel-ski.co.uk; www.hemel-ski.co.uk.

High Wycombe: Wickham Summit Ski and Snowboard Center, Abbey Barn Lane, High Wycombe, Bucks HP10 9QQ; ☎01494 474711; info@wycombesummit.com; www.wycombesummit.co.uk.

Ipswich: Suffolk Ski Centre, Bourne Hill, Wherestead, Ipswich, Suffolk IP2 8NQ; ☎01473-602347; 01473-602260.

Kendal: Kendal Ski Club: Thorny Hills, Kendal, Cumbria; ☎01539-733031; sec@kendalski.co.uk.

Llandudno: John Nike Leisuresport, Wyddfyd Road, Great Orme, Llandudno, Gwynedd, LL30 2QL; ☎01492-874707; www.jnl.co.uk.

Llanelli: Ski Pembrey, Pembrey Country Park, Llanelli, Carmarthenshire SA16 OEJ; ☎01554-834443..

London Docklands: Beckton Alpine Ski Centre, Alpine Way, London Docklands E6 4LA; ☎0207-511 0351; ski@becktonalps.co.uk.

Milton Keynes: Snozone, Xscape, 602 Marlborough Gate, Central Milton Keynes MK9 3XS; tel01908-230260; www.snozonemk.co.uk.

Norwich: Norfolk Ski Club, Whitlingham Lane, Trowse, Norwich NR14 8TW; ☎01603-662781; info@norfolkskiclub.co.uk; www.norfolkskiclub.co.uk.

Orpington: Bromley Ski Centre, Sandy Lane, St. Pauls Cray, Orpington, Kent BR5 3HY; ☎01689-876812; bromski@lineone.net.

Pendle: Pendle Ski Club, Clitheroe Road, Clitheroe, Lancs BB7 9HN; ☎0200-425222.

Plas-y-Brenin: National Centre for Mountain Activities, Capel Curig, Gwynedd LL24 OET; ☎01690-720214.

Plymouth: Plymouth Ski Centre, John Nike Leisuresport, Alpine Park, Marsh Mills, Plymouth PL6 8LQ; ☎01752-600220; www.nikegroup.co.uk/jnl/plymouth.htm.

Polmonthill: Polmonthill Ski Centre, Polmont, Falkirk FK2 OYE; ☎01324 503835.

Pontypool: Pontypool Leisure Park, Pontypool, Gwent NP4 8AT; ☎01495-756955.

Rossendale: Ski Rossendale, Haslingden Old Road, Rawtenstall, Rossendale, Lancs. BB4 8RR; ☎01706-226457; info@ski-rossendale.co.uk; www.skirossendale.co.uk.

Royston: Bassingbourn Ski Centre, 1 Rose Villas, Jacksons Lane Reed, Nr. Royston, Herts. SGB 8AB; ☎0763-848114; bassingbourn@community.co.uk.

Runcorn: Runcorn Ski/Snowboard Centre: Town Park, Palacefields, Runcorn, Cheshire WA7 2PS; ☎01928-701965; info@runcornskicentre.co.uk.

Rushden: Skew Bridge Ski Slope, Northampton Road, Rushden, Northants. NN10 9NP; ☎01933-359939.

Sheffield: Sheffield Ski Village, Vale Road, Parkwood Springs, Sheffield S3 9SJ; ☎0114-2769459; info@sheffieldskivillage.co.uk; www.sheffieldskivillage.co.uk.

Silksworth: Silksworth Ski Centre, Silksworth Sports Complex, Silksworth, Tyne and Wear SR2 3AW; ☎0191-5535785.

Southampton: Calshot Activities Centre: Calshot Spit, Fawley, Southampton, Hampshire SO4 1BR; ☎023-8089 2077; calshot.ac@hants.gov.uk; www.hants.gove.uk/calshot.

Southampton: Southampton Ski and Snowboard Centre, Sports Centre, Bassett, Southampton S016 7AY; ☎023-8079 0970; ski.centre@southampton.gov.uk.

Stamford: Tallington Ski and Snowboard Centre, Tallington Lakes Leisure Park, Barholm Road, Nr Stamford, Lincolnshire PE9 4RJ; ☎01778-346342; www.waspdirect.com.

Stoke-on-Trent: Festival Park, Stoke-on-Trent, Staffs ST1 5PU; ☎01782-204159.

Stoke-on-Trent: Kidsgrove Centre, Kidsgrove, Stoke-on-Trent ST7 4EF; ☎01782-784908; www.ski-kidsgrove.co.uk.

Tamworth: Tamworth Snowdome Ltd, Castle Grounds, River Drive, Tamworth, Staffs.

B79 7ND; ☎01827 67905; info@snowdome.co.uk; www.snowdome.co.uk.

Swansea: Dan-yr-Ogof Ski Slopes, Abercrave, Upper Swansea Valley, Powys SA9 1GL; ☎01639-730284. Telford: Telford Ski Centre, Court Centre, Madeley, Telford, Shropshire TF7 5DZ; ☎01952-586862.

Tillycoultry: Firpark Ski Centre, Tillycoultry, Clackmannanshire, FK13 6PL; ☎01259-751772.

Torquay: Alpine Ski Club, Barton Hall, Kinkerswell Lane, Torquay, Devon; ☎01803-313350; info@skitorquay.co.uk

Tunbridge Wells: Bowles Outdoor Centre, Eridge Green, Tunbridge Wells, Kent TN3 9LW; ☎01892-665665; admin@bowles.ac.; www.bowles.ac.

Warmwell: Warmwell Snow-Zone. Warmwell Leisure Resort, Warmwell, Dorset, DT2 8JE; ☎01305-853245.

Wellington: Wellington Sports Centre, Corams Lane, Wellington, Somerset TA21 8LL; ☎01823-663010; wellington.sportscentre@tauntondeane.gov.uk; www.tauntondeaneleisure.co.uk.

Weardale Ski Club: Swinchope Moor, B6293, Westgate, Weardale; ☎01388-517402.

Welwyn Garden City: Gosling Ski Centre, Gosling Stadium, Stanborough Road, Welwyn Garden City, Herts AL8 6XE; ☎01707-384384; www.goslingsport.co.uk.

Yeovil: Yeovil Ski Centre, Addlewell Lane, Nine Springs, Yeovil, Somerset BA20 1QW; ☎01935-21702.

OTHER OPPORTUNITIES

ALPINE ANSWERS
Specialist Ski Travel Agency, The Business Village, 3-9 Broomhill Road, London SW18 4JQ; ☎020-8871 4656; fax 020-8871 9676; ski@alpineanswers. co.uk; www.alpineanswers.co.uk.

Alpine answers brokers holidays for 70-80 ski tour operators' programmes in Europe and North America. They do not employ staff in the resorts but they do employ 4 seasonal sales staff at their London offices for eight months for about 16.5K per annum. All staff are entitled to a free skiing holiday, usually in a catered chalet, at the end of the season in a top Alpine resort e.g. Zermatt, Courchevel etc.

A typical applicant would be a young graduate with a great interest in skiing (and preferably at least one season under their belt). The job involves advising and selling ski holidays on the telephone and via e-mail. The employment period is from August to March. Applications in April/July to Hannah Savory at the above address.

FREE RADICALS SKI RECRUITMENT: ☎ 07968 183 848; Claire@freeradicals. co.uk; www.freeradicals.co.uk
Free Radicals is an independent ski recruitment specialist. One application form will open the gateway to all the UK's top independent ski companies. Your details are matched to the ideal company and registration with Ski Radicals is free. There are jobs for Chalet Chefs, Hosts, Helpers, Drivers, Ski Guides, Resort Management, Nannies and Mother's Helps. Contact Free Radicals at the above website.

HARRI'S BAR
Evolution 2, Hotel Le Lavachet, 73320 Tignes, France; ☎+33 4 79 06 48 11; fax +33 4 79 06 57 13; info@skibarjobs.com; www.skibarjobs.com.
Evolution 2 is a French company based in Tignes and runs Harri's Bar, one of the resort's biggest and liveliest bars with a large British clientele. They recruit:
Bar staff: must be enthusiastic, presentable, outgoing and fun-loving personalities. Previous experience not essential but must be hard-working and able to fit into a team

quickly.

Chefs: should have experience of ordering for and setting up three-course menus for up to 100 hotel guests for the pre-season period. During the main season the chef will run a pub-food menu, prepare local speciality meals for up to 100 people several times a week and provide staff meals each evening.

Kitchen hands: for cleaning and washing up; also to fill in for the chef with the pub-food menu on days off.

Staff should be willing to work as a team and infuse the bar with a positive and enthusiastic spirit. December to April hours of work are 3.30pm-1.30am with a meal break, and there are two full days off per week. Pay starts at £300 net per month not including tips and there is a discretionary end of season bonus. Good quality shared accommodation, daily evening meal and the usual ski perks. Chance to ski every day.

Apply from 7th October to Jeremy Goodall.

HOTEL BELLES PISTES
56 Route du Pernand, Les Carroz, 74300 Cluses, France; ☎+33 450 90 00 17; fax +33 450 90 30 70; www.hotelbellespistes.com; jobs@hotelbellespistes. com.

Hotel Belles Pistes is a British, family-owned, two star hotel near the centre of the ski resort of Les Carroz and 50 metres from the lift to the Grand Massif skiing area. They recruit up to seven staff: **Chamber staff** (2), **bar staff** (2), **waiting person, washing-up person** and a **kitchen assistant**.

All applicants must be aged 20+ and have a reasonable standard of the French language. Ski perks include free board and lodging, return travel, ski pass and equipment and €120 weekly pocket money.

Applications with a CV and photo should be sent from the 1st September to Darren Faulkner at the above address.

JOBS IN THE ALPS
www.jobs-in-the-alps.co.uk; e-mail info@jobs-in-the-alps.co.uk

Anyone looking for work in a hotel in a ski resort in France or Switzerland should consider contacting the employment agency Jobs in the Alps which has been arranging jobs in Alpine hotels since 1972. They recruit about 200 staff for various positions in Swiss ski resorts, for which good German or French is usually required. There are normally many more applicants than jobs and Jobs in the Alps applies high standards in its selection process. They often find workers for the same employers year after year and so it is in their own interests to make sure employers are satisfied with the employees they get.

Working in any locally-owned Austrian, Swiss, German or French hotel is quite different from work in a hotel in France leased by a British tour operator and run with an entirely British team for entirely British guests. The former are run to the exacting standards of professional hoteliers for reasonable pay and conditions and every opportunity to speak French or German. The latter are more informal with a relaxed ambience and nothing but English spoken, one day off per week and less pay than in a Swiss or French hotel.

Jobs in the Alps does not impose pre-conditions on applicants except that they must be over 18 and available for the whole season from December to April. However, knowledge of French or German and/or real hotel experience enables applicants to compete for the more interesting jobs in these hotels.

Most of the jobs are in Switzerland. Under the name Alpotels, the agency carries out aptitude testing on on behalf of German and French hotels for the winter season. The employers ask for workers to fill vacancies for set periods with languages/experience required. Some jobs are in formal hotels with a rigid hierarchy, others in family hotels with a small versatile team, some in informal restaurants or cafés with a local clientele. Jobs in the Alps reckon that they place twice as many girls as boys because that is the way the aptitude of applicants turns out.

All jobs are with known employers on the correct conditions giving a wide berth to those who seek to recruit and exploit cheap labour. Currently in Switzerland, the normal working day is 8/9 hours (excluding meals) which makes a 45-hour week with two free days per week. However, as in all seasonal work this schedule tends to be ignored at Christmas and other peak periods and is compensated for when the pressure eases. The minimum salaries are about £545 net with board and lodging provided. This compares with salaries of about £180-£200 per month in British tour operators' hotels in France.

Jobs in the Alps visit every employer and worker every other season, sometimes every season. Thus they know well what each job entails and can select the right person for it. They also learn how each individual is getting on and, if something is going wrong, can take steps to correct it.

Jobs in the Alps charge a flat fee of £30 plus £20 for each month they work, up to a maximum of £110. No fee is charged for those who wish to work again for the same employer. Many who have enjoyed a winter season return the following summer – and often enjoy it more. The closing date for applications and interviews are 30 September (winter) and 30 April (summer) but aptitude tests are carried out in October for late applicants, who may come in as reserves in due course. The main job offers are made in October for the winter and May for the summer to give employers ample time to obtain the essential work permits.

MACDONALD AVIEMORE MOUNTAIN RESORT
Aviemore, Inverness-shire PH22 1PN; ☎0845 608 3783; www. AviemoreHighlandResort.com.
In the autumn of 2005 a year-long independent study was concluded into how Aviemore could be turned into a world class mountain resort. Macdonald Hotels led the consortium to redevelop Aviemore and spent 80 million pounds on regenerating the resort including the outdated Aviemore Centre facilities, which now including a state-of-the-art swimming pool, a health spa and beauty complex, and it also owns several Aviemore hotels including Macdonalds Highlands hotel and the Macdonalds Four Seasons. There is also a training Academy in resort, based in the hotels and business centres which offers one day courses and nationally recognised qualifications such as Scottish Vocational Qualifications (SVQs) for people working in the hospitality and tourism sector. The Academy is run in conjunction with the North Highland College.

The Ski School (☎07881-988484) is the only ski school based on Cairngorm Mountain. The ticket office is located in ski hire in the Day Lodge on Cairngorm. Together these organisations offer hospitality training courses, jobs for catering and bar staff, as well as ski technicians, ski instructors, ticket vendors, etc. A reasonable proportion of these jobs are open to North Americans and Australians in possession of the appropriate working visas. For further information see the *Scotland* section.

PAMPER OFF PISTE
42 Aglionby Street, Carlisle, Cumbria CA1 1JP; ☎07950038353; fax 01697-476606; e-mail enquiry@pamperoffpiste.com; www.pamperoffpiste.com.
Pamper off Piste is a mobile massage and beauty service that operates in the French ski resorts of Courchevel, Méribel-Motteret, La Tania, Val d'Isère and Morzine as well as in London. Staff visit clients in their chalets. They employ **Massage Therapists (8), Beauty Therapists (5)** and **Reflexologists (3).**

The company is owned by Anna Sanderson who is always interested to hear from suitable applicants. You should have the relevant qualifications and be over 18 years old. All staff get accommodation, and a lift pass included in their employment package. Pay is competitive and related to age and experience. Employment dates are from 1 December to 1 May. Apply through the website above or contact her at the above address.

PIERRE ET VACANCES HEAD OFFICE
L'Artois – Espace Port de Flandre, 11 rue Cambrai, 75019 Paris, Cedex 19; ☎+33 (0)1 58 21 5821; pvtrecrutement@pierre-vacances.com.
Large French holiday and property company which has hotels and self-catering apartments in most French ski resorts. They employ **resort representatives** from different EU countries. Applicants must be aged 23+ and be fluent in French. This is a demanding job, which requires a lot of initiative. Salary is commensurate with experience, accommodation and meal vouchers provided, plus ski perks. Applications should be made (with a hand-written letter letter of application), to the Personnel Department at the above address.

PRECISION SKI
BP 110, 73320 Tignes Cedex, France; ☎+33 (0)4 79 40 07 43; fax +33 (0)4 79 06 49 43; in Val d'Isére at BP 313, 73150 Val d'Isére; staff@precision-ski.com and info@favresports.com; www.precision-ski.fr.
Precision has award winning ski and board shops in Val d'Isère and Tignes and recruits staff to work in them. Enthusiastic skiers and boarders are needed to work in its rental departments as **ski fitters** and to look after clients. Knowledgeable individuals are needed for **sales positions** in the equipment, clothing and accessories departments and **cashiers** are required for all areas of the shops. There are also positions in the workshops and for drivers.

Applicants should be aged 21+. Good English is essential and good French is very advantageous. Previous retail experience is beneficial. All staff undergo intensive training at the beginning of the season. Applications by e-mail to info@favresports.com. More information on the website www.precision-ski.fr.

SKI HIGHER
La Vieille Scierie, 73550 Les Allues Méribel, France; ☎+33 (0)4 79 00 51 70; e-mail skihigher@wanadoo.fr; www.skihigher.com.
Ski Higher is a ski equipment and ski rental business with four shops in Les Allues, La Tania, Courchevel 1850, Le Praz 1300 and a mobile ski rental service for fitting boots and skis, which operates in the Les Gets, Portes du Soleil skiing area. During the season they employ a total of about 30-35 staff based in the French Alps at their five centres. Staff tend to be either French or British passport holders.

Applications are welcomed for **Retail** and **Ski Technician** positions. Candidates should have extensive experience and a good level of French. Workshop technicians should have experience with Winterstiger or similar machines. Salaries are very competitive at £1,000 per month with accommodation provided. The work period begins 1 December. Contact Simon Hooper, Recruitment Manager at the above address.

SNOW-FUN
BP 110, Le Grand Tichot, Val Claret, 73322 Tignes Cedex, France.
For nearly 25 years, Snow-Fun have been at the forefront of the ski and board scene in the Espace Killy and have expanded to fifteen shops located throughout Tignes and Val d' Isère. Staff are recruited to work in these shops:
Sales staff: for ski, board, clothing and accessory departments. Must be knowledgeable.
Ski tecs: for the rental department. Responsible for ski, board and boot rental. Training will be provided on how to fit boots and adjust bindings.
Workshop technicians: responsible for tuning skis and boards and carrying out repairs. Full training provided.

Previous experience is beneficial for all positions. All applicants must speak good English and the ability to speak French as well is even better. Applicants can be residents of the EU or other nationalities with a working visa. Apply by e-mail to jobs@snowfunsport.com attaching a CV and photo, or visit www.snowfunsport.com for further information.

UK OVERSEAS HANDLING (UKOH) TRAINEE PLACEMENTS
Third Floor, Link Line House, 65 Church Road, Hove, East Sussex BN3 2BD; ☎0870 220 2148; ukoh@ukoh.co.uk; www.ukoh.co.uk
UKOH recruit all kinds of resort/hotel staff for its clients in France, but also offers a number of management, management trainee and student placement roles involved in all aspects of the resort and hotel management.

UPHILL SKI CLUB
Part of Disability Snowsport UK, Cairngorm Mountain, via Aviemore, Inverness-shire PH22 1RB; 01479-861272; www.disabilitysnowsport.org.uk
Disability Snowsport is a charity committed to providing skiing holidays for children and adults who have a wide range of mental and physical disabilities. They vary the resorts from season to season, but obviously select those with hotels or accommodation appropriate for groups of clients. A variety of specially adapted equipment such as sit-skis for wheelchair clients is used. It costs the clients about £500 for a week all inclusive holiday. Able-bodied volunteer helpers (one to every two skiers),qualified instructors and medical staff accompany each group. For further details of help required go to the above website and download information packs for different volunteer jobs.

VILLAGE CAMPS SA.
rue de la Morache, 1260 Nyon, Switzerland; ☎022-990 9405/fax 022-990 9494; personnel@villagecamps.ch
Village Camps was founded in 1972 by Robert McCausland and Roger Ratner, to organise leisure camps for children. In winter there are camps in Anzère and Leysin in Switzerland. Many of the programmes are educational as well as recreational and include other activities besides skiing. The staff and children are multinational with English being the common language. Several types of staff are taken on for the winter, predominantly ski counsellors of which 100 are hired annually.

Ski counsellors: age 21+. Must hold an internationally recognised Ski Instructor certificate.

Skiing nurses, house staff: age: 19+ for house staff, 21+ for nurses.

Ski counsellors get about SFr 385-435 per week, room and board, ski pass and insurance. Nurses get SFr 150 and the above. House-staff wages depend on experience. Contracts can be as short as ten days, but a few season-long contracts are issued to exceptional candidates.

As Village Camps also run summer multi-activity, language camps in Switzerland, France, Austria, Germany and England, there are possibilities for winter staff to be taken on in the summer as well. Applicants must be bilingual in English and one other language. Nurses, tennis coaches, swimming, art, canoeing instructors and a rock climbing specialist. Age 21+. EFL teachers with a minimum of three years' experience.

EUROPE

Finding a Job on the Spot

Reports from the Resorts

Where the jobs are
How to get them
Cheap Accommodation
Skiing and nightlife

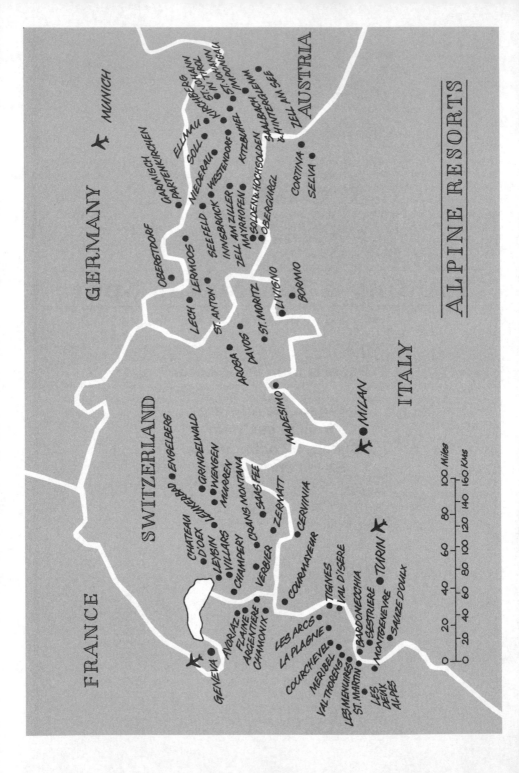

Some Hints For Independent Ski Resort Workers

TRAVEL

Getting within range of most ski resorts presents no problem. Many are near major cities like Lyon, Geneva, Salzburg, Innsbruck, Munich, Milan or Turin, which are all easily accessible by rail, coach or hitching. Most of them are also reachable by with frills, and no frills airlines, and charter flights.

Since the last edition of this book the budget airline industry has continued to expand its wings (!) to such an extent it seems there is barely a city in Italy or France, if not Europe, that cannot be reached by EasyJet or Ryan Air, plus a growing number of smaller no frills operators which have sprung up in almost every European country. These operators fly to destinations in useful proximity to ski areas such as BMI Baby's route from East Midlands airport to Bergamo in northern Italy. The airline scene is in a constant state of flux: route changes and additions, appearing and disappearing airline names, giveaway flights on new routes and so on, therefore the internet is a vital tool for up-to-date information. In 2006, Jet2.com was offering one-way fares from £9 on its new service to Salzburg. It is also worth checking out national carriers such as BA and Swiss Air who are cutting their prices to compete in the budget market. At the time of press EasyJet destinations included Geneva, Zurich, Munich, Milan and Lyon; while Ryan Air was flying to dozens of European cities. British Airways has some splendid offers such as the current £35 for a one-way fare (including taxes) from Birmingham to Geneva.

Useful contacts:
Ski.OneTime.com. Searches for the cheapest ski flights
Jet2.com; www.jet2.com/ski/. Fares from £9 to Geneva, Milan, Salzburg.
British Airways: www.ba.connect.com. Regular bargains and decreasing fares.
Ryanair: ☎0871 246 000; www.ryanair.com. Flights to Turin, Lyon etc.

Also useful to those heading independently to ski resorts are tour operators unfilled flights, which are being sold increasingly on the internet. For instance Ski Power (www.skipower.co.uk) were offering oneway flights from Gatwick to Chambery (for the French Alps) from £15 in 2006. Although flights to Geneva are available every day of the week, the prices are lower at weekends because this is when most charter flights operate. Departure times are normally early in the morning. One-way flight prices vary during the season; the most expensive times are Christmas and February half term. In general, ski charter flights begin in early December and end at Easter.

Sources for finding out what the lowest fares are, as usual via the internet. Try googling 'ski flights' or look on one of the well known sites for finding the cheapest fares to anywhere, eg. www.opodo.com, www.cheap-flights.co.uk, www.lastminute.com etc, where you log in to your chosen destination and get a list of prices and companies. Transfers from the airports to the ski resorts can be arranged with the tour operators on arrival by approaching their reps at the airport for a seat on their coaches at a cost of £20-£35.

It is once the journey from the cities to the mountains starts that the problems of travelling around ski areas become apparent. Because of their location high in the Alpine valleys, travel between resorts can be limited to infrequent buses or cog railways and it can take at least a day to check out each resort – an expensive proposition if visiting many small ski areas in a country like Switzerland. On the other hand, some ski resorts, especially the more modern areas, are starting to link together with shuttle systems, so it can be a good idea to pick out clusters of resorts in one valley and try all the areas before moving on to the next.

For example, the valley above Moûtiers in France contains the major resorts of the Trois Vallées, La Plagne, Les Arcs, Tignes and Val d'Isère – all accessible from Moûtiers and a normally fertile hunting ground. However, hitching from there to the relatively nearby resorts of Flaine, Megève and Argentière can be a major undertaking on the lightly travelled roads.

Other clusters of resorts include the areas along the N9 between Aigle and Brig in Switzerland (Verbier, Crans, Montana, Saas Fee, Saas Grund, Zermatt and Leukerbad) and the towns above Interlaken in the Bernese Oberland, also in Switzerland.

However, do not rule out smaller towns and less well-known resorts. They may be more difficult to get to but that means there will be less competition for jobs. However, while this is recommended for those who can speak the local language it is on the whole much less feasible for those who speak only English.

Once the winter season has started, another very cheap way to get to the resort is to make a 'travel only' arrangement with a tour operator. It is not generally known that many operators are only too pleased to sell off spare seats on an aircraft or coach to individual travellers at sharply discounted rates. During January you can even get bargain basement prices on a week's bed and breakfast in a western European resort. According to the Ski Council Representative in Belfast there are usually many bargain ski offers available out of Belfast with reputable ski companies.

Dealing direct with the company has the added advantage that, if you fly out you will have the benefit of their transfer coach from the airport to the resort itself. Ring round all the tour operators serving your chosen destination, or check on the internet, to get the best possible deal. This method of travel can also work on the return journey; company representatives in the resort are often empowered to sell off spare seats notified to them by head office. Similarly if you only want a transfer from the resort to the airport (or vice versa), you can usually buy a seat on a tour operator's coach.

If you are capable of sheer effrontery you can get a free coach ride from Dover to the resort on a tour operator's bus taking the staff out a week before the season starts. Div, from Scotland could only afford a fare as far as Dover where he hopped aboard such a coach, mingled with the staff on board, mentioned a few names of company head office staff and bluffed a free ride to Morzine, where thankfully he managed to get work before he had to demonstrate even more desperate survival techniques.

Another way of getting out to the resort from the UK is to log on to Natives.com where you can find motorised lift shares advertised. You are expected to pay your share of the costs (mainly petrol) of getting there.

REFERENCES

Collect as many references from previous jobs as you can. It does not matter what kind of job they are for – after all, you never know what you will be offered – and if an engineering apprenticeship may not be strictly relevant to a kitchen porter's job, at least it shows that you have work experience and a former employer who is willing to recommend you. If you can get a translation made into the languages of the countries in which you are looking for work, so much the better.

JOBS

One of the best rules for job-hunters is to accept anything you are offered. The pay may be minimal and the hours may be rotten but at least it will give you a chance to settle into a place and look around for something else.

It is not likely that you will be able to walk into a town and immediately fix up a good job as a wait person or bartender so you are anyway more likely to be offered a menial post in the first instance.

As in holiday resorts everywhere, the service industries in ski resorts offer the best prospects for jobs. Hotels and restaurants open only for the summer and the winter in many ski towns and, with a seasonal staff, often have openings at the beginning of the season. These offer one of the best deals for travelling workers as wages are often higher in mainland Europe for this type of work than in comparable positions in Britain or Ireland. In a prosperous country like Switzerland, there is minimal competition from locals for jobs like dishwasher or janitor; but you will probably be up against migrant workers from Portugal, eastern Europe and Turkey. Larger hotels often have openings for chamber staff.

If you have any cooking experience, then you stand a fair chance of getting a kitchen job and can eventually find yourself with a good degree of responsibility, as there seems to be a continual shortage of qualified kitchen personnel.

Another job you may find in a larger hotel is that of porter, where the duties range from carrying bags to shovelling snow. If you are lucky, you may be promoted to bartender or waiter. Obviously knowledge of the local language is a prerequisite.

Ski lift companies also offer good prospects. Again, you must be able to communicate in the local language and if you have this ability then there are jobs for ticket collectors, lift operators or mechanics with the possibility in some cases of being retained for summer work. One perk of these jobs is the free ski pass that goes with the position, not a bad deal in areas where a season's pass can set you back £600+.

Ski schools are sometimes on the look out for staff – but in most places these jobs are taken by locals and any work you get is likely to be of a temporary nature. The exception is in the British-run ski schools of which there are now a handful in the French Alps (see *Types of Job Available*). If you really want to be an instructor it is far better to get a job with one of these schools or a British tour operator. Some people have managed to get work by setting themselves up as a private tutor – usually through contacts with other foreign hotel workers or chalet girls – but this is frowned upon by local ski schools and the lift companies, who will not give you the queue-jumping privileges granted to official teachers; it may also be illegal in some resorts.

You should also check out the local version of estate agents and letting agencies. They often hold holiday flats and chalets and may need people for maintenance, cleaning or snow clearing duties. In fact, snow-shovelling driveways or roofs in some of the higher resorts can prove profitable as private enterprise – just put up a notice in the local tourist office, supermarket or town hall after a particularly heavy fall. The same goes for babysitting for foreign tourists in private chalets or pensions.

The other main ski-related activity is in winter sports shops as a sales clerk, a fitter for skis and boots and/or or ski maintenance or repair man (often referred to as a ski-man). Lack of expertise in a foreign language may not be too much of a problem, as many shops like to have English-speaking staff. For the maintenance jobs, previous experience is preferable but not strictly necessary for someone who has a good skiing background. The specialised skills involved in mounting bindings and waxing skis are quickly learned and representatives from the major ski and binding companies often hold certification courses for their products in the resorts. Be sure to hold on to these qualifications – they will stand you in good stead if you decide to spend another winter in the Alps. Jobs in the ski shops are popular even though they tend to offer lower than normal wages and often involve day work thus cutting down your skiing time. One reason for their popularity is the staff discount offered on ski equipment and clothing – often cost price for employees as it is a good advertisement.

SUMMER JOBS

Many ski resorts are in the business of marketing themselves as year-round resorts, but the fact is that employment prospects are geared mainly towards the winter and are considerably diminished during the summer. One problem you will face when trying to work year-round is the off season – usually about eight weeks from the middle of April when the lifts close and with a comparable autumn break from mid-September to mid-December. During this time hotels, restaurants and bars close down and a town which may have been host to 10,000 tourists in the winter contracts to its stable population of 1,000 farmers and construction workers. Even if they are not running a summer programme in the Alps, tour operators often refurbish their chalets and other buildings during summer in readiness for the winter season and it may be possible to enquire with them about work connected with this. In the spring issue of the BASI News (the newsletter of the British Association of Ski Instructors), the big operator First Choice was advertising for qualified painters, decorators, electricians, carpenters and plasterers to work a five-day week in the Alps.

It is still possible to get ski-related jobs in those resorts that are lucky enough to have a nearby glacier. These few resorts play host to specialist training camps for activities like ski-ballet, slalom and downhill racing or mogul and free-style skiing. The summer snow conditions are an acquired taste and range from ice in the morning to something approaching melting sorbet in the afternoon.

Other lower resorts specialise in summer sports. For example, Champéry in Switzerland is a centre for tennis. Tignes in France offers sailing and windsurfing and Garmisch-Partenkirchen in Germany attracts kayakers and mountaineers. There will be jobs available in hotels and restaurants and as instructors and sales clerks for people with the relevant skills. However, tourist traffic tends to be more from the home country than in the winter and so there is less demand for English-speakers.

One effect of the growing popularity of skiing and boarding has been the expansion programmes of existing resorts – and as a result the construction industry is one of the best areas to look for a job. There is also constant renovation and upgrading of existing accommodation.

Try estate agents or, better still, tour round the building sites and ask the foreman if any jobs are going. Wages are high for this kind of work and well they might be, for hours are often long and the work can be brutal to an unhardened physique. You will, in many resorts, be competing with workers from eastern Europe and the Mediterranean countries for jobs which start, for example, in Switzerland at about SFr 1,700 take home pay. Occasionally you may be able to combine a construction or renovation job with work as a caretaker/security person – giving you a free or cheap place to stay.

ACCOMMODATION

One of the perennial problems in the ski resorts, summer or winter, is the shortage of accommodation. Those high-rise apartment complexes are meant and priced for the affluent tourist, not the impoverished foreign worker – and because of the planned nature of some of the purpose-built resorts there is a lack of older and smaller living areas normally available to the transient employees.

The housing shortage will hit you at two times – when you look for a job and when you have found one. The best idea when on a job search is to use the network of youth hostels – there is normally one in the nearest major town and they are also good places to pick up hints about job possibilities. Some job seekers travel in camper-vans but this can be miserable – imagine spending the night in the supermarket carpark with the outside temperature at -6C as Nick Earl did in Pas de la Casa, Andorra.

If you have found a job in a hotel then you will normally get a place to stay in the building. Larger enterprises, such as ski-lift companies or sizeable sports shops also sometimes offer a chalet rented for seasonal employees. But if there is no work-related accommodation or you are self-employed then get up to the resort as early as possible and start checking out the possibilities. Throw yourself on the mercy of anyone you meet and trudge around the town. Quite often, the best areas to look are on the outskirts of the town or in nearby satellite villages. One final point, be careful about being drawn into a lease which ends in June, a common ploy with landlords who are trying to get revenue for the dead months of the off season when the lifts close.

Useful Contacts

Alpine Elements, Seasons on Snow (Alpine Elements Ltd, 1 Risborough Street, London SE1 OHF; 08700-111360; www.alpineelements.co.uk; info@alpineelements.co.uk). Seasons on Snow offers excellent grade accommodation for one to six months for snowboarders, skiers, ski bums, resort professionals, seasonaires and other like-minded snow fanatics, working or otherwise, in Tignes, Whistler, Morzine-Avoriaz, Serre Chevalier and Chamonix from £73 per week. Catered accommodation or self-catered available. The company tries to put compatible clients with similar interests and of similar ages together in the same chalet/apartment. Age range is mostly 18 to 36 but can be older.

www.seasonaires.com offers accommodation for one to six months of the ski season in many resorts worldwide including many French resorts and Whistler and Fernie in Canada and Breckenridge and Mammouth (USA) and Wannaka (New Zealand). By booking the accommodation before you travel you have a safe secure base from which to look for work. Contact info@seasonaires.com or ☎0870 068 4545.

www.planetsubzero.com are seasonal accommodation specialists, offering affordable accommodation for the ski season throughout the French Alps and in North America. Shared chalets or your own pad in all the main resorts, and stays from 3 weeks to the whole season. Resorts include: Les Arcs/Paradiski, Méribel, Courchevel, Chamonix, Tignes, Val d'Isère, Val Thorens and the Canadian resorts of Banff and Whistler. Aimed at anyone who wants to spend a winter in the mountains: skiers, boarders, young, old, gap year, sabbatical, want to work away from home etc. Contact info@planetsubzero. com or ☎+33 (0)6 79 17 85 78.

MOUNTAIN SAFETY

Safety is probably the last thing any seasonal ski worker thinks about, but according to ski instructor Rob Fowler who worked in the French Alps ignorance very definitely kills in the mountains. There were several fatalities due to avalanches that were barely reported outside the resort where he was working as a ski host. He says that it is essential to have a snowpack including a transceiver, and to know how to use it. Mobile phones can disrupt signals from transceivers and at least one resort last season was insisting that off piste skiers should leave theirs behind. The 2005/06 season in the French Alps produced a record number of avalanche fatalities (55) blamed on the type of snow conditions, but triggered by the victims or people they were skiing with. There is at least one case of manslaughter being brought against some skiers who started an avalanche that killed another skier. The

American Institute for Avalanche Research and Education (www.avtraining.org) is one of the leading authorities and course providers for avalanche training at Levels 1, 2, and 3 and also offers Instructor Training Courses. Level I is a good basic course for those who ski adventurously off piste and who want to stay safe. Avalanche courses are widely available in the European Alps for instance Chamonix Experience (info@chamex.com) offer one-day Avalanche Awareness courses for about €80. There are avalanche training courses held in the UK by amongst other bodies, the The Mountaineering Council of Scotland (www. mountaineering-scotland.org.uk), which runs one-day Avalanche Awareness courses in the Cairngorms (in 2007 these will will be on the 13th, 14th and 20th January) and cost £35. The Ski Club of Great Britain holds seminars including one on transceiver usage and hires out transceivers. Fresh Tracks (the skiing company that is part of SCGB) organises Mountain Safety Courses, as does Mountain Tracks (www.mountaintracks.co.uk). It is also worth asking in your resort about courses as it could be a lifesaver for yourself and others.

Useful Publications

The Avalanche Handbook: by David McLung and Peter Schaerer (£13.95). Try Amazon. co.uk for a discount price.

Avalanche Safety for Skiers, Climbers and Snowboarders: by Tony Daffern. Available from outdoor sports shops (not bookshops). Try also Amazon.com, which has new and used editions from $15.95.

Andorra

For those with limited pockets and ambitions the tiny independent principality (470 sq. kms) of Andorra, situated high in the Pyrenees between France and Spain, can provide marvellous, cheap skiing although its popularity has dropped recently as the requirement for even cheaper skiing has been satisfied by the new Eastern European countries of the European Union. Although this duty-free principality is not as cheap as it was some years ago, cameras, hi-fi equipment etc are slightly cheaper than the major UK discount stores. Leather goods, designer fashions and other luxury goods are all good value in the main shopping centres in the capital Andorra La Vella. Eating out is considerably cheaper than the French and Swiss resorts and if you stick to the menu of the day, a three-course dinner is still as little as £10 in a good restaurant.

After nearly a quarter of a century, Andorra has become very well known in Britain as a ski resort and there are five ski areas in the country. Pas de la Casa/Grau Roig, Soldeu/El Tartar, Arinsal, Pal and Aracalis. The main ones catering for the British tourist are Pas de la Casa/Grau Roig, Soldeu and Arinsal. Soldeu has aimed itself steadily upmarket over the last few years and is no longer a cheap resort. British tour operators including Inghams, First Choice, Thomson Ski and Snowboard and Crystal and increasing numbers of British skiers prefer the resorts of Andorra to their counterparts in the European Alps, so much so that there is a shortage of accommodation in the resorts themselves and many skiers find themselves lodged in La Massana or Andorra La Vella inconveniently distant from the slopes.

The nearest airport is Girona, which is one of Ryanair's busiest hubs and there are flights there from many UK airports, and Thomsonfly (www.thomsonfly.com) also fly there from the UK. Otherwise Barcelona airport is the nearest; Jet2.com (www.jet2.com) have cheap flights there from the UK. From France Carcassonne, Perpignan and Toulouse airports are the nearest options.

There are seven or eight skiing areas in the country (population approx. 70,000) but they are counted as five resorts: Pas de la Casa/Grau Roig, Soldeu/El Tarter, Arinsal, Pal and Arcalis. However, only two of these really count as resorts with associated accommodation, nightlife and opportunities for work: these are Soldeu/El Tarter and the smaller, newer Arinsal. Pas de la Casa, which lies just inside the country's eastern border with France, was until recently exclusively geared to French skiers who flood across at weekends. There are plenty of shops, bars, restaurants and discos and accommodation for about 6,000 in hotels and self-catering apartments. Unless you speak French, opportunities for work in Pas de la Casa are extremely limited but the demand for English speakers is present and definitely worth pursuing.

Pas de la Casa/Grau Roig

Pas de la Casa/Grau Roig (www.pas_grau.andorramania.com) is a small village, which has grown into a sizeable town fuelled by the French buying apartments there since about 1979. Skiing is very convenient as ski lifts go from the middle of the town up to the peak of the mountain and down the other side to Grau Roig. Several large British tour operators including Panorama and Airtours now offer holidays there. As this is the most recent resort to attract the British market, there should be more opportunities for work than in Soldeu and Arinsal where there are many people who return each year to the same job.

Soldeu

Soldeu (www.soldeuonline.com) was the original ski station in Andorra to be marketed to the British. Soldeu is linked to El Tartar and the majority of accommodation has either been in apartments or in small hotels. Josep Calbo, one of Soldeu's local entrepreneurs built the superb Sport Hotel Village, which greatly raised the standard of accommodation in Soldeu. Nobody need now look to Andorra as being 'cheap and cheerful' as the Sport compares very favourably with hotels in any of the Alpine resorts.

The Soldeu Ski School (☎+376 890591) is highly thought of and has a large English section. Skiers coming to Andorra will benefit from the high standard of teaching in English, which makes the resort particularly suitable for beginners.

The road from Soldeu descends through Canillo, Encamp and down to the capital Andorra la Vella. This town, the highest capital in Europe, is full of shops and supermarkets and also some very high quality shops such as Le Pyrenees (Andorra's answer to Harrods) which is a large store, full of merchandise with particular emphasis on designer items, all at competitive prices.

From Andorra la Vella the roads divide. The main road descends down into Spain, where the first town is La Seu d'Urgell, site of international Canoe and Kayak competitions including for the 1992 Olympic Games. To the right is the road to the La Massana Valley, which rises up some 1,500 feet in five miles and passes through La Massana and on to Arinsal and Pal.

Pal/Arinsal

Pal and Arinsal (www.arinsal.com) both belong to the Commune of La Massana. Arinsal was newly-created as a ski resort in the 1970s. For several years, combining Pal and Arinsal into one ski area was talked about, until finally in 2000/01 a 50-person cable-car was inaugurated and the two resorts were linked. This made Pal/Arinsal a superb skiing area with the contrast of Pal, which is slightly lower and heavily wooded, with Arinsal, which is in a large northeast-facing bowl.

Pal/Arinsal

Pal is a ski station without any accommodation nearby and it is mostly aimed at the Spanish weekend market. Arinsal is one of the main centres for the British skier in Andorra, The pistes have been expanded over the last decade and an extensive snow making plant has been installed. Once again Arinsal has a large part of its ski school devoted to the British market with a considerable number of British, Australian and other English- speaking nationalities working as instructors.

There are 11 mountain restaurants Arinsal/Pal. Arinsal village has developed over the last few years and is now linked to Pal by skilift. There are many new hotels and many new apartment blocks. The village also has some ten bars, two discos and half a dozen good restaurants. Among the places which should not be missed are Cisco's located in a woodland setting, which is a bar/disco/Tex Mex restaurant, while Frankfurt Joan's located in the shopping centre at the foot of the slopes is a classic which serves hot sandwiches and pizzas as well as more traditional fare. Rocky Mountain (+376 837 532) is a particularly lively place in the evenings and packed at breakfast and lunchtimes too. For sunbathers there is Restaurant El Refugi (+376 836 767) where can enjoy your food on the terrace at the food of the slopes. If you want to hear yourself speak try the bar at the Arinsal Hotel.

Arcalis

Arcalis ski station is about 15kms from La Massana. It is a superb ski area with rugged, bold mountainous country. It has the best snow record in Andorra but like Pal has no accommodation nearby. However there is a good ski school which now has several English-speaking instructors. Public transport by bus is steadily improving but it is still not easy to get from Arinsal to Arcalis. A car is therefore a great asset particularly if you want to ski at any of the other ski stations.

The whole area carries an atmosphere of relaxed charm. It has none of the sophisticated jet-set glamour other resorts have and is quite content to do without it. The locals are reserved but friendly and anxious for you to have a good time in their country, so visitors rapidly drop their guard. Nearly all the English-speaking workers are British, a high proportion of them Scots. The resorts are small enough for them all to get to know each other well, and a considerable group spirit develops by the end of the season, so that many of them make plans to return the following season.

WORK

Nearly all of the seasonal workers have jobs arranged either from the previous year or before they arrive. Tour operators' representatives are nowadays likely to be career jobs rather than seasonal but for details contact the companies concerned.

The Red Rock, in Arinsal and the Sport Hotel in Soldeu are still the best places to meet the local English-speaking workers and tap into the local grapevine, listen for jobs and put your name about.

Nick Earl who worked a season in the sports shop Ski Evasio in Pas de la Casa, said that there are plenty of British skiers in the resort all season so there is a demand for English-speaking staff in many establishments. He suggests turning up at the end of the season and arranging a job for the following season. According to Nick, the best places to try for work are the bars, clubs, hotels and ski shops that deal with British skiers and which include: the Marseilles bar/restaurant, Milwauke bar, El Mexicano bar and Bilbord Club. He recommends that you speak some French/Spanish as this will greatly improve your chances as will previous relevant experience.

Nick Earl explains how he landed sports shop in Pas de la Casa
I graduated from Southampton University and went to Andorra in November to look for work, i.e. before the season started. I got the job by asking around everywhere and getting to know a few people around the resort. I had never worked in a ski resort before but my knowledge of snowboarding and ability to speak good French helped me get the job at Ski Evasio. A guy at the shop left, and because I was known there they employed me. I also had to learn to speak Spanish while I was there. Luckily, the agency which owned the shop arranged a flat for my two friends and myself at a subsidised monthly rent. While looking for jobs we had been sleeping in our van at the supermarket car park – not an enjoyable experience with the freezing temperatures outside. I had one and a half days off a week plus two hours at lunchtimes and spent most of my free time snowboarding. The shop specialised in snowboarding equipment for rent or sale. The regular trade was in renting skiing and snowboarding equipment, which was my main area of work. On the whole I enjoyed my job, not least because I could use the repair facilities at the shop for my own equipment and make use of the hire equipment there. I also found my employers and the other guys in the shop congenial. The only irritation was that I needed a work/residence permit, which is obligatory for foreigners as Andorra is not in the EU. Once you have arranged a job you then arrange the permit. It is not difficult to obtain but is very complicated and time-consuming. I had to make at least four trips down to Andorra la Vella to Immigration and the hospital for the medical examinations.

After the season in Andorra, Nick returned to London to begin a commission in the Royal Navy but he looks back on his time in Andorra with happy memories
I personally enjoyed making loads of friends who weren't English. Overall I had a fantastic season and although I worked very hard, had plenty of time for snowboarding and every evening free to enjoy myself. I would recommend it to anyone.

Keith Meaden, aged 22, also worked the same season in Pas de la Casa as a night security guard. He is a friend of Nick Earl's (see above) whose employers also owned an apartment block in the town. When they sacked the incumbent security guard in December, Nick was able to suggest Keith for the job. The employers wanted someone physically robust and English-speaking as most of the clients in the apartments were Brits. Keith had been trying to get a job in the resort from the end of November, but without the relevant foreign languages he found it difficult. The security job was reasonably paid at approximately £500 per month, but either 'pretty boring' (most of the time) or sometimes annoying for instance when he had to deal with inebriated clients breaking the noise regulations late at night. However, he did have all day free and though he had to catch up on his sleep he still found plenty of time for snowboarding. Tiredness did however become a consistent problem. After Andorra, Keith knew he could get a summer job teaching watersports and then spend another season working in a ski resort.

Another possibility in Pas de la Casa is in the supermarket. Andrew Morton, aged 28, got a job there as an assistant after arriving in the resort after the season had started in mid-December. He was taken on because the employer needed someone to deal with the British clients. Andrew also spoke Spanish having spent the previous summer working in Seville. Before that he was in banking in the UK for five years. His wages were good, about £700 monthly, but there was no accommodation provided. He shared a flat with some other British workers in the resort. His hours were very flexible and he managed to ski for a few hours every day. Other time off could always be arranged with the employer who would tell him when he was definitely needed and gave him plenty of choice for time off. The supermarket was open until 8 p.m. every evening and Andrew was expected to be there in the evenings, which were the busiest time. Despite the flexibility, he did not enjoy the work and was planning to return to London and the banking profession at the end of the season.

Andrew's girlfriend, Julie Mowat, aged 24, who speaks Spanish, managed to get a hotel job working in the laundry, disco and as a chambermaid with board and lodging included.

Lifts and Ski shops, Restaurants and Bars

Without exception the lift-operating, piste-bashing and snow-clearing is done by Andorrans. There are a few possible vacancies in the ski shops. There are also opportunities in bars, restaurants and discos particularly in Arinsal and Soldeu. The English bar is The Aspen in Soldeu, which is a combined bar/restaurant/club is almost entirely staffed by Brits. The club at Le Duc Hotel also employs English-speakers. The Hotel Rock in Soldeu has been known to employ English girls.

Ski Schools

All the ski schools are part of ENSISA, which is the national body that sets the standards and represents all the ski schools. Each Andorran resort organises its own recruitment and has a local manager. Arinsal and Soldeu are the biggest schools and employ the most British instructors. Instructors wishing to apply for work in Andorra should write enclosing details of their BASI or equivalent qualifications to the following:
Escola d'Esqui: Arinsal, La Massana, Principat d'Andorra (☎836135).
Escola d'Esqui: Soldeu, Principat d'Andorra (☎851269).

Over the past few years most Andorrans who deal with the holidaymakers have learned to speak good English as well as Spanish, French and Catalan, all of which the majority of Andorrans speak. There is therefore not as great a demand for imported English speakers as there once was.

Austria

REGULATIONS

Austria is in the EU so any job seeker from another EU country can turn up in Austria with just their passport to look for work. It has one of the lowest unemployment rates in Europe (4.5%). There is no shortage of hotel work, much of it is done by foreigners from Eastern Europe, particularly the countries that have recently become part of the EU, as well as by large numbers from Turkey and Bosnia. Immigrants from these countries are often preferred to ski bums as they are perceived as hard working and willing to do long hours. Many of them are supporting their families back home. The largest concentration of hotels and guesthouses etc is in the Tirol, and the Voralberg in western Austria is another good area. Those coming from outside the European Union are required to arrange a work permit before taking up work there but in reality this may be impractical. The national employment service is the *Arbeitmarktservice* though if you do not speak German they will find it virtually impossible to help you. If you do speak German you may find their website (www.ams.or.at) useful. Offices that specialise in seasonal work are called *BerufsInfoZentren* or BIZ. There are about 60 of these including eight in the Tirol. Many hotel and catering vacancies in the South Tirol are registered with the Euro BIZ Jobcentre at Schöpfstrasse 5, 6020 Innsbruck (eurobiz.innsbruck@702.ams.or.at). Most *Saisonstellen im Hotel und Gastwerbe* (seasonal hotel jobs) for the winter season are notified to the BIZ in time for the start of the season in November. Bars, shops and ski shops are other possible sources of work.

Au pairs from outside the EU have to have both a residence and work permit (*Beschäftigunsbewilligung*) which can be applied for outside Austria.

If you are working legally, expect to have about 16% of your gross wage deducted for compulsory contributions to the Health and Security Scheme (not au pairs). The government website www.help.gv.at/Content.Node/144/Seite.1440000.html gives information about immigration and social security procedures for those working in Austria.

As regards the job situation generally, Austria is still integrating refugees from former Yugoslavia and eastern Europe and this is affecting the employment situation for seasonal work. The *Arbeitsamt* (employment office) in Kitzbühel even went so far as to say it was nearly impossible to get because finding employment for refugees, particularly those from former-Yugoslavia, took precedence.

'Nearly impossible' may be a slight exaggeration. As many a seasoned alpine worker will tell you the situation is always changing and at Christmas time there is usually a healthy list of vacancies for the menial hotel jobs. By and large, it seems that a work permit (for those nationalities that require them) will be issued if staff is badly needed. Even if work permits are not forthcoming hoteliers are usually willing to take on workers part-time or even full-time in exchange for accommodation, meals and pocket money. If you manage to fix up a job with an Austrian employer in advance and you come from outside the EU you are supposed to have a permit sent to you before you enter Austria. In practice however, many workers find that the work permit materialises after they have started work. Wages in hotels and restaurants are not as high as in Switzerland.

There is also the possibility of obtaining a Volunteer Permit, which allows you to receive board and lodging with a family and a small amount of pocket money per week. Many 'volunteer workers' are discreetly paid more. Americans, Canadians and Australasians need a visa for staying longer than three months.

Many of the Tourist Offices in resorts act as unofficial employment or information centres and some have a proper employment agency (*Arbeitsamt*) where jobs are registered.

Up to the mid-1980s, Austria was the number one destination for British skiers. In the early 1990s, it lost out to France in the popularity stakes. It has never regained its supremacy with the Brits, 36% of whom take their skiing holidays in France while 20% choose Austria. Austria is not unexpectedly, Europe's biggest destination for German skiers. Britons nevertheless still rate many Austrian resorts highly and a couple of hundred thousand British package holidays skiers and boarders go there annually with British tour operators including Inghams, First Choice, Alpine Tours, Snowcoach, Thomson, Club Europe and Crystal and there is a considerable demand for English speaking staff of all types except ski instructors: Austrian ski resorts may have hundreds of ski schools and thousands of instructors but the Austrian National Ski School is particularly hard to penetrate and only about four in a hundred instructors are non-Austrian. Deutsch-Institut Tirol, based in Kitzbühel offer a course that combines ski and snowboard instruction with German language and is especially designed for gap year students wishing to study towards Austrian Instructor qualifications. More details in the *Kitzbühel* section.

As elsewhere, it is better for the independent worker with no languages to stick to the resorts where there is a demand for English-speakers. But for those with German, there is the whole wide range of resorts and ski areas to choose from: the Voralberg west of Innsbruck has St. Anton, Lech, St. Christoph, Zürs, Stüben and Ischgl; in the vicinity of Innsbruck itself resorts include Fulpmes, Zell am Ziller and Mayrhofen; further east, the next cluster of resorts form part of the Kitbüheler Alpen and include Kitzbühel, Alpbach, Niederau, Westendorf, Hopfgarten, Kirchberg, St. Johann in Tirol, Leogang, Saalbach and Zell am See. Yet further east near the Dachstein Glacier are resorts, which have barely been discovered by the British skiing fraternity: St. Johann im Pongau, Eben, Radstadt,

Altenmarkt, Ramsau, Schladming and Obertauern. There are dozens more resorts, many of them tiny villages, which may be worth the effort of exploration if all else fails.

In larger resorts it should be possible to find babysitting jobs though it is essential to have a base where you can be contacted. Ask the larger hotels if you can put up notices.

> ### Global Warming
> *There is a general scientific consensus that global warming is melting the Alps (i.e. the great mountains' icing of permafrost, which literally holds the mountains' crumbly edges together). This is giving rise to more frequent and devastating avalanches. Some of Austria's most popular resorts including Kitzbühel and Grindelwald are very low lying (below 1,000 metres) while the snowline in the Alps is steadily rising with global warming. This means that serious ski bums may wish to head for resorts above 1,800 metres (the height towards which the snowline is heading according to a recent UN report on global warming).*

Brand

Off the motorway from Feldkirch, on the way to St. Anton and west of Klösterle, is the small resort of Brand. Camilla Lambert, when a modern languages student at Bristol University, worked a summer season in the biggest hotel in the resort. This enabled her to find out about ski jobs for the following season. Her job waiting tables entailed a 10-hour day with two days off per week. Her hours were generally 9am to 2pm and 5pm to 10pm but she had to eat her lunch at 11am and supper at 5.30pm 'which took some getting used to'. She had pleasant shared staff accommodation in a 'little, typical Austrian House'.

> ### Camilla suggests other possibilities for work
> *Once you are in a place like Brand, which in high season accommodates 600 permanent residents, 2000 staff and 5000 guests, it is easy to find out about jobs in hotels, shops, as an au pair, or in specialist areas like the* Skiverleih *(ski hire) as a technician, or on the drag lifts. If you arrived without a job at the beginning of the skiing season, the tourist office would be the best source of local info. Also most of the bar staff in the various cafés and the 'British Pub'. I was offered several jobs for the coming winter as there is usually difficulty getting staff for such a remote place. If you don't mind hard work, I would certainly recommend this place.*

Kitzbühel

Kitzbühel is an international resort and an extremely attractive base for anyone wanting to sample the delights of skiing in the Tirol. It is one of the larger resorts – its population of 8,000 virtually doubles during the winter season – but this does not detract from its charm. A leading alpine centre since before the First World War, Kitzbühel has developed around its skiing (though the village dates back centuries), consequently the facilities are excellent and the tourist trade well catered for, whilst at the same time it has a reputation for being more relaxed in its approach than some of the more puritanical Swiss and French *ski-evolutif* resorts.

THE SKIING

The aesthetic appeal of the town might be seen as a caveat for the quality of the skiing but Kitzbühel has the best of both. Even though it may not appeal to some, there is no denying the quality of the skiing which caters for all levels from beginners to experts. What is more, there is now snowmaking on Streif, Steinbergkogel, Pengelstein and down to Kirchberg which makes the season longer and more reliable than in the past. Every year Kitzbühel plays host to the Men's World Cup Series which takes place on the Hahnenkamm, while at the bottom of the Streif downhill run, children and beginners get their ski legs. There are skiing areas on both sides of the town and the area is linked to Kirchberg and Aschau in the neighbouring valley. Skiing in these areas is extensive, varied and well served by over 60 lifts. The easier slopes start where the town centre finishes with a cable-car, high-speed gondola and a chairlift serving the large skiing areas of the Hahnnenkamm and the Kitzbüheler Horn which face each other across the town. Beginners can progress quickly from the nursery slopes at the bottom of the Hahnenkamm to the more challenging areas: the bowl beneath the Kitzbüheler Horn, which centres on the Trattalm lift is particularly good. Enclosed within this easily accessible area are several different standards of slope ranging from a baby lift through two blue runs to several quite demanding and varied red runs and a black run, providing everybody with the opportunity of improvement. The Hahnenkamm area is not as self-contained but covers a wider variety of slopes, including the World Championship Run for the more intrepid skier.

An efficient bus service links Kitzbühel to the neighbouring villages. It takes about 25 minutes to reach Pass Thurn at the head of the valley. The combined area of Pass Thurn-Jochberg has a total of 14 lifts and is extensive and suitable for intermediates. The villages of Aurach, Kirchberg and Ashcau, each with a few good long lifts, provide variety. One lift pass includes free bus travel between them. The striking characteristics of this centralisation are evident: efficient, co-ordinated lift and bus services, beautifully designed and prepared pistes and a wide diversity of skiing. Certainly with 60+ lifts and 160km of pistes, even if you spend the whole season in Kitzbühel you will never need to seek skiing elsewhere.

Off-piste skiing combined with ski-walking is growing in popularity in Kitzbühel. You climb up the mountains in skis with back-release bindings and then ski downhill where there are no lifts at all. The ski area Bichlalm has trails set up for walking up, and it is possible to buy a single touring or hiking lift ticket which allows you to get up into the area quickly.

A season's ski pass will be your first concern after a job and a bed. If you show the Bergbahn A.G. representative your resort worker's pass you will get a resident's discount which is about 50%. To obtain a worker's pass you need an *Ausweiss*. You get this from the *Gemeinde* (town council); you need a proof of National Insurance (*Gebietkrankenkass*) and a photograph. If there is a delay getting your *Ausweiss* (green card) you can buy the more expensive pass and get a refund when it arrives. Next comes skiing equipment. Kitzbühel is very expensive, so you should buy all your clothing before you go. Second-hand skis on the other hand are readily available, as the locals follow fashions avidly and often sell skis, which are just about run in if they are superseded by a new model. For boots, sticks and skis you should try asking the advice of shops which hire such equipment and who will probably sell you ex-hire stock. Initial surprise may greet you, but if you persist you should end up with real bargains.

The town offers other recreational facilities for the days when the snow is bad, or at the end of a hard day on the slopes. The ski pass entitles you to free access to the Aquarena swimming pool as well as reductions on some of the other amenities housed within this leisure complex, such as saunas, massages or mudpacks. Cross-country skiing is very good, with a special ski school and 35km of prepared pistes.

Ice-skating, tobogganing and curling are favourite sports in the area too and indoor facilities extend to squash, table tennis, tennis and riding.

Kitzbühel boasts a lively nightlife: it is tourist oriented and therefore pricey, but there are several discotheques, a casino and a cinema. Try and steer clear of this side of Kitzbühel and find instead the bars inhabited by locals. Younger locals tend to hit the tourist bars in particular 'Big Ben' and 'The Londoner' which are big and English-speaking.

ACCOMMODATION

If you arrange a job before you go, you should try to find a bedsit as close to the town centre as your income will permit, as this will provide you with the best access to the skiing and the skibus facility. Starting work at the beginning of the season, you will probably succeed in finding accommodation quite easily. For the best choice arrive early and look during late November, early December. Austrian houses are enormous and sub-divided, and many residents have well-equipped bedsits under the eaves or with private bathrooms, kitchenettes and entrances, which will be fine for a few months; as well as giving you more independence, it should prove cheaper than the alternative of a guesthouse. The Tourist Office (+43 5356 62155; www.kitzbuehel.com; info@kitzbuehel.com) will be able to give you a list of such bedsits. Also, it is worth being aware that many of the bigger employers (e.g. some ski schools) keep large houses for their staff. If you get a job with them, you will have accommodation as well so it is advisable to take temporary accommodation until you know what you will be doing, rather than commit yourself to a long, expensive lease on arrival. Other sources of accommodation include estate agents and the local papers for adverts of flats and rooms.

If you go to Kitzbühel in search of a job, a guesthouse is a better bet than a hotel with the cheapest at about £20 a night and again the Tourist Office will help. Finding someone sympathetic already there who might put you up for a while is another alternative, and as there are lots of English and Australian people in the town it might be easier than it sounds. Unfortunately, there is no Youth Hostel, although if you are desperate and of the Scott and Oates school, there is a winter camping site by by the Schwarzsee.

It should be mentioned that the cost of living in Austria is about 25% higher than in Britain and whilst hopefully your wage will reflect this, do bear in mind the extra cost of food and drink when deciding how much you can afford to pay in rent. Another alternative should accommodation in Kitzbühel prove difficult to find or to afford would be to live in one of the smaller nearby villages and make use of the regular ski buses: although this would not be as convenient the skiing in the surrounding area is good and it might be worth considering if you encounter problems.

WORK

The seasonal and unskilled nature of much of the work available in Kitzbühel is good news for anyone planning a working holiday in the town. Better still, there is a department in the local employment office, which exists solely to cater for foreigners seeking work. Arbeitsamt Kitzbühel, (Wagnerstrasse 17, 6370 Kitzbühel). The Arbeitsamt publishes a comprehensive list of local vacancies, which is updated every few days thus providing an excellent basis from which to start looking for a job. A personal visit to their office is more likely to achieve a result than writing.

The skiing season starts in mid-December and ends in mid-April although obviously at these extremes opportunities are scarcer. Nevertheless a three-month contract in the middle of the season probably covers the best skiing period. It is possible to pick up casual work too, but on a more ad hoc basis, particularly over the Christmas and New Year period and during February which is also busy. One of the most pleasant surprises for people working in Kitzbühel is that they are well protected from exploitation by unscrupulous employers. An employer is not allowed by law to pay foreign members of his staff less than the statutory minimum wage which is quite a respectable sum. In a country with low unemployment and virtually none in the prosperous, tourist enriched Tirol, Austrians tend

to avoid just those jobs which are suitable for foreigners who want to ski, because they often involve unsociable hours.

The types of employment that we encountered fell into several categories in Kitzbühel. Catering is predominant, encompassing hotels, restaurants and bars. At the height of the season the town has about 8,000 visitors, so demand for people to work in these areas is high. The hours may be long for waiting or bar staff and the pay is not particularly good. If your main aim is skiing you may be disinclined to catch the first ski lift after getting to bed in the early hours of the morning. This is true of such work in most places although Kitzbühel is so close to the skiing slopes that the situation is not as bad here as elsewhere. If you live in the town and do not wear make-up or insist on a bath every morning, you could conceivably be starting your first run half an hour after the alarm clock wakes you. For these sorts of job ask at the employment agency, or for more casual work in busy periods make enquiries at the larger hotels and restaurants.

Work is often available in the sports shops, which dominate Kitzbühel. Several of the places visited said they are willing to employ foreigners who have a basic knowledge of German, some skiing experience and an understanding of the equipment. An Australian who worked in Ski Hausl in Joseph Herold Strasse found his job convenient for skiing and for socialising with the large English-speaking community in Kitzbühel. His hours were 8am till 12 noon and 3pm till 6pm. with regular days off, but the long lunch hour combined with the fact that his shop was next to Hahnenkamm cable car enabled him to ski at lunch time as well. An additional perk of being a shop assistant may be good equipment at a discount, although once again the pay is not very high.

It is possible to get a job as a ski instructor, if you are prepared to be badly paid, frequently insulted by frustrated novices and continually exposed as a second-rate skier by the Austrian instructors who have a finely developed sense of one-upmanship. Austrians tend to regard instructing as something of a menial occupation, along the lines of cowherding, and are contemptuous of the skiing abilities of many of Kitzbühel's 220 'Red Devils'. In some years it has been estimated that 50-60% of ski instructors were foreign because of the pay and the lack of respect for instructors. The upside is that this does open up opportunities for work, particularly as there are now five ski schools in Kitzbühel (see addresses below). However, as an inexperienced skier in Austria is one who started skiing at the age of five rather than four, foreigners should not expect an easy time. The basic requirements are a working knowledge of German to use in classes of mixed nationalities, a good grasp of the fundamentals of the sport and a degree of patience. Instructors are hired just before the beginning of the season when your German and your skiing are tested and if you are competent enough to be hired, you will be trained for a fortnight. Ask at the following ski schools:

Skischule Kitzbühel- Rote Teufel (Red Devils): Museumkeller (05356 62500).
Skischule Kitzbüheler ☎05356 73323 (off piste).
Skischule Jochberg: ☎05355 5342.
Skischule Hahnenkamm Egger: Waldorf 1; ☎05356 63177.
Skischule Total: Schwarzseestrasse; ☎05356 72011.

There are more openings over the peak period of Christmas and the New Year than at any other times and during these weeks anyone will be hired temporarily who can say 'snow-plough' and 'in a line' in German, and knows that the curved end of the ski should point forward. The pay is also higher during this part of the season and tips throughout the winter are a useful source of income.

Kitz, as it is known to its fans, is a great resort in which to ski and hang out and Deutsch-Institut Tirol (Am Sandhügel 2, 6370 Kitzbühel, Austria; ☎53-56 712 74; fax 53 56 723 63; office@deutschinstitut.com; www.gap-year.at) offers a combination of German language and ski and snowboard instruction (preparation for Austrian ski/snowboard instructor exams) in a course specially aimed at gap year people. Courses last 12 weeks from the end of September to just before Christmas and include 8 weeks intensive German at DIT in Kitzbühel, interspersed with eight, 3-day weekends sking/snowboarding on the glacier at Kaprun and a 7-day trip to Eastern Europe. The price of €8000 (£5,500) is inclusive except for travel to Kitzbühel and insurance.

Some TEFL teachers have tried to find work in Kitzbühel. However, since there is a year round population of English-speakers in the resort finding work as a teacher of English will not be easy. One English teacher tried putting an advert in the local paper with some success. However, her income from this was not sufficient to pay her rent. Richard Williams, a modern language graduate from Oxford University got an assistant post at the local secondary school for a year and believed it had allowed him the most leisure time possible consistent with a good standard of living. His skiing was only limited by the snow conditions: even so, he found the slopes in this area easily extensive enough for a whole season. The job allowed Richard to get to know the many residents of Kitzbühel and his social life revolved around the pleasant local haunts especially those popular with Austrian students.

In Kitzbühel there is only one post for an assistant, but across the Tirol there are a couple in Zell am See, about nine in Innsbruck, a couple in Saalfelden, one in Imst and so on. If you have or are studying for a degree in modern languages, have a reasonable grasp of German and would like nine months abroad before with access to skiing, this is a very good way of arranging a job before you go: apply to the British Council who will provide you more information. As these positions are very oversubscribed, it is essential that you fulfil the appropriate entry requirements and that you make it perfectly clear to the British Council that your primary motivation is the teaching work and that the proximity of good skiing is a lucky coincidence.

Another good possibility for combining skiing with work would be to work for a company called 'Foto Flash' (Traunsteinerweg 2; ☎05356 71443), which employs foreigners to take photographs of tourists while they ski. The photos are then displayed in the town for those narcissistic enough to buy them.

Kirchberg in Tirol

Kirchberg (www.kirchberg.at; ☎+43 (0)5357 2309) is situated 6km from the town of Kitzbühel, and uses the same ski area and pass. It is effectively the centre of the Kitzbühel skiing circus and the village has 8,000 tourist beds. The computerised, six-seater Fleckalm gondola system, just outside Kirchberg can move 2,400 skiers an hour up to the Ehrenbachhohe station from which a vast part of the Kitzbühel skiing area is accessible. Skiers from Kitzbühel often drive out to use the Fleckalm as it is quicker to get to the ski region. A few tour operators go there including First Choice, Flexiski and Neilson.

Mayrhofen

Mayrhofen (www.mayrhofen.at), the third largest parish in the Tirol, lies at an altitude of 630 metres above sea level and has 3,600 inhabitants. It is a quiet, traditional village but at the same time a lively holiday centre in both winter and summer as its 8,000 tourist beds testify. It is situated at the end of the Ziller Valley and is a starting point for the four subsidiary valleys – the Zillergrund, Stilluptal, Zemmgrund and the Tuxertal known as 'Grunde'. All are easily accessible if you want a change from skiing in Mayrhofen.

With its four million square metres of excellently prepared and marked downhill runs and slopes, as well as numerous amenities, Mayrhofen has been an international sports resort for many years. Due to the altitude of the Ahorn, Penken and Horberg/Gerent skiing areas (1,600-2,250 metres) good snow conditions are guaranteed until April.

THE SKIING

Together the Penken, Rastkogel, Eggalm, Ahorn and Horberg/Gerent runs provide 143kms of varied skiing. The Penken ski area has a cable-car, gondola, one treble chairlift, two double chairlifts and four draglifts which give access to numerous ski runs for beginners and proficient beginners. The Ahorn skiing area has one cable car and six drag lifts; due to its easy runs, the Ahorn is especially suitable for beginners and children, although good skiers too can enjoy a variety of pistes. The Horberg/Gerent skiing area has one gondola cableway, three double chairlifts and three drag lifts. The Lärchwald double chairlift connects the Horberg ski area with the Penken. A skibus service, running every 15 minutes, brings you directly to the bottom stations of the cable cars free of charge. The ski pass covering the entire Ziller valley gives access to 142 lifts with over 460kms of runs.

Although Mayrhofen provides good skiing facilities, regulars found that during the peak season it was worthwhile going to Hippach, Zell am Ziller or Hintertux where the slopes and lifts are less crowded. All are easily accessible by train or bus.

The Zillertalpass is valid on all 148 lifts in the Ziller Valley and includes all rides on the Zillertal railway and the regularly scheduled Zillertal bus line between Mayrhofen and Jenbach. The pass is valid from the 12th December until 10th April. Cheap skiing insurance can be obtained in Mayrhofen and you can pick up second-hand skis for reasonable prices.

Mayrhofen is not rated highly as a place to learn snowboarding. However, enthusiasts will know that it hosts the boarders' annual Brit Games and the Hintertux Glacier further up the valley calls to the advanced boarders.

Mayrhofen has also a lot to offer the cross-country skier with its nine well-prepared and marked trails, total length 20kms; two floodlit ski trails ensure that enthusiasts can enjoy the fun of cross-country skiing in the evening too. You can ride with the Postbus on its scheduled route between Mayrhofen and Hintertux for alpine and cross-country skiing free of charge. Other winter activities on offer include: horse riding, tobogganing, ice-skating and curling. In addition there are indoor swimming pools, saunas, solaria, turkish baths, bowling alleys, four squash courts and indoor tennis courts.

APRÈS SKI

Recommended restaurants include: Mamma Mia for good pizza, noodles and wine, Gasthof Rose for cheap three course meals and Grill Kuchl is also a very popular fast food restaurant for ski bums. The best of the nightclubs and pubs are probably the Scotland Yard, the usual haunt for alpine workers and very crowded in high season, Sporthotel disco, with good ski videos and reasonable prices. Little Gery's, a small cosy bar with music which is very popular with the locals, Schlüssel and the Hotel Bergerhof Bar/Disco.

ACCOMMODATION

A major problem on arrival in Mayrhofen is finding accommodation, which will last for the season. It is therefore essential to arrive early, preferably before the season begins. It may be quite easy to find a room in a pension which offers a slightly reduced rate if you are there for the season, but make sure they are not going to move you out at peak season. Four ski bums who arrived in January spent their first three weeks sleeping in an ex-ambulance (which they had driven from London) as they could not find rooms at reasonable prices. Luckily they could have a shower at a nearby pension for a small charge. With many jobs, accommodation is provided although sometimes a small fee is required. Among the places worth investigation are Ludwig Kroll's Rosengartl, opposite the Scotland Yard Pub. Europa house is also very helpful. A rented room usually comes with shared bathroom and no kitchen facilities. Bed and breakfast accommodation starts from about £20 per night. Contact the tourist office (☎+43 5285 6760; www.mayrhofen. at), can offer further help.

WORK

As Mayrhofen is a small resort, jobs are quite difficult to obtain, although there are usually 30+ ski bums working in the village. The majority, tend to be British with a smattering of Australasians or Swedes. A lot of tourists who come to Mayrhofen are from English-speaking countries so it is not essential to speak German although for reps, bar/table waiting jobs it is definitely an asset.

To get a job in Mayrhofen it is essential to be in the right place at the right time; jobs are there if you arrive early enough in the season and can afford to stay around until the peak period starts just before Christmas; you need to persevere and not give up hope. Socialising with ski bums and locals is also important: when a job comes up word spreads like wildfire and it is usually a matter of first there, first served. Another way of securing a job for the season is to look the previous summer and with luck an employer may keep a job open for you. You should visit the tourist office (Postfach 21, 6290 Mayrhofen; ☎+43 5285, 6760; www.mayrhofen.com) when you arrive as they have a list of job vacancies in Mayrhofen; another possibility is to look in the newspaper *Tiroler Zeitung* especially on Fridays.

The ski bums' haunt is the Scotland Yard Pub, the only place in Mayrhofen where you can play darts, listen to the jam, borrow a pair of boots or even get the odd ski lesson if your uphill leg is not coming on as it should, so it too is worth a visit when you arrive.

There are over 100 ski and board instructors in Mayrhofen working out of three schools: Ski and Board (5285-63800), Max Rahm's SMT (5285-63939), and Mount Everest run by Peter Habeler (5285-62829). Competition is stiff and there is usually only a handful of foreigners employed there. However, you might get taken on at peak periods for two or three weeks. An alternative is to try for a job in the Hippach Ski School. Hippach is a less regimented ski school about five minutes from Mayrhofen by train, which usually employs about half a dozen foreigners.

To get a place at the Hippach Ski School, you should arrive by 1 December. You will undergo a week of ski tests for which you will pay a fee. At the end of the week the better skiers/instructors will be chosen to work for the season. Even then work is not guaranteed as local ski instructors always get preference, but you should get at least six weeks work. Dave White, a Briton who worked for the Hippach School found that as an *Auslander* or foreign worker you will always be the last to get a group, so that as the season draws to a close the work will become less certain. You may also be limited to English-speaking beginners or two-week ski groups depending on your language and skiing abilities. For Hippach Ski School you usually work four hours a day. The maximum hours you can work per week is usually 24; you must attend a prize-giving one night a week (usually lasts 3 hours) for which you will be paid and must also pay for the servicing of your own skis. The perks of the job are free or cheap lunch and a lift pass for the season if you are a full-time instructor.

Brett Earle after spending the summer in Greece as a windsurfing instructor went back to Mayrhofen for his second season. He started work in a ski-hire shop on 12 December. He worked from 8am to 11am and from 4pm to 6pm every day, with Thursday off. On Fridays and Saturdays he had to work whatever hours were needed but his weekly rate of pay was fixed and included free accommodation and breakfast. His work involved servicing skis, giving out boots, and being in the shop generally to deal with any problems. He stayed for the season. He says:

> *Working in ski hire means weekends are hard especially if there has not been much snow; when the skis come back they must be serviced, waxed and repaired for the new people coming in.*
>
> *However, this is one of the better jobs as I get free use of skis, can ski five times a week and get provided with free accommodation German is not essential for this job, although, again it is an advantage if you can speak a little.*

Lorraine Blackwell spent her first season in Mayrhofen working as a transfer rep. Although she arrived in Mayrhofen on 8 December she did not get her first transfer until the first week in January. She did one or two transfers a week from Mayrhofen to the airport. Her starting time for work varied; she worked anything between six and 24 hours a day doing one transfer. Her salary is fixed and she received a standard wage for each transfer; if flights were delayed she was brought food and drinks at the airport. Lorraine was lucky in that she got a free flight home at the end of the season and another advantage was that she could participate in tobogganing evenings free of charge or get a free lift on another transfer to another part of the valley.

To get a job as a part-time rep it is important to get to know the other reps when you arrive. You are at an advantage if you have wheels as you can travel to neighbouring resorts and it helps if you can speak German. Vacancies for transfer reps always come up at peak season when the tour companies always need extra people. Tour operators that go to Mayrhofen include Inghams, Crystal, Equity, First Choice Ski Activity, Total and Thomson.

Lorraine supplemented her income by working part-time as a cloakroom attendant at the Schlüssel Discotheque. They usually employ one full-time and one part-time worker in the cloakroom each season. Lorraine worked from 8pm until it closed (which varied from 3am to 6am) and received £15+ per night; on prize-giving night she started work an hour earlier. You need to be able to speak German as the clientele is largely German. Perks of her job included a meal before she started work, a snack at the end of the night, plus half-price drinks while on duty.

Lorraine found the job very tiring and never knew when she would finish work; despite this it was a job in which you were not under any pressure and got to meet lots of people.

Lorraine was in Mayrhofen for four weeks before she got a job; her advice is not to get downhearted if you have not found a job for the first few weeks. If an employer says no

– keep going back and trying again; in a sense they can just be testing you. If possible arrange a telephone number where you can easily be contacted if a job arises.

Nick, Kirk and Colin (stagename 'The Cellmates') took advantage of an opportunity to visit Mayrhofen after they read an advertisement in *Melody Maker* in mid-November. They fixed up a contract playing in the Scotland Yard pub until mid-January, with one night off a week. They were lucky in that they had a job fixed up, a free flight, free accommodation, free three-course meal and three free drinks a day. They were only paid pocket money had a whip round the pub after playing. Kirk feels that:

> *Although we had guaranteed gigs, it got a bit monotonous playing the same audiences; you felt as though you were going through the motions a bit after the third week and we played two and a half to three hours each night. Skiing was limited as we had to be back by 4pm for après ski and we were playing peak season which meant queues for the lifts were bad.*

When their contract terminated the Cellmates returned to the UK for a month. They decided to return to Mayrhofen on 15 February, confident they could get work through contacts they had made and the reputation they had built throughout the valley. They played at a variety of sport hotels and nightclubs up and down the valley, on average playing about four or five gigs a week. They earned about £100 per week plus a free meal before their gigs started.

Kirk would not recommend musicians to turn up on spec unless they have contacts.

> *You must be good as the competition is very tough and be prepared to work when hung over or suffering with a skiing injury. You have got a much better rate of pay playing a few gigs per week but without transport there's a problem; it also costs a lot if equipment breaks down as music shops are few and far between.*

The Sportshotel Strauss, Schlüssel and Scotland Yard pubs are a few places for musicians to investigate.

Peter Kerridge from Caloundra, Australia worked his first season in Mayrhofen at Vroni's a mountain restaurant on the Penken. In recent years there have been up to six jobs available for ski bums in Vroni's (sometimes they are non-EU citizens like Peter and have been working black), three as dishwashers and three as dish/glass collectors. Full-time hours are: 8.30am to 5 pm (seven days a week); part-time, 11.30am to 4.30pm (average three to four days a week). Wages are: full-time, £22 per day; Part-time £3.50 an hour. Perks include: cost of lift pass reimbursed to full-time workers at the end of the season, free lunch and free drinks while working.

Peter feels that his part-time job at Vroni's was more suitable for a skiing beginner than a serious one. He managed to ski from 8am to 11am every morning but could not plan his working days or his days off as they were dependent on the weather. Although the job itself was quite boring and monotonous he met lots of people which provided useful links for further travels.

Sue Hall was 21 when she spent her second season working as a chambermaid at Ludwig Kroll's Rosenhof. Originally she turned up in Mayrhofen mid-November and got the job after one and a half weeks. Although it is only one job, she decided to share it with a friend so she worked three mornings a week from 7.15am to 11am and on Saturdays from 7.15am to 1pm, and received £40 per week. Sue felt lucky because she could ski six days a week and the work was good fun because in the nicest possible way Ludwig was slightly eccentric. She got free breakfast every morning and after her first season received a Dirndl (see glossary) for her hard work.

Sue also worked waiting tables in the Scotland Yard Pub. She obtained a volunteer work permit, which officially limited her earnings and consequently she only worked a few evenings a week. The management treated their staff really well and on race days they were all taken out for the day, all expenses paid.

Sue managed to further supplement her wages in the peak season when the Mayrhofen Ski School were short of instructors on the Ahorn. She instructed for one week receiving £24 per day for four hours work. She also managed to do some babysitting on her nights off for which the going rate is about £6 an hour).

Kevin Du-Puy first went to Mayrhofen when he was 19 years old; nine years later he was back again having spent seven winter seasons there. Kevin has has various jobs in Mayrhofen ranging from dishwasher in Vroni's, ski instructor (four seasons) and transfer rep to ski guide and photographer. He feels that the easiest way to get a job in Mayrhofen is to be there and make yourself known; reputation is 80% of getting work. If you are willing to do anything and to hang around you will find work. Jobs for ski guides only exist if you get a large number of people in the resort. Thomson and Neilson normally have ski guides in Mayrhofen and Kevin worked part-time. Ski guides have the advantage that they do a lot of skiing with intermediate and above skiers although they must follow stipulations and are certainly not allowed to take people off piste.

Kevin also supplemented his finances by working a few days a week for a photography shop, 'Photo Willy'. Part-time jobs existed for one day a week and there was one full-time job for three days a week. You are at an advantage if you have your own camera. You get all your films free and on any photographs you take and sell you receive a percentage. On average Kevin earned £25-£30 per day.

St. Anton am Arlberg/Klösterle

St. Anton (www.stantonamarlberg.com) is the largest of the Arlberg region ski resorts, the others being St. Christoph, Zürs, Stüben and the super-chic Lech/Oberlech.

St. Anton can best be described as a big village since despite being sprawled out the atmosphere is cosy and everywhere is within reasonable walking distance. St Anton has excellent road and rail links. In fact the mainline railway station is in the centre of the town. Although you could spend a fortune in St. Anton on clothes and slap-up meals at the St. Antonerhof, there are plenty of good meals to be had in lively inexpensive surroundings: the Krazy Känguruh (www.krazykanguruh.com), considered one of the better haunts is reasonably inexpensive.

With its reputation as one of the classic international alpine centres seems to go a general air of politeness, not only from the locals but also the skiers. There is virtually no shoving to get on the ski-buses and lifts where Germans, Swedes, Belgians, Americans etc. queue in as orderly a fashion as only the British are supposed to do.

THE SKIING

The skiing area of which St. Anton is a part, is enormous. The lift pass covers St. Anton, St. Christoph, Stuben, Sonnenkopf, Lech, Oberlech and Zürs. There are 86 lifts and over 200 km of marked pistes, plus an abundant amount (180 km) of off-piste and ski touring. In St. Anton itself there are four principal ski areas: Gampen and Kapall where the World Cup downhill races take place; the Valluga mountain, which is the main skiing area, and whose summit can be reached by a three-stage cable car; Galzig which can be reached from the Valluga lift system or from St. Christoph; lastly Rendl, the newest ski area on the other side of the valley which is reached by a most dramatic gondola ride which finishes up at the excellent Rendl restaurant where you can sunbathe in a deck chair on the veranda known as Rendl 'beach'. St. Anton skiing favours intermediate to advanced skiers. For expert skiers the Valluga mountain is justly recommended – several black runs and plenty of off piste and mogul skiing. There are nursery slopes on Gampen and Kapall. Rendl is also used for beginners who should however beware the terrifying drop off the precipice from which the T-bar lift starts. Generally, St. Anton is not a beginners' resort. Rendl is also a powder skier's paradise.

The Arlberg ski school will take expert skiers on the more adventurous off piste tours. You could find yourself skiing on the North Face of Rendl to the small village of Pettneu, 6 km east of St. Anton, or going over the back at Stüben to Langan. It is even possible to ski from the very top cable car on the Valluga into the neighbouring resort of Zürs. At Zürs you can pick up a route known as the White Circle, a one-way circuit covering 40km which goes from Zürs to Zug, into Lech, then Oberlech and back to Zürs. It makes a wonderful day's skiing and is possible for most standards of skier as the pistes are well-bashed and wide open without very steep sections. The season starts at the end of November and ends officially on May 1st when the lifts close, although the tour operators usually finish a week before this.

APRÈS SKI

There is no shortage of lively spots in St. Anton. Popular mountain bars include the cosy Rodle Alm at the head of the toboggan run. The manager of the Rodle Alm is Robert Alber who owns the Alt St. Anton Hotel in Nasserein and also manages the Schlosshof chalet usually rented out to British tour companies like Crystal. He is therefore a good contact for employment, although his staff do not seem to stay long. The Krazy Kanguruh is another popular bar at lunch times and for après ski. It is slightly up the slopes and therefore less accessible in the evening though you can get there by car/taxi. A lot of Australians work there in cramped conditions. The Mooserwert bar, just over the road from the KK, is popular with resort staff, particularly on Monday night around 4 pm when there is a live band. It has become the regular meeting point for British staff in the resort and would be an ideal place for anyone looking for work to go.

In the town centre, the bars most frequented by resort staff are the Piccadilly, Hazienda, Underground, Stanton and Drop In. If you are looking for work on the off chance, go to these bars from 10.30pm. onwards and talk to the people already working in the resort. They know exactly what is going on and will almost certainly try to help. Most bars charge admission and/or a coat check fee. The Underground charged double after 11pm. Once you are established in the resort as someone looking for work or with work, and you have established contact with the doormen, they will allow you in for free.

The bowling alley in Nasserein is also worth a visit. Not only can you get the cheapest beer in St. Anton there, but it is frequented by all the resort reps. Bowling is a popular après ski activity and therefore every night one or other of the holiday companies' reps with be there with their guests.

CHEAP ACCOMMODATION

Finding cheap accommodation in St. Anton is difficult even for the British tour companies looking for staff accommodation. George Dellar, a graphic designer from London, who worked as a ski guide tells his story:

> *I had a job and was in the resort at the beginning of the season without accommodation. My employers agreed that it was their responsibility and they were prepared to pay £15 per night, but there was nothing available. I was put in a guestroom for the first three weeks, as there was a spare, then on a mattress on the floor with two chalet girls in a tiny room. This saga went on for most of the season. I never had a permanent room of my own and moved every two weeks.*

Although it is difficult to find cheap accommodation in St. Anton itself, there are cheaper places out of the centre in St. Jakob and Nasserine. The information office in St. Anton (☎+43 5446 22690; fax +43 5446 253215; www.stantonamarlberg.com; st.anton@netway. at), posts details at the beginning of the season about available worker's rooms. There is a phone you can use for free in the information office for calling B & B's, hotels etc.

WORK

A useful place to hang around is the Spar supermarket in the centre of town. This is where all the chalet staff buy their weekly shop; a chalet catering for 20 people means anything up to 15 trolleys. It is a good place to meet not only the large UK company staff, but people that run private chalets, small hotels etc. and pick up jobs. Start by offering to carry shopping home, which is a major problem for some. Also, in Austria, rubbish is divided into five categories: food, tin, plastic, glass and paper. Collection points are dotted around the resort but the only rubbish collected is the good waste. It is thus a hassle to dispose of the other categories of rubbish. Therefore a good job for the energetic is to take bottles back to the Spar where an automatic collection point gives refunds. This is not a gold mine as the refunds are small, but they can mount up.

British Tour Operators

There are reasonable possibilities for work with British tour companies as St. Anton is extremely popular with British skiers and there are clients from about two dozen British companies; these include Crystal and Crystal Finest, First Choice, Flexiski, Lotus Supertravel, Mark Warner, Neilson, Ski Activity, Ski Club of Great Briton, Ski Val and Thomson The pay ranges from £60-£100 per week in the UK, but all accommodation and food is free.

Kelly was a ski guide with Mark Warner after she graduated from Heriot-Watt where she was a pillar of their ski club. Before being accepted by MW she had to have a dry slope ski test in the UK. She and the other MW staff arrived in St. Anton in mid-December, a week before the first MW clients. In addition to free skiing including equipment if necessary, and full board and lodging, Mark Warner personnel get anoraks and T-shirts. The representatives and ski guides eat dinner with the guests, progressing through the chalets so that they meet all the company's clients in the resort. They also organise inter-chalet slalom competitions and preside over the prize-givings. Teams that rely heavily on Dutch courage are known as SOS (Shot of Schnapps) teams.

Amanda Jagot and Louise Campbell together cooked, cleared tables and washed up for 18 guests in Mark Warner's Haus Kossler. Lunch is not provided for the guests and the girls get one full day off a week when the guests get their own breakfast and make their own arrangements for supper. 'It helps if you know it takes six minutes to soft-boil an egg at this altitude' says Amanda. 'It also helps' retorts one of the guests who on the girls' day off put salt instead of sugar into her tea, 'if you know what's what in the kitchen'! The girls always seem to be good-humoured and they both enjoyed their first season as chalet girls.

George Dellar, whose accommodation problems are described above, otherwise enjoyed being a ski guide.

George Dellar describes how he got his job and what it's like being a ski guide

I applied for the job in the UK in June. I had no previous experience. I realised they were not looking for boy racers but for people with a friendly outlook, that were able skiers. You needed to have at least 20 weeks' skiing under your belt and a good knowledge of ski equipment. I was offered the job subject to passing the ten-day training course at Sandy Balls Camp, set for November. There was no guarantee that I would pass as it was subject to getting a mountain First Aid Certificate and having my skiing ability approved on a dry slope. It was rather nerve-racking as

> *there were more people on the course than there were jobs so you knew that some would be disappointed.*
>
> *I was paid a weekly bonus payable at the end of the season as an incentive for staff to stay to the end. After the training course we went to the resort on 12 December. Actually I was transferred from France to Austria a few weeks later due to some mix-up over staffing levels in each resort, hence my accommodation problems. The season ended in mid-April.*
>
> *The job entailed guiding three days a week. Other duties were doing airport transfers, shopping for and cooking a barbecue on Friday night for 50 people, taking guests bowling one night a week, and tobogganing on another. I was also responsible for the maintenance of three chalets, disposing of the rubbish and generally helping out where necessary.*
>
> *I used to ski every day except Saturday fitting my other jobs around this most vital activity. I enjoyed the job because I was able to ski a lot. However some guests are fun; others a nightmare. Being nice to the obnoxious ones is difficult. I hated being tired all the time, but after a while you get used to that. It was hard work; a lot of people think you are on a jolly holiday for four months. When you actually do the work, you soon realise it's not all skiing and partying.*

Working for Austrians

As you would expect from a resort with accommodation for 8,000 tourists, there is a variety of work in hotels, pensions etc. You can start looking for jobs as early as September as there is lots of demand for casuals to clean and spruce up the accommodation for the first influx. This kind of work begins in late November. If you prove yourself doing this you will be offered a job for the season as domestic and cleaning staff. Boys not generally keen on this kind of work will have to wait until mid-December for other employment as hoteliers are obliged to offer the jobs to Austrians and generally refugees first. There are also snow-shovelling jobs available on a casual basis.

It stands to reason that most people will have to do more than one job to survive. A lot of B&Bs need staff to serve breakfast, which is a good job as it leaves the rest of the day free for skiing. Again for the same reason a number of bars need staff to cope with the early evening rush.

Susan Toft (Toftie), who is British, did two jobs. In the mornings she cleaned in Pension Bacherspitz from 9.30 am-11.30 am and for four hours on a Saturday morning. In the evenings she worked in a restaurant clearing tables and serving in the bar from 6pm to 10 pm, six days a week. Neither of these jobs paid more than £50 a week but the total was enough to live on and included meals while on duty. It also left Susan free to ski every afternoon.

Susan Christie from Australia trained as a financial analyst before coming to St. Anton.

Susan Christie explains how she landed her job at the Grieswirt restaurant

I arrived late October and booked in at the Tyroler Frieden where many Australians stay while they are looking for work as the proprietor Frieda speaks English and has a reputation for friendliness. After knocking on doors around the town, I was lucky enough to be offered a cleaning job for four days. That employer's mother-in-law runs the Grieswirt and he got me a job here, though I had to wait until December 1st to start. For the first month I worked seven days a week then went on for five days for the same remuneration when they employed another hand.

As well as her pay, three good meals daily were provided at the restaurant. She enjoyed the work because of the variety: preparing food, dishwashing, serving at the bar and washing the glasses. The working hours 5pm to 1am meant she had plenty of time for skiing.

Of Austrians as employers Susan says it can be a strain because they have to make a living in a short season and so the pressure is always on, and it's difficult to be more than perfect all the time. There are Australians, Swedes and Americans working regularly at restaurants Alt St. Anton and Rodelbahn.

Sports Shops

These are another possible source of jobs. In St. Anton, the three main ones are Schneiders, Fauner and Pangratz all situated in the town centre on the main drag. They employ ski bums to mend skis or to hire out equipment. Wages per hour plus room and board. Judging from the reluctance of those so employed to talk much about it 'are you from Interpol or something?' most are unofficial workers and wish to remain incognito. The cost of hiring boots and skis for a season can be reduced by taking your tax forms to the nearest border and getting them stamped, thus avoiding 18% VAT.

Ski Instructors

Not only does St. Anton have some of the oldest ski instructors, but it also has one of the oldest ski schools which was founded in 1902 by the celebrated Hannes Schneider whose family still predominates in St. Anton where there is a monument to him; and the neighbouring villages, where several businesses bear the family name. There are over 300 instructors at peak season (Christmas to the end of February) in St. Anton alone, and together with the other Arlberg resorts where there are another four schools, the total reaches 600. But, if you harbour great expectations of being among their number you might well be disappointed as apparently there is great difficulty involved for foreigners trying to permeate a body that is devoted to abundant home-grown talent. But those nationalities, albeit still in small numbers, which have managed to do so include Swedish, Danish, Australian and American. You could always try the newer Piste to Powder (+43 664 174 6382; UK 01661 824318), which offers different levels of off piste tuition and ski guiding and is run by Briton Graham Austick.

A ski instructor works on a commission basis, which means that their income varies depending on the number of pupils passing through the school. Basic pay depends on what grade of instructor you are. There are no independent instructors in St. Anton. One instructor of the lowest grade, an Australian girl, had been earning about £500 a month. Instructors have to pay for their own accommodation and insurance, but can usually get free meals at grateful restaurants where they take their pupils. In the summer they do other jobs – one was a lorry driver – and even in the winter they do other jobs; one Danish instructor was to be found every night in charge of a take-away burger stand.

Klösterle

On the Arlberg Valley floor, some 26 km from St. Anton is the small resort of Klösterle (1075 m) which is served by both rail and motorway from Feldkirch, near the Swiss border. The village itself, strung out along the river beneath the steep forests of the valley sides, is peaceful enough, and has one ski shop, a couple of friendly bars (the more atmospheric being the Keller Bar in the centre). There is also one quality restaurant. Two of the four or five hotel/pensions, the Arlberger Hof and the Blisadona, are run by the genial Peter Rettenhaber, who speaks English with an Austro-Geordie accent, having spent several years on Tyneside. The chief beauty of the place is that it is inexpensive, being off the fashionable tourist track.

THE SKIING

The skiing itself takes place at Sonnenkopf, a little known gem of Austria, less than 2 km by free ski bus from the village. The ski school, a ski shop and a useful bar for the end of the day are at the bottom of the covered chair which takes you up to a broad bowl with skiing mainly at 1600 and 2300 m. The runs are mainly reds and blues with one long and exhilerating black bump run which goes nominally off piste. Being north-facing, but still sunny, the snow-holding is exceptional and usually skiable until June. In some poor snow years, Sonnenkopf has managed to be one of the few functioning ski areas in Austria. Under normal circumstances however, it is blissfully uncrowded. One or two British school/teenage groups have discovered it, but otherwise it has a local feel. At the end of the day, or earlier if you wish, in reasonable conditions there are two beautiful tree runs all the way back down to the valley floor, one of which takes you back to the village itself, just behind the Arlbergerhof.

WORK

The main way of getting work is to apply on spec to the ski school, which has a few regular non-Austrians and local, friendly students who help out during the vacations. Being a small resort, they are fairly laid-back, and Vorarlbergers tend to be cosmopolitan. Otherwise, it would be worth asking at the one mountain restaurant, the ski shops, or Peter's hotel. The drawbacks are that it could soon become boring for a good skier, but it is a worthwhile place. Another option nearby with some real local characters and a flexible and sometimes understaffed ski school, with more limited skiing than Sonnenkopf, is Laterns, above Rankweil on the north-west edge of the Alps, which does however, have fantastic views. Just ask for Gerhardt Fleisch. The ski shop has the inventor of the fast-selling 'flip clip' for hanging your skis, Egon Heinzle, who may need some help.

St. Johann im Pongau

St. Johann im Pongau is a market town with a population of 8,000. It is situated south-east of Salzburg and 38 kms due east of Zell am See. The town lies in a snow pocket (the meaning of im Pongau), surrounded by the Tauern mountains. It is a traditional and friendly place, and the locals are trying to retain as much of the atmosphere as possible as their home becomes increasingly popular as a winter resort. Although there are over 3,000 beds available for visitors, the town is never swamped with tourists – it doesn't double in size as other ski resorts do.

Over the last few years St. Johann im Pongau has developed its facilities to attract more skiers.

THE SKIING

St. Johann im Pongau has long been underrated as a ski resort, which is wonderful for those who have just discovered it. The resort has an excellent snow record because it is too far north to be affected by the warm Mediterranean winds. The town lies at 2,460 feet and the highest station in the ski complex is at 7,177 feet. There has been a ski school in St. Johann since 1925, but the resort's increasing popularity is due to the linking of three towns (St. Johann, Wagrain and Flachau) and associated valleys with ski lifts to form a ski area called Die Drei Täler (The Three Valleys) in 1978. The three valleys are also linked to the Altenmarkt ski area (the next valley to Flachau) which also includes Zauchensee and Radstadt. In all about a dozen resorts with 350 km of linked skiing with 130 lifts. The whole area covered by one lift pass encompasses 25 ski stations and is known as the

Skiverbund Amadé with total of 270 lifts and 860 kms of pistes. The villages in the area are all easily accessible which is another plus point. There are also 160 km of cross-country trails.

There are a couple of black runs but most of the runs are graded intermediate which means St. Johann is a good choice for mixed ability groups. One of the reps assured us that there is an abundance of off piste black runs, but these are not mentioned in the publicity brochures. There is also an FIS-racing slope and an electronically timed racecourse.

Beginners are taught on the nursery slopes at St. Johann itself. These slopes are conveniently situated on the edge of the town, but are the first to suffer if the weather is warm. Intermediate skiers take a five-minute free bus ride to the Alpendorf gondola. One of the joys of skiing in St. Johann is the number of cosy restaurants scattered along the tops of the mountains offering refuge, good food and a range of warming drinks including the local specialities – tea or chocolate with rum!

As in most Austrian resorts, the season's lift pass is cheaper for residents. Apparently a local address is enough to qualify for the reduction. Beginners interested in buying second-hand skis will find a good selection in the ski hire shops.

Other facilities in St. Johann include tobogganing tracks, curling, ice skating, snowboard renting, horse-sleigh rides, nine-pin bowling, squash, indoor tennis, indoor swimming pools and a fitness centre. The best treat after a day of skiing was a trip to the hot spas at Bad Hofgastein, a half-hour drive from St. Johann. Facilities at the 'Bad' included saunas, massage, jacuzzis and sun-beds. The experience of looking up at the snow-capped mountains, the black night and the stars from the steamy mineral bath was unforgettable.

Nightlife in St. Johann could best be described as cosy. No throbbing all-night discos here. Pubs frequented by visitors were Amadeus and Bar'adox. A couple of discos operate in the Tennerhof Gasthof and the Alpenland hotel about once a week.

WORK

Unemployment tends to be higher in the smaller towns where many residents rely on the seasonal tourist trade for work. St. Johann is a farming community, and most of the seasonal work is taken by farmers, their employees and their families. However the locals do recognise a need for a sprinkling of English-speaking employees to help if there are problems with guests. This explains why anglophones are more likely to find work in St. Johann, where 70% of the visitors are British, rather than nearby Alpendorf, Wagrain and Flachau, where the visitors are still predominantly northern Europeans.

The Austrians seem to be doing their best to protect themselves against the establishment of chalet-type holidays, which are so popular in France and Switzerland. To quote the owner of one Gasthof 'The chalets are no good for Austrian business unless we have control of them. It is no good when chalet operators bring their own workers and import all their own food from England or Germany'. Consequently chalets are few and far between and there is no quick way of finding work in them.

Normally, about 30 *Ausländer* (foreigners) find employment in St. Johann every year including Thomson ski staff. However the investment in Alpendorf is expected to attract more up-market English visitors, which should in turn provide jobs for English speakers.

It seems that one ski school goes to the trouble of getting work permits for those of its foreign ski instructors (e.g. Australians) that need them. There is a total of four ski schools in St. Johann.

The number of foreigners getting jobs is carefully monitored by the locals; it is they, and not the authorities that prospective employers have to answer to. If there is an obvious reason why a foreigner is employed (the ability to speak English in a position which requires frequent contact with British visitors) it is accepted by the locals.

To find work in St. Johann, you should arrive in early December. The most efficient way to travel there is by train; the railway station is a very easy walk from the centre of the village. Go to the tourist information office (+43 6412 6030; www.sanktjohann.

com; info@stjohann.co.at) for the information about accommodation. They have a list of gasthofs and rooms to let; there is also a youth hostel. Next, make yourself acquainted with any representatives of British companies. The reps wield considerable power within the gasthofs where their guests are accommodated, and if they suggested that an English-speaking person would be useful to help in the kitchen, the gasthof would be likely to take their advice, if only to keep the rep's clients happy.

Ask particularly about work in the ski hire shops, restaurants and anything that might be going at the Sporthotel Alpenland (+43 6412 70210), one of the more international hotels. If you are any good at tennis you might find out if there are any vacancies for teaching tennis – the hotel has two resident pros, and takes on more people if they are particularly busy. If you speak German, your chances will be better.

To have any hope of a position as a ski instructor you have to be very organised. The ski schools are predisposed to employing a few foreign ski instructors and employs about half a dozen out of a ski school of 70 instructors every year. The tourist office can supply the addresses. To be considered for a position you should send a written application in about June, saying how much skiing you have done and enclosing references and a photograph. If you appear suitable enough you will be put through your paces by the Austrian Ski Instructors Association. If successful, you will become a member of the Association, which is fairly prestigious and will stand you in good stead when applying for ski instructor jobs in America, Australia and the rest of Europe. You should then be ready to start instructing in mid-December. You will also need to find accommodation, sort out work permits if you are from outside the EU, and arrange the required medical examination.

It is possible to supplement this income by taking private lessons, the going rate for these is about £20 an hour, plus £6 for any extra person in the group. There is a small increase in salary for the second season. It is illegal to teach skiing without being a member of the Austrian Ski Association.

Gail Pemberton, a modern languages student from the University of Southampton had an excellent job as an *Austauschassistantin* (English conversationalist). The position was well paid (about £125 per week) and gave her masses of free time. She had arranged the job through the Central Bureau for Educational Visits and Exchanges in London. She was obliged to be available for 15 hours a week to talk to students in English. She said that invariably, this ended up as between eight and ten hours a week, because of exams, sick teachers and other school activities. The only requirement of participants in this scheme is that English is their mother tongue. There is no upper age limit – Gail said that one of the teachers was a middle-aged woman who wanted a job in Austria to be near her daughter. Participants are obliged to be available from October to mid-June. Candidates were given a crash course in teaching which Gail said was great fun, and helped them all with structuring lessons. There are two English teachers based at St. Johann im Pongau, one at Zell am See and once at St. Johann in Tirol.

There is also room for entrepreneurs eg mobile discos. The deal is that you take the door money (usually about £100) and the hotel takes the drinks money.

Another possibility of employment not in St. Johann, but in the nearby resort of Altenmarkt is the Pension Lugs ins Land whose Welsh proprietor sometimes employs English-speakers.

St. Johann in Tirol

St. Johann in Tirol (www.st.johann.tirol.at; +43 (0)5352 6335) is a medium-sized resort situated in a wide sunny valley in the Tirol between the Kitzbühler Horn and the majestic Kaisergebirge ridge of mountains. Although less well-known than its neighbour Kitzbühel (only 15 minutes away by road) it nevertheless provides an attractive base for a skiing holiday. Its charm lies in its lack of sophistication, for although the facilities are very good, the approach is reliable rather than glamorous. One feels that it is a town first and a tourist centre second; it does after all have an income from light industry although heavy traffic is confined to the outskirts of the town. In many ways it is a refreshing change after the razzle-dazzle of some of the other resorts. St. Johann is situated on a main railway line with regular trains from Munich, Innsbruck and Salzburg passing through.

SKIING

For the skier, St. Johann has a lot to offer: the resort's top station Harschbichl is at 6,233 feet and the N, NE and West facing slopes usually ensure snow to the very end of the season. The lift pass here is cheaper than in Kitzbühel, although it does not give access to such extensive skiing. Nevertheless, the lift system in St. Johann encompasses a total of 17 lifts, the funicular railway and one cable car and 60kms of prepared pistes as well as allowing access to a limited range of off-piste terrain. The Pensing-Sauregg black run provides a challenge to the expert skier on its 900m descent, but it is fair to say that for accomplished skiers St. Johann is limited; it does however cater extremely well for the beginner or intermediate skier and snowboarder. There are several good long red runs and a whole host of beginner and intermediate lifts above Eichenhof, where first-time skiers can make rapid progress on a series of graded lifts. The other main nursery area is at Buchwies, just above the main village.

St. Johann is excellent for the cross-country skier, providing better facilities than most of the other resorts in the area. There are over 210 km of trails and the terrain is ideally suited to the sport. In addition there are another four lifts at Eichenhof on the same mountain, and half an hour away the famous Steinplatte provides higher extensive skiing.

If you feel like a day away from the strenuous activity of the slopes there is a wide range of other leisure facilities to choose from: an indoor swimming pool (where swimming hats must be worn!), a sauna, a steam bath, a solarium to even out the 'skiing tan', or a massage room to help ease your creaking and protesting joints. If you are still feeling energetic, there is the possibility of indoor tennis and riding; and for the real masochists, a weights room. Tobogganing and ice-skating are other outdoor options.

APRÈS SKI

It has to be said that the nightlife in St. Johann is friendly rather than spectacular, but the town does provide a reasonable variety. The Traublingerhof has a good discotheque which is very popular, and the Café Rainer and the Café Klausner often have live music. St. Johann also boasts another of the infamous Londoner pubs, in case you are feeling homesick; although the surroundings are not at all salubrious, the pub does provide a good meeting place.

WORK

Jobs are not so readily available as in Kitzbühel but that is not to say it is impossible to find employment in the town. Good starting places are the Tourist Office (+43 5352 6333; www.st.johann.tirol.at; info@st.johann.tirol.at), which will give you a list of hotels, guesthouses, restaurants and bars, as well as advice on which of them offer the most casual jobs; and the employment office in Kitzbühel (see Kitzbühel) which also covers St. Johann. There is a department here, which caters solely for foreigners seeking work, and a visit to it should more than reward the bus journey, as the office produces a comprehensive list of the vacancies in the region, which is updated frequently. This will provide a sound basis for a job hunt.

The skiing season runs from mid-December to mid-April and the longer commitment you can make, the more likely you are to be given a job. A three-month contract is probably the best one to aim for – few employers will ask you to work the whole season, but on the other hand they will not be too keen on showing you the ropes if they know that you only intend to stay for a few weeks. The middle of the season is normally the best skiing period as well as being the time when demand for casual labour is at its peak. If you need a work permit, you should have no difficulty once you have an offer of a job and have passed the medical that your prospective employer will pay for.

Working in one of the 90 hotels and guest houses that St. Johann boasts is probably your best bet. The pay is not high but that is often alleviated by the offer of free board and lodging: the high cost of rented accommodation and the relatively expensive food makes this a good answer in many ways, and whilst it restricts your independence it means that you will not have to think about cooking and cleaning. Avoid chambermaid work if you can, as this will not allow you many skiing hours. One English girl found a job as a waitress in one of the larger hotels having been a chambermaid in a guesthouse for the previous six weeks where she had worked from early in the morning until mid-afternoon and had only had one day off per week; although she knew the waitressing hours were going to be long and unsociable, she felt that at least she would have most of the day in which to ski.

There are several sports shops in St. Johann and the owners may be amenable to the idea of foreign people working for them, particularly English-speakers as they are good for business. A Canadian who worked there knew only basic German, but had a lot of skiing experience, and was very familiar with the technicalities of the equipment. The hours were regular and he had about one and a half days off per week on average, with reasonable pay. He did, however, feel that the skiing opportunities were restricted in the resort if you skied there a whole season and preferred to travel further afield for variety.

There are normally over 100 ski instructors at the two ski schools in St. Johann and there is a requirement for about 50 English-speaking instructors per season. Be warned that Austrian standards of competence are very high and being an instructor requires not only a firm grasp of the basics but a very high standard indeed. Being an instructor also requires an even temper, a reasonable grasp of German and the ability to inspire confidence in your class:

Stefan, a local hotel keeper, reports:

Although the Austrian Ski School is very unfriendly to English people who come out to instruct, they often have too much work at high season periods, and have to take on foreign instructors from about December 20th to mid-January. You must write direct to Salzburg, Innsbruck or Kitzbühel Ski Schools, as they will know where and when help is needed. Setting yourself up as an instructor to rival their business is illegal.

The address of the St. Johann Ski School is Hornweg 15, 6380 St. Johann in Tirol. As with any job application, whether it involves calling in person or writing, you should communicate in German. Do not consider applying unless you have BASI qualifications. In the summer, the equivalent is the Wanderschule, specialising in mountain walks, climbing and general mountaincraft; if you have experience, the address to write to is Internationale Berg- und Wanderschule, Velbenstrasse 30, 6380 St. Johann in Tirol. The other opening in this area is the Freizeitzentrum between Achenallee and Pass-Thurn-Strasse, which has large sports and leisure facilities; again you only really stand a chance of work if you have something to offer which is specialised or if you show that you don't mind being given menial jobs.

Other avenues worth exploring would be the kindergarten run by the Ski School for non-skiing children, the factories on the edge of the town (which make St. Johann the most carcinogenic area in Austria), or on a very casual basis teaching and conversation lessons at £8+ an hour.

It is possible that some of the tour operators will need additional staff: those with operations in the resort include Crystal and Thomson.

Lech

Forty minutes bus-ride from St. Anton, having passed through the skiing hamlet of St. Christoph and the ultra modern Zürs, you come to the picture-postcard village of Lech (www.lech-zuers.at; +43 (0)5583 2161 229). Conveniently situated on the main railway line the village also has a river running through the centre and an abundance of horse-drawn sleighs. The sleigh station is near the Post Hotel. Just above the main village is the purpose-built extension of Oberlech, and two kilometres westwards the rather bleak outpost of Zug completes the skiing area. Lech/Zürs has a reputation for sophistication and exclusiveness. The kings and queens of Sweden and Holland and Prince Edward are amongst the regulars, and film stars like Ali McGraw ski here. No one shows much interest when you remark that you stood next to Princess Caroline in the lift queue. Newer types of clientele include the 'Russian mafia' or at least recently monied Russians.

THE SKIING

The Lech skiing area, which incorporates Oberlech, Zürs and Zug has 34 lifts and offers extensive skiing for all standards. Lech is part of the Arlberg skiing area and the ski pass also covers St. Anton, St. Christoph and Stüben to which it is linked by a further 53 lifts. The main skiing area above Oberlech has a range of blue runs and red mogul areas; for black runs try the runs from the Rüfikopf back to Lech which are for the very experienced. The other main skiing area of Zürs can be reached either via the Rüfikopf cable car followed by a 5 kms run into Zürs. Alternatively a five-minute ride to Zürs by Postbus may help to avoid the queues for the cable-car at weekends. Afficionados comment that piste maintenance in Lech is remarkably thorough. In addition to piste-bashing, snow cannon prolong the season, though the granulated consistency of artificial snow is not nearly as good as the real thing.

As another attraction, Lech boasts a permanent ski-race course with electronic timing, near the Hinterweis ski lift. Chips for the automatic timer have to be bought at the ski school and you have the satisfaction or otherwise of seeing your course time displayed on a board near the finish.

WORK

With the tourist authorities claiming a total of over 6,700 beds for visitors and over 3,000 people looking after the holiday makers in Lech, it may seem surprising that so few of them are English-speaking foreigners. Research reveals that hotels have employed Australians and Britons in the unskilled jobs of kitchen hand, plongeur, cloakroom attendant and chambermaid. Brett Archer, a New Zealander worked in the small (30 beds) hotel Verwell in Lech. He and a friend began looking for work in mid-November and landed a job quite easily after two days. They started in St. Anton where there was no work but masses of people trying to get jobs. They decided to try the smaller villages where there was likely to be less competition and after being told the names of a few likely hotels quickly hit the jackpot. Brett got a job as a kitchen helper (or as he calls it a 'dish-pig'). He and his girlfriend who worked at the same hotel were provided with free accommodation and all meals, even on their days off. Brett takes up the story:

Brett Archer explains how the necessity of working cut into his skiing time

The work permit was dealt with by our employer along with medical cover – at least we assumed it was, though we never actually saw any paperwork. My working hours were 8am to 1pm and 6pm to 10pm. Normally we got one day off together per week, but this could be changed at the last moment whenever work demands dictated. I can't honestly say I enjoyed the work, mainly because of demanding employers whose needs conflicted with skiing time, but I learned a bit about cooking and a little German and I was grateful to have a heated room with my girlfriend. I don't know how ski bums who don't have accommodation manage to find anywhere.

A keen skier, Brett was however elated by the skiing which he said made everything worthwhile:
We had to buy our own ski passes, but we got them at the local (residents') rate, which was about half-price. One ski hire shop would lend tourist staff equipment free in the afternoons. Others charged about half-price for the day. We also got 35% discount on new equipment. Combine this with getting the VAT back and it worked out at about 50% discount. To get our VAT back, we took our skis and boots etc. over the border with customs tax forms, to get them stamped and inspected by customs. In the event, they stamped our forms, didn't look at anything and wished us a happy journey back to Lech. We then took the forms back to the shop where we bought our boots and skis and got cash on the spot. I was lucky and managed to ski for 4-5 hours a day. My girlfriend only managed to ski for about 3 hours a day.

According to Brett, when there is no snow, as happened in the season he worked, the trouble tends to start as the employers adopt a 'no snow, no pay' policy. While he was in Lech, nine staff left (were sacked?) from one hotel in January and in another hotel seven staff 'walked out' on the same day. Had he known about this Brett thinks he would have tried to work in Switzerland where working conditions tend to be better regulated. In the event however his job lasted the season and both he and his girlfriend were able to save enough money from their jobs in Lech to go inter-railing around Europe. After a spell back in New Zealand, Brett planned to be a ski bum in the USA for the following season.

Glenda Folpp, an Australian who was a hotel receptionist in Sydney and Perth, was a chambermaid at the Hotel Theodul. She shared a bedroom with two Australian friends whom she recommended to the proprietor for similar work. She got the job originally by knocking on doors. In addition to cleaning the bedrooms and the rest of the hotel except the restaurant, they also had to keep the balconies clear of snow, which usually meant sweeping it off several times while it was falling. Full-time workers who complete the season get a bonus of one and a half month's pay. Glenda mentioned other reasons why it is better to have a full-time, rather than a part-time job:

Part-time workers are getting half the wages but doing more than half the hours, only around two and a half hours less per day; also you may not get accommodation or a day off if you are part-time.

In addition to board and accommodation the girls' fringe benefits included half-price ski school and lift pass, and 15% discount on ski equipment, clothes and hairdressers.

There is also the possibility of baby-sitting work and anyone interested should enquire in the big hotels about putting up an advertisement.

Tour operators in Lech include, Alpine Tracks, Crystal, Lotus Supertravel, Ski Activity and Ski Club Travel Service.

Zell am See

Zell am See (www.europa-sport-region.info; +43 (0)6542 770) is a small, attractive resort in the Pinzgau region of Salzburger Land, set on the edge of the Zellersee at the foot of the Schmittenhöhe mountain which also provides the town's main skiing area. By day, the charm of the resort can be felt both on the slopes and in the town, but by night, the idyll is somewhat interrupted by the throb of the Zell nightlife.

Zell is more than just a seasonal tourist resort. With a permanent population of about 7000, it is large enough to offer a number of working possibilities and free time pursuits, while being small enough to allow you to 'get in with' some of the locals. The local government teams up very successfully with the tourist board to offer a range of festivals, concerts and shows all year round. This, combined with the extensive local amenities make Zell a place in which you could pass more time than just a ski season.

Salzburg, the nearest airport is about 80km (50 miles) distant).

THE SKIING

The Schmittenhöhe ski region descends from 1,993m to 756m at resort level, with 28 lifts and 75km of pistes of which 20 are blue, 35 red and 15 black. In good snow conditions the possibilities are excellent for both skiers and riders alike. The main attraction then, is the extensive tree skiing and riding on and off piste. When the conditions are less propitious, it is time to take full advantage of your lift pass and bus the 12km to the neighbouring resort of Kaprun which, together with Zell is marketed as the Europa Sport ski area which includes the magnificent Kitzsteinhorn glacier. The Europa Sport region pass doubles the km of piste available, but more importantly it gives access to the Kitzsteinhorn at Kaprun. This glacier offers skiing up to a height of 3,029 m, including a cable car, gondola, chair lift and six T-bars; the six or seven runs up here are nearly all blue and the snow excellent and long lasting. For these reasons the glacier attracts Austrians in thousands, particularly when there is no good snow elsewhere. Another attraction is the restaurant at the top of the glacier with breathtaking views of Austria's highest mountain, the Grossglockner (3798m). Both areas offer snowboard parks to brush up on those 'grabs' and 'cossacks'. For off piste guiding, you should speak to the British reps who will undoubtedly have deals with local guides.

APRÈS SKI

There are many bars and nightclubs, but some stand out. There are fewer English-speaking workers here than in some of the other Austrian resorts, so it is not possible to pinpoint one as the main haunt for them. Liveliest bars are the Crazy Daisy on the Brückner Bundesstrasse, Pinzgauer Diele (which is also a disco, and where British people are usually to be found), and next to it in the Kirchengasse, the Viva nightclub is a hotspot, and the disco is good; the Pinzgauer Diele is free, but both insist on you buying a drink (not too exorbitant). The Hirshen Keller and the Lebzeltkeller (the latter is part of the Zellerhotel) are also lively at night. The Karambar is a cocktail bar with a Latin flavour and dance music only rivalled by B-17 on BB Strasse which is US-style cocktail bar, complete with juggling bartender and is decked out like an aircraft hanger. Reasonably priced restaurants include Octopussy, and the Italian/Greek eatery Zum Ceäsar; otherwise try the Weinerwald, a cheap restaurant specialising in chicken (as is obvious from their sign), or the snack bars Kupferkessel (Brückner Bundestrasse) and Centro (by the station).

WORK

Finding work with a tour company via their UK head offices, is a surefire way to secure a season of work. They all offer inclusive lift passes, ski hire, accommodation and between £50 and £200 per week depending on whether you are washing up or managing in the resort. Operators in the region include: Crystal, Thomson, First Choice, Skibound, Inghams and Neilson. For chalet operators, qualified chefs are always in biggest demand and once here have a variety of hotels on offer for more long-term possibilities. Karen was a rep in Zell and said of the hectic lifestyle:

Honestly, we didn't stop all season, up at 7.57am for 8am duties, Ski guiding from 9.30am until 4ish, then drinks with the guests until 6pm, a quick shower then duties again, then dinner with the guests followed by the entertainments, all rounded off with Daisy's until the early hours. Then up again at 7.57am.....

Other chalet jobs include washer uppers, hostesses, qualified NNEB nannies and maintenance people. As far as repping goes, Zell is one of the best Austrian resorts to make money, especially because of its year round potential. Karen went on to complete a very successful summer there, working for a local tour bus company Steger Niederer.

Most companies are also on the lookout for on the spot replacement staff. The above mentioned jobs can be found through contacts best made in bars like the Crazy Daisy (+43 6542 76359) or in rep office hours. If you drop in at some of the larger hotels such as the Tiroler Hof or the Grand you will be able to surreptitiously glean information from tour operators' notice-boards for their contact times, their names and even to see what they look like. Crystal would probably be the first port of call (contact the resort manager, care of the Crazy Daisy) who said they are always on the look out for transfer reps.

As far as ski instructor jobs go, Doris Zisler of Zell/Thumersbach has been a ski instructor for many years who comments:

The only way you can get taken on here is to take the ten-day Anwaerter Skilehrer course which costs a few hundred euros). With that you can begin to teach, but to make a good living you have to do the next three stages.

As Zell is very much a self-sufficient community, there is a full range of jobs you would find back home. Check out the tourist office website (www.zellamsee.com) for more details.

Lawrence Brundell who worked for several tour companies before working in Zell as a Neilson senior rep says:

The job is not too well paid, so job satisfaction is the most important thing, and I get that. Every day is different, and the work is not like any nine-to-five job; you don't stop work and go home each evening. The other thing is, it's not as glamorous as it looks. I can ski three or four times a week, maybe more. If you're looking for work, come out in October or November, and go round the bars, restaurants and hotels; they can always find something. It's a question of being in the right place at the right time, and being persistent. Come in summer if you possibly can because even by mid-November it can be too late.

When looking round the hotels, don't expect too much from the big ones – if you are worried about work permits. The most hopeful avenue to explore would be the middle-sized ones, still big enough to need help, but not quite so concerned about taking on non EU foreigners. Obviously you need to be able to speak some German in order to find work. If you want to start at the top of the list and work down, Grand Hotel, Salzburger Hof and the Hotel Katharina are the biggest. You can get a list of the hotels in Zell from the Information Office (☎ +43 6542 770; fax +43 6542 2032), and it will give you the names of the *Pensionen*, the bed and breakfast houses which will put you up for as little as £15 per night. There are hordes of *Pensionen* in Zell to choose from.

You should also make use of the station personnel's knowledge of the resort – it may save hours or days of laborious searching to ask them as soon as you arrive. There is also a large sports complex (*Hallenbad*) with pool, skating etc. If you have the relevant experience, your chances of getting work here go up significantly. Otherwise, try one of the ski shops by offering to work as a ski technician. The British tour companies operating here include: Crystal, Equity, First Choice, Inghams, Panorama, Neilson and Thomson.

Eastern Europe & Slovenia

The growth of interest in skiing has developed no less in Eastern Europe, in Bulgaria, Romania the Czech and Slovak Republics and Poland, than it has in the western European countries. These nations have fine terrain for downhill skiing or langlauf and are anxious to continue attracting larger numbers of foreign tourists to boost their newly capitalist economies. Prices for skiing packages to these countries are generally cheaper than elsewhere in Europe, despite the extra travelling distance. But a skiing holiday in the eastern part of Europe is not everyone's cup of tea. Even in the best resorts of Bulgaria, one of the most tourist oriented eastern nations, the skiing possibilities are less extensive than the average Alpine resort. Equipment tends to be decrepit, après ski facilities limited and hotels of poor standard or even downright dangerous.

The only work opportunities are with tour operators as representatives (including in the case of Balkan Holidays) or children's reps. Given the still unpredictable nature of eastern European bureaucracies, these jobs tend to go only to experienced representatives or those fluent in the local language. But for low-cost skiing especially good for novices, and a chance to visit a still little-known area, eastern Europe is well worth considering, even if your ski instructor is paid a pittance and pesters you to find him a job back in your home country. In 2004 another ten countries, most of them Eastern European, joined the EU but it hasn't made finding a job in Eastern Europe for all EU nationals easier. Instead it has, as predicted, produced a flood of backpackers and working travellers from Eastern Europe looking for jobs in Western Europe, particularly Britain.

WORK

There are no casual jobs, in ski resorts or elsewhere, as the upheaval in the economies of these countries caused by the overthrow of communism fifteen or so years ago, has resulted in massive unemployment. The only opportunity for legal employment is as a rep working for a tour operator. As with other repping work, this involves a season of three to five months based at a resort, looking after clients of the company. Normally only seasoned reps are sent to these countries. For the most part it is not considered necessary to speak Bulgarian, Romanian, Czech or Polish, but you will obviously improve your reception locally if you do. Even Italian and Russian can be useful. Slovenia, which was the first of the former Yugoslavian areas to remove itself from Balkan turmoils, has managed business as usual for several years at its two resorts of Kranjska Gora and Bled which are both in the north of the republic on the Austrian border. Not surprisingly it attracts large numbers of skiers from Austria and Italy. Operators who go to resorts in Slovenia include Thomson, Inghams and Alpine Tours; Bulgaria: Balkan Holidays, First Choice and Crystal; Romania: Crystal, Balkan Holidays and First Choice. Tour operators admit that their reps do not want to be sent to eastern European countries as conditions are difficult, the nightlife is limited and they get paid less for working in these countries than in the Alps etc.

With the upset of communism came the end of compulsory Russian lessons at school and a sudden surge of interest in learning English over other European languages. This presents another possibility for anyone wanting to enjoy skiing in eastern Europe: by getting a job near the ski areas you will probably be better paid than if you were working in a ski resort. For instance Vitosha mountain, one of the main Bulgarian ski areas, rises from the suburbs of the capital Sofia. Although there may be little difficulty finding such work, accommodation is usually in short supply.

While many of the former sinister problems of working in Slovenia and eastern Europe have disappeared, namely being mistaken for a spy or being caught selling western goods or changing money on the black market, they have been replaced by others: unemployment, creaking infrastructure, poor communications and general uncertainty about the future in some of the Eastern European nations, Poland being the possible exception. It is therefore unlikely that many ski bums will want to work there when they have the European Alps or the resorts of North America to choose from.

France

For several reasons France ought to be the best of all countries in Europe for British people to find jobs in ski resorts: it is easy and cheap to get to, and France is the number one destination for British skiers with over 100 top resorts and an estimated 350,000 British skiers going there every season, two-thirds of these with British tour operators. Furthermore, there has been a sharp increase in the availability of jobs with French employers in the resorts and an enormous shortfall of applicants to fill the vacancies. During one past season only 2,000 people applied for over 7,000 vacancies offered in the Grenoble area including ones on ski lifts and in hotels, prompting the employment service for the region to advertise the vacancies in English on its website.

France tends to attract more ambitious skiers, than Austria, which is favoured by beginners and novices. Most of the big French resorts are high enough to ensure fairly reliable snow throughout the season. The drawback is that many of the top resorts are purpose-built and a high proportion of the accommodation is in self-catering apartments or designed for chalet parties. This is fine if you want to work as a chalet person or rep for a tour company but there is less scope generally for the full après ski infrastructure of bars, tea-rooms, restaurants and night clubs found in the older resorts of Austria and Switzerland and which is so often the mainstay of casual work for ski bums and others. This is not to say there are no jobs – on the contrary there are an estimated 7,000 in *l'hôtellerie restauration* (hotels and restaurants) throughout the French Alps. About a third of these are for unskilled workers. It is generally agreed that if you're going out on spec, it may well be better to head for one of the older alpine resorts like Chamonix or Morzine than somewhere like Avoriaz or La Plagne. If you want to go to a newer resort choose somewhere like Méribel which has some variety of accommodation and a very large UK skiing clientele – but go early, before the season starts. ANPEs (The French national employment offices) in the area are keen on British applicants because of the increasing numbers of English-speaking guests skiing in the area. Note that finding long-term accommodation is likely to be easier in the less trendy resorts, for example Risoul or Bourg-St-Maurice. However, as the British are still a fairly rare sight in such resorts it will be essential to have some French at your command to negotiate your way into a job with a French employer. The disadvantage of working in a mainly French resort is that, unless your French is up to it, you will miss the socialising that goes on amongst the British alpine workers in the big international resorts; you will however, probably be better paid. If you hold professional qualifications in hotel catering, or tourism you could try the ANPE in Albertville (45 avenue Jean Jaurés, BP 96, 73200 Albertville; ☎04 79 32 03; ale.albertville@anpe.fr), which has a centralised placement service for vacancies in hotels throughout the French Alps (Morzine, Avoriaz, La Clusaz, Chamonix, Megève, St.-Jean-de- Maurienne, Bourg-St.-Maurice, Les Arcs, Tignes, Val d'Isère, Les Deux Alpes, Courchevel, Méribel, Chamrousse and L'Alpe d'Huez). Vacancies can also be found through MINITEL 36.14 Alpes. If you are in France and have access to a Minitel terminal you could try registering your application directly. In theory, you will be informed directly of vacancies suitable for your qualifications. The Albertville ANPE also operates in the summer as well for a different selection of resorts including thermal spas like Thonon-les-Bains and Aix-les-Bains.

AGENCES LOCALES POUR L'EMPLOI (FRENCH WORK BUREAUX)

SAVOIE

Opening periods may vary, except year-round offices.

Agence d'Aix les Bains: 12 rue Isaline, B.P. 301, 73103 Aix les Bains; ☎04 79 88 48 49; fax 04 79 61 15 35. e-mail ale.aix-les-bains@anpe.fr.Open all year.
Agence d'Albertville: 45 Ave Jean-Jaurès, B.P. 96, 73203 Albertville Cedex; ☎04 79 32 20 03; fax 04 79 31 28 55; e-mail ale.Albertville@anpe.fr .
Agence de Chambéry: Parc Joppet, 32 rue Paulette Besson, 73000 Chambéry; ☎04 79 60 24 70; fax 04 79 60 46 88; e-mail ale.chambery@anpe.fr.
Agence de Montmélian: 17 avenue de la Gare, 73899 Montmélian; ☎04 79 84 78 20; fax 04 79 84 78 21; e-mail ale.montmelian@anpe.fry.

ANTENNES SAISON HIVER
(Seasonal Work Bureaux for Winter Jobs)

Opening dates may vary from year to year

Bourg Saint Maurice: Immeuble La Croisette, Les Arcs 1800, 73700 Bourg Saint Maurice; ☎06 22 85 15 07.
Courchevel: Maison de Moriond, 73120 Courchevel 1650; ☎04 79 00 01 01; e-mail www.mairie-courchevel.com

Les Menuires: Galerie de l'Adret, 73440 Les Ménuires; ☎04 79 00 23 20; open November to the end of April.
Méribel: Office de tourisme, 73550 Méribel; ☎04 79 00 51 75. Open from the beginning of October to mid-December.
La Plagne: Maison des Saisonniers de la Plagne, Salle Omnisports, 73210 Plagne Centre; ☎04 79 09 20 85; fax 04 79 55 77 84; e-mail maison-des-saisonniers@mairie-smb.com. Open from the beginning of October to mid-December.
Tignes: Immeuble Glattier, 73320 Tignes; ☎04 79 40 09 89; open from beginning October to mid-December.
Val d'Isère: Immeuble Jardin d'Enfants, 73150 Val d'Isère; tel: 04 79 06 84 78. Open from the beginning of October to the end of March.
Val Thorens: Immeuble Eskival, 73440 Val Thorens; 04 79 00 22 11. Open from the beginning of October to the end of March.

Argentière

Ask any hardened skier where they go for the best powder in Europe and chances are that they will say Argentière. Situated in the incredible Mont Blanc region 5km down the valley from Chamonix (www.compagniedumontblanc.com), Argentière is the experts' resort.

The resort itself is mostly old, unpretentious and a bit higgledy-piggledy. The single main street consists of old fashioned, chalet-style buildings while further down more modern types of apartments like the Grand Roc are to be found.

The skiing at Argentière is mainly for the better skier. One of the runs, the Pas de Chèvre is famed for its steepness. As Konrad Bartelski put it: 'It was the single most spectacular run I've ever done...When you get down to the bottom and look back, and where you started is almost overhanging, there is real satisfaction'. On the Grand Montets glacier are acres of unmarked powder, and you must take a guide for safety. For those not wishing to get their satisfaction in the same way as Mr. Bartelski, there is easier skiing at Le Tour, a short bus ride down the valley. The pass for the area, the Mont Blanc pass, also includes the other resorts in the Chamonix Valley including Chamonix itself, La Flègère, Les Houches, La Praz and St. Gervais.

The local ski school vies with the Ecole du Ski Français. There is also an off piste ski school run by the French 'impossible' skier Patrick Vallencant. There is a complex system of priorities for different ski schools on the lifts at different times in the hour. If you are not with a group it can take 30-40 minutes to get up from Argentière. New lifts may help to reduce this.

NIGHTLIFE
Après ski not very exciting in Argentière, mainly because everyone is tucked up early resting for the battle of the next day. However there are some lively bars and restaurants and a handful of discos full of the super fit and chic: The Office bar is small and friendly and patronised by English-speakers (see also *Work* below) as is the Stones Bar; La Trace offers pinball and video games. The Savoie Bar is much more popular with the French than the foreign workers and specialises in good beers and even has a yard of ale glass; the 'beat' can be found in the plush Night Roc nightclub.

ACCOMMODATION
Accommodation is usually found by word of mouth, though there are several agencies in Chamonix which offer a rental service. The cheapest temporary accommodation is at Le Chamoniard, and Le Belvedere gîtes. The Belvedere gîte (www.gitebelvedere.com)

charges from £98 per week self catering, accommodation, of 14 euros for a bed only for one night.

WORK

It is unlikely that you will find work at the ski school even with qualifications and speaking French, as there is plenty of tough competition from the locals. However, due to the enormous amount of glacier skiing around Argentière, guides are always in demand, and the high price of professional guides creates many opportunities for private guiding of skiers; research the area very thoroughly before taking responsibility for anyone, as the glaciers are very dangerous for the unprepared.

The lift company has employed Americans and in this job you usually get plenty of time to ski and a free pass; accommodation may or may not be provided. The work is usually menial, e.g. maintaining tow pathways. Knowledge of engineering may well be a handy asset for ski tows tend to break down quite often. It is essential to speak French. Bruno Stevens from London worked for the chairlift company for three seasons, being promoted from snow-clearing and general handyman to operating the emergency stop at the top of the chair. This last was particularly tedious as there is no one to talk to, but the free ski pass, free lunch and two days off a week were good compensation, and he was able to jump all the lift queues (which are actually not too bad) as he knew all the other employees.

Sports stores are also worth trying. The 'Centre Commercial' contains a number of sports shops, but most are family run (e.g. Stamos Sports). Mont Blanc Sports (Centre Commercial, 74430 Argentière, France), may take on foreign workers during the peak season. As competition for such jobs is stiff – you need a thorough technical knowledge of ski equipment and French. Namaste, Fontaine and Devousassoux Sports may also be worth trying. Sports shops' employees usually have to work full-time but they do get a proper wage. Ideal Snowboard, also in the Centre Commercial, will provide a meeting place and jobs for friends of the guys who founded it – worth cultivating. They also hire out mountain bikes.

As in Chamonix, most of the jobs in Argentière available to foreigners are in bars and restaurants. Though most bars prefer French-speakers, many people manage to find work without any knowledge of the language. A good place to try is Le Samoyède, run by Lawrence Stein and his French wife. They have been known to employ those who do not speak French. It's also worth trying the Video Bar, and The Office bar on route Charlet-Straton, run by Simon Norris. Sven Llewellyn, who originally worked for a computer company in Britain, worked as a barman there for three seasons. Employees at the Office Bar do not work strict hours so that all of them have plenty of time to ski. Accommodation is not provided but the work is said to be very enjoyable. The manager is often asked if he knows of anyone available for a particular job, so he is worth keeping in with. The bar also has a notice-board where jobs and accommodation are regularly advertised. La Piano bar also employs English-speakers.

It is also possible to find bar and table waiting jobs in the mountain restaurants, in particular Le Grand Mottet and La Flègere have been known to employ Brits.

Most of the hotels in the area require cheap labour to wash up, clear snow and clean, but pay is low. You must be in the resort no later than November to look for work. EU nationals will probably find it easier than Americans, Australians etc. who need work permits. It is essential to speak French. The pay is reasonable and most people get enough time to ski in the afternoons. Accommodation is usually paid out of wages but is not expensive. Another hotel to try is the Hotel Olympic at Le Tour.

A considerable number of jobs are registered with the official job centre in nearby Chamonix: (Agence National Pour L'Emploi, Résidence le Mummery, 27 Avenue du Savoy, 74400 Chamonix; ☎04 50 53 15 31; fax 04 50 55 86 79) which is open all year.

Avoriaz

Avoriaz (www.avoriaz.com; tourist office ☎+33 450 74 02 11) is a purpose-built resort whose wood-faced, high-rise terraced buildings are typical of such resorts built in the 1960s and 70s. Set high at 5,904 feet and located above Morzine, Avoriaz is surrounded by yet higher peaks. It has an excellent snow record on its mainly north-facing slopes. Traffic is allowed to the edge of the resort, but cars and other traffic are banned from the resort itself. However, the term 'traffic free' is used rather loosely here with the streets clogged with horse-drawn sleighs, ratracs, 4x4 nimbus taxis and skiers. There are two main shopping areas in the resort, which provide all the temporary inhabitants of the residences (apartment blocks) with the necessities. Owing to its relatively traffic free status and excellent children's facilities including a self-contained children's village (Village des Enfants) which takes 3-16 year olds and Les P'tits Loups (04 50 74 00 38) ski kindergarten and the Club Med family village, Avoriaz is popular with families.

THE SKIING

As the gateway to the famous Portes du Soleil circuit of 13 interlinked ski resorts (eight in France and five in Switzerland), Avoriaz offers skiers of all standards varied and testing possibilities. The Portes du Soleil Circuit is very worthwhile and can easily be skied in a day by an intermediate skier.

The skiing begins and ends literally at your doorstep. All the resorts are on the main Portes du Soleil Ski Pass which allows access to seemingly limitless runs (actually 650 km of marked piste) served by over 205 lifts and you need only your passport and lift pass to ski over the frontier. There is also an Avoriaz only pass, and beginners pass for the lifts and cable-car to the Plateau Les Linderets where the nursery slopes are located.

Whether a beginner learning to ski on the Plateau, an intermediate skiing the open pistes of the Chavanette or Les Marmottes, or an advanced skier tackling the infamous Wall on the Swiss border or the World Cup Downhill Course from the top of Les Hauts Forts to Les Prodains, Avoriaz provides extensive opportunities. However, you must be careful to avoid being stranded on the Swiss side of the area when the lifts are shut around 4.30pm each day as there are often major queues for the last lifts back, both from Les Crosets and up from Les Lindarets. Although there is a bus to ferry you back to the comfort of the resort it can be an unsettling experience, especially if you have failed to take the precaution of carrying some Swiss Francs with you!

Off the slopes, Avoriaz has two squash courts, a gym and fitness centre and a turkish bath. There is also a two-lane bowling alley (fully electronic) and an outdoor ice rink. Toboggans and snowshoes can be hired. Husky dog teams are another exciting way of getting around. Hang gliding, parapente and helicopter trips are also available.

APRÈS SKI

Although the ski opportunities are limitless, après ski entertainment is less varied and on the expensive side. It is centred on the bars, restaurants and discos in the resort, but somehow they all lack the panache of Courchevel or St. Moritz. There are also two cinemas showing English films.

The bar Le Choucas which has the best live music is always crowded. The best bars otherwise are Le Pub Tavaillon, Le Tar-Zoon and Le Fantastique. The best restaurants are Le Bistro, Pizzeria, Lac d'Intrets, Le Savoyarde, La Boule de Neige and L'Igloo. Le Tavaillon usually employs an English bartender. Le Petit Vatel (next to the top station of the cable car) is also excellent.

WORK

The nature of the resort as a major complex has developed over the years as have the opportunities for employment. With its reputation as an international resort, Avoriaz has considerable potential for Brits to find jobs alongside the French. The season is long, extending from mid-November to mid-April:

Tour Operators

Major tour operators Airtours, First Choice and Neilson operate in the resort as do Erna Low and Ski Weekend.

Lipika Mandal from Cheshire, worked as a rep. She applied in writing to the (now defunct) Enterprise after seeing an advert in the *Manchester Evening News*. She had no previous experience of repping but spoke basic French and was interested in the long-term prospects of working in tourism. She earned a basic monthly salary, paid in the UK and earned commission on ski packs and après ski in the resort. She was provided with free accommodation only. She was free to ski most afternoons, which she enjoyed. Other aspects of the job she liked were living abroad, meeting lots of new people and broadening her experiences. The worst part of the job was dealing with unreasonable clients, long stretches of unsociable hours, lack of sleep, being always on duty and being far from family and friends in England. However, the drawbacks were insufficient to deter her from working a summer season for the same company as a rep in Turkey and Majorca.

Ski Schools

Although the militant attitude of the local ski instructors towards their foreign counterparts, particularly British qualified ones, has at last been breached now that the French recognise those with the *Equivalence* or European Speed Test (see *Types of Job Available*), there are still only limited opportunities for British ski instructors. There are very few if any British instructors at the ESF (French ski school, ☎4-50 74 05 65). The British Alpine Ski and Snowboard School (BASS) in Avoriaz, is probably a better bet.

Anthea Brown (an Essex girl!) got a job teaching 3-6 year olds to ski at the Jardin des Enfants. She had previously worked in Courchevel as a resort manager for the defunct Ski Whizz and as a rep/ski guide in Avoriaz the previous season for another company. During the course of the latter job she approached the director of the ski school to ask for a job for the following season. She said that no special qualifications were needed for teaching children but French and previous experience with children was essential. The fact that she was already known in Avoriaz was a considerable factor in her getting the job. In addition to over £100 per week after tax, she got accommodation, lunch and supper. Her hours were 9.30am to 4pm/5.30pm and she found the work tiring but enjoyable. The worst part was having to teach snivelling and bawling children but she found observing progress in her pupils very rewarding. She was also able to ski free during the period of employment but as she only got Saturdays off this did not amount to much time for her own skiing.

Other Jobs

For the British workers staying in Avoriaz, chalet cleaning appeared the area offering most potential. Karen Houghton, who works in the Serius Apartment Complex, applied for her job on arrival after she had approached the *Directrice de Multivacances*. She said that the ski tour representatives were most helpful in directing her towards possible job vacancies. She told us:

> The ability to speak French is desirable since I work as part of a cleaning team, which is predominantly French. The work is hard but well paid and gives me time off to ski.

Karen earned over £100 per week and also received perks such as free accommodation and ski-pass reductions. The accommodation provided by the employing hotel was quite basic, but gratefully received since there is very little in the way of cheap accommodation or hostels. Most jobs provide accommodation, but the standard depends upon luck and initiative.

Karen McPhilemy worked with the bakery at Les Ruches and delivered bread to the eager skiers in the early hours of the morning. She says 'charm, wit and confidence' are the qualities needed to perform this job which can bring in over £300 a week! She finished delivering the croissants at 8.30am, just in time for the opening of the ski lifts and so had the whole of the day free to ski.

She enjoyed her job, saying 'It's a great crack – a surprise waits behind every door!' But Karen also offers some sound advice for non-EU nationals:

It is better to obtain a permit that classes you as an independent worker, which enables you to do a variety of different jobs. The bakers, Marie Brioche, require this from their delivery staff.

The tourist office in Avoriaz (Maison d'Avoriaz, 74110 Avoriaz; ☎4-50 740211; fax 4-50 741825; www.avoriaz.com) are very helpful with advice about permits. Work is available in the supermarkets Genty, Codec and Ducef throughout the season; also weekend repping for the tour groups taking parties to and from the airport in Geneva and helping with the supervision of the ski-lifts may also be possible. Mark Pearson turned up on spec in the resort at the end of January and managed to survive on a range of odd jobs, which kept him going until he left on April 1st. These included clearing snow, nannying, clearing glasses in bars, carrying luggage, and helping at Ski Fun (ski hire). His earnings could be up to £30-£40 a day; at other times he managed on about £15 plus meals. He was paid mostly in cash so he paid no taxes. He had a free lift pass but it was shared amongst a group of friends. He had to find his own accommodation, which was thankfully cheap (when split between five occupants) but cramped. He managed to ski four days a week. After finishing in the resort he planned to travel round Europe then move on.

Chamonix

Nestling at the foot of the awesome Mont Blanc Massif dominated by Europe's highest peak, Mont Blanc (15,800 feet), lies the sprawling, old village of Chamonix (www.chamonix.com; tourist office ☎+33 (0)4 50 53 00 24). Here the locals will remind you, Alpinism was born with the first ascent of Mont Blanc in 1786, and also the Winter Olympics, which were staged for the first time in Chamonix in 1924. Many of the original lifts and ski jumps built for this event are still in operation. The lift system also contains some of the most spectacular gondola rides in Europe including the haul up to the Aiguille du Midi from which the views are breathtaking and the even more heart-stopping gondola from the Aiguille across to Helbronner on the Italian border.

The village is reached from Geneva in under two hours. Chamonix is also on the railway line from St. Gervais-le-Fayet which links up with major European cities like, Geneva, Lyon, Paris etc. The Mont Blanc tunnel gives access to nearby Italy with Courmayeur just the other side.

THE SKIING

The skiing is divided into five main areas: Les Houches, Le Brévent, Argentière, La Flégère and Le Tour. La Flégère and Le Brévent are linked by a short gondola ride with some spectacular views. Ski buses links the rest. With the exception of Les Houches the fare is included in the Mont Blanc area ski pass. Skiing at Mègeve and Courmayeur (Italy) are also covered by this ski pass.

Chamonix's most famous run, La Vallée Blanche is 20km long and involves a 2,770 metre descent from the Aiguille into Chamonix. Understandably, it attracts skiers from all over the world. It is only open intermittently early in the season, but is more reliably in use from February onwards. It is compulsory to take a guide as the first part of the descent involves a roped walk down onto the glacier from the cable car station. The run itself is off piste and full of hidden snags for the unsuspecting, but is a must if you are there for the whole season.

Do not think however that Chamonix is only for the out and out expert: beginners may not be particularly well catered for but there are nursery slopes in the village at the bottom of the Brévent lift and just outside the village at Les Planards. The area is suited above all to intermediates and good skiers who have a huge range of runs up and down the valley: take the lifts up to La Flégère or Le Brévent to find easier, more gentle skiing. Also down at Le Tour and up at Les Houches, very pleasant skiing can be found. The experienced skier can try the challenging runs of Les Grand Montets at Argentière, which can be reached by bus. Other wonderful runs are also to be found, but go with a guide, it can be dangerous. Although Chamonix is not renowned for its summer skiing, it is possible to ski during the summer months at Col du Geant, accessible via l'Aiguille du Midi.

Chamonix is also one of the top resorts for experienced snowboarders.

Skiing is not Chamonix's only appeal; there is plenty for non-skiers. Apart from the numerous cafés and bars scattered around the town centre, there is a triplex cinema, 2 ice rinks, swimming pools, a bowling alley and a sports centre. Non-skiers can also go on excursions to Italy (out by cablecar, back by bus). For the more cultured visitor there is a museum, an observatory and even a bridge club. The resort also attracts mountaineers in both winter and summer.

APRÈS SKI

Chamonix has a charm of its own. A mixture of Victorian-type hotels like the Astoria rub shoulders with modern ones like the Alpina. The streets are narrow and not suited to the traffic that pours through the village; but there is a buzz you can feel from one of mountaineering and skiing's oldest resorts. From the Pub and Wild Wallabies to the grandeur of the Casino, there is something to suit everyone's taste, so boredom should not arise. Live music is popular in he bars and dancing in clubs like the Arbate will loosen ski sore muscles. Live and popular bars include La Choucas, Le Brévent, Mill Street Bar and Bar du Moulins. Chamonix's restaurants cater well for its international clientele, from the locally renowned L'Impossible and L'Atmosphere to Mexican, Chinese and Italian.

WORK

The first place most people go when looking for work in Chamonix is the ANPE (*Agence National Pour L'Emploi*) in the centre of town. However, most jobs in Chamonix, especially those available through the ANPE require good, spoken French and they tend to go to locals. Unlike many of France's purpose-built ski stations, Chamonix is a proper town with a life outside the ski season. It also has a thriving summer tourist trade. Most of the hotels and restaurants get their staff through the ANPE. Some hotels do employ foreigners and you could try approaching them direct: try Hotel Vallée Blanche (04 50 53 04 50) and the rather larger modern Alpina (04 50 53 47 77).

While the majority of staff working in the hotels or serving the Savoyarde fare in the restaurants, appear to be locals, there are other jobs that foreigners can create for themselves: musicians, wearing traditional costumes who concentrated on wowing female diners before handing round the hat, have been seen playing around the restaurants; evidently they had some deal going with local restaurateurs. Another candlelight entrepreneur was a photographer offering to snap diners as they chomped. This kind of work involves hustling and charm and is not for the shy and retiring. If you have the knack it can be reasonably lucrative. However, wannabe singers and musicians should note that it is essential to have good voices and be reasonably talented as an audience will not pay you just to get rid of you!

The time to start applying for jobs is in June and July. Non-French nationals who speak some French may get work if they apply early enough, i.e. in the summer or right at the beginning of the season. Early in the season, there is often a demand for people to paint, decorate and refit buildings ready for the winter. Tony Locust from Essex got work refurbishing and doing some maintenance work for the restaurant La Bourrique Endiablée at the beginning of the season and was then offered a job there when it opened.

Most of the dozen or so sports shops have adequate local labour, but some employ Brits, Australians, Americans and other English-speakers though most require ski techs who are French-speakers. One Swedish ski tech, who spoke both excellent French and English, pointed out however, that although he would return to Chamonix, he would find a different job, as he preferred to spend daylight hours on the slopes, not behind a counter.

Some ski shops will train you to be a ski tech, but this is more the exception than the rule. Bert Conneely, from Coventry, was one of the lucky ones. He was employed by Perillat Sports/Chamonix Mountain Bikes as a bike mechanic and ski tech. His only previous experience was restoring scooters and paint-spraying back in the UK. His hours were midday to 4pm daily, and he was paid about £500 monthly including ski equipment but not accommodation.

The ski schools (which include ESF, Sensation Ski Ecole Internationale, Evolution 2 and Summit Ski Montagne) and the lift company take on very few foreign staff. If you speak French and have a ski instructor qualification it might be worth asking. Sensation Ski Ecole Internationale, which can be found each evening in the reception of the Gustavia Hotel (opposite the train station), has employed Irish and Australian instructors in the past. Competition is strong however, not only from locals, but from other French instructors who have found the lure of Chamonix irresistible: as Philippe, born and bred in Alpe d'Huez but translocated to Chamonix put it: *'Just look around you'* and he pointed to snow-capped needles silhouetted against a cobalt sky, and tree-lined slopes above the awesome drop to the valley floor, *'this is what skiing is about'*; and who could disagree?

The Panda Club (a kind of junior ski school) does employ Brits. Emma, from Newcastle was given a job there doing general administration and taking bookings for lessons.

Not surprisingly there is a wide range of companies operating in the resort including, Club Med, Collineige, Crystal, Esprit Ski, Flexiski, Huski, Inghams, Rush Adventures, Ski France, Ski Weekend, Thomson and Total.

The majority of job opportunities for English-speakers are in bars and clubs. Talented Martyn Mulhere entertained in the Irish bar Jekyll and Hyde. It was an on spec appointment. Martin had been in Paris working and fancied a holiday. His wages paid for his accommodation and the Jekyll and Hyde provided his meals. Frank Hennessey, the young and flairful owner of the bar does take on British bar staff, but emphasised the need for early application (May or June), and more importantly, a professional attitude. The same message came from Jonas, owner of The Pub (215 rue Paccard) who looks for French-speakers with plenty of bar-tending experience. You must also be happy to wait tables, which many British bar staff are not used to. Both these bars are also excellent for making contacts with other staff in the resort. You can also check out the notice board outside the Hotel de Ville (opposite the Tourist Office).

Just a word or two of warning: Chamonix is spread out along the valley and although the ski bus links the different areas, visitors and staff alike are agreed that a car is extremely useful. If you take a vehicle you may find you are more attractive to employers, particularly tour operators (but make sure you check out rates for mileage/petrol allowances) before you get hired. Also if possible, whether they will help towards your outward journey. The kind of mobile job you could get is as maintenance person, but for this you would need skills and your own tool kit. With initiative, it is possible to organise a delivery service. Note that for fee-paying passengers, the regulations are different and you should not be tempted without checking regulations with the French authorities first. Usually there are many more people seeking jobs than there are vacancies in Chamonix and you may find your chances are better if you try the less publicised resorts in the valley. If only Chamonix will suffice then dig out your French dictionary, hone your language skills (French and other languages), and highlight the most likely selling points on your CV that will appeal to Chamonix employers.

ACCOMMODATION

The cheapest accommodation is at the Chalet Ski Station by the Brévent ski-lift, the Belvedere gîte and Le Chamoniard in Argentière (see *Accommodation* under that resort). Hotel attics are also worth asking for as are any tour operators in the resort. Centrally located Le Vagabond hostel (www.gitevagabond.com) is well thought of for the good, inexpensive accommodation it provides from €14.40 per night for the bunkhouse. The British business Planet Subzero (07905 097 087;info@planetsubzero.com) provides affordable long stay and seasonal accommodation in resorts including Chamonix; you can e-mail for a brochure and information pack or check out the link on Natives.com). The tourist office (☎0450 530024; fax 0450 535890); www.chamonix.com) can provide other accommodation contacts.

Courchevel

Courchevel (www.courchevel.com; tourist office ☎+33 (0)4 79 08 00 29), consists of four villages spread over a mountain side at different heights: 1300, 1550. 1650 and 1850m. Courchevel 1300 is the old village of Le Praz and also the site of the 1992 Winter Olympics ski jump. After Le Praz, Courchevel 1850 is the oldest and probably the nicest of the newer resorts and dates from the 1940s. It is attractively laid out and many of the buildings have wooden facades and balconies and chalet-style roofs. All four stations are linked by a free bus service. Courchevel is part of the Trois Vallées ski area (famous after the 1992 Olympics), which includes about a dozen linked resorts including the two Méribel resorts and LaTania in the next valley and Les Menuires, St. Martin-de-Belleville and Val Thorens (the highest resort in Europe) in the valley after that.

When people talk of Courchevel they generally mean 1850, and being one of the smartest resorts in the Alps means that it is expensive. It attracts a rich and cosmopolitan clientele, which seems to mean few British. There are far fewer English-speakers here than in Méribel or Val Thorens, probably because 1850 tends to have more hotels than self-catering apartments. Apart from the obvious trappings of wealth, including the clothes shops stuffed with designer labels and very expensive nightclubs like La Grange and Le St. Nicholas, Courchevel has also been in the forefront of all new ski-oriented fads from hang-gliding and parascending from cliffs to heli-skiing. Rich Parisiens arrive by air direct to the Altiport beside the pistes. For the less fortunate the journey takes three hours from Lyon or Geneva airports, Courchevel is reached by heading up the mountain from Moûtiers. There is dual carriageway from Albertville to Moûtiers, which helps prevent traffic congestion on Saturdays. Trains run from Paris to Moûtiers from where buses go to Courchevel.

THE SKIING

Courchevel 1850, the largest and most popular village, is perfectly adapted for all standards of skier with the easiest runs near the village, and runs that can test even the most experienced skier further up the mountain – try the notorious couloirs at La Saulire to make your hair stand on end. There are also testing runs in Méribel and Val Thorens. There is a choice of lift passes: the Vallée de Courchevel Pass which covers all four Courchevel resorts comprising over 160 km of pistes and 68 lifts. While the Trois Vallées pass gives you access to the 600 km and over 200 lifts of the area and should be seriously considered by anyone spending a season here. However, it is a fast day's skiing to get over to Val Thorens and back – it is important to avoid being stuck in the wrong valley when the lifts close. You can also get day supplements for the skiing areas outside Courchevel. There is a ski bus service linking all four villages of Courchevel, the cost of which is covered by the ski pass.

Although Courchevel is not as modern as some French resorts, all the lifts are kept in immaculate condition, and new lifts are always being planned or built. Ater heavy snowfalls, the piste patrollers are quick to start blowing up avalanches and the highest runs are sometimes open surprisingly early. Runs that are still dangerous are always ostentatiously shut. All in all, Courchevel has a very good safety record.

The resort has an excellent assortment of ski schools: The Ski Académie is run by independent French instructors but classes in 1850 are mainly taught in French. Ski Supreme is owned and run by British Instructors. New Generation/Le Ski School is another British school with the pick of young British instructors and operates in 1650 and 1850 (and Méribel). New Generation/Le Ski School is a fairly recent addition but has acquired an excellent reputation. Foreign ski instructors must have their *equivalence* or the newer European Speed Test in order to be allowed to teach in France permanently (see *Types of Job Available*).

APRÈS SKI

It is not only the pistes which are well-groomed in this resort: Courchevel 1850, the main residential area of the resort, attracts an up-market clientele of all nationalities, especially in the form of executive conferences. Fur coats and champagne are *de rigeur*. All the flash gear will be seen as well as snowboards and *ski evolutif* paraphernalia. There are plenty of roving photographers waiting to snap the designer-dressed skiers on the slopes. The restaurants Chabichou and La Chouca are highly rated and pricey and the Chalet des Pierres up on the pistes and out in the sun, is the place to be for lunch. It's cocktails at Le Mangeoire, Le Tremplin or Le Barbare, transvestite floor shows at Le St. Nicholas and dancing the night away at Les Caves or you can throw your money away at La Grange nightclub.

Other Courchevel highlights include a superb ice-rink, saunas, cinemas and a concert hall, aerobics classes, language courses and flying lessons.

But you do not have to be one of the jet set to enjoy or afford Courchevel. This is thanks mainly to the British companies out there in force who offer holidays at much the same price as anywhere else. Crystal go to 1850/1650/1550 and all the usual big companies and more than a dozen chalet companies including Inghams, Esprit, Equity, Finlays, First Choice, Flexiski, Le Ski, Lotus Supertravel, Mark Warner (1850), Neilson, Ski Olympic, Powder Byrne, Crystal Finest, Silver Ski, Ski Activity, Ski France, Ski Val, Thomson and Total. Most of the tour operators organise their own social life – fancy dress parties, torchlight descents etc – but have also spawned a wealth of attractive options for the less well-heeled. La Saulire (Jack's Bar) and the Ski Lodge in 1850, beneath the neon sign of La Catina, are usually packed out. The Bubble Bar in the centre of 1650 is an all day all night spot with internet access.

Courchevel is noisy, lively and fun. The more money you have the better, but for impoverished job seekers the opportunities to capitalise on the affluence of others are quite good and varied.

ACCOMMODATION

Once in Courchevel accommodation ought to be quite easy to find, and it is if you keep away from 1850. Most British companies will provide ski reps, chalet staff and all their other employees with free accommodation on a short-term basis, 1650 is probably your best bet. Alex Lock was sharing a flat with three others. He was there for the whole season and was often looking to fill up the other three beds. Simon Isdel-Carpenter spent his first week living in a car with a friend. He soon found a flat for about £50 a week. Anything over that is expensive, and you can even find free beds in chalet parties especially in the low season if you can find a sympathetic chalet host; alternatively, you can ad hoc (i.e. stay as an unscheduled guest) in an unfilled chalet bed for £8-10 per night. Cheap accommodation can also be found down the mountain at Brides les Bains. However, a good way to discover what is available is to call in at the Ski Lodge Bar in a British-run hotel. It is not only the hub of life for the British workers, but for the French workers too. Planet Subzero (www.planetsubzero) also has affordable long-term or season's accommodation in Courchevel; e-mail info@planetsubzero for a brochure. Don't go to estate agents unless you are desperate.

WORK

The first people to get to know about jobs are the reps from the British tour companies operating in Courchevel. They are not only the largest employers of Brits, but the ones with the highest turnovers of staff – you would be amazed how many chalet staff break a limb, rush back pining for the other half, get sacked or any of the other things you shouldn't do if you want to survive in the Alps.

Some of the tour operators that employ British workers in the resort are listed above. The reps have office hours either from 5.30 to 6.30pm or 6.30 to 7.30pm depending on the company. At one time or another, most reps can be found having a drink at the Ski Lodge Bar. Inghams reps can be found up the road in the bar of the Hotel St. Louis. In 1650 the popular bar for British workers is at the Hotel Les Avals. In 1550 the popular Glacier bar is run by the British company Ski Chamois and La Taverne (a.k.a. The Scabby Dog) is run by two Frenchman.

Once you have made one contact you will find a network opening up. Give the reps your name and address and with any luck they will offer you a job rather than fly someone out from the UK if a replacement is needed for sick or injured staff. With luck you should get something within a fortnight.

The Employment Office among the shops and offices of La Croisette, underneath the main gondola lifts at 1850, is only useful for people who can speak French. Courchevel is however, a resort full of possibilities. Advice to job hunters is neatly summarised by Nick Davies from London: 'Go where the workers go and persevere'. Finding life in London as an accounts manager too stressful, Nick Davies drove to Courchevel in a camper van with his Canadian girlfriend. They asked everywhere and got to know the manager of the Ski Lodge. Through this contact, after ten days, Nick's girlfriend found a job as a chalet girl with Bladon Lines. Nick found part-time work standing in for sick employees and lived in the van for three weeks. As a result, Bladon Lines finally gave him a full-time job as a chalet boy. Bladon Lines do not require chalet staff to speak French, but it is helpful. Nick got a small weekly wage with free ski perks and accommodation. He had ample free time for skiing.

Ian Parkinson who has a diploma in hotel management and catering and is the manager of the Ski Lodge, says that he would take people on in the resort when vacancies arose, although Ski Val had waiting lists in Britain. Workers for these companies live on site at the Ski Lodge in shared rooms. Ian worked for Bladon Lines for two winters and a summer season before being offered the Ski Lodge position by Ski Val. He earns £120 per week and finds the work hard but enjoyable ('It's what you make it'). His hours are 7am to 11.30am and 6pm to 11pm with one day off per week. Hotel managers and reps must be able to speak French.

Another worker, Jasper Valence wrote to 30 companies and had six interviews from which he was offered three jobs: rep, driver and bartender. He chose the bartender job. His success at interview was no doubt due to his obvious ability to get on well with people. His experience in the Territorial Army and two holiday jobs on a kibbutz taught him teamwork. He has a degree in estate mangagement, speaks French and has a skiing qualification. He told us that he can double his weekly wage from tips and cigarettes and chooses to prepare vegetables rather than ski all day. His ambition was to run his own chalet.

In Courchevel, most British workers agreed that it is essential to work as a team and speak enough French to get by. Richard Irving worked for Ski Val two days a week as a ski guide and the rest of the time as a rep. He landed this job having worked in previous years as a barman and assistant chef in Méribel. Before this he had been a bond trader and a journalist. He reported that Ski Val interviews nearly everyone who applied in Britain. Personally, he had already found 12 people work in Courchevel by the end of January. He said he loved the resort because of its 'Frenchness' and the good atmosphere of cooperation between the tour operators.

Julie Fowler from Hampshire applied for a job by writing to British operators in May and June. She worked as a hostess. No special qualifications were needed. Her duties included bed-making, serving meals and tidying up. Her basic wage was about £40 per week. She had lots of time for skiing and enjoyed the job although the accommodation was 'a bit like boarding school'. She thought that Courchevel was an especially good resort for meeting the French.

When Bladon Lines made Tana Rowe redundant as a graphic designer, she asked if she could be a chalet girl. She worked six days out of seven from 7am to midday and 5pm to 10.30pm in a chalet that sleeps 12. She said that it was neither the job nor the skiing that attracted her, but spending six months with people her own age. There is a good team spirit at BL and it is valuable experience to work with all types of clients from toddlers upwards. She sums it up as 'good practice for running a home'. Tana spoke enough French to do the shopping in Moûtiers. She reported that to get a job as a chalet girl you need to be an outgoing personality as well as being able to cook.

Hannah Wade, aged 30 worked for customer services at Oxford University Press for ten years. She was a chalet host in Méribel Mottaret for Ski World. Two weeks before the start of the ski season she looked for a job on the website Natives.com where she made applications online to several ski companies advertising last minute vacancies. Ski World was the first to reply and ask her to come for an interview.

Hannah Wade tells how she maximised her minimal cooking skills at interview and spent two seasons as a chalet host progressing from rookie to veteran with attitude.

My interview for the job lasted about half an hour during which I elevated my cooking experience to dinner parties for fifteen, when in fact I had never cooked for more than four guests at a time. I mentioned some fancy dishes and that was it. To be honest, personality and character go a long way towards getting you the job.

We had a week's training in Courchevel and then I had a week to prepare my chalet in Méribel before the first guests arrived. The first week of guests is a period of great anxiety as you have not fully established your routine. For the first four weeks of your chalet job you should realistically not expect to get out too much, as this period embraces the run up to Christmas and New Year when guests are paying top dollar and have very high expectations. I actually found Christmas Day the most miserable Christmas of my life as I spent the whole day cooking. But after Christmas things calmed down and I got into the swing of partying all night, skiboarding in the day and living with exhaustion.

My second season was quite different. I again worked for Ski World, and as a returnee they let me choose my resort, St Anton in Austria. I ran a chalet for 16-18 guests with my boyfriend Simon Morris who had formerly run his own restaurant. A word of advice to couples thinking of running a chalet togther – it is a big strain on a relationship particularly if you have both run your own chalets individually before and have different ideas of how to organise the kitchen. Many couples split up under the strain – fortunately we didn't.

Another useful tip involves making sure that you know all your guests by name. I used to have this routine where I would sit them all down at the start and ask them to say their name for the benefit of all the others. I would then go through all the names again indicating who was who. This was enough for me to remember their names for the rest of the week and it worked wonders for how they viewed you from then on.

My final tip is one it took me a season to learn: don't be afraid to say NO. I used to get incensed with guests turning up late for dinner after other guests had already started and I told them that they had to arrive on time unless they had given me prior warning. Believe me, if you lay down the law in a sensible way, they will behave. Otherwise, if you let mealtimes slide you will be taken advantage of, as many chalet hosts are, and then find the guests have complained to the company that their meals are overcooked when it is really the guests' fault, not yours.

Hannah was paid £65 per week in her first season and £70 for the second one. Hers were standard chalets; staff in luxury chalets usually get a little more. She says you can easily save the money and live off the tips if you don't go drinking every night – which she did less of second time around. She and Simon are planning to take a year off to travel and Hannah wants to spend a season in Queenstown ski resort, in New Zealand and do a Snowboard Instructor Course there with the Rookie Academy (www.rookieacademy. co.nz). From there she hopes to go to the USA where the NZ qualification is recognised – unfortunately it is not recognised in Europe.

There are other kinds of vacation work to be found in Courchevel. Mike Smith, a Canadian, was the top skidoo driver at Courcheneige Evasion. John Morgan from Britain, was playing the piano at the Dacota Bar for the second consecutive season.

If you speak understandable French, you may get a job with a French employer. French law stipulates a minimum rate of pay for full-time work, the SMIC (*Salaire Minimum Interprofessionel de Croissance*) which increases about twice a year. This is why those working for French employers are generally reasonably well paid.

Hotel La Croisette/Bar Le Jump (Place du Forum, BP65 73120, Courchevel; www. hoteldelacroisette.com) is a small (18 beds), friendly hotel that employs staff with EU passports and good French. Positions include nanny/child carer, chef, assistant chef, waiting/breakfast person, bartender, reception etc.

French law forbids freelance ski instructing, although for fully certificated BASI instructors prepared to take the European Speeed Test, employment with French ski schools or starting their own, is now recognised thanks to EU regulations governing the mutual recognition of qualifications though the French still operate a tough protectionism (see *Types of Job Available – Ski Instructor*). Where protectionism still operates, it is almost certainly in contravention of EU regulations. Those with lesser BASI qualifications are still more likely to get a job ski guiding with a British company than at the French ski school in Courchevel.

Simon Isdell-Carpenter spent three weeks washing up in a mountain hut but gave up because he got very little skiing as a result. Stuart Morrison and his partner Jean-Pierre were operating a company called Une Premiere Production out of Chalet Fosse in 1550, charging about £50 for two hours filming. Last heard of, they had won a BBC contract.......

All the workers interviewed agreed there were few better places in Europe than Courchevel to work and ski.

Flaine

The horseshoe-shaped resort of Flaine is situated at the heart of the Avre-Giffe Massif in the Haute Savoie region of the French Alps. It dates from 1969 and is built on three levels, the main one being Flaine Forum, which is traffic free and contains the main area of shops, bars and restaurants. Above is Flaine Fôret, which is more residential and has a smaller commercial centre. Below is the newer, attractive chalet-style satellite Hameau de Flaine. The levels are joined by the free Red Devil cable car, which operates 24 hours. The middle level also has a useful supermarket that takes credit cards. You can also use your plastic in several international payphones around the resort, should you wish to check in with your spouse/boss/broker or analyst.

Flaine resort has now become part of the Compagnie des Alpes which is itself part-owned by the Canadian company Intrawest whose portfolio also includes Whistler/Blackcomb. The biggest news in Flaine is that it is once again in the throes of expansion thanks to the Canadian company Intrawest which, through its partner Compagnie des Alpes, is creating two and a half thousand beds worth of property units. The first to be ready units below the new Scandinavian style complex were on sale in 2006, and the rest will be completed in stages (2008 and 2012). They are probably an excellent investment for any ski worker who can afford to buy one.

THE SKIING

Postcards of Flaine tended not to make it look very attractive (they usually show the concrete buildings in the background, half-hidden behind some obliging trees). However, attempts have been made in recent years to make the facades of older apartment blocks more aesthetically pleasing and newer buildings are constructed to harmonise with the surroundings where possible but despite such cosmetic improvements, Flaine will probably retain its 'ugly but functional' reputation. Flaine is very well-positioned in a bowl at 5,500 feet and has an excellent snow record. Flaine on its own has 150 km of pistes but together with its neighbouring linked resorts of Les Samöens, Morillon, Les Carroz and Sixt it forms part of the Grand Massif circuit of 265 km of pistes serviced by 75 lifts. The resort is excellent for beginners who can learn by the *ski evolutif* method of beginning on short skis and progressing by stages to full length ones, and there are no fewer than seven nursery slopes including a green run from the top of Les Grandes Platières all the way down to the village. Beginners soon tire of the three nursery slopes and are quick to join the intermediates that make up the bulk of Flaine's clientele on the varied blue and red runs. The few black runs are fairly short and this resort is best suited to intermediates, especially those that fancy their hand at snowboarding or surf-skiing.

The basic Flaine ski pass allows access to three main areas – Grandes Platières, Grands Vans and the Aujon area – but for the competent skier it is well worth paying the small premium for the more expensive Grand Massif pass which will allow you to ski back from the four delightful linked villages already mentioned. The pistes down to these old Savoyard villages are narrow, wooded, exciting and surprisingly free from other lunchtime trippers. When you arrive, a pizza, chips, crêpe and beer on a café terrace costs about £8 and makes a delicious reward after your two-hour trek.

Most of the skiers at Flaine are British or French, but you could well find yourself talking to a German or Italian on some of the chairlifts. Indeed, when you see a young guy sporting a fluorescent headband and strapped on to a surfski, it's odds on he's Italian.

Most intermediate skiers opt for two hours ski school in the morning. There are two or three schools to choose from: ESF, The International School (very good) and small Super Ski which specialises in small classes with high quality instruction. Arranging private lessons or even video teaching presents no problems. All the instructors speak English, but also manage to retain a few Clouseau-like phrases for your amusement!

APRÈS SKI

Since Flaine is one of those resorts patronised by the serious intermediate, the nightlife tends to cease around 10.30pm when all serious skiers go to bed. However, from around 7pm to 10pm all the restaurants, bars and cafés are pretty lively. Most Brits head initially for the White Grouse Pub where you can obtain bottles of Newcastle Brown and other UK brews. There is also La Perdrix Noire (Black Partridge) which serves cocktails and has a restaurant. Some of the smaller restaurants are worth seeking out and traditional Savoyard meat and cheese fondues can be enjoyed for about £12-£15.

The main nightclub in Flaine is the sophisticated but expensive Shelby, but this is generally not as well patronised as the much cheaper and less chic discos staged four times a week in one of the hotels. Flaine also boasts an indoor swimming pool, a cinema and a natural ice-rink and there is also the weekly dinner/dance in a mountain-top restaurant, followed by a potentially lethal torchlight descent on skis. For a romantic candlelit dinner, the traditional old Chalet Bissac offers an unforgettable menu and ambiance.

ACCOMMODATION

Most of the accommodation in Flaine comprises purpose-built apartment blocks, hotels and chalets. There is unfortunately a distinct lack of any reasonably-priced accommodation, i.e. youth hostels or bed and breakfast equivalents. However, some of the chalets are locally owned and vacant and it is probable that should you manage to land a job in the resort, you will be given free accommodation. Indeed most of the job-hunters interviewed who had turned up on spec had been given chalet rooms by their employers.

Unfortunately, since Flaine is a modern resort, the vast majority of rooms are let to tour operators, who ensure maximum utilisation of the available spaces. Probably the only way of finding any accommodation is by striking up a firm friendship with one of the locals and then relying on the local grapevine. The outlying villages mentioned earlier may well be a source of accommodation, since they are lived in by local families and are far less commercialised, with few tourists to be seen. You could also try Planet Subzero (www.planetsubzero.com) which specialises in finding affordable long-stay and seasonal accommodation in top ski resorts.

WORK

We had to look hard to find any foreign casual workers in the resort. There are possibilities with the tour companies including: Club Med, Crystal, Erna Low, Action Vacances (UCPA), Inghams, Ski Club of GB, Neilson, Ski Weekend and Thomson, who have a range of staff including ski guides/ reps in Flaine. Carole Iddon from Northampton, worked as a chalet host. She had arranged the job in advance and earned a small wage for approximately a 30-hour week. Although she had free board and lodging and plenty of time to ski, she would have preferred to have had access to a car, since the local bus service was pretty poor, with at best one scheduled stop daily. She planned to work until early May and then to take an Inter-rail holiday around Europe before returning to the UK to arrange a summer job in the Mediterranean. She strenuously denied that her life was just one long holiday!

The dulcet tones of Australian Greg Harris could clearly be heard in Flaine Sport ski shop. Greg arrived in Flaine soon after Christmas, with no job arranged, but was fortunate in that one of the shop's French employees had just broken his leg (not in a skiing accident) and they were temporarily short-staffed. He learned all this talking with the shop's owner in the White Grouse Pub and managed to convince him that he was a good skier (true), spoke reasonable French (exaggeration) and had previously worked in an Australian ski shop (shamelessly untrue). After a few hearty Australian skiing stories and even more beers, he landed the job. Since most of the shop's clientele spoke English, he rarely needed to speak French. He was given free accommodation, skis and boots and a wage of £120 per week for a 36-hour, six-day week. Although he was greatly enjoying the skiing, he planned to leave France around the end of April and spend a month in London before flying back to Australia, to contemplate his next (first?) career move. He said that he overcame his lack of ski retail experience by saying simply 'of course, that's not how we do it down under!'

Peter Hill from Staines worked in Eve's Bar. He came out to Flaine just before Christmas and spent over a week looking for work in the resort and sleeping in a friend's van at night. After much pleading with café owners, he was offered the bar job in Eve's at a wage of £3 per hour. He chose to work about 40 hours a week, spread over five days. His friend also had difficulty finding casual work, but was earning over £4 an hour washing up in a small restaurant. His boss had arranged a small room for him in a friend's house and had also allowed Peter to live there as well. However, after they paid for ski hire, lift passes and beer they were not quite breaking even and both planned to return to the UK within the month.

The only other Brits encountered were two reps, Alison and Sarah, who admitted that they really enjoyed their jobs. Both had graduated some two to three years earlier and now spent half the year in ski resorts and half as reps in Greek resorts. While agreeing that their permanent suntans did nothing for their complexions, they also said that it was nice to go home to the UK occasionally and make their friends jealous.

Overall we estimate that there were fewer than 20 foreign workers employed in Flaine. Clearly, the best policy here is to try to arrange a job through an agency or other contact before leaving the UK, unless you have sufficient funds to buy several café owners vast quantities of ale while you regale them with stories of how you just missed being selected for the British or Australian Ski Team and try to talk them into giving you a job.

L'Alpe d'Huez

L'Alpe d'Huez (www.alpedhuez.com) is located high in the Grandes Rousses mountains in the southern Alps, about one hour from Grenoble by road. The neighbouring resorts are Deux Alpes, La Grave, Serre Chevalier and Montgenèvre. Among the Parisian French, L'Alpe d'Huez is considered one of the more chic resorts and it is increasingly popular with the Brits. The town is fairly modern but the centre is old and traditional. In recent years the Eclose and Bergère areas have been built, both of which are about five minutes walk from the centre of town. There is a superb modern sports centre, an outdoor swimming pool and a skating rink. The town is mostly full of British and French, though Belgian and Danish companies also operate there.

THE SKIING

The skiing has something for all levels (literally since it has plenty of high altitude snowsure skiing and summer glacier skiing). The area above the town is ideal for beginners, and the resort offers terrific scope for progression. Above all though, Alpe d'Huez is known for two of its black runs, The Tunnel and The Sarenne. Both start from the top of the Pic Blanc, where it is worth stopping to take in the view of the Massif des Ecrins and Deux Alps. The Tunnel descends steeply for 300 metres before, as its name would suggest, taking you through a dimly lit tunnel cut through the mountainside. The descent from there is very steep and mogully and there is often a tailback into the tunnel while skiers try to pluck up courage to make the first slide on to the final descent. The Sarenne is reputedly the longest black run in Europe at 16 km and is steep and fairly narrow for the first km of its length. After this difficult start however, it is not a great challenge for the good skier. From the Pic Blanc there are also a number of difficult off piste descents, the most famous being the Pyramid.

L'Alpe d'Huez is now connected to the villages of Vaujany, Oz and Auris and this means that the ski area is quite extensive and varied. In addition a book of tickets is supplied with your season lift pass which allows you to ski for a specified number of days per season in Deux Alps, Serre Chevalier, The Milky Way (Montgenèvre, Sestriere etc.) and a small resort called Puy St. Vincent.

NIGHTLIFE

Many British resort staff have such a good time in their first season in L'Alpe d'Huez that they come back for more. Some reps have been known to stay for four or more seasons. Though the skiing is good, it is for the most part the friendliness of the resort and the raging nightlife that people return for. There are three British-style pubs in town, the Lincoln, The Underground and the Apples and Pears which doubles as a nightclub. Many of the French bars are also frequented by the Brits, in particular the P'tit Bar and the Avalanche, both on the main street. There is a singer/entertainer in the Avalanche called John St. John who is a veteran of many seasons and a well-known local character, as is Olivier, the bartender. The nightlife of the town is addictive and tends to run a fairly set pattern, with a tour of the bars followed by a bop in the Apples and Pears, followed by a final munchies stop in the Crémaillère – a pizza restaurant in the old town which is open until 7am!

ACCOMMODATION

All three British bars supply accommodation with jobs. If you are coming on spec, there is a youth hostel (Auberge de Jeunesse) in the old part of the town. Probably the cheapest apartment-letting agency is the Agence Signal, next to the cinema. The tourist office in Place Paganon (☎4-76 11 44 44; www.alpedhuez.com) may also be able to help as can Planet Subzero (www.planetsubzero.com).

WORK

Tour operators in L'Alpe d'Huez include Airtours, Club Med, Crystal, Equity, First Choice, Inghams, Mark Warner, Neilson, Ski Activity, Skibound, Ski Miquel, Skiworld, Tops and Thomson. All employ reps and some guides, while Neilson and Crystal also employ chalet staff. As already mentioned, many reps return for a second or third season so getting a foot in the door is not easy.

The three British bars (Apples and Pears, Lincoln and Underground) employ exclusively English-speaking staff. All take on bar staff, the Lincoln also takes waiting staff and bouncers and the Apples sometimes disc jockeys and cloakroom attendants.

Some of the French hotels and apartment agencies will also employ British staff. For most of these jobs you will need to be bilingual or have at least a reasonable level of French with the exception of plongeurs (washer-uppers). The Vallée Blanche Hotel, Dumez Agency and Pierre et Vacances Agency have all employed British nationals in the past.

It is possible that the Lincoln or the Apples would employ a live band at certain times during the season. The sports centre and SATA, the lift pass office, have been known to take on bilingual staff as has the Ecole de Ski International.

Owing to the fact that L'Alpe d'Huez does not tend to attract a large number of ski bums, those who do turn up tend to find it relatively easy to find something. Babysitters always do well, particularly if they are known to the reps in town. Transfer reps are also much in demand. Ian, who worked in L'Alpe d'Huez as a rep for Crystal holidays said that most reps would recommend English-speakers before the local crèche service. People have also made good money by offering a video service to clients.

La Plagne

La Plagne is a group of high altitude, purpose built villages: Aime 2000, Plagne 1800, Plagne Villages, Bellecôte, Belle Plagne, Plagne Centre and the newest: Plagne Soleil which is a fifteen minute walk from Plagne Centre. Altogether there are ten ski centres making a big resort capabable of providing accommodation for over 50,000 tourists which makes it the second biggest ski resort (by tourist bed capacity) in the world after Chamonix. The resorts are all self-contained as far as amenities are concerned but by and large the main centres are Plagne Centre and and Plagne Bellcôte. A frequent shuttle bus service links the villages and is free with the lift pass. The resort is about three hours from Geneva airport and close to Val d'Isère, Les Arcs, Tignes and Courchevel. Despite its massive and invariably rather ugly appearance, La Plagne lacks nothing as far as convenience for the skier is concerned. Its apartment blocks provide a wide range of accommodation from 'A' Grade' luxury flats to studios and the ski lifts are literally on the doorstep.

Although La Plagne rates as one of the the top ski resorts worldwide (beating even the resorts of L'Espace Killy and the Trois Vallées areas), La Plagne lacks the individuality which is associated with the older resorts. It has little to distinguish itself from any other purpose-built 'ski-paradise'. It is totally ski-oriented and there is little for the non-skier apart from skating, swimming and squash. Adrenaline junkies can get high on the Olympic Bobsleigh run at La Roche (below Plagne 1800), which is open for tourist rides, at a price. Or you can literally get high at the parascending school if the views from the cable cars are not good enough for you.

THE SKIING

La Plagne is linked with four lower level ski villages: Les Coches, Plagne Montalbert, Montchavin and Champagny. The combined area boasts over 200 km of piste and 119 lifts. The La Plagne system has something for all standards but is particularly good for beginners and intermediates including some extremely attractive runs down through the trees to the villages of Montchavin and Montalbert. Advanced skiers have only six black runs that are not particularly challenging, but there is off-piste skiing including the Friolin from the Dôme de Bellecôte Glacier at 3250 m. There is also summer skiing on the Bellecôte Glacier. The La Plagne system is linked to Les Arcs by cable-car and together they form one of the largest ski areas in the world marketed under the brand name Paradiski.

The La Plagne Lift Pass entitles you to a day's skiing at Tignes/Val d'Isère or Les Arcs. The double-decker cable car, the Vanoise Express, ferries skiers across the gorge that separates La Plagne and Les Arcs. Intermediate and advanced skiers can take advantage of the services of the ski school (one in each resort) to explore the vast areas of off-piste skiing that La Plagne is known for.

APRÈS SKI

La Plagne is less than renowned for its nightlife, which is limited to a few pubs and clubs where a gathering of more than five people can be called a party. King Café is a popular venue attracting custom with a big screen showing satellite sport channels. The spread out nature of the resort means that a lot of partying time can be lost moving between venues. However, it is worth making a trip to Colour Café in Plagne 1800, if only for the draught Guiness. Not surprisingly this is a favourite meeting place for British workers and tourists alike.

Other favourites worth checking out for contacts are Mat's Pub in Belle Plagne, the Lincoln Inn in Plagne Soleil and the bar in the Mark Warner Hotel Christina at Plagne Centre. The Showtime Café, Bellecôte is lively and a good laugh with live music and karaoke. Under the same ownership as the Showtime, the neighbouring Jet 73 is the best nightclub, attracting both French and foreigners alike. Entry and drinks are expensive, but a free bus home is provided after 2am when the shuttle bus has stopped.

The cinema at Bellecôte shows two different films per day, with a selection in English throughout the season and there is a bowling alley (expensive) in the Belle Plagne Sports Centre. There are swimming pools in both Plagne Centre and Bellecôte and there are the usual sauna and massage providers to wind down after a hard day on the piste.

WORK

Almost all British workers in La Plagne are hired in the UK and there is little opportunity for on-site employment unless you are fluent in French. Most Brits work for the tour operators of which there are an inordinate number with big names: First Choice and Crystal run extensive operations. Others include Ski Beat, Airtours, Ski Amis, Club Med, Esprit, Silver Ski, Ski France, Skiworld, Mark Warner, Thomson, Tops, Inghams and Neilson. The tour operators are based mainly in Belle Plagne, Plagne Soleil and Plagne 1800. As reported in previous years, the other workers in La Plagne are almost entirely French except for staff in the bars popular with English-speakers.

Mark Warner run the Hotel Christina, which employs about 40 British staff but these are recruited in the UK and Club Med has a village there.

Philip McMillan who worked for First Choice as a chalet manager estimated that there were as many as 300 people working for British tour operators in La Plagne. His accommodation, which was shared with one other, was arranged by the company. The cost of this and of food, travel to and from the resort and the ski pass was deducted from his wages leaving him around £300 per month. He got one day off a week and has plenty of free time for skiing every day other than the Saturday changeover day when guests leave and arrive.

The only independently-owned establishment which employs any considerable number of British workers is the Lincoln Inn Aparthotel in Plagne Soleil. They recruit 15-20 chamber and waiting staff and chefs per season. Accommodation and food are provided. The posts are advertised in *The Lady* magazine or you can apply direct to BP 64, Plagne Soleil, 73210 La Plagne. When short-staffed they have been known to advertise on the local radio station.

Positions as ski instructors are almost impossible to get with the Ecole du Ski Français, although private ski schools do employ non-French ones. There has been the occasional Brit working for the Ecole de Ski Oxygene (+33 4-79 09 03 99) and you can try Evolution 2 (+33 4-79 07 81 85).

British entrepreneurs might be tempted to sell goods in the outdoor market at Plagne Centre where stalls sell clothes, sunglasses, dried fruits, sweets, cheeses and *sauscissons,* but be warned – stall holders have to apply to the local council offices in Aime for permits and these are limited and so almost impossible for foreigners to obtain.

Ski season jobs are advertised at various local ANPE offices (see list at the beginning of this chapter). Some are open seasonally (as in La Plagne +33 4-79 09 01 14), but fluent French is essential for any of the jobs advertised there. For late arrivals, it is certainly worth doing a tour of the bars and shops as confirmed by people who got jobs locally by this method. There is also a notice board under the stairs to the Grande Rochette cable car in Plagne Centre where you might get a lucky lead.

The tourist office in Aime (04-79 09 79 79; www.la-plagne.com) may be able to give ideas of job vacancies before the season starts. For late arrivals, it is certainly worth doing a tour of the bars and shops to see if extra staff are needed. In addition, the receptions of accommodation agencies such as Pierre et Vacances and the Hotel Eldorador in Belle Plagne and Mark Warner's Hotel Christina should be checked out. Although they have a full personnel quota at the start of the season, a few will inevitably crack under the strain by Christmas.

A big problem for those who have not arranged jobs in advance with tour operators is that there is nowhere cheap to stay while looking for work. Probably the cheapest option is to book a holiday with one of the tour operators and make friends with the locals as quickly as possible. Also contact Planet Subzero (www.planetsubzero.com; info@planetsubzero.com) as they can deal with specific requests for long-term/seasonal accommodation.

Les Arcs

Les Arcs is a group of three self-contained purpose-built villages that make up the Les Arcs skiing area in the Savoie region: Arc 1600 (Arc Pierre Blanche), Arc 1800 (Arc Chantel), and Arc 2000 which is located over the ridge from the other two Arcs and is the quietest of the three. The Canadian company Intrawest is responsible for the new development just below Arc 2000.

Les Arcs can be reached from Lyon or Geneva airports and is 12 km (8 miles) from Bourg-St.-Maurice, which is on the main railway line. From Bourg there is a funicular, which connects with Les Arcs 1600 day and evening; the journey takes 10 minutes. The resorts themselves are traffic-free. Les Arcs is the home of Ski Evolutif where beginners are taught on short skis which are gradually exchanged for ones of increasing length as confidence improves.

Arc 1600.
Arc 1600 is the lowest and smallest of the Les Arcs stations and is popularly considered to be the least trendy. The centre is small, although offering all the main services and amenities and is set around a suntrap where you can sit out on café terraces when the weather is fine. Frequented mostly by the French, most of whom have their own apartments there, and some British families, Arc 1600 is more leisurely than the other two villages with picturesque paths through the woods up to 1800.

Arc 1800.
'The Smart Arc' is how the tourist guide describes Arc 1800. And smart it is too. This is what a purpose-built resort should be. A delightful shopping and restaurant arcade, all decked out in wood, blends into the woods beyond, and the apartments are cleverly built into the hillside so that they are not obtrusive to the eye.

Most of the accommodation is in apartments but there are some hotels including the Latitude and the very plush Hotel du Golf.

Arc 2000.
Although out on a limb from the other Arcs, 2000 has developed as a serious ski resort for those who like to be half way up a mountain (the 3225 metre Aiguille Rouge) near the powder. Consisting of a few hotels including Les Melezes, a Club Med 'village' and blocks of self-catering studios, it is possible to find everything you need in the way of provisions, restaurants and entertainment in 2000 and it has a reputation for being good value.

THE SKIING
Having made its reputation and a place to learn skiing, Les Arcs seems to have branched into every permutation invented and has something for everyone from beginners to advanced. It is also one of the most popular resorts in France for snowboarding. There are also possibilities for variations such as mono-skiing, sail skiing, parapente and speed skiing. This last on the Flying Kilometre speed track open to the public from January. There are over 200 km of piste served by 62 lifts. The nursery slopes, of which there are four in Arc 1800, and the ski school is excellent with about three dozen instructors who

speak English. There are however very few foreign instructors. For intermediate skiers there is a vast choice of red and blue runs starting from Arc 1800 where drag lifts and the Transarc gondola whisk you up into the system from where you can ski back into 1800, 1600 or 2000. For advanced skiers there are some real challenges: There is a black run of almost 11 miles from the top of the Aiguille Rouge (3226 metres) along the ridge of the mountain down to Villaroger (1100 metres). Speed freaks can try the 1km Olympic course (the 'Flying Kilometer') on the Aiguille Rouge. For a fee you get equipment, and a printout of your time. The aim is to get down in eighteen seconds (the current record). Also for the racer are the French national ski tests: Flèche (Grand Slalom), Chamois (Super Slalom) and Fusée (Downhill).

There are also excellent opportunities for off piste skiing and for the expert there are vast areas of 'Ski Total' off piste which you can ski with a guide. In Arc 2000 'Ski New Way' lets you have a go at mono-skiing, Skiing at Val d'Isère, La Plagne and Tignes one day a week is included in the Les Arcs lift pass. Experienced skiers can ski as far as Val or Tignes from Les Arcs though it is essential to take a guide. There is a link between the Les Arcs system and La Plagne with a Savoy lift pass to cover both areas.

APRÈS SKI

It is generally agreed that 1800 provides the best nightlife with its 30 plus odd bars, cafés and restaurants – not to mention the odd nightclub. Popular places with the British include L'Arc-en-Ciel Pub, Pub Russell, Le Salon and Gargantus. The Fairway nightclub under the Golf Hotel, the Carré Blanc and the Rock Hill Club are where the eardrum abusers congregate while foodies can sample the delights of L'Auberge.

ACCOMMODATION

Cheap accommodation is not easy to find. There is a small youth hostel in Séez (seez-les-arcs@fuaj.org; 04 79 41 01 93), just outside Bourg-St.-Maurice which is empty out of season, but often full of holiday makers during the season. Matthew Binns recommends trying the Red Cross hostel in Bourg-St.-Maurice, which he says is free for a few days to those looking for work. There is also a winter campsite in Bourg-St.-Maurice itself. One group of New Zealanders lived in a camper van parked outside the hotel in which they had all got jobs. It is usually possible for most employees (except lift operators) to get board and lodging with the job, so if possible try to do this. Planet Subzero (www.planetsubzero) can arrange seasonal/long-term accommodation in Les Arcs.

WORK

Most of the shops and restaurants employ only French nationals, but some of the bars including L'Arc-en-Ciel employ English-speakers. There is a good children's centre and if you are qualified in child welfare and speak French it is worth trying to get work there.

As elsewhere, the best time to look for jobs in bars, hotels and restaurants etc. is at the beginning of the season or earlier if you can manage it, but another good time is just after the New Year when French students have to go back to college which can often leave seasonal vacancies for others. There are reports that a number of hotels (including the Hotel du Golf) are prepared to take on English-speakers for about four hours a day in exchange for board and lodging only. This can be an excellent arrangement for the worker whose main concern is to get maximum skiing time.

Matthew Binns got a job in a hotel in Arc 1600 on a job hunt, which took him by car through the Haute-Savoie in mid-November. He was amazed to get offered a job on his first afternoon of trying. The next day he went to Val d'Isère, just to see what was going there and found 'everything there was either closed or full'. Back in Arc 1600 he found his hotel job very varied:

Matthew Binns gives details of the variety of jobs the hotel in Arc 1600 gave him and his views on the resort

I started painting rooms in early December, then went on to be at various times: a storeman working in l'economat (stores) of the hotel, a receptionist, a night-porter, a bartender, a cook, a waiter, a snow-shoveller, an errand-boy and a chamberman all of which were pretty enjoyable, apart from the last which was mind-numbing. I generally worked about 35 hours a week in exchange for board, lodging and French national wage per month and a season's ski pass and Carte Neige (insurance). I had every afternoon free for skiing. Most French nationals were working full-time for the SMIC (minimum wage)with board and lodging provided.

There were a few other English, Australian and New Zealand workers in the resort, especially at the main bar L'Abreuvoir. Everywhere at 1600 seemed to be willing to take on foreigners ready to work on the black market. The work inspectors came round twice in the season, during which time anyone working illegally was given the morning off. The second time their visit was prompted by a deranged communist working at our hotel, incensed by the fact that foreigners working illegally were betraying the French working class.

1600 is fine if you're not bothered about nightclubs (although there is one) and are happy with skiing and drinking. But in the evenings, without a car you are restricted to your own resort. Drinks are however served to resort workers at reduced prices.

The main hotels in Arc 1600 are Les Trois Arcs and Hôtel de la Cachette, which are worth trying for jobs. Apparently however, waiting tables at La Rive restaurant (part of Hôtel de la Cachette) is particularly gruelling. According to Matthew Binns 1600 is small enough for all the workers to know each other and the management are very pleasant. Most people tend to congregate in L'Abreuvoir bar in the evenings and the landlord gives a warm welcome to any bands willing to play there in return for board, lodging and ski pass and probably a small wage. Matthew also recommends hitching through the Haute Savoie, if you don't have your own wheels as this is a good way of picking up useful information about possible jobs. Of course, it helps if your French is reasonable.

British workers also in evidence are tour company reps and ski guides. Crystal, Ski Club of GB, Inghams, Skiworld and Thomson are some of the main companies spread throughout the three Arcs. So if your powers of persuasion are exceptionally good your main chance lies in getting a job with a tour company.

Caroline Cowper, a graduate in social sciences from Edinburgh, wanted to go abroad to get some experience and went to Les Arcs where she had a friend working. After two weeks of looking, she managed to find a job serving behind the bar of a restaurant in Arc 1800. She was given accommodation and board and about £55 a week for working from 6pm to 10.30pm daily. She subsequently found another job in addition to the first: washing up in a restaurant in the ski area. For two and a half hours each lunch-time she was paid about £30 a week. She still had time to ski in the mornings and made a lot of friends among her French colleagues. At the end of the season, as Les Arcs closed around April 15th, Caroline managed to get in two extra weeks' work at Les Menuires with a ski company.

Perhaps because the resort has developed so rapidly, there was quite a lot of dissatisfaction among UK tour companies' staff and a disproportionate number seemed to have left mid-season and taken other jobs. Alison Martin had switched to the French company Touralp soon after Christmas and was much happier with the job she had with them as an information clerk, while Joanne Wilkinson, who had enjoyed working with her tour company previously in France and Kranjska Gora (Slovenia), did not like it in Les Arcs and in December landed an alternative job with the Société de la Montagne de l'Arc (SMA) the adminstrating body of the resort. Her job was in the tourist office as a *hôtesse d'accueil* (welcome hostess) and she worked 35 hours a week for £150 per month plus free accommodation and meals. The job was seven days a week but as she could choose whether she worked mornings or afternoons it was ideal for skiing and nightlife.

Joanne was asked to come back the following year when she would have been paid double. Besides Joanne, a Dutch girl, Paula, a student from Amsterdam also managed to get a job in the tourist office. She wrote a speculative letter, was called to an interview in Paris and finished up with a job in Radio Les Arcs making announcements about forthcoming activities in the resort and reading the weather forecasts.

Les Carroz

Although Flaine is the highest and best-known of the Grand Massif resorts, Les Carroz (www.lescarroz.com), a few kilometres less far up the winding road from Cluses, is in many respects a much better bet for the visitor. Les Carroz stands at the head of the Partiel Massif, a southern part of the Grand Massif that also includes the resorts of Morillon, Samoëns and Sixt. Where Flaine is purpose-built and essentially ugly, Les Carroz is Alpine architecture at its most traditional and picturesque; indeed, the locals have enjoyed skiing there since 1936. It is larger than Flaine, and offers a greater variety of après ski activity, and most importantly it has more jobs available for English-speaking ski bums. It is accessible from Geneva airport 50km/31miles distant, and Cluses rail station (13km/8miles).

THE SKIING

'Probably the most underrated skiing in the Alps,' was how one Briton described this area. A single pass gives the skier access to any of the numerous lifts which link the above-mentioned resorts together, while a relatively small extra premium grants access to the Flaine slopes. There are some excellent long and varied runs through the wooded slopes, notably at Carroz and Morillon, and a total of some 267 kms of piste in all.

NIGHTLIFE

There is a plentiful choice of eating and drinking places in the town, many of them round the central square, but none is cheap. Undoubtedly the most unusual is Gron's Pub – a red double-decker London bus; try a hamburger and chips on the top deck for your memoirs. Gron's Club (no connection; the Gron is a river) is one of three discos in town. It is rated cheaper and more atmospheric than Club 74, which is crowded with teenyboppers and the Loup Blanc (a cavern rather than a nightclub) but each to his own. There is also a two-screen cinema, Le Choucas.

ACCOMMODATION

It is usually possible to find a season's accommodation if you come early enough. Try to come in September and pick up a functional apartment flat, which will take up to four people for about £100 a week. By the time December arrives the prices will double for the same amount of space, if you can find it. If you do choose to turn up on spec for a job, you will probably find a room, but it will not be cheap.

WORK

Les Carroz is a bustling resort with several hotels, numerous apartments and chalets and a host of pubs and restaurants and there are plenty of jobs. There are usually assorted English-speaking winter workers in the resort, including Brits, Aussies and Americans. The Front de Neige hotel, which used to be leased by Skibound is now run by a French tour operator, but might still be worth trying if you speak French. The hotel is convenient for the telecabins up at the top of the town. Accommodation and food are provided for all staff.

A smaller hotel, Les Belles Pistes (see entry in *Working Through Other Organisations*, is also well situated at the higher end of town and which advertises once a year in *The Lady* magazine, and receives 150+ responses. They only hire staff after taking up references and they said they would never hire anyone who turned up on the doorstep, though many hopefuls do. They provide food, accommodation and ski passes for all their staff, who are free to ski in the afternoons.

There are two ski schools in Les Carroz. There are usually a couple of English-speakers working for the Ecole de Ski Français (+33 4-50 90 02 38) but regulations are very tight. You need the right ski instructor's accreditation: French, Swiss, German and Austrian are acceptable, but US and British are not, unless you have the Equivalence or the newer European Speed Test qualification. All instructors in France are self-employed and pay tax from their earnings as opposed to being taxed at source.

Further information on the resorts can be obtained from the tourist office (4-50 90 80 01; www.carroz.com).

Les Deux Alpes

Les Deux Alpes (www.les2alpes.com; 04 76 79 22 00) is located in the southern Alps, about one hour's drive from Grenoble via the RN91 in the direction of Briançon (63 km) and is 77 km from the Italian border. Nearby resorts include L'Alpe d'Huez, one hour's drive away and La Grave. Probably no one would describe Les Deux Alpes as a pretty resort consisting as it does of an old mountain village (Venosc), and modern hotels and apartment blocks only some of which are built in traditional style. However for a purpose-built resort there is a conspicuous absence of multi-storied monstrosities. Plans for extending the resort arc likely to place emphasis on traditional style buildings. Les Deux Alpes is a resort that caters for both skiers and non-skiers and offers a wide and varied choice of après-ski activities.

THE SKIING

Les Deux Alpes has 200 km of pistes served by 63 lifts. An express gondola (the Jandri Express) whisks skiers up to the eastern side of the resort which is the main skiing area including the Glacier du Mont de Lans and an underground funicular transports skiers even higher up to the top of the Glacier de la Girose, a vast skiing area with mostly easy runs where it is possible to ski all year round above 2,800 metres. This ski area is also linked to the resort of La Grave. On the western side of the valley the Pied Moutet area has mostly easy runs but there is a red or black run back into the village. You can also take a gondola ride down to the traditional old village of Venosc. The resort has something for all standards but is most suited to beginners and intermediates. Beginners learn on slopes in the village or on the glacier. Advanced skiers can enjoy Le Diable, a well-known downhill racing slope down into the village or off-piste skiing from the top of the glacier. The Grande Galaxie lift pass also includes one day's skiing in Alpe d'Huez, Serre Chevalier, Puy St. Vincent, and some of the Italian resorts of the 'Milky Way' ski area including Clavières, Cèzanne, Sansicario, Sestrières and Sauze d'Oulx. There is a helicopter service between Les Deux Alpes and Alpe d'Huez.

APRÈS SKI

The evening of the truly dedicated skier ends at around 10.30pm. After that only the more gregarious holidaymakers and the resort workers are to be found out and about. The main nightlife is to be found in the live music bars such as Le Baron. Other popular meeting places are Mike's Bar (= La Belle Epoque) and the discos L'Avalanche and L'Opera. Most of the resort workers tend to congregate at the cheaper bars such as Le Baron and Smokey Joe's. Le Brésilien is good for live music.

The majority of foreign workers try to avoid eating out as it is rather expensive. If they can't arrange a lift, they take the bus down the mountain to shop in Bourg d'Oisans. However, if a meal out is the order of the day, then L'Étable and Smokey Joe's are good value for money.

ACCOMMODATION

Accommodation is expensive; however, the youth hostel Foyer St. Benoit offers accommodation and three meals a day for about £20 a day with the meals being optional. A cheaper option is to stay in Bourg d'Oisans. The bus ride to Les Deux Alpes takes 30 minutes but, when in Bourg d'Oisans you are also well placed for a visit to the resort of Alpe d'Huez. If you are lucky enough to find employment, free accommodation is often provided. Planet Subzero (www.planetsubzero.com) has apartments for the season in Les Deux Alpes.

WORK

Les Deux Alpes has both a winter and a summer season; the winter season starts in early December and ends in late-April, the summer season lasts from June to September. Seasonal workers are more in demand in winter than summer; very few work for any two consecutive seasons.

The first British tour operator arrived in Les Deux Alpes in 1983/84 and since then it has become a regular fixture in mainstream operators' brochures: Inghams, Airtours, Crystal, First Choice, Neilson and Thomson, plus a few smaller companies like Skiworld, now operate here. The presence of large numbers of British skiers has brought with it a demand for English-speaking workers. This is not confined to the reps and ski guides in the operators' employ; the number of British workers who have arrived on spec or through an agency has increased, as indeed has the capacity of the resort.

As in many resorts, live music is very much the thing. Kevin O'Donnell played the guitar and sang in the Baron. He started an hour's aperitif spot at 6pm and then worked from 10pm to 1.30am. The pay was excellent: £50 a night plus accommodation. During the day he was at liberty to ski to his heart's content. For a job like this one needs to be quite an accomplished performer.

Sven Gay, a graduate in economics and music, most certainly fell on his feet when he went into a photographic shop clutching his camera. With some well-chosen words he secured a job as a ski photographer. In high season he earned about £200 per week and an apartment was provided by his employers, Photo Neige.

About half a dozen workers in Les Deux Alpes found their positions mainly as chamber staff or washing dishes, through Jobs in the Alps. Typically these people ski for up to three hours a day, work six days a week and earn £100 per week. The majority of them were taking a year off between school and university.

The most intrepid British worker to be found in Les Deux Alpes must have been Michael Jenkins. He gave up his job as a bricklayer when he was 17 and, for the next four years travelled around Europe taking work as he found it. Having completed his second season as a ski lift mechanic he strongly advocates applying for seasonal work in early September.

Michael skied for at least an hour every working day. He needed no qualifications for the job, not even basic French. He received about £150 a week, free accommodation and lift pass; in every two weeks there are three non-working days.

By all accounts casual work is quite easy to come by but, often, it is very temporary. Au pair jobs seem to be a bit haphazard with wages and hours varying greatly between households. In preference to turning up on spec try to arrange a job beforehand. There are 40 plus hotels, 20 plus ski shops, 40 plus restaurants and 120 plus clothes, gifts and food shops in Les Deux Alpes. Most useful information can be gleaned from the tourist office website www.les2alpes.com or phone +33 4 76 79 22 00. At the beginning of the summer and winter season, the ANPE (job centre) has an office in Les Deux Alpes, situated at the town hall (Mairie Annexe de Mont de Lans, Antenne ANPE, Les Deux Alpes 38860; ☎04 76 79 50 94). This will give you the names and addresses of all potential employers. Better still, go out there in late summer and try to fix up a job in advance by applying in person.

Méribel

Méribel is situated at the heart of the Trois Vallées area, with Les Menuires and Val Thorens on one side and the newer La Tania on the other. One of the first things the newcomer to Méribel notices is the abundance of cars with British registration plates. Occasionally French-registered cars are spotted, slotted into the tank formations of 4x4's from the shires and sporty-looking GTIs from metropolitan London. Méribel is very much a 'British' resort and has been so ever since it was conceived: in the nineteen thirties, military Scotsman, Peter Lindsay recreated a typical Tyrolean village in France after Hitler's annexation of Austria forced him to ski elsewhere. In fact Méribel is two villages. The orginal one, sometimes called Méribel-les-Allues at 1450/1600 metres, and the newer and higher satellite of Méribel-Mottaret at 1700 metres.

Despite its attractive appearance and appeal to the British visitor, there are nonetheless, certain disadvantages for those who spend more than a few weeks in Méribel. It is spread on a steep mountainside so that if anyone is living or working at level 1600, it is half an hour's walk (via about 12 bends in the road) down to the centre. Some chalets are a long way from the slopes and many people are employed just to drive mini-buses to and from the centre. If at all possible, own transport or use of an employer's car is recommended. There is a bus service but it stops mid-evening which is a blow to anyone keen on nightlife. In the popular bars (see below) one can find bevies of chalet girls, ski guides and plongeurs discussing their day's work and the skiing they have cunningly fitted into their busy schedule of cooking dinners or washing-up. In addition you can skate, swim, have a sauna and see films. However, as Méribel principally consists of chalets and apartment blocks, the nightlife of the tourists tends to revolve around the individual chalets and flats.

THE SKIING

As the skiing literature hyperbole never fails to remind you, the skiing area of Les Trois Vallées of which Méribel is a part, is the largest in Europe. The ski area in Méribel itself covers 100 kms and together with its neighbouring resorts (see above) the ski area covers an impressive 600 kms (linked by 200 lifts), which even for dedicated speed maniacs is hard to cover in much under a fortnight.

As you might expect from the main clientele, there is skiing for all grades and the resort is awash with British-run ski schools including Ski Principles, New Generation, Magic in Motion, Parallel Lines and Snow Systems (www.snow-systems.com); and even the ESF school has British instructors. Beginners use the nursery slopes beside the resort or above 1600 at the Altiport. For intermediates the choice is seemingly endless: the gondola lift up Mont Vallon provides two challenging and long red runs: the Campagnol and the Combe de Vallon and for the advanced skier there is every permutation: on the east (Tougnete) side of the resort there is La Face – a black run used for the Women's Olympic downhill, also a glacier to conquer at Val Thorens and plenty of off-piste including the treacherous, steep, narrow couloirs down from La Saulire into either Méribel or Courchevel, and exhilerating schusses through the trees. Furthermore, Méribel is in a sunny bowl, and has many good vantage points on the mountainside doubling as restaurants. There is also the Trois Vallées Rally – a tour of all three valleys in a day.

There are of course one or two drawbacks. The sun does not just melt away the pallid complexion inherited from a British winter, but quite a lot of the snow as well. Earlier in the season the pistes can be icy, and later the lower slopes can bloom into spring flowers rather prematurely. Storms and avalanche danger can often cause the Val Thorens section of the area to shut down. And of course, you must be sure you end up in the right valley when the lifts close; taxis are prone to unbridled extortion when confronted with stranded skiers so you must be organised, or else camp on a friend's floor.

APRÈS SKI

Méribel is known for its rampant nightlife. Evenings usually begin in the Rond Point where there is often a live band. Jack's bar near the lift stations is also very popular. Things are fairly quiet around suppertime because of the large proportion of chalets in the resort. The centre livens up again from about 10.30 p.m. when The Pub is the place to see and be seen in. This is probably the most famous British-style pub in the Alps and is certainly obligatory for the homesick.

Up the hill in Mottaret, the nightlife is slightly different with many punters eating out and staying out to make their own entertainment. Le Rastro is probably the most celebrated bar. It is situated at the far end of the pistes, next to the Mont Vallon Hotel and has a rustic atmosphere. Guests and staff are often to be seen stomping on the tables. Le Plein Soleil is another retreat from the calm. Great food is served nightly and top live bands perform every evening from about 10 p.m. There are over 100 whiskies to be sampled. If however, you prefer the typical French atmosphere then the Downtown Cellar bar in the centre of Mottaret is the place. It has a giant video screen, pool tables and many *flipper* (pinball) machines.

ACCOMMODATION

Cheap accommodation is not readily available in Méribel and if you do find something expect it to be cramped. For information on what accommodation is going you can try the *hebergement* (lodging) department of the tourist office (Office du Tourisme, 73551 Méribel; ☎4-79 08 60 01; info@meribel.net). There is a notice board outside the office and another one in Le Pub that sometimes carry offers of places to stay. You can also ask around – tour company reps and ski guides usually know what's going. The best time to meet them is in their informal office hour between 5.15 pm and 6.15 pm in the bars where they make themselves available to their clients. Spotting the rep is made easy by the various company logos emblazoned on their jackets: those you are likely to see include: Airtours, Club Med, Crystal, Inghams, Scott Dunn, First Choice, Ski Club of GB, Mark Warner, Meriski, Neilson, Ski Activity, Crystal Finest, Skiworld and Thomson. Probably only Val d'Isère can boast a greater tour company presence than Méribel. Reps are the best source of information for accommodation, work and cheap flights home. There is no Youth Hostel in Méribel.

While you may be told there are a couple of cheap hotels in Méribel it is worth noting that one of them: Jeunesse/Famille is strictly for families only.

The solution many people come up with is to rent a studio or apartment and then fit as many people in as will bring the rent down to an affordable level. The prices start at about £15 per night for a one-person studio into which, at a pinch, you could get three people. It is easier to secure this sort of accommodation at the start of the season, though apartments do become vacant during the season. Once again reps and guides will know the up-to-the-minute situation or you can try Planet Subzero (www.planetsubzero.com) as they handle seasonal lettings in Meribel/Mottaret and enable you to secure your accommodation in advance if you wish. The tourist office may be able to supply you with particulars of other agents but these are likely to be much more expensive than Planet Subzero.

The standard price for a room or bed in a chalet is not cheap at about £25+ per person. However, due to cancellations or slack periods some will have beds or rooms they want filled and it is worth trying to negotiate a lower price, and perhaps doing without the meals. Again, you will have to ask around to see what's going.

Moûtiers is the nearest town to Méribel (8 km) and as well as being the railhead is the connecting point by road to the other three resorts in the area. You can get a reasonably cheap room in a hotel there. A coach service runs to Méribel but is expensive (about £6 return). There is also a campsite in Moûtiers.

WORK

Many workers return to Méribel for a number of years. Add to this the familiarity of most British skiers with Méribel and you begin to see why the resort is awash with people looking for jobs at the beginning of the season. About 200-300 English-speaking people find jobs in Méribel during the skiing season, which makes it one of the most concentrated spots for work in the Alps. The majority are from Britain with most of the rest coming from Australia and New Zealand. The jobs available here are mostly with the 25+ British tour companies that operate in Méribel. The alternatives are working in a privately-owned chalet or finding casual work in bars and restaurants. No-one seems to bother about work permits for the non-EU nationals but those from outside the EU may find it pays to discreet about the fact that they are working.

Most of the tour companies run chalets and apartments in Méribel which are filled up each Saturday with a new set of paying guests. Staff are employed to see to the guests' every need and the range of jobs is quite wide, including: chefs, managers, skiing hosts, chalet cook/hosts, bar and laundry staff, washer-uppers, local reps, maintenance persons etc.

Operators, Meriski and Purple Ski operate exclusively in Méribel and there are numerous other small businesses running just one or two chalets there including Alpine Action (01273-597940), Bonne Neige (01270-256966), Cooltip Mountain Holidays (01964-563563), Ski Blanc (based in Les Allues 020-8520 9082) and Ski Cuisine (01702-589543). Méribel is one of the few areas where good spoken French will not necessarily be a requirement, but often guides will be expected to have at least a holiday knowledge of the Trois Vallées ski area.

As in any resort if you wish to start your own enterprise you are advised to get yourself known by as many people as possible (with the exception of *gendarmes*) The Ski Rock café is used by many reps for their office hours and many ski bums trying to build up an illegal guiding or teaching clientele. Reps are often looking for gofers (dogsbodies) to work for them on Saturdays and Sundays. This can be a job for the whole season and if you are lucky you may be employed on other days of the week to guide or do other jobs. Will came to the resort at the beginning of the season and rented a house in a hamlet called Le Raffort, between Méribel and Les Allues. He rented out rooms to ski bums, and found a job snow clearing and cleaning for a small ski company. He also did a weekly transfer for Inghams and worked in the bar underneath Mont Vallon Hotel collecting glasses in the evenings. Despite this apparent heavy workload, he also had time to ski!

Most people who go out to Méribel to find work turn up just before the start of the season, around mid-November, when jobs and accommodation are in greater supply. The best places to start are the British-style bars. In Les Allues, the Sept Tor has been known to employ Brits *en masse*. Mike and Tony came over from Australia especially to spend the season skiing in Méribel. They wanted to find some part-time work so as not to dig any further into their savings. They both found washing-up jobs in different restaurants. 'You just have to go around asking at every single place', they say. They say French is not needed for this work but probably would be for waiting or bar work where there is contact with customers. They worked just two hours daily, leaving plenty of time for skiing. They did not have work permits and kept quiet about their jobs. They planned to return to Australia in time to catch the start of the skiing season over there.

Helen Mackay and Alison Bates, who worked as chalet hosts, were able to ski from 11am to 4pm every day except Saturday when they often had to wait for new guests to arrive at the chalets. They also said, that whereas it was impossible (or at least unlikely) for a girl to go out and find a job as a chalet girl as all the vacancies were arranged from the UK, on the other hand, it was particularly advisable for those wishing to work in bars, restaurants or hotels to go out and search for jobs on the spot, as many of the hotel and restaurant owners simply expect British people to turn up and claim jobs for the season. There are over 65 restaurants and bars in Méribel and more than 20 hotels in the whole of the Méribel Valley which includes Méribel-Mottaret the large, purpose-built complex 4 km up the valley from Méribel itself). Many of these will take on staff but good places to start as they have been known to employ English-speakers include the restaurants Cro Magnon, Santa Marina and of course Le Pub which one year had four English-speakers. There are some smart new hotels at the Rond-Point area (1600) including Le Chalet, Antares and Aspen Park, which might be worth trying. The best time to go out would be before the season starts in November, just after Christmas or high season in February and March when the weather gets better and Easter approaches. Mike Scott-Watson and Charles Swabey turned up in late December and, with little difficulty, had secured jobs as a porter and a bartender in one of Méribel's leading hotels. They did say, however, that it was wise to go with a friend in order to share a flat, or to know someone who has already rented a flat or owns one, since it can be very expensive staying in a hotel while you look for a job.

Maureen turned up in Méribel from Grenoble, after failing to find work there (before that she was a secretary in Birmingham). The Tourist Office put her on to a French family who had a vacancy for a chalet girl. She got a comparatively high wage (£100) per week as well as skis and a lift pass. During spells when her family was away she spent her time skiing and improving her cooking.

There may be some scope for ski instructors at one of the ski schools which are firmly established here. Despite the threat of mafia-like repercussions, private teaching does go on and if you limit yourself to one or two clients and are discreet, (i.e. don't exchange money on the slopes) you will probably be all right. Chalet staff can be a good source of clients.

Geoff Banks from Surrey got a job as a skiing host with a UK tour company. He found his job through someone he worked with in a summer resort where he had a job as a cocktail barman. He says:

> To be a ski host you have to be able to ski well, French is helpful and common sense essential. The job isn't well paid but I got discounts to restaurants and ski shops, free skis and pass and accommodation. Becoming a skiing host is difficult, it's a bit of a closed shop. People tend to do the job year after year so openings are few and lots of people apply for them.

Annabel Hawkins ran a luxurious chalet in le Villard, a village just outside Méribel. Her employers were an English couple and she had the job of running the chalet and cooking for them, their children and guests. Annabel is a trained nurse from Australia and was travelling and working in Europe. She was offered the job while working in a shooting lodge in Scotland! But such jobs are also advertised in *The Times* and *The Lady*. Free skis, lift pass and use of a car compensated for a rather small wage. She got time to ski every afternoon and had one full day off per week. She started the job after Christmas and it lasted the season.

Annette d'Arc is also Australian and she managed to obtain a job as a cleaner for the resort Agence (in charge of the apartments of the various residences). She was employed on a part-time basis, working mornings for about three hours a day and was paid about £4 an hour. She was quite happy with her situation because working for the agency offered better conditions and the guarantee of employment; she also got a cheap ski pass.

Méribel is something of an oddity in the Alps – a large resort with a huge colony of

British companies and skiers, but strangely unpretentious and homely. Everyone agrees it is one of the best places to work, ski and enjoy yourself in the evenings, and despite a large number of interested people, and with a little luck and forward planning you should be able to find a job quickly if you are not fussed what you do.

Potentially useful telephone numbers: Méribel Tourist Office (4-79 08 60 01); Mottaret Tourist Office (4-79 00 42 34) and Radio Méribel(4-79 08 59 07).

Montgenèvre

6,000 feet up on the French/Italian border, Montgenèvre can be reached from the French side via Briançon, or the Frejus Tunnel via Oulx. Situated at one end of the Milky Way area which runs down to Sauze d'Oulx in Italy, Montgenèvre therefore shares a ski area with a number of Italian resorts the nearest being Clavière and Cesana Torinese. The village of Montgenèvre is a delightful combination of rustic village and purpose-built resort and is quite elongated. You can actually walk across the border into Clavière. The historic small town and nearest rail station are at Briançon 10km/6 miles away from where you can get a bus to Montgenèvre. The airport access is from Turin 98km/61miles distant.

THE SKIING

Montgenèvre has 100 kms of skiing and 39 lifts. There are two main skiing areas either side of the village. On the eastern side there is La Bergerie and the area below the summit of La Chalvet, while on the other side a more extensive area includes the Col du Soleil (les Anges) and the Rocher d'Aigle (Eagle's Rock). From Colletto Verde there is a fairly easy run down into Clavière. You can buy daily lift pass extensions for La Voie Lactée (The Milky Way) area which will enable you to ski the areas around Sansicario, Sestrières towards Sauze d'Oulx in Italy which are linked to Montgenèvre, making an impressive total of 400 kms of piste served by over 100 lifts.

For beginners and ambitious intermediates there is a large ski school, catering for five proficiency levels, and a third of the native instructors speak good English. The nursery slopes are right in the village centre. There is a long and flattering green run right from the top of Les Anges down into the village. Intermediates have a huge choice of runs while advanced skiers can test their mettle on off-piste and powder at Eagle's Rock and Col de L'Alpet on the other side of the valley. Snowboarding is also well catered for with a fenced off snowpark above the town and the open bowls of the Milky Way.

Despite its impressive snow record and a variety of skiing to suit all standards, Montgenèvre is relatively little known to British skiers. It is a very convenient resort linked into a vast ski area and it seldom has long lift queues.

WORK

With such obvious advantages and opportunities, Montgenèvre is becoming increasingly popular with skiers and and therefore the possibilities for employment are also growing.

Elaine Whitehead and Andy Richie arrived in Montgenèvre at the beginning of December from Gibraltar where the former had been waitressing and the latter had been finding ample work and earning good money as a builder. Elaine had already arranged a waitressing job at Montgenèvre's only mountain restaurant, through a family with whom she had worked in Cap d'Agde the previous summer. Working from 9am to 4.30pm with one day off a week she could only ski on her day off, but was earning £125 weekly plus tips and given free lodgings. Having no pre-arranged job, Andy began a regular daily round of visiting the local bars, restaurants and hotels and asking the tour company reps for work. He found the Town Hall (*Mairie*), rather than the tourist office, a very useful place to make enquiries as they often knew of employers needing staff. He eventually found a job as a barman at Stevie Nicks, one of the resort's two nightclubs, which enabled him to go skiing every day. In searching for a job Andy stressed the importance of not only getting your face known locally but also being friendly and approachable and demonstrating knowledge of the French language. He received offers of help and advice from the employers he approached and indeed the consensus of opinion amongst all those who worked in Montgenèvre was that it was a very friendly and amicable resort in which to live and work.

Debbie Moss had arranged a waitressing job at Le Chalet café during the previous summer whilst visiting some friends in Montgenèvre whose parents owned the café. She was especially busy, as indeed were all the establishments, over the peak holiday periods of Christmas, New Year, February and Easter and it is just before those times that anyone seeking work should arrive as it is then that employers are most likely to need extra staff. In February, for instance the Hotel Le Chalvet took on extra chamber staff. Unfortunately there is no youth hostel in Montgenèvre or nearby, where you can stay cheaply while you look for work but the Chalet des Sports (4-92 21 90 17) and Hotel Le Boom (4-92 21 92 59) are both cheap places to stay but Boom is especially cramped.

On arriving in the resort, one will find most of the resident British workers in the popular bars like Le Graal, Le Refuge and Ca de Sol (the last two also serve excellent food) or Stevie Nicks and the Playboy nightclubs in the evenings. The nightclubs often employ British DJs. and the bars are good places to pick up information about possible jobs. Another opportunity to meet company reps is at the weekly slalom race for British tour clients held every Wednesday at 6pm. Companies represented include Airtours, Crystal, Equity, First Choice and Thomson. While staying in Montgenèvre you can also make excursions to the neighbouring resort of Clavière where smaller companies like Equity operate along with Crystal, First Choice and Ncilson. The resort of Serre Chevalier where many British companies operate is only 20 minutes away by road and most importantly it has a youth hostel (serre-chevalier@fuaj.org) where you can stay, although it is likely to be full at peak times.

In Montgenèvre the ESF ski school and the ski lift operators' jobs are so firmly established as the locals' prerogative that there have been no instances of illicit guiding or instructing, both of which carry a heavy fine. One enterprising woman had set up her own video-on-the-piste business for skiers who wanted a souvenir capturing the action of their holiday.

Morzine

Morzine (www.morzine-avoriaz.com; e-mail touristoffice@morzine-avoriaz.com) is one of the twelve resorts that make up the huge Portes du Soleil circuit – reputedly the largest international skiable domain in Europe. It has long been established as a ski resort and has an authentic feel in the village centre, which despite the largeness of the resort, manages to retain a friendly atmosphere. Morzine lies in proximity to the Swiss border and the architecture looks appropriately Alpine in the traditional way.

There are two main parts to the village – the shops, bars and hotels around the Pléney télécabine and the lower part of the town, which contains the hallmarks of traditional French provincial life – the pavement cafés frequented by the locals, the *mairie* (town hall), post office etc. Also in the lower part of the town is the Palais des Sports which houses an olympic-sized skating rink and hosts international competitions. The resort is 80km/50 miles from Geneva airport and the nearest rail station is Cluses/Thonon 39km/24 miles.

THE SKIING

Morzine is a regular host of World Cup events, which in particular utilise the black slalom run which runs parallel to the Pléney télécabine. At the top of the Pléney is the meeting point for all ski school lessons. Ski schools include the ESF, The British Alpine Ski and Snowboard School (04 50 74 78 59). There is a useful plateau for beginners and a hotel and panorama restaurant with marvellous views over to the next resort of Avoriaz. This is also a good place to get to know the hordes of French instructors who hang out there in between classes. For the relaxed skier there is a pleasing rustic chalet-cum-bar with a terrace which looks down the other side of the plateau to Les Gets. From the top of the Pléney, it is possible for the intermediate skier to cross over either to Les Gets, or on the other side of Nyon via red runs, or to take the chairlift and gaze undistracted at the stunning scenery.

An alternative to the chairlifts or skiing the area around Morzine, is to jump aboard one of the regular free bus services which run from just outside the Maison de Tourisme in the centre of town. There are three main destinations: Avoriaz, Les Gets and Nyon/La Chamossiere. The buses run until 6 pm. According to Skibound rep, Heather Parry, skiers can be caught out like some of her clients who made a frantic telephone call because they had missed the last bus and were stranded at Ardent.

Avoiding the queues can become rather an obsession although there have been some large improvements including a six-seater chairlift at Les Lindarets. There are several other ways you can spare yourself if you are so minded. In order to get from Morzine to Avoriaz, instead of taking the bus you can use the Super Morzine gondola and then take connecting chairlifts. At the height of the season you take the Prodains télécabine at your peril as this is where the French flock especially after a fresh snowfall. The chairlift that runs from the bottom of Les Prodains is another good alternative to the télécabine, but beware the tricky red run directly at the top which can give some people a nasty surprise. If your plan is to escape the madding crowd then consider the free shuttle buses to Chatel or Ardent which are normally a good bet.

Skiing the Portes du Soleil is exhilerating. For the advanced skier there is the challenge of the Swiss Wall (which is hair-whitening stuff) and then there is the thrill of being able to ski down into Switzerland (but remember to take your passport).

Morzine's only discernible drawback is its low altitude – the lift range is 975-2460 m which means the quality of the snow on the Pléney slopes suffers relatively quickly if there is no replacement snow for a few weeks. However, when there has been a dire lack of snow the Pléney remained open with the help of snow cannons and the artificial snow, which had been laid down earlier.

NIGHTLIFE

If you are one of the many hopefuls who turn up in Morzine looking for a job, you will soon find out the best places to go in the evening where the action is. A typical evening will begin with a few drinks in Dixie's, Le Crépuscule or the Bowling Bar. From there, if you can take the pace, on to Opera Rock which, unusually for a French nightclub, has no door charge.

The number and diversity of those who frequent Dixie's and the other bars means that you should make for them straight away after your arrival as they will be useful places to make contacts and find out about likely jobs up for grabs in the resort. The large number of bars in Morzine is also a likely source of jobs. If you speak French, head for the Irish Coffee bar where the young bloods of the ski school hang out.

WORK

A number of tour operators are present in Morzine and they include: First Choice, Crystal and Thomson as well as the medium-sized and small companies such as Ski Chamois, Chalet Snowboard, Esprit, Mountain Highs, Ski Purple Goat, Snowline, Trail Alpine and

Ski Weekend. The jobs they offer, as always, are best applied for in the usual way, back in the UK. However opportunities will also arise to work for them during the season as Will Downing found out when he arrived on spec in Morzine. He got a job as a *girlie* (Skibound speak for a waiter/bed-maker). He got the job when he heard by chance that someone was leaving. Even if you have been rejected by the company after applying too late in the UK, there may be hope if you keep your name on a waiting list albeit at the expense of some highly unfortunate individual who has been put out of commission by an accident: In such an instance, Laura Bolton who was having a gap year between school and university got called out to work in France in the New Year as a sous-chef.

Morzine is a fairly child friendly resort, partly due to the Cheeky Monkeys Childcare (Chalet le Roncherai; +33(0)4 50 75 05 48; www.cheekymonkeysmorzine.com) service that hires qualified nannies to take care of skiers' children in their own chalets.

Heather Perry took a year out between finishing her degree in French and starting teacher training, to work as a Skibound representative in Morzine. She describes how she got the job and what it entailed:

Heather Perry worked as a Skibound representative

Barely had I finished finals than I saw a Skibound staff advert in The Guardian and I sent a CV and covering letter as requested. I had previously worked two summers for Canvas Holidays and this was helpful in getting me as far as the interview, which took all day and was held in Brighton. I also had to chat with a French-speaker to prove my competence. After the interview I was offered a job on the spot and the formal written offer arrived a few days later. I was surprised that the company required a £100 'bond' to cover the Company's expenditure to date on seasonal insurance, travel and accommodation deposit. It was returnable at the end of the season minus any deductions for damage to company property and financial loss to the company caused by the employee. In addition I was asked for a non-refundable £50 toward the cost of the uniform. There was a week's training course, which struck me as an amateurish affair. We travelled for 24 hours by coach to the French office unaccompanied by any company staff. I found out later, that to their credit, two stowaways had managed to get a free trip out to France! The training course gave a very scanty idea of what the work really involved, especially in the matter of smoothing relations with the other company staff working in the resort hotel. Reps, as you know, earn commission, which they split with the company. The hotel workers, on the other hand, are paid small wages and have no access to commission and this inevitably causes a barrier however carefully you try to disguise the fact. The training seemed to focus on daily aerobics at 7.30 am followed by two sessions in the morning and the afternoon, and towards the end of the week, in the evening as well. The aim was to prepare us physically for the long hours and endless socialising.

Two things that are not made clear from the outset are firstly, the amount of time and energy that school parties (a speciality of Skibound) take up. If you are not used to children and the energy required to control their exuberance, you will find it a shock to the system. Secondly, the extent to which you have to nursemaid some adult clients, even to the extent of waking them up in the morning so they get to ski school on time. Ideally a rep has to combine work and socialising – after all most clients are hell bent on enjoying themselves and will expect you to get swept along by their enthusiasm or vice versa. But you never get a whole day off and you have to be cheerful at all times of the day or night. It can be a serious case of no sleep until April. However, if you are a budding Miss World and love working with children, travelling and meeting the public, this is definitely your vocation.

Risoul

Located in the southern French Alps, Risoul 1850 is a small, purpose-built but attractive resort set on a high, south-facing plateau above the village of that name. Risoul itself may be small, but it is part of an extensive ski area, La Fôret Blanche. Together with the neighbouring and interlinked resort of Vars it has 57 lifts and offers 180 kms of piste and extensive off piste skiing. Montgenèvre is 45 minutes away by road. The Fôret Blanche lift pass covers both the Risoul and the Vars regions. With a wide range of runs for all abilities Risoul is suitable for mixed ability groups and families. It also has the Surfland Park for snow boarders which hosts a high jump contest every Thursday. Risoul is a long way from any major airport: you can take your choice from Turin three and a half hours away or Marseille, 250km/155 miles. The nearest rail station is Montdauphin-Guillestre 15km/9 miles.

APRÈS SKI

There are no great extremes of prices in Risoul and the nightlife tends to be typically French, even the pizzerias are French-run. Popular bars include La Licorne, Bar Rock (disco/nightclub) and le Morgan. Hungry skiers can get a main course pasta dish for about £7 and a three-course meal from £12 and the Assiette Gourmande and La Cherine restaurants are very popular.

WORK

There are fewer possibilities for casual work in Risoul, which does not have the massive English-speaking clientele of some of the big-name resorts. However, although there are few jobs there is also not much competition for them. Those who speak French reasonably well stand the best chance. Risoul is patronised above all by the French but also Italians, Belgians, Dutch and British skiers. There are a number of jobs with tour companies: Airtours, Crystal, First Choice, Neilson and Thomson are all represented and a Dutch company Sportura go there and have reps and/or ski guides in the resort.Louise Bentley, taking a year out before studying modern languages at Oxford, was enjoying a summer holiday in Risoul with her parents. She was dining in le Cherine restaurant when she noticed the proprietor having communication difficulties with some Spanish guests and she offered to interpret. Louise takes up the story:

Louise Bentley on how she got her job opportunistically
Just before we finished our holiday I asked the proprietor of le Cherine, Alain Fournier, if I could work for him next season and he agreed. I wrote to him when I got back to England to confirm our agreement and he replied that the job would begin on December 15th. He also asked me to reconfirm in October, which I duly did and to make doubly sure I also phoned him. In the end I left for France on December 10th as he wanted me a bit earlier. The journey was a nightmare. I went by National Express coach to Lyon; that bit was all right. I then took a train from Lyon to Valence, changed trains and got another from Valence to Gap. From Gap I took a bus to La Gare de Montdauphin where I telephoned the Fourniers and thankfully Mrs. Fournier came to collect me.

I was employed as a waitress. There were 'slack periods' when we worked normal hours i.e. 9am to 3pm and 6pm to midnight. The period over Christmas involved longer hours and at New Year we didn't finish until 5.30 am on New Year's Day. I only got two days off in five weeks and on those days I skied. There were three British boys also working at le Cherine. Waiting staff were paid about £100 net per week and we got a Christmas bonus of about £80. In addition I got free

> accommodation in a rather dilapidated apartment in Risoul village above the Bar
> Rock which I shared with two French female employees. I also got all my meals
> provided at le Cherine. I also got a subsidised lift pass for the season and ski and
> boot hire for a nominal sum for the same period.

Unfortunately Louise broke her wrist, not on the ski slopes, but by falling over near the restaurant in early January. This meant a visit to the hospital in Gap and a few weeks of convalescence back in the UK before resuming her job at le Cherine on February 19th. Her injury was classified (with a little licence) as an 'accident at work' which was therefore covered by her employer's insurance. This was a kind gesture on the part of the employer as normally Louise would have had to have rely on her EHIC (European Heatlth Insurance Card), backed up by private medical insurance cover – both of which she had arranged before leaving the UK. For her return to the UK after the accident, she got a free coach transfer from the resort to Lyon airport courtesy of the Skibound rep. Once at the airport the Skibound area manager sold her a one-way flight to Gatwick for £80 cash. By contacting the Skibound head office in Brighton she hoped to get a cheap fare in the other direction (Gatwick to Lyon) when she returned to Risoul. She was lucky to get to know the Skibound reps so well as they used le Cherine restaurant for their clients.

I must say I was exceptionally lucky to find such a nice bunch of reps in Risoul. I would always recommend making friends with the British reps in any resort as they can help out a lot with travel arrangements.

After finishing in Risoul, Louise had plans to work in an orphanage in Santiago, Chile (arranged informally through the Anglo-Chilean Society – based at the Chilean Embassy in London). She says that she got an introduction to the Embassy through her father's contacts. The secretary at the embassy has contacts with the orphanage. She thinks other potential volunteers might be able to do the same. The work will be unpaid and she will also have to pay for her own board and lodging with a family. She hopes her earnings from the ski resort will cover all her expenses for the Chilean trip.

St Martin de Belleville

Situated at 1400m in the Vallée de Belleville, St Martin is a traditional, picturesque resort that forms part of the immense Trois Vallées ski area. The village is compact, with everything you need within five minutes' walking distance. Although the original village has been expanded and developed the traditional style of building has been maintained in sharp contrast to the neighbouring tower-block resort of Les Menuires. St Martin is half an hour from Moûtiers, where you can pick up the Eurostar, and two and a half hours from Lyon and Geneva airports.

The Skiing
St Martin is lift-linked to the slopes of Méribel and Les Menuires and is firmly on the Trois Vallées map. In less than 20 minutes (via two lifts) you reach Tougnette at 2434m. From there you can ski directly to Méribel, Les Menuires, La Masse or Mont Vallon. If you want to stay local, the two reds off the top, Pramint and Jerusalem are excellent, and tend to be firm favourites amongst *saisonniers*. There is also plenty of off piste back way down to the resort. On sunny afternoons, the snow in St Martin tends to stay in better condition than that of Méribel. Another bonus of local skiing is that the queues are few and far between, which is more than can be said for the battlefield up the road at Val

Thorens.

If the unthinkable occurs – a season with no snow, there is guaranteed glacier skiing at Val Thorens.

In summary, St Martin is a brilliant gateway to the Three Valleys, and has plenty of entertainment for a great season.

Après Ski

Francis Booth, who worked as a rep in St. Martin describes the social life there.
St Martin is small, close-knit and a lot of fun to work in. The saisonnier scene has an international feel to it. Seasonal workers come from New Zealand, Australia, Holland, Denmark, Sweden, Canada, Germany, France and the UK. Everyone tends to know everyone, and hang out in either the Piano Bar or Brewskis (www.brewskis.fr).

The Piano Bar is the more civilised option, with sofas, dimmed lighting and candles. After the tourists have gone to bed, it can be quickly transformed into a mini nightclub. Karaoke nights there are usually packed. Brewskis, notorious across the Three Valleys, is ideal to ski into for an après ski drink. A live band plays there twice weekly, there is a pool table for quiet nights and you'll find a party going on whenever you least expect it.

Fondue nights followed by a drunken ski home take place in La Loi, a mountain restaurant on the last run back to the resort. One other bar that deserves a mention is the Joker. This is probably the smallest bar in the whole Three Valleys. It's very French and perfect for a glass of red wine, some homemade paté and a chat, with Eric the owner.

The bars go quiet for a few hours while guests go back to their chalets for dinner, and the saisonniers go back to work. Things get going again about 10pm. There is no nightclub so after 2am the options are limited to house parties or a trip to Val Thorens.

There are lots of fancy restaurants in St Martin, and neighbouring St Marcel. However, most seasonal workers don't experience much more than La Voute, an essential haunt for those on a staple diet of takeaway pizza.

Accommodation

If you are working for a tour operator your accommodation is provided. Other seasonal workers rent rooms or apartments in St Martin or nearby Villarabout or St Marcel. Get there before the start of the season to find a room. Alternatively, check out the resort website. St Martin is supposed to be one of the cheapest villages in the Three Valleys in terms of cost of living. If you are cooking for yourself, or frantically buying ingredients for your chalet guests' dinner, 'Huit a huit' supermarket is the best place in town to shop.

Work

Seasonal jobs in St Martin are centred on chalet, hotel and bar work. Thomson, Equity and Total are a few of the UK tour companies that operate here, employing people as chalet hosts, reps and serving staff. Small company Les Chalets de St Martin (Chalet Alice Velut 04-79 08 97 80; UK: 01202-473255) employs about six staff in the resort. See the Tour Operator Section for details of all these companies. Both the Piano bar (ask for Simon) and Brewskis (ask for Steve), employ bar staff. Brewskis offer some of the best paid bar jobs in the Alps. In St Martin, chalet staff and reps are the next best paid, at about £300-£400 a month basic salary. Skilled jobs such as ski technician can sometimes be found with local French businesses, such as Twinner Ski Shop. There are also a number of privately-run chalets. This makes baby-sitting an easy way to earn money (about 10 euros an hour).

Most seasonal workers arrange their jobs in advance, either by applying directly to tour operators, or by finding jobs on the websites such as Natives and Voovs. Vacancies occasionally arise on the spot due to broken bones, etc. or people who can't take the pace. You'll quickly hear about any work going from saisonniers in Brewskis or the Piano. You can also ask the reps, who tend to know if any jobs are going in the resort. Equity reps duty 'hour' is 5.30-7pm Hotel Altitude bar. You can find out about jobs in Méribel or Val Thorens from tour operators who also have staff there. If your French is up to it, another source of job information is the local taxi drivers.

Beware though, many St Martin saisonniers have no intention whatsoever of working. There is a hardcore of ski bums there, whose working day consists of having a lie-in, skiing/boarding and then drinking to excess. Most of them end up doing some form of work for occasional cash. This contributes to a laid-back atmosphere, lots of social skiing and drinking, and everyone who actually does have a job trying to do as little as possible!

Tignes

Tignes has an international reputation as a serious skiers' and boarders' paradise. The main resort is dominated by the Grande Motte glacier and surrounded by majestic jagged peaks. Although a modern, purpose-built resort, the magnificent setting makes up for the unappealing (though improving) architecture; while the skiing more than makes up for it. Tignes is comprised, like many serious French resorts, of a clutch of villages; in this case five. The main resort, consisting of Lavachet, Lac and Val Claret is found in a high valley at 2100m. A free shuttle bus connects these three areas of very different character. Val Claret is busy, touristy but impersonal, whilst Lavachet has a quieter feel but a strong community spirit, especially among the seasonal staff. Below, are the other villages: Tignes-les-Boisses (1850m) and the old village of Tignes-les-Brevières (1550m). Tignes is also one of the major European summer skiing resorts. If you are lucky you may be able to find a job that will allow you to spend the summer in the mountains too.

THE SKIING

Together with Val d'Isère, with which it shares a lift system, Tignes forms part of the vast ski area known as L'Espace Killy named after local-boy-made-good Jean-Claude Killy. The whole area is made up of 300 kms of piste and over a 100 lifts and extends from Les Brevières up to La Grande Motte (3656 metres) which offers year round glacier skiing. Not really a beginner's resort, Tignes provides best scope for intermediates and advanced skiers. There are three main skiing areas: Tovière (which connects with Val d'Isère, La Grande Motte (from Val Claret up to the glacier) and Col du Palet/Aiguille Percé on the other side of lake. One of the most enjoyable runs for intermediates is from Aiguille Percé down to Tignes Les Brevières while the off piste possibilities are just endless. There are mogul slopes and a wide variety of red and blue pistes as well as one of the longest blacks in the Alps, the Sache. Snowboarders are well catered for in Tignes, whether shredding the piste, or playing in one of the famous board parks, there is something for everyone. The full area lift pass includes a day in Les Arcs, La Plagnes and Les Trois Vallées. If you are in Tignes for any length of time, make sure that you get a pass for the whole of the Espace Killy so that you really make the most of the whole area.

Tignes is popular with English-speakers as well as the French. At weekends it is invaded by the Jean-Pierre Loony brigade who ski the way they drive, without consideration, but even so the lift queues are remarkably short. The only bottlenecks tend to be the *télécabine* from Le Lac to Tovière, especially when the instructors are taking large groups up (groups have priority on the lifts); and on good days, the cable-car to the top of La Grande Motte. However to be on top of La Grande Motte on a nice day is well worth waiting for.

The season is exceptionally long – from the beginning of October to mid-May. National teams, ski clubs and trainee instructors fill the glacier all autumn as the resort gets going early for the winter. The summer season runs from mid-June to the end of August with skiing on the glacier alongside a host of other activities such as mountain biking, climbing, white water rafting and paragliding, to name but a few.

ACCOMMODATION

As with most resorts, finding accommodation can be more of a problem than finding a job as Camilla Lambert found when she looked for work in Tignes while on holiday there 'if it's not a live-in arrangement, you pay nearly holiday prices. However, even during peak season there will be unoccupied rooms due to dropouts and injuries, so before paying the full price for somewhere, ask the reps if they have any space to fill. Most reps hold their office hours in the early evening, between 5.30 and 8 pm, to answer the frequently inane questions of their flock. They are the people to speak to and know; if you know the resort well, ask for guiding work and you may well get accommodation thrown in. As in any resort, the more you put yourself around and ask, the more chance you have of getting work quickly and solving the accommodation problem. As one bartender in Tignes put it 'Always keep trying. One company may flatly refuse you, and the next may fit you up for the rest of the season.'

APRÈS SKI

Although Val d'Isère might not like to admit it, Tignes does have après ski to be proud of. Harri's Bar (www.skibarjobs.com) in Lavachet remains the busiest and longest etablished of the 'British' bars with regular theme parties and live music and its outdoor pool that opens each March. Others in an ever-increasing list include TC's in Lavachet, the Loop, the Red Lion and the Café de la Poste in Lac and the Fish Tank and the Crowded House in Val Claret, plus plenty of Dutch, Danish and French establishments. Tignes is very much based around the bar scene with the thought of fresh powder the nest morning. If you fancy partying that bit later, head for one of the late night spots, Les Caves in Lac or Sub-Zero or the Blue Girl in Val Claret.

WORK

There has been a big increase in recent years of the number of British tour operators running hotels and chalets in Tignes as the companies focus more and more on the snow-sure altitude of the resort. This has resulted in a bigger workers' community and increased odds that there will be mid-season vacancies due to injury and homesickness.

Camilla Lambert who was on a skiing holiday in Tignes managed to make a deal with a chalet girl – if Camilla wanted to she could return at Easter and look after the chalet for a week while the chalet girl went home for a break, in return for her lift-pass, and £55 wages. Unfortunately Camilla couldn't take up the offer as she had other plans for Easter. Camilla also managed to find vacancies for cleaning and being a supermarket cashier.

Companies which have operations in Tignes include: Inghams, Crystal, Mark Warner, Ski Olympic, Neilson, Ski World, Ski Val and Thomson. Club Med are based Val Claret where they have two hotels: the Val Claret and Les Montilles. If you contact their local manager you might just be lucky, though all their recruitment is officially done centrally (see Club Med entry in the *Ski Tour Operators* section).

This extra activity has led to a corresponding increase in the number of British bars and restaurants which in turn has increased the demand for bar and waiting staff and especially chefs. Reasonable French for the locally run establishments is needed, but you will also find your English a real bonus as there are so many English-speaking holidaymakers.

Work on the lifts is largely the preserve of the locals so not much chance there. However, if you already have accommodation, there is a steady demand for Saturday transfer reps and cleaners. Wages are good, and a day's hard work can keep you in food and drink for a week. Radio Tignes takes on an English-speaking news-reader each season for morning and evening broadcasts, for which they donate a ski pass. If you have equine experience and don't mind the smells, the stables employ people to muck out. There are always a couple of jobs shelf-stacking in the supermarkets too. The local launderettes also take on people to provide their full wash and iron service. With the rise in British client numbers it is no longer unheard of to get jobs in shops, but you still need some French. Try the kindergartens, which care for under-tens during the skiing day: Les Marmottes in Le Lac and Val Claret, takes two to eight-year-olds and Les Petits Lutins, which takes children from three months to three years.

There are many ski and board shops throughout Tignes offering seasonal work as a ski tech or sales assistant; in some cases with accommodation. Snowfun and Favre Sports are one of the biggest employing over 50 people in ten shops. Good English is essential, good French and previous retail expeience are major advantages. The season normally starts at the beginning of December, e-mail your CV to tignes@snowfunsport.com in October or visit www.snowfunsport.com for more details.

Many people prepared to flirt with tax evasion have also tried home-hairdressing, airport car-runs, or taking and selling photos or videos of punters falling off kickers. Bear in mind, though that there are bona-fide locals who make their livings with such activities and have to pay their taxes. They will have no scruples about pressing charges if you undercut them or take their business. The same applies to ski-instructing on the quiet; it is bad for your health when the official instructors find out, as they inevitably will. If you have the French *equivalence*/European Speed Test, and go through the proper channels there are opportunities for employment with the ski schools. Evolution 2 (www.evolutions.com) employ hundreds of instructors, and the ESF (Ecole du Ski Français) also has the odd foreign instructor.

Val d'Isère

Val d'Isère lies at the head of the Isère Valley, about 40 minutes of hairpin driving from Bourg-St.-Maurice. Surrounded by the spectacular Savoie Alps, it is probably the most famous of all French ski resorts. Originally the hunting village of the Dukes of Savoie, but now swamped by modern apartments, hotels and tourist complexes. 'Val Village' legacy of the 1992 Winter Olympics, and just behind it is the historic heart of Val d'Isère, which still manages to retain its Alpine charm due to the strict building regulations requiring all new buildings to be built in traditional style. Buses run throughout the winter from Bourg up to Val d'Isère and its neighbour Tignes (www.autocars-martin.com).

Val d'Isère stretches from La Daille (a satellite of the main village) at one end, to le Fornet at the other end, some three miles away. Connecting all areas is a regular and free bus service 'Le train rouge' which in peak season runs through to the early hours. 'Val Proper' is an intense and frenetic place, crammed with people who like to ski hard and drink hard. The resort continues to be a firm favourite with Brits and Scandies.

THE SKIING

Val d'Isère is linked by an extensive lift system to its neighbouring resort of Tignes. With 320 km of pistes and 100 lifts, it forms one of the largest skiing areas in the world. Val d'Isère's three main areas, Le Fornet, Solaise and Bellevarde join up with Tignes to make the Espace Killy (named after the local, former Olympic champion).

Le Fornet, situated at one of the area's extremities, stays relatively quiet all season. Its pistes are for the most part sprawling and unchallenging. On the plus side however, it generally proves snow sure, especially on the glacier 'Les Pissailles'. Treat yourself to lunch at Le Signal; definitely one of the best mountain restaurants in the area.

By contrast, the Solaise is an immensely popular area ideal for beginners and intermediates. The various routes 'home' offer some challenging skiing and riding as with all home runs, it can get crowded at lunch time and the day's end.

The centrally located area of the Bellevarde offers a full range of pistes from gentle and meandering to steep and bumpy. The Olympic black run, the 'Face' (pronounced fass) is for many intermediates, the ultimate goal at the end of a hard week's skiing and many a Friday is filled with stories to that effect.

A season's lift pass for Espace Killy costs about 850 euros. Resort workers are able to benefit from a scheme where you buy a monthly pass for about £150, buy four of these and your fifth month is free. Bear in mind that you need to be organised and take your contract, pay slips and passes from the previous months to benefit from this scheme.

APRÈS SKI

Val d'Isère has some of the most amazing nightlife in the Alps. There are numerous bars in Val, the Pacific (www.pacificbar.co.uk), Moris pub, the Lounge Bar and Bananas are popular season worker haunts and for a more Scandinavian feel check out the Saloon Bar (www.saloonbar.com), Le Petit Danois (www.letpetitdanois.com) and Victor's – and a season in Val would not be up to much without a visit to the legendary Dick's Tea Bar (www.dicksteabar.com). Most of the popular staff bars do seasonnaire drinks prices – make sure you get your face known at the start of the season.

ACCOMMODATION

Accommodation is expensive in Val. If you are planning to stay for the whole season and have not made prior arrangements then it is worth organising some temporary accommodation until you find out where the good deals are.

For temporary or ad hoc accommodation, it is worth asking the tour operators' staff as they may have vacant beds for as little as £10 per night. Contact the reps in their office hour, or go direct to the accommodation. A little old-fashioned bargaining will not go amiss.

For the mid- and long-term, apartments are available through commercial agencies such as Val Agence (www.valdisere-agence.com) and Savoie Immobilier (www.savoieimmobilier. fr) both located on the main street. Their prices do however include a sizeable commission. Apartments may be available through www.planetsubzero.com which offers affordable accommodation in many resorts for the season.

For other accommodation possibilities check out the notice boards around town (in the supermarkets, internet cafés, bars etc) and keep asking – someone always needs a new flatmate. Another option is to go through 'agents' who organise staff digs. This can be a good option if you are going to Val by yourself and don't mind sharing with a couple of strangers, although sometimes the prices can be rather high. For more information call Pierdor (+33 (0)6 80 47 11 70 in France or 01264-861251 in the UK). If you are desperate, there is a youth hostel in Bourg.

WORK

The season runs from the last week of November to the first week in May, but if you are looking for work in Val then it is advisable to be there as early as the end of October. Not much will be up-and-running, but you will get a chance to meet people and get your face known. The Pacific bar will be open and is probably the best place to make contacts with resort staff and possible employers. It is also the time when major refurbishments will be going on in readiness for the winter, so 'chippies' (carpenters) and 'sparkies' (electricians), may well be able to establish themselves a base for an entire winter's work.

If you can't make it out there that early, and decide to go out with the hordes of hopefuls, you need to possess qualities of persistence and a sense of humour. As the manager of the infamous Dick's Tea Bar (☎04-79 06 14 87; fax 04-79 41 92 46) put it, 'just keep trying, ask everywhere, discover the meaning of *une cherche* and don't take no for an answer except from me'. The best way to stand out from the crowd of job seekers is to treat each prospective job as a professional undertaking. A well-presented candidate with a CV at hand, who has made an appointment to see the employer, will make more of an impression than one who has not made an effort. Contrary to popular belief, being able to speak French, even in Val d'Isère, is a great advantage. It is also vital to have a number you can be contacted on immediately. If a bartender or a chalet cook breaks a leg, their employers will want you to start the same day.

By far the largest number of British workers have gone through the conventional channels arranging their work prior to leaving the UK, with one of the many ski companies. The obvious benefits are job security, free travel to and from the resort, accommodation, food, free loan of ski equipment and a season's lift pass, not to mention loads of time off to be on the slopes. Some of three dozen or so tour companies with a presence in Val are First Choice, Crystal, Crystal Finest, Finlays, Inghams, Le Ski, Supertravel, Mark Warner, Silver Ski, Ski Beat, Ski Scott Dunn, Ski Total, Ski Val, Ski World, Snowline, Thomson, VIP and YSE.

The average working day at the chalet starts at about 7am with preparing and serving breakfast followed by lots of cleaning including the loos and maintenance and some advance food preparation for the evening. Most chalet staff are on the slopes (or back in bed) by 11am. Work resumes at about 6pm (sometimes 4pm) depending on your job.

Owing to the high turnover of staff in these jobs, with the right timing you can get employed on the spot. Their head reps or resort managers will always be on the look out for potential replacement staff. They hold 'office hours', generally around 6pm, in bars such as Dick's, Pacific and Le Petit Danois, or in the bar of one of their clients' hotels; for Mark Warner it is the Moris Pub.

Qualified chefs and chalet staff with proven cooking skills are usually in the greatest demand. Other jobs include weekend transfer repping, ski guiding, chamber person, waiting staff, maintenance staff and washer-uppers. Zak Emerson from Norwich arrived in Val in December to visit his rep friend Chris. Chris found him accommodation and food and work in a British-run chalet hotel and then Zak did some transfer repping for extra cash. For more senior positions however, employment is only possible through the UK head offices.

Trying for employment with French companies has the obvious advantage that you will be paid the French minimum wage. You should have a French version of your CV. Apart from the bars, shops, hotels and restaurants too numerous to list here which all need staff – a good place to begin is the tourist office resort guide which has most of the resort restaurants and bars listed in it. English is normally essential and good French will be a big advantage although inability to speak fluent French is not such a stumbling block in Val as it would be in Tignes or St. Foy where immersion into French life is more likely.

As you would expect there is a plethora of ski and board equipment shops in Val. Precision Ski (www.precision-ski.com) and Snow Fun (www.snowfunsport.com), attract much of the British and Scandinavian clientele so the majority of their staff is English-speaking. Previous retail experience is advantageous although full training is normally given. Jobs range from sales people to rental technicians and cashiers to workshop technicians, the recruitment process for these positions usually starts in August; visit their websites for more details.

If you are not qualified to teach skiing or boarding in France then don't do it. Teaching without the relevant qualifications is illegal and has led to people being arrested on the mountain. If, however, you are one of the chosen few and hold the French equivalence/European Speed Test, instructor qualification, then contact Evolution 2 (www.evolutions.com; ☎04 79 21 16 72) for employment opportunities. A BASI (British Association of Snowsport Instructors) training centre has been set up in Val d'Isère and is called The International Centre of Excellence for Snowsport Instructors. ICE (www.icesi.org) is one of the first franchised centres in the Alps licensed to train and grade BASI instructors to the same high standards as are expected on BASI run courses. From now on, courses will be available to BASI students in Val. Students can form their own courses, take part in modular based courses over a period of time if they are based in the area for the season or join one of the packaged courses which includes the BASI course and training towards that end.

A season behind a bar is one of the obvious choices for the would-be Val *saisonnier* (seasonal worker). Everybody wants to know you; you are in the middle of the action and there are no early mornings. There are far too many pubs and bars to list but good starting places include, the Pacific bar, The Moris Pub, Bananas, Café Fats, and of course Dicks Tea Bar (www.dicksteabar.com). There are also vacancies for door security, cloakroom and floor boys in most of these and other establishments. The Internet is fast becoming the essential way of accessing useful information about Val d'Isère, potential employers and their contact details.

For those who want a less structured working life in Val, there are plenty of entrepreneurial possibilities. If you are musically talented, you can pay your way through the season playing music in bars or DJ-ing in clubs like Dick's Café Face and new club The Graal (NB you have to be pretty good to do this). Other past success stories include designing and selling T-shirts and hoodies to resort staff, baby-sitting, child-minding, ski servicing, photography and filming for large ski groups and tour operator clients and once upon a time Val d'Isère even had its own magician!

Whatever your choice for employment for the forthcoming season, remember that each employer is inundated every year with applications at a very busy time of year. If you are not immediately successful, then keep your ear to ground and be patient for an opening.

Val Thorens

Val Thorens, the highest resort in Europe at 2300m, is part of the Trois Vallées ski area. Though not renowned for its beauty (some call it bleak), it is an excellent base from which to ski the area often having the best snow in France. The link to Méribel and Les Menuires is made via one chair lift and Courchevel is just two lifts away. The resort has a cosmopolitan feel to it having as many resident Scandinavian, German and Dutch companies as British ones. This is also reflected in the nightlife with bars such as the Viking and the Frog and Roastbeef.

THE SKIING

Many *saisonniers* are more than happy to buy or be bought the Val Thorens ski pass. It gives access to 32 lifts and over 1400 kms of piste, not to mention the fantastic off piste in the immediate area. There are many off piste routes (*itinéraires*) from the Cîme de Caron and the Péclet glacier. The great advantage of Val Thorens is its height, which means that most runs do not descend below 1800 m. Access to the glacier guarantees the snow year round.

For those intent on doing a high ski mileage, a Three Valleys pass is a must for access to 600km of piste and 200 lifts. Access to the superb Mont Vallon area of the Méribel Valley and La Masse remains relatively queue-free, even during the February French school holidays.

NIGHTLIFE

Val Thorens is, for the most part, a hotel and self-catering resort. There are relatively few chalets and thus the majority of the nightlife revolves around the bars and clubs in town.

The bars are many and varied in both clientele and atmosphere: Scandinavian (the Viking Pub), English (Sherlock) and French (The Monde). If you like to bop, you will always find a rocking pub and a live band somewhere. English-speaking staff tend to congregate in the Lincoln and the Frog and Roast Beef at the top of the town. The resort reps are often to be found doing office hours in the Ski Rock Café at the entrance to the resort or the Choucas, opposite the Centre de Caron.

ACCOMMODATION

Many job seekers stay in Moûtiers, which is one hour away while looking for work. It also has a free Catholic doss house should you be able to convince the monks that you are sufficiently destitute. Lights are out by 10pm and you are back on the street by 6am. Great value for no money provided that it is not -30C and blowing a blizzard.

While Moûtiers is obviously cheaper, you stand a much better chance of hearing of work if you are in the resort and known as a serious job hunter. Accommodation is not cheap in VT because agencies can guarantee occupancy through the season. Many ski bums kipped down in their VW vans for a few weeks at the beginning of the season but as Christmas approached this became a problem as VT is officially a car free resort and anything parked in town runs the risk of being towed away with the levy of a hefty cash fine to boot.

Anyone with reasonable funds, can live virtually rent-free by renting a good-sized apartment for the season and sub-letting to workers, or even better, holidaymakers. If you do not have the wherewithal for this then the cheapest hotel accommodation in VT is the UCPA at the entrance to town.

Tips on accommodation can be sought pre-season at the tourist office but also check out the job/accommodation noticeboards in the English pubs including the Frog and Roastbeef.

Jobs with accommodation are much sought after. Both the Lincoln and the Chantaco have staff accommodation as do most of the hotels, though it is invariably of the fairly squalid, dormitory type.

WORK

The Tourist Office in Val Thorens (www.valthorens.com; 4-79 00 08 08) publishes a comprehensive guide to the resort or look on the web as it contains the telephone numbers of more or less every business in the town. It is always worth examining the job possibilities for the next winter from April onwards by phoning round the hotels, bars and shops and then following up by sending a CV and letter, preferably in French. For menial hotel and bar work, little or no French is required.

Some British tour operators in Val Thorens are Airtours, Action Vacances (UCPA), Crystal, Equity, Erna Low, First Choice, Inghams, Neilson, Panorama, Ski Activity, Ski Club of Great Britain, Ski France, Skiworld and Thomson. All employ reps and some rep/ guides and Crystal also has chalet staff in the resort. Guides and reps will nearly always be given a Three Valleys lift pass, but some of the reps have such heavy workloads they rarely get the chance to ski.

As far as the bars go, apart from those already mentioned under *Nightlife*, El Gringos and Champagne Charlie's are your best bets if you speak little or no French. Other larger bars and nightclubs include the Agora, the Mirage and the Malaysia. Some of the hotels take on British staff but these are best contacted in the summer (July and August). Some of the sports shops will also employ qualified English-speaking ski tecs. The apartment agencies such as Domaines du Soleil which owns the Altineige, Valset and Silvalp residences in Val Thorens will consider bilingual English/French applicants but jobs should be applied for through the head offices of these agencies (see *Types of Job Available*).

Over the Christmas and New Year peak times, the British tour operators are often looking for gofers to be transfer reps. The going rate is about £30 per day. Well-organised gofers use the opportunity to sell their other services (see *Free Enterprise*). One enterprising group of lads managed to sell beer to clients on the coach. They undercut the resort price and made a profit of around £100 per week by buying up beer in Moûtiers. It is always advisable to agree with the rep, before promoting your own enterprise.

Karine arrived in VT at the beginning of December. At first she and two friends stayed in a four-person studio. Her first job as a chambermaid did not allow her enough time off for skiing so she changed to nannying for one of the bar owners and doing a regular transfer for Crystal on Sundays. Her nanny job was live-in, although she had to share with two others. She was paid £250 monthly plus food but had to pay £100 towards accommodation. She worked about five hours a day, but had plenty of time to ski and one whole day off a week.

Mairi was employed as a rep/ski guide with Crystal. She applied to the company in July and started a week's training course at the end of November. She boosted her earnings with commission on any services sold such as lift passes, ski school and fondue evenings. She guided 3/4 days a week and was on duty for much of the rest of the time, with no day off. In order to get the job she had to demonstrate her skiing skills on the training course.

George worked for Altiself, one of the mountain restaurants. He arrived on spec in the resort in early December and was told by one of the reps that some people wanted a flatmate. He paid £50 per week for accommodation which lasted the season, but on some peak season weeks they all had to move out on to other people's floors. He was given a lift pass and earned the SMIC rate per hour. The job depended on demand, so some days he worked from dawn to dusk and sometimes only for two hours a day. He learned to speak French and supplemented his income doing a Crystal transfer on Saturdays. He also worked voluntarily in a ski shop in his spare time, learning how to be a ski tech, which will stand him in good stead when he applies for ski jobs next season.

Germany

Germany has very high unemployment, which is currently over 10% and is the result of a combination of factors. Liberal asylum laws have allowed thousands of east Europeans and war refugees from former Yugoslavia to flood into the reunited Germany. Accession to the EU by some of Germany's impoverished East European neighbours in 2004 caused another influx of impoverished, job hungry migrants who are now filling most of the menial and seasonal vacancies in Germany. It would seem, that German ski resorts, and in particular Garmisch-Partenkirchen are not still good places to pick up jobs. After the collapse of communism, thousands were left un- or under-employed in the eastern part of the country. It is therefore perhaps not surprising considering the high rate of unemployment in Germany, that there are fewer prospects for seasonal casual work in the mountain resorts.

The withdrawal of a large part of the NATO forces from Germany following the end of the Cold War is all but complete. However, there will still be contingents of various armies on German soil for training and other collaboration exercises. The American army's vast rest and recreation infrastructure at Garmisch (the American Forces Recreation Centre), which includes winter and summer sports will remain and with it, hundreds of casual jobs. It is however very difficult for non-Americans to work at the AFRC. If you are thinking of trying, the season begins around mid-December.

Britons can try the organisation Jobs in the Alps (see *Working Through Other*

Organisations) which helps German resort hotels recruit about 25 British staff for the winter.

Apart from the Harz Mountains south of Braunschweig (Brunswick), and the Black Forest where the skiing is often disparaged as being totally uninspiring, it is generally agreed that German skiing is underrated and that the best skiing areas are all on the Austrian border. To the west of Garmisch is Oberstdorf south of Kempten and about 20 miles north of St. Anton; while to the east of Garmisch and south of Salzburg in a portion of Germany that juts into Austria, is the winter and summer resort of Berchtesgaden.

REGULATIONS

Although EU citizens are free to look for work in Germany, anyone intending to stay longer than three months has to apply for a residence permit (*Aufenthaltserlaubnis*) from the aliens' authority (*Ausländerbehorde*). You normally have to surrender your passport for up to six weeks while this is being processed. Many casual workers try to avoid becoming embroiled in the labyrinthine German bureaucracy if at all possible. There is one document you will not be able to do without if you are planning to work in a bar or restaurant or as an au pair: you must acquire a certificate of health (*Gesundheitzeugnis*) obtained from the local health department (*Gesundheitsamt*). Whilst employers may turn a blind eye to other regulations they are liable for a big fine if their workers do not have a certificate of health.

Garmisch-Partenkirchen

The twin towns of Garmisch and Partenkirchen, divided by the Loisach river actually form one whole sizeable town, spread over a broad, flat valley bottom and surrounded by majestic scenery. Generally Garmisch is the glitzy part with its smart shops while Partenkirchen manages to retain a more traditional alpine atmosphere. Twenty years ago Garmisch-Partenkirchen was the answer to a ski bum's prayer: plenty of jobs, cheap or even free job-related accommodation and no worries about immigration or work visas if you are from the EU. While the job situation may have deteriorated, there are still a dozen or so large hotels in the resort and they may be worth trying to approach directly.

This year-round vacation resort is dominated by Germany's highest mountain, the 3000 metre Zugspitz, just a few miles from the the Austrian border. It is Germany's largest ski area but it boasts a lot more than that; the site of the 1936 Winter Olympics and an annual venue for some of the World Cup Races, it has a reputation as a top ski-jumping, cross-country skiing and ice-hockey centre, and when the snow starts to melt away, the summer tourists arrive in their hordes to sample the mountaineering, trekking and kayaking possibilities of the area.

With such fine skiing and other diverse possibilities it is perhaps surprising that British tour companies virtually ignore Garmisch. Only Moswin Tours (www.moswin.com), the operator for independent skiers, goes there. Garmisch has not remained entirely one of the Alps' hidden secrets: a glance at the ritzy Spielbank (casino) in the centre of town will tell you what kind of tourist the town attracts. You are more than likely to see a group of conspicuously well-heeled and fur-wrapped Berliners strolling down the streets.

There is another side of the town as well, and one that isn't universally popular with either locals or travelling workers. The strategically important area of southern Bavaria has been host to the military since Hitler chose to build his mountain hideaway at nearby Berchtesgaden. Garmisch hosts a massive American army presence – vacationing GIs lured by the presence of a military recreation area – as well as a German mountain regiment's barracks and a further large base in neighbouring Mitterwald.

The experience of being mistaken for a dollar-laden GI can become tiring for other English-speakers. But when the Bavarian conservatism or American brashness gets too much there's always an escape to the peace and solitude of the surrounding mountains and lakes in the summer, and the isolated cross-country trails of nearby villages when the snow finally arrives. Or if you are missing city lights, music and action, then there are excursions to Munich (an easy hitch up the autobahn) or, in the other direction is Innsbruck, which lies at the centre of the Tyrolean ski area.

THE SKIING

Garmisch is a sizeable resort with 120km of piste and 38 lifts. The Happy Ski Card which covers Garmisch-Partenkirchen is also valid for the nearby Austrian resorts of Heiterwang, Berwang, Bichlbach, Bierwier, Lermoos, Ehrwald, Reith and Seefeld. Garmisch is probably best for intermediates but advanced skiers will not be bored by a couple of world famous runs and beginners are also encouraged; there are several ski schools from which to choose. Unfortunately, one of Garmisch's main problems is that it is only 90 km from Munich and when the snow conditions are at their peak the resort is packed out, so the best time to ski is on week days which is fine for resort workers as they are more likely to get a day off during the week. There are four separate ski areas: the Zugspitze reached by a fifty-year-old cog railway which takes an hour to reach the Zugspitzplatt where there are red runs galore and marvellous views over Austria; alternatively the faster gondola from Eibsee which goes right to the summit from whence you take another lift down to the skiing area. The less high Hausberg area includes the Kreuzeck and Osterfeld lifts and the Kandahar and the Horn runs for advanced skiers. There are two black runs down to the town but Swiss and French resorts would scoff at their designation and expert skiers will have to wait for decent snow cover to sample their dubious delights. Another area, the unfortunately named Wank-Gebiet is reached by the Wankbahn gondola at the top of which there are some long red runs. The least high area, the Eckbauergebiet has some red runs and is not particularly demanding.

Enthusiasts used to the wide-open expanses of France and Switzerland may be disappointed by what Garmisch has to offer. On the other hand the skiing season, running from October to May, is one of the longest in Europe. The first area to open and the last to close is the high glacier just below the peak of the Zugspitz.

Garmisch's other main problem is snow, or rather lack of it. In a bad season, it seems that Munich gets more precipitation than the mountains. As the longer runs to lower elevation close down, the shorter and higher lifts become packed and the peace and harmony of the peaks is shattered by the bustle on the lifts reminiscent of Oxford Street on the last Saturday before Christmas. Then the only remedy is to rise early and ride up to the Zugspitze – or to take a day or two and head off to the nearest reliably snow-covered area in Austria.

Once a year, skiers will have the chance to see the best in the world when Garmisch plays host to the World Cup Downhill race; and avid ski-jumpers will be interested in the championship held at New Year.

WORK

As usual the best times to look for work are at the beginning of the winter or summer seasons. However the American army base and some German hotels have vacancies throughout the year and anyone who has the time, money and patience to stick around is the most likely to find something eventually. In order to get the residence permit (mentioned above) you need a local address. Don't worry about this red tape too much though; ask another worker to use the number of his or her apartment, or make one up. The *Rathaus* (town hall) officials sometimes turn surly if you do not have a job but persevere: they are obliged to issue the permits to EU nationals.

If you are looking for a job on an American base, you will probably have to go through the civilian recruitment office in Garmisch aka the AFRC (short for American Forces

Recreational Centre). The bureaucracy involved however can be infuriating and you may feel discouraged. It can smooth your path somewhat if you can track down some GIs at their favourite watering places in the town and befriend them and find out exactly how the system works. The American army has closed its resorts at Chiemsee and Berchtesgaden and also the ageing hotels in Garmisch-Partenkirchen including the General Patton and the Von Steuben and replaced them with a state of the art lodge and resort (the Edelweiss) in Ga-P. The Edelweiss lodge has 330 rooms. More details on the AFRC website (www. AFRCEurope.com). After you have established yourself, there may be more enjoyable work and higher pay as a waiter, childcare attendant or even ski instructor. Normally accommodation goes with the job. Although it will probably resemble a seedy college dorm it will be extremely cheap.

If you are put off by the prospect of working for the military or find the routine of an Army operation unbearable after a while, the other option is to get a job with a local German employer. Again, there is no guarantee that there will be a shortage of employees at the right time of year.

There have been mixed reports of the helpfulness of the local *Arbeitsamt* (employment office) and in any case the better route is to use the tried and trusted method of trudging round the hotels and restaurants in person.

Amanda Smallwood worked at the Ramada Sporthotel. She first visited the resort in August and tried to get a job then, but had no luck. Undaunted, she collected brochures with the details of all the hotels in Garmisch and on her return to the UK wrote to 20 of them; she got fifteen replies and seven offered her a job. Having scrutinised the offers, she decided the Ramada's offer of a chambermaid's post was the best based on pay, hours etc. Of her job Amanda says:

> *There are a lot of foreigners working here. In the housekeeping department there are four Hungarians, two Spaniards and myself. Admittedly it is hard work and has to be well done as the housekeeper is very strict. So far my hours are 8.30am to 5pm and I work a five-day week on a rota-basis. I share accommodation with the two Spanish girls, which I prefer to being on my own – there is little chance to feel homesick. It's a great way to spend the winter and to see another country. I can really recommend Garmisch-Partenkirchen and the Ramada Hotel for English-speakers.*

Other places to try include the Hotel Wittelsbach, often on the lookout for dishwashers, the plus Post Hotel on Marienplatz in the centre of Garmisch, or the Holiday Inn in Partenkirchen which hires chambermaids. Somewhat out of town is Eibsee Hotel, at the foot of the Zugspitz and set on a beautiful lake, and on the ski slopes you can try at the Garmischer Haus.

These are only some of the best prospects and there are many other restaurants, hotels and guesthouses who may be on the look out for staff. Ask around and keep trying, the job will come eventually.

ACCOMMODATION

Accommodation can sometimes be a problem here while looking for a job. You may be offered a doss (i.e. a place on the floor or couch) in army housing – however you should be aware that this common practice carries with it the possibility of arrest and a stiff fine for trespassing if discovered.

There is a youth hostel (☎08821-2980), somewhat inconveniently located in the village of Burgrain just 3km down the road and with an age limit of 27. You could also try the cheap Naturfreundehaus hostel situated at the foot of the Wank mountain.

Other than that, your best bet is to hunt around the various guesthouses, or head out to the camping ground, about a mile past the Sheridan Caserne on the Grainau road. Free camping is also possible, although illegal, in the hills around the town – be discreet and do not light any fires.

The village of Mittenwald about 20 km from Garmisch on the Innsbruck road is a more peaceful and accurate reflection of Bavarian culture. There is some limited skiing there – limited, that is by the snow cover on the lower slopes and the avalanche danger on the one high run off the peak above the town. If you are interested in looking for a job there, try the Hotel Post, the Gasthof Hotel, the Gröbl-Alm above the town, the Hotel Rieger or the Hotel Alpenrose.

Oberstdorf

Oberstdorf is a picturesque resort located in the Allgäu region of Germany that dips down into Austria. It is a spa town famous for its *Kurs* (cures) as well as a well-known skiing resort, home to the World Nordic Skiing Championships in 2005. As well as nordic skiing the resort is known for ski-jumping and other winter sports and as a summer resort. With over 300 hotels and pensions there are reasonably good employment prospects. However K McCausland who worked there took a rather dim view of the employers. He had a lot of contact with other foreigners working in the resort and many complained of being shabbily treated, underpaid and overworked though the beauty of the area offered some compensations.

There are also jobs available in other resort hotels in the Allgäu; About 20 km from Oberstdorf in the town of Hindelang, the Bad-Hotel Sonne (8973 Hindeland/Oberallgäu; ☎8324 8970) run by the Schneider family, likes to employ English-speakers. It is not quite so convenient for the skiing though.

Italy

The advantage of Italy compared with France, Austria and Switzerland used to be that it was cheaper. However, eastern European resorts have long taken over from Italy as the really cheap alternative to other European resorts and this is still the case. Italian resorts are no less expensive than their counterparts in France and Switzerland but it is true to say that there are some variations: for instance upmarket Cortina and Cervinia are more expensive than say Sauze d'Oulx, Arabba, Bormio, Livigno and Canezi. However, in the less exclusive resorts the costs for accommodation and food for the job seeker while he or she looks around for work will almost certainly be a lot less than in Switzerland or Germany. It is true also true that the value for money coupled with good quality in the eateries of Italian resorts is better than elsewhere in the European Alps.

The other advantage for the job hunter is that fewer English-speakers will be trying to find jobs in Italian ski resorts because of the language deficiency on both sides. Italians generally do not speak English and although many British people learn some French or German at school, far fewer learn Italian. Anyone who does have a grasp of the language will therefore have a distinct advantage and a chance to improve their Italian as they will be able to speak little else unless they are looking for a job in the Alta Badia region in the province of Bolzano where you may be able to get by with German. Resorts here include La Villa, San Cassiano, Pedraces, Corvara and Colfosco. German may also be useful in other resorts since many skiers in Italy come from Germany and Austria. If on the other hand you are working for a British tour operator or in a resort swamped by British skiers (Sauze d'Oulx springs to mind), you can probably get by with less Italian.

REGULATIONS

Although anyone from an EU country does not need a work permit, a residence permit (*permesso di soggiorno*) is required by those staying longer than three months. Unfortunately Italian bureaucracy outdoes any in Europe for convolution. For jobs lasting longer than three months a residence permit is obligatory and if you are intending to work for longer than this period you should contact the police at the *questura, commissariato* or *stazione di carabinieri* and get a *libretto di lavoro* (worker registration card) from the town hall or *municipio* and, if desired (for opening a bank account etc.) a resident's card, by applying to the *Ufficio Anagrafe* (registry office).

Once you have all the paperwork your employer will have to pay the usual contributions on your behalf and you will be covered by the Italian State Health Service (*Servizio Sanitorio Nazionale/SSN*). At local level you deal with the ASL (*Azienda Sanitoria Locale*), which is often referred to by its old name (*Unitaria Sanitaria Locale* or USL) in some parts. If your employer is not paying contributions you should ensure that you have private medical insurance. SAI is a big Italian insurance company with branches everywhere if you have not already taken out insurance in your home country.

If you are working legally in a hotel, you also need to have a medical examination (similar to Switzerland) which is done free of charge at the local *ufficio igiene* in order to get a *libretto sanitario* (health certificate).

Anyone who is working in the food and beverage department, even if they are not actually handling the food themselves, has to have a *Tessere Sanitaria* (hygiene certificate). Employers can find themselves in serious trouble from the authorities if they employ people without this and so most are insistent. To obtain the certificate you have to call at the nearest ASL (see above) office with your *permesso di soggiorno*, passport photos and a receipt from the post office for the fee paid into the appropriate ASL account and submit to a routine medical examination and injections. Note that procedures and the fee for this are bound to vary a little depending on the area.

If you have not been totally deranged by the paperwork you may feel ecstatic on having dealt with it successfully. Your employer however will not, as he or she has to pay contributions on your behalf, which can be very substantial in Italy. However, you should not be too discouraged by the regulations since there is a great deal of unofficial, cash-in-hand work or *lavoro nero* in Italy, not just among foreigners but also among moonlighting natives. It has been estimated that the black economy adds 25% to Italy's economic output.

Lara Giavi, an Italian from the Veneto region which includes the Dolomite mountain resorts of Cortina d'Ampezzo (near Belluno), Asiage, Canazei, Alleghe, S. Stefano di Codore etc. says it is easy to find work in tourism in her region. The winter season lasts from Christmas to Easter and most mountain resorts have a summer season, usually of two months (July and August). After working in a ski resort she recommends looking for a summer job at the seaside resorts near Venice: Tesolo, Bibione, Lignano, Carorle, Cavallino, Chiaggia, Venezia Lido etc., where the season lasts from May to mid-September. If you speak Italian she suggests you call in person or contact the local *Associazione Albergatori* (hotels association) via the internet for jobs which can be applied for online. Or you can consult the job offers in the papers in the local *ufficio di collocamento* (the official government employment service) before the season begins. Most of the jobs advertised are for waiting staff and if your Italian is up to it, there are usually receptionist jobs as well. Salaries for such jobs may have a deduction for board and lodging, which is usually provided by the employer. Some employers give a day off a week.

Bormio

Bormio is positioned at the foot of the Stelvio pass, which separates 'Italian' Italy from the German-speaking Dolomite area of Italy. Its origins as a spa town go back to Roman times and from its historic centre it has spread out into a thriving resort, which manages to cater for tourist demands yet remain unmistakably Italian. The population of about 4,000 enjoy a steady prosperity, and increasing trade and tourism from improvements to the valley road between Sondrio and the Stelvio pass in late 1998. Via Roma, the main street through Bormio, is narrow and cobbled with an incongruous alternation of Armani and *salami locali* filling the windows of the numerous shops and boutiques. Bormio also boasts a fifteenth-century church in an attractive square with great views of the mountains from the cafés. The locals are generally very friendly and can be seen every evening on their *passegiata*, no doubt invigorated by a visit to the Bagnio Vechio spa, which also supplies the olympic-size swimming pool.

THE SKIING

Bormio hosts an annual World Cup race, and it was host to the (first) Alpine Skiing World Championships in 1995 and they were held there again in 2005. You can ski the downhill course. This all takes place on the tall but narrow north-west facing slopes of the Monte Valecetta reached from lifts near the centre of town. The cable car and gondola take you to either side of what is an intermediates' paradise with not much for the expert to test themselves against bar a good mogul run and some interesting off piste possiblities.

Alternatively, there are the nearby resorts of Livigno (one hour) and Santa Caterina (30 minutes by bus) and the summer glacier skiing at Stelvio offer a huge range of possibilities for all ranges on and off piste. There is also cross-country skiing.

ACCOMMODATION

Most of the accommodation is in the form of hotels or *alberghi* (inns) of which there is a great variety in standard and price; only those nearest the cable car and gondola are disproportionately expensive. All the accommodation appears on the list provided by the Associazione Albergatore (Bormio Hotels Association) or the private CAB list (see below). The tourist office (+39 0342 903300; www.valtellinaonline.it) will provide a list of self-catering accommodation and there are also privately owned apartments to be had. These latter are at a premium and have to be booked for a season in advance.

APRÈS SKI

Bormio is not renowned for its nightlife, but there are plenty of friendly bars open until 3am, restaurants and one potentially happening nightclub. Some of the bars are clearly aimed at attracting foreigners by being pub-like with Guiness and karaoke, but the typical Italian bars are usually the busiest. An exception to this is the Shangri-La, a popular haunt for the reps, which used to be a club and plays good music.

WORK

The resort of Bormio is predominantly used by Italian tourists and its working population reflects this. However, there is a sizeable contingent of British and Irish punters throughout both the winter and summer seasons with a large flow of Germans particularly at Christmas and Easter.

The first British arrived in 1971 and now there is a constant presence thanks to the regular operations of a handful of operators including Equity, Interhome, and the Irish agent Directski. All those interviewed spoke of their job satisfaction and remarked on the very high standards of accommodation compared with other countries they had worked in.

They advised anyone wanting to rep in Bormio to apply a year in advance.

For reps and most other staff the winter season starts in early December and continues through to the first or second week of April. The summer season is busier in Bormio than in most other alpine resorts because of the proximity of the Passo Stelvio glacier which is open to skiing from mid-June to early September and attracts a lot of American tourists.

At present, there are plenty of Anglophone tourists and lots of scope for English-speaking and other foreign staff to seek employment in Bormio and the neighbouring resorts of Santa Caterina and Livigno. Some areas of work, e.g. ski instruction, lift installations and sports shops seem exclusively Italian with locals and family businesses dominating the staffing of these. Qualified, and very determined ski instructors can also try one of the ski schools:

Alta Valtellina: via Roma 85, Bormio; ☎+39 0342 911010.
Bormio 2000: via Funiva 16, Bormio; ☎+39 0342 903135.
Capitani: via Vittoria 36, Bormio; ☎+39 0342 910130
Nazionale: via Funivia, Bormio; ☎+39 0342 901553.
Sertorelli: via Piave 3, Bormio; ☎+39 0342 903060.

However, there are encouraging signs of growing foreign employment in other areas, with Britons, New Zealanders, Irish, Poles, Croats and Serbs all having worked or settled to live and work in Bormio. Elizabeth Cantoni, of Irish origin, has lived in Bormio for over 30 years and used to co-run the Hotel Girasole (Bormio 2000, 23032 Bormio, SO, Italy; ☎0342-904652). She has employed Scottish and Irish staff with Italian language skills and proper technical qualifications for hotel work. Most of her staff were recruited from a local hotel training school. However, it is worth seeing if the new management are carrying on the tradition of taking applications from catering students or similar for bar, dining room, kitchen and reception/secretarial work, but only with the qualifications as above. She said the police were very strict about imposing fines for working without a residence permit (see *Regulations* above), but other foreign staff had managed to get one or found a way round the problem.

The best place to ask about this and anything else about accommodation or work is the Tourist Office (☎+39 0342 903300; www.valtellinaonline.com) which shares offices with the Associazione Albergatore (Bormio Hotels Association). There you can obtain names and addresses of all the hotels in the area and their managers' names. The hotels owned by Mr Antonioli (about seven of them) are separate and you can find information on them over the road at the private association (called CAB) in via Peccedi, where they recommended writing to him a season in advance with references. Chef and receptionist are the best paid jobs but you have to be suitably qualified and skilled. Bed and board is provided and while work is often seven days a week, afternoons are usually free for skiing.

Your chances of getting work in hotels are largely down to persistence and are helped by the fact that employers are realising the need for at least one English-speaker on their staff to satisfy clients' needs. Fulvio, a local waiter said that more and more young people are trying to learn English because of its importance in tourism and said that *stranieri* (foreigners) were welcome. At the Capitani chain of hotels located in Livigno, Stelvio and Bormio, they welcomed applications from English-speakers. Write a season in advance to Alberghi Capitani s.r.l (Via Funiva 15, 230323 Bormio). However, Georgio Pellos, manager of the Hotel Posta in Via Roma is reluctant to take on foreigners because he thinks they only stay for one season and then move on.

If you are planning on staying for both seasons and need work in the interim period, there are plenty of opportunities in the many bars. Lynn, from New Zealand, worked at Café Mozart for six seasons with the very friendly Sergio Mozart (via Fiera 2; ☎+39 342 901201) who asks for experienced staff who are prepared to find their own food and board. Katerina from Germany, worked at the popular Clem pub (☎+39 0342 903109) on the same street and gets accommodation but only because she knows the manager from her five years as a rep in Bormio and recommends getting your face well known around town as the best way of getting bar work. She gets food while at work. Despite bar work not being her chosen career, she is happy for the time being and loves Bormio and its people. Once again she stressed the need for Italian as 75% of her customers are Italian.

More non-seasonal employment which could be handy for extra income anytime during the year could be found for mother-tongue English-speakers teaching or translating either privately or through Nadia dei Cas and Giovanna Pedrana at the Studio Organiser agency (via Roma 113, 23032 Bormio(SO); tel/fax +39 0342 910771) who also teach French and German to both school children and adults. They are part of a rapidly expanding business and might take on staff for part-time work.

Other evidence of Britons in the resort manifests itself in Leslie from Scotland, who works as a beautician at the Swimming Pool and Maggie who is a permanent resident in Bormio, but works as a rep in the winter.

There is plenty of room in Bormio for entrepreneurs. Try selling ski photos and videos or run private taxi services for the punters staying in isolated hotels. Finally, if you are still stuck for work, it might be worth scanning through the jobs at the state employment office (*ufficio collocamento*), via de Simone 16; ☎+39 0342 901470), which has a noticeboard divided into two sections: jobs vacant and services offered. A spot check revealed a need for a chef, hotel waiter, cleaner and secretaries.

Cervinia

At 2052m/6,764ft, Cervinia is one of the highest resorts in the Italian Alps. It is dominated by the mighty Matterhorn mountain (4478m), which it shares with Switzerland. In fact you can ski over the Matterhorn into Switzerland. As you do so, you may contemplate that its roughly triangular shape was reputedly the inspiration for Toblerone chocolate. Cervinia, has a tradition of accommodating visitors to the grand peaks of the region formerly known as Breuil. Local villagers acted as guides for those travellers and climbers that came from all over Europe to explore the area in the nineteenth century. By 1911, hotels and travellers' refuges were being built, and the Ski Club Breuil was formed signifying the beginnings of a tourist resort. In 1936 Breuil was changed to Cervinia and there is still some disagreement over whether the name came from the Servinia wood at the foot of the valley or, more likely Il Cervino, the Italian name for the Matterhorn. However while the centre of the resort is traditionally pretty, expansion has taken the form of functional apartment blocks and hotels which are not at all pleasing to the eye. The resort is about two hours' drive from Turin.

THE SKIING

To this day, Breuil-Cervinia remains one of Italy's top ski resorts. The skiing area extends right up to 3500m/11,500ft most of which is well above the tree line. There are good connections with the resorts of Val Tournenche and Zermatt. The 30 or so lifts are capable of carrying more than 25,000 people per hour to sport on 200 km of pistes. The glacier at Plateau Rosa guarantees snow on upper slopes throughout the season, and there are good artificial snow facilities on the lower slopes. It is rare to be unable to ski back down into the village. Cervinia boasts the seemingly incompatible combination of long hours of sunshine and outstanding snow conditions and is ideal for spring skiing.

Skiing in Cervinia offers wide scope for beginners and intermediates, offering a large area of gentle, open pistes. The extensive wide, undulating slopes are also ideal for snowboarders. There is however, little that the advanced skier will find challenging, particularly later on in the season. The five runs designated black are dotted about the resort, skiers must search to find them and they are usually the first to suffer from poor snow conditions. Most routes can be expected to lead you at some point to Plan Maison, the central lift station of the ski area, from which there is easy access to nursery slopes and a selection of blue and easy red runs. Needless to say the central station becomes very crowded in high season because so many routes coverge there. Venturing up to the summit of Plateau Rosa is rewarded by stunning views thanks to spectacular scenery. However, the winds can be biting in this exposed area. If it is the slightest bit breezy anywhere in Cervinia, you can be sure it will be blowing a hurrricane on Plateau Rosa. From there skiers can choose a number of different runs from the gentle blue run off to the left which goes across the Swiss T-bar before branching back into Italy and where you have to keep to the left to avoid being swept down into Zermatt and billed for a Swiss lift pass. To the right, the famous Ventina run offers a splendid 11km run that begins at the glacier and takes you right down to the village.

Cervinia's high altitude makes it an ideal place for spring skiing and the season extends well into April with almost all pistes open. However, in warm weather, the best conditions can be round around the area of the Lago Goillet (the spectacular dammed lake). This area offers a challenging mogul run if your knees can take it. Lago Goillet also offers access to the pistes of Val Tournenche, a separate resort, slightly lower down the valley, which is included in the normal Cervinia lift pass. Skiing down to Val Tournenche provides a pleasant gentle excursion, and takes you to just about the only place in the area, which does not have a view of the Matterhorn.

APRÈS SKI

Despite being a fairly compact village, Cervinia offers plenty of activity off the slopes. There is a large variety of bars, clubs, cafés and restaurants in the lively centre of the village offering something to suit most tastes from cheap and cheerful to romantic chic. Try the 'Matterhorn' for mouth-watering steaks and fondues, or the speciality mixed grill at La Bricole. Casse Croute, high above the village serves the most enormous pizzas and has featured in the *Sunday Times*. It is also worth visiting La Pavia and La Grotta, offering a wide selection of pasta dishes, meat, fish, seafood, salad and local specialities. One of the reps, spending a second season in Cervina said the Tiramisu at La Grotta was the best in the valley and their homemade Glüwein is a must. For a slightly different night out, spend the evening at Baita Cretaz in a rustic mountain cabin.

Lively bars in the village include the Yeti Bar, the Grivola, the Scotch (underneath Hotel des Guides), the Copa Pan and White Rose. The Dragon pub has English beers and karaoke and Linos (adjacent to the ice rink) is a good Glüwein stop at the end of a day's skiing or, Cocktails at the Ymelerob followed by La Chimera and Garage discos for those with any energy left over for clubbing.

WORK

With many of Cervinia's skiers coming from Britain, working for British tour companies offers reasonable prospects for work arranged in advance. Crystal, First Choice, Inghams and Thomson all run operations there. Crystal has four reps there, with some doubling up as ski escorts.

Stories from the reps varied. Most claimed to be well satisfied with their jobs citing their improved language skills and career prospects as 'fringe benefits' One ski escort resented the fact that his ski escort duties meant having to ski well below his true ability for most of the week and then finding himself too busy with administrative duties on his non-skiing days to enjoy any free time on the slopes.

For casual jobs, foreigners could try the Copa Pan, which not only takes on foreigners to run the bar, but is also the hanging out place for ski bums and foreign workers and a good place to catch up on job vacancy gossip. It might also be worth trying any of the shops and small businesses of which Cervinia has a large number. Clearly proficiency in Italian would be pretty much essential. There are ski-wear shops, a chemist, bakery, delicatessen, small green grocer and a range of cafés.

There are also ski hire shops, which recruit casual staff with the appropriate technical experience. Most employees are locals, but there always seems to be scope for a small number of foreigners to be taken on, especially at the beginning of the season. Try La Genzisnella Sport Shop or Herrin Ski Hire Shop on the main street in the centre of the village. If you are after a real ski job in the mountains, look out for the Union Jack flying from the roof of the Igloo bar as you ski down the lower section (Cime Blanche) of the Ventina run. Pauline, who runs the restaurant often has kitchen and serving work available. Chalet Etoile mountain restaurant near Plan Maison will also take on foreigners who speak passable Italian.

It might be worth contacting the regional tourist board of the Aosta Valley (Valle d'Aosta Azienda di Promozione Turistica) for news of employment opportunities in the area: in Cervinia : 11021 via Carrel 29; ☎+39 0166 94 91 36; fax +39 0166 94 97 31; www. montecervino.it; in Val Tournenche: 11028 via Roma; ☎+39 0166 92 029; fax +39 0166 92430.

Cortina d'Ampezzo

The town of Cortina d'Ampezzo in the eastern Dolomites, nestles at the head of a valley enclosed by three blocks of mountains: the Cristallo, Sorapis and Tofane, whose spectacular peaks glow pink-gold at sunset; and when Il Corso, Cortina's upmarket 'High Street', is transformed into a Noah's Ark parade of tigers, beavers, foxes, lynxes, sables and chinchillas, you know the season has started. This is no place for ski bums. The town, bathed in its big-spender atmosphere, drips with designer labels: Gucci, St. Laurent, Cartier, Armani, Cacharel etc. which append the clothes displayed in shop windows and on the backs of the resort's clientele of wealthy Romani, Venetians and Bolognese. For the record Alberto Tomba 'La Bomba' the Italian double gold-medallist of the 1988 Calgary Olympics, learned to ski here.

THE SKIING

Host to the 1956 Olympics, Cortina is the most famous and one of the largest of Italy's winter sports centres, as well as being a popular year-round resort. Ranging from 3200m down to 2000m, the pistes offer roughly 140kms of downhill skiing served by over 51 lifts. By going over the top of Lagazuoi (2778m) you can link into the Alta Badia area (Cassiano, La Villa, Corvara etc.) with 460 lifts and about 1,200 km of piste which is covered by the Superski Dolomiti Pass. The skiing in Cortina is best suited to the intermediate and more experienced skier. There are also 58 km of cross-country tracks. The superb Olympia piste up on Tofane and the unforgettable Dobbiaco-Cortina cross-country run of 35 kms are highly recommended. There are plenty of opportunities for off-piste skiing when the snow is good, and for the jet-set, heli-skiing is possible 8 km down the valley at San Vito (Cortina is off limits) and don't forget bob-sleighing and ski-jumping are also possible. Three ski schools with about 160 qualified instructors cater for all levels of skier, although the sighting of a complete beginner not under the age of five is a rare event and English is not a language much possessed by ski instructors in Cortina. Access to some of the slopes is possible from the town itself, by getting a cable car at the bottom of Sorapis up to Faloria or at the Freccia del Cielo up to Col Druscie. But a word of warning: you really do need your own transport. Buses to lifts further afield are just non-existent, the town, for a resort, is large and if you have only got a few hours free time, you don't want to spend most of them in a queue.

If you tire of skiing but your body still hankers after exercise, you may be tempted by one of the many other attractions on offer: the Olympic ice-rink, the swimming pool, riding stables (open all year). And there's always the après ski...

APRÈS SKI

More and more people seem to come to Cortina just for the après ski. The afternoon is spent taking the sun on the terrace of the Faloria refuge or at El Camineto on the other side of the valley. Then the *bella gente* stream down into town for tea at the Embassy or the slightly cheaper and less snobby Lovat. Then an aperatif at the Hotel La Poste or the Cristallino Bar.

There is no shortage of top-class restaurants with prices to match: Melon, Tivoli and El Camineto, the last two on the road up to Pocol. Cheaper places are Da Franco (pizzas or pasta) and the Spaghetti house, at either end of Il Corso; and Il Buco del Diavolo on the top side of town just below the ring-road and along from the ski-lift up to Faloria.

Towards midnight the bars clear and the discos begin to fill: VIP, L'Area and the Hippopotomus are the 'in' night clubs and at weekends are wildly overpriced; in the high season you won't get in at all unless they know you.

ACCOMMODATION

Unless you are lucky enough to fix up a job with board and lodging thrown in (before you go), finding somewhere cheap to stay while job hunting can be quite a problem. There is no youth hostel and prices for a small apartment are prohibitive at over £800 per month. Your best bet would be to stay down the valley at San Vito (8km) or Borca di Cadore (13km) and make forays into Cortina from there. A good bus service connects along the main road up to Cortina. Bed and breakfast is available at the Albergo Cavallino in Cortina but will almost certainly be cheaper outside. Look for signs saying *camere* or *Zimmer* by the roadside. Go off the main road a bit and you are bound to find something cheaper. Do avoid timing your arrival for a Friday or Saturday as the whole area is inundated pretty much all year round, by weekenders escaping from the smog-filled cities of northern Italy.

WORK

All the usual jobs associated with a ski resort are there for the determined hunter; determined underlined. Cortina is very proud of its exclusivity and lack of foreign tourists. You will be marooned without a good smattering of Italian. The town's all year round popularity means that unlike many other resorts there is no grand scale seasonal turnover.

There are several ways of securing a job before arrival. You can check th Associazione Albergatori (Hotel Owners' Association) websites as they hire people on behalf of the hotels. They are organised regionally and offer you a chance to apply for jobs online and email your CV to potential employers. This would be totally legal work but don't forget your *ricevuta* (see *Regulations* above). Alternatively, contact the Tourist Office (0436 866252; www.cortina.dolomiti.org) and via them get in touch directly with the hotels and see what openings are available. Either way you should get room and board. For details of tour operators that take on chalet staff/ski escorts (see section at the beginning of this book) for which you must be an excellent cook as well as doing the bedmaking. British companies in Cortina include Crystal, Inghams, Ski Equipe and The Ski Club of GB.

Another way of getting a job is to turn up and do the rounds. We spoke to one hardened American ski bum who has many years' experience of Cortina. His advice was to come before November:

December is too late and this goes for all jobs. Otherwise turn up just before Christmas or Easter when high season means places are often desperate for the occasional extra hand.

This is especially true for waitressing or baby-sitting. You can get child-minding jobs though the hotels by giving a 10% to 15% commission to the *portiere* (caretakers) who'll find the work for you. It is best to do this via the better hotels. They won't hire illegally, but a little charm in the right direction will go a long way. Knocking on doors is the surest way of getting jobs and some places also need extra washer-uppers at peak periods. You'd be unlikely to get room and board with any of these jobs, but bar work up at the refuges would provide accommodation. For this kind of work you need to get there by the beginning of the season. You can often work without papers; however one ski bum stressed that the finance police do impose stringent controls and if you are caught, your employer, and possibly you too, face heavy fines. You spend the season from November through to mid-April up on the mountain, but can take the last lift of the day down and stay a night at Cortina, to be back at 9 am the following morning, with one day off a week.

Courmayeur

The attractive old village of Courmayeur (www.aiat-monte-bianco.com) is tucked into the north-west corner of the Aosta Valley, just inside Italy and at the foot of Mont Blanc (Monte Bianco if you're Italian) Massif. It is also conveniently situated at the opening of the Mont Blanc tunnel, which burrows through 11 km to Chamonix on the other side. You can also travel to Chamonix above ground via connecting cable cars. Although now in Italy, Courmayeur was, as its name suggests once French. It is part of an area that became Italian in 1918 and the inhabitants speak Italian with a French accent. This does not mean however that they speak French any better – that comes with an Italian twang.

Courmayeur is the smartest of the Aosta resorts and popular with British tour operators some of which also go to the neighbouring resort of La Thuile (Italy). The town itself is not purpose-built but has been there for centuries, and hence has a lot of local atmosphere and attractive architecture. Several villages down the road to Aosta use the Courmayeur slopes, some as much as six miles away, and one of the most attractive of these is Pré Saint Didier.

THE SKIING

Although Courmayeur at 1224m (4,015 ft) is quite low, the first cable car starts at 1800 m with a top station (Plan Checrouit) at 3,000 m so the snow at Courmayeur is generally reliable. With about 100 km of piste served by 23 lifts Courmayeur offers a surprisingly varied range of runs, probably best suited to low intermediates. There is however a very good school for beginners, and despite there only being one black run there are plenty of opportunities for off piste e.g. from the Cresta d'Arp.

The main ski areas are: to the north-east the slopes of the Checrouit which also provides the nursery slopes at the top of the first chairlift, and the Val Veny slopes which face northwest and are sunny in the afternoon and also the Mont Blanc area. One thing not to be missed for competent skiers is skiing on Mont Blanc itself: you go up with a guide to 3400m, and then ski down the glacier called Mer de Glace, on a 20 km run into Chamonix in France. This is the so-called Vallée Blanche. It is an unbelievably exhilerating experience and offers some of the most astounding mountain scenery anywhere.

APRÈS SKI

Courmayeur is a lively place – the large number of Italians coming up from Turin and Milan see to that. As well as Italians, there are large numbers of French, quite a few Belgians and a good international mix including Brits. Courmayeur has about 45 restaurants all good value in their class. Mont-Frety, La Terraza and Margherita are good quality and value for pizzas and simple pasta meals. Après ski drinking usually starts with a *vino caldo* or hot chocolate up the mountain and then continues at the bottom in the American Bar, Le Privé, Poppy's or the Bar Roma. For later there is a good selection of discos, of which perhaps the most attractive for English people is the Tiger Club where the entrance fee includes the first drink and the opportunity to dance all night, plus a free lift home in the disco's minibus. If you can get there, Va Cherie a nightclub in a converted cowshed, just outside the town is also rated highly. Attractive, lively with good snow and skiing, Courmayeur is an excellent place to go, either on holiday or to work.

ACCOMMODATION

If you go out to the resort with no job, you'll need somewhere to stay while you are waiting. This is usually quite easy; rooms for the night or else flats at a variety of prices. These can be rented for the whole season or at weekly rates, which are negotiable. Ask at the tourist office (☎+39 0165 842060; www.courmayeur.net) in the main square.

WORK

Step number one when looking for a job in Courmayeur is to go to one of the bars where British staff are employed, for instance the American Bar and find out as much as you can about what is on offer, who to ask, who to get to know, who the reps are this year, and so on.

Having said that, there are several ways of going about it. Courmayeur is the most popular Italian resort with British tour operators. The companies out there who give a lot of jobs to British people include: Airtours, Crystal, First Choice, Interski, Inghams, Mark Warner, Neilson, Skiworld and Thomson. All of them employ reps or ski guides, although in some cases these roles are doubled up. You'd need to apply for the whole season the previous April, and probably be 25 with experience of being responsible for others.

John Anderson, was a 29-year-old from Scotland working as a rep-cum-ski-guide for Interski. He feels the job was a tough one, on call 24 hours a day, and active for at least twelve of them, but he kept the job as a good way of getting to know people with a view to setting up his own ski-teaching company. Bladon Lines (Inghams) employ chalet staff and Crystal a ski escort in Courmayeur. Again, apply in April, and come equipped with the relevant qualifications and or experience, and preferably knowledge of Italian, although French will usually do. Ben Bathurst was the odd-job man for Bladon Lines/Inghams, and his duties included mending anything that went wrong, delivering bread in the mornings. He also doubled-up as a ski guide accompanying guests on their days out skiing. MBOs are given all living expenses and free skiing plus pocket money. Ben loved it because he had lots of time to ski and enjoy himself and got on particularly well with the people he found in the resort.

More British companies would like to run chalets, but Italian regulations are extremely strict about how they should be kept. They see chalets as hotels and demand high standards of hygiene, a strict control on work permits and expect someone to be on the premises at all times.

There are no rules about getting work on the spot, except to keep asking. Knocking on doors can prove successful. Alison Brady found work in a mountain restaurant that way. She was a waitress, working during lift hours (usually 9am to 4.30pm), with a day and an afternoon off and was paid £60 a week including accommodation. She enjoyed it, particularly as working outside on sunny days gave her a good tan. Chris Belling worked in a butcher's shop next to the American Bar; he got one day off, accommodation and £70 per week. He was particularly happy about his boss, but regretted being stuck indoors at the resort for so much of the time. It is worth trying the lift operators, the restaurants, discos and shops. For all these, and the jobs described above, Italian is pretty much essential.

There is scope for private enterprise. With so many spread-out villages and an infrequent bus service, there is always room for a taxi service, especially in the evening out of Courmayeur. Ben Bathurst did it in his spare time sometimes, and earned up to £40 a day. He used the company bus; if you do it yourself you obviously need your own transport but earnings can be higher than £70 a day.

Courmayeur is quite an easy resort to find work in, it seems, as there is a high turnover of staff. But if you have no luck, you can take the bus through the Mont Blanc Tunnel to Chamonix, or a little further to Argentière and Megève. None of these is far away, and they offer lots more job possibilities. But stay in Courmayeur if you can – the snow and the skiing are better, and it's a great place to spend all or part of the season.

Folgarida

The purpose-built resort of Folgarida was opened in 1964 and rests 1250m up in the Brenta Dolomites surrounded by breathtaking scenery. Strangely, it has managed to keep its vast skiing area under wraps and therefore relatively few tour operators seem to have caught on to this excellent ski location. So it seems that school group organisers like Equity, PGL, Ski Europe etc. have the monopoly of bringing Britons to this lovely village for the time being. The village itself is fairly quiet although it provides the essentials: pizzerias, cafés, bars, cinema and an assortment of shops. There is also a skating rink and a few more hotel bars, which can be reached by a shuttle bus that will take you to upper Folgarida.

Folgarida can be reached from the UK by flights to Verona leaving from Gatwick, Stanstead and Manchester. Alitalia has numerous flights from Heathrow to Milan from where there are onward connections to Verona. For a cheap flight and transfer, look into cheap deals with the schools companies that go there. It is possible to travel to the resort by train: take the Verona-Brennero line to Trento, transfering to the trenino line to Malé and then there is a bus service that links the whole valley.

THE SKIING

Folgarida/Marilleva provides a vast skiing area for skiers of all standards but is especially good for beginners and intermediates, providing many wide blue and red runs. Advanced skiers are challenged by three black runs, off pistes and powder skiing through fabulous larch and pine forests. The lift system is very modern and efficient, transporting skiers by télécabine to a network of 30 lifts. Marked pistes span 160km including Madonna di Campiglio. Both Folgarida and Marilleva are included on the ski pass, but in addition an extension to Madonna di Campiglio can be arranged. From the beginning of the season in December until its end in April, the snow conditions are always good and new pressure cannons ensure the black run to the village is always open.

APRÈS SKI

Folgarida is not what you would describe as a haven for happening bars and wild nights out, but there are numerous hotel bars as well as the 'TNT'. The 'TNT' is a dark, sultry, candle-lit den whose walls are covered in artwork and also visitors' graffiti. It has live music, stays open until 3am but drinks are pricey. The village has an amusement arcade, cinema, bowling alley and skating rink. The stylish and lively resort of Madonna di Campiglio is only a 15-minute taxi ride away, offering an exuberant nightlife and shopping area.

WORK

At the moment employment in Folgarida is essentially the preserve of Italians, but with the continuing rise in the number of British guests staying in the village there is definitely an opening in the future for more English-speaking staff in the resort. Presently there are two reps and one ski tech working for Equity and one Thomson rep working in the village. If you want a job in this friendly village contact one of the tour operators mentioned. Deciding to turn up in a resort looking for work is a bit risky, so contact hotels and bars in advance. It is possible to get information from the staff at the tourist office who are very friendly, but remember it is not their job to find you employment (Information Office, 3820 Folgarida (TN), Italy; fax +39 0463 986594). Also check out the website of the local *Associazione Albergatori Provincia di Trento* (local branch of the hotels association).

Gary Mullet graduated from Birmingham University with a degree in French and Italian. He found his rep job with Equity through an advertisement on the Department of Italian notice board. It was his first season as a rep and he was moved around four resorts before spending the last six weeks of the season in Folgarida. He described being a rep as a 24-hours a day, seven days a week job. His life as a rep involved picking clients up from the airport, making sure that as much relevant information as possible is given to the guests on the coach journey to the resort. This includes resort information, hotel activities, ski school, lift passes, duty hours and a ski fitting which is organised as soon as possible on arrival. Each rep is responsible for booking ski school and arranging ski pass extensions to Madonna di Campiglio for their clients. According to Gary you basically get back what you put into the job. He also described it as 'the best thing since sliced bread' and 'getting paid to have fun'. The work is varied, dealing with anyone from families to school parties. As a first time rep you can expect about £80 a week, free ski perks and accommodation and meals at one of the hotels. Bonuses depend on the circumstances that occur throughout the season.

Ali Park is a ski instructor with both ASSI and BASI qualifications. He worked in Folgarida several seasons ago as a part-time ski tech for Equity. Ali previously worked in Méribeland in Scotland with juniors. The snow in Scotland did not last, so he contacted Equity who gave him a week-long job as a rep two weeks before the end of the season. During the second week, Ali arranged an interview with an Italian ski school and was successful in obtaining a job for the next season subject to references from his previous employer and confirmation of his skiing qualifications. Ali was the first British Instructor to be employed by the school, apart from a snowboarding instructor, originally from England. There are not many instructors who speak fluent English so there may be job opportunities in the future for British instructors, but check with the ski school (Scuola Italia, Sci Folgarida Dimaro 38025, Folgarida di Dimaro TN) before arriving in Folgarida.

After qualifying as a hairdresser in Ireland, Stella Lawlor went to work as a waitress in her brother's restaurant on the Italian island of Elba. The restaurant's cook told her about working in Italian ski resorts and gave her an introduction to the Vecchia America hotel in Folgarida where she subsequently worked as head waitress. She arrived at the start of the season and her hours were 7am to 11.30am, free time from midday to 6pm and then work until 10.30pm. Stella's meals and accommodation were free and she was paid about £95 per week. She made lots of useful contacts through which she arranged a winter job waitressing in the Caribbean. The Vecchia America is exclusive to Equity clients. This proved advantageous for Stella because she was able to join the Equity guests on their regular evenings out in the nearby lively resort of Madonna di Campiglio. Stella's advice to people seeking employment in Folgarida is that hotels are probably your best bet, speaking Italian is important and if possible, organise employment before arriving in Folgarida.

Livigno

About 40-odd years ago, Livigno was a tiny farming community based around the hamlets of S. Antonio, Sta. Maria and S. Rocco. Since then it has been developed into the most important Alpine resort in northwest Italy. Situated far from urban areas, isolated between northern and Southern Alps, Livigno's closest airport is Bergamo, five hours away. Daylight permitting, the long journey provides ample opportunity to witness the stunning scenery surrounding Livigno which makes up part of both the Swiss national park and the Stelvio National Park, the largest conserved areas of their kind in Europe. Geographical location has led to Livigno's history as a territorial pawn in a chess game played by rural Bormio and the Swiss Grigione, resulting in eventual independence and duty-free status. The latter has ensured that there are a vast number of shops selling clothes, electrical goods and alcohol. These have not quite managed to obliterate the still traditional feel of the town whose 12km provide many examples of the typical Livigno house (known as a *bait*) made of stone and wood and providing the focal point for the preservation of traditional mountain life.

The first hotel, the Alpina, opened in 1880, solely for summer use, while the first road from Bormio opened in 1914 and from St. Moritz in 1937 and it was 1952 before the Bormio road was opened for the winter season. The first ski lift was built in 1960 and a tunnel from Livigno to Switzerland opened in 1964, which explains the high proportion of tourists from northern Europe in evidence. Livigno's growth from having only four hotels and a single ski lift in 1964 has been rapid. In 1996, it could boast 94 hotels, 900 apartments for rental (sleeping accommodation for 4,500 people), 30 ski lifts, 110km of downhill piste and 30km of cross-country tracks. The main road around Livigno's 'traffic-free' centre buzzes continually with vehicles arriving for the duty-free shopping which further swells the numbers of visitors. The local bus services, operating on three-colour coded routes, are free and frequent (if overcrowded at peak times), and stop running in the early evening.

The locals, as with most locals, are courteous and pleasant if treated similarly, but like to think of some places in the resort as tourist-free sanctuaries. The overriding familial feel of the resort means that most people will feel comfortable, if not inspired by the town's atmosphere. Although it has some interesting slopes, more advanced skiers would appreciate the day trip to glitzy St. Moritz with its wider range of slopes. This fact, coupled with the lack of an open-all-hours party atmosphere (and therefore no abundance of flexible working hours) means that the typical ski bum is thin on the ground.

THE SKIING

At an altitude of 1800m (highest point near 3000m) and with snow machines maintaining the lower slopes, Livigno is considered a guaranteed snow resort. The season can last from November to May with 32 lifts hoicking 40,000 people up the slopes every hour. Livigno competes well with other affordable resorts for its variety of skiing. Most of the 115km of it appeals to beginners and intermediates who can choose from three main areas, allowing the sun to be located all day long. You can ski around 2,500m most of the time, and the snow machines of Mottolino and Costaccia offset the lack of a nearby glacier. The three main areas of Costaccia, Mottolino and Carosello have a greater accessibility due to the recent addition of a gondola, plus attached chairs running from Teola up the Mottolino ridge. As well as northwest facing runs back towards Livigno from Nonte della Neva, there are north-east facing pistes and lifts on the other side of the ridge, above Trepalle, on the road to Bormio. On the other side of the valley, close to town, chairs in the middle of a row of nursery slopes take you up to Costaccia (2340m), where a long high-speed quad chair-lift now goes along the ridge towards the Carosello sector. The linking run beyond this lift to mid-station of the Carosello gondola and (more especially) the linking run back from Carosello, are not runs you would ski for pleasure in the wind. Carosello skiing is usually reached by the Carosello 3000 gondola at San Rocco, which reaches a height of 2750. Most of the runs travel back towards the valley, but there are a couple of runs on the back of the mountain, on the west-facing slopes of Bal Federia. The 110km of piste tend to be wide open with little vegetation but are seldom more than *gentile* in their challenge to the skier. Gentle slopes around the lower Costaccia make Livigno very attractive for novices, though the northern nurseries can be steep, but for variety, many of the longer runs are also suitable for the beginner.

For intermediates, the challenge of a near direct fall-line is rare, so learning the techniques of off-piste skiing is, in the presence of a guide, a good option. The runs on the back of Carosello down to Federia are more challenging than most, and can develop some interesting natural moguls. Moderate skiers have a free run of the area, with the long red under the Mottolino gondola being a must-ski. For the skier who likes to be in cruise control, Passo d'Eira-Teola, Note dell Neve-Sponda drag, and Costaccia's easy skiing all provide a long cruise. For those lacking confidence, the run underneath the new Vetta chair, at the top of the Costaccia sector is very relaxed, dropping only 260m in 1.5km of skiing.

The advanced skier will find the black runs unsatisfying, and moreover, that these runs can be left open despite very poor snow on the lower slopes.

Snowboarders of all levels have access to 70km of slopes and as with skiers, could contact the Scuola Sci Livigno Invernoestate who have instructors for all levels of competence.

Alternatives to skiing include a 50-minute skiddoo run, horse riding along the river and paragliding.

APRÈS SKI

There is a profusion of bars and restaurants to choose from in Livigno, and a few discos to move on to for a good evening's conclusion. People expecting a blatant and exuberant night life will be disappointed however, as some of the town's atmosphere is eroded by the disparate nature of the popular spots. However, the tour companies all organise party nights, which will introduce you to the main pubs and clubs in which Brits often congregate. There are several decent early evening video bars, many of which also run novelty evenings, like Galli's fun pub, Marco's bar, or Foxi's Cellar, which are a good precursor to the disco's, which have extremes represented by the predominantly Italian, Art is stylish and expensive and the cheap and cheerful 'Kokodi's', a particular favourite of Livigno's British working community. The reps and guides tend to let their hair down in a limited number of places, so it is worth trying these establishments in order to get connected. The slopes are well serviced by mountain restaurants, where self-service is often worth considering. The Tea del Medal, at the bottom of Mottolino is a popular choice but can get crowded at tea-time. While in Livigno, be sure to try the local specialities which include the sturdy pasta/potatoes dish called Pizzocheri, the Bombardino (Advocaat with whisky or brandy, topped with cream) and the red Valtellina wine.

ACCOMMODATION

Livigno's accommodation comprises mainly hotels and apartments. Many of the apartments are owned by Fausto Galli so it is worth going to his Fun pub (he also owns the restaurant Il Cenacolo below Hotel Galli) in order to check out availability, or to see if there are any opportunities to house-sit. The tourist office (☎+39 342 996881) is always a good stand-by for accommodation. Likewise, the tour operators have affordable accommodation, but make sure the frequent description 'convenient for the lifts' means the lifts you are interested in. New skiers should avoid the Carosello end of town, because your ski school may be a bus ride to San Antonio. The type of hotels range from the large and expensive Itermonti, complete with indoor swimming facilities, through the typical Steinbock which is well-placed for nursery but not the major runs, to the basic but handy Silvestri.

WORK

To get work in Livigno, as in other resorts you have to be adaptable and flexible and if this means longer hours and less skiing than you want, so be it. There may be scope for opportunists with tour operators: Livigno is patronised by Airtours, First Choice, Inghams, Panorama and the Ski Club of GB. Italian is a must – imagine a transfer rep trying to deal with an Italian coach driver and 30 delayed passengers. Most of the jobs are of course arranged in advance. Adam, a ski guide/chalet hand with Crystal said his work meant 'a lot of early starts and the occasional 10-hour transfer, but you can make time for skiing and the perks help the wallet'. As with the rest of the chalet staff, Adam earned £60 a week plus occasional tips from satisfied guests. A resort rep is not necessarily better paid but can expect £100+ in tips. George, a resort rep, was on this kind of package. He commented 'it certainly helps if you enjoy meeting new people not only for the job but also for the social life – all the tour company people know each other and do pretty similar things.'

Those seeking work on spec will find it hard going, as the commercial structure from tertiary services to providing wood for more building, is dominated by one family. Fausto Galli is the man in charge, and he employs an Englishman, John Carter, to manage all of Livigno's watering and recreational places. John Carter himself started as a waiter and progressed from there to general management. He says Livigno is a closed shop as far as entrepreneurial activity is concerned, apart from the most imaginative and discreet. Every activity that the tour companies offer is related to the Galli network from après ski entertainments (ice-skating, night-time descent of a floodlit piste, horse riding, cinema etc) to taking photos on the slopes. The people who run these activities for Fausto Galli tend to come back several years consecutively, so you have to bide your time. If however, you can show the kind of qualities that can drum up business for a themed night in one of the Galli pubs, you will probably be able to find work handing out the tickets and accosting people during the day. There will also be occasional vacancies for experienced bar and waiting staff but the hours will be considerably more restricting than working for a tour operator as the atmosphere is very work-oriented. Perks of working for the Galli empire include full board accommodation and free taxi rides (in Galli taxis) so you can expect to leave Livigno at the end of the season with a reasonable sum of money in your pocket. John Carter said he was always looking for DJs to run karaoke theme nights as well as the other usual DJ activities. However, such people must be prepared to spend their daylight hours drumming up business for the fun and games in the evening. The organisational hub of these activities is Galli's Fun pub.

While in Livigno, it is also worth trying the bars mentioned in the apres ski section for contacts but it would be wise to pre-arrange this kind of work. You can contact John Carter/Fausto Galli c/o Dani Smith (fax: +39 0342 996922). You can also write to Fausto Galli (Hotel Galli sport, Via Fontana 58, Livigno 23030 (S0), Italy. or check out *Loot* magazine for job adverts.

Sauze d'Oulx

The village of Sauze d'Oulx lies at about 5000 feet (1,650 metres) above the Susa Valley in the Piemonte region 80 km/50 miles to the west of Turin. The French border and the Frejus Tunnel are nearby, about ten miles further to the west. A bus connects the modern, purpose-built resort of Sauze d'Oulx with the attractive old town of Oulx a short way down the mountain, and from Oulx there is a train connection to Turin, which takes approximately 90 minutes. After Courmayeur, Sauze is the most popular destination for British skiers.

Although it has been dubbed 'Benidorm on snow' on account of its popularity with a young, British clientele of the lager lout on skis variety, Sauze is no longer as cheap and slightly less yobbish than it used to be.

In the village there is an ice rink, a covered tennis court, several excellent shops and a market held weekly on Fridays.

THE SKIING

The Sauze ski area offers 40 km of piste and 28 lifts and is excellent for first time and intermediate skiers. Sauze is linked by lift to the neighbouring resort of Sestriere (combined pistes 120 km), and if that still doesn't give you enough skiing, Sauze is the gateway to the vast Via Lattea (Milky Way) lift system (92 lifts) via Sansicario. The Milky Way ski circus (400 km of piste) also includes the resorts of Sestrières and Clavière and extends to Montgenèvre in France. A series of drag lifts all within easy walking distance in the main town access the main ski areas of Sportinia, Clotes and Genevris where there are plenty of easy runs for beginners. Intermediates have a vast amount of choice: Triplex (2507m) and the even higher Rocce Nere (2424m) have a varied selection of red runs.

APRÈS SKI

The nightlife in Sauze has something of a reputation for being one of the most lively in the Alps. There are numerous bars and restaurants and one of the most attractive aspects of Sauze is the variety of charming and inexpensive restaurant/bars found up on the slopes tucked in amongst the woods. Paddy McGinty's bar is a good place to meet resort staff. There are also discos including the ever-popular Schuss and the Bandito.

WORK

Sauze is reportedly a good place to find work during the winter season. Jane Ingles from Leytonstone worked two seasons in Sauze in the very friendly Scacco Matto bar. Her first season was spent as a chambermaid, and the time between seasons she spent temping back in the UK Having improved her Italian she intended to stay in Italy at the end of this season and had a job lined up as a representative for Eurocamp (a camping and mobile home holiday company) in southern Italy. She enjoyed her job at the Scacco, which involved general bar work in the evenings, and cooking English breakfasts in the mornings. Italian hotels only give you bread and coffee for breakfast so when the bar's owners caught a whiff of freshly sizzling bacon and eggs they knew they had a winner. Jane's afternoons were free for skiing. She originally found the job by going from bar to bar and asking. Since just about every bar in the village employs an English-speaker during the season, it is easy to find work in this way provided you turn up early enough. The season commences round the beginning of December and lasts until about mid-April.

Apart from bar work, the most plentiful jobs are for chamber staff and dishwashers in hotels and restaurants. Terms of employment for these sorts of jobs including bar work seem to be negotiable but in general one can expect to earn between £300 and £600 per month plus some meals.

'Freddie' (Amanda Griffiths) turned up in Sauze on 6 November with five other British friends and speaking no Italian but determined to find work to finance a season's skiing there. They chose Sauze because they knew from the tourist 'brochures' that it was popular with British skiers and they reasoned correctly that there would be a demand for English-speakers although they wanted to work for Italians rather than British tour companies.

Since they arrived with almost no money, it was fortunate for Freddie that her expectations of a job were soon realised. After knocking on a few doors she quickly got work in a shoe shop where they found it useful to have someone who spoke English. It was a good job and paid about £100 a week but the drawback was that it left little time for skiing.

Soon Freddie and her friend Julian found a replacement job in a mountain restaurant the Pian della Rocca which turned out to be ideal. Their hours were usually 9 am to 11 am and midday to 3 pm, when everything was a mad rush as skiers stopped for their midday meal, then again for an hour or two after 5 pm serving mulled wine and other drinks before the skiers returned to their hotels. The rest of the day was free for skiing and as the restaurant was right by the lifts there was no time wasted.

Because of their locality, mountain restaurants have certain peculiarities not suffered by other catering establishments. This becomes painfully clear when you have spent a morning trying to clear out loos, which have frozen solid overnight and are no longer able to disgorge their contents into the neighbouring ravine. Luckily for Freddie it was Julian who got the bar and general maintenance job, not her.

Sometimes she would stay the night in the restaurant, at other times she would descend to the village in the evening armed with an enormous shopping list and spend the night in the flat they had all rented for the season. Next morning she would bring groceries up on the chairlift and ski precariously from one lift to the other weighed down with pasta and tomatoes. Electric sleigh-bobs were used to cart away the rubbish and sometimes provisions were brought up by dog-sleigh.

All in all it was a wonderful experience and I stayed until May 1st. The family who owned the restaurant were the nicest people who really seemed to appreciate any catering experience. I shall never forget the beauty of the early morning before the lifts were officially open and seeing the wild deer wandering across the piste as I skied past laden with provisions.

Tom Whitehead from Salisbury worked as a ski technician at Eydallin Sports, an equipment and hire shop opposite the nursery slope in the village. A fair number of the resort's ski technicians were from English-speaking countries because, as in the bars, a large proportion of the clientele is British. A ski-tech deals with repair, maintenance, fitting, sale and hire of ski equipment. As you might expect, this comparatively interesting work requires experience and qualifications. Before coming to Sauze, Tom had trained in London as a ski mechanic and had also trained as a dry ski slope instructor. He wanted the opportunity of doing more skiing, so he answered an advertisement for the ski technician's job in *Ski and Board* (the official magazine of the Ski Club of Great Britain). He was called for an interview, which took place in London, and was hired.

However, when we met Tom he was rather unhappy since the job had not turned out entirely as expected. Originally he was hired to work a six-day week from 8 am to 12.30 pm in the morning and 4 pm to 7.30 pm. Thus, he should have been free to ski for about four hours a day either in the morning or afternoon. But the second ski-tech, who should have been working at the shop had left, and Tom was now expected to work virtually all day with no time to ski. Tom felt that the more menial jobs were subject to less hassle since not so much was expected of you. Tom's basic wage was about £500 per month but he did have the opportunity to earn commission from sales of equipment. He had to find his own accommodation and food.

Getting work as an instructor is always difficult. Roger Goodfellow, an Arbroath farmer in the offseason, had qualified as an instructor in Scotland before coming to Sauze regularly for several years. He considered becoming a 'face' to be the most important factor in his gaining acceptance as an instructor at one of Sauze's ski schools, which include Scuola Italiana Ski Sauze Sportinia (+39 0122-850218) located at Via Clotes, and Scuola Ski Sauze d'Oulx (+39 0122-858084) in via Monfol. The rate of pay for a ski instructor depends on the hours worked. If the demand for individual tuition is low, and you are not assigned to take one of the group classes, there may be no wages at all. Roger found he averaged three/four hours instructing a day, and supplemented his income by working as a ski-tech from 3.30 pm to 7.30 pm in the evenings at Lo Sportivo, a large equipment and hire shop situated in Sauze's main square.

Perhaps the surest way of making certain that you get plenty of skiing, and a job lined up in advance, is to become the ski guide/representative for one of the tour operators such as Thomson or Airtours. A ski guide's role is to introduce clients to the various ski runs of the resort, and also the neighbouring resort of Sestrières or even as far along the Milky Way as Montgenèvre. It is a gruelling outing skiing to France and back in one day, but many people enjoy the challenge, and the guide is responsible for leading the party.

Chris was one of the Thomson reps/ski guides in Sauze and he was finding it very enjoyable. He pointed out that it is not necessary to ski in order to become a rep, but you do need to speak the local language. Thomson reps are selected after attending two interviews. The first is a group interview, which is usually held at one of a number of regional centres in the UK. The second is an individual interview held in London. Chris told me that he thought a good personality was the most important factor in getting through the selection procedure i.e. you need to get along well with other people and be fairly outgoing (love that fondue!). Having succeeded at the interviews the new rep is given a week of training and can look forward to a basic wage of £350 a month with accommodation and food provided.

Few local employers in Sauze d'Oulx provide accommodation, so most seasonal workers share rented apartments. A one-bedroomed apartment costs £1,500-£1,750 for the season. But it is possible to share one of these between three or four people. For example, Tom the ski-tech was spending £120 a month on accommodation, or roughly one quarter of his income.

Officially, a permit to stay *(permesso di soggiorno)* is needed to work in Italy, but the procedure is to get the job first and the permit afterwards. So it is not really a problem. Having obtained a letter from your employer stating that he/she is employing you, you take it to be endorsed by the *brigadero* (i.e. the chief at the local police station or *carabinieri*. This letter together with your passport is then submitted to the *ufficio stranieri* (foreign workers office) at the *questura* (police station), which is affiliated to the *carabinieri* in Turin. The permit has to be collected in person, your employer has to pay tax on your behalf, hence there are many delays and several people are usually working illegally. Play it by ear though and bear in mind that police swoops for illegal foreign workers are more common in the mountain resorts than elsewhere in Italy.

Besides the various jobs available with UK tour companies; apart from those already mentioned Crystal, Equity, The Ski Club of GB, Inghams, Neilson and Panorama have operations there. Generally, there appears to be a wealth of opportunities for casual work in Sauze. Amanda Griffiths found the Italians overwhelmingly friendly and came home with a few hundred pounds in her pocket, new skis, boots, a wicked sun tan and a good working knowledge of Italian which helped her land a job as a chalet girl in Selva for the following season.

Norway

Generally speaking, non-Scandinavian, would-be skiers do not head to Norway during the winter months. The resorts, which in any case bear little resemblance to the crowded, tourist-oriented villages of the Alps, are almost exclusively populated by Norwegians, Swedes and Danes. An English phrase may occasionally be heard, but it is more likely to be spoken by a Norwegian to a Dane than by one Brit to another. Such parochialism was briefly shattered, in Lillehammer at least, when the Winter Olympics were held there in 1994 leaving a legacy of a greatly expanded ski village and facilities. The Men's Downhill course at Kvitfjell, 19 miles from Lillehammer was specially built for the Games. The rest of the Games took place at Hafjell, which takes 20 minutes to reach by ski bus from Lillehammer.

Norway has several undeniable advantages, not the least of which is this very lack of popularity with other Europeans, but it is expensive, it is comparatively uncommercialised and its scenery remains spectacularly unspoiled. It boasts an unprecedented area of ski slope per skier, as well as a complete network of cross-country trails (over 500 km of it), and though access to the hotels is often up twisting, ice-covered roads, the journey's end is well worth the effort – the first sight of jagged sunlit peaks against the brilliant Easter sky is unforgettable. Originally best known for cross-country (i.e. Nordic) skiing, one of the best centres for it is at Oyer, about 15 miles from Lillehammer, Norwegian resorts for downhill skiing are of recent construction with state of the art lift systems and a great quality and quantity of pistes.

Although Lillehammer is the one Norwegian resort that many skiers have heard of, it is neither the biggest, nor in the estimate of experts, the best. The others are Oppdal, the most northerly resort (which therefore has the shortest day) and which is about two hours drive south of Trondheim. Oppdal has over twice as much prepared piste as Lillehammer as has Trysil three hours from Oslo. Geilo, about half-way between Oslo and Bergen, has 25 km of runs, but they are for the most part short ones. Voss, about one hour from Bergen is one of the smallest resorts. Hemsedal, an hour's drive from Geilo, between Oslo and Bergen is reckoned by officianados to be the best Norwegian resort with 16 lifts and 45km of pistes and, thanks to its latitude, a better snow record than the lower Alpine resorts. There are also 130km of marked cross-country trails.

Since there are so few British-based tour companies which arrange downhill skiing in Norway (a few arrange cross-country adventures) the only chances for the potential worker are either to fix a job up by correspondence, or to go there on spec and hope to get lucky. To fix work in advance, your best plan would be to get a list of the tourist offices in Norway's ski resorts from the Norwegian National Tourist Office in London and then write to them asking for a list of hotels, ski hire shops etc. Those prepared to chance their luck and go looking stand a reasonable chance of success. Two things work strongly in their favour: firstly the natural hospitality and desire to help of the Norwegians, secondly a rarity value; few English-speakers go round knocking on doors looking for work.

Although Norway declined to join the European Union, it is a member of the European Economic Area, which includes the countries of the European Union and so work permit regulations relating to those coming from EU countries are now similar to those of the European Union. This means that any EU national can enter Norway to look for work and if successful can apply for a residence permit (*oppholdstillatelse*). For non-EU citizens there are stringent work permit regulations which mean that, strictly speaking, aliens are not allowed to enter the country to look for work and both job and work permit must be fixed up before you arrive, so any employment you do find is likely to be of a part-time and unofficial nature. Reports indicate there are an increasing number of hotels, shops etc. who are happy to provide board and accommodation, or perhaps a small wage in return for part-time work. They do not however, advertise this and often the best approach may be through another member of the staff. You will be at a great advantage if you speak some Norwegian, but a high proportion of Norwegians speak excellent English.

Travelling from the UK to Oslo by ferry, rather than flying, gives potential job seekers the opportunity to supplement funds by a little judicious trading in duty free cigarettes or cognac, both of which cost a small fortune in Norway. The journey also gives you the chance to tout for possible job opportunities. Neil Tallantire reports:

> *With a modicum of charm, ingenuity and luck you should get some job offers. I was offered work on a pig farm for pocket money plus board and accommodation, or alternatively a job teaching English to a couple's children. Both jobs were in resort areas and left plenty of time free for skiing!*

Other possibilities likely to yield fruit revolve around individual resourcefulness: there are plenty of odd jobs like snow clearing while DJing is a definite possibility as Britons are thought to know their way around the music scene and there is always au pairing.

Another possibility open to all nationalities is to try to get a job through Atlantis (Kirkegata 32, 0153 Oslo; tel/fax 22 47 7179; post@atlantis.no; www.atlantis.no), the Norwegian foundation for Youth Exchange, which generally means 18-30 year-olds working in a rural part of Norway for two to six months (three months if you are non-EU). You can request a certain area as the scheme covers placements in family-run tourist accommodation (for European nationals). The scheme's organiser's try to take into account applicants' preferences on the matter so you can ask for work in a ski resort.

Gausdal

The tiny village of Gausdal lies approximately 130 miles north of Oslo in the same region as Lillehammer. Gausdal scarcely merits the title 'village', consisting as it does of two large, luxurious and attractive hotels, a trailer camp and a general store tucked at the foot of the mountain, with summer cabins scattered sparingly over the lower slopes.

THE SKIING

Despite its lack of size, or perhaps because of it, the skiing facilities are, quite simply, superb. The season begins at Christmas and lasts until Easter. One of the hotels has a small ski lift practically on its doorstep, while further away there's a larger T-bar; both of these extend halfway up the mountain to a small (but exceedingly expensive) café, from which another lift reaches the summit. Excepting the most popular times, queues are short or non-existent – though at Easter watch out for the Norwegian children, who have some very strange ideas about queuing!

The area also offers a variety of cross-country trails: in a country where skiing is a way of life these are well-used by Norwegian families in particular, and in peak times there are many races, fancy-dress competitions and other events laid on specifically for the cross country addicts. However, the alpine skiers are certainly not neglected, with frequent slalom competitions in which almost every entrant is guaranteed to win a prize.

Because of the nature of Gausdal, après ski activity tends to be based around the two hotels, and is rather low key. The general trend seems to be early to bed, early to rise – after all the vast majority is there for the skiing, and rightly so.

WORK

A work permit is a necessity. It used to be the case that you could arrive looking for work, and once you had secured a job there was no problem in obtaining a permit. However reports indicate that from about 1990, the Norwegian authorities' concern about unemployment (a mere 3.7% in April 2006) prompted a strict enforcement of the law about obtaining the permit in advance of your arrival. However, in practice, since many Norwegians don't want to do the kind of casual jobs that foreigners are willing to do, there is still plenty of demand for workers in ski resorts. The only job a foreigner is not likely to find is that of ski instructor; in a country where practically everyone can ski there is simply no demand for foreign instructors. The only possibilities in Gausdal would be the shop and the Hotel Skeikampen. The other hotel, the Gausdal Hoifijellshotel, which has been run by the same family for several decades is unlikely to employ English-speakers. The Skeikampen hotel usually employs Norwegians and Swedes but also considers British students (providing they have the necessary qualifications) and would provide accommodation for them. Fluency in Norwegian is not necessary unless a job in reception is required, but obviously any experience in waiter/waitressing or chambermaiding would be a valuable asset when applying for these jobs. Employees work a 6½-hour day, but this would leave plenty of time for skiing, especially for those working in the dining room, who work till 1.30 pm one day, and don't start until 2 pm on the following day.

The shop in the trailer camp is run by a husband and wife together with two full-time assistants and an assortment of students and local schoolchildren as temporary help over the winter. A working knowledge of Norwegian would be an absolute necessity here, but even then the proprietor would give preference to Norwegians. However, don't be deterred from trying other larger resorts, such as Voss and Hemsedal, where the job opportunities are considerably better. After the noisy, school-party crowded slopes of France and Italy, the majesty and serenity of Norway come as a breath of fresh air.

Lillehammer

Lillehammer on the banks of the scenic lake Mjosa, is situated in the heart of southern Norway, though 'southern' here is well north of John O'Groats, at the entrance to the mountainous Gudbrandsdalen region. It has an international reputation as a winter resort, and was a serious contender for hosting the 1992 Winter Olympics; it got the honour for 1994 instead. As a result there was a spate of construction including new runs, lifts, hotels and a railway/bus station. Even though it is, in Norwegian terms, a major tourist centre, the main source of income remains industry. Despite being of fairly recent origin, founded in 1827, the main street, Storgahen has been successfully conserved and in places restored to give an impression of typical small-town Norway. The natives are never unfriendly, and most, if not all speak exellent English, putting the typical tourist as usual, to shame.

Sporting facilities are impressive. The town has an excellent swimming pool and two ice rinks, plus sledging, curling and the ubiquitous sleighriding and everything else to be expected of a major winter resort. There is also the Spiker, a cross between sledge and bobsleigh, steered standing up, and great fun, and the skiing facilities are superb, Lillehammer being the centre of a whole web of runs and tracks. Slalom is the old Norwegian word for downhill skiing and enthusiasts will find runs with varying degrees of difficulty from simple nursery slopes to those of international standard. Recently some demanding new downhill runs have been opened up.

If you come to Norway, however, you should try cross-country skiing which is where Norway can be seen at its very best. Lillehammer offers more than 400km of skiing tracks, some floodlit, and all well tended. All the tracks are route colour-coded.

Lillehammer is no St. Moritz, but there are several lively discos and the hotels arrange frequent live bands. Nonetheless, the Norwegians are an outdoor race and excessive drinking seems to be frowned upon – liquor purchase is heavily controlled and prices are exorbitant with the consequently high proportion of moonshine distillers. A measure of spirits in a hotel will cost you more than £6, a small beer £4 and a bottle of indifferent plonk £17! If you need a glittering nightlife, avoid Norway; there are no crowds of beautiful people here, but if you want to ski and have a good time, you will find yourself welcomed with open arms and come back feeling Norway was the best thing to ever happen to you.

ACCOMMODATION

When you arrive either at the bus garage or station which are next door to each other, you will need somewhere to stay unless your're fortunate enough to have hospitable friends. Your best bet will be the Youth Hostel (☎06 25 09 87), about 1km easy walk and right next door to the ski centre. Here however, you will discover, if you didn't do so at the Oslo station coffee bar, that the stories of the high cost of living, are no exaggeration. The Youth Hostel, far and away the cheapest place to stay is still expensive by the standards of other European countries at about 100 kroner for a dorm bed. Failing that you could try the Bellevue Sportell, whose proprietor has a reputation for helping young job seekers. Whether or not you actually stay here it should certainly be one of your ports of call. After the youth hostel, the cheapest bed in a Lillehammer hotel would probably cost about 400 kroner (£40 approximately) per night without breakfast. If you are very lucky, look respectable, and at the same time sufficiently downcast, then you may be offered a bed in a private house for the Norwegians are a generous race. Of the guest-houses and hotels Gjestehuset Ersgaard is probably the cheapest followed by the Dolaheim. The ladies in the Tourist Information Centre know of locals who are willing to put people up at rates somewhere between the hostel and a hotel. It is also possible to rent a flat, but this will normally only make financial sense if you are one of a group.

WORK

If you choose to come job hunting on spec in Norway, you must realise that it is no easy task, not least because of the the the endless expense. You'll need determination and an ability to survive on a shoestring. First do the rounds of the hotels, starting with the Lillehammer, the Bellevue and the Rica Victoria; there are more than a dozen hotels in central Lillehammer, plus more at Susjoen, Nordseter and Tretten, many totally ski-oriented and all willing to employ foreign workers who appear at the right time in any capacity from chambermaid to bartender. Of the central hotels, only the Oppland Twinthotel and the Lillehammer and Rica Victoria Hotels have bars. The hotels at Nordseter, and particularly the Hoifijellshotel all seem helpful and keen to offer or suggest something. If you are big and burly, you can offer yourself as a bouncer at one of the discos on the high street.

You might well be sensible to throw yourself on people's mercy if your pride will stand it to at least ensure accommodation. Your best prospect for these 'jobs for keep' will be the small shops on the high street and also the garages, which are often on the look out for people to serve at the pumps. The restaurants and cafeterias are also a good bet, particularly 61 Café, Din Café and El Gaucho; the mountain restaurants will supply accommodation as well as wages. There are several sports shops, which would probably employ foreigners including Breidergarden Sports, Hakon Brusveen Sports, Intersport and Rustachtuen, plus clothes shops, which may be willing. Moreover, with the predominance of British music Rilla Plalebar, the local record shop, might well be willing to employ a foreign worker in some capacity. If you have a lifesaving qualification, try the swimming pool, or the stables up at Sasjoen if you know about horses.

Check the noticeboards for adverts – take a dictionary with you! Possibly you could place one yourself, either on a board or in one of the two local papers. Talk to both the Tourist Information Centre next to the Gudbranchdal Sparebank and to the local job centre, which is nearby on the corner of Jernbot and Stortorget.

Your task will be easiest if you are qualified as a ski instructor. All the ski schools employ English and American instructors. Susjoen alone employed six last season. Again there are openings for foreign language speakers as lift operators, and ski guides cum track tenders. On the whole you will find employers will bend over backwards to help despite language problems and permit restrictions. Foreign workers are unusual enough to be something of a novelty.

Lucy worked as a waitress in Nordseter. She had skied extensively in the Alps and had worked a season in Val d'Isère, before getting fed up with the crowds and heading north. She had not regretted it, indeed was so taken that she overstayed and thus needed work. Having studied German and French she said the language wasn't hard and quite similar to German. She only earned about £30 per week plus tips but had two full days off to ski and got full board and lodging. Since Nordseter was bang on the tracks it was easy to make full use of the time. Lucy found the job by getting friendly with one of the other waitresses and getting her to put her name forward, since the hotel had been scared when she approached them direct.

John worked at the Neverfjell Turisthotel. Again short on cash he had just asked around and been overwhelmed at the help he got. The hotel did not pay him but supplied full board and in return he spent every morning clearing the carpark, carrying garbage etc.

Rosalie Green had spent a season working at Val d'Isère and chose Norway for the simple reason that she had always wanted to go there. She had gained experience as a waitress in Val, and within a couple of days of her arrival she was told by someone else staying at her hotel, of a hotel as Susjoen that might employ her. She said:

The work's hard but fun and there is a constant turnover of guests. I get accommodation and all meals, plus about £80 per week, and have four afternoons off a week, for skiing. I was just lucky and turned up at the right time.

David Moor was simply intending to spend a month on holiday. However he saw an advert in a local supermarket for a native English teacher to teach for a month and he jumped at the chance. It was a first visit to Norway to ski.

A teacher put me up and fed me. I'd intended to stay in the hostel or a cheap hotel, but was finding Norway expensive. I was just working for keep, but only teaching three days a week, so I had lots of spare-time, I had a fantastic time, much better than a normal holiday.

Michael Hunting made a fine living going round clearing paths and roofs of the copious quantities of snow they collect. He commented:

I was stuck for a job and badly in need of money, when I saw two guys clearing a roof and thought it was something I might do. I just started knocking on doors. It was easy – nearly all Norwegians speak good English and they paid well. Thirty minutes work gets about £7. So I easily covered all costs for food and accommodation.

There is a considerable demand for British disc jockeys since they are thought to know their way around the music scene; most of the discos in Lillehammer have English-speaking DJs and it would certainly be worth trying your luck at Marcellos or Amadeus, though most of the jobs are for the full season and fixed up well in advance.

Jonathan Lewis worked as a DJ at the Rica Victoria. He got his job through a job agency in the UK and worked six-month stints. Obviously he was supplying all his own records. The money was excellent although mitigated by the high Norwegian prices, and included full board at the hotel. He was enjoying the work very much and it was his first experience of Norwegian work. He did comment that he was fed up with requests for Michael Jackson and that music-wise Norway was a bit behind the UK (though not as bad as the rest of Europe). There was plenty of time off to ski since the job was very much a night one and he was an early riser.

Another DJ, Mike worked at Amadeus and echoed Jonathan's comments except that that he found his job in a music mag. Both held permits. Marcello's too employed an English-speaking DJ, an American who turned up on spec and got the job.

Scotland

The topography and climate of Britain dictate that a true snow skiing industry can exist only in Scotland. There are some areas in Wales and England that can offer skiing when conditions permit, but snow cannot be relied on; those companies which offer skiing on their holidays include it as just one of their package of holiday activities.

Cross-country skiing is promoted by the Youth Hostels Association in Edale in Derbyshire and in also in Wales. However both these are for the keen enthusiast: there is no organised accommodation or instruction. The YMCA's High Plains Lodge in Alston, Cumbria will organise an instructor for groups of five or more booking together for downhill skiing in the Pennines but only from January to March and in a good snow season.

There are five significant ski centres in Scotland: Aviemore (Cairngorm), Glenshee, The Lecht and the last area to be opened (in 1989) Aonach Mor (The Nevis Range). It is worth obtaining a copy of the brochure *Ski Scotland* from the Scottish Tourist Board (Bridge House, 20 Bridge Street, Inverness IV1 1QR; ☎0131-332 2433) or look on the website www.ski-scotland.com, which gives details of the facilities and vital statistics of the main areas. Aviemore overshadows the others in terms of the number of tourists it receives (even though it possesses just 16 ski lifts to Glenshee's 23), and the opportunities for work it presents. However the newer resort of Aonach Mor is also a purpose-built resort like Aviemore and thus presents good employment prospects in its range of facilities. The other skiing areas of Glenshee, the Lecht and Glencoe are traditional Highland areas and offer a less commercialised atmosphere. They may perhaps envy the substantial financial backing that has enabled Aviemore and Aonach Mor to offer resort attractions including swimming, ice skating, cinemas, year round activities and a plethora of bars and discotheques. The relative lack of tourist amenities at Glenshee, the Lecht and Glencoe not only limits their appeal for tourists but also means that there are fewer peripheral jobs available outside the hotels and ski slopes themselves.

WORK PERMITS

Nationals of EU countries can work freely in Britain. American students wishing to work in Britain may do so under the Work in Britain Program, which allows about 3,500 full-time college students over the age of 18 to look for work after arriving in Britain. They must obtain a blue card for a fee of $225, which is recognised by the British Home Office as a valid substitute for a work permit. They may arrive at any time of the year and work for up to six months. Candidates must be US citizens residing in the USA and able to prove that they have at least $600. For further information contact the Council (Council on International Educational Exchange/CIEE), 7 Custom House Street, 3rd Floor, Portland, Maine 04101;(toll-free 1-800-40-Study); 207-553-7600; fax 207-553-7699). The Work in Britain Program is the counterpart of British Universities North America Club (BUNAC) Work America Programme for British students (see chapter on North America).

Like the Australian working holiday visa available to British young people, 'working holidaymaker' status may be obtained by members of Commonwealth countries between the ages of 17 and 27 inclusive with no dependants. This entitles the holder to work in Britain with the primary intention of funding a holiday, for an initial six-month period, with the possibility of extending it up to a maximum of two continuous years. It is essential to apply in the country of origin rather than at the point of entry. You must however also be able to prove that you have enough money to support yourself and fund a return airfare; for New Zealanders, the suggested sum is £2,000.

Canadian students who want the security of a package arrangement may participate in the Student Work Abroad Programme (SWAP) which is comparable to the Work in Britain Programme. It is administered by the Canadian Universities Travel Service (CUTS) which has 30 offices in Canada. After paying the registration fee and showing that they have support funds of C$1,000, eligible students aged 18-27 are entitled to work in Britain for up to six months at any time of year. As on the American Work in Britain Programme, the facilities of BUNAC in London are available to SWAPPERs.

Aviemore

A little over 45 years ago, Aviemore was a small Speyside village with a few bed and breakfasts and one hotel. In 1961 a chairlift was built on Cairn Gorm mountain which was the beginning of commercial ski development in the area. In 1966 the ambitious Aviemore mountain resort was opened with theoretical accommodation for 2000 visitors. Other hotels, self-catering accommodation and even time-share developments gradually followed, so that Aviemore became an important and bustling resort. Some of the older locals resent the dramatic changes, which have taken place, and dislike the idea that one or two large companies control most of the tourist amenities. On the other hand, the most recent developments, led by the Macdonald Hotels consortium, which has spent an estimated 80 million pounds on creating state-of-the–art facilities and accommodation at Aviemore and the Aviemore Centre have created a great many employment prospects, which the locals are not slow to pursue.

The village of Aviemore is nine miles from the ski slopes at Cairngorm, so that those without a car must rely on a ski bus.

Aviemore is a year-round destination and most of the tourist enterprises operate on this basis. This means that the staffing arrangements are less seasonal than those of the European Alpine resorts. Unemployment is sufficiently serious throughout Scotland that year-round jobs (for example in Pizzaland next to the station) are never empty for long. May and particularly November are notably slack periods, when staff are in danger of being laid off, so these times are recommended for job hunting for the season to follow.

The skiing season officially opens around December 20th and closes in the first week of May although this is merely a working fiction. Quite often there is snow in November, thereby rescuing the Valley – as it is always referred to (including the Spey villages between approximately Grantown and Kingussie) – from a period of extreme quietness. In October 1992, freak, abundant snowfalls caused the lifts to open in October for only the second time in 30 years. For several recent winters there has been a dearth of snow throughout the season, but in March 2006 huge snowfalls ensured seven weeks of excellent skiing and boarding conditions.

There are three peak periods when there is usually a shortage of staff in most categories: Christmas/New Year, school mid-term (usually the middle two weeks in February) and then Easter. Also, weekends are invariably hectic, and most employees must take their days off during the week. The peak season is February 1st to Easter. Some seasonal staff are taken on in time to help with the Christmas rush, but many others don't begin until late January.

After the winter, those who do not want to stay on in Aviemore generally head for warmer climes. One favourite destination among Aviemore itinerants is the Channel Islands. Others go abroad, such as Kim an 18-year-old Scottish receptionist who was heading for a receptionist job in Majorca. Several of her fellow workers in the Aviemore Mountain Resort were clearly tempted to accompany her on the off chance that they too would find work in a more congenial climate.

Job seekers can try the Scottish Tourist Board for leads. The Tourist Information Centre in Aviemore (Grampian Road, Aviemore, Inverness-shire, PH22 1PP; ☎01479-810363) can be helpful as they can and send the general brochure on Aviemore and Spey Valley which lists the addresses of all the hotels etc. to which people may apply directly.

SKI BUMS

As in many ski resorts, there are a number of ski bums, groupies and hangers-on who lurk in the shadows of Aviemore ready to pounce on any jobs, which come up. The majority are looking for evening jobs which would allow them to ski, but these are in such demand that it is difficult to get one and when you do, you will be paid a very low wage. It is probably easier to pick up casual jobs before the ski season gets underway; Kim Fletcher travelled up to Aviemore from the Isle of Wight in October and had no trouble stringing together some temporary jobs in restaurants, which kept her solvent.

THE MAJOR EMPLOYERS

The big employers in Aviemore rely very heavily on speculative applications and off-the-street job seekers to fill their vacancies both before the season begins and during it. They also make use of the Inverness Jobcentre (33 High Street, Inverness; ☎01463-888200), especially before Christmas for the New Year rush. The job centre has two ways of accessing job information. You can either telephone their Job Seekers Direct local rate telephone line on 0845-6060234 and speak to an advisor or you can find all job information on the website www.jobcentreplus.gov.uk. According to the Inverness Jobcentre Aviemore does not merit a job centre of its own as vacancies there are registered with them. Any jobs which the Inverness Jobcentre thinks will be hard to fill, such as chefs, silver service waiting staff or experienced hotel receptionists, are likely to be entered on the central computer which links jobcentres throughout the country. Although there are always vacancies coming up because of the high turnover of catering staff generally, most vacancies are filled promptly.

For hotel jobs, you can also apply direct to Macdonald Aviemore Highland Resorts (Aviemore, Inverness-shire PH22 1PJ; ☎01479-810771; fax 01479-811576; e-mail hr.aviehighlands@macdonald-hotels.co.uk) for work in Aviemore hotels, also the Golf and Country Club. Jobs include live-in positions such as housekeeping, waiting and bar work and you can apply at any time of year according to the Human Resources manager.

Another method of publicising vacancies is through the columns of the local weekly paper *The Strathspey and Badenoch Herald* published every Thursday. The situations vacant column always lists a wide range of jobs mostly in catering.

Providing accommodation for staff is a serious problem facing employers, since staff cannot afford to pay the market rate for rooms. Some of the big employers have rented whole houses, which they let out to their staff at favourable rates.

According to an informal survey carried out by the staff themselves, about half the employees at the Cairngorm Mountain resort stay for more than a year. Nevertheless, turnover is high in the busy seasons and it is well worth contacting hotels in Aviemore. Applications may well be kept on file for up to three months, and are often reactivated at frantic periods. This is what happened in the case of Alyson Slane from the Scottish borders who was surprised to be phoned up weeks after she had submitted her application in the summer, about a vacancy in reception, one of the most sought after jobs.

Complaints about the levels of wages are universal. Furthermore there is almost no overtime available beyond the standard 39 hours a week, though it is not unusual for staff to get a second job working behind a bar or in a disco a few evenings a week. Live-in hotel staff are paid a lower rate than staff who live out. The availability of on-site accommodation for about 120 workers is a distinct advantage, though many find sharing a room irksome. (There are some singles, but you have to be relatively 'senior' to qualify for one). The low cost of accommodation with free meals as well means that it is possible to save money despite the low wages.

There are very few complaints about the nightlife. Most people are there to have a good time and Aviemore seems a place where that is easily possible, not just because of the abundance of bars and discos, but because it it is full of people pursuing the same ends.

People working at the Cairngorm Mountain resort can be found in all the bars at most times of day, though they tend to congregate in the early evening at Crofters Show Bar which has entertainment ranging from live bands to sumo wrestling with a happy hour from 9pm to 10.30pm.

Most people who go to Aviemore intend to do plenty of skiing. Many end up doing very little, partly due to a lack of time but mostly because of the expense. Most employees (except those working for ski hirers) have to pay for ski hire and instruction.

Staff benefits at the Cairngorm Mountain resort include a pension scheme for employees who have worked a full financial year and are over 25, free or reduced skating, swimming and cinema/disco admission.

There is an impressive range of nationalities working at the centre including, Italians, French, Spanish and Australians. The average age of workers is about 21.

Seasonal jobs are limited. Non-local staff tend to be employed on the catering side, where there is a fairly large percentage of repeats from previous seasons.

The Mountain also owns and runs the Day Lodge (at car park level, at the bottom of the chairlift) and the mountain restaurant and snack bars. They normally have plenty of applicants without needing to advertise, except in the case of chefs.

Joanna Keys from Fowey, Cornwall decided to take a year off before starting her degree at Bradford University. In the autumn she telephoned the Aviemore Information Centre (01479-810624) and asked them to advise her on finding a winter job. There is no fixed finishing date; a great deal depends on how long the snow stays. The Company owns a house in the village, which provides dormitory accommodation for about 16. There is a small weekly charge for accommodation.

BARRETTS

Barretts International Resort (☎01479-811244) has been in Aviemore for about about fifteen years. They have expanded at the north end of the village where the Dalfaber Country Club and timeshare estate are situated. The Club has various facilities including a restaurant and a range of staff is employed. Like other Aviemore employers, Barretts receives a constant trickle of speculative applications throughout the season and also makes use of the Inverness Jobcentre.

SKI HIRE

Before looking at the skilled requirements for ski instructors, ski hire outlets are potential sources of employment for the unskilled. There are of course several ski hire outlets in Aviemore with similar requirements. The task of fitting boots safely on to skis can be taught to a novice in a couple of hours. They should, perhaps, have some mechanical aptitude but they need not be skiers (though most of them are). The·seasonal staff work in ski hire rather than in the shops where permanent local staff are preferred. The ski hire shops open seven days a week and weekend work is compulsory. Working hours are 8.30 am-6 pm. The cost of rental to the customer varies. Aviemore ski hire (01479-811711) charges from £14 per day; £48 for six days.

SKI INSTRUCTION

Ski instructing is a tenuous existence at the best of times but when things in Scotland are bad they tend to be worse than in the Alps. Snow can appear and disappear in the space of a few days; unlike in the Alps where there is always snow if you go high enough.

This means that instructors would prefer to work in the European Alps if they can, since the weather, the range of skiing and nightlife are generally considered superior to anything the Cairngorms can offer. The quarterly *BASI News* magazine carries advertisements for jobs in Scotland, Europe (usually with British tour companies) Canada, the USA, New Zealand and even Chile (in the summer). The magazine is circulated among BASI members of which there are over 2000. BASI (☎01479-861717) is located in Glenmore next to Glenmore Lodge, the Scottish National Sports Centre near Loch Morlich.

Addresses of the 14 ski schools which operate in the Valley – five of which are based in Aviemore – can be obtained on a single printed sheet from the tourist office. Alternatively, they are listed in the Ski Scotland brochure available from the Scottish Tourist Board. Anyone with a BASI or other internationally recognised instructor qualification should be able to find work at one of these schools.

Ski schools are always looking for new instructors to add to their list of contacts. A school can expect to get an average of three seasons from an instructor before he or she heads away. Prospective instructors are usually invited to attend a clinic early in the season, which weeds out the talent. Ski school managers will assess your standard of skiing, and send you out with a trusted instructor who will report back on whether or not you have potential. Standards have to be kept as high as possible since competition among the ski schools is fierce, and holidaymakers are paying good money for lessons: £15 a day for a group lesson, though seven-day residential packages including equipment, lift pass and instruction start at about £265 for adults. There are special lower rates for under 17s.

In past years there has been a shortage of ski instructors at peak times and skiers who have had no BASI training have been hired. This practice is resented by the qualified instructors who worry that ski instruction is too dangerous an activity, especially in the fickle weather conditions of the Cairngorms, to entrust to novices who are unfamiliar with the Scottish mountains. One instructor, who regularly takes four months off from his job with an engineering firm in Carlisle to teach skiing in Aviemore, claims that these emergency instructors are very often 'rich kids' whose families have funded their skiing holidays in the Alps since infancy and whose independent finances mean that they are willing to work for exploitative wages. Any non-BASI skier who considers looking for work in Scotland should be aware of the possible hostility, but the fact remains that work does exist for competent skiers.

The Aviemore Ski School (tel/fax 01479-810296; glenmore@talk21.com) is the largest ski school in the area and employs up to 60 instructors at busy times in good snow years. About 20 instructors are usually employed full-time. The part-timers usually hold down other jobs, anything from acting in London to being a civil engineer in Glasgow. The manager of the ski school said they keep a list of names of possible instructors. They circularise them at the beginning of the season and ask them to nominate weekends or weeks when they might be able to come up and help out. The main attraction seems to be free accommodation as well as a chance to get out on the slopes.

In past years they have also recruited by telephoning round the dry ski slopes of the UK (most of whose managers) they know personally. You have to be more technically precise to teach on dry slopes, and it is an excellent and strenuous training for snow skiing (though some say the skills required are quite different). Many snow instructors go to one of the 90-odd dry slopes in the summer to instruct. The busy season for plastic slopes is October to January.

The standard wage for a lowest grade instructor is about £20 per day although this varies from school to school. One instructor commented:

I am virtually funding myself to be up here instructing. I certainly don't do it for the money, but because I love it. Some of the younger ski instructors get bored teaching beginners but I get a real sense of accomplishment teaching a complete beginner to ski down the mountain by the end of the week.

Hours are shorter than in mainland Europe, but this is for a good reason. In the dead of winter, daylight may last no longer than 10 am to 3 pm. A visiting instructor from Andorra (where instructors normally work an eight-hour day) once hinted that he thought Scottish instructors have it easy. But in adverse weather (which is much of the time) four hours is as much as anyone can stand.

Most full-time instructors don't seem to have too much trouble surviving through the summers. As mentioned already, some are employed on the plastic slopes. Many also teach sailing, windsurfing and other summer activities either locally (on Loch Morlich) or elsewhere. One instructor who originally came from the Isle of Wight, worked regularly in Aviemore in winter. She qualified in America as a Ski Instructor for the disabled (the only country so far to offer such a qualification) and plans to promote the service in Britain. In good years, many schools are prepared to employ one or two foreign instructors. In order for a school to be willing to support an application for a work permit (if needed), the applicant would have to have an impeccable record and have a strong recommendation from a recognised ski school. Application procedures for work permits should begin in August/September in order to be completed for the beginning of the season.

By the same token, if an 'old hand' from Aviemore wants to work a season abroad, he asks his manager for advice and for a good reference. There are also occasional exchange visits between European alpine resorts, which provide a good opportunity to gain contacts.

OTHER VILLAGES BY CAIRNGORM

In addition to Aviemore, the villages in the Spey Valley include Newtonmore, Kingussie, Kincraig, Boat of Garten, Carrbridge, Nethy Bridge and Grantown-on-Spey, all of which have a number of hotels, restaurants, ski rental shops etc. Grantown has the highest concentration of tourist facilities including golf clubs, watersports centres etc. inlcuding the Ben Mhor Hotel and the Coppice hotel which have 24 and 26 bedrooms respectively and the Grant Arms Hotel (62 bedrooms). A full list of hotels and guest houses can be found in the *Ski Scotland* brochure (see above).If you are looking for somewhere to stay while you look for work there are numerous bed and breakfasts (listed in the same brochure), many of them for around £16 per night.

The Scottish Youth Hostel Association offers ski instruction from the the Scottish Sports Council run Glenmore Lodge Youth Hostel (01479-861256).

Barretts have a time-share development in Carrbridge called Lochanully Woodlands Cottages (☎01479-841234). The resort manager says that most of their staff are locals but they occasionally have one or two jobs for live-in catering staff. The positions tend to be long-term, rather than seasonal.

Nevis Range (Aonach Mor)

Nevis range is the newest of Scotland's ski areas and is built on Aonach Mor, the mountain next to Ben Nevis. The car park and base station are seven miles from the centre of Fort William, which is where you find the accommodation and ancillary tourist services.

A six-seater Gondola (which runs for 11 months of the year) provides access from the car park at 300 ft to the bottom of the skiing at 2150 ft and this is also where the main Snowgoose restaurant, bar, shop and ski school meeting place are situated. Ski hire, crèche, ticket offices and main offices are all at car park level. In addition to the Gondola there are 11 ski lifts giving access to all standards of skiing to a height of 3950 ft). The most recent developments include an extension of the lift system into a second corrie (mountain bowl) giving access to many more red and black runs and some of the more spectacular skiing in Scotland.

There is a permanent staff of approximately 55, but this increases to about 100 in winter. The season usually starts around Christmas/New Year and finishes early May, but employment tails off after Easter. Additional winter staff include three ticket office/general office staff; catering staff for the base station café, the Snowgoose restaurant and bar and the mountain snack huts; 20 ski and/or snowboard instructors (BASI or equivalent qualified); five ski patrollers (BASP or equivalent qualified); a crèche supervisor, six ski hire staff and 12 lift operators. Some staff return year after year, so not all these posts are available every season. Many, but by no means all jobs go to locals. Seasonal staff have to find their own accommodation in or near Fort William.

Application forms are available from Nevis Range Development Company, Torlundy, Fort William, PH33 6SW; ☎01397-705825; fax 01397-705854; nevisrange@sol.co.uk; www.nevis-range.co.uk. Applicants should state which job(s) they are interested in.

Other jobs may be found in the hotels, bars, shops and ski hire outlets in and around Fort William.

Glencoe, Glenshee, The Lecht

These areas differ from Aviemore in that they do not offer such a concentration of hotels around the ski slopes. For example, hotels offering skiing packages on the Glenshee slopes are scattered around the villages of Ballater, Blairgowrie, Braemar, Bridge of Cally, Glenisla, Kirkmichael, and Spittal of Glenshee, which are up to 26 miles from the slopes themselves. Skiing is only part of Glenshee's year-round tourist programme that includes in summer: pony-trekking, sailing, shooting, golf, hang gliding, fishing and hill-walking.

Further discouragement for the job seeker lies in the fact that all these areas have a high local rate of unemployment, and so there is no shortage of local unskilled labour to work on the chairlifts and in hotels and restaurants. Few hotels ever need to use their local employment centre. Apart from tourism, the main local industries are farming, which employs few people, and the distilleries, which employ mainly locals.

A centre such as Aviemore which depends solely on tourism finds it necessary to attract casual labour from outside to help them cope with their busiest times of year: Glenshee, Glencoe and the Lecht also need to do so; there are up to 80 seasonal employees in Glenshee, ten to 15 in the Glencoe and a handful in the Lecht.

However, because there is no particular tradition of skiing in these areas skilled instructors have to be imported. One ski school proprietor said with exasperation that local schools seemed keener to organise skiing holidays abroad for their pupils than to send them to the local slopes. Admittedly, most instructors tend to be Scots, but there is no particular discrimination involved. It is simply that Scots have more opportunities to ski (for example, the Lecht is only 50 miles from Aberdeen), and are therefore more likely to have reached a high standard of skiing, and to have made themselves known to ski school proprietors. The nature of the tourist industry is also a factor: these slopes are at their most busy over weekends and snow is an unpredictable commodity, so extra staff must be prepared to come at short notice for short bursts. This kind of arrangement is therefore suited to staff who are comparatively local.

GLENCOE SKI CENTRE

Glencoe was Scotland's first ski centre; there was a ski tow there in 1955. It used to be essentially a weekend resort. However, the ever-growing popularity of skiing and a recent partnership with Nevis Range to provide multi-centre skiing has brought an upsurge of skiers into the area. The resulting demand for more local facilities has led to an improvement in hotel and dining establishments in nearby areas. Novice skiers are also being enticed to Glencoe by new long tows to a spectacular nursery area. For better skiers the Flypaper and the Haggis Trap are the two best known runs. Glencoe remains Scotland's most scenically beautiful resort and on a clear day you can see Ben Nevis from the summit.

Accommodation can be found in Ballachulish 12 miles distant and Fort William which is 26 miles. Glencoe does not offer that much prospect for job seekers but it may be worth contacting the Glencoe Ski Centre Kingshouse, Glencoe, Argyll PA39 4HZ; ☎01855 851226; fax 01855 851 233; info@ski-glencoe.co.uk; www.ski-glencoe.co.uk) or the Glencoe Ski School (Glencoe, Argyll, PA49 4HZ; ☎01855-851233; www.ski-glencoe.co.uk; info@ski-glencoe.co.uk). For a list of hotels in the area contact Ballachulish tourist office (01855-811866).

GLENSHEE

Glenshee is impressive with its 23 lifts capable of handling 17,000 skiers an hour. It has 40km/25 miles of downhill runs making it the most extensive ski area in Britain. In 1995, it was also the venue for the very first British Snowboarding championships whose legacy is the snowboarding school there (☎013397-41320). The skiing is on either side of the road between Braemar (9 miles) and Blairgowrie (24 miles). There are 38 pistes in three different valleys. Probably Scotland's most famous difficult run, The Tiger is on Cairnwell (3059 feet). Glenshee's highest peak for skiing is Glas Maol at 3500 ft, the highest peak of the station and the site of a 2km long red run. You really need your own transport to get to Glenshee, which is five miles from the nearest village (Spittal of Glenshee). Possibilities for employment at the slopes include lift operators, catering staff for the main restaurant at car park level, or the Cairnwell Mountain Restaurant or the Meall Odhhar licensed café. Ski patrollers, ski and board instructors and experienced groomer drivers are also employed.

The main employer at Glenshee is the Glenshee Ski Centre (Cairnwell Mountain, by Braemar, Aberdeenshire AB35 5XU; ☎013397-41320; fax 01339-741665; info@ski-glenshee.co.uk; www.ski-glenshee.co.uk). Over the winter a total of about 180 staff are employed. There are around 20 full-time staff who work year round, but a large number of extra people are taken on for the skiing season, weather permitting. There are approximately 50 lift operators, about ten staff in the Ski and Board Hire, four experienced groomer drivers and about eight ski patrollers. Ski Patrol applicants should have the BASP (British Association of Ski Patrollers) qualification or equivalent. The Glenshee Ski School employs about 35 ski and board instructors. Numerous catering staff are also taken on for the three café/restaurants at the Ski Centre. No accommodation is provided for employees. Non-local staff must find their own accommodation in hotels and guesthouses in Blairgowrie, Kirkmichael and Braemar. Usually it is possible to do a deal with a hotel whereby you do some evening work at the hotel in return for lower rates for board and lodging. Having your own transport may be desirable, but not necessarily essential as the company provides transport from Blairgowrie, Kirkmichael and Braemar to the Ski Centre.

Ski instructors could try the independent Cairnwell Ski and Snowboard School located at Gulabin Lodge (Glenshee PH10 7QE; ☎01250-885255) which is a year round activity centre. Any ski instructor qualified to teach other sports may also be able to get work instructing multi activities for groups in May and June.

People looking for hotel work around Glenshee will not find the situation entirely hopeless. There are just a few large hotels that are so isolated that local people are unwilling or unable to commute every day and some residential workers are needed. However as there are no hotels at the ski station, people should not harbour visions of being able to walk to the ski lifts during their few hours off.

Fortuitously, prospects seem reasonable around Spittal of Glenshee (the nearest village to the slopes) itself. The Dalmunzie House Hotel (☎01250-885224; dalmunzie@aol.com) even advertises six vacancies for winter and summer for general hotel staff in the book *Summer Jobs in Britain*. Catherine Ryder, a temporary worker at the Dalmunzie House Hotel, pointed out that one of the negative aspects of working in an isolated hotel is the difficulty of reaching 'civilisation': her nearest post office was the Bridge of Cally, over fifteen miles away. Owning a car would be a definite advantage.

There is a Youth Hostel in Braemar (☎013397-41659) that is open all year round. The hostel offers skiing packages in winter: self-catering accommodation and ski instruction and hire for £95 a week. Booking a package might give you time to ask about job possibilities on the mountain during the day while indulging your passion for the white stuff.

THE LECHT

The Lecht ski area was opened in 1979. The Scottish Tourist Board's brochure describes it as 'absolutely ideal for (skiing) families, especially those with young children'. Its ski crèche facilities are an excellent way to get post toddlers onto skis while the limited skiing (only 21 short runs served by 15 lifts), plus very easy access from the car park make it ideal for families. The slopes are a combination of gentle nursery and intermediate slopes. The skiing is too limited to attract ambitious skiers but for beginners it has excellent facilities. The main problem is with the snow conditions, however snowmaking machines introduced in 1997 on three runs make a big difference. A floodlit dry ski slope at the ski station means the Lecht is equipped to train beginners to ski all year round.

The Lecht Ski and Multi-Activity Centre (Strathdon, Aberdeenshire AB36 8YP; ☎019756-51440; fax 019756 51426; info@lecht.co.uk; www.lecht.co.uk/wap; www.ski-scotland.com.) is the biggest employer. The manager of the Lecht Ski Centre, the company's base, admits trying to improve the local high level of unemployment by favouring locals for jobs on the chairlift and tows and in the equipment hire shop and cafeteria. But outsiders may be able to find a job as an instructor in the Lecht ski school if they have BASI qualifications. There are usually 20-25 permanent ski instructors but ten or more part-timers are taken on for busy times i.e. weekends. The Company also employs three ski patrollers and the odd Australian has been taken on for this.

Also worth trying for employment are the hotels in nearby villages: Ballater, Strathdon, Tomintoul and Grantown-on-Spey. A list of these can be obtained from the Braemar Tourist Office (01339-741600).

Spain

Although a comparatively recent addition to the list of countries with ski resorts patronised by British skiers. Spain offers very competitive prices when packages are booked with tour operator. Unfortunately, few of these are British and are represented at present by Thomson and Ski Miquel. The main resorts are: Cerler, La Molina, Baqueira, El Formigal and Panticosa in the Pyrenees and Sierra Nevada (formerly Sol y Nieve) in the mountains of that name. The best known Spanish resort is Sierra Nevada. The Alpine World Championships were held there in 1996 for which preparations included a new lift system and snow making equipment. Only a few resorts including Formigal and Baqueira have featured with British companies.

REGULATIONS

The procedure for those coming from other EU countries has followed that of France in that you no longer have to apply for a residence permit *(Tarjeta de Residencia)* to work there for longer than three months. However, it may be useful to apply voluntarily as it acts as a form of ID that you can carry around with you and is useful for opening a bank account or using the Spanish National Health Service, should you want or need to. Application should be made to a regional police headquarters *(Comisaria de Policia)* or a Foreigners' Registration Office (*Oficina de Extranjera*). The central one in Madrid is at Calle Madrazo 9. The documents required for the *residencia* are a contract of employment, three photographs, a passport and (sometimes) a medical certificate. Spain is infamous for the complexity of its bureaucracy but the regulations above come from the handouts supplied by the Spanish Embassy in London (20 Peel Street, London W8 7PD; 020-7221 0098 spanlabo@globalnet.co.uk) and in the leaflet 'Settling in Spain' from the British Consulate General in Spain.

For non-EU nationals the procedures have not changed and the legendary complexity of the process leads many temporary workers from North America, Australia etc. to simply cross the border when their tourist visa expires and re-enter with another three months stamped in their passport. If you do decide to go legitimate you have to obtain a *visado especial* from the Spanish embassy in your own country after submitting a copy of your job contract, medical certificate in duplicate and usually also authenticated duplicates of your qualifications. Sometimes a certificate from the police is also needed. The whole procedure takes months to accomplish and when the visa is issued you have to collect it in your home country. There can therefore be months of delay before you start work – hopeless for those hoping to pick up work on spec in a Spanish resort.

Needless to say only those with a reasonable knowledge of Spanish are likely to be successful in a speculative job search, knocking on doors in the resorts. If you don't speak Spanish but are still determined, Sierra Nevada with a sizeable British clientele is probably your best bet.

Sierra Nevada

Formerly known by the tacky name of Sol y Nieve (Sun and Snow) Sierra Nevada has acquired more gravitas since its successful hosting of the World Championships in 1997. This gave the resort a whole new infrastructure and a boost in popularity. Sierra Nevada now figures in the worlds top 100 ski resorts. It is the most southerly ski resort of mainland Europe (the same latitude as Rhodes and Tunis), Sierra Nevada is only 20 miles from the beautiful city of Granada and 100 miles from the coast, making it possible for holidaymakers to combine a week's skiing with a week by the sea. The resort village where most skiers are accommodated is called Pradollano. It is not particularly attractive but very convenient for the lifts and facilities. Unfortunately, it is so convenient that it is under constant siege from daytrippers and weekenders undeterred by the vertiginous road that leads from Granada. Its most notable feature is that it is higher than most ski resorts. In fact, the Pic de Veleta, the road, which goes to the resort and beyond is the highest in Europe reaching 3470m.

THE SKIING

The main part of the resort, Pradollano, is at 2100m, with most of the skiing based around the Borreguiles complex 650m higher. A happy consequence of the altitude is that you can usually rely upon good snow: early in 1988, Sol y Nieve was virtually the only western European resort with good ski conditions. But it can be unreliable: the World Championships were supposed to take place in there in 1995 but were postponed for lack of the stuff. Optimistically, the resort bid to host the 2010 Winter Olympics. A more permanent drawback is that the thinness of the air can be tiring, and attempting to smoke at such an altitude is no fun at all.

The altitude of the resort means that the season is one of the longest in Europe, running from December to mid-May. Be warned that weekend skiing is best avoided since the entire population of Andalusia seems to drive to Sierra Nevada at weekends. The queues for the lifts are long, and when you finally get to ski you run a high risk of collisions with inept but totally fearless Spanish school children.

Even without the aggravation of kamikaze adolescents, Sierra Nevada has runs to terrify everyone but the most experienced skiers. Beginners tend to travel both to and from the mid-station at Borreguiles by cabin, avoiding the difficult run down from Borreguiles to the resort. Unfortunately the morning queues for the *telecabina* are long, averaging 40 minutes during the week and over an hour at weekends. From Borreguiles there is a selection of green runs, but each has a tricky stretch or two. Beginners who are tempted by a blue run straight down to Pradollano should be warned that the last section is of at least red-run standard, and a popular sport at the end of the day is drinking in the sunshine outside the Telecabina Hotel watching hapless beginners trudge down. A safer, but much longer bet is the 3900m Loma Dilmar run.

Intermediates can get their thrills on some of the precipitous runs on the far side of the mountain, taking in the remarkable scenery while trying to keep on the narrow ledges hugging the mountain.

The resort has about 30 independent ski school set up by individuals or groups of instructors, most of whom have trained and qualified with the Spanish Ski Federation (RFEDI). There are however, very few English-speaking instructors, which is why Giles Birch and Jonathan Buzzard set up the British Ski Centre (+34 646 178406) in 2002/03 after working in the resort since 1996 and 1991 respectively. They both have the highest Spanish instructor qualification (the Diplomado).

Sierra Nevada has 65 km of piste and 20 lifts and the skiing is enjoyable for all standards although it suits ambitious intermediates best. The lift pass and ski school are very good value.

APRÈS SKI

As elsewhere in Spain, the cost of eating and drinking is low: to cut costs to a minimum, seek out the bars frequented by the Spanish workers. Holidaymakers, both Spanish and foreign have pushed prices up in fancier bars and restaurants (such as Cunini's, where the King has dined while skiing in the resort). It will not take you long to exhaust the limited possibilities offered in Sierra Nevada itself, and you may well be tempted to sample the inviting and extensive possibilities of Granada or go looking for a winter job on the Costa del Sol. Be warned however that there is only one bus a day between Granada and Sierra Nevada running to the resort early in the morning and returning at about 5 pm. Hitching is only really feasible at weekends.

WORK

The hosting of the World Cup Championships in 1997 was a big publicity coup for the resort and Thomson, once the only British tour operator to go there was joined by the likes of Airtours and First Choice even though these two have now stopped going there. There has been some kind of employment spin off with more catering jobs and opportunities for snow clearers, reps and ski instructors. Much of this demand is however still assimilated by local people, so to stand a chance a good grasp of the language is essential. Do not expect accommodation to be provided automatically, since there will probably be a room shortage, particularly in the Championship season. Don't be surprised if you're obliged to find a cheap *pensione* in Granada (32km away), and travel up each day on the early bus.

Baqueira

Baqueira/Beret founded in 1965, is Spain's smartest ski resort; it has to be, the King of

Spain goes there to ski. Situated high (1500m) in the Pyrenees, Baqueira is a purpose-built resort located in the Aran Valley. The British tour operator Ski Miquel flies its guests to Toulouse airport, which is 160kms (about 2hours) distant from Baqueira. The resort was thought out by champion Spanish skier Luis Arias and the lift system is well-designed and fast and the ski areas of Baqueira and adjacent Beret are linked. High tech snow making by 109 cannons guarantees the best possible skiing conditions.

THE SKIING

The well-groomed slopes of Baqueira are rarely crowded, thanks to a lift system with several entry points. The chairlift near the Hotel Tuc Blanc takes you up to Baqueira 1800 where there are slopes suitable for beginners and where there is a large self-service restaurant. There are lifts up higher to Cap de Baqueira (2500m) where a variety of pistes keep all grades of skier happy. The Mirador Express four-seater chairlift takes you to the top in seven minutes. For high adrenalin skiers there are mogul fields (Luis Arias) or black runs to challenge even the most blasé including the graphically named Escornabrabes (tumbling mountain goat).

WORK

As with most Spanish resorts, the labour demands are largely satisfied by the locals themselves. If Baqueira catches on with British skiers then there will more chance of getting a job. At the moment Ski Miquel are the lone representatives of the British companies. They own and run their own chalet hotel, Chalet Salana which has fourteen bedrooms. Staff include resort managers, chef, chalet person and bar person/ski guide.

Switzerland

REGULATIONS AND WORK PERMITS

Switzerland is not a member of the European Union but since the Bilateral Agreement between Switzerland and the European Union was concluded, the free entry for nationals of the EU into Switzerland to look for seasonal work has been possible. EU job-seekers can enter Switzerland for up to three months (extendable) to look for work. If they succeed, they must show a contract of employment to the authorities and are then eligible for a short-term residence permit (valid for up to one year and renewable) or a long-term permit (up to five years) depending on the contract. The L-EC/EFTA permit (*Kurzaufenhalter/ Autorisation de Courte Durée*) is the short-term residence permit and a B-EC is long-term permit valid up to five years depending on the contract. The *Controle de l'Habitant/ Fremdenpolizei* (Aliens Police) are still in the process of adjusting their systems and regulations. Employers are obliged to give EC applicants equal consideration with Swiss nationals. A useful document entitled *European Nationals in Switzerland* can be found on the website www.europa.admin.ch Further details on the newly introduced freedom of movement for foreign jobseekers in Switzerland can be found in the document *European Nationals* www.europa.admin.ch. For non-European Union nationals the situation is a lot tougher as they have to find an employer willing to sponsor their application, and all the paperwork this entails puts most alpine employers off. The best chance of employment is to apply for a temporary trainee (*stagiare*) placement. More information on participating organisations in different countries can be obtained from the Swiss Federal Office for Migration, Emigration and Trainees (Quellenweg 15, 3003 Bern (031-322 42 02; swiss. emigration@bfm.admin.ch; www.swissemigration.ch/elias.en). The trainee positions must be in the applicant's vocational field; for ski resorts this is most likely to be in catering. The age limits are 18-30. Successful applicants can stay in Switzerland for up to 18 months after completing their studies. Further information in the UK can be obtained from the Overseas Labour Service of the Department of Employment (W5, Moorfoot, Sheffield S1 4PQ).

Although Switzerland has very low unemployment (under 4%), the percentage is double that of five years ago. Switzerland also has a high proportion of foreign workers (approximately 20% of the population) and it is understandable that the Swiss want to proceed with caution towards further integration with Europe.

With a residence permit you become eligible for the state insurance scheme, for the Swiss minimum wage for the area you are working in and the excellent legal tribunal for foreign workers which arbitrates in disputes over working conditions, pay and dismissals. Accident insurance is compulsory for all foreign workers and the employer pays the bulk of the premium. If you have paid contributions (approximately 15% of your wage) for at least 150 days you become eligible for unemployment benefit irrespective of your nationality. Also, temporary and long-term residence permit holders, in most of the resort areas, become eligible for travel on public transport at a subsidised rate and also to obtain a reduced price lift pass. So there are many advantages to acquiring legal status by means of a stay permit.

A Swiss company that has been advertising for resort staff and ski instructors in recent seasons is Viamonde, Personnel Department, Viamonde, Case Postale, CH-1972 Anzère, Switzerland (027 398 4882; fax 027 398 4883; personnel@viamonde.com), which runs ski and snowboard programmes for international schools.

Many of the Swiss Tourist Offices in the Alps compile lists of vacancies from September onwards for the coming winter season. The lists will be frequently updated and there is no charge for someone who gets a job by this means.

SWISS SKI RESORT TOURIST OFFICES

Resort	Website	Telephone numbers
Adelboden	www.adelboden.ch	033 673 80 80
Andermatt	www.andermatt.ch	041 887 14 54
Anzère	www.anzere.ch	027 399 28 00
Arosa	www.arosa.ch	081 378 70 20
Bettmeralp	www.bettmeralp.ch	027 928 60 60
Champéry	www.champery.ch	024 479 20 20
Champex-Lac	www.champex.ch	27 783 12 27
Château d'Oex	www.château-doex.ch	026 924 25 25
Chur	www.churtourismus.ch	081 252 18 18
Crans Montana	www.crans-montana.ch	027 485 04 04
Davos	www.davos.ch	081 415 21 21
Les Diablerets	www.diablerets.ch	024 492 33 58
Engelberg-Titlis	www.engelberg.ch	041 639 77 77
Flims	www.alpenarena.ch	081 920 92 00
Grächen	www.graechen.ch	027 955 60 60
Grindelwald	www.grindelwald.ch	033 854 12 12
Gstaad	www.gstaad.ch	033 748 81 81
Kandersteg	www.kandersteg.ch	033 675 80 80

Klosters	www.klosters.ch	081 410 20 20
Lenk	www.lenk.ch	033 733 31 31
Leukerbad/Loèche-les-Bains	www.leukerbad.ch	027 472 71 71
Mürren	www.wengen-muerren.ch	033 856 86 86
Pontresina	www.pontresina.com	081 838 83 80
St Moritz	www.stmoritz.ch	081 837 33 33
Saas-Fee	www.saas-fee.ch	027 958 18 58
Silvaplana	www.silvaplana.ch	081 838 60 00
Verbier	www.verbier.ch	027 775 38 88
Villars	www.villars.ch	024 495 32 32
Wengen	www.wengen-muerren.ch	033 855 14 14
Zermatt	www.zermatt.ch	027 966 81 00

Another excellent source of jobs for those with catering qualifications is the trade newspaper of the hospitality industry *Hotel and Tourismus Revue,* published every Thursday. It is full of vacancies for hotel and catering industries also well worth looking at are *La Suisse* and *24 Heures.* Also check notice boards and adverts in local papers like *l'Est Vaudois* for the Montreux region.

Working for Swiss hoteliers is no picnic as they expect high standards and will often demand longer hours than contracted for and expect employees to take on extra duties when necessary. Over Christmas and New Year forget about time off. In theory extra hours will be paid or repaid with extra time off but if things are not going well and they are having a bad season this is not always guaranteed. By and large the accommodation provided will be pretty good but the food can at best be described as 'variable'.

With typical efficiency, Swiss hoteliers are experts in the fine art of balancing the number of staff they have with the number of guests expected. This can have unfortunate consequences for prospective employees who have been offered and have accepted a job only to hear, literally days before the starting date, that the job has been cancelled due to low bookings. Alternatively, if the snow is bad a winter job can be cut short two thirds of the way through the season and an employee given notice to leave early.

Another feature which can be unnerving is the hotel trade's practice of expecting people to arrive on day one, start work on day one, and be at top efficiency by day two. The winter skiing season starts with a rush at the beginning of the Christmas holidays and there is often no time to ease gently into a job. The resorts listed below are only a selection of the Swiss resorts where work can be found but are intended to give a good idea of the range of jobs available and the general conditions and life of a winter season worker in Switzerland

Arosa

Arosa (www.arosa.ch) is situated at the head of the Schanfigg Valley in the Graubünden (Grisons) in German-speaking east Switzerland, about 10 miles from Davos and 20 miles from St. Moritz. Unlike St. Moritz and Davos, Arosa has remained uncommercialised and retains its atmosphere of a typical Swiss mountain village. Before the growth in the popularity of skiing, the village was famous as a health resort and doctors in cities all over Europe sent their patients to the sanitoria there (many are now hotels) to benefit from the fresh Alpine air. Nowadays, although primarily a ski resort, many still go there purely for a healthy holiday. The leisurely pace of life coupled with the lack of really challenging runs attracts those who want a restful break rather than those who are avid skiers. Arosa is thoroughly civilised in every way; there is none of the mad rushing about associated with the purpose-built ski resorts in France; the gobbled breakfast and frantic race to the lifts at 8am is disregarded in favour of a buffet breakfast in the hotel and a gentle stroll down the main street.

The wealthy and privileged are very much in evidence and fleets of white Cadillacs ferry fur-clad figures from their hotels to the village where the shops tend towards designer boutiques and old-style cafés rather than souvenir shops and snack bars offering chips with everything. There are over 70 hotels, but even the cheaper ones are rather expensive and this is reflected by the fact that relatively few British tour companies offer holidays there: Powder Byrne, Ski Weekend and Swiss Travel Service are the usual providers of holidays there plus a few tailor-made holiday specialists including Momentum and White Roc. Generally speaking, a skiing holiday in Arosa seems to be beyond the means of the average British punter. If Arosa is relaxing, however, it is certainly neither dead nor deserted.

THE SKIING

None of the skiing in Arosa is particularly challenging. Having said that, the resort has a good snow record, 43 miles/70 km of piste and an efficient system of fourteen lifts that connects the three main ski areas. The summit of the highest, Weisshorn (8,700 ft) is reached by two-stage cable car. There is a black run from the top to the Carmenna. The first stage of the cable car takes you to Tschuggen in six minutes. There are two other access routes to the Tschuggen so lift queues are minimal. From the Inner Arosa area you can take the six-seater gondola up to Hörnli where there are some superb wide easy runs back down to Inner Arosa; or you can ski across to the Plattenhorn. Cross-country skiing takes place in the Maran area and down at the Isla. There are also two toboggan runs from Tschuggen and from Prätschli.

A lot of visitors seem to be very attached to the place and the skiing is extensive enough to make a holiday there enjoyable. It is ideal for the first-timer, though by the end of a season working there it may begin to pall. The runs are mostly blues and reds and there are plenty of lifts and few queues. To compensate for the often unexciting pistes there is some excellent off piste skiing. Arosa also has 27km of beautiful cross-country skiing tracks, one of which is actually upon a frozen lake. There are also 37 miles of cleared and marked walking paths and horse-drawn sleighs that can take you into the mountains.

The ski school has an excellent reputation. Beginners meet at the nursery slopes in Inner Arosa or at Tschuggen. Intermediate skiers should get in touch with the Ski Club of Great Britain, which has a representative in Arosa who can be contacted through the Tourist Office (+41 81 378 7020; www.arosa.ch). The rep will act as a guide and will take you anywhere on or off piste.

Apart from skiing there are of course all the standard resort sports: two natural and two artificial skating rinks and an ice hockey team about which the whole resort is crazy. Toboganning is popular – a favourite run with the seasonal workers was the torchlit descent from Tschuggen.

The Fun Park at the Tschuggen is for good snowboarders only, but with its bar and deck chairs it attracts all kinds of young people. There is a specialist snowboarding school.

ACCOMMODATION

If your job was not arranged from Britain as the majority here are, then there will be the usual first priority of finding somewhere to stay upon your arrival. There are over 70 hotels, one it is said for each of the bends in the narrow twisting road from Chur. These range from the formal, luxurious international five star hotels such as the Kulm (+41 81 378 8888) and Tschuggen (+41 81 378 9999) to small, homely pensions. In between, there are many varied hotels, usually occupied mainly by couples and families – amongst these are the Waldhotel, Hof Maran, Sporthotel, Valsana, Parkhotel and Hotel Eden. If you insist on a chalet-type holiday bang on the piste, the Batin is lovely. Most of the hotels operate on a half-board basis.

As usual the first stop for the budget traveller should be the 176-bed Jugenherberge (Youth Hostel) run by the family Josef Wagger (☎081 377 13 97; arosa@youthhostel.ch) which is friendly, efficient and spotlessly clean and charges SFr27 for a dorm bed. There is a notice board, which may help with job hunting. If the youth hostel is full, or you have outstayed your welcome, try Haus am Wald (081 377 31 38) which costs SFr 70 per person per night. It is described at homely and comfortable.

WORK

Being a fairly large resort, there are usually quite a number of English-speaking workers around, most of whom seem to congregate in the Expresso Bar or in the Waldeck. They may well be able to give some valuable pointers for jobs, particularly early on in the season when a number of those sent out by agencies to work for the season find they can't take the pace, despite having undergone careful vetting, and having endless warnings that it isn't all fun and skiing. This often leaves worthwhile employers in dire need of workers, and you will find them willing to employ you, maybe at a better rate than the previous worker.

Generally speaking, the casual work to be picked up is similar to other resorts; try the hotels, shops, bars, night clubs, mountain restaurants (Weisshornhütte, Alpenblick, Carmennahütte) and tea-rooms (Kaiser, Weber). As is so often the case your chances of finding work will depend upon your appearance, linguistic ability and persuasive powers. One British girl managed to get a job looking after the sleigh horses, so anything is possible.

Many of the British working in Arosa are from Jobs in the Alps but Peter Hatfield, who was unemployed, saw an advert for a pianist for a hotel in Arosa, applied for and got the job. He spent the season there and had a wonderful time. To save hassles over work permits, he worked for his keep only but got pocket money, free skiing gear and so on.

It was dead easy. All I had to do was to play the piano in the bar for two or three hours per night. People bought me lots of drinks and I had a fantastic time. I'd nothing else to do and felt very pleased to have the job.

Peter had never skied before but reckoned he was now fairly proficient. The Carmenna Hotel by the ice rink has a lively piano bar.

Jane Stewart, a student from New Zealand was spending her summer travelling round Europe and enquired more on impulse than anything else at a mountain restaurant and found she had a job as a waitress.

I had a wonderful time – I started off a complete non-skier and I reckon Arosa is a perfect place to learn. I don't think I'd choose Arosa to return to even if I could though, now my skiing is better I feel I'd want something more demanding. Still Arosa is a nice friendly place.

She was working as a waitress earning about £80 a week plus generous tips, with one and a half days off a week.

Philippa Sumner working in the Waldhotel comments:

If it hadn't been for the foreign work force, Arosa would have ground to a halt. The Tschuggen Grand Hotel employed Italian waiters as did the Prätschli and the Kulm. Apart from the 12 Jobs in the Alps workers there were about a dozen other British workers whom I met including an Irish girl working as a waitress in the Orelli, a Scots cook in the Eden and an English disc-jockey in Nuts Disco, the most popular night club. So, plenty of opportunities for British workers in Arosa. With some 70 hotels, guest houses and bed and breakfasts, not to mention the bars and restaurants, all needing waiters, washer-uppers and chambermaids, it must be relatively easy to find jobs.

Champéry

Ask most snowsports enthusiasts to name the great winter sports resorts and they will probably wax lyrical about the Val d'Isères and Zermatts of this world. Ask them about Champéry and nine out of ten times you'll get back a blank stare. Yet this tiny mountain village is the kind of place skiers dream about going to when they die.

Part of the Portes du Soleil complex (650 km of piste spread amongst 12 French and Swiss resorts and 24 mountains), Champéry offers access to some of the finest skiing in Europe. Somehow though, the village has managed to avoid the tourist invasion that has marred many of its more popular neighbours. The village is picture-postcard Switzerland. Reached by a winding and sometimes treacherous road or on the mountain cog railway, the chalets and hotels nestle under the jagged peaks of the Dents du Midi (Teeth of Midday) so-called because for most of the winter the sun won't hit the village until late morning.

THE SKIING

There is something to suit every grade of skier. Beginners are not well catered for as the nursery slopes are on Planachaux and are reached by cable car from the Sports Centre, or by chairlift from Grand-Paradis village, just outside Champéry and reached by ski bus. But it's the slopes on the other side of the village which are the attraction for the serious skier. Avoriaz, the next door resort is in France. To get there you have to take the chairlift up the Chavanette or Crosets-Mossettes or Grand Conche. Chavanette (is famous for its black run 'The Wall', which is the border, and ski down an intermediate run into Avoriaz. Day trips can be made to nearby Châtel and Morzine or further afield. The huge Portes du Soleil area is engaged in a war of words with the Trois Vallées of France for the title of largest ski area in the world. The statistics are impressive in both cases. The realities are equally telling. It's impossible, for example, for even the strongest skier to get from one side of the area and back again in the same day. And you'd be pushing it if you managed to sample every run in the region in a season.

APRÈS SKI

Given the scope for strenuous skiing, it's not surprising to find that Champéry doesn't rate as one of the more sophisticated après ski hangouts. Bodies tend to be too tired at the end of the day for heavy-duty nightlife. What action there is will be centred on the live music at the Mines d'Or ('le Min'), Bar le Levant, Bar des Guides, Vieux Chalet, Le Pub and Mitchell's Irish/Swedish Bar. You'll probably find most of the foreign workers in one of those six, or at a hotel bar with liberal attitudes to closing hours. Even so, the style for seasonal staff is to make your own fun – whether it's a torchlight descent from the slopes above the town, a fancy dress invasion of a bar, or a quiet fondue evening at someone's apartment. Locals, too, reject the tinsel-town aspect of nightlife in many ski resorts. Traditional family feuds smoulder among the four or five clans that control most things in the town and, in an area where religion continues to play a strong part in people's lives, it's still frowned upon to work outdoors on a Sunday. So party if you want or are able to – but a lot of nights there will come a point where people will look outside, see the snow falling and slip away to bed to rest and prepare for the main attraction, the skiing.

WORK

The first problem is finding somewhere to base yourself while you look around. If you come in low season you could try the tourist office for low priced guest houses – but even these start at about SFr 50 a night per person with breakfast. If you are extremely lucky then a seasonal worker already there might offer to put you up for the night – but don't count on it – they get inundated throughout the season by friends and acquaintances sleeping on floors and landings. Your best bet is probably the youth hostel just outside Montreux in Territet (☎021/963 49 34) which costs SFr36.50 per night (six francs less for members) from where the train journey up to Champéry isn't too long and it's a good base from which to visit other ski resorts at the eastern end of Lac Leman.

Anyone heading up to Champéry to look for work should get used to the idea that a job search here is far more difficult than in other resorts. Count on about 80 to 100 jobs for foreign workers a winter and consider that a lot of these are handed on a friend-to-friend basis or hired for outside the resort by a tour company in the UK.

The largest employers in town are the hotels and restaurants. The ski-lift company which is now semi-independent, has been known to hire French-speaking foreigners, although they have been more reluctant to do this in recent years. The sports shops Borgeat Sports and Holiday Sport – also have foreign employees.

The smaller British tour companies tend to operate in Champéry and some of them are fairly transitory but Ski Weekend are established regulars.

The late night bars and discos also have a few jobs going every year. The hotel situation is in a permanent state of flux, due to a continuous process of takeovers by local consortia, but try the following hotels who have hired foreigners in the past: Hotel Suisse (024 479 07 07), Hotel de Champéry (Grande Rue, 1874 Champéry, ☎024 479 10 71), Hotel Beau Séjour (1874 Champéry; ☎024 479 17 01) and Hotel des Alpes (Grand Rue, 1874 Champéry; ☎024 479 12 22). The Hotel de la Paix was bought by the owner of Champneys health spa and given a million pound refurbishment in English country house style, a few years ago. It caters for the corporate end of the market and the owner's own house parties. Most of the regular hotels will have a couple of jobs open to people who turn up at the right moment.

Opportunities for casual jobs are few and far between – although you might be lucky enough to find a regular babysitting job or to be hired on a very temporary and very casual basis by the ski school. Normally however, the local teachers are fighting among themselves for classes. Other possibilities in the area include the Hotel-Restaurant Grand Paradis (☎024 479 11 67) in the nearby village of the same name, the Sundance Saloon in Les Crosets and Planachaux. If you are lucky enough to find a job, you'll normally get a temporary stay permit and a place to stay, which is essential as apartments are expensive and difficult to find.

La Cravasse (1874, Champéry, Switzerland; ☎+41 79 434 8980; fax +41 24 479 3489; andymac@pisteartiste.com) is a near-legendary bar in Champéry owned by extreme skier Andy MacMillan who employs a bartender for the winter season. Non-British nationals can apply. Andy MacMillan is also a guide/instructor at the Freeride Company (info@ freeridecompany.com; 02 44 79 10 00) ski and boarding school in Champéry.

Crans Montana

Crans Montana is made up of two resorts set on a high plateau amongst pine trees and it overlooks the Rhône Valley. The resort is reached by funicular, or road from Sierre, a busy market town. French-speaking Sierre lies near the linguistic boundary between Suisse Romande and Schweizerdeutsch, German-speaking areas. The hills surrounding Crans Montana were formed by a gigantic rockfall in prehistoric times. At an altitude of 1500 m (nearly 5,000 feet), the overall effect of the resort is a sophisticated complex in stunning surroundings: it faces a majestic view of the Valais Alps across the Valley. Along with the neighbouring villages of Bluche, Aminona and Vermala, it forms the largest skiing area in Switzerland.

Although a modern-looking resort, the first hotel (originally a sanitorium) was built there in 1893 on the strength of the acclaimed health giving properties of the region, with its mild, dry mountain climate. The first ski lift arrived in 1936. As a sports centre it provided golf, ice skating, swimming, tennis, riding and fishing – but it is best known for skiing, especially since hosting World Championships in 1987.

SKIING

Apart from providing one of the most beautiful settings in Europe in which to ski Crans Montana offers 160 km of piste and 35 lifts. The resort is suitable for all levels of skier and as it has no through traffic it is popular with families. About 60% of the runs are suitable for intermediates. There is summer skiing on the glacier on the highest mountain, Plaine Morte (3000m). For novices there are wide, easy runs from Cry d'Err and beginners will also find a wide choice of gentle slopes on Mt. Bonvin and the Aminona. The Aminona area is included in the Crans Montana lift pass. Advanced skiers can hire a guide and go for miles off-piste. There is a ski shuttle bus, which runs every 30 minutes between Crans Montana, Les Barzettes and Aminona bottom lift stations. Other points in Crans Montana's favour include the area's microclimate, which claims the most sun and the least rain of any Swiss ski area. Snow is usually reliable, despite the sun!

From the Café Restaurant du Cervin you can have a panoramic view of the Rhône Valley and the Weisshorn – forming a backdrop.

ACCOMMODATION

In Montana with its international ambience and plethora of upmarket hotels there is not much chance of finding a cheap place to stay while job hunting: unless you already have contacts there, it may be wise to make daily forays into town from another base. The how and why of this depends of course on your budget: prices of hotels started at SFr 50 a night for the cheapest guesthouse. There is a dormitory (☎027 481 28 51) at the camping place (La Moubra) in Montana. Unfortunately the Montana Youth Hostel became a hotel some years ago, so this leaves winter job seekers with the Montreux hostel (☎021/963 49 34; fax 021/963 27 29) as the best base, or Sion, (closed from 22 January to 2 February and from 21 October to 20 December) which can be reached on (☎027/323. 74 70; fax 027/323 7438) as the nearest bases.

WORK

Foreigners living and working in Switzerland now account for more than 20% of the population, and of these an estimated 100,000 are seasonal workers, employed in the types of jobs that have long been spurned by the indigenous population. While such statistics may make Switzerland seem a job hunter's paradise, in reality, finding a job on the spot depends on a combination of linguistic ability, contacts made through the international grapevine of transient workers, and persistence.

Crans Montana is one of the largest resorts in Switzerland, with a very high turnover of labour. The chances of finding a job here are good, especially during September and October when the tourist offices are inundated with job vacancies. The tourist offices in Crans: (☎027 485 0800) or Montana (☎027 485 04 04) should be able to help. You can get some additional information about the resort at www.crans-montana.ch.

Hotel work in a town with 54+ hotels, may seem the most obvious area to base a job hunt, but it may not prove the most accommodating as the long hours demanded of employees often precludes much time off for skiing.

Mark Stephenson did a variety of jobs in Crans Montana

Apply early for hotel jobs, unless you are confident that you will find something to tide you over, as I did: before working in Montana, I worked in a hotel in the much smaller resort Les Diablerets in the Vaudois Alps. The interim period between the summer and winter seasons is a quiet one, and it was at that time that I was employed for six half days a week in return for the legal minimum Swiss salary, plus accommodation and board. My job entailed weeding the garden, tiling the roof and some inside chores like washing up. I secured this job by knocking on the door of every likely establishment until I received an offer.

By the time snow started falling in December I was being employed to clear snow in Crans Montana: this was in answer to an advertisement for 'un homme pour déblayer la neige' *which I saw in the tourist office which also keeps copies of local papers which contain job adverts.*

The job had its attractions, despite the failure of the snow-clearing machine to function: fresh air, healthy exercise and tots of alcohol supplied by sympathetic residents. Last but not least was the offer of a flat to rent at the reduced rate of SFr380 per month in the apartment block whose concierge employed me.

However, I was already installed in a chalet which was the raison d'être of my other, concurrent job: redecorating a ski chalet at the rate of SFr10 an hour, and at the low rent of SFr6 per day. I shared this job with Paul, an American who later found employment as a ski instructor.

Mark's skilful arrangement of hours of work could allow time off for skiing: the main obstacles being the landlord's frequent visits to ensure that work was in progress, and the need to clear snow as and when it fell. The impending deadline on the job of painting and wallpapering helped curtail extra-mural activities. Intensive labour on both jobs enabled him to save enough money to be used in the pursuit of skiing as well as après ski once work was completed.

Social life in the resort is centred on bars- such as Cuban Punch, Le Monki's, Amadeus, Pub Georges and Dragon and la Grange and Indiana Café, each developing an international ambience as the season takes off. The (largely female) bar staff originate from as far afield as Glasgow, Sweden, Austria and Spain; some of them returning season after season. The job is recommended for those who like late nights, hard work and as compensation – time to ski during the day. Those with languages, especially German and French are naturally more in demand here, as they are with other smaller employers such as the many local sports shops.

An excellent source of summer jobs is the International Summer Camp Montana (La Moubra, 3962 Montana. ☎027 481 56 63; www.campmontana.ch). The Moubra Sports Centre has been organising sporting holidays for young people from all over the world since 1961 at their Summer Camps. There are a lot of jobs available in the summer but sadly, they no longer operate winter ski camps. However, working for the summer camp would give you a chance to fix up a job for the winter well in advance of other job seekers. You could try Les Elfes International based in Verbier (CP 174, Verbier 1936, Switzerland; ☎07 95 46 70 74), which recruit ski/snowboard instructors/camp counsellors children's ski and snowboarding camps in Crans Montana. Duties include instructing in the daytime and managing après ski or evening activities, helping out in the hotel with domestic duties

Louise Brown and Denise Gardini were secretaries to the two directors of La Moubra, one in charge of administration, and the other of publicity and personnel. Their jobs were typical of any secretaries involving correspondence, typing, arranging appointments, answering enquiries, the telephone etc. Denise worked at La Moubra for four years and then married an Italian who also worked at the Camp. She saw the job advertised in *The Guardian*. Louise saw the advertisement in *The Times*, started work initially for the summer season and returned the next year. As most of the clients at La Moubra camp are

English-speaking children, the common language in the Camp is English.

The winter season lasts from mid-December to mid-April. It is also worth trying Le Chaperon Rouge International School in Crans (☎027 481 25 00; fax 027 481 25 02). Susanna Macmillan from Cornwall arrived at the beginning of November having hitched a lift from a Rolls Royce! After three days of asking around in Crans Montana she was offered a job at the School which takes children from the ages of six to 16 years. Her relief was immense especially as accommodation was provided.

It was lucky the job came with a room as up to then we had been camping in a forest with our thermal insulation aluminium foil. My job in the school was as a monitrice, and teaching English and sport. My salary was SFr 850 net monthly after room and food.

Susanna's boyfriend Mark got a job at the Hotel Les Hauts de Crans, where his job earned him about SFr 1,700 net for a 40-hour week. Some weeks he only worked three or four days but for the same money. The hotel charged him SFr 3.60 per meal. Both Susanna and Mark got their jobs by asking around but emphasised that the tourist office was the best place to start as they hand out photo-copies of the jobs available and start advertising summer jobs before the winter season has finished.

Kim Dewhurst worked as a waitress at the Centre de Tennis La Moubra, which is a privately owned indoor (outdoor in summer) tennis club, which has a very good restaurant. She usually worked as a plate waitress, but sometimes also as bartender, especially in the afternoons, between lunch and dinner. The tennis club has nothing to do with La Moubra summer and ski camp but is named similarly due to the proximity of both etablishments to the Lac de Moubra in Montana. The club is expensive and rather exclusive.

Kim started working in Switzerland at La Moubra Camp. She worked there for a number of summer seasons as an assistant riding instructor, and as a waitress in the winter, until she wanted a change, and asked the Swiss-German owners of the tennis club if they needed any staff, before the club opened. Having earned herself a good name at La Moubra, she had no trouble persuading them to take her on.

Kim was paid the official Swiss minimum salary for catering staff (currently about SFr 2,790 monthly gross) plus meals on duty. Accommodation was not provided. However, as long as you arrive in the resort early enough at the beginning of the season, there is never much of a problem finding a cheap studio, with one main living/bed/dining room, kitchenette and bathroom for about SFr 500 monthly.

It is pretty essential to be able to speak some French or German. Even if you only have a basic knowledge of either language you will almost certainly find that it will improve tremendously once you are working in an establishment where you use a foreign language constantly. It also helps when searching for jobs to have evidence of previous experience of bar or waiting work.

There may be job possibilities mid-season with a UK tour operator. Crystal, Erna Low, First Choice, Inghams, Oxford Ski Company, Swiss Travel and others currently have a presence in Crans Montana.

John Norris was a ski instructor employed by the *Ecole Suisse de Ski* which has a school in Crans (Ski and Board 027 485 9370) and Montana (ESS Montana 027 481 1480). Being employed by a local organisation, he enjoyed exactly the same benefits and pay as the Swiss instructors. All group lessons take place in the morning and John was allowed to teach groups in classes 1 to 4, though not 5 and 6 (the top two) for which one has to have earned the *patente*, and this qualification cannot be held by anyone who has lived in the Valais for less than two years. In the afternoons, the ski instructors give private lessons, also organised by the school; they can give as many of these lessons as they wish, or can get.

The previous winter, John worked for a British tour operator as head of the skiing department for the resort. At the end of the season, he applied directly to the Swiss Ski

School for a job. No written reply was given to him until October, when he was told that there would be no possibility of a job due to difficulty with obtaining a stay permit. After Christmas, another British instructor left the school prematurely, thus John was able to obtain the former's place in the school.

It is usually very difficult to obtain a job directly with the local ski school, due to intense competition. However, in order to stand a chance, one must have at least BASI III. It is also necessary to be able to teach in several languages, even though one may be teaching mostly British people. In Crans Montana, a stiff training is obligatory each December for all instructors, after which each must take an examination to prove their capability in teaching. Incidentally, John himself spoke French fluently and Italian passably.

John was paid a high wage, but for this type of job you have to arrange your own food and accommodation, and John rented an apartment for the season. The training period takes place normally in the first week of December: therefore, instructors have to be in the resort by December 1st. All ski-related accidents are insured by the Swiss Ski School. Ski instructors seem to do everything under the sun during the rest of the year, from tending their family vineyard to lighting manager for an opera house. John himself was the owner of an estate agency in Torquay, which he was more than happy to leave for five months of the year.

Davos

Davos is situated in the far-easterly canton of Graubünden (Grisons) on the Landwasser River and is the heart of one of Switzerland's largest skiing areas. A bustling resort divided into two parts, Davos Dorf and Davos Platz, it is also Switzerland's highest town at 5,000 feet. Although its origins go back centuries, it only acquired an international reputation at the end of the nineteenth century as a spa town for tubercular patients (as immortalised in Thomas Mann's novel *The Magic Mountain*). In the intervening years the valley floor from the neighbouring resort of Klosters up as far as Davos Platz has become cluttered with hotel after hotel, pension after pension, and shop after shop so Davos itself is by no means an attractive town, although most of the buildings are painted in pastel hues, some with murals on the walls. The Promenade runs the length of the two areas of Davos Dorf and Davos Platz (main centre).

But it is not the scenery, the clean dry air, or the ritzy hotels that attract people from all over the world, but the pistes of what is generally acknowledged to be one of the world's top resorts. Davos has more than 20,000 beds and 100 hotels to accommodate the flocks of skiers and non-skiers alike. The height of the top station (2843m) is virtually guaranteed deep snow on the slopes for the whole of the winter season with the occasional avalanche in February. Ski equipment is cheaper and more varied than in the UK and there are usually quite a few adverts in shops selling second hand equipment, as seemingly, the Swiss can afford to get a new set for each season.

Davos is reputedly a rich person's resort, but don't let that stop you from working there. Swiss wages are higher than British wages for the equivalent work; tips reflect the affluence of the clientele; meals and accommodation will be included in your contract if you are working in a hotel; and there are discounts for residents. Don't forget that if you have a contract and temporary residence permit you will be entitled to discounts at some shops, cheaper swimming, reductions on the Swiss train (Rhaetische Bahn), and most importantly a *Legitimationskarte* from one of the the the ski stations which in turn entitles you to buy half price ski passes. This covers unlimited skiing on the seven mountains surrounding Davos and Klosters, and free travel on the trains in the area. You can buy a season ticket for the local buses, which entitles you to free travel thereafter.

THE SKIING

People come from all over the world to the vast and excellently serviced skiing regions surrounding Davos. Probably the best known of these is the Parsenn-Weissfluh. The Parsenn funicular (the original one is being entirely rebuilt in stages) goes from Davos Dorf to the Weissfluhjoch. Those runs from the Weissflujoch regarded as the most interesting are those going down to Klosters, Serneus, Saas or the 14km Küblis. From Klosters a fifteen-minute train journey will bring you back into Davos. For advanced skiers there are even longer possibilities off piste. Probably the next most important area is the Jakobshorn area with cableway access near the Davos Platz station. The wide variety of runs from the Jakobshorn are mainly intermediate but watch the steep beginnings of the runs. The popular blacks are the Jakobshorn Nord, which starts off black and gets more intermediate and the more demanding Brama. The 4km run down to Teufi descends almost 3000 feet. 'The sun always shines at Pischa' – the Pischa area, 5 minutes away by free ski bus, is a self-contained ski area. It is not possible to ski from here back to Davos but the slopes are good for intermediates and tend to be less crowded than the other, higher profile areas. A cable car whisks you to the southwest-facing slope in ten minutes. For those with more testing skiing in mind there is some interesting off-piste skiing behind the Pischahorn. Another quieter area is the Rinerhorn reached by car along the Plaz to Glaris road, or via the Rhatische Bahn (a ten-minute train journey). There is something for all standards on the Rinerhorn but the runs are not as spectacularly long as elsewhere although skiing through the trees has a beauty of its own. The Schatzalp-Strelpass area is no longer included in the Rega lift pass.

To summarise: the Davos Klosters area has 320 km of marked runs and 54 lifts. There is something for every grade of skier and 30% of the runs are suitable for beginners who can also benefit from the outstanding ski school where most instructors speak English.

Less widely known in the UK, Davos is very popular with the cross-country skiers. Over 75 kms of prepared trails through stunning scenery make up a varying and ideal terrain for Nordic skiers and there is a cross-country ski school on the edge of town.

APRÈS SKI

If you are going to spend a whole season in the Alps, there will be times when the weather is bad, when you have only a short break during the day, or when you want a rest from skiing. So it is an advantage to stay in a large resort, which offers alternative facilities. Davos boasts a cinema, numerous teashops, bars, cafés, restaurants, discos, a slot-machine casino and several nightclubs. If you want to try a different sport to skiing you can try ice-skating – Europe's largest natural outdoor ice rink and the ice stadium are not only home to the Davos Ice Hockey team, but are open to the public morning and afternoon. Alternatively, there is a large public indoor swimming pool, saunas and tennis and squash courts, two toboggan runs (6km), curling rinks and two fitness clubs provide yet more variety.

Nightlife is very varied. Everyone has their own favourite spot. The English-speaking workers tend to meet at Café Carlo's, Chämi Bar or Bolganschanze (snowboard crowd), before going on to the Pöstli nightclub at the Posthotel Morosani which has live groups as well as a disco. But there is also the Cabanna Club (in the Hotel Europe), a fashionable nightclub with video screen, the Cave Grishcha – a rustic beer cellar, the Pizzerias, and even a striptease club.

WORK

By virtue of its size Davos offers many possibilities for work. Few of the hotel workers in the 100+ hotels are Swiss and the hotel managers are in general willing to take on English employees. Some knowledge of German is definitely an asset since the majority of tourists are German or Swiss. However, there is such a diverse nationality of workers that other European languages such as French and Italian may be spoken.

Jobs in the Alps sends over about ten people a season to Davos. Alternatively, order a copy of the *Swiss Hotel Guide* from www.swisshotels.ch for 15 euros and contact the hotel managers direct. Most of the British boys worked as night porters but some worked as waiters, day porters and mini-bus drivers (International Driving Licence required). The girls were waitresses or buffet servers. The minimum age for these jobs was 18. For one season only it is virtually impossible to work as a ski instructor, because you would have to qualify and then be available for a long course before even contemplating work.

At the beginning of the season it is possible to find a job simply by knocking on doors. Jobs are advertised in shops: Migros Supermarket on the promenade of Davos Platz or the Eurospar Supermarket on the promenade in Davos Dorf are the two best options. The local newspaper has a section for job hunters. If you were to try to find a job on the spot in the resort, you could stay in a bed and breakfast dormitory. The local tourist office is a good place to start when looking for a place to sleep.

The season lasts from the beginning of December to the end of April. Fines for working without a temporary residence permit are very high and also entail a black mark stamped in your passport preventing you from entering the country again. One of the hazards of trying to work for a while without the necessary documents: the police do make random checks particularly at the beginning of the season.

Sue Pike obtained a list of hotels in Davos through the tourist office and then wrote to about ten hotel managers for service work leaving the options as wide as possible. Any exams taken in German or time spent in German-speaking countries was mentioned along with any experience she had in restaurants in the UK. All of the hotels replied and in fact she ended up with a choice of work. The best time to write is at the end of the previous ski season or mid-way through the summer season. Sue reports:

Sue Pike explains how she found herself a job

Finding a job for yourself cuts out the expenses of an agency's fees, but be prepared to write a lot of letters. Make sure that your employer has not written into the work contract a clause preventing you from skiing. This is not unknown in some hotels where the manager has not enough staff to cover for people with possible ski injuries. Also, if you are going to work in Switzerland make sure you get a work contract from the enmployer. You will have to show this in order to get a temporary residence permit Another thing to check is that you have medical insurance. The employer will have accident insurance to cover you only while you are at work.

In Switzerland the wages of hotel staff are regulated. £1,500 per month approximately is what most foreign students earn after deductions for board, accommodation and tax. Not only the wages but the hours worked are regulated. It is standard to work nine hours per day with a half-hour break for every mealtime worked and alternately one day or one and a half days free per week worked. These free days may be given on a weekly basis or as a holiday during the quieter time of the season.

And how it was working as a waitress

As a buffet server/waitress I worked in the mornings from 8 am to 11.30 am making teas and coffees and generally overseeing the buffet breakfast. In the evenings my shift was from 5.30 to 11.30 pm when I worked as a waitress in the fondue Stübli of the hotel. On both shifts it was very hectic. But I was always left time to ski. Swiss hoteliers do not like to see staff standing around: – rather than employ enough staff for mealtimes to run calmly, they employ just enough staff so that even in the quieter periods all staff are active.

John Chivers, now a modern languages student in his final year at Coventry University, took a year out before starting his degree to work as a *chasseur* (general assistant) in the Hotel Kongress in Davos. He went through Jobs in the Alps (see *Other Organisations*). He says he thinks he got the job, largely on the strength of having an excellent grade German 'A' level which he certainly needed for some of his duties which included reception work and translating German menus. He enjoyed the job because of the variety of work involved. He also had to drive the hotel minibus to and from the railway station, act as relief night-porter and clear snow whenever needed which was frequently. Unfortunately this last task sometimes interfered with his skiing:

Normally my hours were from 8 am to 12 pm and 3 to 8.30 pm which gave me three hours in the afternoon for skiing. Unfortunately, if it was snowing I had to stay and clear the snow. Even though I got paid extra or was given more time off later, I got rather annoyed as it snowed a lot that year!

John found his employer 'firm but fair' and rather formal. The job lasted for four and a half months. There was a fellow British worker in the hotel Kongress (☎081 417 11 22; fax 081 417 11 23) who was employed as a waitress. Her boyfriend, who was turned down by Jobs in the Alps came out with her and after much knocking on doors got a job as a waiter when the incumbent left suddenly. During the following summer John worked in another alpine resort as a night porter with the Robinson Club (a kind of German Club Med) at the Hotel Schweizerhof in Vulpera. This is a tiny place near Tarasp and within spitting distance of the Austrian and Italian borders. It is also used as a skiing base in winter. However John would not recommend this except for recluses as it is very quiet.

Another Jobs in the Alps worker, Nicholas Kendrick who worked at the hotel Schweizerhof believes that Davos is a good place for foreign workers and recommends the Migros Supermarket as a good place to chat and ask about work with the many foreign workers, who hang around there drinking coffee and beer. It may also be worth checking out the British tour companies in Davos who may be in need of emergency staff. These include: Crystal, Flexiski, Inghams, Ski Activity, Ski Gower and Swiss Travel Service.

Les Diablerets

The delightful, old village of Les Diablerets nestles at the foot of the Diablerets glacier and at the head of the Ormand Valley in Vaud. In local dialect, Diablerets means 'the little devils', the name given to the glacier that overlooks it, as well as being the name of the first hotel built there at the end of the nineteenth century. It is neither as touristy nor upmarket (and therefore less spoiled) than many other Swiss resorts. A stroll through the village whose resident population is around 1,300 reveals traditional double-balconied chalets dating back over two hundred years, and local walks take you past glacial streams, through gorges and past waterfalls and into uninhabited valleys. Not that the village lacks amenities: there is a co-op and a post office. It is not all picture postcard stuff: Diablerets has an ice-rink, cinema, riding and a range of adventure sports including mud-biking and 'rap' (running down vertical bits of mountain), that make it a year round resort.

Although it is French-speaking, you will need to speak German as well since skiers come from nearby resorts including Gstaad to take advantage of better snow and runs on the Tsanfleuron glacier.

THE SKIING

The resort has nearly 60 km of piste (120 km on the linked lift pass with Villars) and 23 lifts and three separate skiing areas: the Glacier, Meilleret and Isneau. All are being extended and improved enough to impress the large proportion of regular skiers. The Glacier straddles the French/German linguistic border and not only is it the habitat of ibex but it also boasts the steepest cabin lift, 20° off vertical up a cliff-face, and the Quille, a standing rock which defied climbers well into the 20th century and is locally believed to be haunted. Once you have braved the red cabins that dangle over nothingness between the four lift bases, the views and much of the skiing are amazing. There is a restaurant (the Botta) on the peak at 3000m, and Pierre-Pointes is black enough to challenge anyone and the wide reds are sweeping.

Isneau is linked for much of the season by a run down to Pillin, and a PTT (post) bus trundles you back to the telecabins in the village. A good range of runs provide the base for much of the ski school and the off-piste makes the edges satisfying for boarders for whom there is a permanent park there.

Meilleret is the link to the Villars/Gryon skiing area. It includes an Olympic downhill run and a decent mogul section apart from the normal slope. A link into Villars and the Glacier means that even late in the season, respectable snow cover is not too hard to find and both resorts are kept busy around Easter.

APRÈS SKI

Party animals should note that nightlife is not exactly wild in Les Diablerets. There is a bar/disco, but most people are tucked away socialising in chalets and apartments. Since most of the ski workers are local and have families, if not a farm with animals safely tucked up in a barn for the winter, this is hardly surprising. Entertainment provided by the resort includes dinners (expensive) in the mountain restaurants, torchlit descents and at Easter, an egg hunt. If you are desperate for a bit more excitement, add more kirsch to that fondue and sample the wines that Switzerland does not export. That should liven up a few dark winter evenings in a warm chalet, and create a suitable hangover for the blazing sunshine and crisp snowy morning ahead to alleviate.

ACCOMMODATION

There is very little cheap and cheerful accommodation readily available. It would be best to ask your employer to arrange an attic, or to rent an apartment with several friends. The tourist office (024 492 3358; www.diablerets.ch) can supply a list of *chalet et apartements privé*. There is a youth hostel 1 km away at Vers l'Eglise (024 492 3013) but it is quite a walk to the lifts and is only all right for temporary stays.

There is a dormitory-style accommodation (12 beds) with canteen restaurant at Isneau (Ph. Cottier, ☎024 49 23 293). As the base for Isneau skiing runs and next to the telecabins terminus, it is busy and popular. It also serves a mean *géant rosti* (Swiss fried potato cake). Cabanes on the glacier has dormitories (SFr25 for non-members of Alpine Club) and a self-service style restaurant, under the direction of Bernard Lador (☎024 4922 102). Both of these two might also need workers.

WORK

Switzerland is expensive and jobs in Les Diablerets difficult to come by. The enterprises in the resort, as is often the case in Switzerland, are controlled by a few families and so basically the village regulars have it all sewn up. Very few holiday companies (among them Crystal and Ski Gower) do anything there except for booking customers into local hotels. However, if you stare a bit harder, there are opportunities. For instance, a few years ago, there was a ski school for the paraplegic disabled. The 'skis' looked like old-fashioned sidecars with mini ski sticks. This enterprise has now decamped to Villars. However, with this expansion into the area of disabled adventure activities like parapente or camping on the glacier in an igloo, Diablerets might have potential for entrepreneurs in this area.

Regular jobs also exist. The best avenue for obtaining hotel work is by asking. There are two big hotels: Eurotel run by Klaus Wartner (☎024/4923721) and Grand Hotel run by D Biedermann (☎024/4923551); as well as many smaller ones with restaurants and apartment chalets.

The Ski School is run by Eric Liechti (write to Chalet La Finca, 1865 Les Diablerets, Vaud) or contact him through the tourist office (+41 24 492 3358). It would be advisable to contact him in advance of the season, but otherwise February is a very busy month when they have been known to take on 'seasonals'. All instructors need to speak French and German, but in a mixed class the language may be English. Canadian and British instructors have been employed in the past.

Jobs on the lifts (*remontées mecaniques*) are another possiblitity. The lift company office (☎024 4922814) is above the tourist office and hires a batch of fresh workers annually. They prefer that you contact them in August and September for the season beginning mid-December. You can write to or e-mail Remontée Mecaniques (Les Diablerets, PO Box 224, 1865 Les Diablerets; telediablerets@bluewin.ch). The office says applicants must speak French and German but languages were not a problem for one hiree from Vancouver, who could only speak 'three words of French' when she arrived. The pay starts at 1,800 Swiss francs, which is enough to live on, and rises each year of experience you have. The duties, apart from smiling all day every day, are to rescue the accident-prone by skidoo. There is no lunch provided so you have to bring your own. An essential strategy is to make friends with the lift attendants as not only are they a friendly bunch, in general quite bored with the solitary nature of the work, but they will be able to keep you informed as you pass through.

Les Diablotins is a youth-groups accommodation complex on the edges of the village with beds for 180. The groups seem to be mainly Swiss and teenaged, so the manager (☎024 4923 633),who runs it might appreciate offers to help.

Hotel Mon Séjour (024 4923013) at Vers l'Eglise, just down the valley, has 100 dormitory beds and 20 hotel-style rooms. It has a good reputation for its cooking and is handy for a single ski lift that links into the bottom of Meilleret. There was an English girl working there and she was planning to return the following season. If you are interested in working there contact Charly Viret.

Les Diablerets is growing, both in popularity and the activities in terms of sports, that it offers. At present nightlife is virtually non-existent and there is certainly room for some hotel based entertainment. A local entrepreneur has recently started offering physiotherapy-type massage, and services like this for the rising tourist population would do well. What Diablerets has created over the last ten years in terms of enviable skiing is not reflected in the après ski excitement.

Engelberg

Engelberg, meaning 'angel town' in German, was founded by Benedictine Monks in 1120 and the first hotels were built in the 1850s. It has been a winter sports resort since the 1880s. The village still retains its historic Alpine character and is dominated by the vast abbey at one end. The town itself is at 1050m and nestles at the bottom of a large, wide valley. Engelberg is in the German-speaking part of Switzerland and a basic knowledge of German and a commitment to learn is an invaluable asset when looking for a job.

Engelberg is very easily reached by car and is only 20 minutes from the N2 motorway and one hour from Luzern. For those without transport or unwilling to brave the freezing waits of hitch-hiking, a mountain train runs from Luzern (35 km away) to Engelberg. Travel within the village can all be done on foot, but there is a free bus network which covers the village and ski lifts which can be a welcome alternative to walking in ski boots at the end of a day's skiing. If you are feeling rich then you could tour the village in style in a horse-drawn sleigh.

THE SKIING

Engelberg was described by the Swiss poet Conrad Meyer as a 'magnificent Alpine valley glistening with perpetual snow'. This comment was more than apt as summer skiers keep in trim on the glacier at the top of Titlis, the mountain that dominates Engelberg. The skiing areas are on both sides of the village at Brunni-Schonegg and Titlis. Brunni is the smaller section reached from the town itself. The Schonegg ski area only consists of a télécabine and two ski lifts but there are a surprising number of runs, all of which provide good skiing. The larger area of Titlis involves a free three-minute bus ride to the gondola which takes you to the starting point for skiing, the Trubsee (1764m). The Titlis area has something for everyone including the start of a cross-country ski trail. There is the resort's only black run from the top station (9,906 feet). There is approximately 82 km of marked piste in the resort, 12 of which can be skied continuously from the top of Titlis right down to the village. There are 60% red runs in the resort but some of them are very taxing and some of the blue runs would horrify beginners.

ACCOMMODATION

Unlike the more grand and exclusive Swiss resorts, there is a better chance that budget accommodation will be available in Engelberg. First check out the Berghaus which is the official Youth Hostel (☎637 12 92) where a bed costs SFrs. 23-32. Self-catering is also possible here. The warden speaks English, is very helpful and a mine of local information best gleaned over a coffee and schnapps in the evening. The Hostel can be booked in advance and would be worth the telephone call as large groups often book up most of the rooms. If the youth hostel is full then try the bed and breakfast at Matter coffeehouse at SFr 50. Another possibility for cheap accommodation would be to sub-let a room in a private apartment or to housesit for someone whilst they are away. Notices are put up in the information office at the train station. The Tourist Centre (☎041 637 37 37) might also be able to help out.

WORK

Unlike some larger resorts, there is no regular subculture of English-speaking workers in Engelberg. However there are some establishments which have a tradition of taking English-speakers for a season. In one past season there were three British people working at the Hotel Engelberg (☎041 637 11 68) alone and many of the hotels have at least one Brit working for them. Popular meeeting places are the Restaurant Yucatan, Restaurant Matter and the Angel Pub.

Both Hotel Eden (☎041 639 56 39) and Hotel Hess (☎041 637 13 66) have recruited through the agency Jobs in the Alps for several years. Sylvia got her first job in Engelberg this way in order to escape from the Manchester shoe factory where she worked before. She went to the Hotel Engelberg earning the official minimum salary and says:

> *I start at 7 am and work until midday. The afternoon is free until 6 pm and I sometimes finish at 9 pm, sometimes even 2 am! I am very lucky with the hours I work: in some hotels you alternate each week between early and late nights in the restaurant. I work mostly behind the scenes washing-up, looking after the wine cellar and ordering food although I occasionally get the chance to do some waitressing.*

Sylvia learned (Swiss) German on the job and is now fluent for everyday purposes.

Lynda, as a student worked at the Hotel Trübsee which is half way up the mountain right on the ski slopes; a job she heard about from her cousin. She says:

It is absolutely essential to speak German here – even the people doing the washing-up speak German. It is not the same in other hotels though.

Anne, who is English, worked in the management of the Pizzeria on the main street of the town and Chantelle, a South African, was waitressing in the Hotel Hoheneck.

There are very good leisure facilities in Engelberg and they are definitely worth a visit. They prefer to recruit for the whole season so the earlier you can apply the better. The Sportcenter Erlen (☎041 637 34 33) run by Bruno Kühne includes indoor tennis courts, indoor ice rink and a fitness room. If you have any experience training, supervising or maintaining any of these activities then it is well worth applying. There may be possibilities of bar work, cleaning or janitor work. For anyone with the Bronze ASA lifesaving award and a basic knowledge of first aid, there is a possibility of poolside attendant at the Sonnenberg swimming pool. The third leisure centre is near the gondola lift leading towards Titlis and called Sporthalle. Inside there is a large bar which serves light meals, electronic games machines, bowling alleys and a video room. Even if the Sporthalle does not need any more staff when you arrive it is a fun place to spend an evening. Any musicians looking for a venue to earn a few francs should present themselves to the manager: the Sporthalle is ideal with plenty of space for the musicians and dancers.

Another possible job with local employers are the lift companies which also operate the altitude restaurants. There is one company on the Titlis side which is BET (Bergbahnen Engelberg-Trübsee-Titlis). This company needs people to look after the restaurants, run the lifts, bash and mark the pistes and run the emergency stretcher service. However, they only very rarely employ foreigners unless they have a special skill. One Englishman however, was lucky and worked in the souvenir shop at the summit of Titlis where tourists often ascend simply for the view from one of the highest peaks in Switzerland. He was able to find plenty of time to ski and remarked with considerable understatement, 'Well, it's better than being an unemployed landscape gardener in Liverpool'.

British tour companies are not much in evidence though Crystal and the Swiss Travel Service are, and Ski Gower, the school group specialist have groups in the resort intermittently throughout the season. They do not employ any staff in the resort for a whole season but ski teachers accompany the groups from the UK and ski with them for one or two weeks at a time. The groups usually operate from the Engelberg Youth Hostel.

It is worth reiterating the need to either have some basic German or be prepared to learn it as there is a competition for jobs from various immigrants and temporary workers with fluent German.

Grindelwald

Grindelwald is situated in the centre of the Bernese Oberland in one of the most famous regions of Switzerland and the magnificent Eiger, Monch and Jungfrau mountains can be seen from the top of the Lauberhorn skiing area. Grindelwald has not had an entirely trouble free existence. In 1892 a fire destroyed 116 houses (most of Grindelwald at that time) in 24 hours. It took eight years for tourism to recover its confidence and the lovely, traditional wooden buildings that form the centre today, date from this reconstruction. Grindelwald is a fair-sized, but still attractive small town these days and expansion is continuing. New hotels have been built recently making a total of 50. In addition there are nearly a 1,000 chalet flats, and numerous private chalets let for part of the year.

Access from Zurich and Bern is easy and visitors can drive into the centre of town to reach the hotels. There is also a tiny railway station located at the entrance to the village, almost lost amid the surrounding big hotels – in fact one hotel, the Derby, is right on the platform.

THE SKIING

Grindelwald has long been a favourite with British skiers. Today it has 213 km of piste served by 44 lifts. The majority of skiers are sold the resort by the popular tour operators and several specialised companies based in Grindelwald. The train is well-utilised by skiers to get up to the Kleine Scheidegg, the central skiing area for the Lauberhorn runs, the runs to Wengen and also for taking another train up to Eigergletscher. Names of runs like Black Rock, Oh God and Punchbowl show the influence of British skiers. The access to the Mannlichen ski region is by a two-section gondola. This offers another large area, which can be reached from Kleine Scheidegg on runs through the woods.

Grindelwald has another popular skiing, walking and toboganning (70km of runs including Europe's longest at 15km) region known as First, starting a short distance from the centre of the village. A new six-seater gondola, capable of carrying 1,200 skiers an hour has replaced one of the oldest chairlifts in the Alps and has transformed this delightful area. The skiing is suitable mainly for intermediates and is extensive and varied. Lifts have improved the skiing possibilities with the option of skiing right back to the village. The Jungfrau ski pass includes skiing at Interlaken, 35 minutes away by train. It also includes a day trip to Mürren and the Schilthorn.

APRÈS SKI

Grindelwald's admirable selection of bars and restaurants includes many with local folkloric themes and dance evenings. Many hotels have live bands either for dancing or as background. There are two discos, two where the beer is half price on certain nights ensuring a good attendance. Many of the ski workers and reps are to be found there as well as the holidaymakers.

There is a modern Sports Centre with a swimming pool an ice-rink where ice-hockey, for which Grindelwald is famous, is played. Regular après ski activities are: bowling, night ski jumping and evening rides to mountain restaurants using toboggans for the return journey (Bussalp and Grosse Scheidegg). Those who make the trip to Interlaken will find ski equipment can be much cheaper there.

WORK

There are usually more vacancies than applicants in Grindelwald. Most of the jobs are unskilled, i.e. washing up in a bar or hotel, cleaning and general odd jobs in hotels, chalets, shops and bars. The waiters and hotel workers tend to be Italian or Portuguese, although there are some English-speakers, generally in the smaller, family hotels. Accommodation is nearly always provided with such jobs, but if you want something less basic, it is better to rent a place with several friends. It can even work out cheaper than paying the hotel for board and lodging which is otherwise deducted from your wage.

As in many Swiss ski villages, the Tourist Office (☎033 854 12 12) also operates a system similar to an employment agency. They keep a list of vacancies for all types of hotel work and a list of workers who are looking for a job or a change of employment. If you walk in on spec, they charge SFrs.10 for the list of jobs. It is a good idea to carry a bunch of CVs with you so that your details are to hand: include especially any skills and/or experience and any languages you can speak though German is of course the most preferred. However, as English is widely spoken you will almost certainly get offered any menial jobs (i.e. not reception). Remember when considering any job offers to check what time you will have off for skiing. There is little point in taking a boring job if you can only ski once a week or not at all in peak season.

Ideally you should take a week's holiday in Grindelwald at the end of the season before the one you want to work there. This gives you a chance to make contact with the employers and look at the working conditions and accommodation. You should then confirm with your employer during the summer that you still want the job so that he or she can apply for your work permit.

Lisa Hanson who is English and a qualified beauty therapist, was in Grindelwald, when she saw an advert in the Health and Beauty Salon attached to the Grand Hotel Regina (☎033 854 54 55; fax 033 853 47 17). The job was for someone who wanted to set up and run a small operation as the resident beauty therapist. There was already a hairdressing room and a massage room to compliment the sauna and swimming pool there. At first she lived in staff quarters in the hotel, then rented a small apartment in Interlaken. By doing this, her net pay was over SFr 1,800 per month (about £900). She has two days off a week and this is flexible. She has to stay in or near the salon from 10.30 am to 7 pm and brings her snacks with her. The hotel particularly wanted an English person, not just someone who spoke English.

Chris Lamper, a qualified chef, wrote to ten hotels whose addresses he got from the trade publication *Leading Hotels*. He got two offers and started work in Grindelwald in December to work as a chef in the Grand Hotel Regina. His German was non-existent, but luckily for him the other staff spoke English. He liked the hotel but had decided that he wanted to live and work in Interlaken, and moved to the Victoria Lauberhorn Hotel there. Chris found that a quarter of his monthly salary was taken up by tax, insurance (for doctors and emergency treatment for day-to-day occurences and wintersports). However, one invaluable perk of the job was that the hotel paid for him to take German lessons. He suggested that *Hotel and Catering* magazine is another useful publication for hotel jobs abroad.

Kate spent a holiday in Grindelwald and decided she would like to work there. She took a waitressing job but then wanted something better. Having spotted a couple of adverts for au pairs on the noticeboard in the Co-op supermarket she applied and both offered her jobs. As they were part-time, she could do both and found it infinitely preferable to waitressing. She had her own accommodation because for au pair jobs with accommodation, the pay is considerably less.

There are two local papers which are of use to job seekers: The *Echo von Grindelwald* and the *Anzeige von Interlaken*. The Thursday and Friday editions carry employment sections.

Workers from Britain seem to be especially welcome in Grindelwald; perhaps because the British have been faithful visitors for such a long time.

Gstaad

Gstaad, extremely low at 1050 m for what is a world-class resort, is situated at the foot of the Glacier des Diablerets, east of Lake Geneva. It is 93 miles /150km from Geneva airport; a journey of about three and a half hours by road. It has a worldwide reputation for luxury as you might guess from the private jets landing at Saanen, just outside the town and the serried rank of designer shops like Hermes and Cartier which line the traffic-free main street. It has needless to say, been holiday home or vacation spot of the rich and celebrated including Roger Moore, Princess Diana, Michael Jackson etc. The town itself has an ultra smart Swiss atmosphere and there are endless cafés and bars for a pit stop. The railway station is central and the mountain bus and train services are free if you invest in a season pass for the skiing region.

Contrary to what you might expect, Gstaad doesn't even have official status as a town and it is classed as an outlying area of nearby Saanen, a former farming village that has barely been touched by the glittering trappings of commercialism and tourism that have been embraced by Gstaad. Saananland is the name given to region around Saanan, which includes five top ski regions.

THE SKIING

There is an amazing range of skiing in the Gstaad region. The six main areas are Shonried, Saanenmoser, Rougemont, St. Stephan, Chateau-d'Oex and the year-round glacier skiing at Les Diablerets. Gstaad area has a total of 250km of piste and 66 lifts. Gstaad has little in the way of doorstep skiing, but free bus and train rides whisk you to the different areas which are themselves lift-linked to one another. The resort is excellent for both novices and experts for whom the off piste and black runs are suitably challenging. The lift workers are a cheerful bunch as they load you on and off the modern and user friendly equipment. As if this were not enough, all the ski areas have fantastic off piste and beautiful scenery, through trees and with exceptional views.

Season ticket prices are hefty, but there are good deals for separate regions. Workers of course get a discount.

As the resort is low, it can suffer from snow shortage, but the glacier is accessible and useable year round.

There are 60km of cross-country including a stretch between Shonried and Sannanmoser alongside the railway track. For the more adventurous there is ski touring and for the deep-pocketed there is heli-skiing.

NIGHTLIFE

Unlike its celebrated clientele, Gstaad nightlife is concealed in private chalets and suites. If you have the right connections you might be invited. Otherwise you will be left with the dozen or so bars attached to the hotels where the locals are liable to break out into yodelling. Some exceptions might be the English bars such as Richi's or the The Greengo a the Palace Hotel, Club 95 at the Sport Hotel Victoria or the 'Pub of Course' at the Hotel Boo which tend to be more international and contemporary in their choice of disco or live music. For a wilder night out you might have to resort to a trip to nearby Launen, which has a couple of happening night clubs.

ACCOMMODATION

As you would expect, accommodation is not cheap in Gstaad but there are some budget possibilities. The tourist office (033 748 81 81; www.gstaad.ch) will provide youth hostel and B&B information. You can also enquire if there are any rooms in private houses, which you can rent. One couple (☎033 744 1893) interviewed said they would charge about SFr 22 per night per person sharing a room for three people. There are many other such rooms on offer and lists of the places and telephone numbers are available from the tourist office. Some deals will include breakfast. If this fails then the best thing to do would be to stay in one of the surrounding villages and bus in to look for work.

WORK

Gstaad does not have a regular contingent of tour operator staff from Britain except for Ski Weekend so the best way to find work is probably on the spot. If you haven't fixed up anything in advance, you should first check the notices outside the Co-op where jobs like baby-sitting or helpers for private chalets are advertised. Failing this, do a tour of the hotels and bars. The bars that tend to help British job-seekers are the 'Green Girl' in the Gstaad Palace, Club 95, Richi's Pub, which is probably the most useful, and 'The Pub of Course.'

Christina from the UK, came to Gstaad having been working already in Lausanne. She therefore already had a work permit which undoubtedly helped get her job at the Café

Pernet in Gstaad. She did not arrange any appointments in Gstaad, she just turned up on the spot and started asking around. She started as a kind of general help and then progressed to waiting tables. She is proud of having improved her knowledge of languages; first in Lausanne where she expanded her GCSE knowledge of French, now in Gstaad where she is working on her German (albeit with a Swiss accent). She gets free lunches, reduced rate hotel room accommodation and a salary at the minimum Swiss rate. She said it is getting harder to find jobs on the spot in Switzerland, although she herself plans to work in other ski resorts there.

Klosters

Apparently pronounced as if it had an extra 'e' in it (as in 'Klose-ters'), the pretty village of Klosters is entirely surrounded by peaks and is located in Graubünden in the eastern, German-speaking part of Switzerland. Sadly, it is probably better known for its association with Prince Charles and his progeny, than for its excellent skiing. Compared with its neighbour Davos, Klosters is less attractive to mainstream tourism, despite being on the same lift pass. The village is reached from Zurich via the motorway and main road that takes you through Davos. Klosters is in two parts (Dorf and Platz). Klosters Dorf, is the smaller part and has the only genuinely local pub ('Rufinis') not to mention a strip club. Rufinis is the main meeting place for locals as well as seasonal workers from the whole of Klosters and is part pub and part music bar. It is a good starting point for anyone seeking work. Klosters Platz, another km or so up the hill is the commercial part of the village with a couple of shopping streets, banks, co-op etc. A bypass road tunnel links Klosters directly with the Engadine valley (i.e. St. Moritz) in a journey of 45 minutes.

The town of Chur is only 48km away and well worth visiting on days off. Walking and langlauf are other attractions and various rounds of the Swiss langlauf championships are held on three weekends during the season, which results in a sudden rush of visitors.

APRES SKI

Klosters definitely has more of a village atmosphere than a full-blown ski resort air and the evenings can be fairly quiet as well as being expensive. Much of the après ski revolves around socialising in the private chalets and apartments, which make up the majority of the accommodation in the resort. The Steinbock bar is popular with locals and tourists. The night-club 'Casa Antica' charges entry of SFr 20 rising to SFr 45 at Christmas time and with the cheapest drink being mineral water at SFr 18 it is beyond the means of many locals and seasonal workers, but is popular with Prince Harry and his chums.

WORK

Although seasonal work may be hard to find, there are several possibilities. Firstly, check the noticeboard at the Co-op, and also the local newspapers *Klosterer Zeitung* and *Gipfel Zeitung* which both advertise vacancies, especially at the start of the season.

Simon Thompson from Bristol worked in the Robinson Club in Alte Bahnhofstrasse as a night porter having got the job with Jobs in the Alps. He was older than the average seasonal worker at 39.

Simon Thompson was pleasantly surprised that he was hired.
I thought I might be a little old for what is the German equivalent of Club Med, as Rob Club mostly employs young Germans. However, they will employ German-speakers for reception, cooks, ski instructors or in entertainment on personal application.

As you would expect, clients are mostly Germans there for the full in-house entertainment, which the Club provides. This did not present too much problem as long as you are prepared to get involved as much as possible. The Club has a live show and disco every night as well as other 'aktions' as the animation programme is called.

I got the job on the strength of having 'A' level German and having worked in a bank as the duties included closing the day's accounts. I enjoyed my season, but having to work six nights a week without holidays can be quite a strain at times so as long as you get plenty of rest and don't count on skiing every day then it is not such a big problem.

The Robinson Club (☎081 422 61 01) in Klosters is the smallest of four such establishments in Switzerland including Arosa and Saas Fee; there are others in Austria. Anyone interested in working for this organisation can write to the head office (Robinson Club GmbH, Karel-Wiechert-Allee 23, 30625 Hanover, Germany).

Although Klosters has its fair share of visitors, it does not attract hordes of Britons so some knowledge of German is virtually essential to get a job there. The largest hotel in Klosters is the Vereina which is the local meeting place for ski instructors in the evenings. The local rep for the Ski Club of GB has an open night every Thursday in the bar and so could be a good source of information. Other large hotels are the Aldiana, also German-run along the lines of Robinson Club, but has a night club which is open to outsiders, and the Steinbock (081 422 45 45) and Pardenn (☎081 42 21 1 41) are also large establishements.

If you are interested, Prince Charles stays at the Walserhof (081 422 13 40), a small fairly modern Hotel on the main road.

Iain Anderson from London found himself a job playing in the Piano Bar of the Hotel Chesa Grischuna (☎081 422 22 22) run by the Guler family. He played twice nightly from 6-8pm and 10pm to midnight.

Cecila and Mickey from Sweden were working their second season in the Scotch bar and were planning to return for a third. They are here for the skiing and reckon that is the main attraction of Klosters.

Tour operators from Britain in Klosters include Descent International, Inghams, Powder Byrne, Ski Gower and Swiss Travel Service.

Lenzerheide/Valbella

Lenzerheide lies in a valley in the Graubünden canton of German-speaking, southeastern Switzerland, straddling the main road from Chur to St. Moritz. From the early 1880s it was a popular summer resort and still is, but with the growing popularity of winter sports it has also developed a lively trade in the skiing season.

Lenzerheide is usually lumped together with its smaller sister resort of Valbella, about a mile away down the valley and which is on the free bus route, which runs throughout the winter season covering the entire resort. There is also a regular bus service to and from Chur (11 km) where the nearest railway station is and it is also possible to get to the classier and more expensive resorts of Davos and St. Moritz.

Together Lenzerheide/Valbella make up quite a large resort with 45 hotels and plenty of opportunities for the eager holiday worker.

THE SKIING

The Rothorn, Scalottas, Danis and Stätzerhorn are the main peaks surrounding Lenzerheide and offer good, if not top class, skiing opportunities for every standard, although advanced skiers would probably find it a little monotonous. There are over 155 km of runs and the queues are only apparent in high season in mid-February. For those who prefer cross-country skiing, there are 48 km of trails around the Heidsee, a lake that separates Lenzerheide from Valbella. For workers, a season pass is available at a cut rate. It is also worth checking out the best place to get second hand skis. One worker interviewed paid only £80 for skis and boots.

APRÈS SKI

As the bars in Switzerland do not close until 1 am (3 am in hotels) there is always somewhere to go for a welcome half litre or so after work. For most of the resort workers, this tends to be Nino's English-style pub. This bar is the centre of nightlife for seasonal workers of all nationalities and is packed every night between mid-December and late March. Apart from Nino's, there are three nightclubs, which are all over-priced and tawdry and are only worth going to in mid-February. There is also a good smattering of hotel bars and pizza restaurants.

ACCOMMODATION

If you come to Lenzerheide on spec to look for work, there is a youth hostel at Valbella. If the hostel is full, it is worth considering renting an apartment in Lenzerheide if you can find a group to share with. A list of places for rent can be obtained from the tourist office (+41 81 385 11 20; www.lenzerheide.ch). Most workers however, end up living in accommodation provided by the employers, the cost of which is deducted from their rent.

WORK

One thing that the seasonal workers in Lenzerheide agreed on is that there are always job vacancies there in summer or winter. One of the biggest hotels, the Sunstar (081 384 01 21), employs about 60 staff, about six of whom are usually British and have arrived there through Jobs in the Alps (see *Working Through Other Organisations*). According to Liz Hemingway who arranged her job at that hotel in advance through Jobs in the Alps:

Liz Hemingway arranged her job through Jobs in the Alps
There were a lot of foreigners in Lenzerheide, the nationalities most represented were (ex) Yugoslavs, Portuguese, Dutch, Germans and British. There were ten people in the resort who had arranged their jobs through JITA and others from Britain who had found their jobs independently.

I enjoyed working in Lenzerheide immensely, and would do it again at the drop of a hat. I would advise applying early and being prepared for some refusals. Emphasise any experience or languages that you have. Having said that, 90% of the Brits working there had neither. There are plenty of people working in hotels ready to show you their expertise on the slopes and offer some free advice. At the beginning of the season I could just tell one end of a ski from the other; by the end I was skiing red runs, though still spending some time on my backside. During the winter, Lenzerheide is lively and exciting to be in. It certainly doesn't have everything that larger, more fashionable resorts like St. Moritz have, but it is a very friendly resort.

Roland Nash was a waiter in Lenzerheide and had the following advice to those who turn up on spec
There seemed to be plenty of opportunities for work because the turnover of staff was quite high. If you didn't find work one week, you were likely to find some the next. Most seasonal work is to be found in the hotels and the best qualification is a willingness to do anything. Of course languages and experience helps, but a total lack of these is not an insurmountable problem. The hotels known to employ Brits

---

are: the Sunstar, La Palanca (☎081 384 31 31), Pöstli, and Posthotel Valbella (☎081 384 12 12), but all are worth trying. The best place to find out about vacancies is Nino's Bar where you can ask amongst the seasonal workers, most of whom speak English and are only too pleased to meet and talk over a beer.

Despite the hard work there is much to recommend in Lenzerheide as Roland says
The hours I worked as a waiter were horrendous, particularly in the weeks following Christmas and over the New Year. On New Year's Eve I worked over 30 hours without a break, and for the first three weeks I did not have a day off. Working in hotels is not easy, but even with these conditions I still thoroughly enjoyed my four months in Lenzerheide and would recommend the experience to anyone. I could ski a little before I went there, but my skiing improved enormously. The friends I made out there included England under 21 skiers and beginners, all of whom found slopes to please them.

Leukerbad (Loèche-les-Bains)

Leukerbad is a small spa village popular since Roman times, situated in the Valais (Wallis) region of southern Switzerland at an altitude of 1411 m (4,629 feet) about 50 miles from the Italian border, with Mürren to the north and Zermatt to the south. A narrow, winding road lined with picturesque houses and small craft shops runs through the centre from the imposing Hotel Regina to the swimming pool and spa complex at the lower end of the village. The health complex is modern and impressive with warm water jets (water temperature 28C to 41C) and jacuzzis incorporated into the huge half-indoor swimming pool. It also houses the original baths, which although disturbing to the eye, are, we are assured, soothing to body and mind. An attractive square lies in the heart of the village, overlooked by the majestic Hotel les Bains and the quaint old village church. Sadly, a recent costly revamp has taken away some of the old character of the town.

THE SKIING

Although largely uncommercialised and little-known, Leukerbad offers good skiing facilities including 60 km of ski runs and 23 km cross-country trails, 17 ski lifts and a floodlit ski run. The Torrenthorn cable car runs from the centre of the village taking the more energetic members of the holidaymaking community up to the middle station of the main skiing area, the Rinderhütte. There are extensive ski lifts and a good selection of runs including some challenging black runs where major international skiing competitions like the World Cup downhill are regularly held.

APRÈS SKI

The nightlife isn't exactly what you might call pulsating, as the nightspots are tucked away in fairly discreet locations. But the bars are always full: especially the Chinchilla Pub, the Go Crazy and the Face which are the places to be on a Saturday night and a regular meeting place for foreign workers of all nationalities.

WORK

As with many of the older, less commercialised Swiss resorts, hotels are the main source of holiday accommodation. There are 28 in Leukerbad. The larger hotels, such as the Regina, the Grichting, Hotel Maison Blanche and the Hotel de France are staffed almost entirely by foreign workers with the occasional Swiss national cracking the whip in a plum job as housekeeper or head receptionist. Foreign workers are regarded as cheap labour, but the pay is by no means appalling and waiting staff and bartenders get the reasonable minimum wage and tips.

Philippa Sumner got her job at the Hotel Römerhof, which was run by the younger members of the family who owned the four-star Hotel Regina, through Jobs in the Alps, who also arranged jobs for two other Brits as a waitress and a night porter. Nationality seems to be irrelevant to the Swiss as long as you work hard. Philippa's job was highly varied. She waited tables in the hotel dining-room, served lunches and drinks on the terrace, and worked downstairs in the public bar. The hotel was small and consequently she was expected to help with anything if necessary: if no one was on reception she carried round a cordless phone while she cleaned cutlery, made ice-cream and cold snacks and operated a somewhat temperamental meat-slicing machine when preparing the buffet breakfast. She was also called upon to help make the beds when the cleaner had a day off. Philippa says:

> *Working in Leukerbad was fun because of the sheer size of the foreign work force – everyone knew everyone else and we all had a great time. It is, however a good idea to have a job organised before you go out there, as there is nowhere really cheap to stay while you are looking. Most of the people I met had applied directly to hotels and restaurants – the tourist office (Verkehrsverein, 3945 Leukerbad; ☎027-472 71 71)can help with addresses.*

Leysin

Leysin is a fairly large and attractive all-year-round resort situated in the Vaudois Alps. It is easily accessible from Lake Geneva and is twenty minutes drive from Aigle. It is one of the main sports resorts of Switzerland but nevertheless has managed to keep its character and charm. Leysin also has a reputation as a convention centre and because it has a surplus of dormitory accommodation (in the form of former sanitoria for tuberculosis sufferers), it is popular with school and youth skiing trips. The youthful atmosphere is further enhanced by the presence of several colleges including the Leysin American School, The American College of Switzerland, the Kumon Leysin Academy (Japanese/American) and a Swiss Hotel and Tourism School. It is a lively town with lots to do and also offers two large sports centres and an ice rink.

THE SKIING

Leysin at 1200m is not high, the top station La Berneuse is 6658 feet (2048m) and the addition of an excellent sunshine record means that the snow is not particularly reliable late on in the season. The skiing is virtually all on one side of the village. You can take the gondola up to La Berneuse where there is a splendid revolving restaurant with views down the Rhône Valley and of the surrounding peaks. From La Berneuse you can ski down to the Lac d'Aï and take the draglift up the Chaux de Mont (2200m). After skiing down you have to take the draglift back to La Berneuse from where there is a choice of easy and medium runs back to Leysin. Another gondola, near the Berneuse base station goes to the Tour de Mayen ski area. The skiing on 60 km of prepared piste is not in the least demanding and good skiers would have to travel to Les Diablerets (about 25 minutes away) to find any real challenge. The type of skiing makes the resort very suitable for novices.

ACCOMMODATION

The Hiking Sheep Guesthouse (Villa La Joux, 1854 Leysin; tel/fax +41 (0)24 494 3535; hikingsheep@leysin.net) is a useful place to stay and works out around SFr 25 a night.

WORK

Diana Griffiths, practically a professional traveller-worker, arrived in Leysin in January. When she asked people she met in bars about jobs they advised her to go to every single place and ask if there was any work going. This advice she would pass on: 'go early (preferably November or early December) and look around.' Diana found a job washing up at the Buffet de la Gare where she was well paid, well fed and had one and a half days off a week. She returned to Leysin again a year later and this time found work in Restaurant Le Feydey (☎024 494 11 47) which is owned by the same people as her previous place of work. This time she was waitressing instead of washing up; however she left this job part way through the season when a better opportunity came along. This was working for Leysin's largest employer of foreign labour who runs large hotels for school parties. These include the former Grand Hotel and the former sanitoria converted into dormitory style accommodation. Diana received a modest salary, board and lodging and reductions on skiing expenses. There are certainly dozens of English-speaking young people employed in these hotels including Americans, Australians, New Zealanders, Canadians, and even a few from Hawaii. One of the spin offs of the job was the social life with lots of staff parties and discos. But this is by no means a cushy job and can mean working seven days a week. Diana reports that the Berneuse Restaurant situated by the slopes, has employed English-speakers in the past and probably would again.

Leysin does not have a large showing of British tour operators. Coach parties arrive in the summer and winter, and only some of the winter ones come to ski and they vary from year to year.

Saas Fee

Saas Fee claims to be germinal to the history of skiing thanks to a local parish priest, Joseph Imseng who first strapped on a pair of 'skis' on 20 December 1849 to reach his parish of Saas Grund in the valley below. The resort of Saas Fee has grown out of a typical Valaisian farming village, and still contains many quaint old buildings from that time. One of the several points in its favour is that cars have to be parked outside the village and the resort itself is traffic-free. As a thriving resort however, Saas Fee has expanded considerably and is rather spread out necessitating the need for electric taxis. Although these near-silent conveyances help to maintain the tranquility of the resort, they are very nippy and can be a hazard in themselves if you fail to notice their approach in time.

Saas Fee has a spectacular setting surrounded by snowy peaks. Through a gap in the otherwise encircling mountains, the road looks down into the valley below at the rather dull resort of Saas Grund. Despite its popularity the village of Saas Fee has a noticeable absence of large luxury-type hotels and most of the accommodation is in chalet-style buildings. This helps to keep the village atmosphere and create an impression of friendliness.

Saas Fee's smarter neighbour, Zermatt is one and a half hours away by road. The car parks, postbus depot and tourist office, are all to be found at the village entrance. One of the big hotels, the Zurbriggen has an internationally famous name, not from the hotel but because the name Zurbriggen is a local one, a scion of which, Pirmin Zurbriggen won the Olympic Gold Medal at Calgary in 1988. He comes from nearby Saas Almagell.

THE SKIING

Saas Fee must be one of the few resorts which is excellent for beginners and advanced skiers, but has limited skiing for the intermediate. However, with 125 km of piste, it is true to say that everyone can find something to their liking. Of the three main skiing areas two are interconnected: Langfluh-Spielboden can be reached by cable car from the edge of the village via Speilboden. There are spectacular views over the glacier from the top station. From there a long medium run goes down to the village. An alternative is to take the Feechatz skilift across the glacier from where you can ski over to the Felskinn. The Felskinn-Mittelallalin area is reached from the bottom station in Saas Fee on an express gondola (Alpin Express) which climbs up to Maste 4 Section (2550m) in an incredible seven minutes and section two between Maste 4 and Felskinn. There is also a cable car from the edge of the village, which takes you straight up to Felskinn (3000m). From Felskinn you can take the highest underground railway in the world, (the Metro Alpin) which climbs to an amazing 3,500 m (11,500 feet) to the Mitteallalin where the highest revolving restaurant in the world (with prices to match) gives you an unsurpassable panorama of the region. From Felskinn there are a couple of medium runs while the experts can tackle the two black runs from Kamel (3250m) reached by drag lift from Egginerjoch. There are also a couple of black runs from Maste 4. The third area Plattjen, reached by Gondola from the edge of the village is on the opposite side of the valley. Plattjen has both easy and black runs not to mention an excellent restaurant.

If there is any complaint about Saas Fee it's not usually about the skiing but normally about the long treks to the lifts. The village is at least a mile long. There is a ski bus, which costs SFr 3. This is cheaper than taking electric taxis. Like other high resorts, Saas Fee has summer glacier skiing accessed by the Metro Alpin. Saas Fee is also the venue for a number of famous races in the skiing calendar. The annual Allalin Downhill, at 12 km the longest downhill race in the world and with the highest starting point at 3,800 m. It is the Grand National of the skiing world as it is open to anyone from Johannes Bloggs to the World Downhill Champion who has indeed taken part in it.

Snowboarding is big in Saas Fee; not only are there two snowboard bars (Popcorn and Happy), but there is a year round snowboarding park.

APRÈS SKI

The Rendez-vous, situated next to the ski slopes is popular in the afternoon as it has a sunny terrace. Saas Fee has a lively nightlife and the nightclubs: Crazy-Night, Art-Club, Go In or Underground are some of the most patronised. Meeting places for the English ski workers are the Hotel Glacier and the Underground (dive under Benetton), Nesti's Bar, the Why Not pub and the aforementioned Rendez-vous.

WORK

Saas Fee is a popular resort with the Brits and there are about a dozen tour operators here including: Crystal, Erna Low, First Choice, Inghams, Ski Club of GB, Thomson and Swiss Travel Service.

Fran Ashworth, a qualified dietician was a chalet girl for two seasons. She got her first break through one of the classic routes: She was on holiday when the regular chalet girl broke a leg and she offered to take over. She and her colleague Claire Stuttaford, who has a degree in politics and languages think it is important that you apply to work with a friend if possible as there is only a 50/50 chance of a successful working relationship with a total stranger and 'it would be ghastly to spend five months working with someone you couldn't stand'. Claire also mentions the chalet girls' well-known affliction, mid-season blues:

There is a time, about half way through the season when you can't bear the thought of being nice to another punter, and you have to stick an upside-down coat hanger in your mouth every morning until the blues depart.

The girls think it might be a good idea if the chalet cooks had a few days holiday in another resort during the season to refresh them. They had actually been very lucky with their employers and had spent most of the season in another resort before being transferred to Saas Fee.

Karen Barker helped out for the last two weeks at Chalet Claire. She is a friend of theirs and like Fran is a qualified dietician. Karen had spent the rest of season in Flims working as a chalet person with Powder Byrne. She got the job through being a college friend of the director. Fran and Karen both had jobs to go back to in the UK. Claire wanted to save enough money to go round the world.

There is also scope for the enterprising and independent ski bum. Paul Evans and James Westwood from Rutland, came out to Saas Fee in mid-March with flight only and £400 each, intending to stay for the rest of the season (about five to six weeks). Having spent all their money faster than they expected, they survived by washing up and cleaning for chalet staff in return for food. They also got paid for cleaning and tidying chalets on changeover days. Some companies also gave their chalet staff money to pay for cleaners especially for larger chalets. Paul and James also made a bit of money helping out reps with transfers; the rate is about SFr 60 for a Geneva transfer, and SFr 15 for meeting the clients on arrival in the resort. Their accommodation was over a shop and was free but sordid. They got it through an English friend who works in a sports shop. Paul and James were on their year off between school and university. Before coming out to Saas Fee they had been working in the UK. Paul was going to study hotel management and interested in being a rep for a major company. They had both managed to buy second hand skis, bindings, poles and boots quite cheaply in the resort.

There are also opportunities working for the Swiss. Richard James, came to Saas Fee as a rep for a British company, but found he could earn nearly three times as much working in Nesti's bar near the Hotel Christiana earning the statutory Swiss salary. Changing to a Swiss employer also entitled him to reductions on travel in the canton and reductions on ski passes in other resorts as well as Saas Fee. Rick, an Australian ski bum was going to work as a scuba-diving instructor in Bunderberg, on the Sunshine Coast of Queensland, for £580 a week. His girlfriend Carol Wilson, worked at the Hotel Allalin waiting tables. She got the job through Jobs in the Alps. She is half-German and wanted to improve her German and her skiing. She was well paid but she had to work very hard. She had been doing overtime for the last ten weeks. Of the Swiss as employers she was not over enthusiastic:

Some Swiss employers show no mercy; you are expected to turn up for work even when you are ill, and they think a half-day means eight hours work.

However, she earned herself enough to go to Australia with Rick and she hopes to get a part-time job waiting tables in Sydney and Queensland at £12 an hour. After six months in Australia she would like to come back to Saas Fee next season as she likes it very much.

For cheap accommodation while looking for work try the Albana-Mascotte (ask for Doris). However if by the time you arrive any cheap accommodation is taken you could try Saas Grund (seven minutes down the valley by bus) from where you could commute.

SAAS GRUND

Saas Grund is in a wide, flat valley bottom valley below its more famous and attractive neighbour Saas Fee. It has its own ski area on the mountains the opposite side of the valley from Saas Fee: Kreuzboden (2400m) and Hohsaas (3,100m) to which the gondola from Saas Grund provides easy access. Most of the runs are for intermediates but Saas Grund also has its own nursery slopes. The Saas region ski pass also includes nearby Saas Fee to which ski buses run every 15 minutes. Or skiers can take a eight-minute bus ride to Saas

Almagell (1675m) also on the ski pass. Although anyone staying in Saas Grund would probably spend most of their time skiing at Saas Fee, the less glamorous Saas Grund provides cheaper accommodation and entertainment though it has to be said, the nightlife is not that exciting.

WORK

As far as work is concerned, Saas Grund should by no means be written off. It has at least sixteen hotels and several tearooms. Eliane van Rosevelt from the Netherlands worked two seasons in Saas Grund. The first in tearoom La Cabane. She saw the job advertised in a Dutch newspaper, *De Telegraaf*, the Saturday issue of which usually carries adverts for seasonal work in several countries including Switzerland, Germany and Spain. Eliane wanted a change from secretarial work and at La Cabane she earned the statutory Swiss wage plus food and accommodation; the latter above the tearoom. She had a room to herself and shared other facilities. Her hours were noon to 5.30 pm and 7 to 11.30 pm which left her free to ski every morning. Her duties included washing dishes, cleaning the coffee bar and serving customers. She learned to ski during her first season in Saas Grund by teaching herself. The owner of the tearoom also has a similar tearoom/bakery in Saas Fee where she returned to work in the summer. The following winter season found her working again for the Saaser Bäckerei (3910 Saas Grund).

St. Moritz

For over 100 years St. Moritz has been host to the rich and playful. Those wanting to ski, toboggan down the world-famous Cresta Run, bobsleigh, ride horses, play polo, hike, cross-country ski or just enjoy the refreshing mountain air around the upper Engadine Lakes flock in their thousands each winter and summer season. With 13,000 beds for visitors, St. Moritz is one of the largest resorts. Despite its reputation as a jet-setting resort, St. Moritz patrons are not by any means exclusively the super rich; there is also scope for those with modest resources who will find a choice of affordable accommodation readily available. The resort is best reached by the mountain cog railway from Chur. There is a coordinated train service from Zurich.

The town of St. Moritz is divided into two parts, separated by the lake. St. Moritz-Dorf (town) is the older and livelier half. It is at 1,856 m above sea level, which is 50 metres higher than the other half, St. Moritz-Bad (spa). This means that it is a half-hour, uphill walk from Bad to the centre of town. Bad has no public buildings except for the *Hallenbad* (swimming-pool) and the Heilbad Spa. There, if you are feeling a little under the weather, you will find sevices such as peat baths, physiotherapy and a drinking hall where only draught mineral water is served, drawn from a spring whose renown dates back to the Bronze Age.

At the heart of Dorf is the fountain of Mauritius. Near by is a traditional stone building housing the *Rathaus* (town hall) and the Tourist Information Centre (☎081 837 33 33; www.stmoritz.ch). Neither of these hold listings of jobs available but you apply at the former for a temporary resident permit and the latter for town maps.

THE SKIING

St. Moritz is rated one of the top ten ski resorts in the world. It is not difficult to see why. The (Engadine) ski area, of which St. Moritz is the centre is huge: 350 km of piste and 56 lifts. The high altitude and mainly north-facing slopes ensure an excellent snow record. However, the downside is that St. Moritz has a reputation for being one of the coldest skiing areas; the resort itself gets a lot of sunshine. There are five ski areas encircling the resort: From Dorf (Chanterella Station) you can take the Corviglia funicular up to 2488 m from where there are 80 km of runs, mainly easy and intermediate. From Corviglia a cable car takes you up to Piz Nair (3057 m) where intermediates and advanced skiers can find runs to either Marguns (and chairlift back to Corviglia) or a 7 km run to Celerina. To get to the Corvatsch ski area involves a bus ride to the Surlej cable car, a few kilometres outside Bad. From there the cable car rises in two stages to Murtèl and Corvatsch (3451 m) the highest point in the resort where glacial skiing and spectacular scenery provide thrills for both intermediate and advanced skiers. The Furtschellas area on the same mountain can be reached by skiing across from Corvatsch or from the bottom by cable car from Sils Maria. Diavolezza, Piz Lagalp and Muottas Muragl are smaller areas, all reached from the other end of St. Moritz. Piz Lagalp has the most difficult runs while Alp Languard and Muottas Muragl have some blue and red runs.

The costs of the bus rides to the outlying ski areas can mount up but from Corvatsch and Furtschellas you can ski back to St. Moritz. Corvatsch probably has the best skiing and on Fridays 9km of the pistes are floodlit. The télécabine there moves skiers fast enough to avoid the horrendous queues for which Corvatsch was once infamous and there is a brand new, more efficient cable-car from Corviglia to Piz Nair.

St. Moritz also has 150 km of cross-country trails. The Engadine cross-country marathon (42 km) normally held in March has been held in St. Moritz for about 36 years and has made St. Moritz one of the most prestigious cross-country ski resorts in the Alps.

ACCOMMODATION

When you first arrive in St. Moritz, a convenient place to stay is the Hotel Bellaval (☎081 833 32 45) as it is near the railway station. Slightly cheaper is the Bernina (081-833 60 22) which costs from SFr 50 per night). If you are a youth hostel member, you may want to move to the modern youth hostel, (7500 St. Moritz-Bad; ☎081 833 39 69) but it is a good half-hour walk from the centre of town although there is a bus service from the Hotel Sonne, 200 yards away.

WORK

At the youth hostel you may find that half the places are taken by British school children. The hostel is frequently full during the school holidays. The British company Ski Gower is largely responsible for this. Ski Gower employ about one instructor for every 12 children. For instance during February half-term there may be two school groups totalling about 80 school children and eight instructors. The numbers of children change from week to week and so jobs for instructors are usually offered on the basis of nine to ten days' duration. Travel from the UK, ski pass, equipment rental and board and lodging are provided. The number of holiday companies in St. Moritz has fluctuated over the past few years. Among those who operate there are: Club Med, Flexiski, Ski Club of GB, Ski Gower and Swiss Travel Service.

Club Med is a major employer in St. Moritz and owns two hotels: La Reine Victoria and Le Roi Soleil housing about 450 people in each. Both 'villages' (as Club Med call their locations) employ over 100 personnel of whom about 10% are English speaking ranging from plumbers and cooks to swimming-pool attendants and hosts who look after the well being of the guests.

Normally, staff are recruited for the season through the Paris or London offices but a few are recruited for shorter periods. For instance the supervision of children (Kids Club) can be restricted to school holidays. The guests (known as *gentils membres*/GMs) are of many nationalities, but dominated by Francophones. If you are over 20, have an ability with languages especially French and are extrovert and sociable it is worth applying to Club Med. They have thousands of jobs each winter, provide a good wage and fantastic food.

If you are hoping to find a job on arrival in St. Moritz, you probably want to advertise the fact. The local newspaper is the *Engadiner Post*, but a good bet is the trade journal of the hospitality industry *Hotel and Tourismus Revue* (130 Monbijoustr. Case Postale 2657, Berne 3001). Remember that employers advertise in them too and you may find what you are looking for without placing your own advertisement.

This was how Birgit Kratz got a job as a waitress at the Hotel Bären (☎081 833 56 56). She speaks English and German and worked six hours in the morning and three in the evening with the afternoons free from 1.30 pm to 6.30 pm. She worked the full four months of the season and earned over £1,000 a month. She enjoyed it and told us:

I had plenty of time to ski and do what I wanted in the afternoons and then also had time to go out in the evenings. I would certainly do it again if I got the chance.

The focus of social life for the English-speakers is Bobby's Pub in Dorf and then, when the pub closed, the Vivai disco about 50 yards away. These are useful places to visit as you may hear of a vacancy or make contact with potential employers. There are odd-jobs available in St. Moritz but they are usually offered through contacts or friends. In this way you can get a job as an au pair, babysitter or even driving hang-gliders back up the mountain!

There is a consortium of workers (AGOB, Geschäftsstelle, 7500 St. Moritz Bad; ☎081 830 0000) responsible for staffing and maintaining the lifts; the best course may be contacting the individual lift companies direct. If you ask nicely they will e-mail you a list of the dozen or so relevant telephone numbers. A knowledge of German is also required.

St. Moritz is in the German-speaking part of Switzerland and so for any job the applicants with qualifications in German have a better chance of employment than those without. One optimistic worker estimated the number of jobs available to foreigners at over 100, although many of these seem to be taken by Italians. Most of the jobs available are in hotels and their restaurants. The jobs for those who speak English are severely restricted and number around 20 at the most.

The town is very attractive and the skiing is among the best and most reliable in Europe. If you have the good fortune to find employment there, you will certainly not regret it.

Verbier

Verbier, located on a plateau, in the southern part of the Valais region and looking down over the Rhône Valley, is one of the biggest, best resorts with some of the most challenging skiing in the world. Unfortunately, such overt attractions have an all too predictable effect on the length of the lift queues. However, at least the jumbo Funispace gondola from Ruinettes works against bottlenecks. The Verbier area's notoriously expensive lift pass looks better value when the pound is strong. A Verbier only pass is also available.

Verbier was developed as a ski resort after the Second World War and has acquired a reputation for being Sloane Square sur Neige although this is not really fair. Certainly English 'hooray Henry' types are always to be found there, but the social mix also includes the New York jet set, the Lausanne/Geneva brat pack, and a host of German socialites. Verbier is less than two hours from Geneva and has good connections to Bern and Zurich so it is not surprising to find that half Verbier's visitors are Swiss, all of whom speak perfect English or the American version.

Although sprawling, its buildings are for the most part in keeping with the Alpine style so it is more attractive than many newer, purpose-built resorts.

When your ski instructor drops in for tea at the chalet by para-gliding from a nearby peak, you know for certain that you are in a rather special resort. Verbier is just that – full of beautiful people who ski like demons in the day and dance like furies at night. Verbier offers something for everyone whether it be gentle sunny slopes on Savoleyres or the noisy slot machines in Big Ben – the only place where 13-year-olds can drink beer until midnight.

THE SKIING

The Verbier ski area is the Quatre Vallées (Four Valleys) and as the name suggests it provides a vast choice over 400 km of marked piste served by 100 lifts including Le Jumbo, Switzerland's largest cable car with a maximum capacity of 150 passengers. The linked resorts in the Four Valleys, all covered by the area lift pass, include: La Tzoumaz, Nendaz, Veysonnaz and Thyon 2000. The same lift pass provides the opportunity to ski at Bruson across the valley from Verbier and at the nearby resorts of Champex and La Fouly. The ski lifts up from the resort are concentrated in two main areas, Medran and Savoleyres. The resort itself covers a huge area and a regular, comprehensive and free bus service links all of the resort with the two lift stations.

There is something for everyone in Verbier, although it would be true to say it is not a beginners' resort. Above the resort itself, the quiet pistes of the Savoleyres, the sunny, open bowl of La Chaux, the wide runs of Lac des Vaux and the Attelas runs down to Les Ruinettes, all provide plenty of scope for those progressing from the nursery slopes, and intermediates alike.

Further afield, below Tortin, easy runs and lifts lead to Veysonnaz, the host of many World Cup skiing events. For experts there is so much at Verbier that it would be impossible to do it justice here: off piste, and tough black runs and ski tours. From the formidable mogul fields on the glacier of Mont Fort via Col des Gentianes down to Tortin, to the renowed Tortin Wall; not to mention the extreme couloirs of Mont Gelé down to Les Attelas, La Chaux or Tortin, Verbier is an experts' paradise. Best of all, with a guide or a bit of local knowledge, you can discover entire empty valleys.

The skiing is challenging and varied but Verbier is best known for its extreme, off-piste runs: Valon d'Arby, Col de Mouche, the giant reservoir behind Mt. Fort, the Stairway to Heaven between two peaks leading into the Hidden Valley, Marlens sneakily tucked away from the main Savoleyres ski slopes, are just some of the legendary off piste runs which are part of the whispered culture of Verbier which offers peace, pleasure and danger in one package.

NIGHTLIFE

For those who haven't yet heard it – the nightlife of Verbier has reached legendary status. The town has great character, retaining its traditional aspects even though it has expanded over 250% in the last 30 years. Unlike some resorts, Verbier thrives on its nightlife with nearly 60 restaurants, 4 nightclubs and various bars, Verbier has something to suit all tastes. After a fast and furious day on the slopes from the Hotel Rosalp's restaurant with its award-winning chef to the frenetic and crowded atmosphere of the Scotch Club. When you come off the slopes, the options seem endless. You can watch the sun set from the woodland setting of Chez Danny (remembering that you still have to ski a bit further after that), you can go for a milkshake at the Offshore (the surf bar that is cooler than its ice-creams), you can cramp into, or lounge outside, the Fer à Cheval with a beer, or you can head straight for the action at the Hotel Farinet terrace bar at the Place Centrale. There you will find barbecues, live music and people with too much energy from having skied all day. Le Pub Mont Fort (☎ 026 31 48 98) up near the Medran lift station, tends to be the meeting place for many of the resort workers. The Nelson Pub is also a popular rendez-vous in the evening, as is La Luge. The predominantly Swiss 'Bar No Name' also offers a great atmosphere. When the pubs close at 1 am, people head towards the clubs: Marshall's and The Venue are both popular with workers and both have staff nights. The Farm Club, one of the most famous (or infamous) has the gossip columnists' ideal clientele: racing drivers, ex-royal wives and pop stars. Needless to say it is expensive and does not have a staff night. At weekends it is full of rich Germans splashing out SFr 300 a bottle on champagne. Nightlife finishing hours are variable; if business is good, the clubs don't close. Chalet staff, who forget to keep an eye on the time can end up cooking breakfast as soon as they get home.

ACCOMMODATION

Switzerland is known for its high prices and Verbier is no exception. The first major challenge on arrival in Verbier is therefore finding a cheap place to stay while looking for a job. However, a lot of energy might be saved by calling Melissa at Mountain beds (☎020-7924 2650) who can find beds for workers as well as the holiday goers. Shouting your name about in the 'Mont Fort' or the 'No Name' bar on a busy night can also work just as effectively as the locals sometimes have rooms for rent. It took Jason Farrell just 20 minutes using this method to find a whole season's accommodation. Verbier itself has no hostels or guesthouses for the newly-arrived and destitute, so the only option is to stay in one of the cheaper hotels for the first few nights. Les Touristes (☎027 771 21 47) is in the old part of Verbier as you come into the resort and charges SFr 60 per person, per night for bed and breakfast. The Mont Gelé (027 771 30 53), up behind the Médran lift station, charges SFr 65-115 for bed and breakfast. The Rosablanche (027 771 55 55), is a cheap and central hotel, close to the Place Centrale and is an ideal base for those coming out on spec to job hunt in the autumn. Charges are from about SFr 55-75 per night. However, from December to April it is let to a British tour operator and so is out of commission for the public.

Cheaper accommodation can be found in Le Châble, the valley below Verbier. The two places are linked by an inexpensive PTT bus, which takes 30 minutes to climb to the resort. The hotels de la Poste (027 776 11 69), Les Alpes (027 776 14 65) and L'Escale (☎027 776 27 07) all charge similar prices; for instance Hotel de La Poste from SFr 115 (double) including breakfast. The only youth hostel in the area is at Bruson, a ten-minute bus ride from Le Châble. The Auberge de Jeunesse (027 776 23 56) sleeps 40. It is about 50 minutes away from Verbier by bus and you have to change buses in Le Châble.

The Verbier tourist office (☎027 775 3888; fax 027 775 38 89; www.verbier.ch) or the one in Chable/Le Bruson (☎027 776 16 82) can help you search for more permanent accommodation as it keeps a list of apartments for rent. Prices vary but for a basic studio expect to pay SFr 900-1300 per month.

WORK

If you are not employed in advance by a British company and go out on spec, then you should be prepared to be exceptionally persistent. The marketing manager at the tourist office, revealed that 7% unemployment in the Valais canton meant that there was a shortage of jobs for foreign workers and available jobs were often taken by the Swiss. Jobs in hotels, pubs, clubs etc. are often taken by people who return to Verbier year after year.

However, for those coming to Verbier for the first time, it is possible to get a job before the season starts. The tourist office has a small list of jobs available (e.g. waiting staff, ski tech) which is regularly updated and available year round. Also check the noticeboards at Le Pub Mont Fort, The Co-op, the Centre Commercial in the Place Centrale and the Migros supermarket for jobs and put up a notice of your own advertising availability for work. Also displayed on the boards are notices of studios to rent. Another avenue is to look in the recruitment section of the local daily paper *Le Nouvelliste,* which covers the French-speaking areas of the Valais canton including Verbier.

When the season starts in early December, it is worth visiting the Nelson Pub, the Hotel de Verbier bar and Marshall's any day between 5.30 and 6.30 pm as these are where the reps have their office hours. Give them your details including, most importantly a phone number where you can be contacted. Some of the hotels may employ the odd Brit but most of their workers are Swiss, French and Italians who are regulars. If you wanted a hotel job, the best time to arrange it would be as soon as the season is coming to a close for the next season, in person, as employers like to meet their prospective employees. From May onwards many places close, or their owners go away leaving a temporary staff to keep things ticking over. The other best time to try is between September and November. Try asking at Mont Fort, the various clubs, the Café Offshore and the many restaurants including Al Capone's.

Verbier is lined with sports and clothes shops: Danny Sport, Philip Roux Sports and Mountain Air are just some of the many, and they are all disposed to employ Brits proportion of their clientele are British. There are also plenty of boutiques, newsagents/souvenir shops and also a large sports centre, just on the outskirts of the village. The jobs are often taken early, but in such a large village there is always a turnover somewhere. Repeat staff take many of the jobs, but it all seems to work on a hierarchical system where one year someone may be in a dingy shop, the next a bar and so on. Changes also occur mid-season. Hence keeping in touch with existing staff to see if they are moving can increase chances of a breakthrough. Also to ask them how they got their jobs and to get some ideas. The bad news about Verbier is that it has become increasingly anti ski-bum and it is virtually essential to have, or be serious about, getting a full-time employment contract and temporary residence permit.

The safest and surest way to get a job in Verbier used to be in advance with a big tour operator. However, in recent years, several large operators have pulled out or reduced their operations to be replaced by a string of smaller private companies. Some look after the chalets and guests on their own, others look around for extra help. For the serious Verbier chalet person it is advisable to look at among others Ski Verbier (020-7738 0878), Flexiski (020-7352 0044) and Crystal Finest (020-8939 0843) and keep an eye open as others are likely to pop up. British tour companies active in Verbier are many including: Airtours, Crystal, Descent International, Esprit, Equity, Erna Low, First Choice, Flexiski, Ski Club of GB, Inghams, Mark Warner, Neilson, Ski Activity, Ski Peak, Crystal Finest, Skiworld, Thomson, Total and Swiss Travel Service.

There are several ski schools in Verbier, Ecole Suisse du Ski hires a few full-time British Ski Instructors every year and here is also the possibility to work on a temporary basis as over half their 170 instructors are auxiliaries. The school will insist on proper qualifications and unfortunately the school favours French or Austrian before British but it could be worth a try (☎027 775 33 66). The alternative schools are Fantastique (027 771 41 41), who specialise in off-piste and extreme, hence mountain-guiding qualifications are essential and No Limits (027 771 5556) ditto.

Melanie Brown was on her second season in Verbier: the first was as a chalet cook for the now defunct Ski West and the second as an assistant at Ski Service, one of the ski shops. She said that for the first season in Verbier, it is best to get a job with a tour operator and get to know your way around before arranging something independently. She suggested that looking in *The Lady* magazine for jobs from September onwards, would be a good starting point, as positions for nannies, au pairs and chalet girls in ski resorts are often advertised there.

Jackie Harrison was on her sixth season in Verbier. She was a chalet host for two seasons, a rep for another two, an assistant at a hamburger restaurant for a season and then the night receptionist at the 4-star Hotel Montpelier (☎027 771 61 31). She told us that she had been very lucky to get the job as the work she was hoping to do fell through. She then spent the summer prior to the ski season going round all the hotels in Verbier to see if they needed anyone. It was sheer luck that the night receptionist at the Montpelier had just left and so she got the job. The duties included not only looking after the reception but also hoovering the bar and reception area after the guests had gone to bed. She worked from 10 pm to 7 am every night with one day off a week. However, if the hotel was busy she had to forgo her day off for several weeks, which is what happened over Christmas and New Year as well as a three week period in February.

Swiss hotel jobs are renowned for being hard work but do have their compensations. Jackie was paid SFr 2,500 per month and of course had plenty of time for skiing, if she could keep awake! She used to get the first lift up and would then ski until midday. She said that it was vital to speak very good or fluent French for Swiss hotel jobs.

Polly Scott found her job as a chalet cook through an advert in *The Lady*. She found herself in Verbier looking after a chalet, which slept up to 48 guests and was one of four chalet staff looking after them. The job was hard work but she usually managed to ski from 12.30 pm to 5.30 pm most days. She was paid SFr 880 per month and board and lodging was provided as was a free lift pass and ski and boot hire.

If you like working with children, this opens up another option. Try Chez les Schtoumpfs (027 771 6585), Tip Top or the Kids Ski Club (027 775 6333) the last run by the ESS. These are a range of kindergartens that look after youngsters during the day while the parents go skiing.

Verbier is a magnet for young well-heeled couples or single parents (in the case of Fergie) with their small children. Hence, there are always a number of nannies in Verbier and quite often they are English-speaking. The great thing about being a live-in nanny is it solves your accommodation problem; you can find yourself staying in some of the swishest apartments in town.

Kris Laird's company SnowyStaff based in Jindabyne, NSW, Australia recruits Australians for jobs in Verbier. Log on to his website www.snowystaff.com.au for more information.

The pumping nightlife of Verbier combined with a job there and skiing as well is likely to leave you running on sleepless overdrive for at least a month.

Villars

Villars has about twice the tourist bed capacity of Les Diablerets with which it shares a lift linked ski area. It has expanded considerably from its village origins in order to provide expansive amenities for tourists. Despite this is manages to retain some chocolate-box charm in the views and the hamlet peripheries of Barboleuse and Gryon. The village is host to large contingents of school parties and family members of all ages as well as more experienced skiers and boarders. As it has wide appeal to all ages, types and abilities it tends to be busy round the season. The same qualities that make it appeal to visitors, also make it an enjoyable place to work: what better than to spend a ski season with lively company, great skiing and surrounded by the gorgeous scenery of the Rhône Valley.

THE SKIING

Superlatives abound in descriptions of the skiing. The slopes of the Villars-Gryon complex are brilliant: winding and interlocking and extensive. Based around one valley that boasts two restaurants, a baby ski park and a blue button lift, the runs spiral down from all the surrounding peaks, so that all 100 km of skiing can be managed in a day. The challenge is not just from the slopes themselves, but from the varying weather and snow conditions, the slalom competitions in full view of the lunching masses where you will find yourself beaten to the finish by an eight-year-old whizz kid; not to mention the steep drops off piste that simply beg to be launched off.

The privately-operated Paraplegic Ski School is run by an ex-champion who, following a disabling accident in the 1980s, worked on a skiing machine to parallel the paraplegic road or track racing constructions. The result was a range of lightweight, fibre-glass seats, resembling a side-car, then mounted on a single 'ski', with a spring for balance and comfort. A pair of hand-held sticks fitted with 'mini-skis' completes the apparatus. This is a niche in the skiing market that has barely been exploited in Europe and which enables groups of wheelchair disabled skiers to ski together.

Board addicts are not over-served with amenities but can find some hairy cliff edges to waken their interest and powder bowls to freestyle away in. Board instructors may be in demand in future seasons.

Gryon

The hamlet of Gryon is a little further up the valley than Villars and shares its ski area. It is important enough to have its own tourist office (024/498 1422), and a slightly separate set of runs down from Croix des Chaux. The two resorts are linked not only by ski pass and instructors, but by the train that goes up 600m to Bretaye and the main skiing.

It has a range of hotel and apartment chalets, but the centre is less modern than that of Villars, with fewer holiday tour operators in evidence. It is still worth checking for work, but Villars is far more likely to be productive.

WORK

Proximity to the towns and cities of Lac Leman including Lausanne and Montreux means that Villars is well placed for weekend skiers from those places. Villars has a good turnover of clients for its 22 hotels, numerous bars and army of red-clad ski instructors. As with all Swiss ski schools, the instructors tend to be locals, but with the huge number of school groups that swarm noisily around at Christmas and Easter vacations, as well as during the honey-pot month of February, even they require reinforcements. A prerequisite for the job is a love of hard work and the ability to be nice all the time. The Office du Tourisme (025/4953232) will put you in touch with the head of the ski school, preferably at the start of the season.

The lift operators of whom there are about 30, get less sunbathing than in less commercialised resorts owing to the little huts that are provided for them. Ask at the tourist offices if there are any vacancies. You will fare best if they remember you from previous years.

Villars also has myriad opportunities for herding small children about its pistes. There are multitudes of them during holidays. While you can leave the ski instructors to occupy themselves teaching the smallest to ring bells on smurf obstacles, you can probably make a living providing relief guiding so that sleep-deprived teachers and leaders can have some respite.

There is an International School based at Villars which takes on an English 'prof'. Susan Humphries worked for two years as an English teacher here before returning to teach French to the English, which proves that Villars can't be that bad if someone wants to stay on there. Like all teaching posts, a university level education is required and this is not of course a seasonal position.

Club Med operates in Villars and supplies its own chalet staff, reps and ski leaders. See *Club Med* entry in *Ski Tour Operators* section for further details. The Swiss Chalet Company is a firm dealing with chalets and self-catering holidays in Villars.

Accommodation comes with the jobs that are chalet or hotel-based, generally, and the local ski workers are helpful enough with everything else and may be able to help with a temporary arrangement.

Wengen

Wengen is perched on a sunny, south-facing terrace at 4,187 ft overlooking the Lauterbrunnen Valley and is among the most charming of Alpine resorts. Free from cars, buses and towerblocks, it shelters beneath an awe-inspiring trio of peaks – The Eiger, Monch and Jungfrau. It is one of several places which claim to be the place where downhill skiing was invented, when British tourists began using the cog railway to save themselves the walk uphill. Mürren, its near neighbour on the other side of the Lauterbrunnen Valley, was where the pioneer of Alpine skiing, Sir Arnold Lunn, staged the first ever slalom race, in 1922. Some detractors would say that little has changed in the resort since.

Wengen is more British than much of Britain and the same families and holidaymakers will return to their favourite hotels and chalets year after year.

This means that there's a strong and well-recognised need for English-speaking staff in the resort, and language is not the barrier it can be elsewhere. In fact, it is quite easy to get through a day in Wengen without speaking or hearing anything but English. Excellent for work prospects, but sometimes a little claustrophobic, and not very good if you want to brush up your German or French.

Access to the resort is by rail only, a stunning, 14-minute climb from Lauterbrunnen. The trains which also link the skiing areas including Mürren (only on a season pass or with a supplement) and Grindelwald are included on the lift pass and run with clockwork Swiss precision, which can however be an infuriatingly slow process at times.

THE SKIING

Wengen is part of the Jungfrau skiing region, which offers over 213 km of prepared piste and 44 lifts. Wengen is piste and lift linked to Grindelwald and Grund. Beginners are well catered for and there are excellent nursery areas. Intermediates have plenty of scope and advanced skiers can test themselves on the Lauberhorn piste famous as the venue for the annual race in the Men's World Cup Series and the 'Oh God!' off piste run from the foot of the Eiger.

To get to the Kleine Scheidegg area takes 25 minutes on the cog railway and from Scheidegg there is a chairlift up to Lauberhorn (8160 ft) from where there is a choice of runs including the above mentioned. The Kleine Scheidegg has a huge expanse of mainly intermediate runs, with some excellent off-piste runs below the north face of the Eiger.

The Männlichen area is reached by cable car from Wengen in six minutes. As you glide out of the village in the cable car, watch out for the chamois nibbling in the avalanche tracks below. From Männlichen there is an 8 km run down into Grindlewald; alternatively you can ski over to Scheidegg and enter the lift system there.

You can also ski at Mürren, but it's an hour and a half on trains and lifts each way so it's really only feasible for a day's excursion. There are some challenging black runs and a chance to refresh yourself at the revolving Schilthorn restaurant perched at 10,000 feet.

Grindlewald has some easy skiing. The quickest way to the Grindlewald slopes is via the cable car, which departs close the main street in Wengen.

To summarise: Wengen is a good place for the adventurous and the pistes are also gentle enough for the first disastrous attempts and there is good access to suitable lifts.

ACCOMMODATION

Staying in Wengen is not cheap, but many jobs will include some form of accommodation. Looking for work, your best bet in the village itself is the Bernerhof dormitory at the end of the High Street. There are also cheap options at the Mittaghorn or the Falken in their chalet. Also inexpensive by local standards are the Hotel Bären (☎033 855 14 19), the Bergheim YMCA (☎036 55 27 55) and the Edelweiss (☎033 855 23 88) from about SFr 65 a night. They are often used for groups however and may be booked up during certain times of the season. The Valley Hostel in Lauterbrunnen is one alternative that charges about SFr 40 a night. Another is to stay in the Balmers Youth Hostel in Interlaken, about 25 minutes by train from Wengen or in a tent provided at the Balmers campsite with the inclusion of an Italian breakfast. This is a good base for job hunting not only in Wengen, but also Lauterbrunnen and Grindelwald. Furthermore hotel managers in Wengen sometimes ring down if they have a sudden shortage of staff.

APRÈS SKI

Wengen is a small and quiet village with après ski to match. Discos and bars can be expensive. Many British workers can be found in the Tanne Bar (especially after 11pm), which favours quite good music and skiing videos. The Rocks Bar and the bar of the hotel Falken are also popular meeting places, along with Da Sinas restaurant and pub and Rocks café. The Ski Club of Great Britain is well represented in Wengen and the legendary Downhill Only Club meets there. Both are good sources of information about where to find fellow Brits. If you have the time and the energy, there is ice skating, curling, bowling, swimming and long mountain walks. Or you can take the railway up to Allmend or better still Wengernalp and toboggan down to the village. There are also a number of discos, notably The Underground, and Afterburner in the Silberhorn Hotel.

WORK

It's fairly easy to get a job in Wengen, as long as you're persistent and you apply at the right time. It's much, much easier if you apply well in advance. September or October is about the time hotel and restaurant owners start thinking about employing people for the winter. Some vacancies come up throughout the season, but not very many and foreign workers in Wengen warn that, because it's such a small and tight-knit community, the chances of working unofficially or illegally are virtually nil.

Most of the work is in hotels, bars, restaurants and sports shops. The lifts and railways are jealously guarded sources of local employment. Working as a ski instructor is a possibility but ski schools will normally give work to their more experienced, qualified instructors first which is a big problem in your first season as John Thursfield, who was 17, without ski qualifications and with no second-language skills discovered when he was taken on as an assistant instructor during high season:

> **John Thursfield describes his experience working as a ski instructor**
> *My family have always come to Wengen in the Christmas holidays. It was super fun and we met many old friends. After leaving school, I applied for a job at the Swiss Ski & Snowboard School (3823 Wengen; tel/fax +41 33 8552022; ski.school@ wengen.com) and was delighted to obtain one. Unfortunately, the resort turned out to be much quieter outside the school holidays and I found that I was only given clients about one fifth of the time. The unpredictability and scarcity of work resulted in me leaving the resort well before the end of the season. If I return for a second season I would be given more work but the experience of being severely underemployed has discouraged me so much that I do not think that I will bother.*

Working in a ski shop is not as glamorous as guiding on the pistes but it can provide reasonably stable employment. The work is hard and the Swiss expect workers to be conscientious and to pay attention to detail. Steve Dennett describes his experience of working as a ski fitter in a ski shop as hard but satisfying and gave us some insight into life in Wengen and the prospects for work:

> **Steve Dennett describes working as a ski fitter**
> *For fifteen years I had been visiting Wengen as a tourist. Then I was made redundant by the bank I was working for. Rather than face looking for another desk job I approached the boss of Central Sport (Viktor Gertsch ave, 3823 Wengen; +41 33 855 23 23; centralsport@wengen.com)and asked for a job. That was three years ago and now I am still working at the same place.*
> *The Swiss are keen to employ people from the EU as it is easier to obtain work permits for them than it is for other nationals. Furthermore, Wengen is a small,*

friendly community where the Swiss and English get along with each other well so that networking for jobs is easy but fortunately, I am happy where I am and do not have to. I have the joys of testing new skiing and mountain biking equipment in a beautiful environment and dealing with people who are on holiday.

The work is hard. I work from 8am to 7pm and have only one or two days off each week. If I was going to say that we have a motto at work it would be 'The Guest is King' and the standard of work should reflect that. I am treated well and enjoy doing a good job.

Mary Hall, an English nurse who was cycling from north to south across Europe and working along the way, arrived at the Balmer hostel Interlaken (☎033 822 1961) at the beginning of November to look for work for the first time on her trip. Her story points out the pitfalls of not proceeding methodically and not knowing in advance what you expect in wages or agreeing with your employers at the outset what your perks will be:

Mary Hall explains the pitfalls of not thinking things through when obtaining work

I went all round the hotels (in Interlaken) without success. Then a friend advised me to get a phonecard and the yellow pages and ring round. He also advised me to speak with a smile and it seemed to work because I got a couple of offers right away. I completely ignored his third piece of advice, which was to get as many offers as possible and then choose the best and I rushed off to meet the hotel owners. Nothing came of the first offer and the second I accepted without really thinking and found myself in Wengen looking after a hotel owner's spoilt daughter. They asked me to name my price and because I hadn't thought about it, I set it too low, which they obviously accepted pretty smartly. They said they would pay for my train pass, which never happened but they did hire me skis for the season.

The Falken Hotel (3823 Wengen. ☎033 856 51 21; www.hotelfalken.com) run by the Italian Cova family is a long-standing favourite with British visitors and is keen to employ English-speakers. Becky was the senior receptionist at the Hotel Falken for a year. Previous to this she had worked as a chambermaid, a rep for a British tour company, as a barmaid and washing dishes and waiting on tables in various establishments in Wengen. As head receptionist she was reasonably paid and got board and lodging and insurance that covered repatriation in the event of serious accident or illness. Working at the Falken is however no cushy number.

Becky describes her job at the Falken Hotel

I had the choice of working from 7:30am to 12pm or from 3:30pm to 12am and chose the former. I am given two days off a week and go skiing at least four days in the week, which is great. My employer is very reasonable but if the workload demands it I am expected to work two shifts. It comes as a complete shock to many people but it is not usual to be paid for overtime in Switzerland. This leads to some employers taking advantage of seasonal workers in Wengen. For this reason it is important to speak to the people who work at an establishment before applying for work. I would recommend working at the Alpen Rosé hotel, Rocks Café or Central Sport.

I have enjoyed working as head receptionist. The demand of being an interface between suppliers, customers, staff, guests and the boss has made it a bit stressful but I have also enjoyed the contact with people. In that respect, working as a chambermaid was no fun at all.

Wengen has quite a large selection of British tour operators, among them: Crystal, Inghams,

Ski Gower, Ski Club of GB, Thomson and Swiss Travel Service, while the French operator Club Med has a village there in a renovated thirties hotel.

On the whole, Wengen and nearby Grindelwald offer a good chance of success if you're looking for work on a casual basis. People without temporary residence permits are just keeping very quiet about it. Native English-speakers are at an advantage because of the resort's popularity with British skiers. It is however useful to have a working knowledge of German. You may have a few problems initially adapting to the Swiss-German accent. There is no employment office in Wengen, but the website www.wengen.com is extremely useful as it has jobs on it as well as anything else you might want to know about Wengen.

According to Beverley Wood an expatriate who now lives in Wengen permanently:

The bottom line is that young kids with no language skills or any qualifications can only expect to get jobs at the low end of the ladder. Apart from that caveat, it's a great place to live and there are loads of ex-pats here who have made it their home from home for numerous seasons.

Zermatt

Zermatt is dominated by the awe-inspiring Matterhorn mountain and is in the Wallis Canton in the south of Switzerland. The ski area is the largest in the Alps and the winter season lasts well into late spring. Glacier skiing is also possible in the Klein Matterhorn (12,533 feet). Zermatt is car-free and motorists have to leave their cars at Täsch, where the road officially ends three miles from Zermatt and where there are 2,000 parking places. Three is a shuttle train service between Täsch and Zermatt. Access by rail is by the Brig-Visp-Zermatt narrow-gauge railway, which takes approximately two hours to snake its way cautiously through the dramatic landscape to Zermatt. Train journeys from Geneva to Zurich take approximately three and a half to four hours. Zermatt is popular with skiers and mountaineers (a trend started perhaps by the renowned Edward Whymper) but despite this has kept its village character. One main street, Bahnhofstrasse, winds up to the church, and many old traditional wooden buildings are to be seen next to the smart hotels. Althought there are no cars, there are plenty of electric taxis which zip about in an alarming (if pollution free) manner, which is more than can be said for the horse-and-carriage taxis which are the alternative and more romantic mode of transport. There are also electric ski buses; you can buy a carnet of ten tickets for these, which works out cheaper than paying each time. Zermatt like everywhere in Switzerland is expensive by British standards. A simple salad will cost in the region of SFr 10-14, a *rosti* about SFr 14 and the ubiquitous *raclette* (cheese fondue) about SFr 16-18. Apfelstrüdel with vanilla sauce will cost about SFr 7. Set menus offered by a 3 star hotel will cost in the region of SFr 35-45 for a four-course meal. A small beer or a glass of wine will cost anything from SFr 3 to about SFr 9 in a mountain restaurant.

THE SKIING

Zermatt does not really cater for beginners and the only area resembling nursery slopes can be found near the top of the Sunegga Express. There is however plenty of scope for intermediate and advanced skiers. The skiing area is vast with 150 km/93 miles of marked pistes to choose from plus heli- and cross-country skiing. There are 73 lifts including the mountain railway. There are three main skiing areas: Firstly Sunegga Blauherd-Unterrothorn (reached by underground train – the Sunegga Express which takes 10 minutes form bottom to top. The runs in this area offer exceptionally beautiful scenery and challenging skiing for the intermediate and advanced skier. The second ski area is the Stockhorn-Gornergrat Riffleberg area which can be linked from the first. Gornergrat can also be reached by the old rack railway from the village (takes 40 minutes to the top) and has several runs suitable for the less ambitious. For the powder and bump hands there are the northern slops of Stockhorn, RÖte Nase, Ritzengrat and Findelkelle. The third largest ara is nearest to the majestic Matterhorn and offers huge possibilities for ski tours: Schwarzee, Klein Matterhorn, Trockener Steg-Theodul and Testa Grigia. The Klein Matterhorn at 12,533 feet has the highest cable car in Europe and the ride is not recommended for the vertiginous. From the Theodulpass you can ski down into Cervinia in Italy and you can buy a supplementary lift pass for this in Zermatt.

ACCOMMODATION

'Accommodation in Zermatt is not cheap', so says every English-speaking worker. The going rate is about SFr 800+ for a studio. Some workers get accommodation with the job for a small deduction from their salary. Cheap places to stay while looking for work are the Bahnhof Hotel which has shared dormitories (bring your own sleeping bag). Private rooms also available. No meals are served but you can cook your own breakfast snacks in the busy basement kitchen. Frau Biener who has run the hotel for over 45 years is the widow of a well-known mountain guide for whom there is a memorial plaque (from his English friends) on the hotel wall. There is also a Youth Hostel near the Gornergrat Bahn. The Tanenhof Hotel is a 2 star offering comfortable accommodation with breakfast for SFr 45 per night. You could also try the village of Täsch, 3 miles from Zermatt where accommodation is likely to be cheaper than in Zermatt. All workers report that it is much easier to find accommodation for a few nights if one has contacts or friends already working and living in Zermatt.

WORK

Zermatt is a very busy resort with 109 hotels and boarding houses, 30 mountain restaurants and 100 restaurants and eating places in the village. There are other possibilities for work ski equipment/repair shops, the photo-shops or the many pubs. Most years there are several dozen English-speaking people working in Zermatt and many other nationalities including Portuguese, Dutch, Italian and German. The most popular meeting places are the Northwall Bar in the Hotel Rhodania over the river and the Brown Cow bar in the Hotel de la Poste on the main street. Four of the bartenders in the Northwall Bar were British and an American, Karl Ivarsson, who is the owner of the Hotel de la Poste employs staff from several different countries including Britain, in the restaurants, bars and discos within the Hotel de la Poste.

Adrienne Arnott, an arts and law graduate from Sydney was taking a year out to work in Europe. She was employed as nanny to a seven-year-old in a Swiss family. She applied for several jobs advertised in the December issue of *The Lady* and accepted the one that promised the most skiing and because she felt that she corresponded to the requirement for a 'sporty, German-speaking nanny'. She described her job as 'the best on the mountain' as she was given at least two full days off a week to ski and was paid a wage similar to a chalet girl (i.e. not much but with free ski pass, board and lodging and flights).

Des Sheehan who was employed in the electronics field in the UK applied for a ski technician job with Slalom Sports from December to April. He was paid SFr 15 an hour and worked 42 hours a week from 8 am to midday and from 2 pm to 7pm, but had to pay for his own studio and food although help was given with finding accommodation. No particular qualifications were needed, but Des had worked last year as a ski technician and therefore had the necessary expertise. He was happy in the friendly skiing environment but would have preferred more than his two days off to go skiing.

Owing to its international reputation, Zermatt attracts a large number of British skiers and companies. Philip Bamford was working as a ski manager in Zermatt. His responsabilities included airport transfers, accommodation, ski guiding and other representative duties. The job was fairly demanding and required a good level of skiing, excellent communication skills and a bubbly personality. The company provided a personalised service to small groups of clients and Phil found himself 'on call' 24 hours a day at times. This was compensated for by the fact that he had the opportunity to ski with guests most days and he was used to hard work having repped for Thomson the previous year. He got SFr 220 per week, which included shared accommodation, ski pass, equipment and transfer costs. He would like to do it again next season, but may have to return to London to find a more permanent job.

With so many bars and restaurants there are a lot of possibilities for connected jobs. Monique Korterik from the Netherlands knew that there were job opportunities in Zermatt through a friend who had worked there and she dashed off an application in June. This resulted in a bar job in the Hotel Sonne, a friendly and very comfortable 3-star hotel where she worked for the season. She was required to have good knowledge of English and German and previous bar experience, which she had from home and from a summer spent working in St. Moritz. Her hours of work were 4 pm until the last guest left the bar which was great for skiing but really late nights could make her a bit the worse for wear. She was paid the Swiss minimum wage and given a season lift pass. She paid SFr 500 a month for board and lodging. She enjoyed being able to speak to people from different countries and next year whe would like to broaden her experience in the catering field.

Swiss hotels have long been a byword for high standards in the hotel and catering industry and Justin Reeves ended up with free skiing without deviating from his chosen career. A student from Swindon where he is studying catering, he is in Zermatt on a six-month Euro-Studies Module working as a cook at the Hotel Walliserhof. The job was arranged as part of his course by the college in Swindon. He was paid SFr 3000 per week and his board, lodging and insurance came to SFr 1,200. He got two and a half days a week off to ski and is so enamoured of the place that he hopes to work another winter season in Zermatt next year after a summer in Cyprus gaining more experience.

Some workers find that having two or three part time jobs is better than one full-time one. American Jeffrey Steinkamp arrived in Zermatt from California early last season and within three days he had found four jobs. He took three of them: in the Vernisage Cinema, in a hotel and a sports shop. This season he returned to the part-time job as a projectionist at the Zermatt cinema (his only past experience for this was running the theatre at school), and he also works for a few hours at the Staffelalp mountain restaurant which leaves him four full days to ski. He also organised a talent show and a California Beach Party for workers in the resort. His tip for getting a job in Zermatt was 'a good attitude is everthing'. He got about SFr 15 per hour and paid SFr 300 for an apartment, which he shared with four girls. He plans to go rafting in India for the summer before returning for another winter in Zermatt.

Otto Karki from Australia is an expert in getting jobs in ski resorts, which has been doing since the late 1980s. He has worked in resorts in the USA (Heavenly) and Canada (Blackcomb) where he passed the Level II Canadian Ski Instructor examination which helped him get a job instructing in Austria. He visited Zermatt to ski for a day and took the opportunity to ask the owner of Photofast for a job next season. He started work on December 19th working as one of six photographers on the slopes. He is paid on a commission basis and worked 6 days a week, which provided him with a good wage if the weather was good. His hours were 10am-3pm taking photographs on the slopes and then 4.30pm to 7pm in the shop selling the day's efforts. He found it difficult to get accommodation however. His job was flexible enough for him to not work when it snowed so that he could enjoy the skiing instead. He plans to go to Norway and Finland (he comes originally from Finland) next year and hopes to develop his photography skills.

North America

Finding a Job
in the USA
and Canada

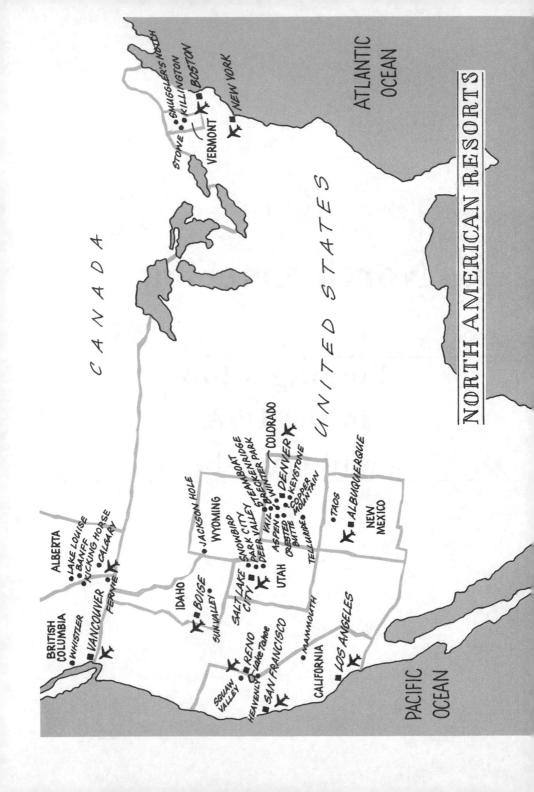

NORTH AMERICAN RESORTS

United States of America

For many British ski bums the idea of spending a season in an American resort seems irresistible: a combination of wider pistes, bigger resorts, more money and more fun than anywhere else. Unfortunately, post 9/11 regulations mean that the 'land of the free and the home of the brave' has some of the most restrictive immigration regulations of any nation and for those seeking temporary jobs, the regulations seem tightest of all. This situation exists despite the fact that by the beginning of the skiing season ski areas are desperate for personnel and have difficulty filling all the vacancies available. In the generally difficult area of getting work in America there are a couple of government approved schemes which allow access to the US ski jobs market. These schemes are organised by IST Plus, the new partner of the CIEE in the UK and the British Universities North America Club (BUNAC), both of which enable thousands of students and others to spend from three to eighteen months in a job related to their studies or on Overseas Practical Training (BUNAC). If you are not eligible for these schemes i.e. you are not a student, graduate, or someone involved in on-the-job-training as a chef, ski instructor, hotelier etc you might feel desperate. Unless you are prepared to go to extremes and emigrate permanently for which you will need a battery of sponsors and qualifications, or to start your own business for which a considerable amount of capital is needed, there are very few approved or legal alternatives. They do however exist and are dealt with later in this section – see *A Job Before You Go*.

Some enthusiasts are prepared to take the risk of working illegally, that is to enter the States on a tourist visa (see below) and then seek work. The laws against such practices are constantly being tightened and involve punitive measures against both the employer who will be heavily fined and the employee who faces certain deportation. Also, without a social security number which among other things gives you redress against unscrupulous employers, you are entirely at employers' mercy as regards, pay, treatment and conditions and consequently exploitation is rife, though not ubiquitous. Those who have done it have become adept at being elusive by changing their place of work and not taking jobs where they are seen every day in the same place i.e. bartender. Contract cleaning and fast food restaurants where the staff is turned over even faster than the food are traditional refuges for such fugitives. Working illegally is however, a desperado existence as one worker put it 'you are always looking over your shoulder and being careful what you say to everyone' and it is advisable to seek exhaustively for a legal way to work in the USA.

By way of preparation for your trip you should set about meeting and making friends with Americans living in your home country. In Britain this could be through universities and colleges or local associations. Look in the telephone directory for the names of American or Anglo-American associations. Start compiling a list of contacts and addresses and home telephone numbers. You will need this for your arrival in the States to provide immigration with evidence that you are planning an extended travelling trip around the country. They must be genuine names and addresses as immigration will not hesitate to call some of them if they are suspicious. If you have relatives in the States then make sure you have a list of these too. Travellers and tourists such as those from the UK may find the new immigration procedures daunting: you will have a digital photograph and an inkless fingerprint taken, before being given permission to enter the USA for up to three months. All incoming visitors on the visa waiver programme (such as those from the UK) have to have a biometric passport (one with a chip that contains all your personal data).

VISA REGULATIONS & TYPES OF VISA

British tourists can wait until arrival to obtain a visa-waiver (1-96) which is however only valid for one entry to the USA for a maximum of three months. Note that in these days of heightened security visas are often given for the minimum (30 days) instead of the maximum (90 days). If you are expecting to stay longer than this, you should obtain the Visitors (B) Visa in advance which entitles you to a maximum stay of six months, though the immigration officer on entry may grant you less especially if turn up with your skis and only a few hundred dollars in your pocket. Obtaining this visa also requires an in-person interview at the US Embassy in your country.

The Visa Branch of the US Embassy (5 Upper Grosvenor Street, London W1A 2JB; www.usembassy.org.uk) can send a brief outline of the non-immigrant visas available, or check the details on their website. The application fee for a non-immigrant visa is about £67. If you live in Northern Ireland you should contact the Visa Branch of the US Embassy, Queen's House, Queen Street, Belfast BT1 6EQ.

TEMPORARY WORK VISAS

The J-1, which is available to participants of government authorised programmes, known as Exchange Visitor Programmes (EVPs). The J-1 Visa is a valuable and coveted addition to a national passport since it entitles the holder to take legal paid employment. You cannot apply for the J-1 without form DS2019 Certificate of Eligibility for Exchange Visitor Status and cannot get form DS2019 without going through a recognised Exchange Visitor Programme which has a sponsoring organisation in the USA. The two main temporary job programmes for the US, run by BUNAC (internship programme OPT USA) and the CIEE are the only ones operating in the winter.

Such programmes are allowed to exist because of their purported educational value, These exchanges and their quotas are reviewed regularly by the Government, though with constant lobbying and proof from employers of staff shortages, the quotas have been increasing. A full list of EVPs and other programmes such as internships, can be obtained by written request to the Fulbright Commission, Educational Advisory Service, 62, Doughty Street, London WC1N 2JZ 020-7404 6994) and enclosing a stamped addressed envelope.

Apart from the J-1 Visa available to those on approved EVPs, there are other possible visas for the prospective ski worker to consider:

○ The Q visa, introduced in 1991, is an International Cultural Exchange Visa, also dubbed the 'Disney Visa' as it was the persistent lobbying by that organisation that helped bring it into existence. This visa is granted where it can be satisfactorily argued that that if you find a job where you will be sharing a practical training or the history, traditions and culture of your country with Americans (e.g. as a nanny, chef, Scottish dancing teacher etc.), you might be eligible to work legally for up to fifteen months. This visa has to be applied for by the employer in the USA and approved in advance by an office of the Immigration and Naturalisation Service.

○ Another possibility is the B-1 Volunteer Visa. Applications for this must be sponsored by a charitable or religious organisation, which is permitted to reimburse your expenses but not to pay you. It is difficult to see how this could be utilised for ski resort work, unless there are any religious organisations that send missionaries to the pistes.

○ The H-1A is available only to nurses and physiotherapists which in theory could be used to get a job in a ski resort.

○ There is also the H-1B Visa which is 'speciality occupation' for professionals with a degree and applies to pre-arranged professional or highly skilled jobs for which there are no suitably qualified Americans.

The H-2B visa is probably the most useful to potential ski workers. This visa is for temporary or seasonal vacancies that employers have difficulty filling with Americans. The maximum duration of the H-2B is ten months but most are issued for around six months. The visa is not transferable so you have to work for the employer who obtained the visa for you. This visa is often used by ski mountains to hire snowboard and ski instructors.

The H-3 'Industrial Trainee' visa is another possibility. Applicants must indicate in detail the breakdown between classroom and on-the-job time, and why equivalent training is not available in their own country. H-visas are rarely relevant to the average traveller, but if you were working for a resort (i.e. one of the companies, which generally own a resort) and learning the job, it might be a possibility. This visa is valid for 18 or 24 months.

INTERNSHIPS

Internship is the American term for traineeship, and provides a chance to get some experience in your career interest while you are still studying or for up to twelve months after graduating. Note that in many cases, internships are unpaid and accommodation may not be provided.

It can however work out an expensive way to get a job as Briton Neil Hibberd found out when he arranged an internship at Steamboat Springs. He had to visit the resort twice: once in August to interview for the job of lift operator, and then back again in October for the start of the season. The whole process including airfares is liable to set you back in the region of £800+.

Several organisations in the UK arrange trainee positions in the US for students and in some cases graduates and non-students. Such placements could be in tourism, catering, ski resort management, snowsports etc. and could be based in a ski resort. Qualifiers are eligible for a J-1 visa. Note that most of the programmes below have a fee.

BUNAC: 16 Bowling Green Lane, London EC1R OQH; 020-7251 3472; www.bunac. org.uk). Mainly known for summer programmes, BUNAC also operates an internship programme open to students and non-students to stay in the USA for three to eighteen months for practical on-the-job-training (NB not just work experience).

CCUSA: (1ˢᵗ Floor North, Devon House, 171/177 Great Portland Street, London NW3 5HT; 020-7637 0779/fax 020-7637 6209); www.ccusaweusa.co.uk.). In addition to their summer camp programme, CCUSA has a work experience programme that is useful to those wanting to work in a US ski resort as it enables qualifying applicants to spend four months working in the USA either in the summer or for a winter ski season. Those accepted on the scheme can arrange their job before they go, or on arrival in the resort. Fixing up a job in advance on the Placement Programme costs £540.

Association for International Practical Training. The UK/US Career Development Programme is administered by the AIPT in Maryland (www.aipt.org). This programme is for people aged 18-35 with relevant qualifications and/or at least a year's experience in their career field. A separate section of this programme is for full-time students in Hospitality and Tourism. A placement assistance service is also available for some participants. The fee is £65 plus a fee ($600-$1000 payable to the US organiser (which the employer sometimes pays).

International Employment Training: 45 High Street, Tunbridge Wells, Kent TN1 1XL; (www.jobsamerica.co.uk) is a division of the Work and Travel Company. IET helps those with a degree and some work experience to find a US placement for three to eighteen months. If you have already arranged a placement yourself you can pay IET for assistance in obtaining the J-1 visa.

IST Plus Ltd: Rosedale House, Rosedale Road, Richmond, Surrey TW9 2SZ (020-8939 9057; info@istplus.com). New UK partner of the CIEE (Council on International Educational Exchange). Organises working programmes in the USA for Britons.

GREEN CARD IMMIGRANT VISA

It is exceedingly difficult to get an immigrant visa (known as a 'green card'), which allows foreigners to live and work in the USA as 'resident aliens'. Generally, they are only given to those who are close relatives of US citizens, which is why some people who want to work in the States are prepared to marry a US citizen just to get one. However, this step is too drastic for most. If you can find an employer willing to state that no American is qualified to do the job you still have to pay out $800-$1,000 for legal fees. Alternatively, if you have enough capital to set up business in the States and offer employment to Americans, you stand a chance of getting a green card.

A JOB BEFORE YOU GO

WORKING FOR A BRITISH-BASED EMPLOYER OR THROUGH A UK ORGANISATION

For those who prefer to organise a job before they go to America the following is a run-down of the companies and types of organisations that can help arrange jobs in US ski resorts:

AU PAIR AND HOMESTAY AGENCIES

Au Pair work has been legal in the United States since 1986 through schemes regulated by the US government. Despite this and the fact that Europeans are regarded as cheap childcare by Americans, anyone wanting to use this as a possible access to a job in a ski resort should not be too dismissive, especially if they like children and have experience of looking after them. Au pairs on recognised schemes can be male or female, aged 18-26 and are normally expected to stay one year. Although none of the agencies mentioned below can guarantee a placement in a ski resort, they will none-the-less try to help with requests for a placement in one and are therefore certainly worth trying:

Au Pair America: 37 Queen's Gate, London SW7 5HR. Au Pair in America is the largest organisation placing thousands of young people in au pair and nanny placements throughout the USA. Brochures and application forms can be downloaded from www.aupairinamerica.com or by telephoning 020-7581 7363. Placements are for a year and departures are in winter or summer.

American Institute for Foreign Study (Au Pair in America): River Plaza, 9 West Broad Street, Stamford CT 06902 (☎800-928-7247/203-399-5000); info@aupairamerica.co.uk; www.aupairinamerica.com).

AuPairCare, Inc. (AYUSA International), California St., 10th Floor, San Francisco, CA 94108 (☎800-428-7247/415-434-8788 ext. 501; www.aupaircare.com.).

*Au Pair International Inc.*3163 S. Columbine Street, Denver, Colorado 80210 (☎720-221-3563; fax 720-221-3563.

EurAupair Intercultural Child Care Programs: 238 North Coast Highway, Laguna Beach, CA 92651, USA (☎800-713 2002/949-494-7355; www.euraupair.com).

Increasingly, au pairs and families are bypassing conventional agencies by using the internet and doing it for themselves. Prospective au pairs can register their details, including age, nationality, relevant experience and usually a photograph to be uploaded on to a website which then becomes accessible to registered families. You can specify that you would like to work in a ski resort. The families then pay the website owners to make contact with suitable au pairs. The job-seeker may have to pay a small fee or none at all. Two internet based agencies currently utilised are www.aupair-agency.com and www.au-pair.aupair-world.net. Note that most placements are for a year.

BRITISH ASSOCIATION OF SNOWSPORT INSTRUCTORS (BASI)
Glenmore, Aviemore, Inverness-shire PH22 1QU; ☎01479-861717; fax 01479-861718; e-mail: basi@basi.or.uk; www.basi.org.uk

BASI has been the training and certifying organisation for ski instructors in Britain for over 40 years. As well as the traditional alpine and nordic skiing, three disciplines have been added more recently: telemark, snowboarding and adaptive skiing.

BASI currently has nearly 4,000 members, only 300 of whom hold the coveted National Ski Teacher international licence and highest qualification. On average, it takes five years to achieve this qualification. Qualified members work in 25 different countries and BASI qualifications are continuing to gain a worldwide reputation.

Anyone wanting to work in North America is dependent on first obtaining a work permit. This is not normally a problem for National Ski Teachers, but lower grades may have more chance of work in the eastern states. Obtaining a work permit to teach as a ski teacher in Canada is difficult.

There is also a possibility of BASI trainees (those who have attended only an initial training course) achieving employment (see *Traineeships* above).

Although BASI has been contacted directly by the resorts (both Park City Mountain Resort and Mount Snow, Vermont were advertising on the BASI website in 2006), it is normally a case of the instructors applying to the resorts. Snowsport Recruitment (www.snowsportrecruitment.com/USA.htm) send about a dozen instructors per season to

Waterville Valley, New Hampshire.

BASI runs training and grading courses year round and anyone interested should contact the above address.

The types of US visa for which a ski instructor might be eligible include the J-1 Exchange Visitor Visa. Ski Instructors may also be eligible for the 'H' (temporary worker) or 'L' (intra-company) visa. To obtain this, the employer in the United States must file a visa petition on form I-129H or I-129L respectively with the nearest office of the INS in the United States.

It is also be possible to do your ski instructor training in North America for a very hefty fee. The International Academy (King's Place, 12-42 Wood Street, Kingston upon Thames, Surrey KT1 1JY; ☎0870 060 1381; fax 020 8939 0411; info@theinternationalacademy. com; www.theinternational-academy.com) organises professional ski and snowboard instructor courses in North America, Chile and New Zealand.

BRITISH TOUR OPERATORS

Over recent years the number of British tour operators going to the United States has been increasing. After a couple of seasons of patchy snow in the European Alps the selling point of the US resorts soon became apparent: their snow is more reliable. Couple this with the fact that many US resorts have only been seriously developed in the last 25 years and that their facilities are state of the art and the resorts themselves are immaculately run by image-conscious, efficient corporations with English-speaking, highly motivated courteous staff and the reason for the migration of British skiers is not hard to find. Some British companies prefer to employ British people who have already got a green card, or local staff. A few British tour companies employ a handful of British staff imported directly from the UK for the season and some are merely agents for US ski holidays and do not employ their own staff in the US. For UK companies using their own staff the types of jobs that are available are usually ski guides/reps and chalet staff. The companies are not involved in the working visa problem, because their staff are working for a British-based company and are paid in sterling in the UK. A number of the companies listed below tend to offer the American jobs to staff who have already worked for them before as they need experienced, reliable-proven employees who can work with a minimum of supervision because of the distance from the parent company headquarters. The addresses of such companies together with their exact staff requirements are listed in the *British Ski Tour Operators* section of this book. The names and contact numbers of some of the relevant ski companies and the American resorts they go to are as follows:

Club Mediterranée: ☎0845 3676767; www.clubmedjobs.com. Club Med has a operation in Crested Butte.

Crystal Holidays: ☎0845 055 0255. Goes to about 20 US resorts including (Aspen, Beaver Creek, Breckenridge, Copper Mountain, Jackson Hole, Park City, Vail and Winter Park). Catered chalets are in Aspen/Snowmass, Breckenridge, Vail and Winter Park. In Canada they operate in several resorts Banff, Jasper, Lake Louise, Tremblant and Whistler and offer catered chalets in Whistler.

Inghams: 10-18 Putney Hill, London SW15 6AX; ☎020-8780 4400; fax 020-8780 4405; e-mail travel@inghams.co.uk;www.inghams.co.uk. Inghams employ reps in the USA (Breckenridge, Vail, Jackson Hole and Killington). They also go to 10 Canadian resorts. Inghams prefer that reps have worked for them first in Europe before they can work in the USA; unless they are already very experienced.

Neilson: ☎0870-241 2901; skijobs@neilson.com, features Breckenridge, Winter Park and Copper Mountain in Colarado and Jackson Hole (Wyoming). Catered chalet in Breckenridge, while all resorts have a Neilson rep from the UK.

Ski Equipe: (0161-439 6955) goes to Vail/Beaver Creek (with catered chalet for up to sixteen guests or two chalets of 8 guests each).

Ski Independence: 5 Thistle Street, Edinburgh EH2 1DF; ☎0845-310-3030; fax 0131-

225-4789; jon@ski-i.com; www.ski-i.com. Specialises in tailor-made holidays to the USA and Canada and employs resort reps and chalet staff), sourced from the UK and also Americans and Canadians. UK-sourced staff are likely to be placed in Vail, Breckenridge, Banff, Whistler and Tremblant. All must have driving licences.

Ski Miquel: (☎01457-820200). Employs four staff in Whistler: resort manager and chalet staff including a chef.

Ski Val: (08707-463030). Employs six chalet staff and a resort manager in Breckenridge.

Skiworld: Overseas Personnel Department, Skiworld House, 3 Vencourt Place, London W6 9NU; 0870 4205912; recruitment@skiworld.ltd.uk; www.skiworld.ltd.uk. Skiworld's US operation covers Vail, Breckenridge, Aspen, Steamboat, Winter Park and Whistler where it has its own staff from the UK including chalet hosts. Minimum age 21 or 25 for chalet hosts for North America depending on the resort. For further details see Skiworld entry in *Work with Ski Tour Operators* section.

Thomson: employ reps in various US resorts. Recruitment is done centrally at www.cantwait4winter.com or telephone 0845-055 0244.

SOURCES OF JOBS

If you are beginning from scratch and have no friends or contacts in the USA who might be able to suggest possible employers then here are a few suggestions:

○ You can write to, or email the individual corporations, which own and run the ski resorts. You will find their titles and postal/e-mail addresses, and some contact names in the *Directory of the Main American Ski Resorts* at the end of this section.

○ Compile a list of other companies, which may have outlets in ski resorts (e.g. large hotel chains like Hilton, Hyatt). You can find out the names of these from American tourist brochures.

○ Write to the Chambers of Commerce in the town or nearest large town where you wish to work for a list of their members in their area. Unfortunately such information is not obtainable from the American Chamber of Commerce in London except to members. The best source of information is probably the City Business Library (1 Brewers Hall Garden, London EC2; 020-7638 8215/480 7638). The nearest tube is Moorgate and opening times are Monday to Friday 9.30 am to 5 pm. There you can consult the *Worldwide Chamber of Commerce Directory* and the library also has American Yellow Pages for most US States.

○ Use the internet. Since the last edition of this book there has been a huge increase in the use of the web for tracking down all kinds of information worldwide. Hunting down jobs in US ski resorts via the internet is the quickest way to contact the companies and get the latest job information and to find out when and where they are holding their recruitment fairs. All you need for the search engine is the name of the resort and once you have the resort home page you can click on 'jobs', 'join the team' etc.

American Skiing Company

The American Skiing Company is a huge ski corporation based in Park City, Utah, that owns seven skiing areas in the USA: Killington, Pico Mountain and Mount Snow (Vermont), The Canyons (Utah), Steamboat Springs (Colorado), Sugar Loaf and Sunday River (Maine) and Attitash (New Hampshire). This makes it an important source of ski jobs which you can find out about through contacting the individual resorts.

American Skiing Company: 136 Heber Avenue, P.O. Box 4552, Park City, Utah 84060; www.peaks.com/employment/html.

Attitash/Bear Park: www.attitash.com

The Canyons: www.thecanyons.com

Killington: www.killington.com

Mount Snow: www.mountsnow.com
Steamboat Springs: www.steamboat-ski.com
Sugarloaf: www.sugarloaf.com
Sunday River: www.sundayriver.com
   More information about some of these resorts can be found in the *Directory of the Main United States Ski Resorts* below.

Useful Website
www.outbreak-adventure.com: a recruitment organisation based in London (36 Staveley Gardens, W4 2SA; mobile 07891-573930) that annually recruits all kinds of staff for US resorts. Candidates should be eligible for H2B Visa status (see *Temporary Work Visas*).

WRITING TO AMERICAN EMPLOYERS

When writing to any potential employer send a one-page covering letter and a CV (known as a résumé in the USA). The CV must be professional looking (i.e. done on a word processor), no more than an A4 page in length and should list your most recent employment first and work backwards in chronological order. If you do not have work experience sufficient to fill a page then list your 'A' levels indicating that these are the equivalent of a high school diploma and/or two-year junior college degree for the subjects taken. If you are applying through a recognised Exchange Visitor Programme then you should also indicate that you have the ability to apply for trainee status and a J-1 visa in your covering letter. The introductory paragraph of your letter should briefly state your reasons for applying for the job and then a couple of paragraphs highlighting relevant excerpts from your résumé.
   Although employers in ski resorts tend to have their main recruitment drive in late summer/ early autumn, it is advisable to write to them early in the summer, especially as you may have to find your own accommodation and the earlier you can arrange this the better.

A JOB ON THE SPOT

DEALING WITH ENTRY AND IMMIGRATION

If you arrive in the USA with a visa, a return ticket and look respectable and confident you will most probably be processed through the formalities without hitches. However, if you create the wrong impression by looking shifty, poverty stricken, clutching skis or snowboard, references from previous employers, a CV and a copy of this book, you are probably in for a hard time at the end of which you are liable to have your passport branded with a two week entry visa.
   Although tourists from Europe in certain categories no longer require visitor visas as part of the 'Visa Waiver Programme', it is still advisable to obtain one (Visitor's Visa B-2) in advance. Otherwise you have to sign a pink visa waiver form (I-791), which allows you to stay for a non-extendable maximum of 90 days. Those planning trips of more than 90 days, including those who wish to work or study, must obtain a Visitor's Visa in advance from the US Embassy. This has become more complicated and involves an in-person interview in the embassy and the completion of a long and complicated form. Although the final decision is taken by the immigration official on your arrival, if you look normal, have a plausible reason for staying in the USA for five months and have a decent amount of funds you should be given the full six months. Post 9/11 America has resorted to tighter security all round. British tourists and travellers to the USA are digitally fingerprinted and

photographed. From October 2006 biometric (i.e. with a smart chip) passports will be compulsory for anyone entering the USA. At the time of press it seems that if your current passport is not a biometric one, you will not have to renew it just to enter the USA, but all passports issued after October 2006 are expected to have a smart chip. Check with the American embassy for the latest entry procedures.

The other reason for applying for a visitor's visa in advance is that otherwise you risk the ordeal of being scrutinised body, soul and baggage by the customs and immigration. This unpleasant experience to which some travellers' have been subjected, including having their diaries read, makes the following precautions sensible and worthwhile:

O   If you are entering the USA on a tourist visa, under no circumstances mention that you have any intention of looking for work in the USA.

O   Do not have on you papers, which may indicate an intention to work such as references, job offers or CVs. Some travellers send these on ahead of them.

O   If you are entering on a tourist visa, immigration must be convinced that you are coming as just that. If you don't have much money, make sure you have prepared a list of names and addresses of Americans who are willing to put you up or letters from them undertaking to put you up and support you for a month. If you have relatives in the States, this would be even better. You should also have an outline of an extensive real or imaginary itinerary of places you wish to visit in America and tourist literature to back it up.

O   Have a reasonable amount of money on you if at all possible. The recommended amount is $500 per month of your stay, plus credit cards e.g. Visa or Americard.

Immigration will probably not take your word for how much money you have so, be prepared to count it out in front of them. One impecunious contributor used an imaginative way of convincing immigration of his affluence: he exploited the fact that many UK building societies are now affiliated to the Link system, which allows card holders to withdraw cash from over 20,000 dispensers in the United States. You can therefore ask friends, family etc. to lend you money for a few days, then have your pass book brought up to date with the new balance, repay the money, and show the passbook and Link card to US immigration. This is not guaranteed to work, but evidently some contributors consider it worth a try.

If, despite your best efforts, you are not granted the full 90 days on arrival, it is still possible to extend your visa when you are there by contacting the local office of the Immigration and Naturalisation Service, before your visa has expired, asking for the form 'Application for Issuance of Extension of Permit to Re-enter the United States.' To get a renewal you will have to show adequate means of support and have a plausible reason for extending your stay. You could say that you wish to travel further or that some relatives are arriving soon and you want to travel with them etc. If you do this more than once it is advisable to apply to a different INS office each time. It is possible in this fashion to legally extend your stay for over a year.

A less laborious way of extending your stay is simply to cross the Canadian or Mexican border and re-cross the border and hope the immigration officer will automatically extend your stay.

SOCIAL SECURITY NUMBERS

If you have arrived in the United States on a J-1 Visa you will have no problem obtaining a Social Security Card with a number when you arrive at the place where you will be working. If you have arrived with the intention of looking for work then your lack of a permit and or social security number can be a severe handicap. To start with, unless you have a social security number there is no official way that your employer can legally pay you which is a big disadvantage because if they have to pay you cash in hand and therefore know you are working illegally, you are at their mercy at are open to exploitation. In any case, regulations are now much more strictly enforced in the United States and employers risk large fines if they are caught employing illegal workers. About the most common arrangement is bed and board plus a few cash handouts for odd jobs if you are lucky, or two week stints here there and everywhere. The object of employing such tactics is to avoid staying long enough in one place for the government to catch up. However, this is obviously easier in a big city than in a ski resort as the latter is a small community where everybody knows everyone's business. More importantly, most of the employment is done through the individual corporations that run the ski resorts and they behave with official correctness.

Despite the risks, reports suggest there are still plenty of travellers who manage to get round the social security number problem though methods are not foolproof or recommended. One of the most common ruses is to exchange social security numbers and names with an American friend who wants to work in the UK, or to 'borrow' their number if they are out of work. That way, anyone paying social security contributions benefits someone they know rather than go into some random account, which is the likely result if you make up a number. The time when the tax authorities usually catch out the false number providers is when the Internal Revenue Service processes the W-4 form which all employees are obliged to complete. Many thousands of illegal workers in the USA, usually leave the country temporarily around this time. Those having finished the ski season working in the USA but who are planning to stay on and work in the summer find themselves having to do the same.

All in all working illegally is far from ideal and no-one recommends it. You should check if there is any way you could get a job through an approved scheme, especially now that the scope of these schemes has widened to embrace more kinds of work and for longer periods.

For full-time students and those on approved Exchange Visitor Programmes tax liability is normally waived.

WORKING LEGALLY WITHOUT A PREARRANGED JOB

It is extremely difficult to get a work permit once you have arrived in the United States, but it is not impossible. The trick is to find an employer who really needs you, particularly if you have some skill that is hard to find amongst American applicants. Englishman James Ogglesbury's employer in Winter Park, Colorado, managed to obtain a work permit on the basis that James spoke French and German; apparently a rare accomplishment amongst young Americans. However, the bureaucracy involved in applying for a permit on the spot is designed to be as tiresome as possible in order to deter both job seekers and employers and James strongly advises fixing up a job and papers in advance if at all possible.

DRIVE-AWAYS

Once you have negotiated your entry to the USA, you may wish to travel around looking for work. If you are not within easy hitching distance of where you want to go and don't fancy the rigid timetable of the Greyhound Bus Service then another possibility is the phenomenon known as drive-away cars that operates widely in the country. This is a service provided for affluent North Americans, usually when they want to have their car on holiday but don't want to drive it there themselves. So they hire a company to move it for them; the companies hire drivers (i.e. you) provide insurance and arbitrate in the event of accidents. All you do is drive the car, pay for the petrol after the first thankful, keep to a delivery schedule and mileage limitation which generally allow some scope for stopping off along the way. The driver also normally pays for the interstate tolls. To find the names of drive-away companies look up 'Automobile Transporters and Driveaway Companies' in the Yellow Pages of any big city or check the internet at www.movecars.com. Widespread companies include Auto Driveaway Company with about 50 offices around the USA.

The normal minimum age for hired drivers is 21 (in some cases 25), but by telephoning round you may find some companies that will take younger ones. Another possibility is to ask around car rental agencies as they often send a batch of cars to areas such as ski resorts, where there is a seasonal demand. The trade jargon for such cars is 'deadheads'.

The only drawback in this otherwise admirable way of covering long distances pleasantly, is that the kind of Americans who can afford this service are not likely to have bottom of the range cars which are economical on gas. You are more likely than not to find yourself saddled with a Cadillac, or some other gas-guzzler. In order to balance the economics a little more in your favour it is permissible to take a co-driver and/or passengers as long as the driveaway company registers them for insurance purposes. You can then split the costs. If you can't find one car going all the way, you can usually arrange several pick-ups that will eventually get you to your destination.

Once you have registered with the drive-away company and they have booked you a car, you have to go to the family or agent's to collect it. It is important to make sure you are aware of any damage or mechanical faults at the outset and have a list of these agreed with the owner as otherwise, you may find yourself liable for existing damage or faults. Any other repairs necessary en route you pay for and reclaim from the recipient of the vehicle. There is usually a ceiling amount for this above which you must call and check with the owner before having the repair carried out.

You should note that there is a maximum speed limit of 65 mph on American freeways, which means you will not be able to give a test run to the Lamborghini that you have just been hired to drive away.

YOUTH HOSTELS & OTHER BUDGET ACCOMMODATION

Unfortunately, although the cost of eating in the United States is cheaper than the UK, accommodation in the resorts while you are looking for work is likely to be expensive. There are youth hostels in some of the main resorts. The Hostelling North America handbook, published by Hostelling International (American Youth Hostels, Dept. 482, P.O.Box 37613, Washington D.C. 20013-7613; ☎202 783-6161; www.hiusa.org) is free to members of the American Youth Hostels Association and gives details of hostels throughout North America and Canada. Membership details can be obtained from the above address. Apart from providing inexpensive accommodation, youth hostels are also a splendid grapevine for information about jobs. Youth hostels and supplemental accommodation (slightly more expensive than a hostel) in ski resorts include:

Colorado
Breckenridge: Supplemental Accommodation: Fireside Inn Bed & Breakfast (HI-AYH), 114 North French Street, P.O.Box 2252, Breckenridge CO 80424; ☎(970) 453-6456; fax (970) 453 9577; info@firesideinn.com; www.firesideinn.com.
The Rocky Mountain Inn: 15 CR 72, Box 600, Winter Park, Fraser, Colorado; ☎(local/ international) 1-970-726-8256; info@rockymountaininn.com.

Idaho
Nr. Grand Targhee (WY): Movin'Sol Hostel, 110 East Little Avenue, Driggs ID 83422; ☎208-354 5454; stay@tetonhostel. 12 miles from Grand Targhee resort, and an hour from Jackson Hole.

New Mexico
Taos (Arroyo Seco): Taos Ski Valley Road, Arroyo Seco, P.O. Box 3271, Taos, NM 87571; ☎505 776 8298.

Wyoming
Jackson Hole: The Hostel X, 3600 McCollister Drive, Box 546, Teton Village, WY 83025; ☎307 733-3415.

Other budget accommodation possibilities include YMCAs and YWCAs, low cost motel chains and even bed and breakfast accommodation, a concept, which has only arrived in the USA in recent years and is a great way to meet Americans. A useful publication listing such facilities is *Bed & Breakfast USA: A Guide to Guest Houses and Tourist Homes* by Peggy Ackerman, published by E P Dutton. Another useful publication is *Peterson's Directory of College Accommodations* by Jay Norman, which carries details of budget accommodation on American and Canadian university campuses.

INSURANCE

Unlike the UK, the United States has no National Health Service that provides free medical treatment whenever it is needed. It is therefore absolutely essential to have insurance that will cover medical costs and repatriation if necessary. If you have arranged your job through one of the approved schemes like the CIEE or AIPT you will almost certainly get insurance as part of the package. In addition, you will also have the back-up of the organisation if you get into difficulty with medical costs i.e. the money for treatment is required upfront and you cannot pay them. If however, you are travelling independently without this safety net you will need to seek out an insurance policy that best covers your needs.

Any travel agent will sell you travel insurance at the drop of a hat, which may or may not be suitable or the best deal. It usually pays to shop around for the best deal and these tend to be on the internet where you can compare prices and what they cover quite easily. Some addresses of well-known companies providing travel and medical insurance are:

Columbus Direct: 17 Devonshire Square EC2M 4SQ; 020-7375 0011; www.columbusdirect. com. Does basic annual medical cover for globetrotters.

Coverworks: 47a Barony Road, Nantwich, Cheshire CW5 7PB; 08702-862828; www. coverworks.com. Policies especially for working travellers.

Endsleigh Insurance: head office: Endsleigh House, Ambrose Street, Cheltenham, Gloucestershire GL50 3NR. Offices in most university towns.

Travel Insurance Agency Ltd.: 775B High Road, North Finchley, London N12 8JY; ☎020-8446 5414; www.travelinsurers.com.

If you want a year's cover then the costs of insurance will run into a few hundred pounds though the actual costs will vary between companies and depend on the levels of cover required. For instance Columbus charge over £300 for a year's cover for those whose main destination is the USA. Other companies' charges range from about £300 to £600+ pounds depending on the level of cover required, for one year's worldwide cover. If you are only going for the skiing season (i.e. five months) then you will probably be able to buy insurance on a monthly basis. You should note that most travel insurance is just that, i.e. it covers you for travelling but not for working. Although it is difficult to see how the companies would actually know how an accident had occurred, it is best to declare your intentions from the outset.

THE JOB HUNT

If you don't have relatives or friends that you can stay with, then surviving on a little money in the States and relying on odd jobs for cash can be extremely difficult. If at all possible, make plenty of American contacts and have several offers of accommodation lined up. Accommodation while looking for work and while working is one of the main problems for ski bums. An Englishman, Simon Melser, who worked in a hotel in Breckenridge recommends coming out to the resort as early as possible and taking anything going in the way of accommodation as you can always move later if something better comes up. Once you have a base and a telephone number that you can give to potential employers who may wish to contact you, you can begin the job hunt.

USEFUL PUBLICATIONS FOR JOBS

The internet has pretty much replaced classified ads in newspapers and magazines as the place to advertise vacancies. In many cases job seekers can find the information they need on vacancies and applying for them on the websites of the various resorts. However some of the publications below may be useful for those on the move or for general information.

You will find the alternative newspapers published in every city and most of the towns in the United States useful for their job sections. These newspapers are free and are distributed to shops, restaurants, offices etc. *Westword* published in Denver (1621 18th Street, 150 Denver, Co 80202; ☎303 296-7744; www.westword.com) could be useful in getting jobs in nearby Telluride. Or job seekers could place an advert of their own. Better still from the jobseekers' point of view are publications that come out in the resorts themselves specifically to publicise ski job vacancies. The local chamber of commerce may be able to advise on the possibilities.

It may also be worth trying the main American skiing magazines of which there are a handful

Cross Country Skier: P O Box 550, Cable, Wisconsin 54821; 715-798-5500; www. crosscountryskier.com.

Ski: Editorial and Online Offices, 929 Pearl Street, Suite 200, Boulder, Colorado 80302; www.skimag.com. Also has useful web links to jobs available in ski resorts; click on *Reader Services* which will give you links to all the resorts. Click on the resort of your choice and then find the employment/jobs section on their website.

Skiing: same editorial address as *Ski* above.

Ski Press Magazine: European, English and American version published. More information at www.skipressworld.com.

Powder Magazine: POB 1028, Dana Point, California 92629-5028; 949-661 5150; www. powdermag.com.

These skiing magazines are published monthly from September to March inclusive, but not during the summer months. The early season editions are likely to be of most use to the job hunter. These magazines are also available in the United Kingdom and other countries. In the UK they can be ordered through newsagents who will obtain them through a UK distributor such as COMAG or Seymour Press. Unfortunately these distributors will not deal directly with individual members of the public.

HOW DO AMERICAN RESORTS RECRUIT?

Most American resorts are owned by a single commercial company, which owns everything including the land and all the facilities provided. It follows therefore that the company or corporation controls a large slice of the employment in the resort. However, some of the hotels (not a big feature in American resorts), restaurants, shops and other businesses will be independently owned. If you are going to try and get a job working for one of the resort corporations then find out when they have their main recruitment drive. Up to two thirds of a typical ski resort's staff are hired just before the winter season for the skiing period only. In some resorts this can start as early as September but the majority like to be open by Thanksgiving in late November. Most ski resorts have several open days or recruitment fairs to attract recruits during the autumn. In many resorts the final push for employees takes place towards the end of October but it pays to arrive earlier. The hiring process may start with a big advertisement in the local newspaper. In past years base lodges of ski resorts have sprouted displays of 'Help Wanted' bills around late autumn. In past years some ski areas were so desperate for help that they began their recruitment drive in June or July: Waterville Valley in New Hampshire distributed leaflets in resorts along the Atlantic coast in summer, inviting job applications for the winter. Although this was in the halcyon days of the 1980s, there are still plenty of jobs going, especially for the early birds. Some ski areas send out recruiting parties who travel to major cities like Denver or Salt Lake City to hold job fairs. Often, recruitment facilities are incorporated into consumer ski shows where ski areas and associated industries promote their wares to the consumer. American resorts will seldom hire on the telephone and will almost certainly want to see you in person so be prepared to attend an interview from September onwards when flights to the USA are much cheaper than during July and August. You should bring references from previous employers and character references from personal contacts, with you to the interview.

TYPES OF JOBS AND CONDITIONS

WHAT KINDS OF JOBS ARE THERE?

The number of employees will vary between resorts but as they all operate along similar lines the types of jobs available in most big resorts are likely to include the following:

Catering and Domestic: Bussers (to clear tables), cafeteria servers, cashiers, chefs, dishwashers, maintenance staff and janitors, waiting staff.

Drivers: for shuttle vans (usually minimum 15 passengers) between resorts.

Emergency/First Aid Staff on the Mountain: Ski Patrollers are responsible for providing first aid to injured skiers on the mountain, and transporting them to the mountain clinic and for avalanche control. Expert skiing essential and advanced first aid minimum requirement.

Hospitality Staff: a combination of domestic and clerical jobs like bell staff, front desk receptionists, housekeepers and night auditors.

Mountain Operations: lift operators, race crew, skier services, snowmakers, snowcat operators & piste bashers.

Office Staff: clerical staff to help with accounts and cash receipts.

Shop Staff: shop assistants, ski technicians for rental and repair, ski storage attendants.

Resort Operations: grounds maintenance, guest attendants, parking attendants, security staff, cabin hosts.

Ski School: Alpine, Nordic and Snowboard Instructors, Children's instructors, childcare and nursery staff, snowmobile guides.

Ticket Operations: ticket reservation staff for private and group lessons, ticket checkers and ticket collectors.

WHAT KINDS OF PEOPLE ARE RECRUITED?

The types of jobs likely to be on offer include many menial jobs like waiters, kitchen helpers, chambermaids, office staff, cashiers, lift attendants, parking attendants and snow makers. Condominiums which feature heavily in many US resorts are also usually a good bet for jobs including maintenance men, drivers and chambermaids. Most of these jobs mean long hours for low pay and if outdoors, then ability to work in all weathers, so flexibility and a cheerful disposition under stress are essential. As well as US college graduates, local competition is likely to come from outdoor types who spend the summer working in the American national parks and are used to working with tourists.

The kind of people (human resources) that American resorts want to recruit is unequivocal; the American term 'people-oriented' people probably says it all. Necessary aptitude for the job includes being naturally positive and cheerful as well as hard working and a 'team-player' who gets along well with his or her colleagues. In some American resorts (as in some European ones), employees are not allowed to ski during the peak times. This is to emphasise that employees are not there to ski and have a good time partying the night away, they are there to enhance the resort's reputation. When applying for a job with a resort, it is necessary to show a keen interest in the company you are applying to work for and to give the interviewer the impression that you are just what they are looking for.

WHAT ABOUT PAY, PERKS AND CONDITIONS?

The pay at first glance does not amount to much: depending on the job it is generally in the region of $6 to $8 an hour. The federal minimum is lower than this, but individual states set their own higher rates, which varies amongst states and goes up every few years. If you are working illegally it can be much less. The minimum for catering work is about $5.15 an hour though some employers get away with paying about $6 for an evening shift because they know you will do handsomely out of tips if you are a waitress/waiter ('wait person') or bartender. One worker who worked in a Colorado ski resort only made $100 per month after paying for room, board, ski pass and ski hire. In a few instances ski areas pay graded increments depending on how long you stay: for instance pay goes up by 25% after a month or, as is the case in Heavenly, an end of season bonus is paid (based on the number of hours worked). According to one seasonal worker two of the best jobs to get are bartender or 'wait person' as Americans always tip and generously if they are enjoying themselves. An average weekly total of tips for waiting staff would be $120; more at peak periods of the season. Bar staff do even better and an English accent can be a big asset.

Employee perks provided by the ski areas include free or discounted skiing. As in some European resorts other facilities may also be available at a discount, for instance at Sun Valley resort employees even get discounts on opera tickets at the resort's Opera House. In addition most ski areas will give employees a discount on food and beverages, and ski rental. Housing is however a more random provision for employees. Some ski areas do not provide housing for employees, who have to find their own, which means usually arriving in the ski area no later than August to arrange something. Other resorts provide subsidised accommodation, usually in dorms. Kirkwood in California has employee accommodation for average rents of $200-$400 per month including utilities, but you have to provide your own bedding and utensils. If the ski area of your choice does not provide accommodation you should request a list of places to stay, but the arrive early rule applies if you want to find the cheapest place to stay. Some companies are sympathetic enough to allow you to postpone payment of your rent until your first pay cheque arrives, but don't count on it and be prepared to pay money up-front when you finally find somewhere, for the deposit or retainer and other costs associated with property rental agreements. Running costs will almost certainly include security and a deposit for the telephone.

WHAT ARE THE CHANCES OF STAYING ON?

Although ski areas understandably employ the bulk of their staff just for winter, many are year-round resorts and have a substantial number of summer staff as well. If you have made a good impression over the winter your chances of staying on, particularly in the catering department are reasonable. However chances of moving up the corporate ladder are fairly minimal as there is not a high turnover of staff in the higher echelons of management. If you want to be a boss you will probably have to start your own business which is precisely what some British citizens have done. Simon Melser, a catering graduate, worked in a big hotel in Breckenridge. He managed to get a permit by convincing a US catering company that they needed his particular skills. He now runs his own catering company in Breckenridge, which employs Americans. Needless to say, he now has a green card.

USEFUL WEBSITES

The following websites are useful for tracking down ski resort vacancies in North America:

> www.coolworks.com
> www.backdoorjobs.com/ski
> www.jobmonkey.com/ski
> www.freeradicals.co.uk
> www.skicentral.com
> www.skiingthenet.com
> www.skitownjobs.com

DIRECTORY OF THE MAIN UNITED STATES SKI RESORTS

The following is a directory of the main ski resorts in the United States which are likely to prove the best sources of employment as they each employ hundreds of staff. The most important resorts are dealt with in detail. Names and addresses of other resorts in the same area are listed at the end of each geographical section. As the biggest employer in any resort is the resort itself (i.e. the company that owns or runs it) we have given the name and address of the company and where possible a contact name. Where no name is given it is advisable to address enquiries to the Personnel Department followed by the name and address of the resort. In most American resorts there are usually some independent employers: hotels, restaurants, catering businesses etc.) and where known we have included these as well under the relevant resort. Others may be obtained by contacting the nearest chamber of commerce to the ski resort.

California/Nevada (Lake Tahoe)

HEAVENLY

Mention Californian skiing to anyone and they will probably think of Heavenly before any other resort. Located on the southern shore of the 72-mile-long Lake Tahoe it lies on the border of both California and Nevada. But Heavenly is just one of the international class Lake Tahoe resorts – Squaw Valley, Alpine Meadows, Kirkwood and Northstar are the others. A regular shuttle connects these resorts and an interchangeable lift pass is available. The dark blue waters of the lake, which lies at 4,226 feet above sea level, contrasted with the whiteness of the surrounding Sierras and the bleakness of the Nevada desert make for an inspirational backdrop. The ski area base is about two miles from South Lake Tahoe, which comprises a seemingly random collection of motels, shops, eateries and casinos that runs for miles along the lakeside. This is where most of the accommodation is located. A free shuttle bus links the accommodation with the ski resort's three base lodges,

Stagecoach and Boulder (in Nevada) and the California Base Lodge. From mid-January you can take a Paddle Wheeler across the lake to Tahoe City (Squaw Valley). One of the area's main attractions, apart from skiing of course, is gambling. Reno is about 50 miles away and the casino culture extends to Lake Tahoe. The Nevada stateline is crammed with glitzy casino-hotels where room and board are tantalisingly cheap in order to lure the punters; so if you are up to it, you can ski all day and gamble all night.

A new pedestrian 'village' is growing up around the base of the gondola. This will probably be popular with fans of European-type après ski.

The Skiing
On Heavenly Mountain you can ski in both California and Nevada. The skiing is suitable for all standards. There are 4,800 acres of trails (marked pistes) and 29 lifts. The Heavenly Ski School has 200 instructors. There is a children's ski school, Snow Explorers for children four to seven years old. Mott Canyon, the area for advanced skiers, has double black diamond (black run) chutes and glade skiing (through the trees) accessed through special gates with an average angle of 40 degrees and a 335m vertical drop, it is designated for super experts only.

Main Source of Employment
Heavenly Mountain Resort: Human Resources, P.O. Box 2180, Stateline, Nevada, 89449; ☎530-542 5180; fax 530-541-2643; www.skihcavenly.com/employment. You can also e-mail them at personnel@vailresorts.com. The personnel office is in the California base lodge at the top of Ski Run blvd, South Lake Tahoe and is open Mon-Fri 8am-5pm. Two job fairs are held in the Base Lodge in October, but you can also apply online and on the spot (with a J-1 visa). Heavenly is one of the largest winter employers on the south shore of Lake Tahoe. Apart from food and beverage attendants, lift mechanics etc Heavenly sponsor some qualified ski and snowboard instructors on H2B visas. One ski bum reported that late in the season Heavenly had signs up in the resort advertising other staff vacancies. There is a good supply of reasonably inexpensive accommodation in South Lake Tahoe. Winter hiring fairs are usually held in October at the California Lodge.

MAMMOTH
Mammoth Mountain located in the Eastern Sierras, is the nearest major Californian ski resort to Los Angeles (6 hours by car) and San Francisco from where the majority of its smart clientele come for their weekend skiing. Hitherto, a reputation for overcrowding at weekends has been a drawback. However, Mammoth has invested $18 million in improvements designed to counteract this, including the addition of three high speed quad chairs which move skiers quickly. Midweek skiing has also been heavily promoted with a high level of success and partnership with Intrawest has already led to $130 million being spent on a new pedestrianised ski village.

Custom-built Mammoth has a reputation for sunshine and a long season from November to May. The resort is situated four miles up the mountain from the town of Mammoth and if you are keen on nightlife the best of it takes place downtown. Mammoth is a big resort as US resorts go and in keeping with the scale of the skiing (3500 acres), there is an abundance of facilities. There are at least 50 restaurants in the town catering for all budgets. There is some ski in/ski out accommodation at the resort but the bulk is still in the nearby town of Mammoth Lakes. Mammoth has a sister resort, June Mountain, 20 miles north – a popular day-trip. There is no accommodation there; it is just a skiing area.

The Skiing
As far as skiing goes Mammoth has much to offer all levels of skier. There are over 150 trails and 30 lifts and 3,500 skiable acres of terrain. For experts there are plenty of challenging trails, the best known of which are Cornice Bowl and Dave's Run and much

of the skiing is above the treeline. If the size of the ski school is any indicator, beginners are well provided for with over 300 bronzed Califorian instructors at their service. June Mountain, the sister ski area reached by shuttle provides another 500 acres of mostly intermediate terrain. Mammoth is also one of the USA's top snowboarding resorts.

Main Source of Employment

Mammoth Mountain Ski Area: Human Resources Dept., P.O. Box 24, Mammoth Lakes, CA 93546. ☎760-934 0654 or 800 472 3160; fax: 760-934-0608; personnel@mammoth-mtn.com. Until 1998, Mammoth and June Mountain Ski Areas were owned and run by the McCoy family and were one of the very few resorts to be family, as opposed to corporation owned. That all changed when Canadian ski industry giant Intrawest acquired it through a majority shareholding in 1998. Intrawest then sold it on to Starwood Capital in 2005. The Ski Areas between them employ well over 2,000 staff and the bulk of international recruiting takes place 1 July to 1 September 'to ensure adequate document processing time and to ensure housing'. Company housing for employees is limited to 650 beds.

California is notoriously strict over immigration and harsh on illegal workers, and this therefore complicates the situation for those working illegally at Mammoth. The best approach would be to contact the Ski Area direct. Ski instructors, catering, tourism etc. applicants who receive a favourable reply should apply through one of the Exchange Visitor Programmes or get the employer to apply for an 'H' or 'Q' Visa (see introduction to USA section). Many positions do fall vacant mid-season so it is always worth contacting the resort. About 650 beds in the resort are reserved for staff accommodation and it is advisable to apply as early as possible (the resort recommends applying between 1 July and 1 September in order to secure subsidised accommodation.

SQUAW VALLEY

Squaw Valley is the biggest employer on the north shore of Lake Tahoe and lists 26 different ski-related jobs on its website. It is situated about 5 miles west of Tahoe City. Although skiing in Squaw Valley started with one chairlift and two rope tows in 1949, the resort attracted international acclaim with the arrival of the Olympic Winter Games in 1960. Since then it has grown enormously. Although the majority of skiers are still accommodated in North Lake Tahoe, the resort at Squaw Creek, a massive hotel complex, six miles from North Lake Tahoe. The Squaw Creek development comprises 405 accommodation units, fitness centre, shopping arcade, and restaurants and is right on the slopes of Red Dog Peak, one of the Valley's ski areas.

Potential ski bums should note that it is probably easier and cheaper to find accommodation (and possibly work) in N Lake Tahoe or Truckee and commute to the ski areas. Squaw Valley is located five miles from Tahoe City, ten miles from Truckee and 45 miles from Reno. Having your own transport would make the whole process a lot easier and cheaper.

The Skiing

Squaw Valley is big as American resorts go. It has skiing on six separate mountain peaks, 100 miles of trails spread over 4,000 acres, and 30 lifts. The slopes are rarely crowded and the skiing, a lot of it in wide-open bowls commands views over lake Tahoe. Luckily for beginners, the nursery slopes at High Camp are serviced by the Cable Car, so they do not miss out on the magnificent scenery. For more advanced skiers there are the North and Siberia Bowls, Olympic Lady, Granite Chief, Cornice II, Headwall and KT22. The last is named after an unfortunate skier who was on the mountain before it opened and having experienced a loss of nerve, abandoned technique and got down to the bottom of slope in 22 kick turns.

Main Sources of Employment

Squaw Valley Ski Corporation: P.O. Box 2007, Squaw Valley, California 96146; ☎530-581-

7112 (personnel office); fax 916-581 7202; e-mail personnel@squaw.com; www.squaw.com/winter/jobs.html. Squaw Valley does not provide on-site housing for employees and most of the recruiting is done at hiring clinics starting the last weekend of October through to the first weekend in November. 26+ different categories of winter work including cable car attendant, building maintenance, kids aide and all the other usual ski resort jobs. Applications are accepted from 1 September. If you are unable to apply in person you can download an application form from the website and fax it to the above fax number.

For a list of businesses including hotels in the area, you could try contacting the North Lake Tahoe Chamber of Commerce (P.O. Box 5459, Tahoe City, CA 94145). In North Lake Tahoe there are over 50 bars and restaurants while near the skiing mountain there are about 25 restaurants. Restaurant concessions on the mountain, where you can apply for work direct to the companies that own them, include Olympic Plaza Food & Beverage (☎530-583-1588) Le Chamois (☎530-583-4505), Wildflour Baking Company (☎530-583-1963) and Headwall Café (☎530-583-1983). Le The Ski School has approximately 250 instructors, but as with all ski schools many of them are employed on a daily or weekly basis.

Other Californian Ski Resorts:

Alpine Meadows: Box 5279. Tahoe City, California 96145; ☎530-581 8212; e-mail goodwork@skialpine.com; www.skialpine.com. Alpine is another major employer on Tahoe north shore and they promote themselves as a friendly resort. The resort has the longest season at Tahoe and workers can find accommodation near Tahoe City. Free transport is provided from Lake Tahoe for employees.

Kirkwood: Kirkwood Resort Company, Box 1, Kirkwood California 95646; ☎(employment hotline 209-258-7340; also 209-258-7310 and 209-258-7385; e-mail humanresources@Kirkwood.com; www.kirkwood.com. Those wanting work can call in person at the administration offices of the Red Cliff's Lodge, or download an application form from the website and fax it to 209-258 7368. Kirkwood resort is situated 35 miles south of Lake Tahoe. They nearly always need staff because they are only able to provide limited accommodation at the resort and most employees have to commute from Gardnerville, Nevada or South Lake Tahoe both of which are about 40 miles away from the resort. However, there is limited free transport once a day for employees coming from these towns. There is also an incentive scheme (in the form of vouchers) to offer lifts to other employees from outlying accommodation. These can only be spent in the resort but include the gas station.

Colorado

The State of Colorado (main city Denver) has more famous-name American ski resorts, including probably the most high profiled of them all, Aspen, than any other state. There are ten in all, perched high in the Rockies, a crooked spine of over 50 peaks: Aspen/Snowmass, Beaver Creek, Breckenridge, Crested Butte, Copper Mountain, Keystone/Arapahoe Basin, Steamboat Springs, Telluride, Vail and Winter Park. Early in 1997 Vail Resorts merged with the nearby skiing areas of Breckenridge and Keystone and began a furious marketing campaign to entice tourists to the new giant US ski circus that embraces six ski areas on one lift pass. The result has tended to be the opposite, with traditional skiers diverting to Aspen to avoid what they perceive as the rush of the downmarket hordes to the new conglomerate.

There are other smaller, subsidiary resorts like Purgatory, and Wolf Creek which are both so remote that skiing accommodation for them is in Durango and Pagosa Springs respectively. As a consequence of their size and remoteness such resorts do not recruit on the scale of the major resorts but they are worth contacting as many of the employers in the resorts are ski bums themselves and will appreciate that someone has crossed half the world to get there to look for a job. One you get there the main problem is finding accommodation. The smaller ski areas are listed at the end of this section after the main resorts.

ASPEN/SNOWMASS

Aspen is as well known for its high life as for its skiing. This is the kind of place where Hollywood stars and billionaires jet in to enjoy the slopes and foreign royalty are also afficionados. So anxious was Aspen Skiing Company to maintain the resort's well-groomed image that it tried to ban hirsutism in the form of beards, long hair (in or out of ponytails) and tattoos and earrings amongst its lift attendants. The 2,600 employees of the resort protested and a compromise was reached, with a ban on straggly beards and more than two earrings per ear. It would appear that clean cut job applicants might fare well in Aspen. However, part of Aspen's charm is that as well as elegance, pulsating nightlife and top class facilities it is also a small, late nineteenth-century, mining boomtown whose main street is full of quaint brick residences and clapboard buildings, not to mention horse-drawn carriages. Skiing gave Aspen a new lease of life after mining had long ceased to bring it prosperity. By 1938 when the first tow opened on Ajax (nowadays called Aspen Mountain), the population had dwindled to the last few hundred souls from a peak of 12,000 in 1893. The skiing is described in hyperbolic terms in keeping with the nightlife and clientele: the snow that falls in the Rockies is deemed 'Champagne Powder'. Despite its glitzy image, Aspen has a reputation for friendliness and so less affluent skiers from Europe feel welcome. Although not cheap, the resort has some budget accommodation, for instance the St. Moritz Lodge, which has dormitory accommodation at under $40 a night. However, ski bums, who a decade ago were much in evidence find the exaggerated prices in Aspen have made it well nigh impossible to earn enough odd-jobbing to fund their skiing habit. Aspen Highlands is the new skiing village which opened a couple of years ago and is still expanding. It is a useful alternative base to Aspen proper; especially for the off-piste and snowboarding fraternity.

The purpose-built satellite resort of Snowmass is 12 miles from Aspen, which takes 20 minutes on the free shuttle. With 2,500 acres and 72 runs, Snowmass is a major skiing areas of North America. It has a shopping mall and accommodation but tends to be quiet at night.

The Skiing

Aspen has four separate skiing areas on as many mountains, which between them provide skiing for all levels. Aspen Mountain itself is for advanced skiers with 75 trails (American for pistes) the longest of which is three miles. It is reached by the Silver Queen gondola and has seven other lifts. Aspen Highlands the next-door mountain has a variety of terrain from easy to expert. Beginners will find themselves superbly catered for on Tiehack/Buttermilk Mountain reached by efficient bus from the town of Aspen. Not quite the entire mountain is devoted to easy skiing: about a quarter is for the advanced, but ten of the trails are beginner-dedicated. Snowmass, the furthest ski area from Aspen has big, varied runs. The Big Burn is especially good for cruising. There is also however, some expert skiing like Sam's Knob and the near vertical drops of the Hanging Wall. There are plans to link the Snowmass and Buttermilk areas and work is underway to build a new link station at Snowmass.

Sources of Employment in the Aspens

The four areas of skiing terrain around Aspen are owned by Aspen Skiing Company, which also operates three hotels (Little Nell, The Snowmass Lodge and Club and The Aspen Meadows) which are open all year. There are a variety of positions available in all these operations. Aspen Skiing Company holds two job fairs: usually at the beginning of October and November lasting from 11am to 7pm in the 'Bumps' building, at the base of Buttermilk Mountain. Limited affordable company housing in Aspen/Snowmass.

Aspen Skiing Company: Ski Job Opportunities, P.O. Box 1248, Aspen Co. 81612 – 1248, USA; ☎(970) 920 0945; fax (970) 920-0771; www.aspensnowmass.com.. Aspen starts its ski recruitment early. In 2006 the early ski job fair was held on August 11th. A second one is held in October.

Snowmass Village Resort Association: P.O. Box 5566 Snowmass Village, Co 81615; ☎970-923 2000; 800 598-2006; fax 970-923 5466; www.snowmassvillage.com/ employment.cfm.

COPPER MOUNTAIN

Copper Mountain is one of the younger resorts having been inaugurated in 1971. It is widely regarded as being one of the best designed skiing mountains in that the skiing areas are naturally separated into ability areas so that beginners, intermediates and experts can each enjoy the experience of skiing at their own pace in their own dedicated area. The resort has 2,450 skiable acres but is very high (2925m-3765m) so beware of altitude sickness. Copper Mountain offers reasonable employment possibilities virtually all of them controlled by latest owners Intrawest who have also built an attractive new ski village called New Village. Also new, is West Lake Market, a seven-building complex of pubs, restaurants etc. located around West Lake and next to New Village. Ski schools might be worth trying: there are usually some Australian and New Zealand ski instructors and the occasional Briton. Those with nursing or childcare experience could try the Belly Button Bakery Nursery, which takes children from the age of 2 months (see below).

The Skiing

The Mountain takes in two peaks, Copper Peak and Union Peak and is divided into three areas. There are a total of 118 trails and 21 lifts including three high-speed quad chairlifts. Beginners will find the Union Peak caters to their needs reached from the Union Creek area at the western end of the village. Experienced skiers will find themselves rushing up the Copper Peak via the Storm King lift, after which there is a short hike up to the top of the Copper Peak where there is a double black diamond bowl, called Copper Bowl. Copper Bowl is also served by two lifts of its own, offering over 600 acres of extreme skiing. There are also 25 kms of Nordic tracks best experienced in the moonlight or on an overnight hut trip. The season runs from mid-November to the end of April, depending on snow conditions.

Website: www.coppercolorado.com

Tourist Office: ☎001-970-968-2882.

Employment

Most employees at Copper Mountain will be working for Intrawest the company that owns the mountain. The peak hiring time for the winter season is from September to December with employees usually expected to be available for work from 15 December. Seasonal jobs involve 26 to 40 hours per week and the starting rate is $6 to $10 per hour. Employee housing is available to lease. Copper Human Resources office welcomes drop-ins by prospective job seekers and will try to arrange an interview for you on the spot. According to the HR office approximately 15% of Copper's employees are from abroad including Australia, New Zealand, the UK, Argentina, Czech Republic and Peru.

Sources of Employment

Copper Mountain Resort Inc: P.O. Box 3001, Copper Mountain, Co. 80443; ☎970-968 3060 or 866-841 2481; humanresources@coppercolorado.com. You can also visit the internet site: (www.coppercolorado.com/jobs) where the resort updates its job listings every week.

Belly Button Bakery, Childcare Centre, c/o Copper Mountain Resort; ☎0101 303-968-2822 extension 6345.

Club Med: Have a village at Copper Mountain. (See *Tour Operators* section).

CRESTED BUTTE

Yet another of Colorado's old mining towns, Crested Butte (pronounced to rhyme with suit except on closing day when the locals ski naked) sits in remote valley 'on the road to nowhere except the mountains', a mere 23 miles from Aspen. In American terminology a butte is a solitary, conspicuous peak. Not that Crested Butte Mountain is that lonely, it lies next to other great Rocky Mountains like the imposing Elk range which lies between it and Aspen. The charming old town with a permanent population of 1,500 includes 40 listed buildings which are carefully maintained, contrary to the rickety look of the brightly-painted wooden buildings. The main drag is Elk Street. An ugly new resort village has been built 3 miles further along the valley at the foot of the Crested Butte Mountain and this is where most of the accommodation and Club Med is to be found. A shuttle runs between the old town and the new resort every 15 minutes until midnight. Crested Butte is big on atmosphere and eccentricity as well as historic interest; and the skiing isn't bad either, which is perhaps why a number of Britons have second homes there. There is also a nice local custom of free ski passes for a month at the beginning and two weeks before the end of the season.

Western State College is situated nearby and many of the students work part-time in the resort.

The Skiing

Crested Butte usually gets most of its snow in January and February so the early year skiing is superb. The temperature tends to be colder than other resorts, but the sun is always shining. British skiers have recently woken up to the charms of Crested Butte and several British companies now deliver clients there. Not the least of its attractions is that it has the highest average snowfall of all the Rockies' resorts. Until a few years back, the skiing at Crested Butte was popular with beginners and intermediates. Now experts too are drawn by some of the most extreme skiing in America. For beginners the best areas are around the Keystone and Peachtree lifts. Beginners here can enjoy on or off trail skiing through the trees. Intermediates are spoilt for choice especially if they take the Silver Queen quad. Experts can benefit from the High Lift to Teocalli Bowl. Extreme skiing from the edge of the Banana claims to be the steepest lift-serviced terrain in North America with slopes ranging between 39 and 44 degrees. The best double diamond runs are reckoned to be those off the North Face Lift – The North Face trail, Phoenix Bowl, The Glades (bumps), Spellbound etc. Ski Patrol at Crested Butte is on hand to guide newcomers around these terrific areas. It is hardly surprising that CB is the site of the US Free Extreme Skiing Championships. No doubt the secret will soon be out as to how good Crested Butte is, but until then the only times the resort is crowded is at the beginning of the season when the resort allows all skiers free use of the lifts!

For powder freaks the proximity of Irwin Lodge, at the centre of a vast powder skiing area only accessible by snowcat is a boon. Built by a millionaire with a reputation for eccentricity, this resort can make an interesting day trip from Crested Butte. It is suitable for first-time powder skiers as well as 70 mph. maniacs.

Main Source of Employment

Crested Butte Mountain Resort: Human Resources, PO Box 5700, Mt. Crested Butte, Co 81225; tel. 970-349 4069; fax 970-349-2250; e-mail jobs@cbmr.com. You can e-mail your CV and application to jobs@cbmr.com. Working for CBMR will include jobs like ski school (for which you must be fully qualified), snowclearing/grooming, lift operator, mountain restaurant staff and ski rental. CBMR also runs the Crested Butte Marriott Hotel (five stars) at the base of the mountain. To work for CBMR a work permit or a social security number is essential as you will be asked for proof of legality. Crested Butte regularly takes those on J-1 visas and Ski and Snowboard instructors can be issued with an H-2B visa (see introduction to this chapter). If you have a permit you can almost be guaranteed a job. They do a lot of recruiting at the college in Gunnison, 26 miles away.

Other Sources of Employment
If you do not have a permit then there are even better possibilities in not working for the mountain as you can earn more and work less and so have generous amounts of skiing time. Jobs not associated with the mountain include bartender, waiter, condo cleaner, and retail sales. Waiting staff can earn $60 to $100 a night in tips. Shops in town range from T-shirt shops to ski boutiques but shop hours unfortunately involves working in the day. Most shops in CB however charge you only $150 for a season's ski pass and return this to you at the end of the season so at least the skiing is free. Some condo cleaning companies will ask for proof of legality. Working as a cleaner can be a useful job for ski bums if you can arrange to be paid by the room, rather than the hour. For instance if all your rooms are done by midday, you can ski all afternoon. Cleaners also get tipped by guests at the end of their stay. A ski pass is usually included.

STEAMBOAT SPRINGS
Situated right in the north of the state, away from the other main Colorado resorts which are clustered west and south-west of Denver, is the genuine Wild West town of Steamboat Springs, near the picturesquely named Rabbit Ears Pass in the Yampa Valley. The origin of the quaint name of the resort arose from the first settlers thinking the noise made by the local hot springs was the chugging of a steamboat. Driving in on US-40 from Denver you will be surrounded by what look like gently rolling hills. But if you are used to European-style peaks and are wondering where the mountains are, just remember that the town of Steamboat is as high as many Continental resorts – more than 6,000 feet above sea level – and those rolling hills hide another 4,000 feet of vertical. The area has long been ranching country, and you may easily see a few authentic cattlemen and cowboys among the locals, though the Wild West image seems a little overworked these days since Steamboat ski resort has grown exponentially whereas old Steamboat town has not. The western atmosphere can be tapped into in the form of The Tread of Pioneers Museum. More likely however, you will meet those employed in less traditional Western industries like construction and coal mining, who make up a large portion of the town's population. A short distance from the old town a new resort, Steamboat has been built sprawlingly over the lower slopes of the mountainside, to provide most of the accommodation for skiers – condominiums, American holiday versions of tower blocks, have sprouted in every available field and shops in Ski Time Square will sell you anything from a T-shirt to a multi-thousand dollar fur coat. The old town and the resort are linked by an eight-minute free shuttle bus ride. The nearest aiport is the Yampa Valley Regional Airport in Hayden, 26 miles west of Steamboat Springs. Most major airlines fly direct flights from national hubs to YVRA and there are also several daily commuter flights from Denver International airport (160 miles) which are also used by packaged skiers. There must be something in the atmosphere or snow of Steamboat as it has produced a record 47 Olympic skiers (and counting); one or two of them even work in the resort taking ski clinics and groups of skiers touring. The Ute Indians, original residents there, had a legend about the Yampa Valley – a spell was cast to stop people from leaving the land. That holds true today. If you are here long enough, you will hear stories from ten-year residents about how they originally stopped in town just to change a tyre. You have been warned!

The Skiing
The first double lift (though not the first skiing) arrived in 1962 from which time the resort has grown to be the biggest resort in terms of skiable acres (2,939), in Colorado. There are 142 trails and 21 lifts. Steamboat's famous ski area is Mount Werner, which comprises five distinct peaks: Storm, Sunshine, Christie, Pioneer Ridge and Thunderhead. The skiing is suitable for all levels but 56% is calculated excellent for intermediates. There are beginner-dedicated areas and the instruction is rated excellent. Experts also come to Steamboat for the glade skiing deep in 'champagne' powder or the double black diamonds off Sunshine and Storm peaks and the Pioneer Ridge. The Billy Kidd Performance Center (970-879-6111 ext 543) has ski instructors for the teaching of intermediate and advanced skiers only. Former Olympic medallist Billy Kidd, sporting a stetson, organises a daily, mass fun run from the top of Thunderhead. The traditional ski school teaches everyone including beginners and disabled skiers and also runs women only classes (970-879-6111 ext. 531). Then after skiing you could try relaxing in the outdoor hot springs pool downtown, or the Strawberry Park Natural Hot Springs (which gave the town its name) just outside town.

Nightlife
Steamboat has plenty of good bars like the Steamboat Brewery and Tavern in Steamboat Springs and The Slopeside, the Tugboat Saloon and Dos Amigos, all of which are on the mountain, and have live bands. These bars are also good places to meet people and get the gen on possible jobs and housing. The range of dining options leaves you spoilt for choice. The best are where the locals go like the Double ZBBQ, Cugino's Italian, Mazzolas Italian, The Old West Steak House and Antares restaurants are very popular with the locals; also the Slopeside Grill.

Main Source of Employment
Steamboat Springs Ski and Resort Corporation: 2305 Mt. Werner Circle, Steamboat Springs, Co. 80487; personnel dept. ☎970-871-5132; www.steamboat.com; hr@ steamboat.com. Check the resort website for the dates of the annual job fairs held n the Steamboat Grand Resort and Conference Center (970 871 5500). Will only employ foreigners with visas. If you think you are eligible for the H-2B visa (see introduction to this chapter) contact the Steamboat winter work visa programme (internationalvisas@ steamboat.com) or write to SS&RC International Employment at the above address. The resort hires every category from security staff to daycare attendants for the Kids' Vacation Center. Ski and Snowboard Instructors have to undergo a knee examination at the resort's expense. Earlier interviews are held in the third and fourth weeks of September for the staff of some departments including snowmaking, Kids' Vacation Center, Lift Ticket Office and Ski School Ticket Office.

Other Work Possibilities
The Luxury Sheraton (970-879 222) employs large numbers of non-local staff, but you will need to be on some kind of approved scheme with the correct visa. If you arrive before the start of the season casual jobs in the fast food outlets may be a possibility. If you are up to cutting and chopping wood this is another possiblity while during the season a lot of bums make a tidy sum snow-clearing.

Cheap Accommodation While Looking for Work
Finding accommodation is likely to be a major headache unless you arrive well before the season and check carefully around the local realty companies for cheap apartments. If you arrive in early season the Rabbit Ears Motel has rooms for $20 per night based on six sharing, otherwise the cheapest single is $69. In desperation you could try the low cost public housing on Fish Creek Falls Road above downtown. Housing is also available in outlying areas of Oak Creek, Stagecoach or Hayden, all about 25 miles away. If you are

lucky enough to get a job with the resort, housing is provided close to the lift base area for full-time staff. These are one and two-bedroom units and the bedrooms are shared.

The local Chamber of Commerce (970-879 0880) should be able to help with information on housing.

TELLURIDE

Telluride is the south-western outpost of the Colorado ski resorts, 330 miles from Denver, and right down in the southern Rockies near the New Mexico and Arizona borders. It is named after the rare element once mined here although a popular local myth would have you believe it is a corruption of 'to hell you ride', the discouraging parting shot of the railroad porter as he herded miners onto the train at Denver. The town is registered a national historic landmark and is infamous for having been the place where Butch Cassidy robbed his first bank (his haul was $24,000) in 1889. It is not bank robbers that Telluride has to worry about these days, it is their modern equivalent, real estate agents: in a town with population of about 1,400 there are over 100 real estate offices. The property boom in Telluride was brought about by celebrities and movie people, buying up whole tracts of land, lock, stock and mountains then fencing them in so that a map of the area is beginning to look like a scaled down version of a map of the Balkan territories. This 'Californation' of Telluride and the surrounding area is a comparatively recent phenomenon. Until fifteen years ago, boxed in at the end of geological cul-de-sac, Telluride was popular but not fashionable. At the beginning of the 1990s some of the richer movie stars, Stallone, Nicholson, Cruise etc formed a consortium to invest in (buy up?) Telluride and launched a rush of the rich and famous including Kevin Costner, Donald Trump, Mick Jagger, Ralph Lauren and so on to buy their own piece of the mountain. The slopes are consequently littered with celebs; watch out for Sylvester Stallone (all five feet of him) and his barrage of bodyguards. If glimpses of the starry clientele doesn't make you breathlesss, then the altitude of the resort (8,750 feet) probably will.

For ski bums wanting to work in Telluride for the winter season, none of this is good news. For one thing it has become virtually impossible to find a cheap place to rent as prices have gone through the roof. Reports from last season said that many workers were having to sleep rough or in their cars. Some of them have to camp out in temperatures of -20 to -30 Celsius up to an hour's hike away to avoid being arrested for illegal camping.

Telluride is has expanded with a new 'mountain village' comprising 1200 condominiums and hundreds of residences. Development is planned to extend along the Coonskin Ridge. Skiing facilities have also been vastly improved with new ski lifts (including a 'chondola' combined gondola and chairlift) taking skiers faster, and higher up the mountain.

The Skiing

In keeping with its raffish past, locals claim that skiing in Telluride dates back to the time when Scandinavians, working up the mountain side would ski down the mountain after collecting their pay, thus beating the other, less accomplished miners to the saloons and the pick of the town's former 27 brothels. Commercial skiing arrived in the 1970s and Telluride's reputation as a place for experts soon became established by The Plunge and the Spiral Stairs, two of North America's steepest mogul fields. Nowadays, Telluride's reputation is based on its range of skiing for all levels. The main beginner area is the Meadows where 20% of the area is beginner-dedicated. Corrono Basin and Sunshine Peak are great intermediate territory, while Telluride Face is for the more advanced intermediate. With Telluride a booming ski town it comes as no surprise to find that further developments are opening up more acres of terrain taking it up to a total of 1700 acres (an increase of 70%), and providing 20 new trails. There is a lift link between Telluride Town and the Mountain Ski Village.

Main Source of Information
Telluride Chamber Resort Association: Box 653, Telluride, Co. 81435; ☎970-728-3041.
Telluride Tourist Office: ☎970-728-3041; wwwtelski.com.

Major Employers
Every winter about 250 extra employees are taken on in all categories on and off the mountain. Company listings of employers in Telluride can be found on www.jobmonkey. com/ski/html/telluride.html.
Telluride: contact: Janice Todd, Recruiting Manager, Box 11155 Telluride, Colorado 81435; ☎970-728-7459; www.tellurideskiresort.com.
Doral Telluride Resort and Spa: ☎970-728-6800. One of the several massive complexes providing deluxe guest facilities: the bedrooms all have faxes and guests get maid-service. There are 177 guest rooms plus a world-class spa.

VAIL RESORTS

Vail resorts consists of Vail, Breckenridge and the Keystone/Araphoe Basin. The management company of Vail Resorts includes the smaller resorts of Beaver Creek and Arrowhead Mountain. The resorts' areas are not linked but comprise six ski areas on a 40-mile stretch of Autoroute 70. As they are now owned by one company there will be a joint lift ticket. A subsidised shuttle bus between the resorts is available. In 2002, Vail Resorts acquired the Heavenly ski resort in California.

VAIL/BEAVER CREEK
At first glance, Vail sports a decidedly Tyrolean air that makes you wonder if it might have been transported to Colorado from the Austrian Alps. There is however nothing ersatz about Vail's reputation: it is the biggest and some say the best ski area in the United States. It has been building up its status worldwide since 1962 when the resort was launched with the help of an Indian medicine man (to conjure up a good snowfall). Nowadays, snow cannons are employed to remedy any shortfalls, but these are thankfully rare. Since installing speed traps on its pistes thus making it one of the most rigorously 'policed' resorts in the world, Vail has acquired the 'boring' tag. Vail's main rival in the high profile stakes is Aspen, but whereas Aspen is a town first and a ski area second, in Vail the skiing takes precedence. Luxury, is however a quality common to both resorts and they have buried the rivalry hatchet to the extent that they now share a lift pass (Premier Passport). Vail has a pedestrianised centre, which merges with the neighbouring area of the town known as Lionshead. Both Vail Village and Lionshead are undergoing extensive renovations and improvements at the time of press.
The smaller, functional, but smart resort of Beaver Creek opened in the 1980s and lies ten miles west of Vail. Traffic can approach no further than the end of the private approach road. Here the emphasis is on quiet luxury with exclusive dining clubs like the Saddle Ridge, and smart hotels like the Hyatt. Like Vail the clientele is likely to be very well-heeled if the facilities of the Hyatt Regency Hotel and complex, situated right on the slopes, are anything to go by. From its 10,000 square foot ballroom to its Total Beauty Center, you can be pampered to distraction.
The resorts of Vail/Beaver creek were bought in 1985 by the businessman George Gillett, who set about expanding its existing 1,880 skiing acres and the superlative back bowls, which have long been a Mecca for the powderhounds.

The Skiing
With 193 trails in a 5,289-acre skiable terrain and 33 lifts on three main peaks, Vail has something for everyone. Considerable improvements were made to the already extensive

skiing for the 1989 World Championships, which were held there. The ski school is one of biggest, and some say the best in the world; with 1,200 high quality and friendly instructors and very small classes (usually). Beginners are conveniently catered for near the bottom: Cubs' Way, Lions' Way and other similar runs below the Eagle's Nest Ridge; also suitable for beginners are some trails high up on Far East (11,240 feet) below which is the China Bowl which is part of the advanced skiers' playground also in this area. For intermediates the choice appears endless, while experts tend to head for the six legendary back bowls including Sun Up, Sun Down, Siberia, Outer Mongolia and the mile-wide China bowls. In the words of one ski bum, who was on her seventh season working in Vail 'Once you've skied in Vail, you'll never go anywhere else'. As you would expect with a resort of such high repute, queues are not entirely avoidable, but waits are usually in the region of 10-15 minutes not the 40 minutes you sometimes get in the most popular Alpine resorts. What makes the queuing different here is the cheerfulness and helpfulness of the lift staff, most of them seasonal, many of them students as is the wont of the temporary workers in Vail, they are totally obsessed with skiing.

Beaver Creek offers different attractions to that of its bigger neighbour, and has a lot to offer intermediates in particular. Although both Vail and Beaver Creek cater well for children, Beaver Creek, marketed as a family resort has special mountain adventure programmes for children. It also has a reputation for being very expensive – more so than Vail. The skiable area is 1,625 acres and there are 13 lifts.

Sources of Employment
Vail/Beaver Creek Resort: Attn. Human Resources, P.O. Box 7, Vail, Colorado 81658; ☎970-845-2460; fax 970-845-2645; vbcjobs@VailResorts.com. Vail Resorts owns and runs Vail, Beaver Creak, Breckenridge and Keystone and they recruit hundreds of seasonal workers including, room stewards/chamber staff, equipment rental staff, receptionists, condo and rental agency staff, restaurant/cafeterias and clothing shop staff. The rates of pay start at $8.50 to $9 per hour, averaging 30 to 40 hours a week. Those working in Vail for the resort get affordable employee housing (limited), free skiing and riding, insurance, training and advancement opportunities and local discounts. Some of the best places for meeting locals and resort workers and for finding out about employment prospects generally are: Jackalope Cantina in West Vail, the sleazy-looking, but popular Sundance Saloon in Lionshead Vail patronised in particular by many of the employees of Vail Resorts who run most of the resort. Vendetta's is for cheap filing food and try The Bridge if you want to meet the snowboarding crowd (both in Vail Village).

Other Sources of Employment
The Sonnenalp Hotel: Staff for this hotel are recruited by the management consultancy North Winthrop who can be contacted c/o the hotel (970-476 5656). North Winthrop also recruit for two hotels in Martha's Vineyard (an island summer resort off Boston) for those wanting to stay for the summer season.

The British tour operators *Crystal, Neilson, Thomson* and smaller company Lotus Supertravel operate chalet holidays in Vail for which they import their own staff from the UK.

BRECKENRIDGE
Like several other Colorado ski resorts, Breckenridge owes its origin to the Goldrush and its rebirth to the rush of skiers. Although skiing began there in the 1960s, the town has preserved the buildings and the flavour of those pioneering days, especially in the main street; even an old-fashioned looking bus (Town Trolley) ploughs up and down it. Regular visitors may notice that the number of old buildings in the town is increasing. These are not however Disneyland replicas, but genuine old buildings from the surrounding area for which Breckenridge has become a kind of repository. There are now over 250 of them,

carefully restored and maintained. The Wild West feel of the place is however somewhat illusory unless you count the nightlife which revolves around the 100 or so bars and restaurants. The nightlife can be very boisterous, try Shamus O'Toole's run by a former White House aid turned hell's angel, or Gold Pan, the oldest bar west of the Mississipi. There are over a hundred bars and restaurants in Breckenridge ranging from the homely to the ultra-sophisticated.

The Skiing

The skiing at Breckenridge is spread over four mountains known as Peaks 7, 8, 9 and 10 with 2,208 skiable acres and 26 lifts including four superchairs – quad chairlift with chairs that slow down for convenient loading and unloading, but otherwise travel at twice the velocity of normal lifts at 1000 feet a minute. To reach the main ski area take the Quicksilver chair from the main base area below Peak 9 (beginner areas are at the bottom of Peak 9). Breckenridge claims the highest in-bounds skiing in North America on Peak 8 at 12,998 feet (Imperial Bowl). Although Breckenridge is consistently one of the most popular North American resorts with the British, its skiing has been called not very challenging. This may have changed with he skiing area enlargements of recent years around the North and Way Out chutes. Also, a recent addition to the ski area, Peak 7 is a bowl in which all runs are black or double black and is considered to be some of the most challenging terrain in the country. Breckenridge, Vail and Keystone are all part of the same conglomerate which means you can ski one of the biggest areas on one pass. The ski areas of the resorts are not linked except by a 40-mile stretch of Autoroute 70 along which a free shuttle bus is available.

Main Source of Employment

Breckenridge Ski Resort: Attn. Human Resources, P.O. Box 1058, Breckenridge, Co. 80424; (☎970-453-3238; fax 970-453 3260; e-mail breckjobs@vailresorts.com; www. breckenridge.snow.com/mtn.employment.asp and www.skijob1.com/breckenridge/.

Other Possibilities for Employment

Breckenridge Outdoor Education: Box 697, Breckenridge, Co. 80424; ☎970-453-6422; www.outdoored.com.. Specialises in year-round wilderness and adventure programmes including downhill and cross-country skiing for disabled people. The centre offers Winter Internships (on-the-job-training posts) to instruct disabled people to ski working with various adaptive ski methods.

Other activities include snowshoeing, winter hiking, ropes courses and camping. Candidates for the winter season should be able to stay for 5 months and have previous relevant experience and strong downhill skiing and first aid skills. Remuneration is paid at $50 per month plus free board, lodging and ski pass. Apply by mid-September deadline. For further information about acquiring a ski instructor qualification to teach the disabled, see entry for Crested Butte resort.

River Mountain Lodge: 100 S. Park Street, P.O. Box 7188, Breckenridge, Co. 80424; ☎0101 970-453-4711. Accommodation and facilities for executive retreats, catered banquets etc.

Main Street Sports: 401, South Main Street, Breckenridge, Co 80424: ☎0101 970-453-1777; fax 0101 970 453 4381. British Owners Richard & Kristine Meyer.

KEYSTONE/ARAPAHOE BASIN

Located amidst pine forests Keystone is a reasonably attractive resort that has had a huge revamp over the last few years and has won awards for its family facilities. It is not big on atmosphere as there is no permanent community or history.

Apart from having 13 trails illuminated at night by sodium lamps for skiing until 10 pm, the day skiing in Keystone resort is also fairly dazzling with a choice of four mountains, three at Keystone plus Arapahoe Basin. The total of 150 trails has something for everyone: long, wide motorways for beginners and intermediates are found on Keystone Mountain while North Peak, further back provides mogul fields and runs for both intermediate and advanced. One of the resort mountains, The Outback is carved with steep, pine-gladed trails which provide yet another skiing sensation. The lift system comprising 22 lifts, including two enclosed gondolas is about as efficient as you could imagine.

The Arapahoe Basin is a ski area only, not a resort, and is reached in 10 minutes via shuttle from Keystone Mountain. It has the highest skiing accessible by lift in North America at 3,800 metres (12,450 feet). The top, which is bleak and windswept provides powder skiing comparable to the finest Alpine versions and advanced skiers will find the steep skiing in open bowls above the tree line a satisfying challenge.

Keystone also claims the longest season in the West lasting from October to June; though only in the Arapahoe basin is June skiing possible.

The resort is marketed as a family-friendly one and children under 12 years old stay free when accompanied by their parents in the resort. Excellent children's facilities including the Children's Center are a big attraction. An enormous maintained outdoor ski rink on a lake in Keystone village is open until 10 pm.

Main Employer and Source of Information
Keystone Resort Colorado: Attn. Human Resources, Box 38, Keystone, Co. 80435; ☎970-496 4157; fax 970-496-4310; keystonejobs@vailresorts.com.

WINTER PARK
Winter Park is the nearest skiing to Denver. Winter Park has notched up over 60-odd years as a ski resort. Before that it was a railroad stop known as West Portal, being the point at which the trains emerged from the Moffat Tunnel, just west of the Continental Divide. The trains still stop there, but these days they bring skiers in hordes from Denver (67 miles away), especially at weekends. Winter Park is one of the few US resorts publicly owned. Located in the Arapahoe National Forest it is actually the property of the city and county of Denver and operated by an independent volunteer board of directors. It is therefore run for the benefit of the public and except for the approximately two million dollars that goes back to the city for the enhancement of Denver's parks every year, all other profits from the resort are ploughed back into improving the facilities at Denver Park.

The Skiing
Winter Park resort is comprised of three peaks, Winter Park Mountain, Mary Jane Mountain and Vasquez Peak. Also, new in 1997 is the Vasquez Cirque located west of Parsenn Bowl. This expansion opens up 435 acres with the potential of adding another 250 in the future. The resort has over 120 trails on 2,886 acres and is served by 22 lifts, plus two 'magic carpets', which are similar to moving pavements. Beginners have two areas, Groswold's Discovery Park, a 25-acre beginner area on Winter Park Mountain, and at the base of Mary Jane where the lift pass for the Galloping Goose chairlift is a snip at $5 daily.

Winter park also has a National Sports Centre for the Disabled and therefore caters well for disabled skiers as well as children's skiing as well as the needs of standard skiers of varying abilities.

Main Employer
Winter Park Resort: P.O. Box 36, Winter Park, Colorado 80482; ☎435-647-5406; e-mail jobs@pcski.com; www.skiwinterpark.com. Winter Park seeks enthusiastic, friendly employees as it says on the back of its tourist brochure. According to James Ogglesbury, an Englishman, who worked in Winter Park in a ski hire outlet an English accent is a definite asset. He recommends contacting the resort before the 1st November as the resort is always open by the second week in November. According to him, the work permit is no

problem if the employer really needs you but its better to organise it in advance if you can, as once you are there the bureaucracy can be intimidating. Starting pay rates are $8.25 per hour and seasonal positions average 30-35 hours per week. Most workers are expected to be available from November. There is limited employee housing available.

Other Ski Areas in Colorado
Arrowhead Ski Area: P.O. Box 69, Edwards, Colorado 81632.
Durango Ski Corporation: 175 Beatrice Drive, Durango, Colorado 81301.
Eldora Mountain Resort: P.O. Box 439, Nederland, Colorado 80466.
Hidden Valley Ski Area: P.O. Box 98, Estes Park, Colorado 80517.
Loveland Ski Areas: P.O. Box 899, Georgetown, Colorado 80444;
Monarch Ski Area: General Delivery, Garfield, Colorado 81227.
Peaceful Valley Lodge & Ranch Resort: Dept. CD2, Box 2811 Star Route, Lyons, Colorado 80540.
Powderhorn Ski Area: P.O. Box 1826, Grand Junction, Colorado 81502.
Purgatory Ski Area: P.O. Box 666, Durango, Colorado 81301.
Silver Creek Ski Area: P.O. Box 4001, Silver Creek, Colorado 80446.
Ski Broadmoor: 1 Lake Avenue, Colorado Springs, Colorado 80906.
Ski Cooper: P.O. Box 973, Leadville, Colorado 80461.
Ski Estes Park: P.O. Box 1379, Estes Park, Colorado 80517.
Ski Idlewil: P.O. Box 3, Winter Park, Colorado 80482.
Ski Sunlight: P.O. Box 1061, 10901 Cr. 117, Glenwood Springs, Colorado 81602.
St. Mary's Glacier: P.O. Box 600, Idaho Springs, Colorado 80452.
Wolf Creek Ski Area: P.O. Box 1036, Pagosa Springs, Colorado 81147.

Utah/New Mexico

Salt Lake City in Utah is usually mentioned in the same breath as The Church of Jesus Christ of Latter-Day Saints, otherwise known as the Mormon church of which it is the headquarters. However, this smallish city of 750,000 souls is also at the centre of a cluster of six ski resorts, none of them large in comparison with the resorts of Colorado or California but which nevertheless attract an increasing number of skiers including those from abroad. Such is the growing confidence of Salt Lake City in its skiing credentials, that it launched a successful bid to host the 2002 Winter Olympics for which it was one of the venues. With its improved facilities it therefore deserves to be mentioned in any list of important American ski areas. The most significant resorts are Deer Valley, Park City, Alta and Snowbird. Of these Alta is the smallest and has the most limited accommodation. However, using Salt Lake City as a base and commuting to the ski areas is positively encouraged: buses run from all the major hotels to the larger ski resorts and a free shuttle bus interconnects the clustered resorts like Park City, Park West and Deer Valley.

PARK CITY/DEER VALLEY
Park City 25 miles from Salt Lake City, is one of lovingly restored late nineteenth-century mining towns that form the nucleus of several popular US ski resorts. It has one long main street that looks like a film set for a cowboy picture. On the route from Salt Lake City to Park City there are many modest, wooden weekend homes built by the locals. Accommodation in Park City ranges from the spartan dormitory to the luxury condo and unlike some of the more fashionable resorts it has kept its authentic, unpretentious character. Park City Mountain Resort is the biggest in Utah and is near to the resort of Deer Valley. Most of the employees of Park City and Deer Valley live in the old town of Park City. Visitor

accommodation is spread out between the old Park City and the modern ski village around the base lifts which has been in existence for barely two decades and has a reputation for exclusivity. Deer Valley comprises a huddle of buildings right on the mountain offering ski-in, ski-out accommodation. The centrepiece is the Stein Ericksen Lodge, named after the former Olympic gold medallist who is often around to welcome guests personally. The building is aptly Scandinavian in appearance and the food and service five-star quality, as are the prices.

Deer Valley is not a resort that is big on ski bums but there are possibilities for work as the resort is bristling with staff including ski valets who take care of clients' skis. For the Olympics in 2002 (Snowboard and GS events) major construction was undertaken and there is no doubt that Park City Mountain Resort is world class offering all the amenities associated with such an operation. The skiing is on three mountains including Flagstaff. There is plenty of challenging skiing for intermediates and advanced. The number of skiers on the mountain is regulated so that overcrowding is never a problem.

The Skiing
The skiing at Park City caters for all standards, but for advanced skiers, there is probably nothing better than the off piste experience. You can even hire a guide and do an off piste (the Americans call it 'back-country' skiing), circuit of five resorts in a day. Utah is famous for light powdery snow, which is present in abundance. The resort has 88 designated trails, almost half of which are for intermediates, and 19 lifts. At the top of the Jupiter chairlift are several bowls filled with the aforementioned powder snow. The top station is Jupiter Peak at 10,000 feet (3,049 m). From the top there are marvellous views of the Wasatch Mountains. Park City historic old town is less than 2 kms from Deer Park resort, yet amazingly, these two ski areas are not linked, although the Ski Utah lift pass covers both resorts plus The Canyons.

Main Sources of Employment
Park City Ski Corporation: P.O.Box 39, Park City, Utah 84060: ☎801-649 8111; fax 801-647 5374; www.parkcitymountain.com. The website is the best source of information.
Deer Valley: P.O.Box 889, Park City, Utah 84060, USA; ☎801-649 1000; www.deervalley.com.
Chamber of Commerce: P.O. Box 1630, Park City 84060 Utah. Can provide useful information i.e. addresses of different types of businesses in the ski area.

SNOWBIRD
Snowbird is both a ski and a summer resort and is situated in the heart of the Wasatch-Cache National Forest, 25 miles from Salt Lake City. Along with Alta resort a mile away, it is located in the Little Cottonwood Canyon. The resort, which opened in 1971 is small and self-contained, but unlike its skiing the resort itself lacks pizazz. The only hotel is Cliff Lodge, which is kept company by three blocks of condos (apartment blocks).

Accommodation
Only key personnel are lodged on site. Most other resort workers stay in the friendly little village of Sandy at the bottom of Little Cottonwood Canyon. Salt Lake City itself is a good source of accommodation and then you can commute into the resorts in 30/40 minutes. Snowbird provided a free bus pass to employees.

The Skiing
Reckoned some of the best in the West. Snowbird is internationally known for its abundance of snow. In fact, Snowbird receives an average of over 500 inches of snow annually, which is enough to keep Snowbird open for over 200 days each ski season. The huge mountain reaches 11,000 feet (3,352m) to the summit, Hidden Peak. There is 3,240

feet of continuous skiable terrain. The largest vertical rise in Utah, and it is among the nation's top ten. Snowbird has eight lifts and one of the largest and most powerful aerial tram (Swiss cable car) in the world, which takes 125 passengers up to Hidden Peak in eight minutes. The resort is probably wasted on beginners but they are encouraged to use the Chickadee beginners' lift for free. The resort is best suited to good intermediates and experts. Guides can be hired from the ski school of 200 strong instructors run by Steve Bills. Off piste adventure tours a speciality. The resort also has a complimentary guided mountain tour service for first timers.

Main Source of Employment
Snowbird Ski & Summer Resort: Personnel Dept. P.O. Box 929000, Snowbird, Utah 84092-9000 USA; ☎801-742 2222; 801-943 2243; e-mail employment@snowbird. com; www.snowbird.com.

Other Major Utah Ski Resorts
Alta: Just over a mile from Snowbird. Very limited accommodation, ancient lift system and no nightlife. Legendary snowfalls (about 40 feet) per winter. Roads to the resort often blocked by avalanches. Snowboarders not allowed. Main employer: *Alta Ski Lifts:* Personnel Department, Box 8007, Alta, Utah 80492; ☎801-742 3333.
Solitude: Only Utah resort so far to cater for both alpine and cross-country skiers. New European-style base village (Creekside) under construction at time of press. Applications to Solitude, Box 21350, Salt Lake City, Utah 21350. ☎801-534 1400.
Brian Head Ski Resort: Box 190008, Brian Head, Utah 84719. ☎800-272 7426.

TAOS
Much has been written in the British press about the ski resort of Taos, which seems to have captured the imagination of skiing correspondents. It is a family-owned and operated ski area, which retains an intimacy that has long since vanished from corporate mega resorts. Situated north of Santa Fe and Las Vegas about 3hrs from Albuquerque, in the north of New Mexico near the border with Colorado and close to the New/Mexico/ Colorado border, Taos is certainly different. In the town of Taos, ancient Native American, colonial Spanish and contemporary American heritage are combined, and its remoteness from 'civilisation' is a large part of its attraction. The ski resort of Taos is actually 18 miles from the Old Town and linked Indian pueblo of Taos. It is not normally possible for resort workers to live in the resort as accommodation there is pricey. Most employees find affordable housing in Taos Old Town or in one of the smaller, culturally diverse communities between the ski valley and the town. (Only Native Americans may take up residencc in the Taos Pueblo, where multi-storied adobe (mud and straw brick) dwellings have been continuously inhabited for nearly 1000 years.

The twin problems of lack of accommodation and remoteness are obstacles (though not insurmountable ones) for any ski bum aspiring to work in Taos. Car-pooling and hitch-hiking combine to help the non-auto owners commute between home and the slopes. Taos town provides some of the most imaginative eating places you could wish for.

There is a regular British clientele who arrive through tour companies and booking agents like Ski the American Dream.

As well as its inherent Native American mysticism, Taos has artistic and literary associations. Artists have flocked to the area since around the end of the nineteenth century to experience the unique light effects of the region. Interestingly for Britons, the latter association is provided by the writer D H Lawrence who stayed there in the winter of 1922 and who is buried nearby.

The Skiing
By contrast with the Native Americans, the skiing facilities of Taos have been there less

than fifty years. A pioneering Swiss-German, Ernie Blake founded the area in the 1950s after having worked for American intelligence during World War Two. Although now deceased, his spirit is kept alive by his heirs who still own and manage the resort. The elevation of the ski area ranges from 9,200 to 11,800 feet can leave the unhabituated gasping for breath, though the really keen have been known to ski with an oxygen tank strapped to their backs. Half of the mountain is expert terrain and the other half is equally divided between beginners' and intermediates' terrain. There are eleven lifts that access 72 trails but some of the best skiing is found by hiking from the top lift station. The ultimate Taos experience is hiking to the 12,481 Kachina Peak and skiing the 3000 vertical feet to the base area.

Main Source of Employment
Taos Valley Ski Inc.: work enquiries should be addressed to Human Resources: Dawn Boulware, P.O. Box 90, Taos Ski Valley, New Mexico 87525; ☎+1 505 776 2291; fax +1 505 776 8596; or visit their web site at (http://taoswebb.com/skitaos/). Hiring for the season is done at the end of October and employment usually begins mid-November and continues through to the beginning of April. Such is the carefully preserved ethos of the resort that getting a job is virtually impossible unless you have some connection with the Blake family. Brilliant ski instructors could try. There are five hotels and as many condominiums in the resort.

Other Ski Areas in New Mexico
Angel Fire Ski Resort: Angel Fire, New Mexico 87718.
Enchanted Forest Cross Country Ski Area: West Main Street, Red River, New Mexico 87558.
Red River Ski Area: Box 303, Red River, New Mexico, 87558.
Sandia Peak Ski Area: 10 Tramway Loop, NE Albuquerque, New Mexico 87101.
Ski Apache Resort: Box 220, Ruidoso, New Mexico 88345.
Sipapu Ski Area: Box 29, Vadito, New Mexico 87579.
Santa Fe Ski Basin: Box 2286, Santa Fe, New Mexico 87501.

Idaho/Wyoming

SUN VALLEY
The ski resort of Sun Valley, sometimes called Sun Valley-Ketchum Ski Area, is about 3 hours by road from Boise, the state capital of Idaho and just on the edge of the Sawtooth Recreation Area. Sun Valley is one of America's senior resorts having origins that go back to 1935 when Averell Harriman, the then chairman of the Union Pacific Railroad commissioned an Austrian friend to scour the mountains of the West for a suitable site for a ski resort that would rival the best in the Alps. Union Pacific engineers designed the first chairlift and no expense was spared on architectural detail. The ski resort, based around the old mining town of Ketchum became a very fashionable place, used several times as a film location and patronised by the stars, many of whom built homes there long before Telluride attracted similar star attention. The resort changed hands in 1964 when it became part of the Janss Corporation. The area has lately acquired a cultural centre with the founding of the Sun Valley Center for the Arts and Humanities. The original centre of the resort, Sun Valley Lodge is dominated by Bald Mountain ('Baldy').

The Skiing
Sun Valley skiing on Baldy, rises to 9,150 feet (2,790m) and Dollar Mountain (on the far side of Baldy) to 6,638 feet. The resort has 70 runs/1,275 skiable acres, 22 lifts and is suitable for all levels of skier though beginners and intermediates are best provided for. Only 17% of the terrain is graded most difficult and expert areas with serious mogul fields include the bowls facing Seattle Ridge: Lookout, Easter and Little Easter. The Ski School, under the direction of Rainer Kolb, has around 170 instructors. Sun Valley prides itself on teaching youngsters through its Skiwee programme.

Main Source of Employment
Sun Valley Company: Human Resources, Sun Valley, Idaho 83353; ☎208-622-2078; toll free 800 894 9946; fax 208-622-2082; svpersonnel@sunvalley.com.

JACKSON HOLE/GRAND TARGHEE

Like Aspen and Vail, Jackson Hole in northwest Wyoming is one of America's best-known resorts. Jackson Hole is used to tourists: in summer it is a stopping off point for rubber-neckers going north to Yellowstone National Park. Jackson town remains a typical ol' Wild West town; the saloons have swinging doors and the customary dress is casual cowboy wear, even though many of the 'cowboys' work on the mountain these days. The town of Jackson has its own ski area, Snow King, while the Jackson Hole Ski Resort is served by the new resort of Teton Village located at the foot of Rendezvous and Apres Vous Mountains 12 miles north-west of Jackson town and right on the edge of the Grand Teton mountains (named by the French trappers of former times). The Tetons are in turn are part of the Rockies. Teton Village with three condos, four hotels and a hostel has guest bed capacity for thousands. In Wild West language a 'hole' was a valley ringed by mountains. The ski resort was created in the 1960s as a result of the collaboration of Paul McCollister and Willi Schaeffler and by 1967 it had become sufficiently established to host a World Cup event. The resort changed hands in the early 1990's and is presently owned by JH Ski Management headed by Jay Kemmerer and John Resor.

On the western side of the Tetons, one hour from Jackson Hole is the small skiing area of Grand Targhee which is a regular excursion from Jackson by free ski bus. The resort has several hundred guest beds.

The Skiing
The skiing at Teton Village may have only ten lifts, but do not be deceived by this it is both expansive and amazing. There are over 60 trails and runs up to 7 miles in length and all amidst the backdrop of the magnificently jagged Tetons. Rendezvous Mountain (10,450 feet) is mainly for experts and its slopes are normally described in suitably respectful terms. The smaller Apres Vous Mountain (8,481 feet) is less demanding and a perfect training ground for beginners and intermediates with 22 miles of novice runs. The Snow King ski area at Jackson town is small with only two double chair lifts and one surface tow, but it offers night skiing Tuesdays to Saturdays until 9 pm. Jackson Hole must be one of the few ski resorts where the brochures point out that when moose wander onto the ski trails (they migrate across them) they should have the right of way.

Skiing at Grand Targhee is on two mountains, one served by 4 lifts and the other reserved for snowcat skiing. It is 47 miles from Jackson Hole.

Main Sources of Employment
Jackson Hole Ski Corporation: Human Resources, P.O. Box 290, Teton Village, Wyoming 83025: ☎307 739-2728; fax 307-739-6255; hr@jacksonhole.com. Has a yearly, two-day recruiting fair in late October, usually held in the Music Festival Hall in Teton Village. Most positions start in the last week of November and run to April 1st or just after. Contact Becky Cohen ☎307-739- 2728 or email to email address given above.

Grand Targhee Resort: Human Resources Office, Grand Targhee Ski and Summer Resort, Box SKI, Alta, Wyoming 83414; ☎307-353-2300 x 1310; fax 307-353-8148; dvanhouten@grandtarghee.com.

Other Ski Areas in Wyoming
Ryan Park Ski Village: Ryan Park, Saratoga, Wyoming 82331.
Flagg Ranch Village: Morna, Wyoming 83013.
Triangle Guest Ranch: Moose, Wyoming 83012.
Eagle Rock Ski Area: Recreation Dept., Town Hall, Evanston, Wyoming 82930.
Hogadon Ski Basin: 1715 East 4th Street, Casper, Wyoming 82601.
Pine Creek Ski Area: P.O. Box 41, Cokeville, Wyoming 83114.
Meadowlark Ski Area: P.O. Box 377, Worland, Wyoming 82401.
Medicine Bowl Ski Resort: P.O. Box 138, Centennial Wyoming 82055.
Sleeping Giant Ski Area: P.O. Box 960, Cody, Wyoming 82414.
White Pine Ski Resort: P.O. Box 833, Pinedale, Wyoming 82941.

Vermont

Although the majority of America's top resorts are concentrated in the West and in particular, the Rockies, New England on the East Coast is not without its own popular ski resorts within easy access of Boston and New York. One of the small New England states, Vermont, famous for its green countryside and its historic battlefields also contains some of the East's best resorts, Killington, Stowe and Smugglers' Notch among them.

KILLINGTON

One of the most noticeable differences between skiing in the western Rockies and skiing in the east is the temperature. Those who like to ski while bathed in warm sunshine will find the cold of the eastern states a bit of a shock. The cold also means that the skiing starts lower in the east, and in the case of Killington, the season lasts longer than in many resorts, from October to June. Killington resort is the biggest eastern ski area and is 158 miles from Boston and 110 miles from Albany. The regular bus service (Vermont Transit) operates between New York and Boston and serves Killington. Further details can be obtained from Killington Tourist Office (802-422 3333; www.killington.com) or Killington Travel Service (802-773-2774). There is a purpose-built village at the ski area and guest accommodation in chalets, condos, country inns, motels etc. in the locality. The resort's nightlife has a reputation for liveliness and variety with several loud music bars with colourful names like Pickle Barrel and Wobbly Barn. The resort gets busy at weekends – recreation time for the city-dwellers of New England. Killington is also known as the St. Moritz of the East, which gives an indication that it specialises in a well-heeled clientele.

Accommodation
The resort hires about 1,000 staff per winter season. Unfortunately Killington does not provide employee housing. The employment office does have a list of available housing, which employees may find useful and also recommended are 'to let' ads in the local newspapers *The Rutland Herald* (www.rutland.herald.com) and *The Mountain Times* (www.mountaintimes.info).

The Skiing
The choice of skiing at Killington is spread over 6 separate mountains; in order of elevation:

Sunrise (2,456 feet), Bear (3,296 feet), Snowdon (3,592 feet), Ram's Head (3,610 feet), Skye (3,800 feet) and Killington (4241 feet), all interconnected by a network of 32 lifts. There are a total of 200 trails making 120km/75 miles of skiing. The longest ski lift in America, the Killington Gondola spans a terrific 3.5 miles. Killington has been carefully planned for all standards though beginners and intermediates have the most choice; only 20% of runs are for experts. What is more, beginners are able to move between the mountains almost immediately as they all have easy runs as well as more difficult ones. This means that skiers of varying abilities do not get the chance to become bored with the view. The best beginner run has to be The Juggernaut – a ten mile cruise. Killington's Ski School is very active in providing tuition at all levels: Accelerated Ski Method for beginners, master clinics, family workshops, private tuition and recreational racing programmes. Expert skiers are by no means neglected with some challenging mogul slopes like Devil's Fiddle and Outer Limits and powder playgrounds like Northstar on Snowdon Mountain.

Main Source of Employment
Killington Resort: 4763 Killington Road, Killington, Vermont 05751; ☎802-422-3333; fax 802-422 6100; apply online at www.killington.com; e-mail humres@killington. com.

SMUGGLERS' NOTCH
Smugglers' Notch is heavily promoted as a family resort and it displays the Family Ski Resorts of the Year Award logo on all its publicity. Somewhat further north than Killington, it is only 30 miles from Burlington airport and an even shorter distance from the other major Vermont ski resort of Stowe. Smugglers' Notch ski resort has been in existence since 1956 and has been planned with the aim of relieving parents of their offspring by providing excellent ski facilities for juniors in age bands 3-5 and 6-12 years, plus snow soccer and mountain adventure programmes for teenagers. Untrammelled parents meanwhile get on with their own skiing leaving junior in the capable hands of Mogul Mouse, Alice's Wonderland Child Enrichment Center and other Smugglers' Notch guardians. The resort is laid out in imitation alpine-style at the foot of the slopes so you can ski to the door.

The Skiing
Smugglers' Notch (or 'Smuggs' to regulars) has three skiing mountains: Morse, Madonna and Sterling with 70 trails between them. Morse Mountain, a modest bump of 685 metres, is dedicated to beginners and children. Madonna (1,109 metres) is the main mountain which has several mogul slopes and from the same base station you can access Sterling Mountain which is classified as intermediate terrain.

The Snow Sport University, deals with both child and adult learning programmes and has more than 250 ski and snowboard instructors.

Main Source of Employment
Smugglers' Notch Resort: Human Resources, 4323 Vermont Route 108 South, Smugglers' Notch, VT 05464-9537; fax: 802-644 8580; www.smuggs.com/jobs/; employment@ smuggs.com. Smugglers' Notch holds its annual recruitment fair in October. The resort has full resort/vacation village which means that they have positions in housekeeping, maintenance, child care, food service, mountain operations (lifts, hosts, ticket selling/ checking as well as ski instructors.

STOWE
Stowe, 170 miles from Boston and 35 from Burlington, is one of America's senior ski areas, and some argue the best known resort in the East. Certainly it has a long (for America) ski tradition, beginning with the Swedish immigrants who took their skis there in the 1920s. The ski school was founded in 1935. The resort itself is based around an attractive

200-year-old New England village consisting of painted clapboard houses and a white, slim-steepled church. Despite it's quaint, antique air, Stowe is classy and its selection of restaurants and a wide range of accommodations from the grand hotels to the modest motels attract an international clientele. The village and the ski area are separated by a few miles though there are additional skiers' accommodations right on the slopes. A shuttle bus runs between the village and mountain every 20 minutes during peak hours, and every hour off-peak.

The Skiing
Stowe has two ski mountains, Mansfield and Spruce. The resort is however, without doubt dominated by Mansfield, Vermont's highest peak and usually referred to as just 'The Mountain'. There are 45 trails and 10 lifts. There is limited terrain for experts although the challenge of the runs known as 'The Front Four' (Goat, National, Lift Line and Starr) which descend from the summit of Mansfield is not exaggerated. However the resort copes best for intermediates, while beginners are accommodated on the less high Spruce Mountain. The cold of New England in wintertime is also not exaggerated, though Stowe has a tradition of offering a complimentary hot drink to skiers in the lift lines. Those with intermediate skills may want to make excursions to other resorts. Smugglers' notch is just over the mountain while Sugarbush and Mad River Glen, the latter highly rated by the locals, are within day excursion distance.

Main Source of Employment
Stowe Mountain Resort: Human Resources, 5781 Mountain Road, Stowe, Vermont 05672. ☎802-253 3541; fax: 802-253 3544; www.stowe.com). Stowe employs about 100 foreign students with visa eligibility per winter season. Accommodation can be rented 15 miles away for about $500-$700 per month.
Useful Information Source: Vermont State Chamber of Commerce, P.O. Box 37, Montpelier, VT 05602; ☎802-223 3443.

OTHER RESORTS IN NEW ENGLAND
Attitash Bear Peak: Human Resources, P.O. Box 308, Bartlett, New Hampshire 03812; ☎603-374 2611; fax 603-374 1960; contact Sandra Woehr (swoehr@attitash.com).
Cannon Mountain: Franconia Notch State Park, Franconia, New Hampshire 03580. ☎603-823 7751; fax: 603-823 8088. 38 Trails and 5 lifts plus a cable-car. Cannon is just a ski area; accommodation is at nearby Franconia or Lincoln.
Loon Mountain: Kamcamagus Highway, Lincoln, New Hampshire 03251; ☎603-745 8111; fax: 603-745 8214. 41 trails and 9 lifts.
Mount Snow/Haystack: Mount Snow, Human Resources, Mountain Road, West Dover, Vermont 05356; ☎802-464 4223; fax: 802-464 4135; www.mountsnowjobs.com; jobs@mountsnow.com. One of the USA's largest resorts is two and a half hours by car from Boston and four hours' drive from New York. It has 135 trails and 26 lifts on two mountains connected by shuttle service.
Sugarbush Resort Human Resourcest: 1840 Sugarbush Access Road, Warren, Vermont 05674; ☎802-583-6380; fax 802-583-6389; e-mail hr@sugarbush.com; www.sugarbush. com. One of the most northern resorts with skiing over two mountain areas (Mt. Ellen and Lincoln) incorporating New England's three highest peaks which are linked by the Slide Brook Express chairlift, the world's fastest, high-speed quad which takes under ten minutes to cover the 11,000 foot length. Has 112 runs and 18 lifts. There is something for all levels for skiers and boarders have their own Mountain Rage park with double half pipe. There are condos in the resort village but most of the accommodation is in Waitsfield, ten minutes drive from the ski area.
Sugarloaf: Sugarloaf Mountain Corporation, Human Resources, 509 Access Road, Carrabassett Valley, Maine 04947; ☎207-237-6778; fax: 207-237-3768; jobs@

sugarloaf.com.. Sugarloaf is a big resort at the foot of Maine's highest mountain, with 101 trails and 15 lifts. Rather isolated. You can stay in Kingfield, 15 miles from the resort.

Sunday River: Human Resources Dept., P.O. Box 450, Bethel, Maine 04217; ☎207-824 5160; jobs@sundayriver.com. Maine's premier ski area with over 120 trails and 18 lifts. Sunday River is spread broadly across a range of eight mountains, all of which are lift-served. There is plenty of accommodation around the base areas or in the town of Bethel, ten minutes away. Is the flagship of the American Skiing Company which also owns Mount Snow.

Waterville Valley Resort: Town Square, Waterville Valley, New Hampshire 03215; ☎603-236-8311; fax: 603-236 4174. Founded by US Olympic skier Tom Corcoran. 48 trails and 13 lifts. Contact: Scott Smith, Manager Human Resources ssmith.wv@boothcreek. com.

Additional United States Ski Resorts

ALASKA

Alyeska Resort: P.O. Box 249, Girdwood, Alaska 99587; ☎907-754 1111; fax: 907-783 2814; www.alyeskaresort.com. As you would expect, the quantity of snow and Alpine, Nordic and heli-skiing opportunities are phenomenal in this area. Luxury year round accommodations are provided at the Westin Alyeska Prince Hotel located 40 miles south of Anchorage. The motto of the resort is 'experience civilised adventure'. The Director of Human Resources accepts applications year round.

NEW YORK

Hunter Mountain Ski Bowl, Inc. Rt. 23A, Hunter, New York 12442; ☎518-263-3704; fax 518-263-3704. 60 trails and 9 lifts over three mountains. The closest resort to New York City 60 miles distant.

OREGON

Mount Bachelor Ski & Summer Resort: P.O. Box 1031, Bend, Oregon 97709; ☎800-829 2442; fax 503-382 6536. 40 trails and 9 lifts. On the western side of the USA, it claims a snow record that usually allows skiing until July.

PENNSYLVANIA

Whitetail: 13805 Blairs Valley Road, Mercersburg, Pennsylvania 17236; ☎717-3289400; fax 717-328 5529. Small resort opened 1991/92 season with 14 trails and 5 lifts open for day and night skiing. About one and a half hours from Washington D.C. Short season from mid-December to end March. Contact: Sally Bray/Craig Altschul.

WASHINGTON

Crystal Mountain Resort: 1 Crystal Mountain Blvd., Crystal Mountain, Washington 98022-8065; ☎206-663-2265; e-mail personnel@crystalmountain.com or contact Gretchen Swanson on ☎231-378-2000, extension 2403. Crystal has 58 trails and 11 lifts. Small resort with lodging for 600 guests at or near the resort. One of the most northwesterly resorts in the States, Crystal is 67 miles from Seattle. It has a reputation amongst afficionados for some of the best back country skiing in the whole USA.

Personal Case Histories – USA

LINDA DOUGLAS – VAIL

Linda Douglas, now in her thirties, worked on and off in the United States for over six years, spending some summers in Martha's Vineyard off Boston and the winters in Vail, Colorado. After graduating with a BSc in Engineering and Geology she went on a BUNAC programme to work that summer in Wisconsin. Although the job fell through, while there she met up with two Scots with whom she agreed to keep in touch. They were on their way to Colorado to work for the winter season and when they asked her to share accommodation that they had already arranged in Vail for the skiing season, she jumped at the chance to join them. She arrived in Vail at the beginning of November when the hiring clinics are being held, usually in the function room of a big hotel, where they have different desks for the various departments, restaurant, guest services etc. and you can be hired on the spot if the selectors think you are suitable. As these are official recruiting fairs, you will not even be considered without the essential social security number. By chance, while in Wisconsin, Linda had met an English girl with the same surname who was returning to England and passed her social security card on to Linda so it was not difficult to get hired as there was a huge demand for employees, and documents are nearly always accepted at face value by desperate employers.

There is apparently, even nowadays no legal requirement for employers to check the validity of your documents, only to see them and photocopy them for their files. According to Linda, many American employers will positively discriminate in favour of foreign workers as they consider them harder workers and more conscientious than their American counterparts, probably because they need the money in order to fund further travels and will do anything to keep a job. After working at one of the big hotels, Linda decided she did not like it and left. In order not to be 'blacklisted around Vail' she reverted to her own name and promptly got another job, this time at an omelette and crêpe bar which was a novelty in the USA at the time. There were about 12 staff employed there from Australia, New Zealand, South Africa and Britain. She got the post by just 'walking round all the cafés and restaurants that were open'. The bar was associated with another café in the Lionshead area of Vail, run by Austrians. She also did shifts in the café for no pay, because the income from tips alone was phenomenal 'anything from $100-$200 per day'. Linda was saving up to go to Australia but also thinking in terms of a career in catering management. Linda recommended offering to work for no pay, just for tips, when approaching employers in ski resorts.

According to Linda another brilliant job for tips is working in a night club as coat check. Again, you get no pay, but tips are usually between $200 and $300 per night though this can drop in low season. When she went back to Vail the following season she worked at the same café and also in the big Austrian hotel Pepi Granshammer which employs a lot of Austrians and Germans and other foreigners to enhance its European ambience. In the hotel Linda worked as a cocktail waitress, complete with Tirolean frilly blouse and flounced skirt. She opined that cocktail waitressing is a lot less arduous than waiting tables but earns the same money. She worked 5 shifts a week, typically: 2 x noon to 6 pm, 2 x 6 pm to midnight and 1 x 4 pm to 10 pm which meant she could ski every day and still work a couple of evenings in the café as well. She had no difficulty whatsoever in getting a job by making up a social security number:

> *Most people choose a number that corresponds to something they can remember easily like their date of birth or telephone number' as long as it falls into the required groups of digits and begins with an area code number.*

For further details see the introduction to the chapter on the USA. As regards other perks, Linda points out that these vary depending on the job and the resort. In Vail, waiting staff did not get free ski passes but their income from tips enabled them to more than afford one. However those jobs which needed some skill, especially kitchen jobs like cook, sous chef etc. which were not in line for gratuities, got their passes at half-price and were reimbursed the other half if they stayed to the end of the season.

The main problem for workers in any resort is finding accommodation, and Vail is no exception. According to Linda, the restrictions on building in the Valley mean that there is never enough accommodation for workers. It is therefore essential to arrange this as early as possible. If you are unable to make a special trip in September to fix yourself up, then early November, at the same time as recruitment is in progress, is the next best time. It is essential to have at least $1,500 for the security deposit and for the first and last month's rent. Ideally find as many people as is comfortable to share with and keep the costs down. Newcomers often pack themselves in two to a room. After a season when you know your way around you can probably afford a room of your own. Linda rented a glorious 3-bedroomed house for $1,000 per month. With three people sharing the rent becomes very reasonable. Averagely people are paying in the region of $300-$450 each. Linda worked the following summer in Martha's Vineyard in a restaurant. As she was intending to return to Vail for the winter, Linda sub-let the house she rented there for the summer.

When Linda had saved enough money, she went to Australia where she remained for a year before returning to London. By this time she had acquired so much expertise in the catering business that she applied for work with the well-known contract caterers J. Lyons (by all accounts a considerable come down in earnings from waiting tables in Vail). As Linda has no formal catering qualifications, she puts her success in getting taken on by so reputable a company as J Lyons to her extensive experience of catering in America. She therefore not only earned a lot of money working in an American Ski resort but also advanced her career and employment prospects.

The cost of living in London finally depleted Linda's financial reserves and she returned yet again to Vail arriving in January. Since her last visit, immigration had brought in tougher regulations regarding documents needed to get employment. This was after there had been ` purges' of the resort, mainly it seems, intended to flush out the illegal Mexican workers. It was no longer sufficient to produce a social security card, you also had to produce a US Drivers Licence or other proof of your identity (i.e. with a photo and your name so that employers could check if your social security card and identity matched up). According to Linda there is no difficulty in obtaining the US drivers licence and it costs about $65: you get it from the local registry of motor vehicles where you are required to take a simple written test on the rules of the road. Additionally, you may be asked to drive 'round the block'. However, Linda advises that you apply for the licence as soon as you get to the resort because if you leave it until just before your tourist visa expires you will be told not to bother.

An alternative to the drivers licence as a form of identification to produce for employers is an ID Card which has only your name, and age and photograph. They cost about $15. Americans use them to prove their age when ordering drinks (you have to be aged 21 to drink in bars in most US states). As a reason for needing one you say that you are staying with friends for a month. For a shorter time, you will be told you do not need one. An ID card is also official enough for employers to cross check your identity.

Forged social security cards have proved another ski bum stand-by. According to Linda some of these are made by Brazilian forgers on the East Coast and good ones are apparently virtually indistinguishable from the real thing. According to Linda, those in need of them get to know 'the right people' (often contacts can be made when working in catering establishments in Boston etc.) and they can cost as little as $30.

For her final two winters in the USA, Linda was working in five-star restaurants in Vail. The lift pass for employees for the last season she was there was $835 (tourist rate $1,400). In the summer she switched to the summer resort of Martha's Vineyard where she was appointed general manager of a new restaurant. She had already worked a previous season in this resort.

A useful legal 'back route' into Vail ski resort, according to Linda is to contact the Management Consultancy, North Winthrop who manage two hotels in Martha's Vineyard, and the grand Sonnenalp Hotel in Vail. North Winthrop recruit personnel for the summer season to work in the hotels in Martha's Vineyard and once you have worked there legally, it is easy to transfer to the Sonnenalp in Vail. They can be contacted c/o The Sonnenalp Hotel.

Linda's plans are to work for her brother's company in the UK, which is acquiring a chain of pubs and eating places and she expects to run the flagship restaurant of the chain.

NEIL HIBBERD – STEAMBOAT SPRINGS

Neil Hibberd worked on an internship programme organised through the Council on International Educational Exchange (CIEE),in Steamboat Springs Colorado. (The CIEE programme has been taken on by IST Plus – see page 272). At the time he applied for the CIEE Internship Programme, Neil was 22-years-old with one year to go in his degree in leisure and recreational management at Thames Valley University. He heard about the programme from the job placement office of his university, which told him that the CIEE was virtually his sole hope for a working visa and internship position in the States. He applied to the CIEE in June, specifying from the outset that he wished to work in a ski resort. The CIEE asked him to name the resort and to verify that he had a job offer. 'The Council's policy is that they need a letter from the employer before giving you the work visa. I first went out to Colorado in August, to look for an internship job and I went to most of the ski resorts in Colorado. Steamboat Ski and Resort Corporation offered me a job as a lift operator if I could obtain a work visa. Once I had obtained a letter from the Steamboat Corporation, I returned to the UK, obtained the work visa through the CIEE and went back to Steamboat in October. Looking back on the process of getting a job and a visa, I realise that there must be an easier way to obtain such a placement.

My job as a lift operator included helping load and unload guests, running safety checks on the lift and clearing snow from the lift access. The lift operator's job is integral to the overall operations of the Ski Resort Corporation. As a part of the lift operations team, I was involved in several aspects of the mountain operations. I attended a number of training sessions in order to understand the policies, procedures and daily operations of the lift system. In the daily operation of the lift, I was exposed to the skiing public probably more than any other category of resort employee. I was obliged to be always courteous and friendly, and also to create a pleasant atmosphere for the guests.

The Ski Corporation provides all its employees with accommodation at a subsidised rent. Employees pay a security deposit of $200 and rent of $190 per month, per person. For this you share a 2-bedroom apartment with two bathrooms. Our employee housing was less than a mile from the base of the ski resort and central to most of Steamboat Springs' amenities. Housing in Steamboat Springs is a major problem as there are never enough apartments to go round. At least 30% of the people who get a job at Steamboat leave after the first month because of the lack of housing. The best way to find accommodation is through the real estate companies or from adverts in the local papers *Steamboat Today* and the *Steamboat Pilot*.

The rate of pay for a lift operator with the Steamboat Corporation is about $8 per hour; as a working student I was exempt from tax. I have to admit that in order to survive in Steamboat, I had to have at least two jobs because the pay rates of $5 and $6 per hour which are paid to newcomers are not enough to live on comfortably.

Anyone looking for a winter job in Steamboat should arrive in early October or November. Those without work visas can pick up jobs as dishwashers, delivery drivers, snow clearers or au pairs for cash in hand. However, those working legally for the Steamboat Corporation get a free ski pass for the season and a 50% discount on food at mountain restaurants. You also get 25% discount on ski hire and ski goods. Travelling twice to the United States and paying for the work visa and insurance came to £650 plus travelling expenses. In all it cost me over £2,500 to go out to the States to work and has exhausted my savings.

As a lift operator my working hours were from 7.30 am to 4.30 pm in winter and 7.30 a.m. to 5.30 p.m. in spring when the mountain stays open longer. I worked a 4-day week with an hour's break per day which left three days off for skiing.

Of Steamboat itself: it has a great Western atmosphere and plenty of amenities. It is a great place to ski and it is also a summer resort. I have been skiing since I was ten, mostly in Europe but I believe that Colorado and particularly Steamboat offers better snow and skiing conditions with more intermediate and extreme skiing runs and I would recommend it to anyone who wants to work in a ski resort in the USA

SEAN HIGNETT – TAOS, NEW MEXICO

The travel writer Sean Hignett worked a winter season for the late owner of Taos Ski Valley in New Mexico as the European Public Relations Manager having made out a good case for employing him (the job didn't exist before his arrival) as the resort has a substantial British following. He later publicised the resort by writing about it for the *Sunday Telegraph*. He worked on the slopes for the Guest Services which encompassed a wide variety of duties from checking lift passes, guiding skiers to less busy areas of the mountain when they were gliding into bottleneck formation and sheep-dogging around the tracks leading off the piste for lost and strayed skiers at the end of the day. He met some interesting characters in the resort including an American lawyer who was on the run from embezzlement charges and was working under a false name and social security number. Canadian and Panamanian nationalities with less colourful pasts were also represented but no British ski bums, except those who were legal residents. Sean had some interesting suggestions for potential ski resort employees. His own daughter once married a Guatemalan American for a couple of months to get a green card, but perhaps that was not one of the suggestions? He also proposed enrolling on the Ski Area Management Course at the Highlands University in Las Vegas or on a ski instructor's course as spending a year working in a ski resort is part of such courses. He also pointed out that you don't have to base yourself in the ski resort; it is cheaper to live and work near a ski resort and commute to the slopes. For instance the gambling town of Reno has dirt cheap accommodation: you can stay in a hotel for $15 a night and stuff yourself with as much food as you can eat for less than that per day and ski at the nearby Lake Tahoe resorts. An alternative base is the town of Stateline Nevada which is on the boundary between Nevada and California and very near Heavenly Ski Area. Sean noticed towards the end of the season that Heavenly had signs up for late season employees for casual work like basket check (left luggage service in which clients dump their shoes and any other small belongings they can't wear or carry on the slopes while they ski). Workers in Taos Ski Valley don't live there because there is only expensive accommodation for clients. They base themselves in Taos town, which is about 14 miles from the resort. There is scope there for work, especially if you can teach something alternative: aromatherapy, massage etc. as Taos is full of flaky people who like that kind of thing. Painting (either to sell or to teach) is another possibility.

Sean Hignett wishes it to be known that he takes no responsibility for anyone who takes any of these suggestions seriously and as result needs to be bailed out.

STEPHANIE WOOD – PURGATORY/CRESTED BUTTE

Stephanie Wood is an American, but while working in the Chamber of Commerce in Durango, Colorado she met a Scot, who was working in America illegally and they are now married and living in the United Kingdom. Stephanie's family live in Durango and being a keen skier she also knows the nearby resort of Crested Butte very well.

'I met my Scottish husband, while he was working illegally as a bartender. He had just come from working in Hawaii and decided to live in the mountains for a while, he ended up in Durango near the ski resort of Purgatory.

When I met him he had been living and working in the States illegally for three years. He originally went to the States to visit his sister in New Mexico. While staying with her he decided to get a US driver's licence. He went down to the Department of Motor Vehicles and took a test, which is very simple, and passed. The girls behind the desk were fascinated by his accent (as are most American women), and asked him questions about Britain. While typing up the licence they asked him what his social security number was. Of course he didn't have one. He quickly made one up and from then on he had his ticket to get a job anywhere in the US. A driver's licence is usually the only form of ID that an employer will ask to see. He then went on to work as a bartender in New Mexico, Colorado, Arizona and Hawaii. While working in the States he never had any problems with the Inland Revenue Service and was never questioned as to why he had never filed an Income Tax Return. It was really as simple as that. Of course, now we are married, he will be working legally in the States.

While working in Durango as a bartender, he was making anywhere from $150 to $200 in tips. That's on top of a wage packet of $825 a month. He worked a combination of nights and days so he could ski. The employer did not provide a free ski pass, but there always seemed to be discount passes that he could use.

One of the best things about bartending is that you can have a job year round. Most ski resort towns have summer activities as well, and you can keep your job. Some of the resorts adapt their chairlifts to carry mountain bikes, so if you work as a lift operator you may be able to stay on through the summer if you choose.

He and I rented a one-bedroom chalet with a loft for $425.00 per month, which included utilities. We stayed there until the end of the season which was April 11th and then we moved to Britain. The bar where he worked didn't pay him a bonus at the end of the season, which is the case with most bars. Normally, only jobs directly associated with the ski resort give end of season bonuses. Jobs in the resort are obtained through the Purgatory Personnel Office (☎303-247 9000). Another useful source of information is the Chamber of Commerce, a kind of visitors' bureau, handy for obtained names and addresses of businesses in the area.

When I was at college in Gunnison, 26 miles from Crested Butte I used to hitch hike regularly to CB during the skiing season. Hitch-hiking between the two towns is common and relatively safe. Crested Butte Mountain Resort and the other businesses start hiring at the beginning of November. I would even suggest arriving sometime in October. Some jobs may require some training or just start early. October, early November, is considered off-season and the rates at the hotels will be cheap. The Old Town Inn is located on the edge of CB, just as you enter the town. It usually has the cheapest rates in town, but it's worth checking around. The least expensive option of all is to rent a place for a month while looking round. That way you can save money by not having to eat out all the time. The best place to look is in the local paper. The bartender at The Talk of the Town Bar also usually knows when there are cheap places going for rent. Most people there for the ski season end up sharing a house. CBMR does have some staff housing but except for key staff, it is located 12 miles out of town in Almont which has a winter population of 25 and a general store that's open when the owner is not skiing.

As a final note, you should bear in mind that both Durango/Purgatory or Crested Butte are extremely small and there isn't a large city within 100 miles. Crested Butte isn't a place where the government will look for illegal aliens. In my four years of living there, I only heard of one incident involving an illegal alien. He was was a Mexican working on a ranch outside of Crested Butte. The local police didn't speak Spanish so they bought him a train ticket back to Mexico.'

Canada

There must be thousands of Britons, particularly Scots, whose relatives emigrated to Canada in the 1960s or earlier. These immigrants have since acquired a high standard of living and amenities, so it is hardly surprising that younger British relatives cannot get out to Canada fast enough to visit them and see the open spaces and easy Canadian lifestyle for themselves.

In order to enter Canada as a tourist for up to 90 days, British citizens need only a valid British passport. Unfortunately, when it comes to getting a work permit, the access for young Britons is less straightforward, even for those with family in Canada. In recent years the Canadian government has had to bring in restrictions on immigration to counteract the rising level of unemployment in Canada and work permits are granted according to strict criteria designed to limit the type and numbers of workers. Not only will those without a work permit not be able to use the national employment bureaux, but also, if caught working illegally the regulations are rigorously enforced and offenders are subject to deportation similar to the system in force in the United States. Although it has to be said that the Canadians are hospitable people and enforced departure goes against the grain to the extent that officials will probably express regret that they have to ask you to leave before you have had a chance to get to know their beautiful country better.

WORKING VISAS

In order to take up employment legally in Canada, you must obtain an Employment Authorisation before you enter the country. It is only since the mid-1980s that the Canadian Government faced with a shortfall of seasonal labour introduced schemes to allow a limited number of foreign students, and more recently, any UK national under 35, to work temporarily in Canada. However, with rising unemployment in Canada, the quotas are subject to fluctuations and there is no guarantee that they will continue. Students can get an idea of the current situation by logging on to www.canada.org.uk/visa-info (click on 'visiting' rather than 'working) or by obtaining the general leaflet 'Student Temporary Employment in Canada' by sending a SAE (bearing a 50p stamp and envelope to be marked SGWHP in the top right corner) to the Canadian High Commission (Immigration Visa Section, 38 Grosvenor St., London W1K 4AA). Note that anyone fixed up with a job in Quebec, e.g. Mont Tremblant has to comply with separate and additional information and immigration requirements for that semi-autonomous region.

Most of the approved schemes for getting a temporary work permit for Canada are operated by the same organisations as for the United States e.g. the CIEE and BUNAC. However, if you already have a written job offer from a Canadian employer, you may well be eligible for programme 'A'. The employer can apply directly to the High Commission in London for an Employment Authorisation valid for a maximum of 12 months and not transferable to any other employment. The more flexible option is BUNAC's scheme for unspecified Employment Authorisation. There are also some schemes, which are particular to Canada such as the 'Live-in Carer Program' for trained child carers (see below). All the schemes applicable to Canada are listed below. Where full details are the same as for American schemes you should refer back to them in the American section.

Americans do not need a passport to visit Canada (only proof of US citizenship if requested), but they are not allowed to enter in order to look for work. Like all foreign nationals, they must fix up a job before arrival, which has been approved by the employer's local Canada Employment Centre. The one difference is that they can apply for employment authorisation at the point of entry, rather than having to apply through a Canadian consulate in the United States.

Australians should write to the Canadian Consulate General, (Immigration Office, Level 5, Quay West, 111 Harrington Street, Sydney, NSW 2000); www.whpcanada.org.au for the latest information on working holiday visa schemes. At the time of writing these were available to young people (including non-students) aged 18-30 who are in Australia at the time of application. Applications open on January 1st annually and close when the quota is reached which is usually in spring. Processing takes about three months.

GETTING A JOB

OFFICIAL WORK PROGRAMMES & GAP YEAR COURSES FOR CANADA
BRITISH UNIVERSITIES NORTH AMERICA CLUB. BUNAC (16, Bowling Green Lane, London EC1R OBD; ☎020-7251 3472) operates a couple of programmes, which could be useful for those interested in working in a ski resort. The main BUNAC programme features departures from February to August and is valid for up to a year from departure. There is also a programme for GAP year students who have a confirmed university place, which enables them to depart in October and work in Canada for up to a year. The student has to produce evidence of sufficient funds plus a letter of sponsorship from a Canadian relative/a firm job offer) and a return ticket.

Eligibility is restricted to those aged 18-35 years who must be either in a gap year or returning to a full time university course in the UK. Proof of acceptance on a course will normally be required. Final year students are also accepted provided that they have proof of personal commitments to return to including a job offer, property or family ties.

BUNAC produces a booklet for Work Canada participants *The Vital Info Handbook,* which contains a directory of past employers of foreign students. Most of the jobs listed are in hotels and tourist attractions in the Rockies, which is a beautiful part of the world any time of year.

CHANGING WORLDS. Changing Worlds (www.changingworlds.co.uk; 01892-770000) arranges paid hotel jobs for students in the two main Canadian ski resorts of Banff and Whistler. The jobs last six months from November and cost about £2000 including airfares. Hotel staff are paid on average $9 per hour and $12 is deducted for board and lodging.

COUNCIL ON INTERNATIONAL EDUCATIONAL EXCHANGE. The CIEE; www. councilexchanges.org, operates a scheme for students and recent graduates from the USA to work in Canada for up to six months starting year round.or for students enrolled in full-time further or higher education to undertake internships (on-the-job training) in Canada lasting for up to a year. The scheme is similar to the one for the USA. Internship candidates should find their own work placements in their field of study, thus hotel and catering students or similar could use the programme to work in a Canadian ski resort. Generally, endorsement by the candidate's tutor of the proposed traineeship is required. Those who qualify for this programme will get an Employment Authorisation for the Canadian High Commission. The programme fee is approximately $350.

GAP CHALLENGE. Gap Challenge (Black Arrow House, 2 Chandos Road, London NW10 6NF; 020-8961-1122; www.world-challenge.co.uk) places a number of British students between school and university in resort jobs in the Rockies in winter and summer. The conditions of eligibility are similar to BUNAC but with higher participation fees. Participants can have a six months working placement and then spend up to a further six months (non-working) in Canada. When time is short it has proved possible in the past to get an Employment Authorisation by queuing all day at the Canadian High Commission.

GAP SPORTS. Willow Bank House, 84 Station Road, Marlow, Bucks SL7 1NX; ☎0870 837 9797; info@gapsports.com; www.gapsports.com. 11-week Ski and Snowboard Instructor Courses in Quebec: Mont Sainte-Anne and British Columbia: Whistler. Includes 2 weeks paid work experience.

LIVE-IN CAREGIVER PROGRAM. British nannies are in demand among affluent families in Canadian cities like Vancouver, Calgary, Ottawa which are very handy for ski resorts: Vancouver is near Whistler, Calgary is convenient for Lake Louise, Banff and Jasper while Ottawa is near the Laurentians, Lake Placid and Blue Mountain. In addition, as part of their city plus outdoors lifestyle many such families own or rent a holiday home in the mountains or lakeside on an annual basis, and skiing with the family is usually a perk of the job. Ideally those interested in skiing should request a job with a family who are involved with running a business in a ski resort which would give them maximum access to the slopes. However, as enabling participants to ski is not the aim of the programme such a placement could only be requested, not insisted upon, but is certainly worth trying as a way of getting a job in a ski resort.

The regulations governing domestic employment in Canada have been carefully formulated and have made it much more difficult to qualify for a permit. It is no longer sufficient to have experience only, prospective nannies must now have at least 6 months full-time training as a child-carer. However the age range is generous: from 18-50 years. A detailed leaflet about the Live-in Caregiver Program can be downloaded from the Canadian High Commission website www.cic.ca/english/pub/caregiver/index.html. Those eligible who have found an employer, probably through a Canadian agency such as ABC Nannies Agency, 11420 95A Ave. Delta, BC, V4C 3V7 (www.abcnannies.org). Nannies can apply for an employment authorisation for Canada valid for one year and renewable once. After that it is possible to apply for 'Landed Residency' and many ex-nannies do indeed apply for this. The procedure for getting an initial authorisation to work usually takes 3-4 months so if you are planning to find a family in or near a ski resort apply in plenty of time so as not to miss the start of the skiing season.

Once you have been matched up with a family, probably via a local Canadian Agency, you will be sent details of the family and an offer of employment validated by the employer's local Canada Employment Office. A copy of this will also be sent to the Canadian High Commission and you will be contacted by them, usually within a few weeks, to arrange an interview. The High Commission charge a processing fee.

INTERNATIONAL EXCHANGE PROGRAMMES. International Exchange Programmes (IEP, GPO 4096, Sydney, NSW 2001)) liaises with the Canadian Consulate in Sydney to administer the Canada Working Holiday Scheme for Australian nationals (www.iep.org.au/workcanada). Applications for the working holiday authorisation can be submitted via IEP with the visa fee of A$170.

SSA/SWAP. SWAP Canada (45 Charles Street, East Suite 100, Toronto M4Y 1S2) also another office in Vancouver, is an approved student scheme for Australian students currently in Australia, for departures in November/December.

OTHER SOURCES OF JOBS

British Tour Operators

The promotion of North American resorts to British skiers frustrated by the queues and undependable snowfalls of the Alps, has led to thousands of them sampling the delights of Whistler, Lake Louise and Banff with Whistler being the most popular. The number of British skiers legging it to Canada has snowballed from a mere 3,500 in 1992-93 to tens of thousands and numbers were up by 30% in the 2005/06 season from the previous season. Although many skiers book their holidays through agents like Ski the American Dream, a small number of British companies employ their own British ski personnel in Canadian resorts, for instance for catered chalets in Whistler. Full details of individual companies' staff requirements may be found in the British Tour Operator section of this book.

Airtours: 0870-2412642 (recruitment line). Now part of MyTravel (www.mytravel.com).

Crystal Holidays: 0845 055 0255. (Whistler, Banff and Lake Louise).

First Choice: 01293-588585; skijobs@firstchoice.co.uk.

Inghams: 020-8780 4400.

Neilson: 0870-241 2901. Has reps in Banff, Lake Louise and Tremblant. Note that reps
     must have worked for Neilson for several seasons before getting posted to Canada.

Ski Independence Ski USA & Canada: 0845 310 3030; jon@ski-i.com. Banff, Whistler
     and Tremblant.

Thomson: 0845 055 0255. Resorts: Banff, Lake Louise and Whistler. May favour Canadian
     employees unless applicants have documentation for working in Canada.

Intrawest

The Canadian Corporation Intrawest is the largest ski resort owner and developer in North America and is in the process of expanding its empire both there and in Europe.

Its Canadian resorts are Whistler/Blackcomb and Panorama (British Columbia), Blue Mountain (in Ontario), Tremblant and Mont Ste. Marie in Quebec. In the United States it owns Copper Mountain, Stratton (Vermont), Snowshoe (W. Virginia), Mountain Creek

(N.Jersey) and Winter Park (Colorado). Until 2005 Intrawest also owned Mammouth Mountain, California, which it sold to Starwood Capital in 2005. In addition it has massive investment projects aimed at developing Keystone (Colorado), Solitude (Utah) and Squaw Valley (Tahoe, California) into world class resorts. In Europe Intrawest has bought a significant share in the Compagnie des Alpes, which is the world's largest ski corporation and has been involved in ski village developments in Flaine Montsoleil in France and Verbier in Switzerland. Intrawest also owns Canadian Mountain Holidays, the largest heli-skiing operation in the world, and an interest in Abercrombie and Kent luxury travel specialists.

Intrawest is therefore a huge source of jobs in Canadian as well as other resorts. Most recruitment takes place at local level (i.e. an Intrawest employment office in the resort) but you can also try contacting Intrawest direct. The corporation has a central jobsite for short and long-term jobs (www.wework2play.com) as well as the sites below.

Intrawest Corporation: Burrard Street, Vancouver, British Columbia, V6C 3L6; www. intrawest.com; www.intrawest.com/employment; www.intrawest.com/applyonline (for seasonal positions).

COMPULSORY MEDICAL EXAMINATION

All prospective workers on approved schemes who are going to be child-carers or food-handlers on an approved scheme must undergo a compulsory medical examination by a doctor who must be on the list provided by the Canadian High Commission. This costs in the region of £130. The examination is very thorough and includes blood tests and a chest X-ray so there is not much point applying if you are not in good health. Once the required document certifying good health has been received by the High Commission, you should receive the work permit within a month.

A JOB ON THE SPOT

As with those who want to work in an American ski resort, it is a fact of life that there will be those who wish to bypass the bureaucracy and pick up casual work, most of it illegal. As in America there is nearly always a demand for casual workers in the big resorts but the lack of an employment authorisation or Social Insurance Number, known as the SIN (the equivalent of the American Social Security Number) is a severe drawback in that the official employment bureaux, the Canada Employment Service will be unwilling to employ you however many vacancies they have. Although many travellers manage to find casual illegal catering work in the big cities by applying directly to employers, in a small community like a ski resort where everyone's business is known to everyone else, there is virtually no chance of being taken on except for very casual jobs like babysitting and snow clearing.

If you are offered a more regular temporary job without proper authorisation, you should be aware that you are breaking the law, which is taken seriously in Canada. If you are working in a ski area known to employ hundreds of casuals, it will almost certainly receive a visit (more of a raid) by immigration officials. If you have insufficient funds you may be deported. Otherwise, you will be served a 'departure notice' requiring you to leave voluntarily via the United States. If caught, you should contact the nearest legal aid lawyer whose services are free.

RATES OF PAY

Wages are fairly good in Canada with statutory minimum wages varying amongst the provinces from $6-$7 or $8 in British Columbia per hour. In Ontario the minimum is C$6.85 per hour though for the lucky few with the expertise and skills required to get technical positions like snowmaking it can rise to C$11. A weekly average is probably in the region of C$300 with C$100 being spent on food and lodging. Although most hotel and catering staff are paid the minimum statutory wage, as with America, wages can be doubled or trebled by tips. Jobs in resorts normally come with subsidised accommodation and meals. In addition employees also get certain 'privileges' such as discounts in food and clothing stores and free or subsidised use of sporting facilities (other than skiing ones) and a free season ski pass.

THE MAIN CANADIAN RESORTS

The best known ski areas, at least to foreigners, are in the Rockies in the western Canadian provinces of British Columbia and Alberta, and include Banff/Lake Louise, Whistler, Jasper. Meanwhile Fernie (also British Columbia) has been developed and is definitely up and coming in the popularity stakes. While over on the eastern side there are other significant resorts in Quebec (capital Montréal) in the Canadian Laurentians centred on St. Agathe and Mont Tremblant. Even nearer to Montréal, about one hour by car, near the American border are at least ten ski mountains although only three are notable: Mount Sutton, Mount Orford and Owls Head. Quebec city also has some major ski centres within proximity including Mont Sainte-Anne and Stoneham developments. Ontario (capital Toronto), also has a few sizeable ski areas including Blue Mountain, Thunder Bay, Collingwood (has Canada's biggest skilifts) and Muskoka. If the ski resorts of New England in the US are reckoned to be cold compared with those in the West of the States, the resorts of the Canadian Rockies are even more so. The warmest months for skiing are March and early April. Before that the cold can be bone-numbing.

FURTHER INFORMATION

The 'Visit Canada Centre' in London deals with walk in customers only, but can supply general information on all the provinces of Canada (including Quebec). For brochures by post on Canada there is a brochure line (0891 715000). In addition, Quebec only, has a separate tourist bureau 'Quebec Destinations' (020-7233 8011) which can help with enquiries about tourism in that province.

Useful Address
Canadian Snowsports Association: Suite 200, 505 8th Avenue SW, Calgary, Alberta T2PP 1G2, Canada; ☎ 403 265-8615; fax 403 777-3213; www.canadaskiandsnowboard.net.

Alberta

BANFF/SUNSHINE/LAKE LOUISE

Banff/Lake Louise is the collective marketing name for a trio of resorts comprising 7558 acres. Banff itself is not a ski resort, but is the main accommodation area; the other being in the nearby resort of Mystic/Mount Norquay. Together with the resort of Lake Louise, Banff is located in one of Canada's prime tourist attractions, Banff National Park. In the whole Park there are 25 peaks over 3000m (9850 feet) mirrored in the startlingly blue lakes which are another feature of the area. Banff itself lies in a valley and has a permanent population of about 4,000 souls. It is also a health resort with hot springs and is open all year. In the early 1930s the first skiers were accommodated in huts. Nowadays there are extensive facilities around the slopes of Mount Norquay in Banff and Sunshine Village, a purpose built resort with minimal accommodation, ten and a half miles west of Banff on

Mount Whitehorn near Lake Louise. The resort's centrepiece is the Banff Springs hotel, built in Scottish baronial style in 1888. With a staff of 750, it could be an excellent source of employment, but probably only those with employment authorisation would be accepted.

Lake Louise is Canada's biggest ski area (4,200 acres) in an inspiring setting 1,700m (5,680 feet) above see level about 35 miles from Banff on the edge of the eponymous turquoise and green lake. The skiing area is served by a discreet modern resort but the lakeside is dominated by the massive 500-roomed Chateau Lake Louise Hotel (☎403-522 3511; fax 403-522 3834) which dates from 1890. Lake Louise has has several excellent restaurants and cosy nightspots including the Lake Louise Inn which incorporates a pub bar and disco. A complimentary shuttle bus transports skiers around the village at night and links the whole skiing area by day.

Goat's Eye/Sunshine Village is included on the Banff skiing's Tri-Area Ski Pass with Mystic/Mount Norquay and Lake Louise, Sunshine Village opened North America's largest ski terrain in 1995 adding runs to the Goat's Eye mountain and claims to have opened the world's fastest chairlift and a long skiing season until the end of May.

The Skiing
There is nothing extreme about Banff skiing which takes place ten minutes from town on the small area of Mount Norquay (SkiBanff@Norquay) where there are plentiful nursery slopes near the base and some intermediate runs. For further skiing it takes about 25 minutes to get to nearby Sunshine where you are whisked up the mountain by gondola to a the purpose-built ski village. Just above the village is a wide snow-bowl with runs to suit everyone, though intermediates have the most choice. There are several runs through the trees including the longest down past the resort to the base level. The combined resorts have 35 miles of pistes and 12 lifts. There is a choice of lift passes: the Tri-Area (includes Mystic Ridge/Mt. Norquay, Sunshine Village and Lake Louise) or the Banff Five-Area ski pass which adds Fortress Mountain and Nakiska. Nakiska was purpose built to stage the 1988 Olympics and has accommodation in Kananakis Village.

Lake Louise the biggest Canadian resort is located high above the town of Banff to which it is linked by free daytime shuttle bus. The Lake Louise ski area comprises four separate faces on Mount Whitehorn which has 50 named ski runs. However one of the pleasures of the area is that it is has even more extensive off piste skiing including the back bowls. There is a total of 4,200 skiable acres served by 12 lifts. The resort is a paradise for intermediate and advanced skiers. Beginners are also encouraged by the attitude of the ski school: if you are not skiing by the end of the first day of instruction, you get an additional free lesson. The skiing season lasts from mid-November to mid-May. The much-publicised friendliness of the resort is due in part to the voluntary 'Friends of Louise' who act as hosts on the slopes and will provide a complimentary tour for newcomers. Further information about the resort can be obtained from: Skiing Louise Ltd. 505, 1550 8th Street, S.W. Calgary, Alberta, T2R 1K1, Canada.

The ski mountains are constantly adding new runs and areas: recently Sunshine opened new runs on Goat's Eye and installed 'the world's fastest chairlift' and Lake Louise has developed an area of tree-skiing in an area called Ptarmigan Glades.

Work
Long known as one of the best resorts for both summer and winter work, Banff has a large number of foreign workers in jobs such as catering and chamber staff, trail cutters etc. The immense Chateau Lake Louise hotel (part of the Canadian Pacific hotel group) and the Lake Louise Inn are worth trying. In July 2006 Ski Banff-Lake Louise-Sunshine were looking for ski and snowboard instructors for five hotel branded ski schools (details from perry@SkiBig3.com).

Finding cheap accommodation while looking for work is however a problem. There is a youth hostel in Banff springs.

Resort addresses
Goat's Eye/Sunshine Village: P.O. Box 1510, Banff, Alberta, T0L OCO; ☎(403) 762
6500; fax (403) 762 6512; www.skibig3.com/dm.
Mystic Ridge/Norquay: P. O. Box 1258, Banff, Alberta T0L OCO; ☎(403) 762 4421; fax
(403) 762 8133; www.banfflakelouise.com.
Ski Lake Louise: P.O. Box 5, Lake Louise, Alberta, Canada T0L 1EO; ☎(403) 522 3555;
fax (403) 522 2095; www.banfflakelouise.com.

Human Resources
Ski Banff-Lake Louise-Sunshine: Human Resources, P.O. Box 1085, Banff AB TIL 1H9;
☎403-762-4561; fax 403-762-8185; employment@skibig3.com.

JASPER

Situated in Jasper National Park which adjoins Banff National Park, the town of Jasper
is located in the Marmot Basin much further north than Banff. Edmonton is the nearest
city. Jasper dates from 1911 and grew out of being a stop on the Grand Trunk Pacific
Railway, though there had already been a modest trappers' settlement for a hundred years
previously. The town is very attractive, remote, and has a permanent population of about
4,500 and lots of itinerant elk. There is plenty of accommodation in the town for guests but
skiers can stay nearer the ski area of Mount Marmot at either the enormous Chateau Jasper
Hotel or the Jasper Park Lodge, a Canadian Pacific resort property with 442 rooms set in
900 acres, located on the Beauvert Lake, and four and a half miles from Jasper town.

The Skiing
Less extensive than Lake Louise, the Jasper ski area at Marmot Basin nevertheless has a
respectable 75 runs on 1500 skiable acres with eight lifts. There is a variety of skiing from
tree-lined trails, steep chutes and high snow bowls and all levels of skier are catered for.
There is also 300 km of cross-country skiing. The resort is constantly expanding and is in
the process of creating more skiable terrain for all levels. The mountain is open from late
November to the end of April.

Accommodation
There are lots of camping grounds in the area, which would do until you managed to
find accommodation. Rental accommodation is cheaper in winter, but in limited supply
and expensive after March. Many employers provide accommodation of the shared or
dormitory type. The local newspaper is *The Jasper Booster* (780-852-3620; www.
jasperbooster.com), which might be worth consulting for the classified ads.

Work
Sadly for ski bums, the best time to find employment is from May to October reflecting
the popularity of Jasper as a summer resort for Canadian families. There is much less
employment during the winter. The best way to try to get a winter job would be to stay for a
year and work from May to May. It is advisable to contact the Jasper Employment Services
(see below) in advance for current job prospects.

Contacts
Ski Jasper: P.O. Box 98, Jasper, Alberta, TOE 1EO, Canada; ☎780-852-5247; e-mail
info@skijaspercanada.com; www.skijaspercanada.com..
Jasper Employment Centre: 622 Connaught Square, Jasper, Alberta TOE 1EO; ☎780-
852-5982; e-mail ability@telus.net or contact Jessica Shaver on the above number.

British Columbia

FERNIE

Fernie is not really one of Canada's main resorts but it is acquiring cult ski status like no other. It lies just inside the BC border and is also near the US Montana border. Some claim it is like Whistler before it expanded. However, two things it does not share with that fast growing ski metropolis are the (more likely) extreme temperatures of the more northerly Rockies, or the rain and fog which sometimes blanket Whistler.

The resort is named for William Fernie, who started a coal-mining boom there on the cusp of the 19th/20th centuries. The town grew and prospered from this activity until most of it was destroyed by fire in 1908, which is somewhat ironic considering its origins. There are a few stone-built buildings from that time and the rest is more modern architecture (skiing started there in 1962) is fairly nondescript but not totally unattractive. The small town of Fernie where most employees live is five km from Fernie Alpine resort where the base ski lift is. There is an hourly bus between the town and the ski village.

The Skiing

Fernie is about great and varied skiing for upper intermediates and lots and lots of powder for experts. Furthermore all this comes at a cost far below any other North American resort. The town is growing, but slowly and the two quad chairs serving the mountain are in need of upgrading. Fernie has potential for development and no doubt a conglomerate will snap it up at some not too distant future date. Enjoy it while you can.

Accommodation

If you manage to find yourself a job you will have to find your own accommodation. You can try the chamber of commerce (250-423-6868;www.ferniechamber.com) or the local newspaper (250-423-4666; www.freepress@monarch.net) or the Fernie online news (www.sterlingnews.com/Fernie) for leads and classified adverts.

Work

Being a little out of the way and with a quiet nightlife the jobs potential is not huge, but there is still a need for lift workers, janitors, food and beverage operatives, guest services, rental and repair staff, ticket checking and parking lot attendants as well as ski patrol and instructors for those with the appropriate qualifications. The winter job fair is in late October.

Useful Contacts

Fernie Alpine Resort: 5339 Fernie Ski Hill Road, Fernie, British Columbia, Canada V0B 1M6; ☎250-423-4655; fax 250-423-6644; www.skifernie.com; employment@skifernie. com.

NonStopSki: ☎0870 241 8070; info@nonstopski.com. Based in London, UK, NonStopSki offers ski and snowboard instructor courses and mountain survival techniques in Fernie Red Mountain and Banff in the Canadian Rockies. Also included is a range of additional courses including mountain safety. The course is aimed mainly at Gap Year students and those taking a sabbatical/career break.

KICKING HORSE

2006/7 will be this new big resort's fifth season. The first was disastrous owing to the worst snow deficit in a quarter of a century. The resort has been built onto Whitetooth, an existing area above the unprepossessing town of Golden, which at present provides most of the accommodation. It is about a twenty-minute drive to the base lodge. The origin of the picturesque name is a tale of a Scottish baronet, a horse that kicked him on the head, his premature burial and a fortunate last minute revival. This event caused his Indian scouts to name the spot Kicking Horse Pass. The baronet was Sir James Hector and he was surveying for a rail route across the Rockies in 1859.

The Skiing
A Dutch corporation is responsible for providing the financial wherewithal of 200 million Canadian dollars to increase the skiing area to 4,000 acres (and growing) of steep skiing in two tree-lined bowls. There are four lifts and more planned. The Golden Eagle Express Gondola whisks 1,200 skiers per hour up to the 8,000 foot summit in twelve minutes. At the top of the Gondola is a restaurant, (Canada's highest). You can even spend the night there for an arm and a leg (about £750) which are however better reserved for the skiing itself.

Accommodation
Staff accommodation is not provided so you have to arrange your own. There is a link from the resort website to Golden's websites for local newspapers, chamber off commerce etc. There is a youth hostel in Golden to stay at while you are looking on the spot.

Work
The skiing season starts about mid December. Their website declares 'We accept applications on an ongoing basis for positions that may become available'.In August 2006 the resort website (www.kickinghorseresort.com) was already advertising for handymen and certified ski and snowboard instructors.

Contacts
Kicking Horse Mountain Resort: Human Resources, Box 330, Golden, British Columbia, VOA 1HO; fax 250-439-5436; employment@kickinghorseresort.com; www. kickinghorseresort.com.

WHISTLER/BLACKCOMB
There is little doubt that the world class resort of Whistler is Canada's best known ski resort. Situated 75 km east of Vancouver, Whistler/Blackcomb were once two rival ski villages, which have merged under the recent ownership of the Intrawest Corporation. Intrawest has big ambitions for Whistler which include acquisition of new terrain to add to its already vast skiing area, huge investment into expanding facilities including the building of an entire new skiing village at Whistler Creek. Whistler will also be the host of the Winter Olympics in 2010. There will also be 25,000 volunteers recruited for work in 2010 at the Winter Olympics. There will be a thorough interviewing process followed by a training programme and applications will be accepted from 2008. Those with previous volunteering experience will have an advantage. No further information is available at present. Anyone interested should contact the resort. Those who have grown fond of Whistler over several skiing seasons are not entirely enthusiastic about the scale of the new developments and it would be true to say that Whistler has lost much of the charm that attracted punters in the first place. However, from a seasonal employment point of view, the massive new development makes it an excellent prospect for finding work.

Whistler has a long history of skiing while the *arriviste* Blackcomb has only been around for just over fifteen years. Where once they were two separate (and rival) ski villages they are now interconnected. Whistler is pedestrianised and has lift access from the village centres. The grandest hotel without doubt is the Chateau Whistler, situated about 5 minutes walk from Whistler Village centre, at the foot of the Blackcomb Mountain. Part of the Canadian Chateau Hotel chain it was built quite recently and combines luxury and old-fashioned style. There is a variety of hotel, lodge, apartment and chalet accommodation and shops. There are over hundreds of bars, nightclubs and restaurants which means nightlife and facilities are excellent.

The Skiing
The skiing is spread across the two mountains of Whistler (7,160 feet) and Blackcomb (7,490 feet). Combined they have a total of 200 marked runs, the majority for intermediates, and the highest vertical drop in North America. 27 lifts serve near 8,000 acres of skiable terrain. The lifts include high-speed quad chairlifts on both mountains. Whistler has acclaimed ski bowls including West, Harmony and Whistler and thousands of acres of off-piste. Blackcomb has three glaciers including Horstman. However there is something for everyone including beginners. For the adventurous heli-skiing can be organised locally-a one day excursion costing in the region of C$400.
Website: www.mywhistler.com and whistlerblackcomb.com.

The Work
There are hundreds of jobs in Whistler for seasonal workers. However, ski bums can get frustrated; as one job seeker put it:

It was very difficult, mainly due to the virtual impossibility of being able to secure work permits and a recent clamp down by immigration on foreign workers. Nevertheless, there are a few jobs available along the lines of babysitting/nannying/tutoring/ cleaning (privately)/snow clearing etc for cash in hand. However I must stress that accommodation here is very expensive and casual babysitting work would not provide enough to live on unless board and lodging were provided.

British Student Robert Heathcote recommends getting to Whistler in mid-September if possible as by the third week of October the 'hiring blitz' (see *contacts* below) is almost over. Although he arrived on the 20th October, Robert still managed to get a job as a cook with Blackcomb Mountain, which came with accommodation.

Almost half the staff of Whistler resort turned out to be Australian or from New Zealand and it's an old joke that the Aussies almost out outnumber the Canadians in the resort.

For further information on job hunting in Whistler see *case history – Bethany Smith* at the end of this section.

Contacts
Dempsey Tours: ☎604-932 5550; www.dempseytours.com, organise offer training courses for a variety of ski and snowboard instructor qualifications. Applicants should have some skiing/boarding experience.

Mountain Memories Accommodation: 4573 Chateau Blvd, Whistler BC VON 1BO; ☎604-905 4144; fax 604-905 4122; humanresources@whistler-memories.com. Needs full-time, seasonal or year round front desk/reservations agents and housekeepers.

Whistler Blackcomb Mountains: Recruiting Office, Whistler Blackcomb Cabin at Base 2, 4896 Glacier Drive, Whistler BC, VON 1B4; ☎604-938-7366; fax 604-938-7838; www.whistlerblackcomb.com//employment/contact/index.htm. Recruitment takes place year round. The recruiting office strongly recommends pre-booking an interview for the recruiting fair. You do this by contacting the office (☎604-938-7366) after 1 October. Note that in the employment notes the mountain company states that men's hair must be no more than mid-ear length and their ears adorned by a single stud or ring (two matching earrings for women). Other facial jewelry or 'exposed body piercings' must not be worn while working. Guide pay at entry level is $8.16-$13.9 CDN per hour.

Accommodation

James Gillespie from Surrey also worked in Blackcomb and says that finding somewhere to stay there in the winter is a major problem. He suggests getting there before September in order to secure. He managed to stay the month of February in the Youth Hostel on 'stunning Lake Alta' which is also a great way of meeting other people who are looking for somewhere to stay. He also suggests that if you hitch hike from Vancouver, you 'talk to the people you hitch lifts from and ask if they have anywhere you could stay or if they know of anywhere'. After a month and a half in the Youth Hostel, James stayed in the Shoestring Lodge. After James got a job as a ticket validator on Blackcomb, he was on a waiting list for staff housing as there is never enough staff accommodation to go round. He finally got a room there 'a very steep five-minute walk up from the Whistler Gondola Station'. He had to pay for this and says 'it wasn't the cheapest way of living in Whistler, but it saved finding a house and people to share it with'.

Local newspapers can also be a source of short and long-term rentals in their classified ads sections. Try the *Pique* (news magazine)www.pique.bc.ca as well as the *Whistler Question* (www.whistlerquestion.com).

Useful contacts

Shoestring Lodge: 604-932-3338; details@shoestringlodge.com. Offers dormitory accommodation from about £15.

Hi Whistler Hostel: 604-932-5492; whistler@hihostels.bc.ca. Cheapest accommodation two and a half miles from the resort. Fills up very quickly. Try to book ahead.

Southside Lodge: 604-938-6477.

UBC Lodge: 604-932-6604.

Whistler Backpackers: 604-932-1177.

OTHER RESORTS IN BRITISH COLUMBIA

British Columbia's other resorts are not on the grand scale of Whistler/Blackcomb. The best known smaller resorts are probably Grouse Mountain less than 20 minutes drive from downtown Vancouver and the even smaller resorts of the Okanagan Valley including Red Mountain, Big White Silver Star and Revelstoke further east.

Resort addresses

Apex Alpine: Apex Resort, 275 Rosetown Avenue, Penticton, British Columbia V2A 3J3; ☎604 4922880; fax 604 493 8677. Apex has just had $20 million's worth of new facilities. May be worth checking out for jobs.

Big White: Big White Ski Resort, P O Box 2039, Station R, Kelowna, V1X 4K5; ☎(250) 765 8888; fax (250) 765 1822. At the time of press was about to spend $45 million on expansion including accommodation and high speed lifts.

Panorama: Panorama Resort, Panorama, British Columbia, VOA 1TO; ☎250 932 3434; fax 250 938 9174. Has skiing for all abilities on 39 km of runs served by eight lifts. Not much in the way of base facilities but there is a ski hotel, The Pine Inn.

Red Mountain: Red Mountain Resort Inc, P.O. Box 670, Rossland, British Columbia, VOG 1YO; ☎250 362 7384; fax 250 362 5833. A large skiing area on two mountains.

Silver Star: P.O.Box 2, Silver Star Mountain, British Columbia VOE 1GO; ☎(250) 542 0224; fax (250) 542 1236. Has a renowned ski school and is of the Western movie set school of appearances. Mostly unchallenging skiing except for the isolated Putnam Creek chutes.

Sun Peaks: Sun Peaks Resort Corporation, P.O. Box 869, Kamloops, British Columbia, V2C 5M8; e-mail: info@sunpeaksresort.com. Sun Peaks is another ski resort in the throes of major expansion and has a new ski lodge and hotels.

Ontario

BLUE MOUNTAIN

Blue Mountain is Ontario's largest ski resort and is an hour and a half's drive from Toronto, and seven miles from the resort of Collingwood on Lake Huron. The resort accommodation areas are based around the three lift base lodges: Blue Mountain Inn Complex, Central Base Lodge and South Base Lodge and there are also various blocks of condos. There is no commercial centre as such and any urge towards a shopping spree entails a drive to nearby Collingwood, which is a small market town, which however lacks the charm of its alpine equivalents.

To get around a car is essential; even if you manage to hitch from Toronto 100 miles away you will still need to get around the resorts as the ski areas are some distance apart.

The Skiing

Blue Mountain has 34 trails over 253 acres with 16 lifts and two areas reserved for beginners. There are over 100 instructors employed in the ski school. Eleven trails are floodlit for skiing at night. The longest trail is less than a mile long and the expert skier would be unlikely to find any of the trails challenging. Indeed the advanced intermediate could well be bored after only a couple of days.

The beginner or early intermediate however would probably regard Blue Mountain as a paradise. Nearly all the trails are blue or easy reds. The facilities compare favourably with any European resort. Wide, well maintained pistes with excellent snow as a result of the cold climate and advanced snow-making equipment.

The trails are spread over a long ridge and there are queues for the lifts at weekends when the resort seems awash with a large part of the population of Ontario.

Work

Blue Mountain employs about 700 staff for the winter season, roughly sixty per cent of which are returnees.

Anyone wanting to work at Blue Mountain needs to have a permit. However, there is not as much problem getting one in Blue Mountain as in some resorts owing to its comparative remoteness and the fact that the local labour pool is limited. Casual workers are in short supply during the ski season and larger employers will accept applications and interview on the spot if their need is great. However, if at all possible it is advisable to contact the resort well in advance of the season (September if possible) and ask for an application form. See the beginning of this chapter for approved working schemes. Note that the resort will not employ anyone without a face-to-face interview.

The main season is at Christmas time, and from then until the week-long March school break they are at maximum capacity and full staff. From post March break onwards the staffing is thinned down towards the end of the season the following month.

Contact

Krista Johnson, Human Resources: Blue Mountain Resorts Ltd, R R 3, Collingwood, Ontario L9Y 3Z2 (☎705 445-0231 ext 6133; fax 705 444 1751; e-mail mail@ bluemountain.ca; www.bluemountain.ca.

OTHER ONTARIO RESORTS

Other good but smaller skiing areas in Ontario include: Thunder Bay and Saulte Ste Marie on Lake Superior and the Ottawa Valley.

Québec

TREMBLANT

Mont-Tremblant, or Tremblant as the resort is now known, is based around a 900 m mountain in the Laurentian Alps about 75 miles/125 km west of Montréal. The transfer time to the resort is little over one hour. There is a shuttle bus or you can share a private taxi which can take 3/4 people and their skis, and split the fare of about C$200. Mont Saint-Saveur (28 runs) is the largest of the small settlements (with a collection of ski lifts aimed at weekend skiers), through which you pass en route to Tremblant.

Tremblant was bought by Intrawest, a resort development company in 1991, and their influence is much in evidence on this always classy resort. There is a new Canadian Pacific chateau hotel and a new village development. The new resort village, at the base of Tremblant, has been meticulously designed to evoke its early Québec heritage with gabled roofs, dormer windows, balconies and decoration all designed to exude an historic effect. The pedestrian is king, and the strolling area, a central square is a pleasant place from which to begin the après ski activity.

Phil Nolan took part in a GAP SPORTS intructor course in Canada, he explains:
Originally, the course was supposed to be at Munt Tremblant. This changed because Tremblant was considered to he a little too commercialised while nearby Mont St. Anne was more secluded and because it is a more personal resort than Tremblant, it was easier to get to know the instructors and locals. We were introduced to the teaching side of being an instructor and we worked on our understanding of the drills and exercises and how they can be used in teaching. The GAP SPORTS programme makes for possibly the best 11 weeks of your life! The mountain allowed us to do so much more than ski and board. We went dog-sledding, snow shoeing, visited an ice hotel, stayed overnight in an igloo, visited the old town of Quebec and saw the annual carnival. This was all included in the course and makes your experience of Canada all the better. The qualification you leave with is internationally recognised and could be the building block for a career in instructing.

The French influence is mixed with a North American one which makes an enjoyable culture clash of French style in the form of boutiques and French cuisine in the restaurants, and North American friendliness in the welcome. Après ski focuses on the central square and the cosy Vieux Tremblant area of huddled chalets.

January and February temperatures can hit -30 Celsius, but the lack of humidity means you are unaware of the cold if you are appropriately clothed.

The Skiing

The name of the resort derives from a Native Indian legend which held that the mountain did indeed do as the name suggests. So far at least, the myth has remained just that. The skiing area occupies both the north and south faces and consists of just over 600 acres served by about a dozen lifts, which means the queues are never very long, even at peak periods like weekends. There is something for everyone from beginner to expert, but beginners and intermediates are the best served. The 'Avalanche' snow-making system is Canada's most powerful and 570 snow guns mean there is never a shortage of the white stuff. At night the piste groomers are out in force with their machines administering the perfect manicure to the slopes.

The resort has an excellent ski school that caters for all standards of adult, and for children there is the Kidz Club supervised by qualified child care staff. Adults can join racing camps held over three days, which are designed to improve personal performances. There are also programmes for women skiers of all abilities marketed as Elle Ski, supervised by women instructors.

For boarders there are award-winning parks on both sides of the mountain and Canada's original learn-to-snowboard park. Floodlit clinics are held in the evenings.

Ski le Gap (www.skilegap.com) operate ski and snowboard instructor courses lasting three months or 4 weeks.

Accommodation
There is every type of accommodation from five-star to cosy bed and breakfasts, but budget accommodation for workers is hard to find and most of them live outside the village and commute daily from places like Vieux Tremblant and St Jorvite. Those working for the big hotels in Tremblant are usually provided with basic, shared, subsidised accommodation.

Work
Tremblant has over 1,700 employees in 100 different categories of job. Qualified child carers could try 'Mother Nature's Day Care'. There is also a demand for after ski supervision of 3 to 12-year-olds and freelance babysitters and personal approaches to families may result in work.

Knowledge of French is required for bar work. Wages can be quite low. C$2 plus tips in hotels and possibly C$6 per hour for bars. The hours allow plenty of time off to ski and some employers provide a free pass while others will provide a pass at a reduced rate.

Main Employers
Tremblant: Tremblant is owned by the giant Intrawest Corporation. It is essential to speak passable French as the job descriptions on the website (www.trembland.ca) are only in French. You can find out more about work there by contacting rh@intrawest.com.

Ecole de Ski: 3005 Chemin Principal, Mont Tremblant, Quebec JOT IZO; ☎+1 819 681 2000; fax +1 819 681 5996. It is not necessary to speak French as many Americans come to the resort and the Quebecois are bilingual. It is possible to find work at peak times such as the January Winter Festival or Washington Week or Ontario Spring Week. Ski instructors can expect tips of C$20-25 per pupil from a five-day ski group.

OTHER RESORTS IN QUÉBEC
Stoneham and Mont Sainte-Anne are both on Québec city's doorstep:

Stoneham
Stoneham is only a stone's (or should that be a stoneham's) throw (30 minutes) from Québec city and is a year-round resort. Snowmaking, night skiing and ski-in, ski-out accommodation, make this a popular if small resort (30 runs and nine lifts spread over four mountains). The ski school has about 150 ski and board instructors. For job enquiries contact: Louise Gagnon, Human Resources, Stoneham Mountain Resort (1420 Avenue du Hibou, Stoneham, Québec, Canada, GOA 4PO; ☎418-848-2411; fax 418-848-1133; lgagnon@ski-stoneham.com).

Mont Sainte-Anne
Just a bit further out of Québec than Stoneham, along the St. Lawrence, is Mont Ste-Anne. Larger than Stoneham, Sainte-Anne boasts 56 pistes over 60km and thirteen lifts including the East's only eight-seater gondola. Monte-Sainte Anne is particularly known as a centre for cross-country skiing with a phenomenal 215 km/134 miles of tracks. For job enquiries contact Parc du Mont Sainte-Anne (Case Postale 400, Beaupré, Québec, Canada, GOA 1EO; ☎418-827-4561; fax 418-827-3121; www.quebecplus.ca/profile/147373/).

Montréal
Montréal also has its doorstep resorts: Bromont, Mont Sutton, Mont Orford and Owl's
Head.
Station Touristique Bromont: 150 rue Champlain, Bromont, Québec, J0E IL0; ☎514-
534-2200; fax 514-534- 1826.
Mont Orford International Tourist Area: C.P. 248 Chemin de la Montagne, Magog J1X
3WG; ☎819-843-6548; fax 819-847-2487.
Mont Sutton: Mont Sutton INC.,671 rue Maple, C.P. 280, Sutton, Québec, J0E 2K0;
☎514-538-2545; fax 514- 538-0080.
Owl's Head: Owl's Head Development INC., C.P. 35, Masonville, Québec J0E 1X0;
☎514-292-3342; fax 514- 292-3067.

OTHER CANADIAN RESORTS

Anyone feeling really adventurous could try the eastern side of Canada where
Newfoundland's own Marble Mountain may be able to offer work possibilities:
Marble Mountain: P.O. Box 252, Steady Brook, Newfoundland A2H 2N2; ☎+1 709 637
7610; fax +1 709 634 1702.

Personal Case Histories – Canada

JAMES GILLESPIE – BLACKCOMB

James Gillespie lived and worked in Whistler over a winter and summer season. Of his experiences he says: 'After taking the beautiful train ride from Vancouver, it soon became clear that getting a place to stay would be a major problem' (see *Accommodation* in Whistler/Blackcomb above for further details).

He got his first job as a ticket validator on Blackcomb mountain which turned out to require certain diplomatic skills as he explained: 'It was an excellent job, and although sometimes mundane it was often livened up by violent and abusive skiers trying to get on the lift for free.' He got a free ski pass and subsidised accommodation with the job.

He also stayed on for the summer season and got a job as a 'telemarketer' selling tours of the Mountainside Lodge's timeshare apartments. For this he got C$7 an hour and commission of C$7 per booking. As he puts it 'I spent many a balmy summer night on the phone to people in Washington State trying to convince them they wanted a place in Whistler'. The hours were 4pm-9pm Sunday to Thursday. This meant he could get another job and he says 'this time I worked in the Wizard Grill at the base of Blackcomb Mountain as a cashier/server'. The job paid the usual C$7 per hour but also came with a free lift pass for summer skiing and hiking. He said that 'Whistler was hot in summer and mostly sunny, but it did actually snow on July 1st'.

Of his experience generally James was very forthcoming: 'Going there was the best thing I've ever done and I hope to live there permanently in a couple of years' time'. I came home with a diary full of experiences a face full of smiles, a bag of dirty washing and pockets full of... well nothing actually. I was in debt, but it was worth it'. In view of this his final piece of advice was logical: 'Don't go to Whistler to make money because you won't; but you'll have a brilliant time.'

BETHANY SMITH – WHISTLER

Bethany Smith worked in Whistler hoping to earn enough money to fund her passion for snowboarding. She went out to Vancouver in November to stay with relatives. Whistler is a large but isolated resort easily reached in one and a half hours from Vancouver from where it is easy to hitch. Bethany, a seasoned ski resort worker having spent a previous winter in Les Arcs, says that unless you have a work permit your chances of getting all but very casual jobs like babysitting and snow-clearing are minimal. Additionally the resorts are full of Australians and New Zealanders whose countries have a reciprocal agreement with Canada and who therefore all have permits. If you are looking for work she recommends the *Whistler Question* newspaper available in Vancouver but comes out in the resort itself on Thursdays. Ideally you wait outside the newspapers' offices so you can grab a copy as soon as it's published. *The Whistler Question* offices are above a café called Moguls which incidentally serves the best hot chocolate in Whistler Village. Bethany arrived in Whistler at the beginning of December to look for a job but found herself distracted from job hunting by the irresistible lure of snowboarding.

Bethany also visited the employment office at Whistler Creek about 6 km miles from Whistler Village by road, but also accessible by gondola. Look carefully for the employment office or you might miss it – a green Portakabin. The employment office told Bethany that she didn't stand a chance without a work permit but suggested that she ask around about nannying or snow-shovelling casual jobs which are paid about $6 or $8 respectively per hour. However she found that employers preferred to employ nannies with work permits as they can claim tax credits for legal employees.

On one of her trips between Vancouver and Whistler she got a lift with a woman, and by chance it turned out that her 8-year-old son wanted to learn snowboarding (Bethany's *raison d'être*) and she got a job teaching him in return for board and lodging, fetching him from school and helping at mealtimes. She was still able to go snowboarding five days a week by herself and she took the boy snowboarding at weekends and Wednesday afternoons when he wasn't at school. She kept this job until she left the resort in mid-March. As she wasn't earning any money at all she made lots of babysitting flyers to post round the resort.

Bethany was lucky in that she met a local executive employed by the mountain corporation who, although she couldn't offer her full-time employment because Bethany lacked a work permit, she nonetheless wanted someone to supervise her 11-year-old's prep time after school because she (the mother), was sometimes too tired after a hard day at work. Bethany usually did this tutoring task two or three evenings a week in return for pocket money ($5) per hour. She also did some babysitting for the same person.

Courtesy of her Canadian relatives Bethany also got to travel round all the Canadian resorts helping escort a school party of 30 children going to five different resorts: Big White, Silver Star, Apex, Red Mountain and Tod Mountain. Everything was paid for except the ski passes. Other small resorts in Vancouver include Grouse, Seymour and Cypresse but they only have three or four lifts apiece and are floodlit at night so that locals can ski after work. They are not really good job prospects for foreigners.

Bethany only met three other British ski bums in Whistler. One of them, an English girl had been in the resort for three years and had survived working in café for cash in hand payment, but unfortunately due to a 'clean out' by immigration she was almost unable to get any casual work at all in the final year despite her many contacts. Employers didn't dare risk taking her on. She was surviving by babysitting.

One of the ways to get babysitting work is to advertise in the *Whistler Book* which comes out every two weeks and is distributed to all the hotels in Whistler. It has details of all the accommodation and restaurants and at the back there is a listing of babysitter services If you want to do babysitting work, you just get your name and telephone number on the list at the start of the season and it costs about $20 a month to keep your name on the list. It's definitely worth the money as nearly everyone who wants a babysitter looks at that list. Bethany got one babysitting job with a British couple who were going through the immigration process to become Canadian citizens. She also got some response to her flyer, which she put up around the village throughout the season.

One possible ray of hope for Brits hoping to get work in Canadian resorts are the official schemes like BUNAC which now cover the winter period. The majority of the lifties (lift workers) were Australians.

If you work for the mountain corporation they pay you some of your salary in Whistler Money which operates like a voucher system which can only be used in the resort for meals etc. Those working for the mountain corps of either Blackcomb or Whistler get half-price accommodation ($500-550 per month to non-workers). The earlier you get there to claim accommodation the better as if you arrive right at the end of November/start of the season the prices are at their highest. Most of those who have worked in Whistler and who know their way around manage to get accommodation pay about $375 a month for shared accommodation.

Whistler has long been considered expensive by Canadian standards but thanks to its success living costs have been creeping up and it is not longer as cheap for Britons. Alcohol is however much more expensive. $5 for a small beer and $7 for a Baccardi and Coke. Canadians are very generous tippers even if they just have a coffee and this makes it even more expensive for them. The other huge expense is the season lift pass which is staggeringly expensive. If you work for the resort (i.e. the Intrawest Corporations which runs Whistler/Blackcomb resort) the pass is free. The corporation also owns most of the cafés and restaurants though many of the shops and some of the restaurants are not corporation owned, so if at all possible you should work for the mountain as this is where the best perks are to be found.

Bethany, who was in between school and university, hoped to return to Whistler on the BUNAC scheme (see chapter introduction). After a winter spent there she anticipated being well organised for the following season. She reckoned the best work to get is as a cocktail waitress because the tips are so good. Cocktail waitresses usually begin work at 7 pm and carry on until 2 am for $8 per hour plus $100 per night in tips 5 days a week. Even in the cheapest place to eat in Whistler the waitresses still bring in $70 in tips a day and over Christmas nearly $200 a day.

A British boy was working on the lifts with a six-month working visa which he got through BUNAC sponsorship which is one of the few ways to get a work permit if you are British.

In the linked but formerly rival resort of Blackcomb, the resort revolves around the Chateau Whistler (The Chateau Hotels are a luxury Canadian chain). The waiters there are rumoured to bring in tips of $200+ a day.

Cheap places to stay while looking for work include the Youth Hostel on the other side of the lake from Whistler Village and the Nordic Estates. The latter is university accommodations and is run like a youth hostel in that it is open to the public. Charges are $15 per night, C$65 per week or $240 per month on a self-catering basis. These accommodations have a fast turnover of birds of passage and consequently can be a bit unsettling for anyone planning to make it their base. Bethany recommended finding accommodation with a family or a shared apartment if possible, though the Nordic Estates are a useful place to stay while you are looking for work.

HAMISH ANDREWS – WHISTLER

Hamish Andrews aged 28, left the British Civil Service after being employed for four years by the MOD. After working in Spain for three years as an estate agent he made a number of North American contacts which led him to Canada. He entered on a five-month tourist visa, which was renewable for a further five months. In order to get the five months extension he bought a season's lift pass for Whistler and said he wanted to ski there for the season. In order to prove that he had sufficient funds to support himself for that long he had an interesting method, which involved buying $1000 in travellers cheques and then claiming he had lost them. This meant that they were replaced by the cheque company and he could then show the authorities that he had $2000, i.e. double the funds he actually possessed. He hastened to point out that the aim of this was not to defraud the cheque company, who would in any case cancel the 'missing' cheques, but they all looked good to the authorities. Hamish got his job in Whistler on the hostel grapevine after getting a lift to the resort from Toronto with a Canadian friend, who was going there in order to look for work. He recommends youth hostels and similar establishments for picking up bits of useful information about jobs in Canada. He worked illegally in Whistler for a contract cleaning company. He was well treated by the company which paid well at $700 per week. As he was working illegally he did not pay tax. As far as the company was concerned he was self-employed and they did not enquire further. His hours were from 6.30 am to 7/8 pm and he worked 12 days out of every 14. He recommends painting and decorating jobs as another excellent money spinner. After the job finished he left for San Diego with a driveaway car for which he had to leave a deposit of $200. Despite the good money and treatment he received, Hamish has his reservations about working illegally in Canada.

Hamish doesn't recommend working without a permit

You know that periodically Immigration carry out sweeps and so you are always looking over your shoulder and you have to very careful about who you talk to and what you say. For instance, the fact that I was paying no tax I explained by telling people I was self-employed and paid my tax at the end of the financial year. You could never let down your guard for a moment. If you get caught you are escorted to Vancouver and put on the first flight and also banned from entering Canada for 2-5 years.

LINDA JAMES – BANFF/LAKE LOUISE

Linda James, an Hnd. Business student from Sussex worked in the Lake Moraine Lodge near Lake Louise from April to October. She got the job through the BUNAC scheme and could have stayed longer. She intends to return and work a skiing season there in the near future. She had previously worked in Canada in Ontario through BUNAC during her first student year. She likes Canada so much she hopes to emigrate. While working at Lake Louise she met a Briton and an Australian who were doing hotel work without visas and says that this is fairly common practice amongst the smaller hotels and businesses. However, illegal work is more common further north in Dawson City. Unfortunately, being so far north, Dawson is not so convenient for those who wish to work in order to ski.

Her job at Lake Moraine Lodge was as a reception supervisor for which she was paid $6 per hour plus an end of season bonus of $1 per hour worked. The practice of paying bonuses at the end of the season is fairly usual in Canada as well as the United States. Linda said that she would have preferred to work as a waitress as the amount you can earn from tips is phenomenal. However, her hours were a very reasonable 7-8 per day, as compared for instance with hours in Swiss hotels during peak times. She thoroughly recommends working in Canada to anyone and says that the service provided by BUNAC was very good. They give all applicants a job directory of employers which was very useful in helping her finding the job.

UK/NORTH AMERICAN GLOSSARY

ENGLISH	AMERICAN
Apartment	*condo*
Bumbag	fannypack
Cable car	*tram*
Black run	*double black diamond*
Queues	*lines*
High speed quad	*4-person chair which slows to let you on and off*
Lavatory	*restrooms*
Ski touring	*back country skiing*
Piste	*trail*
Petrol	*gas*
Pistebasher	*tiller*
Red run	*single black diamond*
On slope lodging	*ski-in, ski-out*

AUSTRALASIA

Finding a Job in Australia and New Zealand

Australasia

As yet there are no ski packages from the UK to the resorts of Australia and New Zealand, which begin their ski season just as those of the Northern Hemisphere are bemoaning the end of theirs. For the hardcore, snow sliding community of instructors and resort staff who have spent the season in the Alps or the Rockies, it is time to pack up and make preparations to go down under to continue the year of white-out. The resorts of Australia and New Zealand are great places not only to live and ski/snowboard, but also to work. According to a 2006 report on the ski industry of Australia by Ski Press Magazine, the ski season there generates a staggering 17,000 employment opportunities. So there is no shortage of work there and the general consensus is that the resorts of Down Under offer a more relaxed atmosphere than their Alpine equivalents and there is less friction between skiers and boarders.

As there are no all-inclusive ski packages, you will have to make your own way there from the airport you decide is nearest to where you want to go. Long distance coaches in Australia are cheap and reliable and go to most of the resorts. In general, cars are banned in the resorts themselves. In New Zealand it is worth investing in a car, otherwise getting around can be difficult.

COMPARISON OF AUSTRALIAN AND NEW ZEALAND RESORTS

Afficionados reckon that for powder hounds, New Zealand is the place. It has vast, uncrowded expanses of snow, long seasons and cheap living. However, there are drawbacks: road approaches to the ski area tend to be rough, unhewn tracks with no safety barriers. The huge quantities of snow too have their downside and when they hit, the storms can often close a mountain for days on end. For these reasons, there is little or no on-mountain accommodation, which is another drawback. Visitors and staff generally inhabit resort towns that can be up to 50 km away. Such places can be pretty quiet, especially during the week (with the notable exception of Queenstown).

Australian resorts on the other hand, tend to be alpine style, with on-mountain accommodation and are generally very commercialised. While this means reasonable living conditions and wages and plenty of employment opportunities, the drawback is the short season. Lack of snow can also be a periodic problem, although the widespread use of artificial snowmaking has made a big difference. There is even skiing on Tasmania, though it would be unwise to depend on it, as even the tourist literature admits the snow is unreliable there.

WORK

In both countries you will find all the usual resort jobs, from instructing to ski hire and bar work. North Americans will be familiar with the fact that the resorts tend to be dominated by the lift companies, sometimes referred to as 'the mountain', and which generally have monopolies on ski instructing and on-piste catering. Sometimes the companies also own the resort's main accommodation complex. Working for 'the mountain' in a resort will generally come with perks including a free or subsidised lift pass, cheap accommodation and so on.

If you work for private employers, the perks are a matter of luck. The most important perk is accommodation (which is generally provided) as it is not only scarce, but beyond the means of many resort employees if they have to try to find their own. The kind of niche entrepreneurial activities that can be a ski bum's mainstay in the Alps (e.g. baby-sitting or selling chocolate to lift queues) tend to be less lucrative in Australasia. This is partly because the resorts are smaller and visitors spend less, but also because there is a fair chance that 'the mountain' or a local entrepreneur has the monopoly. Having said that there are opportunities absent elsewhere: Matt Tomlinson found himself bagging carrots in New Zealand and his friends did building work in Australia. The problem is that such jobs are inclined to leave you with little free time to spend on the slopes.

Another opportunity for ski workers in Australia is that Australasian resorts generally have exchange programmes with the big North American, European, and even, Japanese resorts rather along the lines of the approved schemes listed at the beginning of the North American section, but for Australians. Rebecca Barber from Victoria worked in a Japanese resort (see Japan) through such a scheme. If you are serious about a career in the industry or just fancy being a 'liftie' (lift attendant) in the star-studded resort of Aspen, this is one way of getting a visa and a subsidised airfare. Although such schemes are primarily geared towards instructors, they can also apply to other resort and hotel staff.

WHEN TO APPLY

Once you have decided which resorts you want to work in, the best way to approach the task of getting a job is to do some background research concerning the resort's employers and mail out plenty of applications. This is best done before the end of February. If that does not produce a response, then you should plan to arrive in the resort late in May, to get accommodation and get your name known to all potential employers. There is also scope to arrive in the resort later, as Matt Tomlinson did when he turned up in Mt Buller in Australia on 3 July and eked out an existence, but accommodation was a problem as he could not find anywhere permanent.

AUSTRALIA

Norwegian immigrants are credited with introducing skiing to Australia during the 1860s gold rush there. Since then, Antipodean skiing skills have been re-exported back to Europe via Australasian ski schools. Many a ski school in Europe, North America and beyond, has been glad to employ an instructor who has honed his or her skills on the mountains down under.

Australia's ski industry is concentrated in the far southeast of the country in New South Wales and Victoria. Fly to Sydney for the NSW resorts and Melbourne for Victoria ones. There are also a number of smaller resorts in Tasmania. The season generally starts on the second weekend in June with the Queen's Birthday bank holiday weekend, although lack of snow cover can mean an excuse for a bit of a drinking binge. July is the busiest month, particularly during the school holidays and the various accompanying interschool championships. August is quieter and the season starts to tail off mid-September as the snow melts and people head back to the beaches.

WORKING HOLIDAY VISAS
Australia's immigration service is notoriously strict and you will not find many opportunities to work for cash. However, nationals of selected countries that have working holiday arrangements with Australia including British, German, Irish, Canadian, Danish, Dutch, Estonian and Swedish people between the ages of 18 and 30 are eligible to apply for a working holiday visa valid for one year. The visa is meant for people intending to use any money they earn in Australia to supplement their holiday funds. Working full-time for more than three months for the same employer is not permitted but you are allowed to engage in up to three months of studies/training (which is relevant to ski and board instructors etc.). Although applicants older than 25 are eligible, their applications are scrutinised more closely and they must prove that their stay in Australia will be of benefit not only to them but to Australia. It also helps if they can give a convincing account of why they waited until their early twenties to travel in Australia (e.g. they were in higher education, looking after an ailing relative etc.). There is a similar scheme for Americans aged 18 to 30 but is for four months only. BUNAC (see North American chapter approved schemes) also have a scheme for Australia, 'Work Australia' from Britain and the USA.

The issuing of visas (which have now become paperless and privatized) is now done under the ETA (Electronic Travel Authority). The first step in getting a visa is to contact the High Commission in London (www.australia.org.uk) or the Australian consulate in Manchester. You can also apply at Australian consulates outside the UK. Applying online via www.immi.gov.au is normally straightforward and should result in an e-mailed confirmation within 48 hours or less which is sufficient to get you into the country. To get the visa label in your passport you have have to visit a DIMIA office on arrival in Australia. The fee for the visa at DIMIA offices is A$70. Specialist visa agents such as Visas Australia (www.visas-australia.com) and Travellers Contact Point will add a premium charge.

If you are going to apply for your WHV the non-electronic way, the first step is to get the working holidays information sheet and form 1150 Application for a Working Holiday Maker's (WHM) visa from a specialist travel agent or from a visa agent like Visa Australia in Cheshire (01270-626626) or Consyl Publishing (3 Buckhurst Road, Bexhill on Sea, East Sussex TN40 1QF; ☎01424-223111) enclosing an A4 stamped addressed envelope (66p stamp). The non-refundable processing fee in the UK is about £70; this can be checked online at www.immi.gov.au, website of the Australian Immigration. As with the North American schemes, applicants have to prove they are in possession of reasonable funds (about £2000).

Normally you should allow about eight weeks to have your working holiday maker's visa processed. If you are in a hurry it is now possible to get an electronic paperless visa (see details above) from a specialist agent. However, this can lead to hassle at the other end as you have to take your passport to a Department of Immigration Office on arrival in Australia which can mean hours of hanging around.

A temporary visa (Subclass 462) was introduced in November 2002 for young professionals to work in Australia for up to twelve months (provided their country has signed a bilateral agreement with Australia) but will not be subject to the same restrictions as for the Working Holiday Maker visa; but unlike the WHV it cannot be translated into a resident visa.

Victoria

MOUNT BULLER

Only three hours' drive from Melbourne, Mt Buller is the home of the Australian Ski Institute and gets significant weekend influxes of Melbourne's 'glitterati'. Buller's ski school, which has over 140 instructors, is widely considered to be Australia's best. The Australian Olympic Ski Team also train there.

Buller offers some good skiing on 80km of trails in 180 hectares of mountain served by 25 lifts; roughly two-thirds of the mountain being skiable. Snowboarders are catered for with a half-pipe at the top of the mountain. The main problem with Buller for boarders is that the lift system (until recently split between two companies) was not properly linked, leaving gaps which meant a lot of walking. In the last ten years, A$200 million of investment in the entire resort infrastructure has made Buller bigger and better and thus increasing job prospects including at the new Breathtaker Hotel which offers alpine pampering and spa treatments. Unfortunately there is plenty of competition for these from the 600 students of the Alpine Campus of LaTrobe University.

Buller is a fun place to live, particularly during the University winter vacation. However, getting accommodation in Buller is difficult. The bulk of the lift company staff, which includes the Mt Buller Chalet Hotel, live in two staff hostels in Sawmill Settlement, about 30 minutes away. The bus service is frequent and the fare is taken care of by the employer. However, living outside the resort severely limits your social life.

Full-time staff are eligible for subsidised housing if available. This always means sharing 2-4 with some empoyers providing full board, and others just self-catering facilities. Prices vary from A$60 to A$155 a week (bed only).

If there is no accommodation with the job and you don't want to commute on the bus, you can find a place in one of the few ski lodges (usually run as clubs) which offer rooms to resort staff. According to Matt Tomlinson, to get a place you really need to be in the resort by the beginning of June. Matt 'got by' by alternating between lodges and friends' floors and he says 'it cost me around 150 dollars a week, not to mention a lot of beer for my friends.'

The main employment opportunities other than the lift company and the ski-hire outlets, are the hotels that contain most of the resort's bars and restaurants, namely Mt. Buller Chalet, Arlberg, Ski Club of Victoria, Pension Grimus, Enzian and Kooroora. Some of the larger ski lodges also employ kitchen staff and cleaners. Average hourly pay was about A$10 per hour plus a subsidised lift pass.

Matt Tomlinson describes his experiences of working at Mt Buller

I arrived in the resort hopelessly late and found it very difficult to get work. In the end my resourcefulness called upon my experience a few years back as a 'nanny' and I got some work with the resort's nanny agency looking after the under fours who were too young to go to the Ski School's Ski Kinder. The pay averaged A$10 per hour. I was about the one person to stick with the job for the whole season. Despite the lack of a lift pass or accommodation, I stayed because it suited me to go out boarding when I had no work. I also enjoyed the irony of being paid to build snow people, read stories and go tobogganing. I wouldn't recommend it as ideal though. I got none of the usual ski perks and work was erratic and tailed off after mid-August. If I hadn't anticipated that and worked 60-hour weeks during the school holidays, I'd have been in dire straits. Being a male nanny in Australia was an interesting experience. I got used to being asked if I was a child molester. But on the upside, more than a few parents hired me because I'm a guy as they saw me as a positive role model for their little boys. I was also offered a number of live-in jobs in Melbourne, but I thought the duties might involve more than nannying proficiency. And in case you're wondering, yes, I did get a lot of ribbing from the guys when I told them what job I was doing.

Contact
Mt. Buller Resort: P.O. Box 1, Mt Buller, Vic 3723; ☎03 5777 7800;fax 03 5777 7801; info@skibuller.com.au; www.mtbuller.com.au.

MOUNT HOTHAM

Not only is Mt Hotham Australia's biggest resort, but it is also the country's powder capital. Having recently changed ownership it is still being developed. At 1,861 metres it is the country's highest village. It has 13 lifts, 245 skiable hectares and 35 km of cross country trails. New developments have included three new chairlifts. There is guest accommodation for 4,700 and Hotham has thirteen restaurants. As far as the name goes, Hotham lives up to it by having some of the hottest riders in the country and some great backcountry skiing.

Contact
Mt. Hotham Skiing Company: Mt Hotham Alpine Resort, P O Box 188, Bright, NSW 3741; ☎(03) 5759 4444; fax +61 57 593693; www.mthotham.com.au.

FALLS CREEK

Falls Creek village sits in a natural bowl high in the Australian Alps in northeast Victoria and is privy to some of Australia's most spectacular scenery and some of the nation's best skiing terrain. For several years it has had more snow, (using a combination of natural snow-falls and snow-making than the other Victoria resorts.

Well-known for its unique village atmosphere and a variety of ski runs (96 trails and 20 lifts), Falls Creek is the only true ski-in, ski-out resort in Australia where you can ski right from your door to the slopes and back again in normal snow conditions. The atmosphere is great, and the addition of 38 hectares of off-piste skiing on the back of Mt. McKay has every expert skier rushing to experience the steeps and great tree skiing on offer. Owned by the parent company of Mt. Hotham with which it shares a lift pass, it has had millions of dollars of lavished on it. Mt. Hotham is six minutes away by helicopter and two and a half hours by road.

Contacts
Falls Creek Ski Lifts: The biggest employer is Falls Creek Ski Lifts and details of all their vacancies can be found at www.skifalls.com.au or e-mail queries to the Human

Resources Manager: employment@fallscreek.net
Falls Creek Alpine Resort: P.O. Box 50, Falls Creek, Victoria 3699; www.fallscreek.com.au.

New South Wales

PERISHER BLUE
Perisher Blue was created in 1996 from the almalgamation of four resorts (Perisher, Blue Cow, Smiggins and Guthega) covering seven mountain peaks. It is located in the Snowy Mountains in the Kosciuszko National Park. With over 1250 hectares of terrain, it is easily the largest Australian resort, with over 50 lifts. Perisher is also serviced from Jindabyne and the Ski Tube train connects the resorts. The resort is superb for intermediates with 60% of runs graded at this level. The season runs from June to October.

Perisher is a pygmy possum friendly resort – special underpasses have been constructed to lead them under the pistes so that they will not be mown down by skiers and boarders.

The season lasts from June to October.

Accommodation
Anyone who has found employment in Perisher can get an accommodation needed advert posted on the Perisher Blue Resort Bulletin board – just e-mail the employment office your requirements.

Work
Perisher has approximately 140 full-time permanent staff and has a variety of seasonal vacancies. These vacancies are filled where possible by promoting existing staff. Permanent vacancies are usually advertised on www.monster.com.au. For seasonal vacancies see contact below.

Contact
Perisher Blue Ski Resort: P O Box 42, Perisher Valley, NSW 2624; ☎(02) 6459 4495;
  Some jobs like snow grooming and ski patrol require the relevant experience and qualifications. More information is given on the website www.perisherblue.com.au.

THREDBO
Long regarded as Australia's premiere year-round mountain resort, Thredbo confirmed its ski resort credentials by being given the Australian Best Year Round Alpine Resort in 1997, 1998 and 1999 and the NSW Tourism of the Decade award in 2000. Thredbo has some excellent skiing with some of the country's longest and steepest runs including the 6km from Karel's T-bar. The skiable terrain is over 480 hectares and there are 12 winter lifts plus two Snow Runners.

Apart from being a great alpine village including the Thredbo Alpine Hotel, Thredbo is home to the Australian Institute of Sport's Alpine Training Centre.

Resort staff generally live in Jindabyne, a service town down the Thredbo Valley. Lift company accommodation is rumoured to be very nice apartments, with eight people to an apartment. The closing date for employment is around mid-April with interviews taking place in Sydney in May. Instructors' hiring clinics took place from 16-20 June and cost a whopping A$300.

Contact
Personnel Department, Kosciusko Thredbo Pty Ltd.: P O Box 92, Thredbo Village NSW

2625, Australia; ☎(02) 6459 4100; fax (02) 64 59 41 01; e-mail recruitment@thredbo. com.au; www.thredbo.com.au) enquiries and to download an application form contact recruitment@thredbo.co.au. To check current vacancies go to the recruitment section of the company website. Maureen Roberts is the personnel manager.

NEW ZEALAND

Since New Zealand is a fairly mountainous place, it is not surprising that it has a liberal sprinkling of ski fields ranging from the small club fields serviced by weekend rope tows, to the large world-class resorts with high-speed quad chairlifts. The majority of resorts are on the South Island within reasonable driving distance from Christchurch or Queenstown, while on the North Island Whakapapa and Turoa occupy opposite sides of Mt Ruapehu. The season generally runs from late June to late October.

Apart from the one or two fledged resorts like Treble Cone and Turoa on South and North Islands respectively, the ski areas of New Zealand are in the process of developing from clubs which first build up a loyal following and customer base before being bought up by commercial interests and transformed into a fully commercial resorts.

A good thing about New Zealand is that the cost of living is low. Six ski workers who went to Turoa hired a three-bedroomed chalet for NZ$50 a week. Matt Tomlinson, one of the six described it as basic: 'Heating consisted of a single wood-burning stove and the bathroom was across the veranda; quite chilly when the overnight temperature reached -3 Celsius.

On the downside though, wages are none too high. About NZ$10 per hour is the going rate for casual work in resort catering establishments. Matt Tomlinson says that while this may seem tolerable winter storms meant that the resort was often closed for days on end. So there was no work and no skiing. To add insult to injury, we would have to report to work at 6am even though we knew full well there would be no work that day'.

Getting around could be a problem, especially on the days the ski area is closed owing to adverse weather. Matt Tomlinson advises buying a second hand car at the Sunday morning car auction in the Auckland suburb of Manaku. It cost AS600 (about £250) and he made sure it had enough road tax and MOT to last the season to save major expense. Fortunately, third party insurance is reasonably inexpensive. Snow chains are compulsory on most mountain roads.

Useful Website
www.nzski.com is an excellent source of jobs for New Zealand's seasonal ski resort jobs. Go to the employment section of the website and follow the instructions for online application or use the employment contacts to contact employers directly.

VISA & WORK REGULATIONS

A great advantage of New Zealand is that it allows tourists from the UK to visit New Zealand for up to six months, visa free, while Americans, Canadians and Europeans can stay for up to three months visa free. However, it is better to be organised and apply in advance for a working holiday visa.

The UK and Irish Citizens' Working Holiday Scheme allows Britons and Irish people aged 18-30 to do temporary jobs in New Zealand for up to two years. Applications are welcomed year round. Information can be obtained from the NZ Immigration Service, NZ House, 80 Haymarket, London SW1Y 4TE; www.immigration.govt.nz). Applications for all working holiday schemes have to be done online which means that there is no need to apply from your home country. The fee is about NZ$120/£50 and is payable by credit card at the time of application. The NZ Immigration Service stays in touch with Working Holidayers via email and sends updates on available jobs and requests for feedback about the scheme. This is for Britons. Other nationalities are, UK passport, £60 processing fee, evidence of a return ticket and proof of about £1,400 in funds. A recent new requirement for working holiday applicants from the UK obliges them to undergo a medical check and X-ray. The scheme is open to other nationalities including Japanese, Irish and Canadians, but is limited to one year.

If you can obtain a firm offer of a job before leaving the UK you can dispense with the above and apply instead for a temporary work visa (cost £80 for processing). The temporary work visa does not itself entitle you to work but it facilitates the work permit (valid for 2-3 years) process on arrival.

It is also possible to apply for a work permit at one of seven Immigration Service offices once in New Zealand even if you have arrived in NZ as a visitor and then landed a job. You must have a written job offer from a prospective employer confirming that the position offered is temporary and evidence that you a suitably qualified (original certificates or certified copies). A work permit obtained in this way from one of the several immigration offices in New Zealand is charged at NZ$90.

Special Schemes
BUNAC (downunder@bunac.org.uk) has a Work New Zealand programme with the usual range of services included (flights, stopovers, initial hostel accommodation and back-up during stay) for a year, in association with International Exchange Programs (www.iep. co.nz) in New Zealand.

There is a Work Experience Downunder programme operated by CCUSA (1st Floor North, Devon House, 171/177 Great Portland Street, London W1W 5PQ; 0207637 0779/ fax 020 7580 6209; www.ccusaweusa.co.uk). Application and programme fees start at £320 not including travel, insurance and visas.

Americans aged 18-30 can apply for a year's work exchange visa through certain approved organisations including BUNAC USA (www.bunac.org), CIEE (www.ciee.org/ isp) and CCUSA (www.ccusa.com). Canadians aged 18-35 may obtain a working holiday visa independently or through the Student Work Abroad programme or SWAP (www. swap.ca).

North Island

WHAKAPAPA
Whakapapa bills itself as New Zealand's largest developed ski area and is certainly one of the smartest, attracting substantial weekend custom from the cities of Wellington and Auckland. Terrain-wise, it is definitely a skier's resort, with 400 hectares of skiable area. Whakapapa is fairly unusual for a New Zealand resort in that there is on-mountain accommodation at the Top o'the Bruce base station. Together with the resort Turoa, on the other side of Mt Ruapehu, the area is owned by Ruapehu Alpine Lifts Ltd and the two resorts are marketed as Mt Ruapehu. The ski season typically runs from June to mid-October

The resort is set in the World Heritage National Park and the village of National Park, containing the magnificent Chateau Hotel and a string of motels down the road to Highway 3, provide the rest of the accommodation for the resort.

Work

The resort employs about 40 permanent staff and up to 700 seasonal workers in 65 different job decriptions. The hourly pay rate ranges from A$9.20 to A$14.00 dependent on age and responsibility undertaken in the job.

Contact

Ruapehu Alpine Lifts: Private Bag, Mt. Ruapehu North Island, New Zealand; ☎07 892 3738; fax 07 892 3732; enmployment@mtruapehu.com.

TUROA

Sitting on the opposite side of Mt. Ruapehu from Whakapapa, Turoa tends to be that resort's poorer relation. It is however the second biggest ski area in New Zealand and offers some spectacular skiing, including the 4 km far Sunset Ridge run and a number of gullies that are particularly well-suited to snowboarders. However, as it is particularly exposed to the elements, winter storms often close the resort for days on end. Mt Ruapehu is also an active volcano with a bad sense of timing: it tends to erupt during the skiing season. A conveniently situated ridge stands between the piste and Pompeian catastrophe. Despite the frisson of skiing on a still volatile volcano, its presence is neither good for snow or business, which is probably why the ski area accommodation is based 32 km distant at Ohakune.

Work

Matt Tomlinson spent a season there and had a great time. It is only in recent years that the ski field has become a major contributor to the economy and the area. According to Matt:

> **Matt Tomlinson tells how bagging carrots tided him over until he got bar work**
> *Ohakune has long earned a fair crust as a service centre for the local farms and more recently a huge paper mill. This adds to the employment opportunities and for the first few weeks I got a job bagging carrots to keep myself going. Ohakune is reputedly the 'carrot capital' of the Southern Hemisphere with a ten-metre high carrot on the main road into town to prove it.*
>
> *After seeing more carrots than I ever want to see again in my life, I got a good job working in the bar at the foot of the piste. This was more luck than good judgement as one of my housemates ran an on-piste café and got me an interview. The job paid NZ$8 per hour and I got a ski pass. The main drawback of working on the skifield itself was the 30 minutes commuting, which entailed getting up at 6am every morning. Another was that when bad weather closed the resort, not only did we have no work, but we couldn't go skiing either. Some weeks this was so bad that I worked only 15 hours.*

Other than the lift company and Turoa Cafeterias who run the on-mountain catering, the employers are the town's bars, motels, restaurants and ski hire outlets. Matt advises getting to the resort before late June as all the jobs have usually gone by then and housing is scarce. He recommends getting in touch with Ski Country, who run an accommodation service in the town.

Instructing

Although it is hard, it is not impossible to get your foot in the door as an instructor and get a job on spec. Briton Julian Griffiths did this in Turoa. He turned up with a BASI III qualification having just finished sixth-form college in the UK. He was offered a position just as he was thinking of flying home. As a first year rookie, do not expect to get anything but the most menial of tasks. In his first year at Turoa, Julian was used as a 'human traffic cone' stopping cars from driving off the road in the fog. If the weather is really bad or there are no clients, you may not even get to work at all. An evening job and private funds are just about a must.

South Island

MT HUTT

Known as the snowmaking capital of the Southern Hemisphere, Mt Hutt has the best snow cover and the longest season (late May to October) of any Australasian ski field. The ski field is close by the town of Methven, about 30 minutes away, which in turn is an hour and a half from Christchurch, which is the source of much of the weekend clientele.

The skiing area is big (900 acres) and open with views of the Canterbury Plains to Christchurch and the Pacific Ocean. Your day pass is exchanged if you are not happy after an hour on the slopes.

The resort is owned by Mt. Cook Lines who also own Coronet Peak and The Remarkables (see below).

Contacts
Lift Company's Address: Mount Hutt Ski Area, P.O. Box 14, Methven 8353, New Zealand; ☎03 302 8811/03 308 5074; fax 03 302 8697; e-mail recruit@mthutt.co.nz; www. nzski.com/mthutt/.

TREBLE CONE

Named from the triple rock glacial formation of its summit, and promoted with Cardrona, Treble Cone claims to be the biggest ski field in New Zealand and is certainly unrivalled for the awesome view down to Lake Wanaka. Treble Cone has a new six-seater chair, the first in the southern hemisphere and from the top, you can cruise down Outer Limits. If you want to get to the top you have to hike as lift skiing stops at 2100m. The Norwegian and Canadian ski teams go to Treble Cone to train and the terrain park is also highly rated.

Treble Cone, like its sister resort Cardrona, is serviced by Wanaka, a year-round tourist resort on the edge of the eponymous lake and surrounded by Mount Aspiring National Park. Originally settled during the gold-rush era of the nineteenth century, it is the centre of a busy timber industry during the winter months. Wanaka is a mecca; the skiers and snowboarders' equivalent of the surfers' Waikiki Beach no less. There are the usual employment opportunities and it has the reputation of a nice place to live. If you fancy the bright lights, Queenstown is the place, one hour away.

Contact
Treble Cone Ski Area: P O Box 206, Wanaka, New Zealand; ☎+64 (0)3 443 7443; fax +64 (0)3 443 8401; info@treblecone.co.nz; www.treblecone.co.nz.

CARDRONA

Cardrona has been promoted as a family resort since 1995. It is slightly higher than Treble Cone at 1,180m and lies between Wanaka (30 minutes) and Queenstown (one hour). Access is easy from either centre. Cardrona is renowned for its powder snow and has a very reliable season than runs from June to late October. Its three basins offer wide-open spaces and a mix of terrain that is suitable for both boarders and skiers of all abilities. The resort is perhaps the closest to an alpine resort in New Zealand with three cafés, a bar, and apartments.

Contact
Cadrona Resort: P.O.Box 117, Wanaka, New Zealand; ☎+64 (0)3 443 7411; fax +64 (0)3 443 8818; employment@cardrona.com; www.cardrona.com. Note that applications must be posted by snail mail. Cardrona do not accept an application as an e-mail attachment. Applications should arrive between February and the end of March.

CORONET PEAK

Coronet Peak is the closest ski area to Queenstown 25 minutes away and has been popular with New Zealand's snow addicts for more than 50 years. The skiable terrain of 280 hectares is wide and the piste uncluttered, while the terrain park is to be recommended. The ski field also has a licensed crèche, an additional possibilty for employment. The resort also claims New Zealand's biggest snow-making facility and offers night skiing.

Contact
Coronet Peak Ski Area: P O Box 359, Queenstown; 03 442 4620; fax 03 442 4637; e-mail recruit@nzski.com..

Queenstown
Although not a ski resort, Queenstown is nonetheless, New Zealand's premiere resort town. It is set in a beautiful location beside Lake Wakatipu and is a year-round destination that hums winter, summer and fall. In summer it is host to backpackers and domestic tourists alike. It has pretty much everything going in the way of entertainment and accommodation including nightclubs, restaurants, hotels, campsites and A.J. Hackett's 'world famous' bungy jump. As you would expect of such a place accommodation is at a premium year round, so do not expect to find that or a job here easily.

The town gets especially busy during the week-long Winter Festival, normally held in June, featuring concerts, parades and some very crazy contests such as suitcase races and birdperson flights into the (chilly) lake.

THE REMARKABLES

Serviced by Queenstown, from which it is slightly further than Coronet Peak, The Remarkables ski field is comprised of a number of sheltered bowls linked together by ski lifts. It also has a cat skiing service where you can hitch a ride on a snowcat out to the untracked piste. The Remarkables also has a crèche.

Contacts
The Remarkables Ski Area: P.O. Box 359, Queenstown, New Zealand; ☎03 442 4615; fax +64 03 442 4619; www.nzski.com/remarkables/.

APPENDIX I: WHO GOES TO WHICH RESORT

The following charts indicate which resorts, according to latest information, are the most popular destinations for British-based tour operators. Spain and Eastern Europe have been omitted.

AUSTRIA

	ZELL AM SEE	SOLL	SEEFELD	ST JOHANN IN TIROL	ST ANTON	SCHLADMING	SAALBACH-HINTERGLEMM	OBERTAUERN	OBERGURGL	NIEDERAU	MAYRHOFEN	LECH	KITZBUHEL	KAPRUN	ELLMAU	BAD GASTEIN	ALPBACH
AIRTOURS	●	●			●		●			●	●	●	●	●			
CLUB EUROPE	●						●	●					●	●		●	
CRYSTAL	●	●	●	●	●	●	●		●		●	●	●	●	●		●
CRYSTAL FINEST					●												
ERNA LOW					●		●										
ESPRIT					●				●					●			
FIRST CHOICE	●				●												
FLEXISKI					●							●					
INGHAMS		●	●	●	●		●		●	●	●	●	●		●	●	●
LOTUS SUPERTRAVEL					●						●						
MARK WARNER					●												
NEILSON	●	●					●						●	●	●		
PANORAMA		●					●		●								
SCOTT DUNN					●												
SKI ACTIVITY	●	●			●		●		●				●				
SKIBOUND	●							●	●					●			
SKI CLUB OF GB	●								●				●	●			
SKI MIQUEL																●	
SKI VAL					●												
SKIWORLD					●						●						
THOMSON	●	●	●				●	●	●	●			●	●			
TOTAL HOLIDAYS					●							●					

FRANCE

Operator	VAL THORENS	VALMOREL	VAL D'ISERE	TIGNES	MORZINE	MONTGENEVRE	MERIBEL	LES DEUX ALPES	LES ARCS	LA TANIA	LA ROSIERE	LA PLAGNE	FLAINE	COURCHEVEL	CHAMONIX	AVORIAZ	ARGENTIERE	ALPE D'HUEZ
AIRTOURS						●												●
CLUB MED			●	●			●		●			●	●		●	●	●	●
COLLINEIGE														●				
CRYSTAL	●		●	●	●		●					●		●				●
CRYSTAL FINEST			●				●											
EQUITY					●													●
ERNA LOW									●			●	●		●			
ESPRIT			●	●	●				●		●	●		●				
FINLAYS			●									●						
FIRST CHOICE	●		●	●	●		●		●			●		●		●		●
FLEXISKI														●				
HUSKI															●			
INGHAMS	●		●	●			●		●			●	●	●	●			●
LE SKI			●							●								
LOTUS SUPERTRAVEL							●							●				
MARK WARNER			●	●			●					●		●				●
MERISKI							●											
NEILSON	●		●	●	●		●		●			●	●	●	●	●		●
PANORAMA																		
POWDER BYRNE														●				
SCOTT DUNN							●							●				
SILVER SKI							●					●		●				
SKI ACTIVITY			●						●			●		●				●
SKI AMIS		●																
SKI BEAT							●		●	●								
SKIBOUND			●	●	●							●						●
SKI CLUB OF GB	●		●	●			●		●			●	●		●	●	●	●
SKI FRANCE	●		●	●			●		●		●	●		●	●			●
SKI HILLWOOD																●		
SKI MIQUEL																		●
SKI OLYMPIC			●	●			●		●			●		●				
SKITOPIA/TJM			●			●			●									
SKI VAL			●											●				
SKI WEEKEND	●		●		●								●	●	●		●	
SKIWORLD	●		●					●	●	●								●
SNOWLINE/VIP			●	●						●								
THOMSON	●		●	●								●						●
TOPS TRAVEL																		●
TOTAL HOLIDAYS	●		●	●					●					●	●			

SWITZERLAND

	ZERMATT	WENGEN	VILLARS	VERBIER	ST MORITZ	SAAS FEE	MURREN	KLOSTERS	GRINDELWALD	DAVOS	CRANS MONTANA	AROSA
CLUB MED		●	●		●							
CRYSTAL	●	●	●	●	●	●				●		
CRYSTAL FINEST	●			●								
FIRST CHOICE				●								
FLEXISKI				●								
INGHAMS	●	●	●	●	●	●	●	●	●	●	●	●
LOTUS SUPERTRAVEL	●			●								
PEAK SKI				●								
PGL SKI						●			●		●	●
POWDER BYRNE	●								●			●
SCOTT DUNN	●				●							
SKI ACTIVITY				●								
SKI CLUB OF GB	●	●		●	●	●	●		●	●	●	●
SKI GOWER	●			●	●						●	●
SKI VERBIER				●								
SKIWORLD				●								
THOMSON			●	●						●		
TOTAL HOLIDAYS	●			●		●						

ANDORRA

	SOLDEU	PAS DE LA CASA	ARINSAL
AIRTOURS	●	●	●
CRYSTAL	●	●	●
FIRST CHOICE	●	●	●
INGHAMS	●	●	●
NEILSON	●	●	●
PANORAMA	●	●	●
SKI CLUB OF GB	●		
THOMSON	●	●	●

ITALY

	LA THUILE	SESTRIERE	SELVA/VAL GARDENA	SAUZE D'OULX	PASSO TONALE	LIVIGNO	COURMAYEUR	CORTINA	CERVINIA	BARDONECCIA
AIRTOURS				●	●	●				
CLUB EUROPE					●					
CLUB MED		●								
CRYSTAL	●	●	●	●	●	●	●		●	●
FIRST CHOICE	●	●	●	●	●	●			●	●
INGHAMS	●	●	●	●			●		●	●
INTERSKI	●									
MARK WARNER							●			
NEILSON	●	●	●	●	●	●	●			
PANORAMA				●						
SKIBOUND									●	
SKI CLUB OF GB				●				●	●	
THOMSON	●	●	●	●	●		●		●	●
TOTAL HOLIDAYS			●							

CANADA

	WHISTLER/BLACKCOMB	TREMBLANT	KICKING HORSE	JASPER	FERNIE	BANFF/LAKE LOUISE
AIRTOURS						●
CRYSTAL	●	●	●	●	●	●
INGHAMS	●	●		●	●	●
LOTUS SUPERTRAVEL	●					●
NEILSON	●			●	●	●
SKI ACTIVITY	●			●	●	●
SKI BOUND	●				●	
SKI CLUB OF GB	●				●	●
SKI INDEPENDENCE	●	●	●	●	●	●
SKI MIQUEL	●					
SKIWORLD	●					●
THOMSON	●	●				●
TOTAL HOLIDAYS	●					

USA

Operator	WINTER PARK	VAIL	STOWE	STEAMBOAT	PARK CITY	KILLINGTON	KEYSTONE	JACKSON HOLE	HEAVENLY/LAKE TAHOE/SQUAW VALLEY	CRESTED BUTTE	COPPER MOUNTAIN	BRECKENRIDGE	BEAVER CREEK	ASPEN/SNOWMASS
ALPINE TRACKS												●		
CLUB MED										●				
CRYSTAL	●	●	●	●	●	●	●	●	●	●	●	●	●	●
INGHAMS		●				●		●				●		
LOTUS SUPERTRAVEL	●	●		●				●						●
NEILSON											●	●		
SKI INDEPENDENCE	●	●	●	●	●	●	●	●			●	●	●	●
SKIWORLD						●		●			●			●
THOMSON	●	●	●	●	●	●		●	●					

APPENDIX 2: SKI TALK

Aerial	slope with a jump at the end
ASSI	Artificial Ski Slope Instructor hence ASSI qualification; one qualified to teach on artificial slopes only
BASI	British Association of Snowsport Instructors
BASI I	a very advanced qualification making the holder eligible for top jobs. Many ski school owners are BASI Is.
BASI II	Instructor
BASI III	Assistant Instructor
Black run	see 'pistes'
Blue run	see 'pistes
Chef du Parti	chef in charge of a department: e.g. sauces, fish etc.
Dirndl	female Alpine peasant dress
Fat Boys(Fatsticks/Fats)	extra wide skis which make powder skiing easy. Frowned on by purists who have wasted years perfecting their technique with regular skis.
Freestyle skiing	trick skiing incorporating aerials, moguls etc.
Glüwein	pronounced gluevine) red wine based punch that holds skiers together.
Goofy	snowboarding with the right foot forward
Langlauf	cross-country 'ski walking'. Also called Nordic skiing. Requires different equipment to Alpine (downhill) skiing.
Left Bollock	après ski emetic comprising tequila, vodka and grapefruit juice.
MBO	stands for muscle-bound oaf, a less polite alternative to maintenance and buildings officer. Coined by original chalet company Bladon Lines.
Mogul	large bump found on pistes, usually in groups.
Mono-skiing	skiing on one wide ski with feet parallel
Off piste	unmaintained skiing areas
Para-gliding	Alpine version involves descending from a mountain top by parachute with skis on
Piste-bashing	compression of snow by machine. Colloq. skiing
Pistes	specially prepared and maintained ski slopes marked according to difficulty (blue – beginners, red – intermediate, black – advanced).
Plongeur	originally a washer-upper but in tour company parlance can have wide-ranging duties similar to MBO.
Powder-skiing	skiing on freshly fallen (powder) snow that has not been bashed. Often involves going off piste
Punter	one who pays to ski
Red run	see 'pistes'
Salopettes	waterproof dungarees
Schuss	to ski downhill/a ski run
Silver star	intermediate recreational skier's award. Bronze, one below; gold, one above
Ski ballet	a discipline of freestyle skiing; involves using short skis
Ski Evolutif	(also known as *ski moderne*) a method of learning best suited to adults. Originated in Les Arcs and involves using very short skis which are replaced by ones of increasing lengths as ability develops.
Slalom	downhill race in and out of poles
Slick	icy (for slopes)
Snowboarding	the skiing equivalent of surfing using a snowboard and having one foot in front of the other
Wigglers	speed freaks who make short turns building up a rhythm.
Winterstick	a make of snow surfboard suitable for powder snow only.

Vacation Work Publications

Vacation Work Publications, 9 Park End Street, Oxford OX1 1HH
Tel 01865-241978 Fax 01865-790885

Visit us online for more information on our unrivalled range of titles for work,
travel and gap years, readers' feedback and regular updates:

www.vacationwork.co.uk

Books are available in the USA from
The Globe Pequot Press, Guilford, Connecticut
www.globepequot.com